Georgia Military Commissions
1798 to 1818

Georgia Military Commissions
1798 to 1818

Paul K. Graham

Monoceros Press
Salt Lake City, Utah

Georgia Military Commissions, 1798 to 1818

Copyright © 2017, by Paul K. Graham. All rights reserved

Monoceros Press
Salt Lake City, Utah
www.monocerospress.com

ISBN-10 (paperback): 1-947809-01-6
ISBN-13 (paperback): 978-1-947809-01-7

LCCN: 2017913177

For more information, visit www.georgiamilitarycommissions.com.

Table of Contents

Introduction	i
Georgia Militia Structure	i
Militia Districts	ii
Commission Records	ii
1804-to-1812 Transition	iii
Using This Book	iv
Microfilm References	vi
Works Consulted	vi
Commissions Book 1798–1800	1
Commissions Book 1800–1806	31
Commissions Book 1806–1809	91
Commissions Book 1809–1812	153
Commissions Book 1812–1815	201
Commissions Book 1815–1818	265
Name Index	319
County Index	415
Militia District Index	417
District-to-County Cross Reference	429
County-to-District Cross Reference	439

Introduction

This book documents the name, rank, unit, and commission date of almost ten thousand military officers whose commission certificates are recorded in the Adjutant General of Georgia's Military Commission Books from 15 January 1798 to 13 March 1818. Over thirty-eight thousand men were commissioned as officers of the Georgia Militia from January 1798 to April 1860.

Beyond documenting military service, the names of local officers are the key to correctly interpreting many other historical documents. Prior to the to late-1840s, militia companies were most often described using the name of the officer in command, even following the institution of a unit numbering system in 1804. Using this book, historians and genealogists now have a convenient cross-reference of named officers to numbered units, which will aid in interpretation of early documents such as census enumerations, tax rolls, and land lottery registrations.

Georgia Militia Structure

The Georgia Militia was a citizen force, instituted to protect the civilian population from a multitude of threats confronting the state in its pioneer days. At the top of the militia's organizational structure were divisions, each commanded by a major general. There were five divisions by 1812, each covering a wide geographic area. Divisions contained two or three brigades, each commanded by a brigadier general. Generally, brigades encompassed an area of two counties.

Brigades contained two to four regiments, each commanded by a lieutenant colonel commandant, lieutenant colonel, or colonel. Officers at these ranks all performed the same duties; the title differences reflect changes in naming conventions over time. Populated counties contained one or two regiments; in sparsely populated areas a single regiment could cover multiple counties. Regiments usually contained two battalions, which were commanded by majors. There could be two to four battalions in a county. Each battalion contained two to four companies, which were commanded by a captain, lieutenant, and ensign. Each militia district encompassed one company of men.

In addition to companies organized by physical district, the militia also contained volunteer companies, many of which became famous for their roles in military campaigns. Rifle, specialized infantry, dragoon (mounted infantry), and cavalry companies were attached to battalions, while artillery companies were attached to regiments. Artillery companies were associated with battalions until just prior to the War of 1812, when their senior command was transferred to the regimental level.

In a brief experiment, the cavalry was put into its own organization separate from the regular militia from 1808 to 1818. Cavalry regiments were made up of squadrons (commanded by majors), which in turn contained companies. Commissioned officers in cavalry companies were the captain, first lieutenant, second lieutenant, and cornet.

Georgia Military Commissions, 1798–1818

Militia Districts

The militia's organization based on company-level districts was developed when Georgia was still a colony. The provincial governor was given the power to create company districts and to commission field officers, who in turn would define geographic boundaries for the districts and designate the men constituting a militia company located in the district. The captain of each company was responsible for enrolling every male between age sixteen and sixty, making each of them members of that company. Enlistment was compulsory. When Georgia became part of the United States, the state legislature left the system intact, with only two changes: the minimum eligible age was lowered to fifteen, and the members of each company would elect their officers.

Until the late 1840s, districts were almost always known by the name of the captain in command at the time. Each time a new captain was elected, the district's name designation changed. This is important because historical records like tax lists, census enumerations, and land lottery registrations were organized by district and usually labeled with the captain's name, rather than the district's number. This means that—as was the case for Georgia resident Greenville Henderson—someone could be enumerated in the 1820 U.S. Federal Census in Leonard's District in Morgan County and then participate in the 1827 Georgia Land Lottery as a resident of Sparkes's District in the same county, without moving. The militia district was not different—only the identity of the captain.

Commission Records

Officer commissions recorded in the Adjutant General's Military Commission Books are now by the Georgia Department of Archives and History and available to the general public on microfilm. They are organized in date order and recorded in books containing two printed certificates on each page, similar to most county marriage records.

Commission certificates contain the name of the officer, his rank, the unit of his command, and the commission date. The names of Georgia's governor, the governor's secretary, and the recording clerk are also included in the stock language but only the information concerning the commissioned officer has been transcribed for this book. Each commission book contains its own index of persons receiving a commission. No consolidated name, geographic, or unit index exists for the Military Commission Books.

Prior to 1812, the Register of Military Commissions was instituted, with commissions dating from 1808. The Register is a tabular list of commissions that includes the commissioned officer's name, unit, county, rank, and date of commission, as well as the date of decommission or reference to his promotion. An unpublished name index is available for all commissions in the Register in the form of name files in the card catalog at the Georgia Archives. No geographic or unit index exists for this data.

The information contained in the Register of Military Commissions parallels entries in the Military Commission Books but is far from consistent. Most entries from 1808 to

Introduction

1812 are not included and many later commissions are omitted. Only a small percentage of commissions for volunteer militia companies are included in the Register. For these reasons—and for the purpose of publishing a complete abstract of one record set—only commissions in the Military Commission Books have been transcribed here.

1804-to-1812 Transition

Until 1804, the official naming convention for units was vague and inconsistent. Most commissions describe the associated unit in non-specific terms: "the Company in the Battalion of the Regiment of the Burke County militia." This naming pattern omits any recognition of the existence of multiple unique companies, battalions, and regiments in a single county. The same phenomenon occurs in commissions at the battalion and regimental level.

In most counties, researchers working in the pre-1804 era will find multiple ensigns, lieutenants, and captains in command of what appears to be the same company all at the same time, even though this is not the case. Some separation can be determined by following patterns in the way commissions were recorded in the books. Commissions for a single company issued on the same day were recorded by the clerk in descending order of rank: captain, lieutenant, and then ensign. Using this pattern, it is possible to separate the officers of multiple companies even when the actual company designation cannot be determined. The original arrangement—in book and page order—has been maintained here in order to allow for the correct interpretation of the commissions based on recording order.

The militia in some counties, such as Wilkes County, was established enough to have a well-formed numerical designation system resulting in descriptions such as "the Sixth Company of the First Battalion of the Second Regiment of the Wilkes County militia." While the use of numerals is helpful to a certain extent, the inconsistency in implementation complicates attempts to reconstruct the exact unit association of most commissions prior to the transition to a consistent statewide numbering system.

In 1804, the unit naming convention was changed from vague county-by-county designations to a statewide numbering system, in which all units of the same type were given a unique numeric label. The shift to a consistently implemented and accurate numbering system was not instantaneous, though. The records tell a story of administrative dysfunction, most likely caused by the difficulty of coordinating the communication of the new system's details to all the officers at the local level, as well as the process of developing a reliable system for retrieving those details from the field as individual changes were made.

The first historical document defining a company of the Georgia militia using the new numbering system was a certificate recorded on 2 May 1804 for a retroactive commission dated 13 May 1803. From that date until 1842, the county reference on commission certificates was completely dropped from all but a few units.

Georgia Military Commissions, 1798–1818

On 9 January 1805, general orders were issued that required the sequential numbering of militia units: "The adjutant general will make known to the commanding officer of each regiment the number of his regiment and the number of the battalion and district companies attached to it, by whom the commanding officers of battalions and companies will be made acquainted with the same." (The name of some volunteer companies includes the city or county where they are located, such as the "Savannah Fencibles" or the "Liberty County Light Infantry.")

In late 1807, the Georgia General Assembly passed a law that was necessary to bring Georgia into compliance with recently passed United States militia laws. The militia law of 10 December 1807 states that "every division, brigade, regiment, battalion and company district, shall be numbered throughout the state, by order of the commander in chief, in such manner, that every corps of the same denomination shall bear a different number—by which numbers every district shall be designated in the commissions of officers commanding them."

Approximately 20% of all commissions issued between the beginning of the numbering transition and 20 April 1812 are missing both a county designation and the numerical unit designation, making it impossible to determine the correct association without additional research.

Many commissions recorded early in the transition period were issued retroactively. Certificates during this time are dated at the time of issue and contain the language "to take rank" and the commission date. The first commission certificates specifying the new numbered units were issued 2 May 1804, all for retroactive commissions dated from 13 May 1803 to 22 April 1804. Two "numbered" commissions predate this first round of certificates, but are recorded later. James Alston received a commission for the rank of captain of District 51. His certificate is dated 27 June 1804 and his commission is dated 30 August 1802. This is the earliest dated commission that includes a numeric district designation. The second earliest of these commissions is for Marthew [sic] Scott Montgomery who was commissioned as the captain of District 256 on 22 April 1803 and his certificate is dated 6 December 1805.

Using This Book

In order to locate the district number for a captain's district in a tax roll or other record using the data in this book, simply look up that captain in the index to find his record, which (in the majority of cases) will provide his district number. Check to see that his commission date is prior to the date of the record.

Using the district name from the captain's record, search that district in the "County and Militia District Index" at the end of this book. Review the commission entries for that district on page numbers following the first captain. This will lead to a record of the subsequent captain, from which you can determine whether they took command before or after the creation of the historical record in question. This same technique can also be used to determine the county where a battalion or regiment was located, especially when the only known information is the name of the major or lieutenant colonel in command.

For officers with unique names, an index search usually leads directly to the correct commission. For those with common names, further investigation may be required, but the information contained in this book will dramatically reduce the number of historical possibilities.

This book will be particularly useful to researchers working with the 1807 and 1820 Georgia land lotteries, the 1820 U. S. Federal Census of Georgia, and county tax records from the period 1805 to 1820. Because of the problems associated with the 1804 to 1812 transition as discussed earlier, finding a unit number for captains named in the 1807 Georgia Land Lottery registration process will be difficult if the answer is not immediately clear. Many officers in command at the time of the lottery registration received their commission prior to May 1804 and many commissions received after the transition omitted the unit number, making it impossible to make a match to a specific district.

The 1820 Georgia land lottery registration occurred shortly after the last commission included in this book. However, because officers held their command on average three to five years, many of the commissions for officers in command during the registration period were issued prior to March 1818. Similarly, many captains whose names are used in the 1820 U. S. census received their commissions more than two years prior to the enumeration period.

Note that the district name recorded in land lottery registrations is the name as it was during the *registration period*, not the *lottery draw period*. The registration period for each lottery was established by each lottery law and could be a few months to two years in advance of the date of the lottery drawing. In addition to the initial registration period, the Georgia General Assembly continually extended the registration period, creating the possibility that two individuals living in the same district could be registered under the names of two different captains. See my book *Georgia Land Lottery Research* (published by the Georgia Genealogical Society) for the registration and draw dates for each lottery.

Microfilm References

Commission records can be accessed on microfilm at the Georgia Archives (GA) and the Family History Library (FHL). See the following:

Book	GA Film	FHL Film
Commissions Book 1798–1800	Drawer 60, Box 24	158,997
Commissions Book 1800–1806	Drawer 39, Box 73	158,997
Commissions Book 1806–1809	Drawer 174, Box 29	158,998
Commissions Book 1809–1812	Drawer 174, Box 33	158,999
Commissions Book 1812–1815	Drawer 174, Box 31	159,000
Commissions Book 1815–1818	Drawer 174, Box 34	159,001

Works Consulted

Cadle, Farris W. *Georgia Land Surveying History and Law*. Athens, Ga.: University of Georgia Press, 1991.

Clayton, Augustin S. *A compilation of the laws of the state of Georgia passed by the legislature since the political year 1800, to the year 1810, inclusive....* Augusta, Ga.: Adams & Duyckinck, 1813.

Dawson, William C. *A compilation of the laws of the state of Georgia, passed by the General assembly, since the year 1819 to the year 1829, inclusive....* Milledgeville, Ga.: Grantland and Orme, 1831.

Hitz, Alex M. "Georgia Militia Districts." *Georgia Law Journal*, vol. 18, no. 3 (February 1956).

Lamar, Lucius O. C. *A compilation of the laws of the State of Georgia, passed by the Legislature since the year 1810 to the year 1819, inclusive....* Augusta, Ga.: T. S. Hannon, 1821.

Smith, Gordon Burns. *Campaigns and Generals*. Vol. 1 of *History of the Georgia Militia, 1783-1861*. Milledgeville, Ga.: Boyd Publishing, 2000.

Georgia Military Commissions
Commissions Book 1798–1800

Name, Rank, Unit	Date	Page
John Walton, Lieutenant Colonel Commandant, Lincoln County	15 Jan 1798	p. 1
Gibson Wooldridge, Major, Lincoln County	15 Jan 1798	p. 1
James Thompson, Captain, 1st Company, Oglethorpe County	15 Jan 1798	p. 2
James Martin, Lieutenant, Burke County	15 Jan 1798	p. 2
Thomas Dukes, Captain, Oglethorpe County	16 Jan 1798	p. 3
Peter Wyche, Lieutenant, Elbert County	16 Jan 1798	p. 3
Zachariah Clark, Ensign, Elbert County	16 Jan 1798	p. 4
Holland McTier, Lieutenant, Richmond County	16 Jan 1798	p. 4
Stephen Pilcher, Captain, 2nd Company, Glynn County	16 Jan 1798	p. 5
William Bryan, Ensign, 2nd Company, Glynn County	16 Jan 1798	p. 5
Samuel Barron, Captain, Hancock County	16 Jan 1798	p. 6
Nimrod House, Lieutenant, 3rd Company, Franklin County	18 Jan 1798	p. 6
John Horton, Captain, Wilkes County	25 Jan 1798	p. 7
David Gaddy, Lieutenant, Wilkes County	25 Jan 1798	p. 7
Stokeley Morgan, Ensign, Wilkes County	25 Jan 1798	p. 8
John Loften, Lieutenant, Burke County	25 Jan 1798	p. 8
John Caswell, Ensign, Burke County	25 Jan 1798	p. 9
Henry Wynne, Lieutenant, 4th Company, Battalion 2, Regiment 1, Burke County	25 Jan 1798	p. 9
John Matthews, Ensign, Warren County	27 Jan 1798	p. 10
William Harrill, Ensign, Washington County	27 Jan 1798	p. 10
Shadrick Bivins, Lieutenant, Rifle Company, Hancock County	5 Feb 1798	p. 11
Archilous Ferrell, Ensign, Rifle Company, Hancock County	5 Feb 1798	p. 11
William Yarborough, Captain, Hancock County	6 Feb 1798	p. 12
John Rushing, Lieutenant, Warren County	6 Feb 1798	p. 12
William Wilkinson, Ensign, Warren County	6 Feb 1798	p. 13

Georgia Military Commissions, 1798–1818

Name, Rank, Unit	*Date*	*Page*
John Cox, Captain, Franklin County	10 Feb 1798	p. 13
James Martin, Lieutenant, Franklin County	10 Feb 1798	p. 14
Elijah Martin, Ensign, Franklin County	10 Feb 1798	p. 14
Joseph Carter, Lieutenant, Warren County	13 Feb 1798	p. 15
John Simmons, Ensign, Warren County	13 Feb 1798	p. 15
James Humphries, Ensign, Hancock County	23 Feb 1798	p. 16
Darius Garrison, Lieutenant, Indian Bluff Company, Effingham County	1 Mar 1798	p. 16
Abel Loper, Ensign, Indian Bluff Company, Effingham County	1 Mar 1798	p. 17
John McDonald, Ensign, 6th Company, Battalion 2, Columbia County	3 Mar 1798	p. 17
Amos Brantley, Lieutenant, Hancock County	8 Mar 1798	p. 18
Robert Thornton, Ensign, Hancock County	8 Mar 1798	p. 18
John Lott Jr., Captain, 4th (Ohoopie) Company, Montgomery County	12 Mar 1798	p. 19
James Cockran, Lieutenant, 4th (Ohoopie) Company, Montgomery County	12 Mar 1798	p. 19
William Lott, Ensign, 4th (Ohoopie) Company, Montgomery County	12 Mar 1798	p. 20
John Hobson, Lieutenant, Warren County	19 Mar 1798	p. 20
Thomas Jones, Lieutenant Colonel Commandant, Regiment 2, Burke County	26 Mar 1798	p. 21
William Kendrick, Captain, Washington County	26 Mar 1798	p. 21
Edward Moore, Captain, 9th Company, Jackson County	26 Mar 1798	p. 22
Allen Brazill, Lieutenant, 9th Company, Jackson County	26 Mar 1798	p. 22
John McGee, Ensign, 9th Company, Jackson County	26 Mar 1798	p. 23
John Kogler, Captain, Effingham County	28 Mar 1798	p. 23
Benjamin Dasher, Lieutenant, Effingham County	28 Mar 1798	p. 24
Matthew Whiteman, Ensign, Effingham County	28 Mar 1798	p. 24
John Andrews, Ensign, Hancock County	5 Apr 1798	p. 25
Saymer Lee, Captain, Oglethorpe County	5 Apr 1798	p. 25
Christopher Erwin, Captain, Wilkes County	4 Apr 1798	p. 26
Cerous Billingslea, Lieutenant, Wilkes County	4 Apr 1798	p. 26

Name, Rank, Unit	Date	Page
Caleb Cock, Lieutenant, 1st Company, Battalion 2, Regiment 2, Burke County	11 Apr 1798	p. 27
Elisha Gore, Lieutenant, 2nd Company, Battalion 1, Richmond County	12 Apr 1798	p. 27
Leonard Thompson, Lieutenant, Light Infantry Company, Columbia County	19 Apr 1798	p. 28
William Fussell, Captain, Washington County	12 Apr 1798	p. 28
Frederick Little, Lieutenant, Washington County	20 Apr 1798	p. 29
Simmons Maxwell, Captain, Bryan County	21 Apr 1798	p. 29
John Van Brackle, Lieutenant, Bryan County	21 Apr 1798	p. 30
Green Manley, Ensign, 6th Company, Battalion 1, Oglethorpe County	26 Apr 1798	p. 30
John Barbree, Captain, Big Ohoopie Company, Montgomery County	27 Apr 1798	p. 31
Rowland Williams, Lieutenant, Big Ohoopie Company, Montgomery County	27 Apr 1798	p. 31
Hazel Holly, Ensign, Big Ohoopie Company, Montgomery County	27 Apr 1798	p. 32
Dennis Nobles, Captain, 5th Company, Battalion 2, Regiment 1, Burke County	27 Apr 1798	p. 32
John Thompson, Ensign, 5th Company, Battalion 2, Regiment 1, Burke County	27 Apr 1798	p. 33
Mills Murphie, Major, Battalion 2, Regiment 2, Burke County	1 May 1798	p. 33
Benjamin Posey, Captain, 5th Company, Battalion 2, Greene County	3 May 1798	p. 34
Zachariah Jones, Ensign, 5th Company, Battalion 2, Greene County	3 May 1798	p. 34
John Martin, Ensign, 3rd Company, Battalion 1, Regiment 2, Burke County	3 May 1798	p. 35
John Floyd, Captain, Volunteer Troop of Horse, Oglethorpe County	7 May 1798	p. 35
Chatham D. Scroggin, First Lieutenant, Volunteer Troop of Horse, Oglethorpe County	7 May 1798	p. 36

Georgia Military Commissions, 1798–1818

Name, Rank, Unit	Date	Page
William Collier, Second Lieutenant, Volunteer Troop of Horse, Oglethorpe County	7 May 1798	p. 36
Richard Haines, Cornet, Volunteer Troop of Horse, Oglethorpe County	7 May 1798	p. 37
Peter Aron, Ensign, Lincoln County	8 May 1798	p. 37
Spencer Wilson, Captain, Montgomery County	10 May 1798	p. 38
James Hancock, Lieutenant, Montgomery County	10 May 1798	p. 38
Micajah Bradley, Ensign, Montgomery County	10 May 1798	p. 39
John Gilbert, Captain, Volunteer Troop of Horse, Franklin County	10 May 1798	p. 39
John Easley, First Lieutenant, Volunteer Troop of Horse, Franklin County	10 May 1798	p. 40
William Christian, Second Lieutenant, Volunteer Troop of Horse, Franklin County	10 May 1798	p. 40
Samuel Glenn, Cornet, Volunteer Troop of Horse, Franklin County	10 May 1798	p. 41
Presley Scurlock, Captain, Washington County	10 May 1798	p. 41
Samuel Robinson, Lieutenant, Washington County	10 May 1798	p. 42
Nathaniel Pace Jr., Ensign, Washington County	10 May 1798	p. 42
Solomon Gnann, Lieutenant, Effingham County	12 May 1798	p. 43
John Grovenstine, Ensign, Effingham County	12 May 1798	p. 43
Thacker Vivion Jr., Captain, Battalion 2, Jefferson County	12 May 1798	p. 44
Charles Harvey, Lieutenant, Franklin County	12 May 1798	p. 44
Nathaniel Hally, Ensign, Hancock County	16 May 1798	p. 45
William Hopkins, Captain, Jackson County	17 May 1798	p. 45
William McFarlin, Lieutenant, 4th Company, Battalion 2, Regiment 1, Wilkes County	18 May 1798	p. 46
Thomas Herren, Cornet, Volunteer Troop of Horse, Richmond County	18 May 1798	p. 46
John Cook, Ensign, Richmond County	18 May 1798	p. 47
William Scott, Captain, 2nd Company, McIntosh County	18 May 1798	p. 47
Joseph Joiner, Lieutenant, 2nd Company, McIntosh County	18 May 1798	p. 48

Name, Rank, Unit	*Date*	*Page*
Charles Tharp, Ensign, 2nd Company, McIntosh County	18 May 1798	p. 48
Thomas Davis, Major, Montgomery County	19 May 1798	p. 49
Nicholas Curry, Major, Washington County	23 May 1798	p. 49
William Alford Jr., Captain, Hancock County	23 May 1798	p. 50
Thomas Rutledge, Lieutenant, Oglethorpe County	23 May 1798	p. 50
George G. Gains, Ensign, Richmond County	23 May 1798	p. 51
Arthur Taylor, Ensign, Warren County	28 May 1798	p. 51
Matthew Cox, Lieutenant, 2nd Company, Franklin County	28 May 1798	p. 52
William Hall, Ensign, 2nd Company, Franklin County	28 May 1798	p. 52
William Mathews, Captain, 4th Company, Oglethorpe County	29 May 1798	p. 53
Caleb Stephens, Captain, Warren County	31 May 1798	p. 54
Abraham Pearce, Lieutenant, Jefferson County	31 May 1798	p. 54
Harvey Herrington, Ensign, Jefferson County	31 May 1798	p. 55
James Carr, Lieutenant, Burke County	31 May 1798	p. 55
Peter Ready, Lieutenant, Burke County	2 Jun 1798	p. 56
Samuel Cannon, Ensign, Burke County	2 Jun 1798	p. 56
John Edmonds, Captain, Wilkes County	7 Jun 1798	p. 57
Ebenezer Smith, Lieutenant, Wilkes County	7 Jun 1798	p. 57
William Kennedy, Captain, Volunteer Company of Artillery, Richmond County	11 Jun 1798	p. 58
John Carmichael, Second Lieutenant, Volunteer Company of Artillery, Richmond County	11 Jun 1798	p. 58
Arthur Hamilton, Ensign, 4th Company, Battalion 1, Chatham County	14 Jun 1798	p. 59
William Miller, Captain, Screven County	19 Jun 1798	p. 59
William Mills, Lieutenant, Battalion 1, Hancock County	22 Jun 1798	p. 60
William Foxwell, Ensign, Battalion 1, Hancock County	22 Jun 1798	p. 60
Isaac Farmer, Ensign, Burke County	25 Jun 1798	p. 61
George Padden Read, Captain, Cherokee Hill Company, Battalion 2, Chatham County	26 Jun 1798	p. 61
William Smith, Lieutenant, Cherokee Hill Company, Battalion 2, Chatham County	26 Jun 1798	p. 62

Georgia Military Commissions, 1798–1818

Name, Rank, Unit	Date	Page
Charles Ulmer, Ensign, Cherokee Hill Company, Battalion 2, Chatham County	26 Jun 1798	p. 62
Ambrose Gorden, Captain, Volunteer Troop of Dragoons, Chatham County	26 Jun 1798	p. 63
Thomas Rhodes, Second Lieutenant, Volunteer Troop of Dragoons, Chatham County	26 Jun 1798	p. 63
Thomas Cooper, Lieutenant, Hancock County	26 Jun 1798	p. 64
Richard Warren, Captain, 2nd Company, Battalion 2, Regiment 2, Burke County	26 Jun 1798	p. 64
Burrell Jordan, Captain, Washington County	28 Jun 1798	p. 65
Abraham Jackson, Major, Battalion 1, Regiment 2, Burke County	2 Jul 1798	p. 65
Daniel Ounsell, Ensign, 4th Company, Battalion 2, Regiment 1, Burke County	2 Jul 1798	p. 66
Drury Wamble, Captain, Volunteer Troop of Dragoons, Burke County	2 Jul 1798	p. 66
Robert White, First Lieutenant, Volunteer Troop of Dragoons, Burke County	2 Jul 1798	p. 67
Mordicai Evans, Second Lieutenant, Volunteer Troop of Dragoons, Burke County	2 Jul 1798	p. 67
William White, Cornet, Volunteer Troop of Dragoons, Burke County	2 Jul 1798	p. 68
Stephen Denmark, Captain, 1st Company, Bulloch County	2 Jul 1798	p. 68
David Groover, Lieutenant, 1st Company, Bulloch County	2 Jul 1798	p. 69
John Lane, Ensign, 1st Company, Bulloch County	2 Jul 1798	p. 69
Jacob Raes, Captain, Elbert County	2 Jul 1798	p. 70
Absalom Gray, Lieutenant, Elbert County	2 Jul 1798	p. 70
William Jones, Second Lieutenant, Volunteer Company of Artillery, Wilkes County	10 Jul 1798	p. 71
Augustus Baldwin, First Lieutenant, Volunteer Company of Artillery, Richmond County	10 Jul 1798	p. 71
Thomas Polhill, Major, Effingham County	10 Jul 1798	p. 72
George W. Moore, Ensign, 2nd Company, Battalion 1, Columbia County	10 Jul 1798	p. 72

Name, Rank, Unit	Date	Page
John Eaton, Captain, 3rd Company, Camden County	13 Jul 1798	p. 73
John Campbell, Lieutenant, 3rd Company, Camden County	13 Jul 1798	p. 73
Philip Goodbread, Ensign, 3rd Company, Camden County	13 Jul 1798	p. 74
John Dudley, Captain, 5th Company, Camden County	13 Jul 1798	p. 74
John Brown, Lieutenant, 5th Company, Camden County	13 Jul 1798	p. 75
William Talley, Ensign, 5th Company, Camden County	13 Jul 1798	p. 75
Thomas Robertson, Captain, Light Infantry Company, Battalion 1, Chatham County	16 Jul 1798	p. 76
John Peter Oates, Lieutenant, Light Infantry Company, Battalion 1, Chatham County	16 Jul 1798	p. 76
William Saunders, Ensign, Light Infantry Company, Battalion 1, Chatham County	16 Jul 1798	p. 77
Terrill Higden, Lieutenant, Montgomery County	16 Jul 1798	p. 77
Burrell Higden, Ensign, Montgomery County	16 Jul 1798	p. 78
Randolph McGillis, Captain, Volunteer Troop of Dragoons, Camden County	21 Jul 1798	p. 78
James Jordon, First Lieutenant, Volunteer Troop of Dragoons, Camden County	21 Jul 1798	p. 79
Jacob Mickler, Second Lieutenant, Volunteer Troop of Dragoons, Camden County	21 Jul 1798	p. 79
John King Jr., Cornet, Volunteer Troop of Dragoons, Camden County	21 Jul 1798	p. 80
Francis Smith, Ensign, Hancock County	25 Jul 1798	p. 80
Isaac Woods, Captain, 3rd Company, Battalion 1, Regiment 2, Burke County	21 Jul 1798	p. 81
John Martin, Lieutenant, 3rd Company, Battalion 1, Regiment 2, Burke County	31 Jul 1798	p. 81
John Marshall, Ensign, 3rd Company, Battalion 1, Regiment 2, Burke County	31 Jul 1798	p. 82
Benjamin Blanchard, Captain, 2nd Company, Battalion 1, Regiment 1, Burke County	31 Jul 1798	p. 82
William Smith, Captain, 3rd Company, Battalion 1, Franklin County	1 Aug 1798	p. 83

Georgia Military Commissions, 1798–1818

Name, Rank, Unit	Date	Page
George Durham, Lieutenant, 3rd Company, Battalion 1, Franklin County	1 Aug 1798	p. 83
William Cain, Lieutenant, 1st Company, Battalion 2, Wilkes County	1 Aug 1798	p. 84
Jonathan Oxford, Ensign, 1st Company, Battalion 2, Wilkes County	1 Aug 1798	p. 84
James Box Young, Captain, Volunteer Company of Savannah Rangers, Battalion 1, Chatham County	1 Aug 1798	p. 85
James Johnston, Lieutenant, Volunteer Company of the Savannah Rangers, Battalion 1, Chatham County	1 Aug 1798	p. 85
John Sam'l De Montmollen, Ensign, Volunteer Company of Savannah Rangers, Battalion 1, Chatham County	1 Aug 1798	p. 86
William Smith, Captain, Church Company, Battalion 1, Chatham County	6 Aug 1798	p. 86
Abraham Abrahams, Lieutenant, Church Company, Battalion 1, Chatham County	6 Aug 1798	p. 87
John Jenkins, Ensign, Church Company, Battalion 1, Chatham County	6 Aug 1798	p. 87
John Bethune, Captain, 6th Company, Battalion 1, Regiment 2, Wilkes County	8 Aug 1798	p. 88
Littleburry Little, Ensign, 6th Company, Battalion 1, Regiment 2, Wilkes County	8 Aug 1798	p. 88
Thomas Nelmns, Lieutenant, 4th Company, Liberty County	13 Aug 1798	p. 89
John Lawson, Ensign, 4th Company, Liberty County	13 Aug 1798	p. 89
John King, Captain, Volunteer Troop of Dragoons, Effingham County	13 Aug 1798	p. 90
James Goldwire, First Lieutenant, Volunteer Troop of Dragoons, Effingham County	13 Aug 1798	p. 90
Benjamin Morel, Second Lieutenant, Volunteer Troop of Dragoons, Effingham County	13 Aug 1798	p. 91
William Dupuis, Cornet, Volunteer Troop of Dragoons, Effingham County	13 Aug 1798	p. 91
Benjamin Brack, Ensign, 2nd Company, Battalion 2, Regiment 2, Burke County	15 Aug 1798	p. 92

Commissions Book 1798–1800

Name, Rank, Unit	*Date*	*Page*
Daniel McNiel, Lieutenant, Battalion 2, Columbia County	13 Aug 1798	p. 92
Joseph Dopson, Ensign, Bryan County	22 Aug 1798	p. 93
Barnel Kendrick, Captain, 6th (Silver Bluff) Company, Montgomery County	3 Sep 1798	p. 93
Lewis Hall, Lieutenant, 6th (Silver Bluff) Company, Montgomery County	3 Sep 1798	p. 94
Frederick Jackson, Ensign, 6th (Silver Bluff) Company, Montgomery County	3 Sep 1798	p. 94
Thomas Gibbs, Captain, 8th (Canouchee) Company, Montgomery County	3 Sep 1798	p. 95
Jesse Bird, Lieutenant, 8th (Canouchee) Company, Montgomery County	3 Sep 1798	p. 95
Benjamin Bruton, Ensign, 8th (Canouchee) Company, Montgomery County	3 Sep 1798	p. 96
Rowland Williams, Captain, 3rd (Big Ohoopie) Company, Montgomery County	3 Sep 1798	p. 96
Thomas Powel, Lieutenant, 3rd (Big Ohoopie) Company, Montgomery County	3 Sep 1798	p. 97
Jesse Hutchinson, Ensign, 3rd (Big Ohoopie) Company, Montgomery County	3 Sep 1798	p. 97
Isaac Ledbetter, Lieutenant, 4th (Oconee) Company, Montgomery County	3 Sep 1798	p. 98
John Bash, Ensign, 4th (Oconee) Company, Montgomery County	3 Sep 1798	p. 98
Hardy Wood, Lieutenant, 7th (Saw Mill) Company, Montgomery County	3 Sep 1798	p. 99
Allen Johnston, Ensign, 7th (Saw Mill) Company, Montgomery County	3 Sep 1798	p. 99
John Hogan, Second Lieutenant, Volunteer Troop of Dragoons, Washington County	3 Sep 1798	p. 100
Henry Pearson, Captain, Wilkes County	3 Sep 1798	p. 100
Littleberry Jenkins, Captain, Battalion 1, Greene County	3 Sep 1798	p. 101
Jesse Tucker, Ensign, Battalion 1, Greene County	3 Sep 1798	p. 101
Thomas Buttrill, Ensign, Warren County	3 Sep 1798	p. 102
Daniel Zachary, Ensign, Warren County	6 Sep 1798	p. 102

Georgia Military Commissions, 1798–1818

Name, Rank, Unit	Date	Page
George Low, First Lieutenant, Volunteer Troop of Dragoons, Richmond County	6 Sep 1798	p. 103
Benjamin Stirk, Captain, Effingham County	10 Sep 1798	p. 103
Thomas King, Major, Camden County	10 Sep 1798	p. 104
Isham Cruise, Captain, Liberty County	12 Sep 1798	p. 104
Jacob Moore, Lieutenant, Liberty County	12 Sep 1798	p. 105
Thomas Futch, Ensign, Liberty County	12 Sep 1798	p. 105
John B. Gerardeau, Captain, Volunteer Troop of Dragoons, Liberty County	12 Sep 1798	p. 106
John Bettis, First Lieutenant, Volunteer Troop of Dragoons, Liberty County	12 Sep 1798	p. 106
Joel Walker, Second Lieutenant, Volunteer Troop of Dragoons, Liberty County	12 Sep 1798	p. 107
Saumel S. Low, Cornet, Volunteer Troop of Dragoons, Liberty County	12 Sep 1798	p. 107
Thomas Petters Carnes, Lieutenant Colonel Commandant, Franklin County	17 Sep 1798	p. 108
Thomas Crews, Major, Battalion 1, Franklin County	17 Sep 1798	p. 108
John Holland, Major, Battalion 2, Franklin County	17 Sep 1798	p. 109
Isaac Wilbourn, Captain, Wilkes County	17 Sep 1798	p. 109
George Matthews, Lieutenant, 4th Company, Battalion 2, Oglethorpe County	26 Sep 1798	p. 110
Valentine Meriwether, Ensign, 4th Company, Battalion 2, Oglethorpe County	26 Sep 1798	p. 110
Richardson Hunt, Major, Battalion 3, Elbert County	26 Sep 1798	p. 111
William Parsons, Lieutenant, Battalion 1, Jefferson County	1 Oct 1798	p. 111
Alexander Caswell, Ensign, Battalion 1, Jefferson County	1 Oct 1798	p. 112
Willis Burney, Ensign, Washington County	8 Oct 1798	p. 112
John Rutherford, Lieutenant Colonel Commandant, Washington County	8 Oct 1798	p. 113
Samuel Fulton, Captain, 1st Company, McIntosh County	25 Oct 1798	p. 113
John Floyd, Lieutenant, 1st Company, McIntosh County	25 Oct 1798	p. 114

Name, Rank, Unit	*Date*	*Page*
Norman McDonald, Ensign, 1st Company, McIntosh County	25 Oct 1798	p. 114
Richard Kirkland, Captain, Bulloch County	2 Nov 1798	p. 115
William Mixon, Lieutenant, Bulloch County	2 Nov 1798	p. 115
Joseph Cottins, Ensign, Bulloch County	2 Nov 1798	p. 116
John Caswell, Second Lieutenant, 1st Company, Battalion 1, Regiment 1, Burke County	5 Nov 1798	p. 116
Christopher Bailey, Ensign, Effingham County	5 Nov 1798	p. 117
Leroy Pope, Captain, Elbert County	7 Nov 1798	p. 117
James Coleman, Lieutenant, Elbert County	7 Nov 1798	p. 118
Charles Taylor, Ensign, Elbert County	7 Nov 1798	p. 118
Notley Whitcumbe, Lieutenant, 1st Company, Battalion 1, Columbia County	12 Nov 1798	p. 119
Charles Harvey, Captain, 3rd Company, Battalion 1, Franklin County	15 Nov 1798	p. 119
Ignatius Pursil, Lieutenant, 3rd Company, Battalion 1, Franklin County	15 Nov 1798	p. 120
John A. Baker, Ensign, 3rd Company, Battalion 1, Franklin County	15 Nov 1798	p. 120
Joseph Burden, Lieutenant, Wilkes County	16 Nov 1798	p. 121
William Ford, Captain, 5th Company, Battalion 1, Columbia County	27 Nov 1798	p. 121
David Stanford, Lieutenant, 5th Company, Battalion 1, Columbia County	27 Nov 1798	p. 122
Patrick Casten, Ensign, 5th Company, Battalion 1, Columbia County	27 Nov 1798	p. 122
Lill Sapp, Captain, 5th Company, Battalion 2, Regiment 1, Burke County	8 Dec 1798	p. 123
Reuben Thompson, Lieutenant, 5th Company, Battalion 2, Regiment 1, Burke County	8 Dec 1798	p. 123
Thomas Tipton, Ensign, 5th Company, Battalion 2, Regiment 1, Burke County	8 Dec 1798	p. 124
James Lindsay, Captain, 1st Company, Camden County	10 Nov 1798	p. 124
Josiah Beale, Captain, Hancock County	12 Dec 1798	p. 125

Georgia Military Commissions, 1798–1818

Name, Rank, Unit	*Date*	*Page*
James Brown, Ensign, 1st Company, Battalion 1, Regiment 1, Burke County	12 Dec 1798	p. 125
Ebenezer Baldwin, Ensign, Court House Company, Battalion 1, Chatham County	17 Dec 1798	p. 126
Notby Witcumbe, Captain, 1st Company, Battalion 1, Columbia County	12 Jan 1799	p. 126
James Freeman, Ensign, Oglethorpe County	12 Jan 1799	p. 127
John Mathews, Lieutenant, Warren County	22 Jan 1799	p. 127
John Fletcher, Ensign, Warren County	22 Jan 1799	p. 128
Samuel Bird, Captain, Volunteer Light Infantry Company, Burke County	23 Jan 1799	p. 128
Shadrach Scarborough, Lieutenant, Volunteer Light Infantry Company, Burke County	23 Jan 1799	p. 129
Lawrence Folsom, Ensign, Volunteer Light Infantry Company, Burke County	23 Jan 1799	p. 129
Joseph Miller, Ensign, Columbia County	28 Jan 1799	p. 130
John Boyd, Ensign, Battalion 1, Regiment 1, Burke County	24 Jan 1799	p. 130
John Sargeant, Lieutenant, 1st Company, Battalion 1, Columbia County	7 Feb 1799	p. 131
John Hobson, Captain, Warren County	8 Feb 1799	p. 131
Burrell Bullock, Ensign, Columbia County	12 Feb 1799	p. 132
Henry Wynn, Captain, 4th Company, Battalion 2, Regiment 1, Burke County	14 Feb 1799	p. 132
William Maddox, Ensign, Battalion 2, Hancock County	14 Feb 1799	p. 133
Benjamin Catching, Captain, Volunteer Rifle Company, Hancock County	15 Feb 1799	p. 133
Benjamin Taliaferro, Ensign, Hancock County	15 Feb 1799	p. 134
Thomas Seales, Captain, Battalion 3, Hancock County	15 Feb 1799	p. 134
John Cockran, Lieutenant, Greene County	15 Feb 1799	p. 135
Meshac Towson, Ensign, Greene County	15 Feb 1799	p. 135
Royal Jenkins, Lieutenant, Greene County	15 Feb 1799	p. 136
Thomas Spalding, Captain, 3rd Company, Glynn County	13 Feb 1799	p. 136
Raymond Demere, Ensign, 3rd Company, Glynn County	13 Feb 1799	p. 137

Name, Rank, Unit	Date	Page
James Bird, Captain, Bulloch County	6 Mar 1799	p. 137
George Mekell, Lieutenant, Bulloch County	6 Mar 1799	p. 138
Jesse Jernegan, Ensign, Bulloch County	6 Mar 1799	p. 138
Isaac Willingham, Captain, 4th Company, Battalion 1, Columbia County	6 Mar 1799	p. 139
John Chinault, Lieutenant, 4th Company, Battalion 1, Columbia County	6 Mar 1799	p. 139
Miner Mead, Ensign, 4th Company, Battalion 1, Columbia County	6 Mar 1799	p. 140
David Langston, Ensign, Battalion 2, Columbia County	6 Mar 1799	p. 140
Benjamin Hall, Ensign, Battalion 3, Hancock County	6 Mar 1799	p. 141
Alexander Caswell, Captain, Battalion 1, Jefferson County	6 Mar 1799	p. 141
James Manson, Ensign, Battalion 1, Jefferson County	6 Mar 1799	p. 142
Hustus Sludstill, Captain, Bulloch County	14 Mar 1799	p. 142
Thomas Newbern, Lieutenant, Bulloch County	14 Mar 1799	p. 143
Isham Roberts, Ensign, Bulloch County	14 Mar 1799	p. 143
John Paxton, Captain, 5th Company, Wilkes County	14 Mar 1799	p. 144
Thomas Dillen, Ensign, 3rd Company, Wilkes County	14 Mar 1799	p. 144
Willis Spears, Captain, Screven County	12 Mar 1799	p. 145
Abner Hunter, Lieutenant, Screven County	12 Mar 1799	p. 145
Dennis Colson, Ensign, Screven County	12 Mar 1799	p. 146
John Crozier, Captain, 2nd Company, Battalion 2, Burke County	18 Mar 1799	p. 146
William Gibson, Lieutenant, Camden County	25 Mar 1799	p. 147
Benjamin Landeford, Ensign, Warren County	27 Mar 1799	p. 147
William Cheatham, Lieutenant, Warren County	27 Mar 1799	p. 148
Thomas Wilder, Lieutenant, Screven County	28 Mar 1799	p. 148
Israel Barber, Ensign, Screven County	28 Mar 1799	p. 149
Enoch Everett, Lieutenant, Bulloch County	29 Mar 1799	p. 149
Curtis Wilborn, Captain, 5th Company, Battalion 1, Greene County	6 Apr 1799	p. 150
John Butler, Lieutenant, 5th Company, Battalion 1, Greene County	6 Apr 1799	p. 150

Georgia Military Commissions, 1798–1818

Name, Rank, Unit	Date	Page
Charles Walden, Ensign, 5th Company, Battalion 1, Greene County	6 Apr 1799	p. 151
Byrd Ferrell, Captain, Rifle Company, Battalion 2, Greene County	6 Apr 1799	p. 151
William Stephens, Lieutenant, Rifle Company, Battalion 2, Greene County	6 Apr 1799	p. 152
William Stone, Ensign, Rifle Company, Battalion 2, Greene County	6 Apr 1799	p. 152
William Colbert, Captain, Battalion 2	6 Apr 1799	p. 153
John Bailey, Lieutenant, 5th Company, Battalion 1, Regiment 1, Wilkes County	17 Apr 1799	p. 153
Thomas Richardson, Ensign, 5th Company, Battalion 1, Regiment 1, Wilkes County	17 Apr 1799	p. 154
Pullen Earp, Captain, Washington County	17 Apr 1799	p. 154
Sanders Bush, Ensign, Jefferson County	17 Apr 1799	p. 155
James Farley, Ensign, Hancock County	17 Apr 1799	p. 155
John Montgomery, Captain, Elbert County	17 Apr 1799	p. 156
Jacob Montgomery, Lieutenant, Elbert County	17 Apr 1799	p. 156
Elias Alexander, Ensign, Elbert County	17 Apr 1799	p. 157
James Bevill, Major, Screven County	22 Apr 1799	p. 157
George Norman, Lieutenant, Lincoln County	29 Apr 1799	p. 158
Thomas Forth, Lieutenant, 4th Company, Battalion 2, Regiment 1, Burke County	29 Apr 1799	p. 158
John Waldhour, Captain, 1st Company, Effingham County	29 Apr 1799	p. 159
Timothy Staly, Lieutenant, 1st Company, Effingham County	29 Apr 1799	p. 159
Joshua Kubler, Ensign, 1st Company, Effingham County	29 Apr 1799	p. 160
William Hall, Lieutenant, 3rd (Big Ohoopie) Company, Montgomery County	3 May 1799	p. 160
Hazel Holley, Ensign, 3rd (Big Ohoopie) Company, Montgomery County	3 May 1799	p. 161
Robert Duglass, Lieutenant, 2nd (Little Ohoopie) Company, Montgomery County	3 May 1799	p. 161

Name, Rank, Unit	Date	Page
William Edwards, Ensign, 2nd (Little Ohoopie) Company, Montgomery County	3 May 1799	p. 162
James Carr, Captain, 2nd Company, Battalion 1, Regiment 1, Burke County	3 May 1799	p. 162
Noah Parramore, Captain, Screven County	6 May 1799	p. 163
Osborne Jeffers, Lieutenant, Screven County	6 May 1799	p. 163
John Parks, Captain, 5th Company, Wilkes County	7 May 1799	p. 164
Solomon Thornton, Lieutenant, 5th Company, Wilkes County	7 May 1799	p. 164
Moses Wade, Ensign, 5th Company, Wilkes County	7 May 1799	p. 165
Allen Stewart, Captain, Volunteer Troop of Dragoons, Greene County	8 May 1799	p. 165
Samuel Dale, Cornet, Volunteer Troop of Dragoons, Greene County	8 May 1799	p. 166
James Beaty, Captain, 1st Company, Battalion 1, Regiment 2, Burke County	10 May 1799	p. 166
William Beasley, Lieutenant, 1st Company, Battalion 1, Regiment 2, Burke County	10 May 1799	p. 167
Charles Bishop, Ensign, 1st Company, Battalion 1, Regiment 2, Burke County	10 May 1799	p. 167
Mark Sanders, Major, Battalion 1, Hancock County	11 May 1799	p. 168
Robert Parham, Ensign, Battalion 1, Hancock County	11 May 1799	p. 168
Smith Cotton, Ensign, Hancock County	11 May 1799	p. 169
Timothy Barnard, Captain, Sea Island Company, Chatham County	11 May 1799	p. 169
Moses Allen, Lieutenant, Sea Island Company, Chatham County	11 May 1799	p. 170
Sampson T. Steele, Major, Battalion 2, Columbia County	13 May 1799	p. 170
John Beasley, Lieutenant, Battalion 1, Oglethorpe County	18 May 1799	p. 171
John Hardiman, Captain, Battalion 2, Oglethorpe County	18 May 1799	p. 171
William Patman, Lieutenant, Battalion 2, Oglethorpe County	18 May 1799	p. 172
Samuel Patton, Ensign, Battalion 2, Oglethorpe County	18 May 1799	p. 172
Lott Thomas, Captain, Oglethorpe County	18 May 1799	p. 173

Georgia Military Commissions, 1798–1818

Name, Rank, Unit	*Date*	*Page*
Archibald Crawley, Ensign, Oglethorpe County	18 May 1799	p. 173
John Davis, Lieutenant Colonel Commandant, Regiment 1, Burke County	23 May 1799	p. 174
John Shields, Captain, 8th Company, Jackson County	23 May 1799	p. 174
Thomas Bradshaw, Lieutenant, 8th Company, Jackson County	23 May 1799	p. 175
Henry Bradshaw, Ensign, 8th Company, Jackson County	23 May 1799	p. 175
David Ridgeway, Captain, 12th Company, Jackson County	23 May 1799	p. 176
Robert Diamond, Lieutenant, 12th Company, Jackson County	23 May 1799	p. 176
John McConnell, Ensign, 12th Company, Jackson County	23 May 1799	p. 177
David Terry, Captain, Battalion 1, Jefferson County	23 May 1799	p. 177
Thomas Peabler, Ensign, Jefferson County	23 May 1799	p. 178
Isaac Lacey, Captain, Richmond County	23 May 1799	p. 178
William Scott, Major, McIntosh County	23 May 1799	p. 179
John Howard, Captain, Washington County	15 Jun 1799	p. 179
Preston Rannolds, Captain, 14th Company, Jackson County	15 Jun 1799	p. 180
Isaac Horn, Lieutenant, 14th Company, Jackson County	15 Jun 1799	p. 180
William Harris, Ensign, 14th Company, Jackson County	15 Jun 1799	p. 181
Drury Strickland, Lieutenant, 11th Company, Jackson County	15 Jun 1799	p. 181
Sion Strickland, Ensign, 11th Company, Jackson County	15 Jun 1799	p. 182
David Hillhouse, Captain, Wilkes County	15 Jun 1799	p. 182
Andrew Hamilton, Ensign, Wilkes County	15 Jun 1799	p. 183
Dempsey Justice, Lieutenant, Rifle Company, Battalion 3, Hancock County	15 Jun 1799	p. 183
John Conner, Ensign, Rifle Company, Battalion 3, Hancock County	15 Jun 1799	p. 184
James Martin, Captain, Burke County	15 Jun 1799	p. 184
Henry Gilstrap, Lieutenant, Burke County	15 Jun 1799	p. 185
John Broome, Lieutenant, Battalion 1, Regiment 1, Burke County	15 Jun 1799	p. 185

Commissions Book 1798–1800

Name, Rank, Unit	Date	Page
William Moore, Captain, Lincoln County	15 Jun 1799	p. 186
David Miles, Lieutenant, Lincoln County	15 Jun 1799	p. 186
Asa Keeth, Ensign, Lincoln County	15 Jun 1799	p. 187
Burrill Smith, Lieutenant, Lincoln County	15 Jun 1799	p. 187
Isaac Langdon, Ensign, Lincoln County	15 Jun 1799	p. 188
Holland McTyeire, Captain, Richmond County	19 Jun 1799	p. 188
Robert McTyeire, Lieutenant, Richmond County	19 Jun 1799	p. 189
David Flanneken, Captain, Greene County	19 Jun 1799	p. 189
Dempsey Gaulding, Ensign, 4th Company, Battalion 2, Regiment 1, Burke County	20 Jun 1799	p. 190
Isaac Walker, Captain, Volunteer Company of Artillery, Burke County	20 Jun 1799	p. 190
Edmond Lowe, First Lieutenant, Volunteer Company of Artillery, Burke County	20 Jun 1799	p. 191
Peter Wynne, Second Lieutenant, Volunteer Company of Artillery, Burke County	20 Jun 1799	p. 191
John Cook, Captain, Volunteer Rifle Company, Battalion 1, Hancock County	24 Jun 1799	p. 192
James Simmons, Ensign, Volunteer Rifle Company, Battalion 1, Hancock County	24 Jun 1799	p. 192
Samuel Lockhart, Captain, 1st Company, Battalion 2, Regiment 2, Burke County	24 Jun 1799	p. 193
Drewey Spain, Ensign, 1st Company, Battalion 2, Regiment 2, Burke County	24 Jun 1799	p. 193
Adam Cope, Ensign, 1st Company, Battalion 1, Chatham County	3 Jul 1799	p. 194
Ebenezer Jackson, Second Lieutenant, Volunteer Troop of Dragoons, Chatham County	3 Jul 1799	p. 194
William Hunter, Cornet, Volunteer Troop of Dragoons, Chatham County	3 Jul 1799	p. 195
John Sheuman, Captain, Volunteer Company of Artillery, Jefferson County	8 Jul 1799	p. 195
Peter Johnston Carnes, First Lieutenant, Volunteer Company of Artillery, Jefferson County	8 Jul 1799	p. 196

Georgia Military Commissions, 1798–1818

Name, Rank, Unit	*Date*	*Page*
William Paulett, Second Lieutenant, Volunteer Company of Artillery, Jefferson County	8 Jul 1799	p. 196
William McTyeire, Captain, 1st Company, Richmond County	10 Jul 1799	p. 197
Martin Caswell, Lieutenant, 1st Company, Richmond County	10 Aug 1799	p. 197
Dennis Moriarty, Ensign, 1st Company, Richmond County	10 Jul 1799	p. 198
John Mitchell, Ensign, 3rd Company, Battalion 1, Oglethorpe County	15 Jul 1799	p. 198
James Taylor, Captain, Washington County	17 Jul 1799	p. 199
Jones Windrick, Lieutenant, Washington County	17 Jul 1799	p. 199
Allen McClaine, Ensign, Washington County	17 Jul 1799	p. 200
Peter Dennis, Ensign, Battalion 3, Hancock County	18 Jul 1799	p. 200
Vincent Chance, Captain, Upper Canouchee Company, Montgomery County	13 Jul 1799	p. 201
William Mahaffey, Lieutenant, Canouchie Company, Montgomery County	13 Jul 1799	p. 201
Charles Teakle, Ensign, Upper Canouchee Company, Montgomery County	13 Jul 1799	p. 202
Job Cokron, Lieutenant, Washington County	15 Jul 1799	p. 202
Robert Colquitt, Ensign, Washington County	15 Jul 1799	p. 203
John Beall, Lieutenant, Battalion 1, Columbia County	29 Jul 1799	p. 203
John Barnett, Captain, Franklin County	29 Jul 1799	p. 204
Gabriel Richardson, Lieutenant, Battalion 2, Hancock County	29 Jul 1799	p. 204
James Sandeford, Ensign, Liberty County	29 Jul 1799	p. 205
Francis Pickett, Captain, Lincoln County	29 Jul 1799	p. 205
Joseph Carter, Captain, Warren County	29 Jul 1799	p. 206
Robert Sandford, Lieutenant, Warren County	29 Jul 1799	p. 206
Jack Smith Davenport, Ensign, Warren County	29 Jul 1799	p. 207
Peter C* [*page torn*], Warren County	29 Jul 1799	p. 207
John Martin, Captain, 3rd Company, Battalion 2, Regiment 2, Burke County	29 Jul 1799	p. 208

Commissions Book 1798–1800

Name, Rank, Unit	Date	Page
Wright Duglass, Lieutenant, 3rd Company, Battalion 2, Regiment 2, Burke County	29 Jul 1799	p. 208
Allen Page, Ensign, 3rd Company, Battalion 2, Regiment 2, Burke County	29 Jul 1799	p. 209
Stephen Denmark, Major, Bulloch County	5 Aug 1799	p. 209
Jesse Tucker, Lieutenant, Greene County	5 Aug 1799	p. 210
Nathaniel Mercer, Ensign, Greene County	5 Aug 1799	p. 210
John McMichael, Ensign, Greene County	5 Aug 1799	p. 211
Thomas Woodward, Captain, Elbert County	14 Aug 1799	p. 211
David McCurdy, Lieutenant, Elbert County	14 Aug 1799	p. 212
William Hodge, Ensign, Elbert County	14 Aug 1799	p. 212
Reves Roland, Ensign, Greene County	20 Aug 1799	p. 213
Duglas Watson, Lieutenant, Greene County	20 Aug 1799	p. 213
Jacobus Watts, Lieutenant, Greene County	20 Aug 1799	p. 214
John Shark, Ensign, Greene County	20 Aug 1799	p. 214
John C. Mason, Captain, Hancock County	23 Aug 1799	p. 215
Britton Jones, Lieutenant, Hancock County	20 Aug 1799	p. 215
Warren West, Ensign, Greene County	23 Aug 1799	p. 216
Edward Roberson, Ensign, Burke County	23 Aug 1799	p. 216
Joseph Davis, Lieutenant, Bryan County	23 Aug 1799	p. 217
William Williams, Captain, Wilkes County	30 Aug 1799	p. 217
Fielding Thurmond, Lieutenant, Wilkes County	30 Aug 1799	p. 218
Richard Woodrooff, Ensign, Wilkes County	30 Aug 1799	p. 218
John Cowart, Captain, 1st Company, Battalion 2, Jefferson County	2 Sep 1799	p. 219
Micajah Calhoon, Ensign, 1st Company, Battalion 2, Jefferson County	2 Sep 1799	p. 219
Johnson Clarke, Captain, Jackson County	3 Sep 1799	p. 220
Cornelius McCarty, Captain, Oglethorpe County	6 Sep 1799	p. 220
Hawkins Bulloch, Lieutenant, Oglethorpe County	6 Sep 1799	p. 221
Benjamin Davis, Ensign, Oglethorpe County	6 Sep 1799	p. 221
George Moore, Captain, Volunteer Company of Dragoons, Oglethorpe County	11 Sep 1799	p. 222

Name, Rank, Unit	Date	Page
William Collier, First Lieutenant, Volunteer Company of Dragoons, Oglethorpe County	11 Sep 1799	p. 222
William Lumpkin, Second Lieutenant, Volunteer Company of Dragoons, Oglethorpe County	11 Sep 1799	p. 223
Radford Ellis, Captain, Oglethorpe County	6 Sep 1799	p. 223
John Smith, Lieutenant, Oglethorpe County	11 Sep 1799	p. 224
Alexander White, Ensign, Oglethorpe County	11 Sep 1799	p. 224
Thomas Wooton Jr., Lieutenant, Oglethorpe County	11 Sep 1799	p. 225
Robert Rivers, Captain, Hancock County	11 Sep 1799	p. 225
Mordecai Jacob, Lieutenant, Hancock County	11 Sep 1799	p. 226
John Hammock, Ensign, Hancock County	11 Sep 1799	p. 226
Henry Jackson, Lieutenant, Hancock County	11 Sep 1799	p. 227
Daniel Melson, Ensign, Hancock County	11 Sep 1799	p. 227
Zachariah Booth, Captain, Hancock County	11 Sep 1799	p. 228
Mathew Hawkins, Ensign, Hancock County	11 Sep 1799	p. 228
Cadwallader Raines, Captain, Volunteer Rifle Company, Hancock County	11 Sep 1799	p. 229
Fleming Payne, Ensign, Franklin County	17 Sep 1799	p. 229
William Coats, Lieutenant, Wilkes County	17 Sep 1799	p. 230
John Ayres, Captain, Battalion 2, Columbia County	28 Sep 1799	p. 230
Thomas Runnalds, Captain, Jackson County	28 Sep 1799	p. 231
William Parks, Lieutenant, Jackson County	28 Sep 1799	p. 231
Samuel Bugg, Captain, Volunteer Troop of Dragoons, Richmond County	1 Oct 1799	p. 232
Jody Newsom, Captain, Warren County	4 Oct 1799	p. 232
Jorden Abbott, Lieutenant, Warren County	4 Oct 1799	p. 233
Hardy Harrell, Ensign, Warren County	4 Oct 1799	p. 233
Samuel Briggs, Lieutenant, Battalion 3, Elbert County	10 Oct 1799	p. 234
Ebenezer Tolsome, Lieutenant, Jefferson County	10 Oct 1799	p. 234
James Darsey, Ensign, Jefferson County	10 Oct 1799	p. 235
John Todd, Lieutenant, Wilkes County	10 Oct 1799	p. 235
Joseph Raney, Captain, Little Ohoopie Company, Montgomery County	16 Oct 1799	p. 236

Commissions Book 1798–1800

Name, Rank, Unit	Date	Page
Joseph Spell, Lieutenant, Little Ohoopie Company, Montgomery County	16 Oct 1799	p. 236
William Cavanah, Ensign, Little Ohoopie Company, Montgomery County	16 Oct 1799	p. 237
Samson Ivey, Lieutenant, Warren County	21 Oct 1799	p. 237
James Meikum, Ensign, Warren County	21 Oct 1799	p. 238
Hugh Fruman, Lieutenant, Oglethorpe County	21 Oct 1799	p. 238
James Thompson, Lieutenant, Rifle Company, Hancock County	21 Oct 1799	p. 239
Isaac Ellis, Ensign, Hancock County	21 Oct 1799	p. 239
Josiah Beall, Captain, Hancock County	21 Oct 1799	p. 240
Eleazer Lewis, Lieutenant, 2nd Company, Battalion 2, Regiment 2, Burke County	21 Oct 1799	p. 240
Francis Hillard, Ensign, 2nd Company, Battalion 2, Regiment 2, Burke County	21 Oct 1799	p. 241
Daniel Roberts, Major, Battalion 3, Greene County	21 Oct 1799	p. 241
John Cumming Sr., Captain, Volunteer Company of Rangers, Richmond County	31 Oct 1799	p. 242
Nicholas Ware, Lieutenant, Volunteer Company of Rangers, Richmond County	31 Oct 1799	p. 242
Sterling Grimes, Ensign, Volunteer Company of Rangers, Richmond County	31 Oct 1799	p. 243
Joseph Morrow, Captain, Wilkes County	8 Nov 1799	p. 243
David Martin, Ensign, Oglethorpe County	8 Nov 1799	p. 244
Jeffery Barksdale, Captain, Hancock County	8 Nov 1799	p. 244
Peter Watters, Captain, Volunteer Rifle Company, Battalion 1, Franklin County	8 Nov 1799	p. 245
Frederick Strudlie, Lieutenant, Volunteer Rifle Company, Battalion 1, Franklin County	8 Nov 1799	p. 245
William Cawthorn, Ensign, Volunteer Rifle Company, Battalion 1, Franklin County	8 Nov 1799	p. 246
John Henderson, Captain, Franklin County	8 Nov 1799	p. 246
Benjamin Vaughan, Ensign, Franklin County	8 Nov 1799	p. 247
William Bealle Jr., Ensign, Columbia County	8 Nov 1799	p. 247

Georgia Military Commissions, 1798–1818

Name, Rank, Unit	*Date*	*Page*
Edward Ellerbee, Captain, Bulloch County	8 Nov 1799	p. 248
John Sheffield, Ensign, Bulloch County	8 Nov 1799	p. 248
William Manor, Ensign, Bulloch County	8 Nov 1799	p. 249
Thomas Hummock, Lieutenant, Wilkes County	14 Nov 1799	p. 249
John Jones, Ensign, Wilkes County	14 Nov 1799	p. 250
John McKinne, Captain, Light Infantry Company, Richmond County	16 Nov 1799	p. 250
Reuben Butter, Lieutenant, Light Infantry Company, Richmond County	16 Nov 1799	p. 251
Zachariah Williams, Ensign, Light Infantry Company, Richmond County	16 Nov 1799	p. 251
James Middleton, Captain, McIntosh County	19 Nov 1799	p. 252
James O'Berry, Lieutenant, McIntosh County	19 Nov 1799	p. 252
Andrew Bird, Ensign, McIntosh County	19 Nov 1799	p. 253
Thomas Danely, Lieutenant, Columbia County	21 Nov 1799	p. 253
Thomas Casey, Ensign, Columbia County	21 Nov 1799	p. 254
Thomas Gibbs, Captain, Bulloch County	29 Nov 1799	p. 254
James Monfort, Captain, McIntosh County	4 Dec 1799	p. 255
John Caldwell, Lieutenant, McIntosh County	4 Dec 1799	p. 255
William Machey, Captain, Volunteer Troop of Dragoons, Elbert County	4 Dec 1799	p. 256
Edward Storey, Lieutenant, Volunteer Troop of Dragoons, Elbert County	4 Dec 1799	p. 256
Eliot Hodge, Second Lieutenant, Volunteer Troop of Dragoons, Elbert County	4 Dec 1799	p. 257
Robert Moore, Cornet, Volunteer Troop of Dragoons, Elbert County	4 Dec 1799	p. 257
Caleb Cocke, Captain, Burke County	9 Jan 1800	p. 258
David Fitzjarrel, Lieutenant, Burke County	9 Jan 1800	p. 258
Stephen Cross, Ensign, Burke County	9 Jan 1800	p. 259
Burrel Smith, Captain, Lincoln County	9 Jan 1800	p. 259
Frederick Conner, Lieutenant, Lincoln County	9 Jan 1800	p. 260
Joel Ball, Ensign, Lincoln County	9 Jan 1800	p. 260
Thomas Pace, Captain, Washington County	9 Jan 1800	p. 261

Commissions Book 1798–1800

Name, Rank, Unit	Date	Page
Nathaniel Pace, Ensign, Washington County	9 Jan 1800	p. 261
Robert Jackson, Captain, Washington County	9 Jan 1800	p. 262
Elkanah Briggs, Ensign, Warren County	22 Jan 1800	p. 262
Samuel Montgomery, Lieutenant, Jefferson County	22 Jan 1800	p. 263
Whitehouse Brunson, Ensign, Jefferson County	22 Jan 1800	p. 263
David Thomas, Ensign, Louisville Company, Jefferson County	8 Feb 1800	p. 264
James Patterson, Major, Wilkes County	24 Feb 1800	p. 264
William Ogletree, Captain, Wilkes County	24 Feb 1800	p. 265
Benjamin Edwards, Lieutenant, Wilkes County	24 Feb 1800	p. 265
Nathan Bryant, Ensign, Wilkes County	24 Feb 1800	p. 266
Robert Rayston, Captain, Greene County	24 Feb 1800	p. 266
Epps Duke, Lieutenant, Greene County	24 Feb 1800	p. 267
James McCall, Ensign, Greene County	24 Feb 1800	p. 267
Thomas Haynes, Lieutenant, Greene County	24 Feb 1800	p. 268
James Harvel, Ensign, Greene County	24 Feb 1800	p. 268
Thomas Dickson, Captain, Battalion 3, Hancock County	24 Feb 1800	p. 269
Nehemiah Smith, Lieutenant, Battalion 3, Hancock County	24 Feb 1800	p. 269
Robert McCash, Ensign, Battalion 3, Hancock County	24 Feb 1800	p. 270
Abraham Minis, Lieutenant, Chatham County	7 Mar 1800	p. 270
George M. Troup, Ensign, Chatham County	7 Mar 1800	p. 271
Richard Dennis, Lieutenant, Chatham County	7 Mar 1800	p. 271
Solomon Thornton, Captain, Wilkes County	7 Mar 1800	p. 272
George Gresham, Lieutenant, Wilkes County	7 Mar 1800	p. 272
Robert McKnight, Ensign, Wilkes County	7 Mar 1800	p. 273
William Gerrard, Lieutenant, Wilkes County	7 Mar 1800	p. 273
John Latimer, Captain, Battalion 3, Hancock County	7 Mar 1800	p. 274
John Howell, Lieutenant, Battalion 3, Hancock County	7 Mar 1800	p. 274
Hezekiah Howell, Ensign, Battalion 3, Hancock County	7 Mar 1800	p. 275
William Good, Captain, Elbert County	7 Mar 1800	p. 275
William Hales, Lieutenant, Elbert County	7 Mar 1800	p. 276
Richardson Booker, Ensign, Elbert County	7 Mar 1800	p. 276

Georgia Military Commissions, 1798–1818

Name, Rank, Unit	Date	Page
Shaler Hillger, Lieutenant, Elbert County	7 Mar 1800	p. 277
Rowland Cornelius, Captain, Franklin County	7 Mar 1800	p. 277
David Crews, Lieutenant, Franklin County	7 Mar 1800	p. 278
Abraham Hunter, Captain, Screven County	7 Mar 1800	p. 278
George Owens, Captain, Battalion 3, Greene County	7 Mar 1800	p. 279
John Friar, Lieutenant, Burke County	7 Mar 1800	p. 279
Basdel Sharpe, Ensign, Burke County	7 Mar 1800	p. 280
Freeman Walker, Ensign, Volunteer Company of Rangers, Richmond County	7 Mar 1800	p. 280
Stephen Marshall, Captain, Warren County	7 Mar 1800	p. 281
Archilaus F. Ellen, Lieutenant, Warren County	7 Mar 1800	p. 281
John Seale, Captain, Lincoln County	11 Mar 1800	p. 282
Henry West, Lieutenant, Lincoln County	11 Mar 1800	p. 282
Thomas Gresham, Second Lieutenant, Lincoln County	11 Mar 1800	p. 283
Presley Barton, Cornet, Volunteer Troop of Dragoons	11 Mar 1800	p. 283
Peter Arrant, Lieutenant, Lincoln County	11 Mar 1800	p. 284
Archibald York, Ensign, Lincoln County	11 Mar 1800	p. 284
Alexander McDonald, Lieutenant, Lincoln County	11 Mar 1800	p. 285
Overton Walton, Ensign, Lincoln County	11 Mar 1800	p. 285
Patten Wise, Lieutenant, Oglethorpe County	11 Mar 1800	p. 286
Jacob McCleroy, Ensign, Oglethorpe County	11 Mar 1800	p. 286
William Johnson, Lieutenant Colonel Commandant, Wilkes County	14 Mar 1800	p. 287
Jesse Warren, Captain, 3rd Company, Liberty County	17 Mar 1800	p. 287
John Pigot Jr., Lieutenant, 3rd Company, Liberty County	17 Mar 1800	p. 288
John Largent, Ensign, 4th Company, Liberty County	17 Mar 1800	p. 288
Elisha Matthews, Captain, Battalion 3, Hancock County	19 Mar 1800	p. 289
Allen Jenkins, Lieutenant, Battalion 3, Hancock County	19 Mar 1800	p. 289
Reddich Watson, Ensign, Washington County	20 Mar 1800	p. 290
Stephen Blount, Captain, 1st Company, Battalion 1, Chatham County	25 Mar 1800	p. 290
Henry Barks, Captain, Lincoln County	29 Mar 1800	p. 291

Name, Rank, Unit	Date	Page
James Sandiford, Lieutenant, 2nd Company (Volunteer Troop of Dragoons), Liberty County	31 Mar 1800	p. 291
John Osgood Jr., Ensign, 2nd Company (Volunteer Troop of Dragoons), Liberty County	31 Mar 1800	p. 292
Samuel Sprylaw, Second Lieutenant, Volunteer Troop of Dragoons, Liberty County	31 Mar 1800	p. 292
Paul Grimball, Cornet, Volunteer Troop of Dragoons, Liberty County	31 Mar 1800	p. 293
Thomas Charleton, Ensign, 4th (Church) Company, Battalion 1, Chatham County	31 Mar 1800	p. 293
Richard Dennis, Captain, Chatham Hibernian Fusiliers, Battalion 1, Chatham County	31 Mar 1800	p. 294
Joseph Arnold, Lieutenant, Chatham Hibernian Fusiliers, Battalion 1, Chatham County	31 Mar 1800	p. 294
Thomas Callaghan, Ensign, Chatham Hibernian Fusiliers, Battalion 1, Chatham County	31 Mar 1800	p. 295
Thomas De Mattos Johnson, Major, Jefferson County	3 Apr 1800	p. 295
Thompson Coleman, Captain, Wilkes County	12 Apr 1800	p. 296
Jonathan Oxford, Lieutenant, Wilkes County	12 Apr 1800	p. 296
Garland Cosby, Ensign, Wilkes County	12 Apr 1800	p. 297
Sittleton Reese, First Lieutenant, Volunteer Troop of Dragoons, Hancock County	12 Apr 1800	p. 297
Leonard Abercrombie, Second Lieutenant, Volunteer Troop of Dragoons, Hancock County	12 Apr 1800	p. 298
Michael Schley, Captain, Louisville Company, Jefferson County	14 Apr 1800	p. 298
Moses Daniel, Captain, Washington County	14 Apr 1800	p. 299
Thomas Holland, Ensign, Battalion 3, Greene County	14 Apr 1800	p. 299
Joseph Blackshear, Captain, Washington County	22 Apr 1800	p. 300
William Allen, Lieutenant, Washington County	22 Apr 1800	p. 300
John Marsh, Ensign, 3rd Company, Battalion 2, Regiment 2, Burke County	30 Apr 1800	p. 301
Jacob Robinson, Lieutenant, Louisville Company, Jefferson County	30 Apr 1800	p. 301

Georgia Military Commissions, 1798–1818

Name, Rank, Unit	Date	Page
Peter Wynne, First Lieutenant, Volunteer Company of Artillary, Burke County	30 Apr 1800	p. 302
Elam Yarbrough, Second Lieutenant, Volunteer Company of Artillery, Burke County	30 Apr 1800	p. 302
Nimrod Jones, Ensign, Battalion 1, Columbia County	2 May 1800	p. 303
Thomas J. Presswood, Captain, Dead River Company, Montgomery County	2 May 1800	p. 303
George Vinson, Ensign, Dead River Company, Montgomery County	2 May 1800	p. 304
Thomas Newbern, Lieutenant, Lower Big Ohoopie Company, Montgomery County	2 May 1800	p. 304
Jesse Lott, Ensign, Lower Big Ohoopie Company, Montgomery County	2 May 1800	p. 305
Joseph Burch, Captain, Silver Bluff Company, Montgomery County	2 May 1800	p. 305
Daniel Johnston, Lieutenant, Silver Bluff Company, Montgomery County	2 May 1800	p. 306
Charles Burch, Ensign, Silver Bluff Company, Montgomery County	2 May 1800	p. 306
Zachariah Jirkins, Captain, Lower Canouchie Company, Montgomery County	2 May 1800	p. 307
Caleb McKenny, Lieutenant, Lower Canouchie Company, Montgomery County	2 May 1800	p. 307
Charles Parlin, Lieutenant, Saw Mill Company, Montgomery County	2 May 1800	p. 308
Isaac Mott, Ensign, Saw Mill Company, Montgomery County	2 May 1800	p. 308
Samuel Pinkham, Ensign, Lower Canouchie Company, Montgomery County	2 May 1800	p. 309
James Thomas, Captain, Saw Mill Company, Montgomery County	2 May 1800	p. 309
Edward Ware, Lieutenant Colonel Commandant, Elbert County	7 May 1800	p. 310
Oliver Porter, Major, Battalion 1, Greene County	7 May 1800	p. 310
Samuel Wilborn, Major, Wilkes County	7 May 1800	p. 311

Name, Rank, Unit	**Date**	**Page**
James Wylee, Captain, Wilkes County	7 May 1800	p. 311
James Render, Lieutenant, Wilkes County	7 May 1800	p. 312
Allen Martin, Ensign, Wilkes County	7 May 1800	p. 312
Levi Bush, Ensign, Warren County	12 May 1800	p. 313
Joseph Law Jr., Major, Liberty County	12 May 1800	p. 313
James Montfort, Major, McIntosh County	12 May 1800	p. 314
Joseph B. Chambers, Captain, Hancock County	12 May 1800	p. 314
William Maddox Jr., Lieutenant, Hancock County	12 May 1800	p. 315
Littleton Carter, Ensign, Hancock County	12 May 1800	p. 315
Samuel Davis, Major, Lincoln County	16 May 1800	p. 316
Alexander Reed, Captain, Hancock County	19 May 1800	p. 316
William Barnes, Lieutenant, Hancock County	19 May 1800	p. 317
William Williams, Captain, Hancock County	19 May 1800	p. 317
Nathaniel Halley, Lieutenant, Hancock County	19 May 1800	p. 318
John Hatcher, Major, Warren County	21 May 1800	p. 318
Henry Forth, Lieutenant, 4th Company, Battalion 2, Regiment 1, Burke County	21 May 1800	p. 319
John Hamett, Ensign, 4th Company, Battalion 2, Regiment 1, Burke County	21 May 1800	p. 319
Elijah Grooms, Captain, Washington County	21 May 1800	p. 320
William Kennedey, Lieutenant, Washington County	21 May 1800	p. 320
Isaac Fuller, Ensign, Washington County	21 May 1800	p. 321
Daniel Gillashie, Ensign, Washington County	21 May 1800	p. 321
Joseph Marshall, Ensign, Louisville Company, Jefferson County	3 Jun 1800	p. 322
James Moore, Ensign, Volunteer Company of Light Infantry, Battalion 1, Regiment 2, Burke County	3 Jun 1800	p. 322
Wyott Bettice, Lieutenant, Washington County	3 Jun 1800	p. 323
Thomas Sheppard, Ensign, Washington County	10 Jun 1800	p. 323
John Blake, Captain, Elbert County	11 Jun 1800	p. 324
Robert Kennedy, Lieutenant, Elbert County	11 Jun 1800	p. 324
John Dudley, Ensign, Elbert County	11 Jun 1800	p. 325
Elias Alexander, Lieutenant, Elbert County	11 Jun 1800	p. 325

Georgia Military Commissions, 1798–1818

Name, Rank, Unit	Date	Page
William McKenzie, Ensign, Elbert County	11 Jun 1800	p. 326
Sutton Green, Lieutenant, Volunteer Troop of Dragoons, Franklin County	11 Jun 1800	p. 326
Eli Townsend, Captain, Jackson County	16 Jun 1800	p. 327
James Cunningham, Ensign, Jackson County	16 Jun 1800	p. 327
James Cockran, Captain, Jackson County	16 Jun 1800	p. 328
Daniel Lyle, Ensign, Jackson County	16 Jun 1800	p. 328
Aaron Johnson, Captain, Elbert County	16 Jun 1800	p. 329
Thomas Thompson, Lieutenant, Elbert County	16 Jun 1800	p. 329
Jacob Segraves, Ensign, Elbert County	16 Jun 1800	p. 330
William Coates, Captain, Wilkes County	16 Jun 1800	p. 330
Oliver Prince, Lieutenant, Wilkes County	16 Jun 1800	p. 331
Robert A. Gardner, Ensign, Wilkes County	16 Jun 1800	p. 331
Samuel Spencer, Captain, 1st Company, Liberty County	16 Jun 1800	p. 332
John Bacon, Lieutenant, 1st Company, Liberty County	16 Jun 1800	p. 332
William Flemming, Ensign, 1st Company, Liberty County	16 Jun 1800	p. 333
Andrew Maybank, Captain, 4th Company, Liberty County	16 Jun 1800	p. 333
George Tuggle, Captain, Battalion 3, Greene County	16 Jun 1800	p. 334
Henry Caboness, Lieutenant, Battalion 3, Greene County	16 Jun 1800	p. 334
Jareld Beasley, Ensign, Battalion 3, Greene County	16 Jun 1800	p. 335
Edward Bryan, Major, Battalion 1, Washington County	23 Jun 1800	p. 335
John Jacob Bourguoin, Lieutenant, Chatham County	25 Jun 1800	p. 336
Samuel Hastings Stackhouse, Ensign, Chatham County	25 Jun 1800	p. 336
John Hogan, Captain, Volunteer Troop of Dragoons, Washington County	26 Jun 1800	p. 337
Abraham Colson, Lieutenant, Screven County	26 Jun 1800	p. 337
Joseph Curry, Ensign, Screven County	26 Jun 1800	p. 338
Jesse Lofftley, Lieutenant, Jefferson County	27 Jun 1800	p. 338
Barrett Brewer, Captain, Warren County	27 Jun 1800	p. 339
Thomas Franklin, Lieutenant, Upper Big Ohoopie Company, Montgomery County	2 Jul 1800	p. 339
Stephen Munday, Ensign, Upper Big Ohoopie Company, Montgomery County	2 Jul 1800	p. 340

Name, Rank, Unit	*Date*	*Page*
Furney Holiday, Lieutenant, Burke County	12 Jul 1800	p. 340
Mark Holton, Ensign, Burke County	12 Jul 1800	p. 341
Norman Morrison, Captain, Elbert County	12 Jul 1800	p. 341
Robert Cohorn, Lieutenant, Screven County	12 Jul 1800	p. 342
Charles West, Lieutenant, Washington County	12 Jul 1800	p. 342
Averet Harper, Ensign, Washington County	12 Jul 1800	p. 343
William Smith, Ensign, Washington County	24 Jul 1800	p. 343
Samuel Brady, Lieutenant, Warren County	28 Jul 1800	p. 344
James Durham, Ensign, Warren County	28 Jul 1800	p. 344
Samuel McGehe, Lieutenant, Elbert County	28 Jul 1800	p. 345
Robert Clark, Captain, Hancock County	1 Aug 1800	p. 345
Shadrach Roe, Ensign, Hancock County	1 Aug 1800	p. 346
William Watts, Ensign, Wilkes County	1 Aug 1800	p. 346
William Grimes, Captain, Elbert County	6 Aug 1800	p. 347
John Kilgore, Lieutenant, Elbert County	6 Aug 1800	p. 347
John Appleby, Ensign, Elbert County	6 Aug 1800	p. 348
Jesse Rice, Lieutenant, Columbia County	6 Aug 1800	p. 348
James Moore, Lieutenant, Jackson County	6 Aug 1800	p. 349
George White, Ensign, Jackson County	6 Aug 1800	p. 349
Robert McKeever, Lieutenant, Jackson County	6 Aug 1800	p. 350
Joshua Scurlock, Captain, Jackson County	6 Aug 1800	p. 350
Philip Corker, Lieutenant, Jackson County	6 Aug 1800	p. 351
Bartlet Adkins, Ensign, Jackson County	6 Aug 1800	p. 351
James Hendricks, Captain, Jackson County	6 Aug 1800	p. 352
George Humphries, Lieutenant, Jackson County	6 Aug 1800	p. 352
Isaac Abney, Ensign, Jackson County	6 Aug 1800	p. 353

Georgia Military Commissions
Commissions Book 1800–1806

Name, Rank, Unit	*Date*	*Page*
Joshua Kennedy, Captain, Battalion 1, Washington County	11 Aug 1800	p. 1
James Jackson, Captain, Washington County	11 Aug 1800	p. 1
Isaac Mallett, Lieutenant, Washington County	11 Aug 1800	p. 2
Elisha Renfroe, Ensign, Washington County	11 Aug 1800	p. 2
James Espey, Captain, Lincoln County	15 Aug 1800	p. 3
Jesse Bunkley, Major, Battalion 2, Warren County	13 Aug 1800	p. 3
Henry Trippe, Lieutenant, Volunteer Company of Riflemen, Hancock County	13 Aug 1800	p. 4
William McCoy, Captain, McIntosh County	8 Sep 1800	p. 4
Archibald Campbell, Lieutenant, McIntosh County	8 Sep 1800	p. 5
Donald McDonald, Ensign, McIntosh County	8 Sep 1800	p. 5
John Dozier, Lieutenant, Columbia County	8 Sep 1800	p. 6
David Langston, Lieutenant, Columbia County	8 Sep 1800	p. 6
Alexander Bellamy, Ensign, Hancock Company, Columbia County	8 Sep 1800	p. 7
James Oliver, Captain, Screven County	8 Sep 1800	p. 7
Henry Cragg, Lieutenant, Screven County	8 Sep 1800	p. 8
John Alders, Ensign, Screven County	8 Sep 1800	p. 8
Michael Burke, Captain, Bryan County	15 Sep 1800	p. 9
Thomas Mann, Lieutenant, Bryan County	15 Sep 1800	p. 9
Henry Austin, Ensign, Bryan County	15 Sep 1800	p. 10
Samuel Coleman, Ensign, Greene County	17 Sep 1800	p. 10
Benjamin Gobert Jr., Ensign, Louisville Company, Jefferson County	17 Sep 1800	p. 11
Nicholas Innis, Ensign, Burke County	18 Sep 1800	p. 11
Abel Loper, Captain, Effingham County	22 Sep 1800	p. 12
Thomas Nelms, Lieutenant, Liberty County	29 Sep 1800	p. 12
John Lawson, Ensign, Liberty County	29 Sep 1800	p. 13
Thomas Edmondson, Captain, Battalion 1, Columbia County	29 Sep 1800	p. 13
James Luke, Lieutenant, Battalion 1, Columbia County	29 Sep 1800	p. 14
Richard Roberts, Ensign, Battalion 1, Columbia County	29 Sep 1800	p. 14
James Ramsey, Lieutenant, Battalion 1, Columbia County	29 Sep 1800	p. 15
William Ellis, Ensign, Battalion 1, Columbia County	29 Sep 1800	p. 15

Georgia Military Commissions, 1798–1818

Name, Rank, Unit	*Date*	*Page*
John Lewis, Lieutenant, Hancock County	13 Oct 1800	p. 16
Robert Hudgins, Ensign, Hancock County	13 Oct 1800	p. 16
Archilus Jarrett, Captain, Elbert County	11 Oct 1800	p. 17
Jesse Suttle, Lieutenant, Elbert County	11 Oct 1800	p. 17
Robert Fleming, Lieutenant, Jefferson County	15 Oct 1800	p. 18
Benjamin Browning, Ensign, Jefferson County	15 Oct 1800	p. 18
Charles Dougherty, Major, Regiment 1, Jackson County	7 Nov 1800	p. 19
Roderick Easley, Lieutenant Colonel Commandant, Regiment 1, Jackson County	7 Nov 1800	p. 19
John H. Morel, Ensign, 2nd Company, Chatham County	7 Nov 1800	p. 20
Jesse Evans, Captain, Greene County	7 Nov 1800	p. 20
Thomas Scott, Captain, Hancock County	7 Nov 1800	p. 21
William Hudson, Ensign, Hancock County	7 Nov 1800	p. 21
John Gray, Lieutenant, Hancock County	7 Nov 1800	p. 22
Michael Jolly, Ensign, Lincoln County	7 Nov 1800	p. 22
Luke Moore, Lieutenant, Washington County	7 Nov 1800	p. 23
John Culpepper, Lieutenant, Washington County	7 Nov 1800	p. 23
John Hampton, Major, Battalion 1, Regiment 2, Jackson County	8 Nov 1800	p. 24
Joseph Carson, Major, Battalion 2, Regiment 2, Jackson County	8 Nov 1800	p. 24
Buckner Harris, Lieutenant Colonel Commandant, Regiment 2, Jackson County	8 Nov 1800	p. 25
David Eberhart, Captain, Elbert County	11 Nov 1800	p. 25
James Wood, Lieutenant, Elbert County	11 Nov 1800	p. 26
William Pearson, Ensign, Elbert County	11 Nov 1800	p. 26
Moses Jones, Lieutenant, Lincoln County	13 Nov 1800	p. 27
Burrell Dunefant, Ensign, Lincoln County	13 Nov 1800	p. 27
Robert Nobles, Ensign, Jackson County	13 Nov 1800	p. 28
James Johnston, Captain, Volunteer Corps of Savannah Rangers, Chatham County	20 Nov 1800	p. 28
William Daniel, Captain, Jackson County	26 Nov 1800	p. 29
John Pittman, Lieutenant, Jackson County	26 Nov 1800	p. 29
Burrell Williams, Ensign, Jackson County	26 Nov 1800	p. 30
William Wortham, Captain, Jackson County	26 Nov 1800	p. 30
Joseph Simmonds, Lieutenant, Jackson County	26 Nov 1800	p. 31
George Conner, Ensign, Jackson County	26 Nov 1800	p. 31

Name, Rank, Unit	Date	Page
Aaron Wood, Captain, Jackson County	26 Nov 1800	p. 32
Richard Easley, Ensign, Jackson County	26 Nov 1800	p. 32
Tharpe Spence, Captain, Volunteer Troop of Dragoons, Regiment 2, Burke County	26 Nov 1800	p. 33
James Pugh, First Lieutenant, Volunteer Troop of Dragoons, Regiment 2, Burke County	26 Nov 1800	p. 33
William Patterson, Second Lieutenant, Volunteer Troop of Dragoons, Regiment 2, Burke County	26 Nov 1800	p. 34
Daniel Moxley, Cornet, Volunteer Troop of Dragoons, Regiment 2, Burke County	26 Nov 1800	p. 34
Joshua Zant, Lieutenant, Effingham County	26 Nov 1800	p. 35
Nicholas Pope, Ensign, Battalion 3, Elbert County	26 Nov 1800	p. 35
John Peace, Ensign, Hancock County	26 Nov 1800	p. 36
Robert Flournoy, First Lieutenant, Volunteer Company of Artillery, Jefferson County	26 Nov 1800	p. 36
William Cook, Lieutenant, Volunteer Company of Light Infantry, Richmond County	26 Nov 1800	p. 37
Oliver Sturges, Ensign, Volunteer Troop of Light Infantry, Richmond County	26 Nov 1800	p. 37
Abraham Greeson, Ensign, Warren County	26 Nov 1800	p. 38
Daniel Johnson, Captain, Wilkes County	26 Nov 1800	p. 38
Peter Kent, Lieutenant, Wilkes County	26 Nov 1800	p. 39
William Robey, Ensign, Wilkes County	26 Nov 1800	p. 39
William Weathers, Ensign, Burke County	27 Nov 1800	p. 40
Benjamin Leggett, Ensign, Jefferson County	27 Nov 1800	p. 40
Thomas Scott, Captain, Volunteer Company of Light Infantry, Oglethorpe County	28 Nov 1800	p. 41
John Kidd, Lieutenant, Volunteer Troop of Light Infantry, Oglethorpe County	28 Nov 1800	p. 41
William Wayne, Ensign, Volunteer Company of Light Infantry, Oglethorpe County	28 Nov 1800	p. 42
Vaul Hollingswoth, Lieutenant, Screven County	28 Nov 1800	p. 42
Abram Roberts, Ensign, Screven County	28 Nov 1800	p. 43
Thomas Watts, Lieutenant, Greene County	29 Nov 1800	p. 43
David McIntosh, Lieutenant, Greene County	29 Nov 1800	p. 44
John Reid, Ensign, Greene County	29 Nov 1800	p. 44
Thomas Doles, Ensign, Warren County	1 Dec 1800	p. 45
Randolph Traylor, Captain, Jackson County	1 Dec 1800	p. 45

Georgia Military Commissions, 1798–1818

Name, Rank, Unit	Date	Page
Luke Patrick, Ensign, Jackson County	1 Dec 1800	p. 46
T. L. D. Montmollin, Lieutenant, Volunteer Corps of Savannah Rangers, Chatham County	27 Dec 1800	p. 46
Benjamin Ansley, Ensign, Volunteer Corps of Savannah Rangers, Chatham County	27 Dec 1800	p. 47
James Alston, Captain, Elbert County	27 Dec 1800	p. 47
William Fortson, Lieutenant, Elbert County	27 Dec 1800	p. 48
Wylly Thompson, Ensign, Elbert County	27 Dec 1800	p. 48
Dennis Lindsy, Ensign, Warren County	27 Dec 1800	p. 49
Thomas Carter, Lieutenant, Wilkes County	27 Dec 1800	p. 49
Brooks Modishead, Lieutenant, Jackson County	12 Jan 1801	p. 50
Francis Brown, Lieutenant, Jefferson County	12 Jan 1801	p. 50
Charles Huddlecy, Captain, Franklin County	12 Jan 1801	p. 51
Cornelius Cooper, Lieutenant, Franklin County	12 Jan 1801	p. 51
John Nelson, Ensign, Franklin County	12 Jan 1801	p. 52
William Wilcox, Captain, Franklin County	12 Jan 1801	p. 52
Silas McGrady, Lieutenant, Franklin County	12 Jan 1801	p. 53
William Vaughan, Ensign, Jackson County	12 Jan 1801	p. 53
Bedney Franklin, Captain, Franklin County	12 Jan 1801	p. 54
William Stewart, Captain, Oglethorpe County	12 Jan 1801	p. 54
Thomas Lloyd, Lieutenant, Oglethorpe County	12 Jan 1801	p. 55
Lawrence Briers, Ensign, Oglethorpe County	12 Jan 1801	p. 55
Daniel Smith, Ensign, Oglethorpe County	12 Jan 1801	p. 56
Josiah Jackson, Ensign, Lincoln County	12 Jan 1801	p. 56
Jacob Henton, Ensign, Oglethorpe County	17 Jan 1801	p. 57
Jonathan Richardson, Ensign, Washington County	5 Feb 1801	p. 57
John Cormick, Captain, Volunteer Company of Rangers, Richmond County	5 Feb 1801	p. 58
Allen Daniel, Major, Elbert County	5 Feb 1801	p. 58
Isaac Phillips, Captain, Jackson County	6 Feb 1801	p. 59
Alexander Autrey, Lieutenant, Jackson County	6 Feb 1801	p. 59
John Harris, Ensign, Jackson County	6 Feb 1801	p. 60
James Courson, Ensign, Volunteer Rifle Company, Battalion 3, Hancock County	6 Feb 1801	p. 60
Shadrach Wall, Ensign, Washington County	6 Feb 1801	p. 61
Robert Salters, Lieutenant, Washington County	11 Feb 1801	p. 61
James Walker Jr., Ensign, Washington County	11 Feb 1801	p. 62

Commissions Book 1800–1806

Name, Rank, Unit	*Date*	*Page*
Samuel Garrett, Ensign, Washington County	11 Feb 1801	p. 62
John Stith, Captain, Battalion 2, Columbia County	16 Feb 1801	p. 63
Thomas Forth, Captain, Burke County	16 Feb 1801	p. 63
Furney Holliday, Captain, Burke County	16 Feb 1801	p. 64
Daniel Henderson, Lieutenant, Burke County	16 Feb 1801	p. 64
Thomas Burke, Captain, Burke County	16 Feb 1801	p. 65
Thomas Sykes, Lieutenant, Burke County	16 Feb 1801	p. 65
James Morton, Major, Washington County	19 Feb 1801	p. 66
John Howard, Major, Battalion 3, Washington County	19 Feb 1801	p. 66
William Scott, Lieutenant, Volunteer Company of Rangers, Richmond County	28 Feb 1801	p. 67
Hezekiah Lord, Ensign, Volunteer Company of Rangers, Richmond County	28 Feb 1801	p. 67
Richard Gray, Captain, Jefferson County	6 Mar 1801	p. 68
Mills Murphree, Lieutenant Colonel Commandant, Regiment 2, Burke County	6 Mar 1801	p. 68
Joseph Marshall, Ensign, Jefferson County	9 Mar 1801	p. 69
Charles Cavenah Jenkins, Captain, Volunteer Troop of Dragoons, Jefferson County	9 Mar 1801	p. 69
William Williams, Captain, Wilkes County	9 Mar 1801	p. 70
Fielding L. Thurman, Lieutenant, Wilkes County	9 Mar 1801	p. 70
Thomas Harper, Ensign, Wilkes County	9 Mar 1801	p. 71
William Duncan, Lieutenant, Elbert County	9 Mar 1801	p. 71
Aaron Duncan, Ensign, Elbert County	9 Mar 1801	p. 72
James Gaddy, Captain, Effingham County	12 Mar 1801	p. 72
James King, Ensign, Effingham County	12 Mar 1801	p. 73
John Carswell, Captain, Regiment 1, Burke County	12 Mar 1801	p. 73
Archibald Hatcher, Captain, Richmond County	16 Mar 1801	p. 74
Joel Hill, Lieutenant, Richmond County	16 Mar 1801	p. 74
Dempsey Philips, Ensign, Richmond County	16 Mar 1801	p. 75
Cornelius Murphey, Captain, Battalion 3, Washington County	16 Mar 1801	p. 75
George Prince, Captain, Jefferson County	16 Mar 1801	p. 76
William Blake, Captain, Jackson County	16 Mar 1801	p. 76
James Turner, Lieutenant, Jackson County	16 Mar 1801	p. 77
John Williamson, Ensign, Jackson County	16 Mar 1801	p. 77
Zadock Cook, Captain, Jackson County	16 Mar 1801	p. 78

Georgia Military Commissions, 1798–1818

Name, Rank, Unit	*Date*	*Page*
Silas Downs, Lieutenant, Jackson County	16 Mar 1801	p. 78
Henry Shaw, Ensign, Jackson County	16 Mar 1801	p. 79
Thomas Barnes, Ensign, Hancock County	23 Mar 1801	p. 79
William P. Beal, Lieutenant, Columbia County	23 Mar 1801	p. 80
Thomas Newman, Captain, Lower Big Ohoopie Company, Montgomery County	25 Mar 1801	p. 80
Simon Williams, Lieutenant, Lower Big Ohoopie Company, Montgomery County	25 Mar 1801	p. 81
Abel Cain, Ensign, Lower Big Ohoopie Company, Montgomery County	25 Mar 1801	p. 81
Peter Thomas, Captain, Court House Company, Montgomery County	25 Mar 1801	p. 82
William Hall, Lieutenant, Court House Company, Montgomery County	25 Mar 1801	p. 82
David Mann, Ensign, Court House Company, Montgomery County	25 Mar 1801	p. 83
George Valley, Captain, Saw Mill Company, Montgomery County	25 Mar 1801	p. 83
William Cone, Lieutenant, Saw Mill Company, Montgomery County	25 Mar 1801	p. 84
John Smith, Ensign, Saw Mill Company, Montgomery County	25 Mar 1801	p. 84
Samuel Harrison, Captain, Oconee Company, Montgomery County	25 Mar 1801	p. 85
Samuel Swearingham, Lieutenant, Oconee Company, Montgomery County	25 Mar 1801	p. 85
John Swearingham, Ensign, Oconee Company, Montgomery County	25 Mar 1801	p. 86
Joseph Spell, Captain, Little Ohoopie Company, Montgomery County	25 Mar 1801	p. 86
Henry Jordan, Lieutenant, Little Ohoopie Company, Montgomery County	25 Mar 1801	p. 87
Duncan Thompson, Captain, Silver Bluff Company, Montgomery County	25 Mar 1801	p. 87
Reubin Roland, Ensign, Big Ohoopie Company, Montgomery County	25 Mar 1801	p. 88
Jesse Bird, Captain, Lower Canouchie Company, Montgomery County	25 Mar 1801	p. 88
Gideon Mayo, Lieutenant, Big Ohoopie Company, Montgomery County	25 Mar 1801	p. 89

Commissions Book 1800–1806

Name, Rank, Unit	Date	Page
John McKenney, Lieutenant, Lower Canouchie Company, Montgomery County	25 Mar 1801	p. 89
John Martin, Captain, Franklin County	30 Mar 1801	p. 90
Elijah Martin, Lieutenant, Franklin County	30 Mar 1801	p. 90
Aaron Carathers, Ensign, Franklin County	30 Mar 1801	p. 91
Middleton Fanning, Ensign, Elbert County	1 Apr 1801	p. 91
William Lloyd, Captain, Jackson County	1 Apr 1801	p. 92
Sheppard Williams, Lieutenant, Bulloch County	2 Apr 1801	p. 92
John Lee, Ensign, Bulloch County	2 Apr 1801	p. 93
John McDonald, Ensign, Montgomery County	2 Apr 1801	p. 93
Abner Davis, Major, Montgomery County	2 Apr 1801	p. 94
Jess Embree, Major, Montgomery County	2 Apr 1801	p. 94
Thomas Davis, Lieutenant Colonel Commandant, Montgomery County	2 Apr 1801	p. 95
Hopkins Dye, Major, Burke County	2 Apr 1801	p. 95
Isaac Mallett, Captain, Battalion 3, Washington County	2 Apr 1801	p. 96
John Pray, Major, Bryan County	6 Apr 1801	p. 96
John Sanderford, Captain, Burke County	6 Apr 1801	p. 97
John Almon, Ensign, Burke County	6 Apr 1801	p. 97
Richard Warren, Major, Burke County	16 Apr 1801	p. 98
James Render, Captain, Wilkes County	20 Apr 1801	p. 98
John Heard, Lieutenant, Wilkes County	20 Apr 1801	p. 99
Willis Martin, Ensign, Wilkes County	20 Apr 1801	p. 99
Nathan Chaffin, Captain, Wilkes County	20 Apr 1801	p. 100
William Gartrell, Ensign, Wilkes County	20 Apr 1801	p. 100
Benjamin J. Harper, Lieutenant, Hancock County	20 Apr 1801	p. 101
John Harper, Ensign, Hancock County	20 Apr 1801	p. 101
Archibald Traylor, Ensign, Hancock County	20 Apr 1801	p. 102
Edmond Thomason, Ensign, Elbert County	20 Apr 1801	p. 102
Eleazer Bell, Captain, Effingham County	20 Apr 1801	p. 103
Paul Toossing, Lieutenant, Effingham County	20 Apr 1801	p. 103
David Mitzker, Ensign, Effingham County	20 Apr 1801	p. 104
Henry Peeke, Lieutenant, Columbia County	28 Apr 1801	p. 104
Samuel Germany, Ensign, Columbia County	28 Apr 1801	p. 105
Noah Ramsey, Ensign, Columbia County	28 Apr 1801	p. 105
Elijah Christie, Lieutenant, Jefferson County	28 Apr 1801	p. 106
Joseph Tommy, Ensign, Jefferson County	28 Apr 1801	p. 106

Georgia Military Commissions, 1798–1818

Name, Rank, Unit	Date	Page
William Hanner, Ensign, Jefferson County	28 Apr 1801	p. 107
Jesse Hollingsworth, Lieutenant, Jefferson County	28 Apr 1801	p. 107
John Breed, Captain, Warren County	28 Apr 1801	p. 108
Daniel Dennis, Ensign, Warren County	28 Apr 1801	p. 108
Baynes Carter, Lieutenant, Warren County	28 Apr 1801	p. 109
Edward Green, Ensign, Warren County	28 Apr 1801	p. 109
Isaac Walker, Major, Regiment 1, Burke County	1 May 1801	p. 110
Samuel Devereux, Captain, Volunteer Company of Artillery, Hancock County	1 May 1801	p. 110
Abraham Boreland, First Lieutenant, Volunteer Company of Artillery, Hancock County	1 May 1801	p. 111
James Hamilton, Second Lieutenant, Volunteer Company of Artillery, Hancock County	1 May 1801	p. 111
William Smith, Lieutenant Colonel Commandant, Warren County	5 May 1801	p. 112
John Foster, Lieutenant Colonel Commandant, Columbia County	5 May 1801	p. 112
Jones Kendrick, Captain, Washington County	9 May 1801	p. 113
Robert McDougall, Captain, Volunteer Company of Light Infantry, Battalion 3, Washington County	9 May 1801	p. 113
Tillman S. Dixon, Lieutenant, Volunteer Company of Light Infantry, Washington County	9 May 1801	p. 114
James Harvey, Ensign, Volunteer Company of Light Infantry, Battalion 3, Washington County	9 May 1801	p. 114
Peter Stovall, Lieutenant, Wilkes County	9 May 1801	p. 115
James Phillips, Ensign, Wilkes County	9 May 1801	p. 115
John Brown, Captain, Camden County	9 May 1801	p. 116
David Mezill, Lieutenant, Camden County	9 May 1801	p. 116
Andrew Tucker, Ensign, Camden County	9 May 1801	p. 117
Joseph Morris, Lieutenant, Franklin County	9 May 1801	p. 117
John Wims, Ensign, Franklin County	9 May 1801	p. 118
John Hooper, Captain, Jackson County	9 May 1801	p. 118
Edmond Grissom, Lieutenant, Burke County	9 May 1801	p. 119
William Camp, Captain, Jackson County	9 May 1801	p. 119
Samuel Moor, Lieutenant, Jackson County	9 May 1801	p. 120
Wylee Jones, Ensign, Jackson County	9 May 1801	p. 120
Solomon Carter, Lieutenant, Jackson County	9 May 1801	p. 121
William Kenman, Lieutenant, Washington County	9 May 1801	p. 121

Name, Rank, Unit	*Date*	*Page*
George Stewart, Lieutenant, Jackson County	18 May 1801	p. 122
Thomas Kellough, Ensign, Jackson County	18 May 1801	p. 122
Drewry Brewer, Lieutenant, Battalion 3, Washington County	18 May 1801	p. 123
Shadrick Scarborough, Captain, Volunteer Light Infantry Company, Battalion 1, Regiment 2, Burke County	20 May 1801	p. 123
James Moore, Lieutenant, Volunteer Light Infantry Company, Battalion 1, Regiment 2, Burke County	20 May 1801	p. 124
Jonas Proctor, Ensign, Volunteer Light Infantry Company, Battalion 1, Regiment 2, Burke County	20 May 1801	p. 124
Horatio Walker, Captain, Jackson County	27 May 1801	p. 125
Isaac Pace, Lieutenant, Jackson County	27 May 1801	p. 125
James Pace, Ensign, Jackson County	27 May 1801	p. 126
Eleazer Lewis, Captain, Battalion 2, Regiment 2, Burke County	1 Jun 1801	p. 126
Francis Hillard, Lieutenant, Battalion 2, Regiment 2, Burke County	1 Jun 1801	p. 127
William Pugh, Ensign, Battalion 2, Regiment 2, Burke County	1 Jun 1801	p. 127
Charles Ray, Cornet, Volunteer Troop of Dragoons, Washington County	1 Jun 1801	p. 128
Samuel Barron, Ensign, Louisville Company, Jefferson County	3 Jun 1801	p. 128
John Lamkin, Major, Battalion 1, Columbia County	4 Jun 1801	p. 129
Abiel Schweighoffer, Lieutenant, Effingham County	4 Jun 1801	p. 129
Charles Ulmor, Ensign, Effingham County	4 Jun 1801	p. 130
George Davis, Lieutenant, 1st Company, Bryan County	12 Jun 1801	p. 130
Richard Bennett, Ensign, Bryan County	12 Jun 1801	p. 131
Jesse Hollingsworth, Lieutenant, Jefferson County	12 Jun 1801	p. 131
Samson Slaughter, Ensign, Jefferson County	12 Jun 1801	p. 132
John Gray, Captain, Hancock County	15 Jun 1801	p. 132
Ebenezer Moore, Lieutenant, Hancock County	15 Jun 1801	p. 133
James O'Neal, Ensign, Hancock County	15 Jun 1801	p. 133
Jeremiah Bonner, Captain, Battalion 3, Hancock County	15 Jun 1801	p. 134
Nathan Youngblood, Lieutenant, Battalion 3, Hancock County	15 Jun 1801	p. 134
David Brewer, Ensign, Greene County	15 Jun 1801	p. 135
Morris Harris, Ensign, Greene County	15 Jun 1801	p. 135

Georgia Military Commissions, 1798–1818

Name, Rank, Unit	Date	Page
Edward Bowdre, First Lieutenant, Volunteer Company of Artillery, Columbia County	15 Jun 1801	p. 136
Reubin Reynolds, First Lieutenant, Volunteer Troop of Dragoons, Columbia County	15 Jun 1801	p. 136
Jesse Moore, Second Lieutenant, Volunteer Troop of Dragoons, Columbia County	15 Jun 1801	p. 137
Hezekiah Beall, Cornet, Volunteer Troop of Dragoons, Columbia County	15 Jun 1801	p. 137
Joshua Dodson, Lieutenant, Regiment 2, Jackson County	15 Jun 1801	p. 138
Arthur Bearden, Ensign, Regiment 2, Jackson County	15 Jun 1801	p. 138
William Johnson, Captain, Volunteer Company of Light Infantry, Battalion 1, Regiment 2, Jackson County	15 Jun 1801	p. 139
Poley Rogers, Lieutenant, Volunteer Company of Light Infantry, Battalion 1, Regiment 2, Jackson County	15 Jun 1801	p. 139
Robert Willson, Ensign, Volunteer Company of Light Infantry, Battalion 1, Regiment 2, Jackson County	15 Jun 1801	p. 140
Bowler Moon, Captain, Volunteer Troop of Dragoons, Regiment 2, Jackson County	15 Jun 1801	p. 140
James Ewing, First Lieutenant, Volunteer Troop of Dragoons, Regiment 2, Jackson County	15 Jun 1801	p. 141
Abraham Lindsay, Second Lieutenant, Volunteer Troop of Dragoons, Jackson County	15 Jun 1801	p. 141
Henry Bratcher, Cornet, Volunteer Troop of Dragoons, Regiment 2, Jackson County	15 Jun 1801	p. 142
John Weeks, Lieutenant, Hancock County	17 Jun 1801	p. 142
John B. Rutherford, Captain, Volunteer Troop of Dragoons, Washington County	22 Jun 1801	p. 143
John Irwin, First Lieutenant, Volunteer Troop of Dragoons, Washington County	22 Jun 1801	p. 143
Reid Duprey, Second Lieutenant, Volunteer Troop of Dragoons, Washington County	22 Jun 1801	p. 144
Charles Lowther, Lieutenant, Screven County	25 Jun 1801	p. 144
Benjamin Langston, Ensign, Battalion 3, Washington County	29 Jun 1801	p. 145
Isaac Robinson, First Lieutenant, Volunteer Troop of Dragoons, Jefferson County	3 Jul 1801	p. 145
Williamson Collier, Ensign, Oglethorpe County	7 Jul 1801	p. 146
Solomon Thompson, Lieutenant, Warren County	7 Jul 1801	p. 146
Henry Hadley, Ensign, Warren County	7 Jul 1801	p. 147
Slauter Cowling, Lieutenant, Chatham County	10 Jul 1801	p. 147

Commissions Book 1800–1806

Name, Rank, Unit	Date	Page
Robert Gibson, Ensign, Chatham County	10 Jul 1801	p. 148
Edward Arnett, Lieutenant, Wilkes County	10 Jul 1801	p. 148
George Moreland, Ensign, Wilkes County	10 Jul 1801	p. 149
Henry Tillery, Lieutenant, Oglethorpe County	10 Jul 1801	p. 149
James Cocks, Lieutenant, Washington County	13 Jul 1801	p. 150
Francis Spank, Ensign, Washington County	13 Jun 1801	p. 150
Lewis Moseley, Lieutenant, Elbert County	20 Jul 1801	p. 151
Reuben Slaughter, , Hancock County	20 Jul 1801	p. 151
James Cunningham, Lieutenant, Hancock County	20 Jul 1801	p. 152
Drury Rogers, Ensign, Hancock County	20 Jul 1801	p. 152
Frederick Tucker, , Hancock County	20 Jul 1801	p. 153
James Crowder, Lieutenant, Hancock County	20 Jul 1801	p. 153
John Simms, Ensign, Hancock County	20 Jul 1801	p. 154
John Taylor, Second Lieutenant, Volunteer Troop of Dragoons, Oglethorpe County	20 Jul 1801	p. 154
Thomas Riddle, Cornet, Volunteer Troop of Dragoons, Oglethorpe County	20 Jul 1801	p. 155
Joseph Griffin, Lieutenant, Washington County	20 Jul 1801	p. 155
John Armstead, Lieutenant, Oglethorpe County	21 Jul 1801	p. 156
Reddick Acock, Ensign, Oglethorpe County	21 Jul 1801	p. 156
Perminus English, Lieutenant, Oglethorpe County	21 Jul 1801	p. 157
John Spears, Ensign, Oglethorpe County	21 Jul 1801	p. 157
Elias Hodges, Captain, Volunteer Light Infantry Company, Jefferson County	21 Jul 1801	p. 158
James Derby, First Lieutenant, Volunteer Light Infantry Company, Jefferson County	21 Jul 1801	p. 158
Silas Gates, Ensign, Volunteer Light Infantry Company, Jefferson County	21 Jul 1801	p. 159
William McKinzie, Lieutenant, Elbert County	27 Jul 1801	p. 159
Arthur Cooper, Ensign, Elbert County	27 Jul 1801	p. 160
Enoch Rodgers, Lieutenant, Jackson County	27 Jul 1801	p. 160
Darius Thomas, Captain, Washington County	28 Jul 1801	p. 161
Abraham Abrahams, Captain, Chatham County	30 Jul 1801	p. 161
Elijah Payne, Captain, Dead River Company, Montgomery County	3 Aug 1801	p. 162
Zachariah Payne, Lieutenant, Dead River Company, Montgomery County	3 Aug 1801	p. 162

Georgia Military Commissions, 1798–1818

Name, Rank, Unit	Date	Page
Jacob Alford, Lieutenant, Silver Bluff Company, Montgomery County	3 Aug 1801	p. 163
Absalom Barrow, Ensign, Silver Bluff Company, Montgomery County	3 Aug 1801	p. 163
Needham Cock, Lieutenant, Ogechee Company, Montgomery County	3 Aug 1801	p. 164
Benjamin Wheeler, Ensign, Ogechee Company, Montgomery County	3 Aug 1801	p. 164
William McGriff, Captain, Volunteer Troop of Dragoons, Montgomery County	3 Aug 1801	p. 165
Sherod Swain, First Lieutenant, Volunteer Troop of Dragoons, Montgomery County	3 Aug 1801	p. 165
Alexander Goodgame, Second Lieutenant, Volunteer Troop of Dragoons, Montgomery County	3 Aug 1801	p. 166
Elijah Padget, Cornet, Volunteer Troop of Dragoons, Montgomery County	3 Aug 1801	p. 166
Josiah Horn, Ensign, Jefferson County	3 Aug 1801	p. 167
Levin Wailes, Lieutenant, Elbert County	3 Aug 1801	p. 167
Philip Thomas, Ensign, Elbert County	3 Aug 1801	p. 168
Walton Harris, Captain, Jackson County	3 Aug 1801	p. 168
Martin Hardin, Captain, Franklin County	3 Aug 1801	p. 169
Gadwill Ayres, Lieutenant, Franklin County	3 Aug 1801	p. 169
Samuel Hollingswoth, Lieutenant, Franklin County	3 Aug 1801	p. 170
Benjamin Jackson, Ensign, Franklin County	3 Aug 1801	p. 170
William Grimes, Captain, Elbert County	6 Aug 1801	p. 171
John Kilgore, Lieutenant, Elbert County	6 Aug 1801	p. 171
John Appleby, Ensign, Elbert County	6 Aug 1801	p. 172
Jesse Rice, Lieutenant, Columbia County	6 Aug 1801	p. 172
James Moore, Lieutenant, Jackson County	6 Aug 1801	p. 173
George White, Ensign, Jackson County	6 Aug 1801	p. 173
Robert McKeever, Lieutenant, Jackson County	6 Aug 1801	p. 174
Joshua Scurlock, Captain, Jackson County	6 Aug 1801	p. 174
Philip Coker, Lieutenant, Jackson County	6 Aug 1801	p. 175
Bartlet Adkins, Ensign, Jackson County	6 Aug 1801	p. 175
James Hendrix, Captain, Jackson County	6 Aug 1801	p. 176
George Humphries, Lieutenant, Jackson County	6 Aug 1801	p. 176
Isaac Abney, Ensign, Jackson County	6 Aug 1801	p. 177

Name, Rank, Unit	Date	Page
Josiah Tattnall Jr., Brigadier General, Brigade 1, Division 1	6 Aug 1801	p. 177
Nathaniel Innis, Lieutenant, Burke County	10 Aug 1801	p. 178
John Thomas, Captain, Glynn County	10 Aug 1801	p. 178
John Stewart, Lieutenant, Glynn County	10 Aug 1801	p. 179
Jonathan Brooks, Ensign, Glynn County	10 Aug 1801	p. 179
Abraham T. Powell, Captain, Glynn County	10 Aug 1801	p. 180
Benjamin Sutton, Ensign, Glynn County	10 Aug 1801	p. 180
Alexander Sister, Captain, Oglethorpe County	10 Aug 1801	p. 181
Isom Goss, Lieutenant, Oglethorpe County	10 Aug 1801	p. 181
Richard M. Stiles, Second Lieutenant, Volunteer Company of Artillery, Chatham County	14 Aug 1801	p. 182
Joseph Waters, Major, Battalion 1, Oglethorpe County	14 Aug 1801	p. 182
James Savage, Lieutenant, Columbia County	17 Aug 1801	p. 183
Samuel McNair, Ensign, Columbia County	17 Aug 1801	p. 183
Samuel Cunningham, Captain, Battalion 3, Greene County	17 Aug 1801	p. 184
Asa Cox, Ensign, Battalion 3, Greene County	17 Aug 1801	p. 184
William Hay, Ensign, Wilkes County	25 Aug 1801	p. 185
Robert L. Tate, Captain, Elbert County	25 Aug 1801	p. 185
Mayfield Bell, Lieutenant, Elbert County	25 Aug 1801	p. 186
Stephen Morgan, Ensign, Elbert County	25 Aug 1801	p. 186
Nicholas Meriwether, Captain, Columbia County	29 Aug 1801	p. 187
John Lewis, Captain, Hancock County	31 Aug 1801	p. 187
Thomas Dent, Captain, Volunteer Troop of Dragoons, Warren County	31 Aug 1801	p. 188
Timothy Mathews, First Lieutenant, Volunteer Troop of Dragoons, Warren County	31 Aug 1801	p. 188
Henry Kendall, Second Lieutenant, Volunteer Troop of Dragoons, Warren County	31 Aug 1801	p. 189
Henry Peebles, Cornet, Volunteer Troop of Dragoons, Warren County	31 Aug 1801	p. 189
Henry B. Caboniss, Captain, Greene County	2 Sep 1801	p. 190
Allen Tucker, Lieutenant, Greene County	2 Sep 1801	p. 190
George Caboniss, Ensign, Greene County	2 Sep 1801	p. 191
George W. Foster, Captain, Greene County	2 Sep 1801	p. 191
William Armour, Ensign, Greene County	2 Sep 1801	p. 192
John Straham, Lieutenant, Effingham County	3 Sep 1801	p. 192

Georgia Military Commissions, 1798–1818

Name, Rank, Unit	Date	Page
Septhah Daniel, Ensign, Burke County	3 Sep 1801	p. 193
John Kirkpatrick, Captain, Jackson County	28 Sep 1801	p. 193
Abraham Venable, Lieutenant, Jackson County	28 Sep 1801	p. 194
Nathan Wyche, Ensign, Jackson County	28 Sep 1801	p. 194
William Butler, Lieutenant, Warren County	28 Sep 1801	p. 195
Luke Moore, Captain, Washington County	28 Sep 1801	p. 195
Pallasiah Stallings, Lieutenant, Wilkes County	28 Sep 1801	p. 196
Joseph Gordon, Ensign, Wilkes County	28 Sep 1801	p. 196
John Armstrong, Lieutenant, Jackson County	3 Oct 1801	p. 197
Blassingame Thomas, Ensign, Jefferson County	7 Oct 1801	p. 197
William Gardner, Ensign, Warren County	10 Oct 1801	p. 198
Cary Cox, Ensign, Warren County	10 Oct 1801	p. 198
William King, Lieutenant, Franklin County	10 Oct 1801	p. 199
James Sparks, Ensign, Franklin County	10 Oct 1801	p. 199
John Williford, Lieutenant, Elbert County	19 Oct 1801	p. 200
John Thomason, Ensign, Elbert County	19 Oct 1801	p. 200
James Cunningham, Captain, Jackson County	19 Oct 1801	p. 201
James Hill, Lieutenant, Jackson County	19 Oct 1801	p. 201
William Montgomery, Ensign, Jackson County	19 Oct 1801	p. 202
John Bond, Lieutenant, Hancock County	20 Oct 1801	p. 202
Mathew Rushing, Lieutenant, Effingham County	21 Oct 1801	p. 203
William Mehoffy, Captain, Montgomery County	23 Oct 1801	p. 203
Charles Dekle, Lieutenant, Montgomery County	23 Oct 1801	p. 204
William Durdens, Ensign, Montgomery County	23 Oct 1801	p. 204
John Floyd, Captain, Volunteer Troop of Dragoons, Jackson County	9 Nov 1801	p. 205
Jesse Harris, First Lieutenant, Volunteer Troop of Dragoons, Jackson County	9 Nov 1801	p. 205
Paul Williams, Second Lieutenant, Volunteer Troop of Dragoons, Jackson County	9 Nov 1801	p. 206
John Selman, Cornet, Volunteer Troop of Dragoons, Jackson County	9 Nov 1801	p. 206
Jacobus Watts, Captain, Greene County	10 Nov 1801	p. 207
Benjamin Gypson, Lieutenant, Greene County	10 Nov 1801	p. 207
Thomas Carleton, Ensign, Greene County	10 Nov 1801	p. 208
Thomas Haynes, Captain, Greene County	10 Nov 1801	p. 208
Greene Jackson, Lieutenant, Greene County	10 Nov 1801	p. 209

Name, Rank, Unit	Date	Page
Henry Greer, Ensign, Greene County	10 Nov 1801	p. 209
Epps Dukes, Captain, Greene County	10 Nov 1801	p. 210
Henry Stringfellow, Lieutenant, Greene County	10 Nov 1801	p. 210
Morgan Griffith, Ensign, Greene County	10 Nov 1801	p. 211
Alexander Andrews, Lieutenant, Greene County	10 Nov 1801	p. 211
Robert Reed, Ensign, Greene County	10 Nov 1801	p. 212
Thomas Kimbrough, Lieutenant, Greene County	10 Nov 1801	p. 212
Daniel Hightower, Ensign, Greene County	10 Nov 1801	p. 213
Noel Robertson, Captain, Warren County	10 Nov 1801	p. 213
William Hancock, Ensign, Warren County	10 Nov 1801	p. 214
Thacker Vivion, Major, Jefferson County	11 Nov 1801	p. 214
James Carr, Major, Burke County	11 Nov 1801	p. 215
Francis Flournoy, Lieutenant, Greene County	11 Nov 1801	p. 215
Robert Beasley, Ensign, Greene County	11 Nov 1801	p. 216
Samuel Jackson, Captain, Jackson County	11 Nov 1801	p. 216
Andrew Cunningham, Lieutenant, Jackson County	11 Nov 1801	p. 217
James Shields, Ensign, Jackson County	11 Nov 1801	p. 217
Archibald Campbell, Captain, McIntosh County	11 Nov 1801	p. 218
John Lloyd, Ensign, McIntosh County	11 Nov 1801	p. 218
Peter Arrant, Captain, Lincoln County	11 Nov 1801	p. 219
Thomas Pate, Lieutenant, Lincoln County	11 Nov 1801	p. 219
John R. Reveir, Lieutenant, Wilkes County	11 Nov 1801	p. 220
Leonard Pearson, Ensign, Wilkes County	11 Nov 1801	p. 220
Reuben Luke, Captain, Volunteer Company of Light Infantry, Columbia County	14 Nov 1801	p. 221
Stephen Hoge, Ensign, Columbia County	14 Nov 1801	p. 221
George Mathews, Captain, Oglethorpe County	14 Nov 1801	p. 222
Robert Colquit, Lieutenant, Oglethorpe County	14 Nov 1801	p. 222
Willson Woodruff, Ensign, Oglethorpe County	14 Nov 1801	p. 223
John Hardiman, Captain, Volunteer Company of Light Infantry, Oglethorpe County	14 Nov 1801	p. 223
Littleberry Jenkins, Captain, Greene County	14 Nov 1801	p. 224
Mathew Duncan, Lieutenant, Greene County	14 Nov 1801	p. 224
David Evans, Ensign, Greene County	14 Nov 1801	p. 225
Gilbert Gay, Lieutenant, Greene County	14 Nov 1801	p. 225
William Surrey, Ensign, Greene County	14 Nov 1801	p. 226
Richard Prichard, Captain, Glynn County	16 Nov 1801	p. 226

Georgia Military Commissions, 1798–1818

Name, Rank, Unit	Date	Page
James Powell, Lieutenant, Glynn County	16 Nov 1801	p. 227
William Payne, Ensign, Glynn County	16 Nov 1801	p. 227
Overton Walton, Lieutenant, Lincoln County	16 Nov 1801	p. 228
Needom Overa, Ensign, Lincoln County	16 Nov 1801	p. 228
Jesse Lee, Captain, Oglethorpe County	16 Nov 1801	p. 229
George Cunningham, Lieutenant, Oglethorpe County	16 Nov 1801	p. 229
John Fullerlove, Ensign, Oglethorpe County	16 Nov 1801	p. 230
Philip Colbert, Captain, Oglethorpe County	16 Nov 1801	p. 230
Nicholas Colbert, Lieutenant, Oglethorpe County	16 Nov 1801	p. 231
James Jay, Ensign, Oglethorpe County	16 Nov 1801	p. 231
Robert Reed, Captain, Jefferson County	18 Nov 1801	p. 232
Oliver Sturges, Lieutenant, Augusta Volunteer Company of Light Infantry, Richmond County	21 Nov 1801	p. 232
Thomas Barrott, Ensign, Augusta Volunteer Company of Light Infantry, Richmond County	21 Nov 1801	p. 233
Joseph Waters, Major, Battalion 1, Oglethorpe County	24 Nov 1801	p. 233
Joseph Lamaster, Captain, Jackson County	24 Nov 1801	p. 234
James Martin, Lieutenant, Jackson County	24 Nov 1801	p. 234
James Kellet, Ensign, Jackson County	24 Nov 1801	p. 235
Samuel Braswell, Captain, Jackson County	28 Nov 1801	p. 235
Mathew McMight, Lieutenant, Jackson County	28 Nov 1801	p. 236
Jeremiah Lamar, Ensign, Jackson County	28 Nov 1801	p. 236
Alexander Reed, Captain, Jackson County	28 Nov 1801	p. 237
Stuard McCravy, Ensign, Jackson County	28 Nov 1801	p. 237
David Garlman, Cornet, Volunteer Troop of Dragoons, Jefferson County	28 Nov 1801	p. 238
John Rushen, Captain, Warren County	30 Nov 1801	p. 238
William Robertson, Lieutenant, Warren County	30 Nov 1801	p. 239
William Kellebrew, Ensign, Warren County	30 Nov 1801	p. 239
David Dickson, Brigadier General, Brigade 3, Division 3	10 Dec 1801	p. 240
Elkanah Loften, Captain, Jefferson County	12 Dec 1801	p. 240
Absolam Coursey, Lieutenant, Jefferson County	12 Dec 1801	p. 241
John Acridge, Ensign, Jefferson County	12 Dec 1801	p. 241
William Haddlesey, Lieutenant, Franklin County	17 Dec 1801	p. 242
John Holton, Ensign, Washington County	17 Dec 1801	p. 242
John Broome, Captain, Burke County	18 Dec 1801	p. 243
Willis Chivers, Lieutenant, Hancock County	12 Jan 1802	p. 243

Name, Rank, Unit	Date	Page
John Humphries, Captain, New Company, Hancock County	15 Jan 1802	p. 244
James Humphries, Lieutenant, New Company, Hancock County	15 Jan 1802	p. 244
Ephraim Cohoon, Ensign, New Company, Hancock County	15 Jan 1802	p. 245
James Jones, Lieutenant, Oglethorpe County	20 Jan 1802	p. 245
William Broughton, Ensign, Oglethorpe County	20 Jan 1802	p. 246
William Binns, Ensign, Wilkes County	20 Jan 1802	p. 246
John McKinzie, Lieutenant Colonel Commandant, Regiment 2, Hancock County	4 Feb 1802	p. 247
Jonathan Davis, Major, Battalion 2, Regiment 2, Hancock County	4 Feb 1802	p. 247
John Parks, Major, Wilkes County	4 Feb 1802	p. 248
Stephen Mobley, Captain, Elbert County	4 Feb 1802	p. 248
William Rogers, Lieutenant, Elbert County	4 Feb 1802	p. 249
John H. Morel, Lieutenant, Chatham County	4 Feb 1802	p. 249
Edward Lloyed Davis, Ensign, Volunteer Company of Fusiliers, Chatham County	4 Feb 1802	p. 250
John Harvey, Captain, Volunteer Troop of Dragoons, Regiment 2, Hancock County	6 Feb 1802	p. 250
Nehemiah Harvey, First Lieutenant, Volunteer Troop of Dragoons, Regiment 2, Hancock County	6 Feb 1802	p. 251
John Hall, Second Lieutenant, Volunteer Troop of Dragoons, Regiment 2, Hancock County	6 Feb 1802	p. 251
James Page, Cornet, Volunteer Troop of Dragoons, Regiment 2, Hancock County	6 Feb 1802	p. 252
Nathaniel Payne, Ensign, 2nd Company, Battalion 1, Franklin County	8 Feb 1802	p. 252
Thomas Talbert, Ensign, Regiment 2, Hancock County	9 Feb 1802	p. 253
Henry W. Williams, Lieutenant, Effingham County	11 Feb 1802	p. 253
Frederick Beall, Major, Battalion 2, Franklin County	12 Feb 1802	p. 254
John Easly, Captain, Volunteer Troop of Dragoons, Franklin County	12 Feb 1802	p. 254
Samuel Glenn, Second Lieutenant, Volunteer Troop of Dragoons, Franklin County	12 Feb 1802	p. 255
Andrew McIver, Captain, Volunteer Troop of Dragoons, Elbert County	12 Feb 1802	p. 255

Georgia Military Commissions, 1798–1818

Name, Rank, Unit	Date	Page
Charles Sorrells, First Lieutenant, Volunteer Troop of Dragoons, Elbert County	12 Feb 1802	p. 256
Thomas Thomason, Second Lieutenant, Volunteer Troop of Dragoons, Elbert County	12 Feb 1802	p. 256
William Bowles, Cornet, Volunteer Troop of Dragoons, Elbert County	12 Feb 1802	p. 257
Daniel Dennis, Lieutenant, Warren County	12 Feb 1802	p. 257
John Armore, Captain, Clarke County	18 Feb 1802	p. 258
Joseph Jones, Lieutenant, Clarke County	18 Feb 1802	p. 258
Robert Sims, Ensign, Clarke County	18 Feb 1802	p. 259
Job J. Boles, Ensign, Market Company, Chatham County	19 Feb 1802	p. 259
David Bradie Mitchell, Lieutenant Colonel Commandant, Chatham County	19 Feb 1802	p. 260
Enoch Everitt, Captain, Bulloch County	19 Feb 1802	p. 260
John Thompson, Lieutenant, Bulloch County	19 Feb 1802	p. 261
Andrew Lastinger, Ensign, Bulloch County	19 Feb 1802	p. 261
George Mickell, Captain, Bulloch County	19 Feb 1802	p. 262
Stephen McCoy, Lieutenant, Bulloch County	19 Feb 1802	p. 262
Robert McCall, Ensign, Bulloch County	19 Feb 1802	p. 263
James Moore, Captain, Jackson County	22 Feb 1802	p. 263
Abraham Anderson, Lieutenant, Jackson County	22 Feb 1802	p. 264
William Fanning, Ensign, Jackson County	22 Feb 1802	p. 264
Caleb Cannon, Lieutenant, Washington County	24 Feb 1802	p. 265
John Murkeson, Ensign, Washington County	24 Feb 1802	p. 265
Isaac McCray, Lieutenant, Washington County	24 Feb 1802	p. 266
James Bohannon, Ensign, Jefferson County	26 Feb 1802	p. 266
Solomon Wood, Brigadier General, Brigade 2, Division 1	26 Feb 1802	p. 267
Benjamin Bryan, Second Lieutenant, Volunteer Company of Artillery, Jefferson County	26 Feb 1802	p. 267
Zadock Martin, Ensign, Greene County	26 Feb 1802	p. 268
Garten Backler, Lieutenant, Chatham County	26 Feb 1802	p. 268
John Bourguin, Ensign, Chatham County	26 Feb 1802	p. 269
Samuel Jones, Ensign, McIntosh County	26 Feb 1802	p. 269
George Strother, Captain, Hancock County	2 Mar 1802	p. 270
George Collins, Lieutenant, Hancock County	2 Mar 1802	p. 270
Thomas Hosea, Ensign, Hancock County	2 Mar 1802	p. 271
William Blake, Captain, Battalion 1, Jackson County	4 Mar 1802	p. 271

Name, Rank, Unit	Date	Page
John Callahan, Lieutenant, Battalion 1, Jackson County	4 Mar 1802	p. 272
James McCord, Ensign, Battalion 1, Jackson County	4 Mar 1802	p. 272
Jonathan Fore, Captain, Battalion 1, Jackson County	4 Mar 1802	p. 273
Phiney Robins, Ensign, Battalion 1, Jackson County	4 Mar 1802	p. 273
William Cavenah, Lieutenant, Court House Company, Montgomery County	4 Mar 1802	p. 274
Joshua Houghton, Captain, Greene County	8 Mar 1802	p. 274
Willis Solomon, Ensign, Montgomery County	4 Mar 1802	p. 274
Thomas Dawson, Lieutenant, Greene County	8 Mar 1802	p. 274
William Maxwell, Captain, Battalion 1, Regiment 2, Burke County	6 Mar 1802	p. 275
Solomon Hawkins, Ensign, Battalion 1, Regiment 2, Burke County	6 Mar 1802	p. 275
Archibald Gray, Ensign, Greene County	8 Mar 1802	p. 277
Smith Milner, Captain, Richmond County	8 Mar 1802	p. 277
Randolph Rowell, Lieutenant, Richmond County	8 Mar 1802	p. 278
Robert Wyche, Ensign, Richmond County	8 Mar 1802	p. 278
Richard Sanders, Ensign, Elbert County	8 Mar 1802	p. 279
John R. Ragland, Captain, Volunteer Troop of Dragoons, Elbert County	8 Mar 1802	p. 279
David Greenlaw, First Lieutenant, Volunteer Troop of Dragoons, Elbert County	8 Mar 1802	p. 280
Jeremiah Walker, Second Lieutenant, Volunteer Troop of Dragoons, Elbert County	8 Mar 1802	p. 280
Nathaniel P. Brach, Cornet, Volunteer Troop of Dragoons, Elbert County	8 Mar 1802	p. 281
Daniel Dennis, Lieutenant, Warren County	12 Mar 1802	p. 281
Cowles Mead, Captain, Augusta Volunteer Company of Light Infantry, Richmond County	13 Mar 1802	p. 282
Thomas Barrett, Lieutenant, Augusta Volunteer Company of Light Infantry, Richmond County	13 Mar 1802	p. 282
Barna McKenne, Ensign, Augusta Volunteer Company of Light Infantry, Richmond County	13 Mar 1802	p. 283
Elisha Ward, Ensign, Jefferson County	18 Mar 1802	p. 283
Micajah Whelley, Ensign, Montgomery County	18 Mar 1802	p. 284
Benjamin Allen, Captain, Franklin County	20 Mar 1802	p. 284
Hezekiah Candler, Ensign, Franklin County	20 Mar 1802	p. 285
William Maxwell Jr., Captain, Bryan County	20 Mar 1802	p. 285

Georgia Military Commissions, 1798–1818

Name, Rank, Unit	Date	Page
Richard Sumford, Lieutenant, Bryan County	20 Mar 1802	p. 286
John Sapp, Ensign, Burke County	23 Mar 1802	p. 286
James Smith, Ensign, Camden County	23 Mar 1802	p. 287
Henry G. Caldwell, Lieutenant Colonel Commandant, Jefferson County	27 Mar 1802	p. 287
William Poss, Ensign, Rifle Company, Regiment 1, Hancock County	27 Mar 1802	p. 288
Mund Grass, Captain, Screven County	2 Apr 1802	p. 288
Lewis Collins, Ensign, Richmond County	2 Mar 1802	p. 289
Christopher Snell, Captain, Montgomery County	2 Apr 1802	p. 289
Abraham Lamb, Lieutenant, Montgomery County	2 Apr 1802	p. 290
Jeremiah Coney, Lieutenant, Montgomery County	2 Apr 1802	p. 290
Jonathan Coleman, Ensign, Montgomery County	2 Apr 1802	p. 291
Richard Dennis, Major, Battalion 1, Chatham County	8 Apr 1802	p. 291
Shaler Hilyer, Captain, Elbert County	8 Apr 1802	p. 292
John Lewis, Major, Battalion 1, Regiment 2, Hancock County	8 Feb 1802	p. 292
Wyche Cato, Captain, Hancock County	8 Apr 1802	p. 293
David Shores, Ensign, Jefferson County	8 Apr 1802	p. 293
Thomas Doles, Lieutenant, Warren County	8 Apr 1802	p. 294
Benjamin Christopher, Captain, Greene County	12 Apr 1802	p. 294
Zachariah Jones, Lieutenant, Greene County	12 Apr 1802	p. 295
Ezekiel Lambert, Ensign, Greene County	12 Apr 1802	p. 295
John Alford, Captain, Greene County	12 Apr 1802	p. 296
William Slaughter, Lieutenant, Greene County	12 Apr 1802	p. 296
John Coplin, Ensign, Greene County	12 Apr 1802	p. 297
John Cox, Captain, Greene County	12 Apr 1802	p. 297
Robert Ray, Ensign, Greene County	12 Apr 1802	p. 298
Alexander Carswell, Major, Jefferson County	14 Apr 1802	p. 298
James Walker, Ensign, Volunteer Company of Light Infantry, Washington County	14 Apr 1802	p. 299
Volantine Gates, Captain, Jackson County		p. 299
Simon Williams, Captain, Montgomery County	22 Apr 1802	p. 300
Frederick Rogers, Lieutenant, Montgomery County	22 Apr 1802	p. 300
Joseph Sykes, Ensign, Montgomery County	22 Apr 1802	p. 301
Hezekiah Howell, Lieutenant, Hancock County	24 Apr 1802	p. 301
Willey Hilliard, Ensign, Hancock County	24 Apr 1802	p. 302

Commissions Book 1800–1806

Name, Rank, Unit	*Date*	*Page*
Hardy Hart, Lieutenant, Burke County	24 Apr 1802	p. 302
Jesse Anderson, Ensign, Burke County	24 Apr 1802	p. 303
Samuel Davis, Lieutenant, Burke County	24 Apr 1802	p. 303
Jacob Mock, Ensign, Burke County	24 Apr 1802	p. 304
John Todd, Captain, Wilkes County	24 Apr 1802	p. 304
Philip Cooper, Lieutenant, Wilkes County	24 Apr 1802	p. 305
John Cooper, Ensign, Wilkes County	24 Apr 1802	p. 305
Slauter Cowling, Captain, Chatham County	27 Feb 1802	p. 306
Hardy Mann, Ensign, Burke County	27 Apr 1802	p. 306
Richard Horn, Captain, New Company, Tattnall County	27 Apr 1802	p. 307
James English, Lieutenant, New Company, Tattnall County	27 Apr 1802	p. 307
Reuben Bankston, Ensign, Montgomery County	27 Apr 1802	p. 308
Enoch Daniel, Captain, Ohoopie Company, Montgomery County	27 Apr 1802	p. 308
Robert Whitten, Lieutenant, Ohoopie Company, Tattnall County	27 Apr 1802	p. 309
Elias Whitten, Ensign, Ohoopie Company, Tattnall County	27 Apr 1802	p. 309
John Watson, Lieutenant, Saw Mill Company, Tattnall County	27 Apr 1802	p. 310
John Coarsey, Ensign, Saw Mill Company, Tattnall County	27 Apr 1802	p. 310
Archibald Crafford, Ensign, Canouchie Company, Tattnall County	27 Apr 1802	p. 311
William Paget, Lieutenant, "a new" company, Montgomery County	27 Apr 1802	p. 311
Obediah Garret, Ensign, New Company, Montgomery County	27 Mar 1802	p. 312
William Jones, Lieutenant, Elbert County	27 Apr 1802	p. 313
Thomas McCall, Lieutenant, Camden County	27 Apr 1802	p. 313
Nathaniel R. Greene, , Camden County	27 Apr 1802	p. 314
Noble Jones, Captain, Glynn County	30 Apr 1802	p. 314
John G. Snead, Lieutenant, Glynn County	30 Apr 1802	p. 315
John Harrison, Ensign, Glynn County	30 Apr 1802	p. 315
Jonathan Lewis, Captain, Burke County	6 May 1802	p. 316
Wiley Sharp, Lieutenant, Burke County	6 May 1802	p. 316
James Trice, Lieutenant, Hancock County	7 May 1802	p. 317
David Reddock, Ensign, Hancock County	7 May 1802	p. 317

Georgia Military Commissions, 1798–1818

Name, Rank, Unit	Date	Page
Hyram Hubert, Ensign, Warren County	7 May 1802	p. 318
Henry T. Anthony, Captain, Wilkes County	17 May 1802	p. 318
Thomas W. P. Charlton, Captain, Volunteer Company of Hibernian Fusiliers, Chatham County	14 May 1802	p. 319
John Cumming, Captain, Savannah Volunteer Guards, Chatham County	14 May 1802	p. 319
James Marshall, Lieutenant, Savannah Volunteer Guards, Chatham County	14 May 1802	p. 320
Joseph Machin, Ensign, Savannah Volunteer Guards, Chatham County	14 May 1802	p. 320
Asa Edwards, Captain, Hancock County	14 May 1802	p. 321
John Traywick, Lieutenant, Hancock County	14 May 1802	p. 321
Francis Miller, Ensign, Hancock County	14 May 1802	p. 322
Richard Stokes, First Lieutenant, Volunteer Troop of Dragoons, Lincoln County	17 May 1802	p. 322
Stephen Marchnan, Ensign, Hancock County	21 May 1802	p. 323
William Hatchett, Captain, Oglethorpe County	31 May 1802	p. 323
Stephen Gatlen, Captain, Wilkes County	31 May 1802	p. 324
Joshua Hale, Lieutenant, Wilkes County	31 May 1802	p. 324
Robert Adair, Ensign, Wilkes County	31 May 1802	p. 325
Absalom Coursey, Captain, Jefferson County	3 Jun 1802	p. 325
John McCurdy, Captain, Elbert County	9 Jun 1802	p. 326
Pennell Wood, Lieutenant, Elbert County	9 Jun 1802	p. 326
James Cockran, Ensign, Elbert County	9 Jun 1802	p. 327
James Patton, Captain, Washington County	12 Jun 1802	p. 327
William Smith, Lieutenant, Washington County	12 Jun 1802	p. 328
John Roberds, Lieutenant, Bulloch County	12 Jun 1802	p. 328
Thomas Grines, Ensign, Bulloch County	12 Jun 1802	p. 329
Jesse Roberts, Ensign, Volunteer Company of Light Infantry, Columbia County	12 Jun 1802	p. 329
Charles Moore, Captain, Oglethorpe County	12 Jun 1802	p. 330
George Williamson, Lieutenant, Oglethorpe County	12 Jun 1802	p. 330
William D. Lane, Captain, Oglethorpe County	12 Jun 1802	p. 331
William Bassett, Captain, McIntosh County	12 Jun 1802	p. 331
John L. R. Holzendorf, Lieutenant, McIntosh County	12 Jun 1802	p. 332
Allen B. Powell, Ensign, McIntosh County	12 Jun 1802	p. 332
Richard Wood, Lieutenant, Clarke County	12 Jun 1802	p. 333
Elijah Melton, Ensign, Clarke County	12 Jun 1802	p. 333

Name, Rank, Unit	*Date*	*Page*
Major Henderson, Captain, Wilkes County	12 Jun 1802	p. 334
Thomas Watts, Lieutenant, Wilkes County	12 Jun 1802	p. 334
Elijah Slair, Ensign, Wilkes County	12 Jun 1802	p. 335
Lewis Lanier, Major, Bulloch County	12 Jun 1802	p. 335
James Alexander, Ensign, Volunteer Company of Rangers, Richmond County	12 Jun 1802	p. 336
William Lamkin, Lieutenant, Richmond County	12 Jun 1802	p. 336
Rodham Tallaws, Ensign, Richmond County	12 Jun 1802	p. 337
William Mobley, Ensign, Elbert County	14 Jun 1802	p. 337
Thomas Brixey, Ensign, Clarke County	14 Jun 1802	p. 338
Dempsey Justice, Captain, Rifle Company, Battalion 1, Regiment 2, Hancock County	16 Jun 1802	p. 338
Samuel Kirkpatrick, Ensign, Rifle Company, Battalion 1, Regiment 2, Hancock County	16 Jun 1802	p. 339
Michael Burk, Lieutenant, Volunteer Company of Hibernian Fusiliers, Chatham County	17 Jun 1802	p. 339
Thomas Robertson, Ensign, Volunteer Company of Hibernian Fusiliers, Chatham County	17 Jun 1802	p. 340
Charles Higdon, Major, Battalion 2, Montgomery County	17 Jun 1802	p. 340
Cullen Edwards, Lieutenant, Montgomery County	17 Jun 1802	p. 341
Dempsey Wilkerson, Ensign, Montgomery County	17 Jun 1802	p. 341
Josiah Drew, Lieutenant, Montgomery County	21 Jun 1802	p. 342
James Briggs, Ensign, Montgomery County	21 Jun 1802	p. 342
Thomas Fulton, Captain, Jefferson County	3 Jul 1802	p. 343
Joseph Cooper, First Lieutenant, Volunteer Company of Artillery, Regiment 1, Hancock County	5 Jul 1802	p. 343
Abda Christian, Lieutenant, Franklin County	5 Jul 1802	p. 344
Richard Hooper, Ensign, Franklin County	5 Jul 1802	p. 344
Josiah Cornett, Ensign, 1st Company, Battalion 1, Regiment 2, Burke County	5 Jul 1802	p. 345
Hardy Hobson, Lieutenant, 2nd Company, Battalion 1, Washington County	5 Jul 1802	p. 345
Aventon Griffin, Ensign, 2nd Company, Battalion 1, Washington County	5 Jul 1802	p. 346
Dunstar Blackwell, Captain, Elbert County	5 Jun 1802	p. 346
William McKenzie, Captain, Elbert County	5 Jul 1802	p. 347
John McDonald, Lieutenant, Elbert County	5 Jul 1802	p. 347
Peter Johnson, Ensign, Elbert County	5 Jul 1802	p. 348

Georgia Military Commissions, 1798–1818

Name, Rank, Unit	*Date*	*Page*
Jacob Adair, Captain, New Company, Jackson County	8 Jul 1802	p. 348
Thomas Rutledge, Lieutenant, New Company, Jackson County	8 Jul 1802	p. 349
James McCord, Ensign, New Company, Jackson County	8 Jul 1802	p. 349
Brigs Hopson, Major, Battalion 1, Washington County	9 Jul 1802	p. 350
James Christian, , Elbert County	13 Jul 1802	p. 350
Enoch James, Ensign, Elbert County	13 Jul 1802	p. 351
Joseph McConnell, Captain, Jackson County	13 Jul 1802	p. 351
John Wright, Ensign, Jackson County	13 Jul 1802	p. 352
Thomas Hudson, Captain, Clarke County	10 Aug 1802	p. 352
John Henson, Lieutenant, Clarke County	10 Aug 1802	p. 353
John Holder, Ensign, Clarke County	10 Aug 1802	p. 353
Jeremiah Brown, Captain, Clarke County	10 Aug 1802	p. 354
William Wooten, Lieutenant, Clarke County	10 Aug 1802	p. 354
Pressley Garner, Ensign, Clarke County	10 Aug 1802	p. 355
Thomas Hinsley, Captain, Volunteer Troop of Dragoons, Liberty County	14 Aug 1802	p. 355
John Underwood, Lieutenant, Volunteer Troop of Dragoons, Liberty County	14 Aug 1802	p. 356
John Ratliff, Ensign, Volunteer Troop of Dragoons, Liberty County	14 Aug 1802	p. 356
Joseph Austin, Cornet, Volunteer Troop of Dragoons, Liberty County	14 Aug 1802	p. 357
Elisha Ward, Lieutenant, Jefferson County	15 Aug 1802	p. 357
Becham Dye, Lieutenant, Elbert County	25 Aug 1802	p. 358
Joseph Griffin, Ensign, Elbert County	25 Aug 1802	p. 358
Richard Saunders, Lieutenant, Elbert County	25 Aug 1802	p. 359
James Walker, Ensign, Elbert County	25 Aug 1802	p. 359
William Tait, Lieutenant, Elbert County	25 Aug 1802	p. 360
John Cunningham, Ensign, Elbert County	25 Aug 1802	p. 360
Samuel Ferrels, Captain, Rifle Company, Elbert County	25 Aug 1802	p. 361
William Thomson, Lieutenant, Rifle Company, Elbert County	25 Aug 1802	p. 361
Thomas Williford, Ensign, Elbert County	25 Aug 1802	p. 362
Joseph R. Watkins, Lieutenant, Volunteer Troop of Dragoons, Elbert County	25 Aug 1802	p. 362
William Brown, Lieutenant, Rifle Company, Hancock County	25 Aug 1802	p. 363

Commissions Book 1800–1806

Name, Rank, Unit	*Date*	*Page*
Drury Gilbert, Lieutenant, Washington County	25 Aug 1802	p. 363
Frederick Watson, Ensign, Washington County	25 Aug 1802	p. 364
William Jansan, Captain, Hancock County	25 Aug 1802	p. 364
James G. Handle, Lieutenant, Hancock County	28 Aug 1802	p. 365
William Laurence, Ensign, Columbia County	31 Aug 1802	p. 365
Eli Peacock, Ensign, Jefferson County	1 Sep 1802	p. 366
Timothy Staley, Lieutenant, Jefferson County	15 Sep 1802	p. 366
Robert Fleming, Lieutenant, Jefferson County	15 Sep 1802	p. 367
Moses Loyd, Lieutenant, Hancock County	18 Sep 1802	p. 367
Isac Durham, Ensign, Hancock County	18 Sep 1802	p. 368
Moses Snow, Lieutenant, Jackson County	18 Sep 1802	p. 368
Jesse Lassiter, Captain, New Company, Montgomery County	18 Sep 1802	p. 369
Joshua Stivers, Ensign, Regiment 1, Hancock County	18 Sep 1802	p. 369
Riger Dawson, Ensign, Battalion 3, Washington County	1 Oct 1802	p. 370
Alexander Gordon, Ensign, Regiment 1, Burke County	16 Oct 1802	p. 370
George Pearson, Captain, Franklin County	21 Oct 1802	p. 371
Jesse Keaton, Lieutenant, Battalion 3, Washington County	21 Oct 1802	p. 371
John Fullilove, Ensign, Oglethorpe County	21 Oct 1802	p. 372
John Billingsbea, Captain, Greene County	21 Oct 1802	p. 372
Nathan Gen, Lieutenant, Greene County	21 Oct 1802	p. 373
Nathan Barnette, Ensign, Greene County	21 Oct 1802	p. 373
Jesse Booles, Ensign, Greene County	21 Oct 1802	p. 374
Abraham Greer, Lieutenant, Greene County	21 Oct 1802	p. 374
Thomas Handley, Ensign, Columbia County	22 Oct 1802	p. 375
John Burton, Lieutenant, Jefferson County	26 Oct 1802	p. 375
Burrel Peary, Captain, Warren County	26 Oct 1802	p. 376
Solomon Marshall, Captain, Columbia County	18 Nov 1802	p. 376
Isac Birdsong, Lieutenant, Oglethorpe County	18 Nov 1802	p. 377
Valentine Walker, Captain, Richmond County	28 Nov 1802	p. 377
John Hatcher, Captain, Richmond County	18 Nov 1802	p. 378
William Skimmer, Captain, Volunteer Troop of Dragoons, Screven County	18 Nov 1802	p. 378
John P. Lovett, Lieutenant, Volunteer Troop of Dragoons, Screven County	18 Nov 1802	p. 379

Georgia Military Commissions, 1798–1818

Name, Rank, Unit	*Date*	*Page*
Ebenezer Harding, Second Lieutenant, Volunteer Troop of Dragoons, Screven County	18 Nov 1802	p. 379
Bird Lemar, Cornet, Volunteer Troop of Dragoons, Screven County	18 Nov 1802	p. 380
Beattie McKigny, Captain, Clarke County	26 Nov 1802	p. 380
James Mersson, Lieutenant, Elbert County	26 Nov 1802	p. 381
William Powell, Ensign, Company at the Place of Thomas Hosed, Regiment 2, Hancock County	26 Nov 1802	p. 381
John Spinks, Lieutenant, Lincoln County	26 Nov 1802	p. 382
Elijah Loflin, Ensign, Hancock County	26 Nov 1802	p. 382
Solomon Beckham, Captain, Washington County	26 Nov 1802	p. 383
Zackriah Middleton, Captain, Clarke County	21 Dec 1802	p. 383
Roger Cogle, Lieutenant, Clarke County	21 Dec 1802	p. 384
John Anders, Ensign, Clarke County	21 Dec 1802	p. 384
Aron Boggs, Lieutenant, Clarke County	21 Dec 1802	p. 385
James Wallace, Ensign, Clarke County	21 Dec 1802	p. 385
James Buckannon, Lieutenant, Jefferson County	24 Dec 1802	p. 386
Daniel H. Zachry, Lieutenant, Volunteer Troop of Dragoons, Warren County	17 Dec 1802	p. 386
Atchison Barton, Ensign, Volunteer Troop of Dragoons, Battalion 2, Warren County	17 Dec 1802	p. 387
Timothy Mathews, Captain, Volunteer Troop of Dragoons, Warren County	17 Dec 1802	p. 387
Henry Kendall, Lieutenant, Volunteer Troop of Dragoons, Warren County	17 Dec 1802	p. 388
Ezekiel Alexander, Lieutenant, Volunteer Troop of Dragoons, Warren County	17 Dec 1802	p. 388
Rissle Jones, Lieutenant, Jackson County	30 Dec 1802	p. 389
Bennet Ivey, Ensign, Jackson County	30 Dec 1802	p. 389
Abraham Scott, First Lieutenant, Volunteer Troop of Dragoons, Jackson County	30 Dec 1802	p. 390
John Kinchen, Ensign, Hancock County	31 Dec 1802	p. 390
Josiah Grace, Lieutenant, Company ofRiflemen, Battalion 2, Regiment 1, Hancock County	31 Dec 1802	p. 391
William B. Turnell, Ensign, Company of Riflemen, Battalion 2, Regiment 1, Hancock County	31 Dec 1802	p. 391
Joseph McCullough, Captain, Battalion 2, Montgomery County	31 Dec 1802	p. 392

Name, Rank, Unit	Date	Page
Ashley Wood, Second Lieutenant, Volunteer Troop of Horse, Jefferson County	30 Dec 1802	p. 392
James Jones, Lieutenant, Battalion 2, Montgomery County	31 Dec 1802	p. 393
Francis Trotte, Captain, Richmond County	12 Jan 1803	p. 393
Henry Tate, Lieutenant, Richmond County	12 Jan 1803	p. 394
Richard Ringold, Ensign, Richmond County	12 Jan 1803	p. 394
Jesse Humphry, Lieutenant, Richmond County	12 Jan 1803	p. 395
Jepthat Daniel, Ensign, Richmond County	12 Jan 1803	p. 395
Robert Beale, Captain, Battalion 1, Warren County	12 Jan 1803	p. 396
Robert Oliver, Lieutenant, Battalion 1, Warren County	12 Jan 1803	p. 396
Thomas Flake, Ensign, Battalion 1, Warren County	12 Jan 1803	p. 397
John Downer, Ensign, Jefferson County	22 Jan 1803	p. 397
Samuel Henderson, Major, Jackson County	25 Jan 1803	p. 398
Erwin Wise, Captain, Jackson County	25 Jan 1803	p. 398
John Shellman, Lieutenant Colonel Commandant, Jackson County	10 Feb 1803	p. 399
Abner Hammond, Captain, Louisville Company, Battalion 2, Jefferson County	10 Feb 1803	p. 399
David McCormick, Lieutenant, Louisville Volunteer Guards, Battalion 1, Jefferson County	10 Feb 1803	p. 400
George R. Clayton, Ensign, Louisville Volunteer Guards, Battalion 1, Jefferson County	10 Feb 1803	p. 400
Elkanah Briggs, Captain, Battalion 2, Jefferson County	10 Feb 1803	p. 401
Peter Stoval, Captain, Wilkes County	14 Feb 1803	p. 401
George Wynn, , Wilkes County	14 Feb 1803	p. 402
Allen Hartsfield, Ensign, Wilkes County	14 Feb 1803	p. 402
George Walker, Captain, Volunteer Troop of Horse, Richmond County	8 Mar 1803	p. 403
Zachariah Williams, First Lieutenant, Volunteer Troop of Horse, Richmond County	8 Mar 1803	p. 403
Nicholas Fox, Second Lieutenant, Volunteer Troop of Horse, Richmond County	8 Mar 1803	p. 404
William H. Durkee, Cornet, Volunteer Troop of Horse, Richmond County	8 Mar 1803	p. 404
Mathew Alberton, Ensign, Regiment 2, Burke County	8 Mar 1803	p. 405
Robert Flournoy, Captain, Volunteer Company of Artillery, Jefferson County	11 Mar 1803	p. 405

Georgia Military Commissions, 1798–1818

Name, Rank, Unit	Date	Page
John Bostwick, First Lieutenant, Volunteer Company of Artillery, Jefferson County	11 Mar 1803	p. 406
Elijah Owens, Captain, Elbert County	16 Mar 1803	p. 406
Josiah Dobbs, Lieutenant, Elbert County	16 Mar 1803	p. 407
Abner McGarrity, Ensign, Elbert County	16 Mar 1803	p. 407
Peter Smith, Captain, Elbert County	16 Mar 1803	p. 408
Josiah Powel, Lieutenant, Elbert County	16 Mar 1803	p. 408
Nelson Higginbotham, Ensign, Elbert County	16 Mar 1803	p. 409
William Allen, Captain, Richmond County	16 Mar 1803	p. 409
Waddle Allen, Lieutenant, Richmond County	16 Mar 1803	p. 410
Jesse Connel, Captain, Hancock County	30 Mar 1803	p. 410
Henry Tripp, Captain, Rifle Company, Battalion 1, Hancock County	30 Mar 1803	p. 411
James Ross, Lieutenant, Rifle Company, Battalion 1, Hancock County	30 Mar 1803	p. 411
John M. Dooly, Captain, Hancock County	30 Mar 1803	p. 412
Miles Hardy, Ensign, Hancock County	30 Mar 1803	p. 412
Averton Walton, Captain, Hancock County	30 Mar 1803	p. 413
Needam Avird, Lieutenant, Hancock County	30 Mar 1803	p. 413
Hardy Hunter, Ensign, Hancock County	30 Mar 1803	p. 414
William Wilkins, Captain, Wilkes County	30 Mar 1803	p. 414
Lodowick Brooks, Ensign, Wilkes County	30 Mar 1803	p. 415
Thomas Dawson, Captain, Greene County	30 Mar 1803	p. 415
Abner Semonton, Lieutenant, Greene County	30 Mar 1803	p. 416
James K. Daniel, Captain, Greene County	30 Mar 1803	p. 416
Jonathan Hoge, Lieutenant, Greene County	30 Mar 1803	p. 417
William Wood, Captain, Greene County	30 Mar 1803	p. 417
Robert Sansom, Ensign, Greene County	30 Mar 1803	p. 418
Jesse Berry, Ensign, Rifle Company, Oglethorpe County	30 Mar 1803	p. 418
James Rutledge, Lieutenant, Jackson County	30 Mar 1803	p. 419
John Lindsay, Ensign, Jackson County	30 Mar 1803	p. 419
Fraser Brindley, Lieutenant, Franklin County	30 Mar 1803	p. 420
Lambert King, Ensign, Franklin County	30 Mar 1803	p. 420
Thadeus Beall, Captain, Columbia County	6 May 1803	p. 421
Jonathan Armstong, Lieutenant, Columbia County	6 May 1803	p. 421
James Mikell, Captain, Liberty County	30 Mar 1803	p. 422
Thomas Wilder, Lieutenant, Liberty County	30 Mar 1803	p. 422

Name, Rank, Unit	**Date**	**Page**
William Wilder, Ensign, Liberty County	30 Mar 1803	p. 423
Abner Holliday, Captain, Burke County	30 Mar 1803	p. 423
Noah Griffin, Ensign, Burke County	30 Mar 1803	p. 424
Nathan Bass, Lieutenant, Burke County	30 Mar 1803	p. 424
Jacob Jarves, Ensign, Burke County	30 Mar 1803	p. 425
William Wynne, Captain, Volunteer Troop of Horse, Burke County	30 Mar 1803	p. 425
Blassingame Thomas, Ensign, Volunteer Troop of Dragoons, Jefferson County	30 Mar 1803	p. 426
Isac Roberson, Captain, Volunteer Troop of Dragoons, Jefferson County	30 Mar 1803	p. 426
Jesse Hammock, First Lieutenant, Volunteer Troop of Dragoons, Jefferson County	30 Mar 1803	p. 427
Stephen Gatlin, Captain, Greene County	30 Mar 1803	p. 427
William Harris, Lieutenant, Greene County	5 May 1803	p. 428
John Willson, Ensign, Greene County	5 May 1803	p. 428
Samuel Law, Captain, Volunteer Troop of Dragoons, Liberty County	5 May 1803	p. 429
Daniel Dolly, Captain, Screven County	5 May 1803	p. 429
Samuel Hudson, Lieutenant, Screven County	5 May 1803	p. 430
Gorge Wolf, Ensign, Effingham County	5 May 1803	p. 430
Jacob Cody, Ensign, Jackson County	5 May 1803	p. 431
Ralph Pendral, Lieutenant, Burke County	4 May 1803	p. 431
Burrel Walter, Ensign, Burke County	4 May 1803	p. 432
Moses Jones, Captain, Lincoln County	4 May 1803	p. 432
Joshua Williams, Lieutenant, Lincoln County	4 May 1803	p. 433
Joseph Freeman, Ensign, Lincoln County	4 May 1803	p. 433
John Crosier, Lieutenant, Lincoln County	4 May 1803	p. 434
Owen Holliday, Captain, Wilkes County	4 May 1803	p. 434
Benjamin Hill, Lieutenant, Wilkes County	4 May 1803	p. 435
Henry Jones, Ensign, Wilkes County	4 May 1803	p. 435
John Heard, Captain, Wilkes County	4 May 1803	p. 436
William Smith, Ensign, Wilkes County	4 May 1803	p. 436
Elijah Evans, Lieutenant, Wilkes County	4 May 1803	p. 437
Peter Bennel, Ensign, Wilkes County	4 May 1803	p. 437
Abner Ponder, Captain, Oglethorpe County	4 May 1803	p. 438
William McKleroy, Lieutenant, Oglethorpe County	4 May 1803	p. 438

Georgia Military Commissions, 1798–1818

Name, Rank, Unit	Date	Page
Robert Thomson, Ensign, Oglethorpe County	4 May 1803	p. 439
John Beasly, Captain, Oglethorpe County	4 May 1803	p. 439
Isac Collier, Major, Oglethorpe County	4 May 1803	p. 440
John Carter, Major, Oglethorpe County	4 May 1803	p. 440
John Powel, Ensign, Oglethorpe County	4 May 1803	p. 441
Isac Williams, Ensign, Oglethorpe County	4 May 1803	p. 441
William Clark, Captain, Clarke County	7 May 1803	p. 442
John Elliott, Lieutenant, Clarke County	7 May 1803	p. 442
William Thompson, Ensign, Clarke County	7 May 1803	p. 443
Nathaniel Mires, Captain, Clarke County	7 May 1803	p. 443
Thomas Hooks, Lieutenant, Clarke County	7 May 1803	p. 444
Bryant Williams, Ensign, Clarke County	7 May 1803	p. 444
Aron Buggs, Ensign, Clarke County	7 May 1803	p. 445
Warham Casly, Lieutenant, Clarke County	7 May 1803	p. 445
Thomas McFalls, Ensign, Clarke County	7 May 1803	p. 446
Stephen Neil, Lieutenant, Franklin County	7 May 1803	p. 446
James Haggard, Ensign, Franklin County	7 May 1803	p. 447
George Reid, Captain, Volunteer Troop of Dragoons, Regiment 1, Jackson County	7 May 1803	p. 447
John Smith, First Lieutenant, Volunteer Troop of Dragoons, Regiment 1, Jackson County	7 May 1803	p. 448
Thomas Neblack, Second Lieutenant, Volunteer Troop of Dragoons, Regiment 1, Jackson County	7 May 1803	p. 448
Thomas Black, Cornet, Volunteer Troop of Dragoons, Regiment 1, Franklin County	7 May 1803	p. 449
John Hendrick, Captain, Wilkes County	7 May 1803	p. 449
Solomon Perkins, Lieutenant, Wilkes County	9 Jun 1803	p. 450
Herman Mercer, Ensign, Wilkes County	9 Jun 1803	p. 450
John Pennington, Lieutenant, Jackson County	10 May 1803	p. 451
Henry Graybill, Lieutenant, Hancock County	1 Jun 1803	p. 451
Benjamin Herbert, Ensign, Hancock County	1 Jun 1803	p. 452
William Carel, Captain, Screven County	1 Jun 1803	p. 452
Ephiam Dunn, Ensign, Warren County	1 Jun 1803	p. 453
John Garrett, Captain, Greene County	3 Jun 1803	p. 453
Thomas Adams, Lieutenant, Greene County	3 Jun 1803	p. 454
Samson Neyle, Captain, Chatham County	20 Jun 1803	p. 454

Name, Rank, Unit	Date	Page
John J. Johnson, Lieutenant, Volunteer Troop of Dragoons, Chatham County	20 Jun 1803	p. 455
John Poullen, Ensign, Volunteer Troop of Dragoons, Chatham County	30 Jun 1803	p. 455
Roger McCarty, Lieutenant, Volunteer Troop of Dragoons, Chatham County	20 Jun 1803	p. 456
John Pettilane, Ensign, Volunteer Troop of Dragoons, Chatham County	20 Jun 1803	p. 456
Philip Densler, Lieutenant, Volunteer Troop of Dragoons, Chatham County	20 Jun 1803	p. 457
George Allen, Ensign, Volunteer Troop of Dragoons, Chatham County	20 Jun 1803	p. 457
Peter Shick, First Lieutenant, Volunteer Troop of Dragoons, Chatham County	20 Jun 1803	p. 458
John J. Gray, Second Lieutenant, Volunteer Troop of Dragoons, Chatham County	20 Jun 1803	p. 458
William A. Moore, Cornet, Volunteer Troop of Dragoons, Chatham County	20 Jun 1803	p. 459
Thomas Barron, Ensign, Greene County	23 Jun 1803	p. 459
Daniel Payne, Major, Tattnall County	20 Jul 1803	p. 460
Ishen McClendon, Captain, Montgomery County	20 Jul 1803	p. 460
John Taylor, Captain, Burke County	20 Jul 1803	p. 461
Alexander Godwin, Lieutenant, Burke County	20 Jul 1803	p. 461
Bardle Sharp, Ensign, Burke County	20 Jul 1803	p. 462
Runtin Thomson, Captain, Volunteer Troop of Dragoons, Burke County	20 Jul 1803	p. 462
William Triptell, Lieutenant, Volunteer Troop of Dragoons, Burke County	20 Jul 1803	p. 463
Daniel Maund, Ensign, Volunteer Troop of Dragoons, Burke County	20 Jul 1803	p. 463
Allen Daniel, Lieutenant Colonel Commandant, Elbert County	20 Jul 1803	p. 464
Adam Jones, Ensign, Volunteer Company of Infantry, Battalion 2, Jefferson County	20 Jul 1803	p. 464
Sherod Liles, Captain, Washington County	26 Jul 1803	p. 465
Samuel Ledbetter, Lieutenant, Washington County	26 Jul 1803	p. 465
Henry Smith, Ensign, Washington County	26 Jul 1803	p. 466
Nicholas Sheets, Captain, Wilkes County	26 Jul 1803	p. 466
Thomas Woreham, Ensign, Wilkes County	26 Jul 1803	p. 467

Georgia Military Commissions, 1798–1818

Name, Rank, Unit	Date	Page
John Scriven, Captain, Chatham County	15 Jul 1803	p. 467
William Ogle, Captain, Columbia County	15 Jul 1803	p. 468
John Colbert, Lieutenant, Columbia County	15 Jul 1803	p. 468
Reubin Taylor, First Lieutenant, Volunteer Troop of Dragoons, Effingham County	15 Jul 1803	p. 469
Christian Trutlin, Second Lieutenant, Volunteer Troop of Dragoons, Effingham County	15 Jul 1803	p. 469
John Grovenstine, Cornet, Volunteer Troop of Dragoons, Effingham County	15 Jul 1803	p. 470
William Maguier, Captain, Elbert County	15 Jul 1803	p. 470
Samuel James, Lieutenant, Elbert County	15 Jul 1803	p. 471
Jacob Linsay, Ensign, Elbert County	15 Jul 1803	p. 471
John Shouders, Ensign, Hancock County	15 Jul 1803	p. 472
Robert McCombs, Ensign, Richmond County	15 Jul 1803	p. 472
Roger Lawson, Lieutenant, Washington County	15 Jul 1803	p. 473
James Runsly, Ensign, Wilkes County	15 Jul 1803	p. 473
William Scott, Captain, Volunteer Troop of Rangers, Richmond County	1 Aug 1803	p. 474
John Campbell, Lieutenant, Volunteer Troop of Rangers, Richmond County	1 Aug 1803	p. 474
George M. Evans, Ensign, Volunteer Company of Rangers, Richmond County	1 Aug 1803	p. 475
William Camp, Captain, Jackson County	2 Aug 1803	p. 475
Andrew Camp, Lieutenant, Jackson County	2 Aug 1803	p. 476
More Henly, Ensign, Jackson County	2 Aug 1803	p. 476
William Dunn, Lieutenant, Hancock County	2 Aug 1803	p. 477
Henry D. Stone, Captain, Volunteer Company of Infantry, Glynn County	4 Aug 1803	p. 477
Alen McKinzee, Lieutenant, Volunteer Company of Infantry, Glynn County	4 Aug 1803	p. 478
William Lee Jr., Ensign, Volunteer Company of Infantry, Glynn County	4 Aug 1803	p. 478
Samuel Mongomery, Captain, Jackson County	3 Aug 1803	p. 479
Silas Barron, Lieutenant, Jackson County	3 Aug 1803	p. 479
Joshua Houghton, Major, Greene County	5 Aug 1803	p. 480
David Bush, Major, Volunteer Troop of Dragoons, Regiment 2, Burke County	19 Aug 1803	p. 480
Robert Brasswell, Second Lieutenant, Volunteer Troop of Dragoons, Regiment 2, Burke County	19 Aug 1803	p. 481

Name, Rank, Unit	Date	Page
William King, Second Lieutenant, Volunteer Troop of Dragoons, Camden County	19 Aug 1803	p. 481
Zachriah Sinquefield, Second Lieutenant, Volunteer Troop of Dragoons, Columbia County	19 Aug 1803	p. 482
Abraham Greer, Captain, Greene County	19 Aug 1803	p. 482
Elisha Harrilson, Lieutenant, Greene County	19 Aug 1803	p. 483
William Pennington, Ensign, Hancock County	19 Aug 1803	p. 483
Edward Cox, Ensign, Hancock County	19 Aug 1803	p. 484
Levi Ellis, Ensign, Volunteer Company of Riflemen, Hancock County	19 Aug 1803	p. 484
Solomon Crawford, Ensign, Battalion 1, Jefferson County	19 Aug 1803	p. 485
Rouland Hudson, Captain, Oglethorpe County	19 Aug 1803	p. 485
William Ward, Ensign, Oglethorpe County	19 Aug 1803	p. 486
Chesley Bostwick, Captain, Richmond County	19 Aug 1803	p. 486
Charles Jerrels, Major, Elbert County	29 Aug 1803	p. 487
Charles Ray, First Lieutenant, Volunteer Troop of Dragoons, Washington County	23 Aug 1803	p. 487
Joseph P. Wadkins, Captain, Volunteer Troop of Horse, Battalion 3, Elbert County	27 Aug 1803	p. 488
William Gummage, Captain, Wilkes County	5 Sep 1803	p. 488
Wiley Saxon, Lieutenant, Wilkes County	5 Sep 1803	p. 489
John Pointer, Ensign, Wilkes County	5 Sep 1803	p. 489
Robert Douglass, Lieutenant, Montgomery County	7 Sep 1803	p. 490
John Gresham, Lieutenant Colonel Commandant, Oglethorpe County	10 Sep 1803	p. 490
Singleton Holt, Captain, Hancock County	12 Sep 1803	p. 491
John Dickerson, Ensign, Hancock County	12 Sep 1803	p. 491
James Majors, Ensign, Hancock County	12 Sep 1803	p. 492
Batson Bullock, Ensign, Rifle Company, Hancock County	12 Sep 1803	p. 492
William Sheales, Lieutenant, Clarke County	12 Sep 1803	p. 493
Terry Harris, Ensign, Clarke County	12 Sep 1803	p. 493
William Truman, Lieutenant, Oglethorpe County	12 Sep 1803	p. 494
Edward Harden, Lieutenant, Chatham County	12 Sep 1803	p. 494
George H. Davidson, Ensign, Chatham County	17 Sep 1803	p. 495
Louis B. Cuthbert, Lieutenant, Chatham County	17 Sep 1803	p. 495
James Bryan, Ensign, Chatham County	17 Sep 1803	p. 496
Robert Anderson, Ensign, Burke County	17 Sep 1803	p. 496
James Dozier, Lieutenant, Wilkes County	17 Sep 1803	p. 497

Georgia Military Commissions, 1798–1818

Name, Rank, Unit	Date	Page
Thomas Goffard, Ensign, Wilkes County	17 Sep 1803	p. 497
Littleberry Little, Captain, Wilkes County	20 Sep 1803	p. 498
Joshua Hail, Lieutenant, Wilkes County	20 Sep 1803	p. 498
James Little, Ensign, Wilkes County	20 Sep 1803	p. 499
James Mattison, Captain, Oglethorpe County	24 Sep 1803	p. 499
William Sorrow, Ensign, Oglethorpe County	24 Sep 1803	p. 500
Elias Drake, Captain, Burke County	5 Oct 1803	p. 500
Ichabud Scarboroug, Lieutenant, Burke County	5 Sep 1803	p. 501
Barrel Hutchins, Ensign, Burke County	5 Sep 1803	p. 501
Thomas Sparks, Captain, Greene County	5 Oct 1803	p. 502
Duke Williams, Lieutenant, Greene County	5 Oct 1803	p. 502
Andrew Hamilton, Captain, Wilkes County	5 Oct 1803	p. 503
Thomas Haynes, Major, Greene County	8 Oct 1803	p. 503
Jno Y. White, Captain, Chatham County	8 Oct 1803	p. 504
Joseph A. Scott, Ensign, Chatham County	8 Oct 1803	p. 504
Duncan McNair, Captain, Jefferson County	12 Oct 1803	p. 505
Robert Womack, Ensign, Jefferson County	12 Oct 1803	p. 505
John Chinken, Captain, Hancock County	12 Oct 1803	p. 506
John Hill, Lieutenant, Hancock County	12 Oct 1803	p. 506
Eldrige Hargrove, Lieutenant, Jackson County	12 Oct 1803	p. 507
Calvin Whittenton, Ensign, Jackson County	12 Oct 1803	p. 507
Moses Stallings, Captain, Oglethorpe County	14 Oct 1803	p. 508
Samuel Clay, Lieutenant, Oglethorpe County	14 Oct 1803	p. 508
Noah Ramey, Ensign, Oglethorpe County	14 Oct 1803	p. 509
Greene R. Duke, Lieutenant, Volunteer Troop of Hibernian Fusiliers, Chatham County	14 Oct 1803	p. 509
Richard Stewart, Ensign, Volunteer Company of Hibernian Fusiliers, Chatham County	14 Oct 1803	p. 510
George W. Mare, Captain, Columbia County	19 Oct 1803	p. 510
Phillip Sanders, Lieutenant, Columbia County	19 Oct 1803	p. 511
Edward Sanders, Ensign, Columbia County	19 Oct 1803	p. 511
John Chisolm, First Lieutenant, Volunteer Troop of Dragoons, Elbert County	25 Oct 1803	p. 512
Thomas Smith, Lieutenant, Elbert County	25 Oct 1803	p. 512
Henry Banner, Cornet, Volunteer Troop of Dragoons, Warren County	25 Oct 1803	p. 513
John Collins, Ensign, Richmond County	25 Oct 1803	p. 513

Commissions Book 1800–1806

Name, Rank, Unit	Date	Page
Solomon Shad, Lieutenant Colonel Commandant, Chatham County	12 Nov 1803	p. 514
Alen Berckum, Captain, Washington County	18 Nov 1803	p. 514
Loveless Abott, Ensign, Washington County	18 Nov 1803	p. 515
Jonathan Gauden, Captain, Liberty County	18 Nov 1803	p. 515
Wiley Sharp, Captain, Burke County	23 Nov 1803	p. 516
Daniel Sharp, Lieutenant, Burke County	23 Nov 1803	p. 516
George Washington, Ensign, Burke County	23 Nov 1803	p. 517
William Jones, Lieutenant, Clarke County	23 Nov 1803	p. 517
William Jones Sr., Ensign, Clarke County	23 Nov 1803	p. 518
Joseph Tennel, Ensign, Columbia County	23 Nov 1803	p. 518
Robert Moon, Captain, Elbert County	23 Nov 1803	p. 519
James Long, Lieutenant, Elbert County	23 Nov 1803	p. 519
Patrick C. Buckhaman, Ensign, Elbert County	23 Nov 1803	p. 520
Benjamin Talman, , Elbert County	23 Nov 1803	p. 520
Joshua Tinar, Ensign, Elbert County	23 Nov 1803	p. 521
Neely Dobson, Captain, Franklin County	23 Nov 1803	p. 521
Daniel Wagnon, Lieutenant, Greene County	23 Nov 1803	p. 522
Archibald Wates, Ensign, Greene County	23 Nov 1803	p. 522
William King, Lieutenant, Greene County	23 Nov 1803	p. 523
William Dolvin, Ensign, Greene County	23 Nov 1803	p. 523
Elijah Lamsdin, Ensign, Greene County	23 Nov 1803	p. 524
William Powell, Lieutenant, Hancock County	23 Nov 1803	p. 524
William Buckholts, Lieutenant, Hancock County	23 Nov 1803	p. 525
Daniel Canlor, Ensign, Hancock County	23 Nov 1803	p. 525
Thomas Bell, Captain, Hancock County	23 Nov 1803	p. 526
Joseph Paxton, Captain, Hancock County	23 Nov 1803	p. 526
Benjamin McClusky, Lieutenant, Hancock County	23 Nov 1803	p. 527
William Allison, Ensign, Hancock County	23 Nov 1803	p. 527
Thomas Thomas, Ensign, Lincoln County	23 Nov 1803	p. 528
Richard Stokes, Captain, Volunteer Troop of Dragoons, Lincoln County	23 Nov 1803	p. 528
Thomas Graham, First Lieutenant, Volunteer Troop of Dragoons, Lincoln County	23 Nov 1803	p. 529
Samuel Thomson, Second Lieutenant, Volunteer Troop of Dragoons, Lincoln County	23 Nov 1803	p. 529

Georgia Military Commissions, 1798–1818

Name, Rank, Unit	Date	Page
John Thompson, Cornet, Volunteer Troop of Dragoons, Lincoln County	23 Nov 1803	p. 530
Isham Raney, Captain, Oglethorpe County	23 Nov 1803	p. 530
John Braughton, Second Lieutenant, Oglethorpe County	23 Nov 1803	p. 531
Jesse Slaton, Lieutenant, Screven County	23 Nov 1803	p. 531
James Slaton, Ensign, Screven County	23 Nov 1803	p. 532
John Collins, Captain, Washington County	23 Nov 1803	p. 532
Jesse Colins, Lieutenant, Washington County	23 Nov 1803	p. 533
Epps Brown, Lieutenant Colonel Commandant, Hancock County	3 Dec 1803	p. 533
James Armour, , Greene County	7 Dec 1803	p. 534
John Gaslin, Lieutenant, Greene County	7 Dec 1803	p. 534
Joshua Willson, Ensign, Greene County	7 Dec 1803	p. 535
William Cawsly, Captain, Greene County	7 Dec 1803	p. 535
Little B. Bostwick, Lieutenant, Greene County	7 Dec 1803	p. 536
Nathaniel Holvel, Ensign, Greene County	7 Dec 1803	p. 536
Robert Read, Captain, Greene County	7 Dec 1803	p. 537
Robert Walker, Lieutenant, Greene County	7 Dec 1803	p. 537
Joshua Lester, Ensign, Greene County	7 Dec 1803	p. 538
George Willis, Lieutenant Colonel Commandant, Regiment 2, Greene County	16 Dec 1803	p. 538
William Wiggins, Major, Battalion 2, Regiment 2, Greene County	16 Dec 1803	p. 539
Gilbert Gay, Captain, Clarke County	21 Dec 1803	p. 539
Robert Cole, Lieutenant, Clarke County	21 Dec 1803	p. 540
Nehemah Scrogin, Ensign, Clarke County	21 Dec 1803	p. 540
Elijah Molton, Captain, New Company, Clarke County	9 Dec 1803	p. 541
B. William Thompson, Lieutenant, New Company, Clarke County	9 Dec 1803	p. 541
Micajah Stenson, Ensign, New Company, Clarke County	9 Dec 1803	p. 542
Warham Easly, Captain, Clarke County	9 Dec 1803	p. 542
Richard Laurance, Lieutenant, Clarke County	9 Dec 1803	p. 543
James Hitchcock, Captain, Clarke County	9 Dec 1803	p. 543
James Christian, Captain, Elbert County	9 Dec 1803	p. 544
Henry P. Crittenger, Lieutenant, Elbert County	9 Dec 1803	p. 544
Pryor Crittinger, Ensign, Elbert County	9 Dec 1803	p. 545
Edward Storry, Captain, Volunteer Troop of Dragoons, Elbert County	9 Dec 1803	p. 545

Name, Rank, Unit	Date	Page
James Christian, First Lieutenant, Volunteer Troop of Dragoons, Elbert County	9 Dec 1803	p. 546
Anthony Storry, Second Lieutenant, Volunteer Troop of Dragoons, Elbert County	9 Dec 1803	p. 546
William Thomas, Lieutenant, Franklin County	9 Dec 1803	p. 547
Windsor Dixon, Lieutenant, Screven County	9 Dec 1803	p. 547
David Burke, Ensign, Screven County	14 Jan 1804	p. 548
Sampson Ball, Lieutenant, Liberty County	14 Jan 1804	p. 548
Walton Harris, Lieutenant Colonel Commandant, Jackson County	24 Jan 1804	p. 549
John Bostwick, Captain, Volunteer Company of Artillery, Jefferson County	2 Feb 1804	p. 549
Michall Shelman, First Lieutenant, Volunteer Company of Artillery, Jefferson County	2 Feb 1804	p. 550
Leon H. Marks, Second Lieutenant, Volunteer Company of Artillery, Regiment 0	15 Feb 1804	p. 550
George Rootes Clayton, Lieutenant, Volunteer Company of Infantry (styled the Louisville Guards), Jefferson County	5 Apr 1804	p. 551
James Robinson, Ensign, Volunteer Company of Infantry (styled the Louisville Guards), Jefferson County	5 Apr 1804	p. 551
John Cobbs, Second Lieutenant, Volunteer Company of Artillery, Jefferson County	5 Apr 1804	p. 552
Thacker Vivion Jr., Lieutenant Colonel Commandant, Jefferson County	16 Apr 1804	p. 552
John Scriven, Major, Battalion 2	17 Jan 1804	p. 553
John King, Major, Battalion 3	12 Feb 1804	p. 553
Reubin G. Taylor, Captain, Volunteer Troop of Dragoons, Battalion 3	15 Apr 1804	p. 554
Luke Wilson, First Lieutenant, Volunteer Troop of Dragoons, Battalion 3	15 Apr 1804	p. 554
Isaac Harrell, Ensign, District 17	17 Apr 1804	p. 555
William A. Dunham, Ensign, District 21	15 Apr 1804	p. 555
Jesse H. Harrison, Captain, District 22	9 Feb 1804	p. 556
Bright Baker, Lieutenant, District 22	9 Feb 1804	p. 556
Jesse Campbell, Ensign, District 22	9 Feb 1804	p. 557
John Johnson, Captain, District 28	4 Dec 1803	p. 557
James Jones, Lieutenant, District 28	4 Dec 1803	p. 558
James Smith, Captain, District 29	25 Feb 1804	p. 558

Georgia Military Commissions, 1798–1818

Name, Rank, Unit	Date	Page
Robert Rudolph, Lieutenant, District 29	25 Feb 1804	p. 559
Charles Stohl, Ensign, District 29	25 Feb 1804	p. 559
John Floyd, Captain, District 31	29 Mar 1804	p. 560
Isaac Creny, Lieutenant, District 31	29 Mar 1804	p. 560
John May, Ensign, District 31	29 Mar 1804	p. 561
William Ashly, Captain, District 32	15 May 1803	p. 561
Joseph Raines, Lieutenant, District 32	15 May 1803	p. 562
John Bailey, Ensign, District 32	15 May 1803	p. 562
John Hardy, Captain, District 33	11 Dec 1803	p. 563
John Paris, Lieutenant, District 33	11 Dec 1803	p. 563
Benjamin Turner, Ensign, District 33	11 Dec 1803	p. 564
John Dunwody, Captain, District 36	19 Feb 1804	p. 564
William Williams, Lieutenant, District 46	19 Feb 1804	p. 565
Drury Jones Jr., Ensign, District 46	19 Feb 1804	p. 565
Samuel Lockhart, Captain, District 49	23 Dec 1803	p. 566
Jesse Wiggins, Lieutenant, District 49	22 Apr 1804	p. 566
Elijah Beacham, Ensign, District 49	23 Dec 1803	p. 567
Aaron Rhodes, Lieutenant, District 60	15 Jan 1804	p. 567
James Gunn, Ensign, District 60	15 Jan 1804	p. 568
Robert Moore, Ensign, District 61	22 Apr 1804	p. 568
Gilbert Neyland, Lieutenant, District 70	22 Apr 1804	p. 569
Edmund Robertson, Ensign, District 70	22 Apr 1804	p. 569
William Clark, Captain, District 72	11 Mar 1804	p. 570
Kinchin Hilleard, Ensign, District 74	22 Jan 1804	p. 570
Uz Floyd, Ensign, District 75	13 Mar 1804	p. 571
Edward Moore, Lieutenant Colonel Commandant	11 Mar 1804	p. 571
William Martin, Captain	10 Mar 1804	p. 572
Samuel Bridgewater, Lieutenant	10 Mar 1804	p. 572
John Owen, Ensign	10 Mar 1804	p. 573
John Allen, Ensign	2 Feb 1804	p. 573
Allen Brasswell, First Lieutenant	11 Mar 1804	p. 574
Joseph Clarkson, Major	21 Mar 1804	p. 574
Paul Williams, Captain	18 Dec 1803	p. 575
John Hulsy, Lieutenant	18 Dec 1803	p. 575
Jeremiah Murdock, Captain	11 Dec 1804	p. 576
William Coulter, Lieutenant	11 Dec 1803	p. 576

Name, Rank, Unit	Date	Page
Aquilla Greene, Captain	29 Apr 1804	p. 577
John Brice, Ensign	24 Jul 1803	p. 577
John Gaddis, Lieutenant	11 Dec 1803	p. 578
Elijah Strong, Ensign	19 Dec 1803	p. 578
Jeremiah Darby, Captain	12 Apr 1804	p. 579
Alexander McMillan, Captain	17 Apr 1804	p. 579
Etheldred Fennel, Lieutenant	17 Apr 1804	p. 580
Samuel Martin, Ensign	17 Apr 1804	p. 580
Abraham Tally, Ensign	25 Dec 1803	p. 581
Harbert Dunaven, Lieutenant	25 Dec 1804	p. 581
Henry Evans, Ensign	25 Dec 1803	p. 582
Robert White, Ensign	7 Feb 1804	p. 582
William Gardner, Captain	31 Mar 1804	p. 583
Bartlett Simms, Lieutenant	31 Mar 1804	p. 583
George Dykes, Lieutenant	15 Feb 1804	p. 584
Robert Graves, Ensign	15 Feb 1804	p. 584
Edwin Baker, Captain	13 Mar 1804	p. 585
Barton Achinson, Lieutenant	13 Mar 1804	p. 585
Shemel Drane, Ensign	13 Mar 1804	p. 586
Thomas Mullins, Captain	8 Apr 1804	p. 586
John Hardy, Ensign	8 Apr 1804	p. 587
John Angling Jr., Ensign	20 Dec 1803	p. 587
Isham Fuller, Lieutenant	12 Apr 1804	p. 588
Francis W. Ware, Second Lieutenant	12 Mar 1804	p. 588
Robert Whitefield, Lieutenant	12 Apr 1804	p. 589
Reed Dupree, Captain, Volunteer Troop of Dragoons	14 Jan 1804	p. 589
James Howard, Captain	25 Dec 1803	p. 590
Samuel Hodges, Lieutenant	25 Dec 1803	p. 590
Alexander Reid, Major	26 Feb 1804	p. 591
William Barnes, Captain	15 Mar 1804	p. 591
Stephen Daniel, Lieutenant	15 Mar 1804	p. 592
John Rease, Ensign	15 Mar 1804	p. 592
Henry Graybill, Captain	14 Jan 1804	p. 593
Benjmain Hurbert, Lieutenant	14 Jan 1804	p. 593
Joseph Grimsley, Ensign	14 Jan 1804	p. 594
Henry Huff, Captain	25 Feb 1804	p. 594

Georgia Military Commissions, 1798–1818

Name, Rank, Unit	Date	Page
Edmund Corley, Major	13 Mar 1804	p. 595
William Hudson, Captain	15 Apr 1804	p. 595
Jeremiah Mapp, Lieutenant	10 Mar 1804	p. 596
Benjamin Taliaferro, Major	25 Mar 1804	p. 596
William Brown, Captain	18 Feb 1804	p. 597
Lindsey Thornton, Lieutenant	23 Mar 1804	p. 597
David Irwin, Lieutenant	17 Mar 1804	p. 598
Allen Knight, Ensign	26 Feb 1804	p. 598
Isham S. Fannin, Captain	5 Feb 1804	p. 599
Alexander McCain, Lieutenant	5 Feb 1804	p. 599
William Curry, Ensign	5 Feb 1804	p. 600
Elisha Whatley, Ensign	11 Mar 1804	p. 600
James Mahony, Lieutenant	28 Feb 1804	p. 601
James Russel, Ensign	28 Feb 1804	p. 601
James Tatom, Lieutenant	28 Apr 1804	p. 602
Abner Tatom, Ensign	28 Apr 1804	p. 602
James Smith, Captain	9 Oct 1803	p. 603
William Wayne, Lieutenant	9 Oct 1803	p. 603
John Smith, Ensign	9 Oct 1803	p. 604
Neely Dobson, Major	5 Feb 1804	p. 604
Cabel Griffith, Captain	29 Jan 1804	p. 605
Leonard Keeling, Captain	29 Jan 1804	p. 605
Manly Albriton, Lieutenant	25 Jan 1804	p. 606
Robert Todd, Ensign	25 Jan 1804	p. 606
James Johnson, Lieutenant	24 Feb 1804	p. 607
Benjmain Higginbotham, Ensign	24 Feb 1804	p. 607
George Turman, Lieutenant	27 Apr 1804	p. 608
John Dardin, Ensign	27 Apr 1804	p. 608
Voluntine Smith, Ensign	5 Feb 1804	p. 609
Rice Ellington, Lieutenant	25 Mar 1804	p. 609
James Allen, Ensign	25 Mar 1804	p. 610
Thomas H. Kenan, Captain	2 May 1804	p. 610
James Wells, Lieutenant	2 May 1804	p. 611
Samuel Montgomery, Captain, District 84	7 May 1804	p. 611
Henry Sheppard, Lieutenant, District 84	7 May 1804	p. 612
Thomas B. Horn, Ensign, District 84	7 May 1804	p. 612

Name, Rank, Unit	*Date*	*Page*
John Simmons, Captain, District 106	8 May 1804	p. 613
Henry Brown, Lieutenant, District 106	8 May 1804	p. 613
John Henry, Ensign, District 106	8 May 1804	p. 614
Payne Dexter, Lieutenant	12 May 1804	p. 614
Thomas Thornton, Ensign	12 May 1804	p. 615
James Dees, Captain, District 85	12 May 1804	p. 615
Edwin Mounger, Major, Battalion 19	14 May 1804	p. 616
James Elmore, Captain	14 May 1804	p. 616
Joseph Whorton, Lieutenant	14 May 1804	p. 617
George Ramsey, Ensign	14 May 1804	p. 617
Asa Allen, Captain	14 May 1804	p. 618
Joseph Durrance, Captain, District 44	3 Mar 1804	p. 618
John Rae, Lieutenant, District 44	3 Mar 1804	p. 619
Dempsey Standley, Ensign, District 44	3 Mar 1804	p. 619
William Holloway, Captain, District 45	4 Mar 1804	p. 620
Myal Monk, Lieutenant, District 45	4 Mar 1804	p. 620
John Tellman, Ensign, District 45	4 Mar 1804	p. 621
Seaborn Denmark, Captain, District 47	15 May 1804	p. 621
John Everte, Lieutenant, District 47	15 May 1804	p. 622
David Ruster, Ensign, District 47	15 May 1804	p. 622
Thomas Buckhannon, Ensign	15 May 1804	p. 623
Burwell Jordan, Major	15 May 1804	p. 623
Greenbury Adamson, Captain	15 May 1804	p. 624
John Roric, Ensign	15 May 1804	p. 624
John B. Miner, Captain	22 May 1804	p. 625
John Beard, Captain	22 May 1804	p. 625
William McCall, Captain, District 48	16 May 1804	p. 626
Charles Mikell, Lieutenant, District 48	16 May 1804	p. 626
Thomas Mikell, Ensign, District 48	16 May 1804	p. 627
Miles Gathright, Captain	16 May 1804	p. 627
Francis Dancy, Lieutenant	16 May 1804	p. 628
James Bird, Captain, District 19	16 May 1804	p. 628
John Bull, Lieutenant, District 42	16 May 1804	p. 629
Seth Batson, Ensign, District 42	16 May 1804	p. 629
Jesse Fulgham, Lieutenant	16 May 1804	p. 630
Peter Buckholts, Lieutenant	16 May 1804	p. 630

Georgia Military Commissions, 1798–1818

Name, Rank, Unit	Date	Page
Peterson Smith, Lieutenant	16 May 1804	p. 631
John B. Deering, Ensign	16 May 1804	p. 631
Nathan Williford, Captain	16 May 1804	p. 632
Benjamin Williams, Ensign, District 70	16 May 1804	p. 632
James Willis, Captain	17 May 1804	p. 633
Allen Beddingfield, Lieutenant	17 May 1804	p. 633
William Lynum, Ensign	17 May 1804	p. 634
Daniel Johnson, Captain	17 May 1804	p. 634
Joseph McClester, Lieutenant	17 May 1804	p. 635
James Patterson, Ensign	17 May 1804	p. 635
Aaron Springfield, Captain	17 May 1804	p. 636
James Cash, Lieutenant	17 May 1804	p. 636
Samuel King, Ensign	17 May 1804	p. 637
James Whight, Captain	17 May 1804	p. 637
Greene Winn, Captain, Rifle Company	17 May 1804	p. 638
Batson Bullock, Lieutenant, Rifle Company	17 May 1804	p. 638
John Langford, Ensign, Rifle Company	17 May 1804	p. 639
John Bastie, Captain, District 23	18 May 1804	p. 639
Richard Stokes, Captain, Volunteer Troop of Horse, Lincoln County	17 May 1804	p. 639
Thomas Kirk, Lieutenant, District 23	18 May 1804	p. 639
George Dyall, Ensign, District 23	18 May 1804	p. 640
Jonah Lindsey, Captain	18 May 1804	p. 640
Joseph Taylor, Ensign	18 May 1804	p. 641
Reubin George, Ensign	18 May 1804	p. 641
William McDonald, Ensign	18 May 1804	p. 642a
Winfrey Lockett, Captain	23 Jan 1803	p. 642a
Peter Hilton, Lieutenant	23 Jan 1803	p. 642b
Isaac Bently, Ensign	23 Jan 1803	p. 642b
Clem Allen, Ensign	18 May 1804	p. 643
Jonathan Scarber, Ensign, District 23	18 May 1804	p. 643
Patrick Jack, Brigadier General	18 May 1804	p. 644
Augustine G. Walton, Lieutenant	25 May 1804	p. 644
Simeon Wilder, Ensign	25 May 1804	p. 645
Hezekiah Buison, Ensign	25 May 1804	p. 645
Willis Burney, Captain	30 May 1804	p. 646
William Williams, Captain	30 May 1804	p. 646

Name, Rank, Unit	Date	Page
William McGarlan, Lieutenant	30 May 1804	p. 647
John Kimbro, Lieutenant	30 May 1804	p. 647
Garrett Hudson, Ensign	30 May 1804	p. 648
Joseph Grimerly, Lieutenant	30 May 1804	p. 648
John McGenty, Ensign	30 May 1804	p. 649
Joshua Clarke, Cornet, Volunteer Troop of Horse, Regiment 0	30 May 1804	p. 649
Simson Jones, Ensign, District 65	12 Jun 1804	p. 650
William Jones, Captain, District 65	12 Jun 1804	p. 650
John Cupp, Captain	12 Jun 1804	p. 651
Isaac McCravy, Captain, District 100	15 Jun 1804	p. 651
William Rentfro, Lieutenant, District 100	15 Jun 1804	p. 652
Stephen Rentfro, Ensign, District 100	15 Jun 1804	p. 652
John Hammet, Captain, District 81	18 Jun 1804	p. 653
George Wright, Lieutenant, District 81	18 Jun 1804	p. 653
Needham Bryan, Ensign, District 81	18 Jun 1804	p. 654
George Galphin Nowlan, Ensign, District 9	25 Jun 1804	p. 654
William Wright, Captain, District 82	25 Jun 1804	p. 655
Jesse Hill, Captain	25 Jun 1804	p. 655
Tabard Hearn, Ensign	25 Jun 1804	p. 656
James Stewart, Captain	25 Jun 1804	p. 656
Alexander Devall, Ensign	25 Jun 1804	p. 657
William Durdens, Captain, District 59	26 Jun 1804	p. 657
George Roundtree, Ensign, District 59	26 Jun 1804	p. 658
Abram Jackson, Lieutenant Colonel Commandant, Regiment 8	27 Jun 1804	p. 658
James Alston, Captain, District 51	30 Aug 1802	p. 659
Dempsey Dougherty, Captain, District 58	27 Jun 1804	p. 659
Eli Whiddon, Lieutenant, District 53	27 Jun 1804	p. 660
Brinkley Gandey, Ensign, District 53	27 Jun 1804	p. 660
William Hewell, Captain	30 Jun 1804	p. 661
Howard Allen, Lieutenant	30 Jun 1804	p. 661
Stephen McClendon, Ensign	30 Jun 1804	p. 662
John Stallings, Captain, District 67	12 Jul 1804	p. 662
George Martin, Lieutenant, District 67	12 Jul 1804	p. 663
Anthony Moore, Ensign, District 67	12 Jul 1804	p. 663
Francis Young, Cornet, Troop of Horse, Regiment 3	13 Jul 1804	p. 664

Georgia Military Commissions, 1798–1818

Name, Rank, Unit	Date	Page
Donald Thompkins, Lieutenant, District 30	13 Jul 1804	p. 664
Aquilla Lowe, Lieutenant, District 85	13 Jul 1804	p. 665
Charles Broughton, Ensign, District 108	13 Jul 1804	p. 665
Leonard Jurdine, Captain, District 24	13 Jul 1804	p. 666
Samuel Owens, Ensign, District 24	13 Jul 1804	p. 666
Alexander G. Gordon, Captain, District 66	14 Jul 1804	p. 667
Elijah Powell, Lieutenant, District 66	14 Jul 1804	p. 667
James Barrow, Ensign, District 66	14 Jul 1804	p. 668
George R. Clayton, Captain, Volunteer Company of Infantry (styled the Louisville Guards), Regiment 19	16 Jul 1804	p. 668
James Robinson, Lieutenant, Volunteer Company of infantry (styled the Louisville Guards), Regiment 19	16 Jul 1804	p. 669
Michael Burke, Ensign, Volunteer Company of Infantry (styled the Louisville Guards), Regiment 19	14 Jul 1804	p. 669
Horatio Gates, Lieutenant, District 82	16 Jul 1804	p. 670
Ambrose Wright, Ensign, District 82	16 Jul 1804	p. 670
James Rowland, Captain, District 56	16 Jul 1804	p. 671
Bolin Swearingame, Lieutenant, District 56	16 Jul 1804	p. 671
William Hobson Bacon, Ensign, District 134	24 Jul 1804	p. 672
Terrell Cook Harrison, Captain, District 135	24 Jul 1804	p. 672
Richard Harrison, Lieutenant, District 135	24 Jul 1804	p. 673
Baily Wilkinson, Ensign, District 135	24 Jul 1804	p. 673
Abner Biddle, Captain	24 Jul 1804	p. 674
William Askew, Lieutenant	24 Jul 1804	p. 674
James Price, Ensign	24 Jul 1804	p. 675
William Stephens, Captain	24 Jul 1804	p. 675
Nathaniel Howell, Lieutenant	24 Jul 1804	p. 676
Archibald Watts, Lieutenant	24 Jul 1804	p. 676
Lathland Bethune, Ensign	24 Jul 1804	p. 677
Robert Middlebrook, Lieutenant	24 Jul 1804	p. 677
William Ellis, Ensign	24 Jul 1804	p. 678
Robert Gibson, Captain, District 6	27 Jul 1804	p. 678
George Herb, Lieutenant, District 6	27 Jul 1804	p. 679
William Provost, Ensign, District 6	27 Jul 1804	p. 679
Jordan Taylor, Lieutenant, District 63	30 Jul 1804	p. 680
John Boyakin, Ensign, District 63	30 Jul 1804	p. 680
George Keith, Lieutenant	30 Jul 1804	p. 681

Commissions Book 1800–1806

Name, Rank, Unit	*Date*	*Page*
David Nicholas, Ensign	30 Jul 1804	p. 681
Thomas W. Scott, Major	30 Jul 1804	p. 682
John Arnold, First Lieutenant, Volunteer Troop of Horse	30 Jul 1804	p. 682
Philip Colbert, Captain	30 Jul 1804	p. 683
Merrell Budges, Lieutenant	30 Jul 1804	p. 683
Isaac Meador, Ensign	30 Jul 1804	p. 684
Randal Eads, Ensign	30 Jul 1804	p. 684
Moses Scarborough, Captain, Volunteer Company of Infantry, Battalion 17	31 Jul 1804	p. 685
Alexander Stringer, Lieutenant, District 75	31 Jul 1804	p. 685
James Welch, Major, Battalion 16	17 Aug 1804	p. 686
John Shelman, Captain, Volunteer Troop of Dragoons, Regiment 1	17 Aug 1804	p. 686
Samuel Fee, Captain, District 120	17 Aug 1804	p. 687
William Slater, Lieutenant, District 120	17 Aug 1804	p. 687
Robert Edwards, Ensign, District 120	17 Aug 1804	p. 688
William Son, Ensign, District 132	17 Aug 1804	p. 688
Jeremiah Coney, Captain, District 50	20 Aug 1804	p. 689
Aquilla Coney, Lieutenant, District 50	20 Aug 1804	p. 689
Joseph Denson, Ensign, District 52	20 Aug 1804	p. 690
Dempsey Wilkinson, Lieutenant, District 54	20 Aug 1804	p. 690
Jacob Joiner, Ensign, District 54	20 Aug 1804	p. 691
William McDonald, Captain, District 55	20 Aug 1804	p. 691
John Stansile, Lieutenant, District 55	20 Aug 1804	p. 692
Burrel Yates, Ensign, District 55	20 Aug 1804	p. 692
Burrel Higdon, Captain, District 57	20 Aug 1804	p. 693
James Lewis, Lieutenant, District 59	20 Aug 1804	p. 693
William Maxwell, Major, Battalion 17	20 Aug 1804	p. 694
Charles Lane, Captain	20 Aug 1804	p. 694
David Fain, Lieutenant	8 Sep 1804	p. 695
Jacob Heifner, Ensign	8 Sep 1804	p. 695
Zachariah Candler, Captain	8 Sep 1804	p. 696
Jonathan Conard, Lieutenant	8 Sep 1804	p. 696
Moses Sherley, Ensign	8 Sep 1804	p. 697
Thomas Bulman, Ensign, District 130	11 Sep 1804	p. 697
Jesse Slater, Captain, District 35	11 Sep 1804	p. 698
James Carwell, Lieutenant, District 35	11 Sep 1804	p. 698

Georgia Military Commissions, 1798–1818

Name, Rank, Unit	Date	Page
Robert Dixson, Ensign, District 35	11 Sep 1804	p. 699
Gross Scruggs, Captain, District 13	11 Sep 1804	p. 699
William Hawthorn, Lieutenant, District 13	11 Sep 1804	p. 700
Peter Hawthorn, Ensign, District 13	11 Sep 1804	p. 700
Robert Shrift, Lieutenant, District 96	11 Sep 1804	p. 701
Duke Hammilton, Captain, Volunteer Company of Artillery, Regiment 14	11 Sep 1804	p. 701
Richard Gary, Ensign, District 113	11 Sep 1804	p. 702
Lewis Norman, Ensign	11 Sep 1804	p. 702
Samuel Groves, Captain	11 Sep 1804	p. 703
William Thompson, Lieutenant	11 Sep 1804	p. 703
Jacob Cockran, Ensign	11 Sep 1804	p. 704
Drury Ridgeway, Ensign	11 Sep 1804	p. 704
Benjamin Whitehead, Lieutenant	11 Sep 1804	p. 705
Sheppard Williams, Captain, District 48	11 Sep 1804	p. 705
Lewis Holland, Lieutenant, District 83	13 Sep 1804	p. 706
Moses Mulkey, Captain, District 68	14 Sep 1804	p. 706
William Stobo, Lieutenant, District 68	14 Sep 1804	p. 707
Gabriel Clements, Ensign, District 68	14 Sep 1804	p. 707
David McDonald, Ensign, District 77	14 Sep 1804	p. 708
Alexander Bass, Captain, District 104	14 Sep 1804	p. 708
Rowland Smith, Lieutenant	20 Sep 1804	p. 709
Jacob Martin, Ensign	20 Sep 1804	p. 709
Shadrich McMichael, Ensign	20 Sep 1804	p. 710
William Barnett, Second Lieutenant, Volunteer Troop of Horse	20 Sep 1804	p. 710
John Flemming, Captain	20 Sep 1804	p. 711
Nathan Bursay, Lieutenant	20 Sep 1804	p. 711
Richard Stewart, Captain	20 Sep 1804	p. 712
John Stowart, Lieutenant	20 Sep 1804	p. 712
John Sepp, Ensign	20 Sep 1804	p. 713
Lewis B. Taliaferro, Ensign	20 Sep 1804	p. 713
Snoden Griffin, Captain, Volunteer Company of Infantry, Battalion 28	21 Sep 1804	p. 714
George Whitton, Lieutenant, Volunteer Company of Infantry, Battalion 28	21 Sep 1804	p. 714

Name, Rank, Unit	Date	Page
Curtice Daniel, Ensign, Volunteer Company of Infantry, Battalion 28	21 Sep 1804	p. 715
James Jenkins, Lieutenant, Volunteer Troop of Horse, Regiment 17	21 Sep 1804	p. 715
Winston Bennett, Ensign	21 Sep 1804	p. 716
John Houghtan, Captain, Volunteer Troop of Horse, Regiment 17	21 Sep 1804	p. 716
George W. Dillard, First Lieutenant, Volunteer Troop of Horse, Regiment 17	21 Sep 1804	p. 717
James Stuart, Second Lieutenant, Volunteer Troop of Horse, Regiment 17	21 Sep 1804	p. 717
Charles Miller, Cornet, Volunteer Troop of Horse, Regiment 17	21 Sep 1804	p. 718
Henry Hartsfield, Captain	21 Sep 1804	p. 718
Francis Hilliard, Captain, District 74	24 Sep 1804	p. 719
Thaddeus Beall, Major, Battalion 29	24 Sep 1804	p. 719
Icabod Pitman, Lieutenant, District 127	24 Sep 1804	p. 720
Walker Herndon, Ensign, District 127	24 Sep 1804	p. 720
Thomas Hudson, Lieutenant, District 109	24 Sep 1804	p. 721
George Nelson, Ensign, District 109	24 Sep 1804	p. 721
William Dunham, Ensign	24 Sep 1804	p. 722
Howell Beall, Ensign	24 Sep 1804	p. 722
Joel Hunt, Second Lieutenant, Volunteer Troop of Horse	24 Sep 1804	p. 723
William Pickron, Lieutenant, District 37	25 Sep 1804	p. 723
Hezekiah Broxton, Ensign, District 37	25 Sep 1804	p. 724
Thomas Mangham, Ensign, Volunteer Company of Riflemen, Battalion 23	4 Oct 1804	p. 724
Benjamin Simmons, Ensign, District 101	4 Oct 1804	p. 725
Jesse Lofthy, Captain, District 76	4 Oct 1804	p. 725
Richard Wingate, Lieutenant, District 76	4 Oct 1804	p. 726
Henry Wall, Ensign, District 76	4 Oct 1804	p. 726
William Byne, Captain, District 69	11 Oct 1804	p. 727
John Butler, Captain, District 149	9 Nov 1804	p. 727
Archibald McKissack, Lieutenant, District 149	9 Nov 1804	p. 728
John McKee, Ensign, District 149	9 Nov 1804	p. 728
Mason Jones, Lieutenant, District 185	9 Nov 1804	p. 729
Andrew Maddox, Captain, Volunteer Company of Riflemen, Battalion 49	9 Nov 1804	p. 729

Georgia Military Commissions, 1798–1818

Name, Rank, Unit	Date	Page
William Arnett, Ensign, District 177	9 Nov 1804	p. 730
John Powell, Ensign, District 153	9 Nov 1804	p. 730
William Thadford, Lieutenant, District 247	10 Nov 1804	p. 731
Richard Walker, Lieutenant, District 28	10 Nov 1804	p. 731
Reubin Ross, Ensign, District 28	10 Nov 1804	p. 732
William Smith, Captain, District 98	10 Nov 1804	p. 732
Moses Cox, Lieutenant, District 98	10 Nov 1804	p. 733
Ephraim Cox, Ensign, District 98	10 Nov 1804	p. 733
Benjamin Hurt, Lieutenant, District 156	10 Nov 1804	p. 734
Seth Woolsey, Ensign, District 156	10 Nov 1804	p. 734
Job Tison, Lieutenant, District 27	12 Nov 1804	p. 735
William Nix, Ensign, District 27	12 Nov 1804	p. 735
Jeremiah Baxter, Lieutenant, District 137	12 Nov 1804	p. 736
Johnston Porter, Ensign, District 137	12 Nov 1804	p. 736
John Malone, Ensign, District 146	12 Nov 1804	p. 737
Francis McClendon, Lieutenant, District 166	12 Nov 1804	p. 737
John Prussell, First Lieutenant, Volunteer Troop of Horse, Regiment 25	12 Nov 1804	p. 738
James Love, Second Lieutenant, Volunteer Troop of Horse, Regiment 25	12 Nov 1804	p. 738
Samuel Haden, Captain, District 245	12 Nov 1804	p. 739
James Shields, Ensign, District 245	12 Nov 1804	p. 739
Patrick Glaze, Lieutenant, District 242	12 Nov 1804	p. 740
Kinchen Hillard, Lieutenant, District 74	13 Nov 1804	p. 740
John Coats, Ensign, District 164	13 Nov 1804	p. 741
Richard Hooper, Lieutenant, District 206	13 Nov 1804	p. 741
John Young, Captain, District 173	13 Nov 1804	p. 742
Sherwood Young, Ensign, District 173	13 Nov 1804	p. 742
Shadrick Morris, Ensign, District 248	13 Nov 1804	p. 743
Jesse Standifer, Captain, Volunteer Troop of Horse, Regiment 16	13 Nov 1804	p. 743
Charles Birk, First Lieutenant, Volunteer Troop of Horse, Regiment 16	13 Nov 1804	p. 744
Dudley Peeples, Second Lieutenant, Volunteer Troop of Horse, Regiment 16	13 Nov 1804	p. 744
Jesse Bowles, Cornet, Volunteer Company of Horse, Regiment 16	13 Nov 1804	p. 745
Jacob Wood, Major, Battalion 6	13 Nov 1804	p. 745

Name, Rank, Unit	**Date**	**Page**
Francis Doyle, Major, Battalion 1	14 Nov 1804	p. 746
Benjamin Sessions, Second Lieutenant, Volunteer Troop of Horse, Regiment 13	14 Nov 1804	p. 746
Arthur Burney, Cornet, Troop of Horse, Regiment 13	14 Nov 1804	p. 747
John C. Slocumb, Captain, District 118	14 Nov 1804	p. 747
Curtis Hays, Lieutenant, District 118	14 Nov 1804	p. 748
William Jackson, Ensign, District 118	14 Nov 1804	p. 748
Barrett Farrer, Captain, District 182	14 Nov 1804	p. 749
Abraham Wallace, Ensign, District 182	14 Nov 1804	p. 749
Archibald Drake, Ensign, District 228	14 Nov 1804	p. 750
Pleasant Compton, Lieutenant, District 233	14 Nov 1804	p. 750
John Smith, Captain, District 238	14 Nov 1804	p. 751
William Bailey, Lieutenant, District 238	14 Nov 1804	p. 751
Cornelius Martin, Ensign, District 238	14 Nov 1804	p. 752
Zachariah Williams, Captain, Volunteer Troop of Horse, Regiment 10	15 Nov 1804	p. 752
Nicholas Fox, First Lieutenant, Volunteer Troop of Horse, Regiment 10	15 Nov 1804	p. 753
William Durkee, Second Lieutenant, Volunteer Troop of Horse, Regiment 10	15 Nov 1804	p. 753
James Scott, Cornet, Volunteer Troop of Horse, Regiment 10	15 Nov 1804	p. 754
Jeremiah Gartrill, Captain, District 184	15 Nov 1804	p. 754
Baker Spinks, Lieutenant, District 184	15 Nov 1804	p. 755
Reuben Lockett, Captain, District 220	15 Nov 1804	p. 755
John Pettibone, Captain, District 1	19 Nov 1804	p. 756
Simeon Lane, Captain, District 246	19 Nov 1804	p. 756
Drury Spain, Captain, District 75	30 Nov 1804	p. 757
Newton Perkins, Lieutenant, District 75	30 Nov 1804	p. 757
John B. Flournoy, Captain, District 154	30 Nov 1804	p. 758
Thomas Mounger, Captain, Volunteer Company of Riflemen, Battalion 36	30 Nov 1804	p. 758
Peter Slubblefield, Lieutenant, Volunteer Company of Riflemen, Battalion 36	30 Nov 1804	p. 759
Richmond Terrell, Ensign, Volunteer Company of Riflemen, Battalion 36	30 Nov 1804	p. 759
Hardy Foster, Ensign, District 125	8 Dec 1804	p. 760
Alexander H. Allison, Ensign, District 107	8 Dec 1804	p. 760

Georgia Military Commissions, 1798–1818

Name, Rank, Unit	Date	Page
Richard M. Maxwell, Captain, District 20	3 Dec 1804	p. 761
James Waller, Captain, District 108	3 Dec 1804	p. 761
Levi Ellis, Lieutenant, District 108	3 Dec 1804	p. 762
Thomas Parmore, Ensign, District 108	3 Dec 1804	p. 762
Charles H. Deveaux, Captain, District 151	3 Dec 1804	p. 763
John Spurlin, Lieutenant, District 151	3 Dec 1804	p. 763
Isaac Coleman, Captain, District 79	18 Jan 1805	p. 764
John Vining, Captain, District 76	6 Feb 1805	p. 764
James May, Lieutenant, District 77	6 Feb 1805	p. 765
George Wright, Lieutenant, District 81	6 Feb 1805	p. 765
David Hart, Ensign, District 81	6 Feb 1805	p. 766
William Little, Ensign, District 92	18 Feb 1805	p. 766
John Bacon, Captain, District 15	21 Feb 1805	p. 767
William Fleming, Lieutenant, District 15	21 Feb 1805	p. 767
John Winn, Ensign, District 15	21 Feb 1805	p. 768
Archibald Clark, Cornet, Troop of Horse, Regiment 3	21 Feb 1805	p. 768
John Germany, Ensign, District 125	23 Feb 1805	p. 769
John Fowler, Ensign, District 90	5 Mar 1805	p. 769
Henry Brown, Captain, District 106	5 Mar 1805	p. 770
John Henry, Lieutenant, District 106	5 Mar 1805	p. 770
William P. Burch, Ensign, District 106	5 Mar 1805	p. 771
Chappel Sledge, Lieutenant, District 103	5 Mar 1805	p. 771
John Lary, Ensign, District 112	5 Mar 1805	p. 772
Nathaniel Waller Jr., Ensign, District 116	5 Mar 1805	p. 772
John Weeks, Captain, District 101	6 Mar 1805	p. 773
Adam Jones, Captain, Volunteer Company of Infantry, Battalion 18	2 Apr 1805	p. 773
George Eubanks, Ensign, Volunteer Company of Infantry, Battalion 18	2 Apr 1805	p. 774
Seth S. Langston, Ensign, District 83	10 Apr 1805	p. 774
Seth Fields, Captain, District 73	20 Apr 1805	p. 775
John Hines, Lieutenant, District 73	20 Apr 1805	p. 775
Daniel Mound, Lieutenant, Volunteer Company of Light Infantry, Battalion 17	20 Apr 1805	p. 776
Laurence Folsom, Ensign, Volunteer Company of Light Infantry, Battalion 17	20 Apr 1805	p. 776
Hartwell Ezell, Lieutenant, District 74	18 Apr 1805	p. 777

Commissions Book 1800–1806

Name, Rank, Unit	*Date*	*Page*
Kinchen Curll, Ensign, District 74	18 Apr 1805	p. 777
Thaddeus Holt, Captain, District 99	19 Apr 1805	p. 778
Thomas Edwards, Ensign, District 97	19 Apr 1805	p. 778
Herbert Dunevant, Captain, District 119	25 Apr 1805	p. 779
Thomas Pace, Captain, District 90	26 Apr 1805	p. 779
William Smith Jr., Lieutenant, District 90	26 Apr 1805	p. 780
Charles Terrell, Captain, District 164	26 Apr 1805	p. 780
Bird Tower, Captain, District 84	27 Apr 1805	p. 781
Richard Brackenridge, Lieutenant, District 84	27 Apr 1805	p. 781
John McNeely, Ensign, District 84	27 Apr 1805	p. 782
Mountain Hill, Captain, District 155	6 May 1805	p. 782
James Jones, Captain, District 156	7 May 1805	p. 783
Barnet Fickling, Lieutenant, District 156	7 May 1805	p. 783
Thomas McCall Harris, Lieutenant, District 120	7 May 1805	p. 784
William Sturges, Ensign, District 120	7 May 1805	p. 784
Samuel M. Smyth, Captain, District 122	7 May 1805	p. 785
Samuel Wigfall, Lieutenant, District 122	7 May 1805	p. 785
Charles Lamar, Ensign, District 122	7 May 1805	p. 786
Daniel H. Zachery, Captain, District 157	9 May 1805	p. 786
James Zachry, Lieutenant, District 157	9 May 1805	p. 787
Edward Johnson, Ensign, District 157	9 May 1805	p. 787
Young Gresham, Lieutenant Colonel Commandant, Regiment 16	11 May 1805	p. 788
Constantine Perkins, Lieutenant, District 145	11 May 1805	p. 788
Lewis Jenkins, Ensign, District 145	11 May 1805	p. 789
George Osborne, Ensign, District 154	11 May 1805	p. 789
John Hutchins, Lieutenant, District 154	11 May 1805	p. 790
Thomas Blount, Captain, District 72	4 May 1805	p. 790
Eli Emanuel, Lieutenant, District 72	4 May 1805	p. 791
Robert Bowling, Ensign, District 72	4 Jun 1805	p. 791
John Dean, Ensign, District 217	7 Jun 1805	p. 792
John Irwin, Captain, Volunteer Troop of Dragoons, Regiment 13	26 Jun 1805	p. 792
John E. Dawson, First Lieutenant, Volunteer Troop of Dragoons, Regiment 13	26 Jun 1805	p. 793
William Edward, Captain, District 54	17 Jul 1805	p. 793
James Solomon, Lieutenant, District 54	17 Jul 1805	p. 794

Georgia Military Commissions, 1798–1818

Name, Rank, Unit	Date	Page
Joseph Brantley, Ensign, District 55	17 Jul 1805	p. 794
Sherod G. Swain, Captain, District 55	17 Jul 1805	p. 795
James Fillet Thomas, Captain, District 53	17 Jul 1805	p. 795
Etheldred Hayes, Ensign, District 53	17 Jul 1805	p. 796
Thomas Carter, Captain, District 159	24 Jul 1805	p. 796
John Cooper, Lieutenant, District 159	24 Jul 1805	p. 797
Moore Carter, Lieutenant, District 152	24 Jul 1805	p. 797
William Cook, Lieutenant, District 29	24 Jul 1805	p. 798
Asa Lathrop, Ensign, District 29	24 Jul 1805	p. 798
John Selman, Second Lieutenant, Troop of Horse, Regiment 24	22 Jul 1805	p. 799
James Smith, Ensign, District 216	22 Jul 1805	p. 799
James Helms, Lieutenant, District 217	22 Jul 1805	p. 800
Thomas Appling, Captain, District 220	22 Jul 1805	p. 800
Hardy Sparks, Lieutenant, District 220	22 Jul 1805	p. 801
Gresham Harris, Ensign, District 220	22 Jul 1805	p. 801
Thomas Dickson, Ensign, District 221	22 Jul 1805	p. 802
Daniel Frammell, Lieutenant, District 225	22 Jul 1805	p. 802
Christian Dasher, Captain, District 11	24 Jul 1805	p. 803
Emanuel Siegler, Lieutenant, District 11	24 Jul 1805	p. 803
John Shearhouse, Ensign, District 11	24 Jul 1805	p. 804
Joseph Few, Lieutenant, District 149	25 Jul 1805	p. 804
Benjamin Mosely, Lieutenant, District 184	25 Jul 1805	p. 805
George Husler, Ensign, District 6	26 Jul 1805	p. 805
John Boston, Lieutenant, District 13	26 Jul 1805	p. 806
James Moore, Lieutenant, District 25	26 Jul 1805	p. 806
Rowland Roberts, Captain, District 80	26 Jul 1805	p. 807
Caleb Parker, Ensign, District 80	26 Jul 1805	p. 807
Francis Godfrey, Captain, District 44	30 Jul 1805	p. 808
Thomas Harrel, Lieutenant, District 44	30 Jul 1805	p. 808
Benjamin Wood, Ensign, District 44	30 Jul 1805	p. 809
William Willidrus, Captain, District 46	30 Jul 1805	p. 809
John Dill, Lieutenant, District 46	30 Jul 1805	p. 810
Owen William, Ensign, District 46	30 Jul 1805	p. 810
William Anderson, Lieutenant, District 49	30 Jul 1805	p. 811
Drury Jones Jr., Lieutenant, District 49	30 Jul 1805	p. 811
William Davenport, Captain, District 110	31 Jul 1805	p. 812

Name, Rank, Unit	Date	Page
John Bryan, Lieutenant, District 110	31 Jul 1805	p. 812
Shamme Drake, Ensign, District 110	31 Jul 1805	p. 813
Henry Carleton Jr., Lieutenant, District 143	31 Jul 1805	p. 813
James H. Nicholson, Cornet, Volunteer Troop of Horse, Regiment 17	31 Jul 1805	p. 814
James Jenkins, Captain, District 145	31 Jul 1805	p. 814
William Norman, Captain, District 187	1 Aug 1805	p. 815
John Edmonds, Lieutenant, District 187	1 Aug 1805	p. 815
John Gresham, Ensign, District 187	1 Aug 1805	p. 816
Joseph Madry, Lieutenant, District 72	6 Aug 1805	p. 816
Absalom Turner, Ensign, District 72	6 Aug 1805	p. 817
Jeremiah Walker, Captain, Volunteer Troop of Horse, Regiment 20	16 Aug 1805	p. 817
Samuel Thompson, Lieutenant, Volunteer Troop of Horse, Regiment 20	16 Aug 1805	p. 818
Jonathan Baker, Cornet, Volunteer Troop of Horse, Regiment 20	16 Aug 1805	p. 818
Nathan Bussey, Captain, District 183	28 Aug 1805	p. 819
John Loftlin, Lieutenant, District 183	28 Aug 1805	p. 819
James McCord, Ensign, District 183	28 Aug 1805	p. 820
Josephus Love, Captain, District 142	28 Aug 1805	p. 820
John Copeland, Lieutenant, District 160	28 Aug 1805	p. 821
Archibald McCoy, Captain, District 162	28 Aug 1805	p. 821
James Taylor, Lieutenant, District 162	28 Aug 1805	p. 822
John Rodny, Ensign, District 162	28 Aug 1805	p. 822
Thomas Cole, Ensign, District 163	28 Aug 1805	p. 823
James Hamelton, First Lieutenant, Volunteer Company of Artillery, Regiment 15	30 Aug 1805	p. 823
Peterson Thweat, Second Lieutenant, Volunteer Company of Artillery, Regiment 14	30 Aug 1805	p. 824
John Jeter, Lieutenant, District 101	30 Aug 1805	p. 824
Ezekiel Smith, Lieutenant, District 104	30 Aug 1805	p. 825
John K. Mahone, Ensign, District 104	30 Aug 1805	p. 825
Robert McGinthy, Ensign, District 105	30 Aug 1805	p. 826
Simon Holt, Captain, Volunteer Company of Riflemen, Battalion 24	30 Aug 1805	p. 826
Thomas Turner, Ensign, Volunteer Company of Riflemen, Battalion 24	30 Aug 1805	p. 827

Georgia Military Commissions, 1798–1818

Name, Rank, Unit	*Date*	*Page*
James Powell, Captain, District 26	30 Aug 1805	p. 827
William Payne, Lieutenant, District 26	30 Aug 1805	p. 828
James Wallace, Ensign, District 26	30 Aug 1805	p. 828
James C. Bowler, Captain, District 14	30 Aug 1805	p. 829
John McDorman, Lieutenant, District 14	30 Aug 1805	p. 829
John Forrest, Lieutenant, District 108	30 Aug 1805	p. 830
Jesse Williams, Ensign, District 108	30 Aug 1805	p. 830
John Thompson, Major, Battalion 7	4 Sep 1805	p. 831
John G. Snead, Captain, District 25	5 Sep 1805	p. 831
Jacob More, Ensign, District 25	5 Sep 1805	p. 832
George Williamson Jr., Captain, District 37	16 Sep 1805	p. 832
Robert Allen, Lieutenant, District 1	16 Sep 1805	p. 833
Stephen B. Clark, Ensign, District 1	16 Sep 1805	p. 833
Daniel Johnson, Major, Battalion 53	16 Sep 1805	p. 834
Clement Lanier, Captain, District 259	17 Sep 1805	p. 834
Henry Colson, Lieutenant, District 259	17 Sep 1805	p. 835
Dennis Colson, Ensign, District 259	17 Sep 1805	p. 835
Atton Pemberton, Captain, District 2	17 Sep 1805	p. 836
Thomas Scott, Lieutenant, District 2	17 Sep 1805	p. 836
William Riggs, Ensign, District 2	17 Sep 1805	p. 837
William Hall, Captain, District 42	18 Sep 1805	p. 837
Isaac Kerksy, Lieutenant, District 42	18 Sep 1805	p. 838
Isaac Foreman, Ensign, District 42	18 Sep 1805	p. 838
William Harrison, Lieutenant, District 8	20 Sep 1805	p. 839
Joseph Laurence Bridger, Ensign, District 8	20 Sep 1805	p. 839
Robert Lott, Captain, District 43	20 Sep 1805	p. 840
Andrew Clements, Ensign, District 43	20 Sep 1805	p. 840
Lewis Hutchinson, Captain, District 260	20 Sep 1805	p. 841
William Pickering, Lieutenant, District 260	20 Sep 1805	p. 841
Benjamin Mirell, Lieutenant, District 36	20 Sep 1805	p. 842
William Flake, Ensign, District 36	20 Sep 1805	p. 842
James Caswell, Captain, District 35	20 Sep 1805	p. 843
Joshua Tulloss, Lieutenant, District 35	20 Sep 1805	p. 843
Cally Denson, Lieutenant, District 52	21 Sep 1805	p. 844
Samuel Montgomery, Captain, District 71	27 Sep 1805	p. 844
James M. Hall, Ensign, District 71	27 Sep 1805	p. 845

Commissions Book 1800–1806

Name, Rank, Unit	*Date*	*Page*
Elisha Moreland, Ensign, District 76	20 Sep 1805	p. 845
David Douglass, Lieutenant, District 85	3 Oct 1805	p. 846
Daniel Candler, Captain, District 115	14 Oct 1805	p. 846
John Sanders, Lieutenant, District 82	1 Nov 1805	p. 847
Pleasant Moore, Ensign, District 66	5 Nov 1805	p. 847
Archibald Thompson, Captain, District 51	22 Nov 1805	p. 848
Frederick Hadley, Lieutenant, District 51	22 Nov 1805	p. 848
Neil Munroe, Ensign, District 51	22 Nov 1805	p. 849
Harrey Harrington, Captain, District 58	22 Nov 1805	p. 849
Josiah Collins, Lieutenant, District 58	22 Nov 1805	p. 850
Jesse Collin, Ensign, District 58	22 Nov 1805	p. 850
Eli Bryant, Captain, District 206	24 Jan 1805	p. 851
Sterling Candler, Lieutenant, District 206	24 Jan 1805	p. 851
Joseph Reid, Ensign, District 206	24 Jan 1805	p. 852
Benson Henry, Captain	16 Nov 1804	p. 852
James Denman, Lieutenant	16 Nov 1804	p. 853
James Little, Ensign	20 Jul 1805	p. 853
Samuel Everett, Captain, District 209	19 May 1804	p. 854
Robert Bond, Lieutenant, District 209	9 Nov 1804	p. 854
John Bond, Ensign, District 209	9 Nov 1804	p. 855
Ephraim Dixon, Captain	3 Nov 1804	p. 855
John Garrison, Lieutenant	3 Nov 1804	p. 856
William Craircather, Ensign	3 Nov 1804	p. 856
Boley Conner, Captain, District 214	3 Aug 1805	p. 857
Obediah Wright, Lieutenant, District 214	3 Aug 1805	p. 857
Asa Allen, Captain, District 200	20 Apr 1805	p. 858
William Smith, Ensign, District 210	20 Apr 1805	p. 858
William Wood, Ensign, District 210	27 Apr 1805	p. 859
John Easly, Major	15 Nov 1804	p. 859
Benjamin W. Holliday, Captain, District 172	16 Aug 1804	p. 860
Robert Harrison, Lieutenant, District 172	16 Aug 1804	p. 860
Thomas Johnson, Ensign, District 172	16 Aug 1804	p. 861
Lewis Norman, Captain, District 180	22 Mar 1805	p. 861
Joseph Henderson Jr., Captain, District 171	18 May 1805	p. 862
David Sidwell, Captain, District 176	13 Apr 1805	p. 862
Silas Ballard, Lieutenant, District 176	13 Apr 1805	p. 863

Georgia Military Commissions, 1798–1818

Name, Rank, Unit	Date	Page
Richard Hudspeth, Lieutenant, District 166	19 Nov 1805	p. 863
Jesse Heard, Lieutenant, District 179	22 Jul 1805	p. 864
Stephen Bland, Lieutenant, District 173	10 Aug 1805	p. 864
Shadrach Smith, Ensign, District 173	10 Aug 1805	p. 865
John Welch, Ensign, District 177	1 Aug 1805	p. 865
William Blackley, Ensign, District 170	27 Jul 1805	p. 866
Pitman Milner, Captain, District 168	16 Apr 1805	p. 866
Robert Penman, Lieutenant, District 168	16 Apr 1805	p. 867
Richard Rowton, Ensign, District 168	16 Apr 1805	p. 867
Jacob McClindon, Lieutenant, District 180	20 Apr 1806	p. 868
William Duneway, Ensign, District 180	20 Apr 1806	p. 868
William Park, Lieutenant, District 174	30 Mar 1805	p. 869
William Anderson, Ensign, District 174	30 Mar 1805	p. 869
John Butler, First Lieutenant, Volunteer Troop of Dragoons, Regiment 8	30 Mar 1805	p. 870
William Simpson, Second Lieutenant, Volunteer Troop of Dragoons, Regiment 8	30 Mar 1805	p. 870
Moses Wilcox, Major, Battalion 46	5 Dec 1805	p. 871
John B. Parks, Captain, District 246	5 Dec 1805	p. 871
William Ross, Captain, District 242	9 Mar 1805	p. 872
James McDaniel, Lieutenant, District 242	30 Mar 1805	p. 872
Bennet Ivery, Ensign, District 242	30 Mar 1805	p. 873
Micajah Benge, Captain	18 May 1805	p. 873
Jabez Wilkins, Lieutenant	18 May 1805	p. 874
William Ledbetter, Lieutenant, District 245	18 May 1805	p. 874
Chesley Morris, Ensign, District 245	18 May 1805	p. 875
John W. Shackleford, Captain, District 249	16 Jan 1805	p. 875
Daniel Gillespie, Captain, District 260	13 Apr 1805	p. 876
Mark Hayes, Lieutenant, District 260	13 Apr 1805	p. 876
James Smith, Ensign, District 260	13 Apr 1805	p. 877
William Hendley, Captain, Volunteer Company of Riflemen, Battalion 51	5 Dec 1805	p. 877
Archbalid Nelson, Lieutenant, Volunteer Company of Riflemen, Battalion 51	5 Dec 1805	p. 878
John Tredwell, Ensign, Volunteer Company of Riflemen, Battalion 51	5 Dec 1805	p. 878
David Langston, Captain, District 134	11 May 1805	p. 879

Name, Rank, Unit	Date	Page
Robert Lazenby, Lieutenant, District 134	11 May 1805	p. 879
Thomas Moore Jr., Lieutenant, District 130	22 May 1805	p. 880
Washington Germany, Lieutenant, District 126	30 Jul 1805	p. 880
Charles Burham, Ensign, District 126	6 Dec 1805	p. 881
Adam Heath, Captain, District 126	6 Dec 1805	p. 881
Archibald Peavy, Ensign, District 158	6 Dec 1805	p. 882
Joshua Dodson, Captain, District 251	11 Feb 1805	p. 882
William McKorkle, Lieutenant, District 251	11 Feb 1805	p. 883
William Self, Ensign, District 251	11 Feb 1805	p. 883
Joseph Maddox, Captain, District 254	17 Jul 1805	p. 884
Thomas Bowling, Lieutenant, District 254	17 Jul 1805	p. 884
George Stoncham, Ensign, District 254	17 Jul 1805	p. 885
John G. Pittman, Captain, District 253	5 Jan 1805	p. 885
William Oldfields, Lieutenant, District 253	11 May 1805	p. 886
Williscie Moore, Ensign, District 253	11 May 1805	p. 886
Peleg Rogers, Captain, District 255	6 Jul 1805	p. 887
William Burns, Lieutenant, District 255	15 Sep 1805	p. 887
Alexander Meham, Ensign, District 255	14 Sep 1805	p. 888
James Tuttle, Lieutenant, District 256	24 Nov 1804	p. 888
David Tuttle, Ensign, District 256	22 Apr 1805	p. 889
Larkin Dial, Ensign, District 237	6 Dec 1805	p. 889
Marthew Scott Montgomery, Captain, District 256	22 Apr 1803	p. 890
John Thomason, Ensign, District 256	22 Apr 1805	p. 890
Robert Morable, Lieutenant, District 218	7 Dec 1805	p. 891
James Tye, Ensign, District 218	7 Dec 1805	p. 891
Thomas Mitchel, Captain, District 216	7 Dec 1805	p. 892
Zadock Cook, Captain, District 240	6 Dec 1805	p. 892
William Powell, Lieutenant, District 240	7 Dec 1805	p. 893
James Muckleroy, Ensign, District 240	7 Dec 1805	p. 893
Wiliam Hopkins, Captain, District 22	7 Dec 1805	p. 894
Isaac Funderburgh, Lieutenant, District 22	7 Dec 1805	p. 894
William Brown, Captain, District 221	7 Dec 1805	p. 895
Thomas Dicken, Lieutenant, District 221	7 Dec 1805	p. 895
Cial Camp, Ensign, District 221	7 Dec 1805	p. 896
Samuel Brown, Lieutenant, District 219	7 Dec 1805	p. 896
Isaac Umphries, Captain, Volunteer Company of Riflemen, Battalion 49	7 Dec 1805	p. 897

Georgia Military Commissions, 1798–1818

Name, Rank, Unit	Date	Page
Thomas Stamps, Lieutenant, Volunteer Company of Riflemen, Battalion 49	7 Dec 1805	p. 897
Levi Benton, Ensign, Volunteer Company of Riflemen, Battalion 49	7 Dec 1805	p. 898
John Silman, Second Lieutenant, Volunteer Troop of Horse, Regiment 24	7 Dec 1805	p. 898
Job Tyson, Captain, District 27	7 Dec 1805	p. 899
Benjamin Samuel, Major	7 Dec 1805	p. 899
Joseph Morton, Lieutenant, District 229	7 Dec 1805	p. 900
John Landrum, Ensign, District 229	7 Dec 1805	p. 900
William Berdles, Lieutenant, District 226	7 Dec 1805	p. 901
George Lester, Ensign, District 226	7 Dec 1805	p. 901
George Winn, Captain, District 227	7 Dec 1805	p. 902
George Watter, Lieutenant, District 227	7 Dec 1805	p. 902
Reuben Edward Edwards, Ensign, District 227	7 Dec 1805	p. 903
John Owens, Ensign	7 Dec 1805	p. 903
Jonathan Cooper, Lieutenant, District 237	7 Dec 1805	p. 904
Reuben Weaver, Ensign, District 237	7 Dec 1805	p. 904
Garland T. Watkins, Captain, District 235	7 Dec 1805	p. 905
Thomas Bridges, Lieutenant, District 235	7 Dec 1805	p. 905
John Kidd, Captain, Volunteer Company of Riflemen, Battalion 45	7 Dec 1805	p. 906
Bennet Willson, Lieutenant, Volunteer Company of Riflemen, Battalion 45	7 Dec 1805	p. 906
Cuthbert Smith, Cornet, Volunteer Troop of Horse, Regiment 22	7 Dec 1805	p. 907
James Fox, Lieutenant Colonel, Regiment 10	7 Dec 1805	p. 907
Valentine Walker, Major, Battalion 27	7 Dec 1805	p. 908
Asa Raygan, Captain, District 235	7 Dec 1805	p. 908
Thomas Bridges, Lieutenant, District 235	7 Dec 1805	p. 909
John S. Massey, Lieutenant, District 74	23 Dec 1805	p. 909
Moses Bunn, Ensign, District 74	23 Dec 1805	p. 910
Homer V. Milton, Captain, Volunteer Troop of Dragoons, Regiment 7	11 Jan 1806	p. 910
Mackry McNorel, Lieutenant, Volunteer Troop of Dragoons, Regiment 7	11 Jan 1806	p. 911
John Salsbury, Second Lieutenant, Volunteer Troop of Dragoons, Regiment 7	11 Jan 1806	p. 911

Commissions Book 1800–1806

Name, Rank, Unit	Date	Page
Stephen W. Blount, Cornet, Volunteer Troop of Dragoons, Regiment 7	11 Jan 1806	p. 912
John Powell, Lieutenant, District 153	11 Jan 1806	p. 912
Samuel Lockhart, Major, Battalion 11	22 Jan 1806	p. 913
John Adams, Lieutenant, District 142	22 Jan 1806	p. 913
James Tilly, Ensign, District 142	22 Jan 1806	p. 914
Blassingame Thomas, Lieutenant, District 78	17 Feb 1806	p. 914
Elijah Warner, Lieutenant, District 79	17 Feb 1806	p. 915
Jesse Jones, Ensign, District 79	17 Feb 1806	p. 915
William Hendley, Captain, District 49	27 Feb 1806	p. 916
Samuel Hendley, Lieutenant, District 49	27 Feb 1806	p. 916
Littleton Reese, Captain, Volunteer Troop of Dragoons, Regiment 14	5 Mar 1806	p. 917
Drury Reese, First Lieutenant, Volunteer Troop of Dragoons, Regiment 14	5 Mar 1806	p. 917
William Lewis, Cornet, Volunteer Troop of Dragoons, Regiment 14	5 Mar 1806	p. 918
John Collins, Captain, District 121	11 Mar 1806	p. 918
Benjamin Fudge, Ensign, District 121	11 Mar 1806	p. 919
Isham Ross, Captain, District 57	11 Mar 1806	p. 919
Kindred Brasswell Jr., Lieutenant, District 57	11 Mar 1806	p. 920
John H. Watts, Captain, District 146	12 Mar 1806	p. 920
Robert Tucker, Lieutenant, District 146	12 Mar 1806	p. 921
Thomas Watts, Ensign, District 146	12 Mar 1806	p. 921
Willis Shivers, Captain, District 111	12 Mar 1806	p. 922
Benjamin Humphrey, Lieutenant, District 111	12 Mar 1806	p. 922
Matthew Brake, Ensign, District 111	12 Mar 1806	p. 923
William W. Kemon, Captain, District 182	12 Mar 1806	p. 923
Robert Leverett Jr., Ensign, District 182	12 Mar 1806	p. 924
Samuel Cummingham, Major, Battalion 30	13 Mar 1806	p. 924
Henry Carlton Jr., Captain, District 143	13 Mar 1806	p. 925
William Divine, Lieutenant, District 143	13 Mar 1806	p. 925
Resdon Walton, Ensign, District 143	13 Mar 1806	p. 926
Elisha Crawford, Ensign, District 163	13 Mar 1806	p. 926
Edward Harden, Captain, District 8	21 Mar 1806	p. 927
John B. Mars, Lieutenant, District 4	21 Mar 1806	p. 927
James Pelot, Ensign, District 4	21 Mar 1806	p. 928

Georgia Military Commissions, 1798–1818

Name, Rank, Unit	Date	Page
William A. Moore, Second Lieutenant, Volunteer Troop of Dragoons, Regiment 1	21 Mar 1806	p. 928
Elias Cassels, Captain, District 17	21 Mar 1806	p. 929
Sampson Ball, Lieutenant, District 17	21 Mar 1806	p. 929
Flyming Tynes, Ensign, District 17	21 Mar 1806	p. 930
Ticey Thomas, Captain, District 114	22 Mar 1806	p. 930
George Rachels, Ensign, District 114	22 Mar 1806	p. 931
Isaac Birdsong, Captain, District 112	22 Mar 1806	p. 931
John Hall, First Lieutenant, Volunteer Troop of Dragoons, Regiment 15	22 Mar 1806	p. 932
Thomas Lovett, Cornet, Volunteer Troop of Dragoons, Regiment 15	22 Mar 1806	p. 932
Thomas Ellis, Lieutenant	28 Mar 1806	p. 933
Thomas R. Rigby, Ensign	28 Mar 1806	p. 933
Neil Munroe, Captain, District 57	2 Apr 1806	p. 934
Brinkley Grandy, Lieutenant, District 57	2 Apr 1806	p. 934
William Matthews, Captain, District 52	2 Apr 1806	p. 935
William Nobles, Lieutenant, District 52	2 Apr 1806	p. 935
Philip Hinson, Ensign, District 52	2 Apr 1806	p. 936
Reubin Neil, Captain, District 53	2 Apr 1806	p. 936

Georgia Military Commissions
Commissions Book 1806–1809

Name, Rank, Unit	*Date*	*Page*
Ephraim Willis, Ensign, District 53	4 Feb 1806	p. 1
Joseph Brantley, Captain, District 55	2 Apr 1806	p. 1
Bolen Swearingen, Captain, District 56	2 Apr 1806	p. 2
William Pennington, Lieutenant, District 56	2 Apr 1806	p. 2
Solomon Savedge, Ensign, District 56	2 Apr 1806	p. 3
Ephraim Tapley, First Lieutenant, Volunteer Troop of Horse, Regiment 6	2 Apr 1806	p. 3
William McCall, Cornet, Volunteer Troop of Horse, Regiment 6	2 Apr 1806	p. 4
George Herb, Captain, District 6	3 Apr 1806	p. 4
Richard Wylly, Lieutenant, District 6	3 Apr 1806	p. 5
Robert Bernard, Ensign, District 6	3 Apr 1806	p. 5
Thomas Polhill Jr., Captain, District 9	4 Apr 1806	p. 6
David Milzger, Lieutenant, District 12	4 Apr 1806	p. 6
Frederick Bunch, Ensign, District 12	4 Apr 1806	p. 7
Henry Austin, Captain, District 20	4 Apr 1806	p. 7
Richard T. Keating, Lieutenant, District 20	4 Apr 1806	p. 8
Robert Sherwood, Lieutenant, District 21	4 Apr 1806	p. 8
Elijah Cork, Lieutenant, District 27	4 Apr 1806	p. 9
Ignatius Grantham, Ensign, District 27	4 Apr 1806	p. 9
Robert McCombs, Captain, District 119	5 Apr 1806	p. 10
Joseph Henderson, Lieutenant, District 119	5 Apr 1806	p. 10
Frances Pharoah, Ensign, District 119	5 Apr 1806	p. 11
Abraham Woodside, Ensign, Volunteer Company of Infantry (styled The Savannah Guards), Battalion 1	12 Apr 1806	p. 11
James Crouder, Captain, District 106	12 Apr 1806	p. 12
William Moon, Lieutenant, District 106	12 Apr 1806	p. 12
Daniel Henry, Ensign, District 106	12 Apr 1806	p. 13
Murdock McLeod, Captain, District 21	18 Apr 1806	p. 13
Theophilus Montfort, Lieutenant, District 21	18 Apr 1806	p. 14
John Bassett, Ensign, District 21	18 Apr 1806	p. 14
Stephen B. Clark, Ensign, District 1	25 Apr 1806	p. 15
Raymond Demere Jr., Lieutenant, District 25	27 Apr 1806	p. 15
Joseph Dubignon, Ensign, District 25	29 Apr 1806	p. 16

Name, Rank, Unit	Date	Page
Garland Hardwich, Captain, District 76	29 Apr 1806	p. 16
John Bostwick, Captain, District 81	29 Apr 1806	p. 17
William Harly, Lieutenant, District 81	29 Apr 1806	p. 17
William Shepherd, Ensign, District 81	19 Apr 1806	p. 18
James Beall, Captain, District 124	29 Apr 1806	p. 18
Abraham Fausett, Lieutenant, District 124	29 Apr 1806	p. 19
James Barton, Ensign, District 124	29 Apr 1806	p. 19
Josiah Robbins, Ensign, District 120	29 Apr 1806	p. 20
John Neilson, Captain, Volunteer Company of Artillery (styled the Augusta Rangers)	29 Apr 1806	p. 20
Patrick Kelly, Lieutenant, Volunteer Company of Infantry (styled the Augusta Rangers)	29 Apr 1806	p. 21
John Wright, Major, Battalion 50	29 Apr 1806	p. 21
Thomas King Jr., Lieutenant, District 29	1 May 1806	p. 22
Flavius Waterman, Ensign, District 29	1 May 1806	p. 22
John Duke, Captain, District 218	3 May 1806	p. 23
Nathan Barnett, Lieutenant, District 218	3 May 1806	p. 23
Levin Ballard, Captain, District 67	5 May 1806	p. 24
William Wenthers, Lieutenant, District 67	5 May 1806	p. 24
James Pinkston, Captain, District 118	5 May 1806	p. 25
James McDowell, Lieutenant, District 118	5 May 1806	p. 25
Thomas Forson, Ensign, District 118	5 May 1806	p. 26
John Goodwin, Lieutenant, District 111	5 May 1806	p. 26
William Sanders, Captain, Volunteer Troop of Horse, Regiment 15	5 May 1806	p. 27
John Gilmore, Lieutenant, District 96	7 May 1806	p. 27
Mills Farmer, Ensign, District 96	7 May 1806	p. 28
Gibson Flournoy, Captain, District 140	9 May 1806	p. 28
Avery Wheeler, Lieutenant, District 140	9 May 1806	p. 29
William Stern, Lieutenant, District 217	10 May 1806	p. 29
James Daniel, Ensign, District 216	10 May 1806	p. 30
Harbert Avery, Captain, District 126	22 May 1806	p. 30
Miles Gilliam, Lieutenant, District 82	24 May 1806	p. 31
Edmund Burke Chisolm, Ensign, District 82	24 May 1806	p. 31
Thomas Armstrong, Captain, District 43	28 May 1806	p. 32
William Mobley, Lieutenant, District 43	28 May 1806	p. 32
Richard Joice, Ensign, District 43	28 May 1806	p. 33

Name, Rank, Unit	Date	Page
Valentine Walker, Lieutenant Colonel, Regiment 10	3 Jun 1806	p. 33
William Stafford, Lieutenant	3 Jun 1806	p. 34
Benjamin Davis, Ensign	3 Jun 1806	p. 34
Lewis Moulder, Lieutenant, District 210	21 Jun 1806	p. 35
Champness Arnold, Lieutenant, District 231	21 Jun 1806	p. 35
John Tunnel, Ensign, District 231	21 Jun 1806	p. 36
Elias Beall, Captain, District 230	21 Jun 1806	p. 36
Woody Taylor, Lieutenant, District 231	21 Jun 1806	p. 37
John Arnold, Captain, Volunteer Troop of Horse, Regiment 22	21 Jun 1806	p. 37
William Owen, Lieutenant, District 234	21 Jun 1806	p. 38
Wylly Clouds, Ensign, District 233	21 Jun 1806	p. 38
Thomas Scott, Lieutenant Colonel, Regiment 22	21 Jun 1806	p. 39
Benjamin Thompson, Ensign, District 86	21 Jun 1806	p. 39
William Hillard, Lieutenant, District 89	21 Jun 1806	p. 40
William Holland, Lieutenant, District 93	21 Jun 1806	p. 40
David Griffin, Ensign, District 93	21 Jun 1806	p. 41
John Mathews, Lieutenant, District 94	21 Jun 1806	p. 41
Lemuel Howard, Ensign, District 94	21 Jun 1806	p. 42
Thomas Green, Lieutenant, District 95	21 Jun 1806	p. 42
William Bucks, Lieutenant, District 99	21 Jun 1806	p. 43
Hugh Hickling, Ensign, District 99	21 Jun 1806	p. 43
Charles R. Carter, Major, Battalion 38	21 Jun 1806	p. 44
John Heard, Captain, District 165	21 Jun 1806	p. 44
Adam Loven, Lieutenant, District 165	21 Jun 1806	p. 45
Joshua Render Jr., Ensign, District 165	21 Jun 1806	p. 45
Asa Atkins, Lieutenant, District 171	21 Jun 1806	p. 46
William Parkes, Captain, District 174	21 Jun 1806	p. 46
John H. Triplett, Lieutenant, District 174	21 Jun 1806	p. 47
John B. Slanton, Ensign, District 174	21 Jun 1806	p. 47
James Thorn, Lieutenant, District 179	21 Jun 1806	p. 48
Signor Edmonds, Ensign, District 179	21 Jun 1806	p. 48
Lewis B. Taliaferro, Lieutenant, District 181	21 Jun 1806	p. 49
Quinny Curry, Ensign, District 181	21 Jun 1806	p. 49
John Pearson, Captain	23 Jun 1806	p. 50
Michael Perry, Lieutenant	23 Jun 1806	p. 50
Thomas Bulger, Ensign	23 Jun 1806	p. 51

Georgia Military Commissions, 1798–1818

Name, Rank, Unit	Date	Page
Thomas Stephens, Captain	23 Jun 1806	p. 51
Rowland Mahone, Lieutenant	23 Jun 1806	p. 52
Thomas Rockmore, Ensign	23 Jun 1806	p. 52
Henry Angling, Captain	23 Jun 1806	p. 53
Burrel Bulloch, Lieutenant	23 Jun 1806	p. 53
Joel McClendon, Ensign	23 Jun 1806	p. 54
Winston Bennett, Captain	23 Jun 1806	p. 54
John H. Watley, Lieutenant	23 Jun 1806	p. 55
William Sansom, Ensign	23 Jun 1806	p. 55
Jordon Horn, Captain	23 Jun 1806	p. 56
Samuel Carter, Lieutenant	23 Jun 1806	p. 56
Abemilick Sullon, Ensign	23 Jun 1806	p. 57
William Cowley, Captain	23 Jun 1806	p. 57
John Gilbert, Lieutenant	23 Jun 1806	p. 58
James Thompson, Ensign	23 Jun 1806	p. 58
Benjamin Harvey, Captain	23 Jun 1806	p. 59
Bird Dennard, Lieutenant	23 Jun 1806	p. 59
Isaac Stephens, Ensign	23 Jun 1806	p. 60
William Smith, Captain	23 Jun 1806	p. 60
John Dennard, Lieutenant	23 Jun 1806	p. 61
John Gilmore, Ensign	23 Jun 1806	p. 61
Philip Pitman, Captain	23 Jun 1806	p. 62
Abel Cain, Lieutenant	23 Jun 1806	p. 62
John Crabtree, Ensign	23 Jun 1806	p. 63
Daniel Trammell, Captain, District 225	24 Jun 1806	p. 63
William Beall, Lieutenant, District 225	24 Jun 1806	p. 64
Allen Spurlock, Lieutenant, District 240	24 Jun 1806	p. 64
Aaron Butler, Captain	24 Jun 1806	p. 65
Edward Butler, Lieutenant	24 Jun 1806	p. 65
John Hopkins, Ensign	24 Jun 1806	p. 66
John Martindale, Captain, District 223	24 Jun 1806	p. 66
Gadial Farmborough, Ensign, District 223	24 Jun 1806	p. 67
Tryer Robertson, Captain, District 239	24 Jun 1806	p. 67
Elijah Loyd, Lieutenant, District 239	24 Jun 1806	p. 68
George Loyd, Ensign, District 239	24 Jun 1806	p. 68
Everett Harper, Captain, District 241	24 Jun 1806	p. 69

Name, Rank, Unit	*Date*	*Page*
Haywood Harper, Lieutenant, District 243	24 Jun 1806	p. 69
John Silman, Captain, District 223	24 Jun 1806	p. 70
William Loyd, Lieutenant, District 223	24 Jun 1806	p. 70
Everett McCoy, Ensign, District 223	24 Jun 1806	p. 71
Richard Lewis, Ensign, District 241	24 Jun 1806	p. 71
William McDowell, Second Lieutenant, Volunteer Troop of Horse	24 Jun 1806	p. 72
Wiley Thompson, Captain, District 190	24 Jun 1806	p. 72
James Morrison, Captain, District 191	24 Jun 1806	p. 73
Amos Baker, Lieutenant, District 191	24 Jun 1806	p. 73
Zachariah Baker, Ensign, District 191	24 Jun 1806	p. 74
William Thompson, Captain, District 194	24 Jun 1806	p. 74
Ransom Murrow, Lieutenant, District 194	24 Jun 1806	p. 75
Elijah Baker, Ensign, District 294	24 Jun 1806	p. 75
Larken Clark Jr., Captain, District 195	24 Jun 1806	p. 76
William White, Lieutenant, District 195	24 Jun 1806	p. 76
John Jones, Ensign, District 195	24 Jun 1806	p. 77
Thomas Oliver, Captain, District 197	24 Jun 1806	p. 77
Presley Christian, Lieutenant, District 197	24 Jun 1806	p. 78
Levi Stinchcomb, Ensign, District 197	24 Jun 1806	p. 78
Amos Richardson, Ensign, District 198	24 Jun 1806	p. 79
Joshua Carpenter, Lieutenant, District 200	24 Jun 1806	p. 79
Malcom Johnson, Ensign, District 200	24 Jun 1806	p. 80
Anderson Ive, Lieutenant, District 208	24 Jun 1806	p. 80
Solomon Stephens, Ensign, District 208	24 Jun 1806	p. 81
William Cleghorn, Captain	24 Jun 1806	p. 81
Abednego Robertson, Lieutenant	24 Jun 1806	p. 82
William Byford, Ensign	24 Jun 1806	p. 82
James McDowel, Captain	24 Jun 1806	p. 83
Absalom Trantham, Lieutenant	24 Jun 1806	p. 83
Benjamin Lowry, Ensign	24 Jun 1806	p. 84
Ezekiel Brown, Major, Battalion 35	24 Jun 1806	p. 84
James Stewart, Captain, District 144	24 Jun 1806	p. 85
Jacob Jarrett, Lieutenant, District 144	24 Jun 1806	p. 85
Jeremiah Baxter, Captain, District 137	24 Jun 1806	p. 86
Robert H. Musgrove, Lieutenant, District 137	24 Jun 1806	p. 86
Robert Moore, Captain, District 139	24 Jun 1806	p. 87

Georgia Military Commissions, 1798–1818

Name, Rank, Unit	Date	Page
Douglass Watson, Captain, District 138	24 Jun 1806	p. 87
William Reynolds, Lieutenant, District 138	24 Jun 1806	p. 88
John Duke, Ensign, District 138	24 Jun 1806	p. 88
Silas Littlejohns, Ensign, District 161	24 Jun 1806	p. 89
Gates F. Farley, Lieutenant, District 145	24 Jun 1806	p. 89
James Little, Captain, District 252	24 Jun 1806	p. 90
Robert Wilson, Lieutenant, District 252	25 Jun 1806	p. 90
Joseph Armer, Ensign, District 252	24 Jun 1806	p. 91
Samuel Windham, Captain	24 Jun 1806	p. 91
Willis Windham, Lieutenant	24 Jun 1806	p. 92
Isaac Jackson, Ensign	24 Jun 1806	p. 92
Pheny Robins, Captain, District 257	24 Jun 1806	p. 93
John Engle, Lieutenant, District 257	24 Jun 1806	p. 93
George Roberts, Ensign, District 257	24 Jun 1806	p. 94
Jeremiah Candler, Ensign, District 243	24 Jun 1806	p. 94
John Ramsey, Lieutenant, District 244	24 Jun 1806	p. 95
William Blalock, Ensign, District 249	24 Jun 1806	p. 95
James Smart, Captain, District 18	24 Jun 1806	p. 96
Thomas Griffin, Lieutenant, District 18	24 Jun 1806	p. 96
Abraham Deloath, Ensign, District 18	24 Jun 1806	p. 97
Eli Kennedy, Lieutenant, District 48	25 Jun 1806	p. 97
Charles Mikell, Ensign, District 48	25 Jun 1806	p. 98
John T. Allen, Captain, District 129	25 Jun 1806	p. 98
Peter H. Collins, Lieutenant, District 129	25 Jun 1806	p. 99
Walter Jones, Ensign, District 129	25 Jun 1806	p. 99
Charles Wright, Lieutenant, District 133	25 Jun 1806	p. 100
John Hughs, Lieutenant, District 187	25 Jun 1806	p. 100
Richard Whitley, Ensign, District 187	25 Jun 1806	p. 101
John Gray, Lieutenant, District 182	25 Jun 1806	p. 101
William Dinkins, Ensign, District 183	25 Jun 1806	p. 102
William Poythress, Lieutenant, District 34	25 Jun 1806	p. 102
Uriah Fuller, Ensign, District 34	25 Jun 1806	p. 103
Thomas Haynes Jr., Lieutenant, District 155	25 Jun 1806	p. 103
Francis Resher, Ensign, District 155	25 Jun 1806	p. 104
Benjamin Weatherby, Lieutenant, District 157	25 Jun 1806	p. 104
Henry Bonner, Ensign, District 157	25 Jun 1806	p. 105

Name, Rank, Unit	Date	Page
David Brydie Mitchell, Major General, Division 1	26 Jun 1806	p. 105
John Floyd, Brigadier General, Brigade 1, Division 1	26 Jun 1806	p. 106
Abraham Jackson, Brigadier General, Brigade 2, Division 1	26 Jun 1806	p. 106
Jeremiah McDaniel, Captain, District 41	27 Jun 1806	p. 107
Joseph Sykes, Lieutenant, District 41	27 Jun 1806	p. 107
John McDaniel, Ensign, District 41	27 Jun 1806	p. 108
Ezekiel Stafford, Captain, District 39	27 Jun 1806	p. 108
John Mattocks, Lieutenant, District 39	27 Jun 1806	p. 109
Henry Greenwood, Lieutenant, District 124	10 Jul 1806	p. 109
Armstead Fulcher, Ensign, District 124	10 Jul 1806	p. 110
William McTyree, Captain, District 123	10 Jul 1806	p. 110
Matthew Channel, Lieutenant, District 123	10 Jul 1806	p. 111
Francis Taylor, Ensign, District 123	10 Jul 1806	p. 111
Joseph Ware, Second Lieutenant, Volunteer Troop of Dragoons, Regiment 10	10 Jul 1806	p. 112
Robert Wyche, First Lieutenant, Volunteer Troop of Dragoons, Regiment 7	14 Jul 1806	p. 112
Jesse B. Moore, Lieutenant, District 60	14 Jul 1806	p. 113
Evan Lewis, Ensign, District 60	14 Jul 1806	p. 113
David Gertman, First Lieutenant, Volunteer Troop of Dragoons, Regiment 9	15 Jul 1806	p. 114
George W. Evans, Captain, Volunteer Company of Infantry (styled the Augusta Independent Blues), Battalion 27	14 Jul 1806	p. 114
Shadrack Bogan, Lieutenant, Volunteer Company of Infantry (styled the Augusta Independent Blues), Battalion 27	14 Jul 1806	p. 115
Samuel Lock, Ensign, Volunteer Company of Infantry (styled the Augusta Independent Blues), Battalion 27	14 Jul 1806	p. 115
Barton Atcherson, Lieutenant, District 159	14 Jul 1806	p. 116
John Wilson, Ensign, District 159	14 Jul 1806	p. 116
David Brown, Captain	18 Jul 1806	p. 117
Pheneas Whatley, Lieutenant	18 Jul 1806	p. 117
Philip Jones, Ensign	18 Jul 1806	p. 118
David Thomas, Captain, District 77	24 Jul 1806	p. 118
Tapley Holt, Captain, District 117	25 Jul 1806	p. 119
Nathaniel Ennis, Lieutenant, District 117	25 Jul 1806	p. 119

Georgia Military Commissions, 1798–1818

Name, Rank, Unit	Date	Page
David Parker, Ensign, District 117	25 Jul 1806	p. 120
Abraham Peevy, Lieutenant, District 116	25 Jul 1806	p. 120
Chatten Scroggin, Lieutenant, District 115	25 Jul 1806	p. 121
James Ashly, Ensign, District 115	25 Jul 1806	p. 121
John L. Jones, Captain, Volunteer Company of Riflemen, Battalion 26	25 Jul 1806	p. 122
Easom Franklin, Lieutenant, Volunteer Company of Riflemen, Battalion 26	25 Jul 1806	p. 122
Robert Brown, Ensign, Volunteer Company of Riflemen, Battalion 26	25 Jul 1806	p. 123
William Taylor, Lieutenant, District 63	26 Jul 1806	p. 123
William Brack, Ensign, District 63	26 Jul 1806	p. 124
Archibald Stuart, Lieutenant, District 64	26 Jul 1806	p. 124
Nicholas Thomas, Ensign, District 64	26 Jul 1806	p. 125
James Torrance, Lieutenant, District 75	26 Jul 1806	p. 125
Jonas Proctor, Ensign, District 75	26 Jul 1806	p. 126
James Gaddy, Captain, District 159	30 Jul 1806	p. 126
John Cooper, Captain, District 175	30 Jul 1806	p. 127
Augustine Yager, Lieutenant, District 157	30 Jul 1806	p. 127
John Walker, Ensign, District 175	30 Jul 1806	p. 128
Lunsford Low, Lieutenant, District 71	4 Aug 1806	p. 128
Jonathan Davis, Lieutenant Colonel, Regiment 15	6 Aug 1806	p. 129
William Davis, Ensign, District 62	11 Aug 1806	p. 129
Thomas Burke, Ensign, Volunteer Company of Infantry (styled the Savannah Guards), Battalion 1	15 Aug 1806	p. 130
Joel Chivers, Captain	20 Aug 1806	p. 130
Joseph J. Moore, Captain, District 226	25 Aug 1806	p. 131
John S. Anderson, Lieutenant, District 226	25 Jun 1806	p. 131
Sindney Anderson, Ensign, District 226	25 Aug 1806	p. 132
Michajah Brooks, Lieutenant, District 150	27 Aug 1806	p. 132
Thomas Jones, Ensign, District 150	27 Aug 1806	p. 133
Robert Pope, Captain, District 227	28 Aug 1806	p. 133
James Beal, Major, Battalion 27	29 Aug 1806	p. 134
John McAnnally, Ensign, District 72	30 Aug 1806	p. 134
John Roberts, Captain, District 73	3 Sep 1806	p. 135
Thomas Gordy, Lieutenant, District 73	3 Sep 1806	p. 135
Kinchen Curl, Lieutenant, District 74	3 Sep 1806	p. 136

Name, Rank, Unit	*Date*	*Page*
Washington Montgomery, Ensign, District 256	3 Sep 1806	p. 136
Hardy Strickland, Captain, District 251	3 Sep 1806	p. 137
Stephen Reid, Lieutenant, District 151	3 Sep 1806	p. 137
Laban Rowden, Ensign, District 251	3 Sep 1806	p. 138
James Wright, Captain, District 242	3 Sep 1806	p. 138
Edward McDermont, Lieutenant, District 242	3 Sep 1806	p. 139
Etheldred Ross, Ensign, District 242	3 Sep 1806	p. 139
Ezekiel Seely, Ensign, District 244	3 Sep 1806	p. 140
Mark Snow, Lieutenant, District 258	3 Sep 1806	p. 140
Jesse Dukes, Ensign, District 258	3 Sep 1806	p. 141
Notley Maddox, Lieutenant, District 254	3 Sep 1806	p. 141
William Goode, Ensign, District 254	3 Sep 1806	p. 142
Abner Bagby, Lieutenant, District 246	3 Sep 1806	p. 142
William Darben, Ensign, District 246	4 Sep 1806	p. 143
John Hinson, Captain, District 145	3 Sep 1806	p. 143
John Hinson, Captain, District 245	3 Sep 1806	p. 144
John Gregg, Lieutenant, District 245	3 Aug 1806	p. 144
Martin Boon, Captain, Volunteer Company of Riflemen	3 Aug 1806	p. 145
Andrew Scott, Lieutenant, Volunteer Company of Riflemen	3 Aug 1806	p. 145
John Rorie, Captain, District 164	3 Aug 1806	p. 146
Abraham Ruddell, Lieutenant, District 164	3 Aug 1806	p. 146
John Spear, Ensign, District 164	3 Aug 1806	p. 147
Sherod Malone, Captain, District 169	3 Aug 1806	p. 147
Jarrett Patridge, Lieutenant, District 169	3 Aug 1806	p. 148
David Whatley, Ensign, District 170	3 Aug 1806	p. 148
Joseph Freeman, Ensign, District 180	3 Aug 1806	p. 149
John Coffee, Captain, District 110	3 Aug 1806	p. 149
McKinne Howell, Lieutenant, District 110	3 Aug 1806	p. 150
Thomas Howell, Ensign, District 110	3 Aug 1806	p. 150
Joseph Cooper Jr., Captain, District 107	3 Aug 1806	p. 151
John Cooper, Lieutenant, District 107	3 Aug 1806	p. 151
Robert Bryan, Ensign, District 107	3 Aug 1806	p. 152
Andrew Abercrombie, Lieutenant, District 102	3 Aug 1806	p. 152
Elisha Dodridge, Ensign, District 102	3 Aug 1806	p. 153
Ezekiel Smith, Captain, District 104	3 Aug 1806	p. 153
William Morgan, Lieutenant, District 104	3 Aug 1806	p. 154

Georgia Military Commissions, 1798–1818

Name, Rank, Unit	Date	Page
John Comean, Lieutenant, District 108	3 Aug 1806	p. 154
Frederick Scott, Lieutenant, Volunteer Company of Riflemen, Battalion 24	3 Aug 1806	p. 155
Stephen Marchman, Ensign, Volunteer Company of Riflemen, Battalion 24	3 Aug 1806	p. 155
James Hall, Second Lieutenant, Volunteer Troop of Horse, Regiment 14	3 Aug 1806	p. 156
Jacob Gunn, Captain, District 105	3 Aug 1806	p. 156
Peter Treeney, Lieutenant, District 105	3 Aug 1806	p. 157
Thomas Morris, Ensign, District 105	3 Aug 1806	p. 157
Charles Miller, Lieutenant, Volunteer Company of Riflemen, Battalion 23	3 Aug 1806	p. 158
James Savage, Ensign, Volunteer Company of Riflemen, Battalion 23	3 Aug 1806	p. 158
George Roebuck, Captain, District 119	5 Sep 1806	p. 159
L. King, Lieutenant, District 199	5 Sep 1806	p. 159
J. Brinkley, Ensign, District 199	5 Sep 1806	p. 160
William Faulkner, Captain, District 202	5 Sep 1806	p. 160
George Stovall, Lieutenant, District 202	5 Aug 1806	p. 161
James Hastley, Ensign, District 202	5 Sep 1806	p. 161
Joel Crawford, Lieutenant, District 193	5 Sep 1806	p. 162
Thomas Barrett, Ensign, District 193	5 Sep 1806	p. 162
Isaac I. Barrott, Captain, District 197	5 Sep 1806	p. 163
Jeremiah McMullen, Lieutenant, District 197	5 Sep 1806	p. 163
John Vaughters, Ensign, District 197	5 Sep 1806	p. 164
Youg Moore, Lieutenant, District 139	5 Sep 1806	p. 164
James R. Nelms, Ensign, District 139	5 Sep 1806	p. 165
Zachariah Simms, Lieutenant, District 143	5 Sep 1806	p. 165
Richard M. Sesson, Ensign, District 137	5 Sep 1806	p. 166
Asa Raygan, Major, Battalion 45	5 Sep 1806	p. 166
William Hitchcock, Captain, District 235	5 Sep 1806	p. 167
James H. Ponder, Lieutenant, District 235	5 Sep 1806	p. 167
Exum Lewis, Ensign, District 235	5 Sep 1806	p. 168
Cuthbert Smith, Second Lieutenant, Volunteer Troop of Horse, Regiment 22	5 Sep 1806	p. 168
Nathaniel Smith, Cornet, Volunteer Troop of Horse, Regiment 22	5 Sep 1806	p. 169
Josiah Parish, Captain, District 45	5 Sep 1806	p. 169

Name, Rank, Unit	Date	Page
William Jones, Lieutenant, District 45	5 Sep 1806	p. 170
Henry Simmons, Ensign, District 45	5 Sep 1806	p. 170
Isaac Crews, Captain, District 31	5 Sep 1806	p. 171
Charles Fitchell, Ensign, District 31	5 Sep 1806	p. 171
James Magee, Ensign, District 3	5 Sep 1806	p. 172
George Brooks, Lieutenant, District 2	5 Sep 1806	p. 172
Allen C. Thompson, Ensign, District 2	5 Sep 1806	p. 173
Charles Cope, Ensign, District 1	5 Sep 1806	p. 173
John B. Bacon, Lieutenant, District 16	5 Sep 1806	p. 174
Edmund Adams, Ensign, District 16	5 Sep 1806	p. 174
James Lambright, Cornet, Volunteer Troop of Horse, Battalion 4	5 Sep 1806	p. 175
William Champ, Ensign, District 188	5 Sep 1806	p. 175
James Ware, Lieutenant, District 182	5 Sep 1806	p. 176
Joel Yowell, Captain	5 Sep 1806	p. 176
George Carpenter, Lieutenant	5 Sep 1806	p. 177
John Bryant, Ensign	5 Sep 1806	p. 177
Benjamin Hollingsworth, Captain	5 Sep 1806	p. 178
James Jones, Lieutenant	5 Sep 1806	p. 178
John Meeks, Ensign	5 Sep 1806	p. 179
Peter Mathews, Ensign, District 67	5 Sep 1806	p. 179
Thephulas Thomas, Lieutenant Colonel, Regiment 4	16 Sep 1806	p. 180
Clement Lanier, Major, Battalion 9	16 Sep 1806	p. 180
James Welch, Lieutenant Colonel, Regiment 8	16 Sep 1806	p. 181
John Freeman, Captain	16 Sep 1806	p. 181
Risden Oliver, Lieutenant	16 Sep 1806	p. 182
Archibald Clarke, First Lieutenant, Volunteer Troop of Horse, Battalion 8	16 Sep 1806	p. 182
Francis Young, Cornet, Volunteer Troop of Horse, Battalion 8	16 Sep 1806	p. 183
John Floyd, Major	20 Sep 1806	p. 183
John H. Sims, Captain, District 221	20 Sep 1806	p. 184
Amos Touhand, Lieutenant, District 87	27 Sep 1806	p. 185
Ambrose Yarborough, Ensign, District 87	27 Sep 1806	p. 185
William J. Holmes, Ensign, District 97	27 Sep 1806	p. 186
Samuel Garrett, Captain, District 96	27 Sep 1806	p. 186
William Renfro, Captain, District 100	27 Sep 1806	p. 187

Georgia Military Commissions, 1798–1818

Name, Rank, Unit	Date	Page
Stephen Renfro, Lieutenant, District 100	27 Sep 1806	p. 187
William Hall, Ensign, District 100	27 Sep 1806	p. 188
Joel Smith, Captain, District 99	27 Sep 1806	p. 188
Eli Moffett, Lieutenant, District 99	27 Sep 1806	p. 189
Alexander Smith, Ensign, District 99	27 Sep 1806	p. 189
Vaughflile Howard, Ensign, District 95	27 Sep 1806	p. 190
Elisha Padgett, Ensign, District 91	27 Sep 1806	p. 190
Nathaniel Renfroe, Captain, District 136	27 Sep 1806	p. 191
John Hardy, Lieutenant, District 136	27 Sep 1806	p. 191
John Maning, Ensign, District 136	27 Sep 1806	p. 192
Homer V. Milton, Lieutenant Colonel, Regiment 7	2 Oct 1806	p. 192
Frederick Beal, Lieutenant Colonel	21 Oct 1806	p. 193
Treowetts Wynn, Captain, Rifle Company	29 Sep 1806	p. 193
Lewis Smith, Lieutenant, Rifle Company	29 Oct 1806	p. 194
Peter Hunnells, Ensign, Rifle Company	29 Oct 1806	p. 194
Arthur Bearden, Captain, District 251	8 Nov 1806	p. 195
Vincent Flanigan, Lieutenant, District 251	8 Nov 1806	p. 195
Thomas Black, Captain, District 254	8 Nov 1806	p. 196
Benjamin Hawthorn, Lieutenant, District 254	8 Nov 1806	p. 196
John Mays, Ensign, District 254	8 Nov 1806	p. 197
William Byne, Major, Battalion 16	10 Nov 1806	p. 197
Jesse B. Moore, Captain, District 60	10 Nov 1806	p. 198
William Sexton, Lieutenant, District 60	10 Nov 1806	p. 198
Laird M. Harris, Captain, District 103	12 Nov 1806	p. 199
Morgan Clower, Lieutenant, District 103	12 Nov 1806	p. 199
James Adams, Ensign, District 103	12 Nov 1806	p. 200
Thomas Hudson, Captain, District 109	12 Nov 1806	p. 200
Lovit Smith, Lieutenant, District 142	12 Nov 1806	p. 201
John Turner, Captain, District 113	12 Nov 1806	p. 201
Thomas Gay, Lieutenant, District 113	12 Nov 1806	p. 202
Irby Hudson, Captain, Volunteer Company of Riflemen, Battalion 14	12 Nov 1806	p. 202
John Dillon, First Captain, Engine No. 2 Fire Company (City of Savannah)	12 Nov 1806	p. 203
Ransom Stone, Second Captain, Engine No. 2 Fire Company (City of Savannah)	12 Nov 1806	p. 203
Smith Stringer, Ensign, District 61	13 Nov 1806	p. 204

Name, Rank, Unit	*Date*	*Page*
Asa Allen, Major, Battalion 46	15 Nov 1806	p. 204
John E. Carson, Captain, District 210	15 Nov 1806	p. 205
Joseph Walters, Major	15 Nov 1806	p. 205
William Christian, Captain, District 207	15 Nov 1806	p. 206
Farley Thompson, Captain	15 Nov 1806	p. 206
Moses Ayres, Lieutenant	15 Nov 1806	p. 207
Garland Ayres, Ensign	15 Nov 1806	p. 207
Joedy Newsom, Major, Battalion 3	20 Nov 1806	p. 208
John Powell, Captain, District 153	20 Nov 1806	p. 208
Thomas Williams, Lieutenant, District 153	20 Nov 1806	p. 209
Thomas Maddox, Ensign, District 153	20 Nov 1806	p. 209
John Hughs, Captain, District 187	20 Nov 1806	p. 210
Richard Wheatley, Lieutenant, District 187	20 Nov 1806	p. 210
Joseph Smith, Ensign, District 187	20 Nov 1806	p. 211a
James McDonald, Ensign, District 128	20 Nov 1806	p. 211a
John G. Williamson, Captain, District 127	20 Nov 1806	p. 211b
William Worthy, Lieutenant, District 127	20 Nov 1806	p. 211b
John Tankersley, Ensign, District 127	20 Nov 1806	p. 213
Joseph Binning, Captain, District 135	20 Nov 1806	p. 213
James Casey, Lieutenant, District 135	20 Nov 1806	p. 214
George H. Johnston, Ensign, District 135	20 Nov 1806	p. 214
Nimrod Jones, Lieutenant, District 134	20 Nov 1806	p. 215
Moses Ivey, Ensign, District 134	20 Nov 1806	p. 215
William Mays, Captain, District 186	22 Nov 1806	p. 216
James Turner, Lieutenant, District 186	22 Nov 1806	p. 216
David Murray, Ensign, District 186	22 Nov 1806	p. 217
Richardson Booker, Captain, Volunteer Company of Riflemen, Battalion 38	22 Nov 1806	p. 217
Christopher Brooks, Lieutenant, Volunteer Company of Riflemen, Battalion 38	22 Nov 1806	p. 218
Samuel Brooks, Ensign, Volunteer Company of Riflemen, Battalion 38	22 Nov 1806	p. 218
James Edge, Captain, District 172	22 Nov 1806	p. 219
Henry Hadley, Lieutenant, District 172	22 Nov 1806	p. 219
Abraham Bean, Ensign, District 172	22 Nov 1806	p. 220
Augustine Edwards, Captain, District 167	22 Nov 1806	p. 220
Drurry Cunningham, Lieutenant, District 167	22 Nov 1806	p. 221

Georgia Military Commissions, 1798–1818

Name, Rank, Unit	Date	Page
Tarlton Sheets, Ensign, District 167	22 Nov 1806	p. 221
Robert Martin, Captain, District 220	24 Nov 1806	p. 222
Ephraim Bunyard, Lieutenant, District 220	24 Nov 1806	p. 222
Jesse Scrivener, Ensign, District 220	24 Nov 1806	p. 223
Charles Read, Captain, District 218	24 Nov 1806	p. 223
William Clements, Captain	24 Nov 1806	p. 224
Ignatius Grantham, Lieutenant	24 Nov 1806	p. 224
John McDaniel, Ensign	24 Nov 1806	p. 225
Ezra Jones, Captain	24 Nov 1806	p. 225
Thomas Micham, Lieutenant	24 Nov 1806	p. 226
John C. Harrell, Ensign	24 Nov 1806	p. 226
Richard Walker, Captain	24 Nov 1806	p. 227
Crawford Edmundson, Captain, District 232	24 Nov 1806	p. 227
Thomas R. Stewart, Lieutenant	27 Nov 1806	p. 228
Wiley Pope, Lieutenant, District 227	27 Nov 1806	p. 228
Henry Davis, Ensign, District 227	27 Nov 1806	p. 229
Samuel Bell, Lieutenant, District 237	27 Nov 1806	p. 229
Robert Crawford, Lieutenant, District 128	27 Nov 1806	p. 230
Tapley Holt, Major, Battalion 26	4 Dec 1806	p. 230
Walter Davis, Lieutenant, District 47	4 Dec 1806	p. 231
William King, Captain, District 141	4 Dec 1806	p. 231
William Dolvin, Lieutenant, District 141	5 Dec 1806	p. 232
John Stephenson, Ensign, District 141	5 Dec 1806	p. 232
Nathan Bostick, Captain, District 69	16 Dec 1806	p. 233
James Darby, Lieutenant, Volunteer Troop of Horse, Regiment 9	18 Dec 1806	p. 233
William Fountain, Cornet, Volunteer Troop of Horse, Regiment 9	18 Dec 1806	p. 234
Robert Mountain, Ensign, District 78	18 Dec 1806	p. 234
John Smith, Ensign, District 85	18 Dec 1806	p. 235
Joseph Morton, Captain, District 229	17 Jan 1807	p. 235
Joseph Ector, Captain, District 237	17 Jan 1807	p. 236
Jonathan Palmer, Ensign, District 121	2 Feb 1807	p. 236
James Johnson Jr., Lieutenant Colonel, Regiment 1	9 Feb 1807	p. 237
Ambrose Day, Ensign, Volunteer Company of Infantry (styled the Louisville Guards), Battalion 19	12 Feb 1807	p. 237
Leon H. Marks, Lieutenant, District 82	12 Feb 1807	p. 238

Name, Rank, Unit	*Date*	*Page*
Douglass Watson, Major, Battalion 30	12 Feb 1807	p. 238
Lewis Collins, Captain, District 124	3 Mar 1807	p. 239
James Barton, Lieutenant, District 124	3 Mar 1807	p. 239
Woodward Knight, Ensign, District 124	3 Mar 1807	p. 240
Charles McKenna, Ensign, Volunteer Company of Infantry (styled the Rangers), Battalion 1	6 Mar 1807	p. 240
John S. DeMontmollin, Captain, Volunteer Company of Infantry (styled the Rangers), Battalion 1	6 Mar 1807	p. 241
Benjamin Ansley, Lieutenant, Volunteer Company of Infantry (styled the Rangers), Battalion 1	6 Mar 1807	p. 241
Calvin Baker, Lieutenant, District 4	6 Mar 1807	p. 242
Jesse Peoples, Ensign, District 8	6 Mar 1807	p. 242
John Barnand, Lieutenant, District 6	6 Mar 1807	p. 243
James Barnard, Ensign, District 6	6 Mar 1807	p. 243
John Boog, Second Lieutenant, Volunteer Troop of Horse, Regiment 4	6 Mar 1807	p. 244
Pleasant Compton, Captain, District 233	6 Mar 1807	p. 244
Peter Bennett, Captain, District 169	12 Mar 1807	p. 245
John Chaffin, Lieutenant, District 169	12 Mar 1807	p. 245
Joel Leverett, Ensign, District 169	12 Mar 1807	p. 246
Mossman Houston, Ensign, District 2	12 Mar 1807	p. 246
John B. Mars, Captain, District 4	23 Mar 1807	p. 247
Nathaniel R. Greene, Lieutenant, District 30	23 Mar 1807	p. 247
Thomas H. Miller, Ensign, District 30	23 Mar 1807	p. 248
Josiah Wilson, Captain, District 14	23 Mar 1807	p. 248
Edmund Bacon, Ensign, District 14	23 Mar 1807	p. 249
John Winn, Ensign, District 15	23 Mar 1807	p. 249
Lee Blacksell, Lieutenant, District 20	23 Mar 1807	p. 250
Joseph Stillwell, Ensign, District 20	23 Mar 1807	p. 250
James Martin, Major, Battalion 14	23 Mar 1807	p. 251
John Atkinson, Captain, District 61	23 Mar 1807	p. 251
William Knight, Captain, District 67	23 Mar 1807	p. 252
Thomas B. Thursby, Captain, District 67	23 Mar 1807	p. 252
John Cumming, Major, Battalion 1	25 Mar 1807	p. 253
Josiah Watts, Lieutenant, Infantry Company, Battalion 22	26 Mar 1807	p. 253
Richard Whitaker, Ensign, Infantry Company, Battalion 22	26 Mar 1807	p. 254

Georgia Military Commissions, 1798–1818

Name, Rank, Unit	Date	Page
Jareal Beasley, Captain, District 138	27 Mar 1807	p. 254
William Payne, Lieutenant, District 138	27 Mar 1807	p. 255
Jordan Thornton, Ensign, District 138	27 Mar 1807	p. 255
John Myrick, Captain, District 140	27 Mar 1807	p. 256
Jared Wright, Lieutenant, District 140	27 Mar 1807	p. 256
Caleb Veasy, Ensign, District 140	27 Mar 1807	p. 257
Daniel Mound, Captain, District 75	30 Mar 1807	p. 257
Malichi Mound, Ensign, District 75	30 Mar 1807	p. 258
Martin Harden, Major, Battalion 10	30 Mar 1807	p. 258
John Jones, Lieutenant, District 40	30 Mar 1807	p. 259
Joshua Cathrell, Ensign, District 40	30 Mar 1807	p. 259
William Browning, Major, Battalion 31	3 Apr 1807	p. 260
Tilman S. Dixon, Major, Battalion 22	6 Apr 1807	p. 260
James Gilmore, Captain, District 26	6 Apr 1807	p. 261
Stephen Gilmore, Lieutenant, District 26	6 Apr 1807	p. 261
Cullin L. Mason, Ensign, District 26	6 Apr 1807	p. 262
William Welch, Lieutenant, District 69	7 Apr 1807	p. 262
Joel Gay, Ensign, District 69	7 Apr 1807	p. 263
Edward Harden, Major, Battalion 2	9 Apr 1807	p. 263
William Magee, Ensign, District 4	10 Feb 1807	p. 264
Wylie Clowdis, Lieutenant, District 233	11 Apr 1807	p. 264
Thomas Carter, Major, Battalion 34	13 Apr 1807	p. 265
John White, Lieutenant, District 74	13 Apr 1807	p. 265
James Marshall, Captain, Company of Infantry (styled the Savannah Volunteer Guards), Battalion 1	22 Apr 1807	p. 266
Thomas Burke, Lieutenant, Company of Infantry (styled the Savannah Volunteer Guards), Battalion 1	22 Apr 1807	p. 266
Hezekiah Reynolds, Ensign, Company of Infantry (styled the Savannah Volunteer Guards), Battalion 1	22 Apr 1807	p. 267
John S. Marcey, Ensign, District 82	22 Apr 1807	p. 267
Howel Moreland, Lieutenant, District 76	27 Apr 1807	p. 268
John Morris, Lieutenant, District 79	25 Apr 1807	p. 268
William Alexander, Captain, District 3	30 Apr 1807	p. 269
John M. Woolsey, Ensign, District 3	30 Apr 1807	p. 269
Michael Shelman, Lieutenant Colonel, Regiment 9	30 Apr 1807	p. 270
Benniah McLendon, Ensign, District 188	1 May 1807	p. 270
William Harrison, Captain, District 8	2 May 1807	p. 271

Name, Rank, Unit	*Date*	*Page*
John Peter Oates, Lieutenant, District 2	2 May 1807	p. 271
Christopher Sickington, Lieutenant, District 11	2 May 1807	p. 272
Joseph Brewer, Lieutenant, District 13	2 May 1807	p. 272
Nathaniel Hall, Ensign, District 13	2 May 1807	p. 273
George Nowland, Captain, District 9	2 May 1807	p. 273
Jordon Abbott, Captain, District 150	4 May 1807	p. 274
Benjamin Mathews, Lieutenant, District 150	4 May 1807	p. 274
Gilbert Neyland, Captain, District 69	4 May 1807	p. 275
Bright Baker, Captain, District 22	4 May 1807	p. 275
Jesse Campbell, Lieutenant, District 22	4 May 1807	p. 276
Peter Massie, Lieutenant, District 27	4 May 1807	p. 276
Francis Scarlett, Ensign, District 27	4 May 1807	p. 277
John Poullin, Lieutenant, District 5	4 May 1807	p. 277
Daniel Johnston, Ensign, District 5	4 May 1807	p. 278
John Paulett, Captain, District 71	4 May 1807	p. 278
Samuel Bryant, Ensign, District 71	4 May 1807	p. 279
Jonathan Parish, Second Lieutenant, Volunteer Company of Artillery, Regiment 11	15 May 1807	p. 279
Robert Porter, Lieutenant, District 23	15 May 1807	p. 280
Henry Boles, Ensign, District 23	15 May 1807	p. 280
Job Brooks, Lieutenant	15 May 1807	p. 281
William Askew, Ensign	15 May 1807	p. 281
Abner Slater, Lieutenant, District 156	15 May 1807	p. 282
Gedion Harris, Ensign, District 156	15 May 1807	p. 282
John Gill, Captain, District 146	16 May 1807	p. 283
Samuel Smith, Ensign, District 84	18 May 1807	p. 283
Morris Smith, Lieutenant, District 38	25 May 1807	p. 284
Risden Oliver, Ensign, District 38	25 May 1807	p. 284
George Dougherty, Ensign, District 33	28 May 1807	p. 285
William Magee, Lieutenant, District 3	28 May 1807	p. 285
Jehu E. Harden, Ensign, District 8	28 May 1807	p. 286
William Womack, Lieutenant, District 10	28 May 1807	p. 286
Wright Lofley, Ensign, District 10	28 May 1807	p. 287
Nicholas Childers, Lieutenant, District 106	30 May 1807	p. 287
Richard Simms, Ensign, District 106	30 May 1807	p. 288
Francis Smith, Captain, District 115	30 May 1807	p. 288
Hollinger Brown, Lieutenant, District 105	30 May 1807	p. 289

Georgia Military Commissions, 1798–1818

Name, Rank, Unit	Date	Page
John McRae, Ensign, District 115	30 May 1807	p. 289
Ichabud Thompson, Lieutenant, District 101	30 May 1807	p. 290
Harris Parish, Ensign, District 101	30 May 1807	p. 290
James Finch, Captain, District 109	30 May 1807	p. 291
William Finch, Lieutenant, District 109	30 May 1807	p. 291
Bird Gilbert, Ensign, District 209	30 May 1807	p. 292
Micajah Pickard, Ensign, District 113	30 May 1807	p. 292
Divenport Graves, Ensign, District 114	30 May 1807	p. 293
William Tyus, Captain, Volunteer Company of Infantry, Battalion 24	30 May 1807	p. 293
John Thweat, Lieutenant, Volunteer Company of Infantry, Battalion 24	30 May 1807	p. 294
Robert Dawson, Ensign, Volunteer Company of Infantry, Battalion 36	2 Jun 1807	p. 294
William Smith, Ensign, Volunteer Company of Infantry, Battalion 24	2 Jun 1807	p. 295
Peter Stubblefield, Captain, Volunteer Company of Infantry, Battalion 36	2 Jun 1807	p. 295
Daniel H. Oniel, Captain, District 44	8 Jun 1807	p. 296
John Hilleard, Lieutenant, District 44	8 Jun 1807	p. 296
James Harrell, Ensign, District 44	8 Jun 1807	p. 297
George R. Clayton, Major, Battalion 19	9 Jun 1807	p. 297
Josiah Watts, Captain, Volunteer Company of Infantry, Battalion 22	4 Jun 1807	p. 298
James Daniel, Lieutenant, Volunteer Company of Infantry, Battalion 22	11 Jun 1807	p. 298
Jacob Pinson, Captain	11 Jun 1807	p. 299
Nicholas Perry, Lieutenant	11 Jun 1807	p. 299
James Robert Jenkins, Lieutenant Colonel, Regiment 16	15 Jan 1807	p. 300
James Burrows, Lieutenant, District 161	15 Jun 1807	p. 300
Hiram Glazer, Ensign, District 148	15 Jun 1807	p. 301
Risden Walton, Lieutenant, District 143	15 Jun 1807	p. 301
Churchwell Gather, Lieutenant, District 142	15 May 1807	p. 302
Sterling Carrol, Ensign, District 142	15 Jun 1807	p. 302
William Butler, Captain, District 122	29 Jun 1807	p. 303
Robert Johnson, Lieutenant, District 29	29 Jun 1807	p. 303
George F. Randolph, Ensign, District 122	29 Jun 1807	p. 304
Rodham Tulloss, Captain, District 119	29 Jun 1807	p. 304

Commissions Book 1806–1809

Name, Rank, Unit	Date	Page
John D. Lewis, Lieutenant, District 119	29 Jun 1807	p. 305
Schuyter Richardson, Ensign, District 119	29 Jun 1807	p. 305
Gilbert Longstreet, Ensign, Volunteer Company of Rangers, Battalion 27	29 Jun 1807	p. 306
Zachariah Williams, Captain, Volunteer Troop of Horse, Regiment 10	29 Jun 1807	p. 306
John B. Barnes, First Lieutenant, Volunteer Troop of Horse, Regiment 10	29 Jun 1807	p. 307
Joseph Ware, Second Lieutenant, Volunteer Troop of Horse, Regiment 10	29 Jun 1807	p. 307
William Jones, Cornet, Volunteer Troop of Horse, Regiment 10	29 Jun 1807	p. 308
Jacob Clements, Captain, District 62	7 Jul 1807	p. 308
Charles Wheeler, Captain, District 70	9 Jul 1807	p. 309
William Roberts, Lieutenant, District 70	9 Jul 1807	p. 309
William Gray, Ensign, District 70	9 Jul 1807	p. 310
Noble Glen, Lieutenant, District 6	10 Jul 1807	p. 310
William Lavender, Ensign, District 6	10 Jul 1807	p. 311
Job F. Bolles, Captain	10 Jul 1807	p. 311
Francis Tufts, Lieutenant	10 Jul 1807	p. 312
Thomas Stewart, Ensign	10 Jul 1807	p. 312
Robert Moore, Captain	10 Jul 1807	p. 313
Joseph Hill Clarke, Lieutenant	10 Jul 1807	p. 313
Francis Sage, Ensign	10 Jul 1807	p. 314
Allen B. Powell, Captain	10 Jul 1807	p. 314
John Oneal, Lieutenant	10 Jul 1807	p. 315
John King, Lieutenant Colonel	10 Jul 1807	p. 315
William H. Robinson, Captain, Volunteer Troop of Dragoons, Regiment 9	18 Jul 1807	p. 316
Howell Moreland, Captain, District 76	18 Jul 1807	p. 316
Lancelot Vevrell, Lieutenant, District 76	18 Jul 1807	p. 317
Roderick Joiner, Ensign, District 76	18 Jul 1807	p. 317
William Cowart, Captain, District 83	25 Jul 1807	p. 318
William Eatman, Lieutenant, District 83	25 Jul 1807	p. 318
Stephen Reed, Captain, District 251	27 Jul 1807	p. 319
James M. Morris, Lieutenant, District 251	27 Jul 1807	p. 319
William Watkin, Ensign, District 251	27 Jul 1807	p. 320
Hinchin Warren, Ensign, District 74	28 Jul 1807	p. 320

Georgia Military Commissions, 1798–1818

Name, Rank, Unit	Date	Page
George G. Nowlin, Major, Battalion 2	29 Jul 1807	p. 321
William Barnes, Major, Battalion 23	29 Jul 1807	p. 321
Kenedy Key, Major, Battalion 51	29 Jul 1807	p. 322
Jonathan Scarboroug, Captain, District 73	4 Aug 1807	p. 322
Ephram Bass, Ensign, District 73	4 Aug 1807	p. 323
John A. Cobb, Captain, District 79	4 Aug 1807	p. 323
William Mulkey, Captain, District 67	4 Aug 1807	p. 324
Thomas Tabb, Lieutenant, District 67	4 Aug 1807	p. 324
James T. Thomas, Captain, District 1	11 Aug 1807	p. 325
Deverux Jarratt, Lieutenant, District 1	11 Aug 1807	p. 325
Benjamin Carr, Lieutenant, District 157	15 Aug 1807	p. 326
John Spinks, Ensign, District 157	15 Aug 1807	p. 326
Leon H. Marks, Captain, District 82	15 Aug 1807	p. 327
Hezekiah Gates, Ensign, District 82	20 Aug 1807	p. 327
Benjamin J. Harper, Captain, District 101	21 Aug 1807	p. 328
James Cannon, Lieutenant, District 101	21 Aug 1807	p. 328
Robert H. Musgrove, Captain, District 137	24 Aug 1807	p. 329
James P. Watson, Lieutenant, District 137	24 Aug 1807	p. 329
John W. Towns, Ensign, District 137	24 Aug 1807	p. 330
William Hayles, Captain, District 81	24 Aug 1807	p. 330
Lewis Lee, Lieutenant, District 81	24 Aug 1807	p. 331
Masheck Mathews, Ensign, District 81	24 Aug 1807	p. 331
Daniel Lemle, First Lieutenant, Volunteer Company of Artillary, Regiment 9	25 Aug 1807	p. 332
William Durden, Captain, District 158	26 Aug 1807	p. 332
Thomas Lockett, Lieutenant, District 158	26 Aug 1807	p. 333
Robert Cairey, Ensign, District 158	26 Aug 1807	p. 333
Barton Atchison, Captain, District 159	26 Aug 1807	p. 334
James Seagrove, Captain, Volunteer Company of Artillery	28 Aug 1807	p. 334
Harmon Courter, First Lieutenant, Volunteer Company of Artillery	28 Aug 1807	p. 335
David D. Jones, Ensign, Volunteer Company of Artillery	28 Aug 1807	p. 335
John Winn, Major, Battalion 4	28 Aug 1807	p. 336
William Hendry, Ensign, District 17	28 Aug 1807	p. 336
Ezekiel Wimberly, Captain, District 87	28 Aug 1807	p. 337
William Oates, Lieutenant, District 87	28 Aug 1807	p. 337
Daniel Oliver, Captain, District 38	29 Aug 1807	p. 338

Name, Rank, Unit	Date	Page
David Mizell, Captain, District 49	29 Aug 1807	p. 338
Edward Lane, Lieutenant, District 49	29 Aug 1807	p. 339
Isaac Douglass, Ensign, District 49	29 Aug 1807	p. 339
Thomas Napier, Major	31 Aug 1807	p. 340
Duncan McNair, Captain, District 3	3 Sep 1807	p. 340
Mathew Parker, Lieutenant, District 148	5 Sep 1807	p. 341
Thomas Cantelore, Captain, Lincoln County	28 Sep 1807	p. 341
John Savidge, Captain, District 125	14 Sep 1807	p. 342
James Foster, Lieutenant, District 125	14 Sep 1807	p. 342
Arthur Foster, Ensign, District 125	14 Sep 1807	p. 343
James Ramsey, Captain, District 134	14 Sep 1807	p. 343
William G. Gregory, Lieutenant, District 134	14 Sep 1807	p. 344
Reuben Winfrey, Ensign, District 134	14 Sep 1807	p. 344
Stephen Baker, Ensign, District 128	14 Sep 1807	p. 345
Stephen Hodge, Lieutenant, District 133	14 Sep 1807	p. 345
John Lansdown, Lieutenant, District 127	14 Sep 1807	p. 346
William Johnson, Major	18 Sep 1807	p. 346
John Harris, District 26	18 Sep 1807	p. 347
John Ward, Ensign, District 16	18 Sep 1807	p. 347
Abner Kelly, Ensign, District 112	18 Sep 1807	p. 348
John W. Mendenhall, Ensign	5 Jan 1808	p. 348
Thomas Spencer, Captain, District 193	25 Jan 1808	p. 349
Ezekiel McCrary, Lieutenant, District 245	26 Jan 1808	p. 349
William W. Gray, Lieutenant, District 193	25 Jan 1808	p. 350
Joel Moore, Lieutenant, District 193	25 Jan 1808	p. 350
John Turner, Captain, District 162	25 Jan 1808	p. 351
Jacob D. Hightower, Ensign, District 162	25 Jan 1808	p. 351
Russell Jones Jr., Lieutenant Colonel Commandant, Regiment 26	26 Jan 1808	p. 352
Joseph Hampton, Captain, District 255	26 Jan 1808	p. 352
David H. McCluskey, Captain, District 257	26 Jan 1808	p. 353
Robert Paxton, Lieutenant, District 257	26 Jan 1808	p. 353
Samuel Barnett, Ensign, District 257	26 Jan 1808	p. 354
William Garthright, Captain, District 252	26 Jan 1808	p. 354
John Allen, Captain, District 245	26 Jan 1808	p. 355
Hosea Camp, Captain, Volunteer Troop of Horse, Regiment 25	26 Jan 1808	p. 355

Name, Rank, Unit	Date	Page
Etheldred Ross, Lieutenant, Volunteer Troop of Horse, Regiment 25	26 Jan 1808	p. 356
William Hewett, Second Lieutenant, Volunteer Troop of Horse, Regiment 25	26 Jan 1808	p. 356
Wyley Ross, Cornet, Volunteer Troop of Horse, Regiment 25	26 Jan 1808	p. 357
Steele White, Ensign, Volunteer Troop of Infantry (styled the Savannah Volunteer Guards), Battalion 1	9 Oct 1807	p. 357
John Morehead, Lieutenant, District 4	28 Jan 1808	p. 358
Ephraim Cooper, Ensign, District 1	28 Jan 1808	p. 358
Augustus Baldwin, Captain, Volunteer Company of Artillery, Regiment 10	3 Feb 1808	p. 359
John Wilson Jr., Lieutenant, Volunteer Company of Artillery, Regiment 10	3 Feb 1808	p. 359
Donald McIver, Ensign, Volunteer Company of Artillery, Regiment 10	3 Feb 1808	p. 360
Benjamin Duychinche, Ensign, Volunteer Company of Infantry (styled the Augusta Blues)	4 Feb 1808	p. 360
James Murrey, Lieutenant	4 Feb 1808	p. 361
Thomas Miles, Ensign	4 Feb 1808	p. 361
Gedion Sealey, Ensign, District 124	4 Feb 1808	p. 362
John B. Mars, Major, Battalion 60	6 Feb 1808	p. 362
John W. Cooper, Major, Battalion 38	15 Feb 1808	p. 363
Isaac Funderburg, Captain, District 224	12 Feb 1808	p. 363
Zadock Bonner, Lieutenant, District 224	12 Feb 1808	p. 364
Isaac Stroud, Ensign, District 224	12 Feb 1808	p. 364
Edmund Butler, Captain	12 Feb 1808	p. 365
John Hopkins, Lieutenant	12 Feb 1808	p. 365
John Sawyer, Ensign	12 Feb 1808	p. 366
William Wright, Lieutenant, District 218	12 Feb 1808	p. 366
David Beggs, Ensign, District 218	12 Feb 1808	p. 367
James Morgan, Captain, District 239	12 Feb 1808	p. 367
William Fann, Lieutenant, District 239	12 Feb 1808	p. 368
Benjamin Boon, Lieutenant, District 140	15 Feb 1808	p. 368
William Edmundson, Ensign, District 140	15 Feb 1808	p. 369
George Eubant, Lieutenant, District 82	12 Sep 1807	p. 369
Jesse Robinson, Ensign, District 82	15 Feb 1808	p. 370
Henry L. Revear, Captain, District 176	18 Feb 1808	p. 370

Name, Rank, Unit	Date	Page
Paul T. Willis, Lieutenant, District 176	18 Feb 1808	p. 371
Ambrose Wright, Second Lieutenant, Volunteer Company of Artillary, Regiment 9	18 Feb 1808	p. 371
William Chisolm, Lieutenant Colonel Commandant	20 Feb 1808	p. 372
Archur Barton, Major, Battalion 41	20 Feb 1808	p. 372
Azmon Rucker, Major	20 Feb 1808	p. 373
Edward Story, Captain, District 201	20 Feb 1808	p. 373
Aaron Duncan, Lieutenant, District 201	20 Feb 1808	p. 374
Richard Bond, Ensign, District 201	20 Feb 1808	p. 374
James Long, Captain, District 203	20 Feb 1808	p. 375
William Kirlin, Lieutenant, District 203	20 Feb 1808	p. 375
Henry Shafer, Captain, District 62	23 Feb 1808	p. 376
John Bell, Ensign, District 62	23 Feb 1808	p. 376
Benjamin Hodge, Ensign, District 90	24 Feb 1808	p. 377
James Chappel, Lieutenant, District 136	24 Feb 1808	p. 377
Allen Hardee, Ensign, District 136	24 Feb 1808	p. 378
Richard Long, Lieutenant, District 100	24 Feb 1808	p. 378
Drury Long, Ensign, District 100	24 Feb 1808	p. 379
Allen Took, Lieutenant, District 91	24 Feb 1808	p. 379
William Mason, Ensign, District 86	24 Feb 1808	p. 380
Isaac Wimberly, Major, Battalion 17	24 Feb 1808	p. 380
Joseph Hines, Lieutenant, District 73	24 Feb 1808	p. 381
Thomas Weeks, Ensign, District 72	24 Feb 1808	p. 381
James Pelot, Captain, District 21	25 Feb 1808	p. 382
Thomas Stewart, Captain	1 Feb 1808	p. 382
Henry Crowell, Captain, District 98	1 Mar 1808	p. 383
Henry Kindall, Captain, Troop of Horse, Regiment 12	7 Mar 1808	p. 383
Chruchwell Gibson, First Lieutenant, Troop of Horse, Regiment 12	7 Mar 1808	p. 384
John Gibson, Second Lieutenant, Troop of Horse, Regiment 12	7 Mar 1808	p. 384
Drury Bass, Ensign, District 153	7 Mar 1808	p. 385
James Dozier, Captain, District 174	7 Mar 1808	p. 385
Millington Sparks, Ensign, District 174	7 Mar 1808	p. 386
Raymond Demire Jr., Captain, District 25	7 Mar 1808	p. 386
Joseph Dubignon, Ensign, District 25	7 Mar 1808	p. 387
William Schley, Major, Battalion 19	10 Mar 1808	p. 387

Georgia Military Commissions, 1798–1818

Name, Rank, Unit	Date	Page
Jabez Roberts, Captain	19 Mar 1808	p. 388
Abram Little, Lieutenant	19 Mar 1808	p. 388
John Casey, Ensign	19 Mar 1808	p. 389
Henry Cox, Captain	19 Mar 1808	p. 389
William McDade, Lieutenant	19 Mar 1808	p. 390
Benjamin Cobb, Ensign	19 Mar 1808	p. 390
Thaddeus Holt, Captain	19 Mar 1808	p. 391
Noah Dodridge, Lieutenant	19 Mar 1808	p. 391
John Bender, Ensign	19 Mar 1808	p. 392
Owen H. Kinan, Captain	19 Mar 1808	p. 392
John Yarborough, Ensign	19 Mar 1808	p. 393
Michael Carter, Lieutenant	19 Mar 1808	p. 393
David Gill, Ensign	19 Mar 1808	p. 394
James M. C. Montgomery, Major, Battalion 52	19 Mar 1808	p. 394
Charles Kennion, Captain	21 Mar 1808	p. 395
Hiram Glazier, Lieutenant	21 Mar 1808	p. 395
William Lanear, Ensign	21 Mar 1808	p. 396
Francis Smith, Captain	21 Mar 1808	p. 396
Hollinger Brown, Lieutenant	21 Mar 1808	p. 397
John Stallings, Ensign	21 Mar 1808	p. 397
George W. Dillard, Captain, Volunteer Troop of Dragoons, Regiment 17	22 Mar 1808	p. 398
Jeremiah Early, First Lieutenant, Volunteer Troop of Dragoons, Regiment 17	22 Mar 1808	p. 398
Samuel Nicholson, Second Lieutenant, Volunteer Troop of Dragoons, Regiment 17	22 Mar 1808	p. 399
William Cairy, Cornet, Volunteer Troop of Dragoons, Regiment 17	22 Mar 1808	p. 399
Stephen Dukes, Lieutenant, District 104	30 Mar 1808	p. 400
John Burgay, Ensign, District 104	30 Mar 1808	p. 400
William Pearre, Lieutenant, District 87	30 Mar 1808	p. 401
William Levingston, Ensign, District 87	30 Mar 1808	p. 401
Edward Harris, Lieutenant, District 88	30 Mar 1808	p. 402
Richard D. Carter, Ensign, District 96	30 Mar 1808	p. 402
John Spann, Lieutenant, District 97	30 Mar 1808	p. 403
Samuel Fleming, Captain, District 85	2 Apr 1808	p. 403
James Carr, Captain, District 84	2 Apr 1808	p. 404

Name, Rank, Unit	Date	Page
Pleasant Hargrove, Lieutenant, District 79	2 Apr 1808	p. 404
Leammis Granberry, Lieutenant, District 85	2 Apr 1808	p. 405
Jones Douglass, Ensign, District 85	2 Apr 1808	p. 405
Elnothan Davis, Lieutenant, District 84	2 Apr 1808	p. 406
William Anderson, Ensign, District 84	2 Apr 1808	p. 406
John J. Cottle, Lieutenant, District 83	2 Apr 1808	p. 407
Josiah Calhoun, Ensign, District 83	2 Apr 1808	p. 407
William Reynolds, Captain, District 138	5 Apr 1808	p. 408
Robert Newsom, Lieutenant, District 138	5 Apr 1808	p. 408
David Ray, Ensign, District 138	5 Apr 1808	p. 409
John Hill, Captain	5 Apr 1808	p. 409
Robert Brooks, Lieutenant	5 Apr 1808	p. 410
Jeremiah Warren, Ensign	5 Apr 1808	p. 410
Robert Wallace, Captain	5 Apr 1808	p. 411
Lindsey Thornton, Lieutenant	5 Apr 1808	p. 411
Anthony Butts, Ensign	5 Apr 1808	p. 412
Asa Cox, Captain	11 Apr 1808	p. 412
Benjamin Corley, Lieutenant	11 Apr 1808	p. 413
Allen Hodge, Ensign	11 Apr 1808	p. 413
Isaac Jackson, Captain	12 Apr 1808	p. 414
Ishmeal Davis, Lieutenant	12 Apr 1808	p. 414
William Henderson, Ensign	12 Apr 1808	p. 415
Thomas Ware, Captain, District 163	12 Apr 1808	p. 415
Thomas Riley, Lieutenant, District 163	12 Apr 1808	p. 416
William Baker, Ensign, District 163	12 Apr 1808	p. 416
Lewis Atkinson, Captain, District 111	13 Apr 1808	p. 417
Jesse Lockhart, Lieutenant, District 111	13 Apr 1808	p. 417
Giles Kelly, Ensign, District 111	13 Apr 1808	p. 418
Jeremiah Sanders, Captain, Volunteer Company of Riflemen, Battalion 29	14 Apr 1808	p. 418
Edward Short, Lieutenant, Volunteer Company of Riflemen, Battalion 29	14 Apr 1808	p. 419
John Harden, Ensign, Volunteer Company of Riflemen, Battalion 29	14 Apr 1808	p. 419
Peter H. Collins, Lieutenant, District 130	14 Apr 1808	p. 420
John Collins, Ensign, District 130	14 Apr 1808	p. 420
Randle Jones, Ensign, District 133	14 Apr 1808	p. 421

Georgia Military Commissions, 1798–1818

Name, Rank, Unit	Date	Page
John Benning, Ensign, District 126	14 Apr 1808	p. 421
David Stanford, Captain, District 134	14 Apr 1808	p. 422
William Whitecomb, Ensign, District 125	14 Apr 1808	p. 422
William Collins, Ensign, District 129	14 Apr 1808	p. 423
William Holt, Lieutenant, District 161	15 Apr 1808	p. 423
Abner Wells, Ensign, District 161	15 Apr 1808	p. 424
Joshua Renders, Captain, District 165	15 Apr 1808	p. 424
David Montgomery, Lieutenant, District 165	15 Apr 1808	p. 425
Samuel Northern, Ensign, District 165	15 Apr 1808	p. 425
William Edward, Captain, Volunteer Company of Riflemen, Battalion 45	15 Apr 1808	p. 426
Tilman S. Dixon, Lieutenant Colonel Commandant, Regiment 13	16 Apr 1808	p. 426
James Coldwell, Captain	18 Apr 1808	p. 427
Elijah Rosser, Lieutenant	18 Apr 1808	p. 427
Moses Taylor, Ensign	18 Apr 1808	p. 428
James Hunter, Captain, District 6	20 Apr 1808	p. 428
John W. Barnard, Lieutenant, District 6	20 Apr 1808	p. 429
Wiliam Durkee, Ensign, District 6	20 Apr 1808	p. 429
Charles Machin, Ensign, District 3	20 Apr 1808	p. 430
David Taylor Jr., Captain, District 4	20 Apr 1808	p. 430
Augustus Goember, Ensign, District 5	20 Apr 1808	p. 431
Abner Hicks, Captain	20 Apr 1808	p. 431
Thomas P. Hammilton, Captain, District 102	25 Apr 1808	p. 432
John Studevant, Lieutenant, District 102	25 Apr 1808	p. 432
George Hammilton, Ensign, District 102	25 Apr 1808	p. 433
William Morgan, Captain	26 Apr 1808	p. 433
Edward Cox, Lieutenant	26 Apr 1808	p. 434
Jacob Zuber, Ensign	26 Apr 1808	p. 434
William Walker, Captain	26 Apr 1808	p. 435
James Y. Walker, Lieutenant	26 Apr 1808	p. 435
Julius Cook, Ensign	26 Apr 1808	p. 436
John M. Woolsey, Lieutenant	26 Apr 1808	p. 436
Edward Evans, Ensign	26 Apr 1808	p. 437
George Thrash, Captain, District 231	26 Apr 1808	p. 437
Pinkethman Hawkins, Captain	28 Apr 1808	p. 438
Ford Coulter, Lieutenant	28 Apr 1808	p. 438

Name, Rank, Unit	Date	Page
William Hawkins, Ensign	28 Apr 1808	p. 439
George Nowland, Captain	2 May 1808	p. 439
Alexander Northcut, Lieutenant	2 May 1808	p. 440
John Greene, Ensign	2 May 1808	p. 440
Chappel Sledge, Captain, District 103	2 May 1808	p. 441
Thomas W. Baxter, Lieutenant, District 103	2 May 1808	p. 441
Robert Lucas, Captain, District 107	2 May 1808	p. 442
Joseph Nixon, Lieutenant, District 107	2 May 1808	p. 442
David Carter, Ensign, District 108	2 May 1808	p. 443
John Stith, Lieutenant Colonel Commandant, Regiment 12	11 May 1808	p. 443
John Wilson, Captain, Volunteer Company of Artillary, Regiment 10	11 May 1808	p. 444
Noah Freeman, Captain, District 160	12 May 1808	p. 444
James Ryant, Lieutenant, District 160	12 May 1808	p. 445
William Lucas, Captain, District 36	12 May 1808	p. 445
Simon Sheppard, Lieutenant, District 36	12 May 1808	p. 446
Lodowick Boykin, Ensign, District 36	12 May 1808	p. 446
Hardy Everett, Captain, District 259	12 May 1808	p. 447
Isaac Waters, Lieutenant, District 35	12 May 1808	p. 447
Baxter Smith, Ensign, District 35	12 May 1808	p. 448
Cater B. Harrison, Captain	13 May 1808	p. 448
John Thompson, Lieutenant	13 May 1808	p. 449
William Spraddling, Ensign	13 May 1808	p. 449
Hillery Pratt, Captain	13 May 1808	p. 450
Richard Perkins, Lieutenant	13 May 1808	p. 450
Matthew Watkins, Ensign	13 May 1808	p. 451
David White, Captain	13 May 1808	p. 451
Nathan Fish, Lieutenant	13 May 1808	p. 452
Jacob White, Ensign	13 May 1808	p. 452
Harrison Young, Captain	13 May 1808	p. 453
George Morgan, Lieutenant	13 May 1808	p. 453
William Hearn, Ensign	13 May 1808	p. 454
William C. Patrick, Captain	13 May 1808	p. 454
Levy Martin, Lieutenant	13 May 1808	p. 455
Elijah Martin, Ensign	13 May 1808	p. 455
Isaac Hill, Captain	13 May 1808	p. 456
Abner Durham, Lieutenant	13 Mar 1808	p. 456

Georgia Military Commissions, 1798–1818

Name, Rank, Unit	*Date*	*Page*
Andrew Moore, Ensign	13 May 1808	p. 457
Gedion Harris, Lieutenant, District 156	13 May 1808	p. 457
Littleberry Bagwell, Ensign, District 156	14 May 1808	p. 458
John Thompkins, Captain, District 32	14 May 1808	p. 458
Thomas H. Miller, Captain, District 30	14 May 1808	p. 459
William F. Kelly, Lieutenant, District 30	14 May 1808	p. 459
Garrett Demott, Ensign, District 30	14 May 1808	p. 460
William Cone Jr., Captain	14 May 1808	p. 460
Berry Elsey, Ensign	14 May 1808	p. 461
Isaac Lang, Lieutenant, District 31	14 May 1808	p. 461
Thomas Tucker, Lieutenant, District 33	14 May 1808	p. 462
James Brooks, Ensign, District 33	14 May 1808	p. 462
Jacob Gunn, Captain	14 May 1808	p. 463
Richard Hobkins, Lieutenant	14 May 1808	p. 463
John Jamison, Ensign	14 May 1808	p. 463
James Reddick, Lieutenant	14 May 1808	p. 463
Robert Martin, Ensign	14 May 1808	p. 464
William Watson, Captain	14 May 1808	p. 464
Stephen Rose, Lieutenant	14 May 1808	p. 466
Thaddeus Holt, Lieutenant Colonel Commandant	17 May 1808	p. 466
Harrison Cabaness, Captain	17 May 1808	p. 467
John Jones, Lieutenant	17 May 1808	p. 467
Hardy Mullins, Ensign	17 May 1808	p. 468
Richard Radcliff, Captain	17 May 1808	p. 468
Abram Davis, Lieutenant	17 May 1808	p. 469
James M. Mobley, Ensign	17 May 1808	p. 469
Stafford Williams, Captain	17 May 1808	p. 470
Stephen Ventress, Lieutenant	17 May 1808	p. 470
David Callaway, Ensign	17 May 1808	p. 471
Peyton Bibb, Captain, District 195	17 May 1808	p. 471
James Clarke, Lieutenant, District 195	17 May 1808	p. 472
Barton Rucker, Ensign, District 195	17 May 1808	p. 472
Charles Carter, Captain, District 197	17 May 1808	p. 473
Benjamin G. Higginbothom, Lieutenant, District 197	17 May 1808	p. 473
Michael Smally, Captain, District 127	17 May 1808	p. 474
Archibald Willingham, Lieutenant, District 127	17 May 1808	p. 474

Name, Rank, Unit	*Date*	*Page*
John Briscoe, Ensign, District 127	17 May 1808	p. 475
Thomas Bull, Lieutenant, District 132	17 May 1808	p. 475
John Binion, Ensign, District 132	17 May 1808	p. 476
James Harden, Captain	17 May 1808	p. 476
Jesse Wade, Ensign	17 May 1808	p. 477
Littleton Wyche, Captain, District 40	17 May 1808	p. 477
Grove Shap, Lieutenant, District 40	17 May 1808	p. 478
Arthur Lott Jr., Ensign, District 40	17 May 1808	p. 478
William Ector, Captain, District 237	18 May 1808	p. 479
James Caruthers, Ensign, District 235	18 May 1808	p. 479
John Nix, Lieutenant, District 231	18 May 1808	p. 480
John McMurphy, Ensign, District 231	18 May 1808	p. 480
Thomas Baber, Lieutenant, District 238	18 May 1808	p. 481
Obediah Tally, Ensign, District 238	18 May 1808	p. 481
Thomas B. Landrum, Ensign, District 229	18 May 1808	p. 482
Bradley Harrelson, Captain	21 May 1808	p. 482
Thomas Yarborough, Lieutenant	21 May 1808	p. 483
Matthew Philips, Ensign	21 May 1808	p. 483
William Williamson, Captain	21 May 1808	p. 484
Thomas Bonner, Lieutenant	21 May 1808	p. 484
Thomas Payne, Ensign	21 May 1808	p. 485
Zachariah Butler, Captain	21 May 1808	p. 485
Leroy McCoy, Lieutenant	21 May 1808	p. 486
Baker Mann, Ensign	21 May 1808	p. 486
William Mullins, Captain	21 May 1808	p. 487
James White, Lieutenant	21 May 1808	p. 487
Josiah Harper, Ensign	12 May 1808	p. 488
Thomas Hogg, Captain	21 May 1808	p. 488
Londy Walker, Lieutenant	21 May 1808	p. 489
Walter Mabrey, Ensign	21 May 1808	p. 489
William Wood, Captain	21 May 1808	p. 490
Alexander Heard, Lieutenant	21 May 1808	p. 490
John Pyle, Ensign	21 May 1808	p. 491
John Fort, Major	21 May 1808	p. 491
John C. Harrell, Captain	21 May 1808	p. 492
Samuel Allman, Lieutenant	21 May 1808	p. 492

Name, Rank, Unit	Date	Page
Jesse Corker, Lieutenant	21 May 1808	p. 493
John F. Lovett, Captain, Troop of Horse, Regiment 5	21 May 1808	p. 493
Roger McKinne, First Lieutenant, Troop of Horse, Regiment 5	21 May 1808	p. 494
Richard Miller, Second Lieutenant, Troop of Horse, Regiment 5	21 May 1808	p. 494
William Smith, Cornet, Troop of Horse, Regiment 5	21 May 1808	p. 495
Julius Simms, Captain, District 212	21 May 1808	p. 495
Abraham Adams, Lieutenant, District 212	21 May 1808	p. 496
Thomas Smith, Ensign, District 212	21 May 1808	p. 496
Samuel Burnett, Captain, Troop of Horse	21 May 1808	p. 497
James Moore, First Lieutenant, Troop of Horse	21 May 1808	p. 497
Samuel Piles, Second Lieutenant, Troop of Horse	21 May 1808	p. 498
Jacob Moore, Cornet, Troop of Horse	21 May 1808	p. 498
Robert Leach, Lieutenant, District 27	21 May 1808	p. 499
William Moore, Ensign, District 26	21 May 1808	p. 499
Rizen Swilly, Lieutenant, District 17	21 May 1808	p. 500
Philemon Terrell, Ensign, District 17	21 May 1808	p. 500
John Maxwell, Ensign, District 16	21 May 1808	p. 501
John S. Quarterman, Lieutenant, District 15	21 May 1808	p. 501
Benjamin B. Winn, Ensign, District 15	21 May 1808	p. 502
John W. Butler, Captain, Troop of Horse, Regiment 18	21 May 1808	p. 502
Randolph Bates, First Lieutenant, Troop of Horse, Regiment 18	21 May 1808	p. 503
William Patterson, Captain, Troop of Horse	21 May 1808	p. 503
Sterling Grimes, Captain, Volunteer Infantry Company (styled the Georgia Foresters), Battalion 60	21 May 1808	p. 504
Robert J. Houston, Lieutenant, Volunteer Company of Infantry (styled the Georgia Foresters), Battalion 60	21 May 1808	p. 504
Thomas Telfair, Ensign, Volunteer Company of Infantry (styled the Georgia Foresters), Battalion 60	21 May 1808	p. 505
Green McAfee, Captain	23 May 1808	p. 505
Thomas Coleman, Lieutenant	23 May 1808	p. 506
Meredith Catchen, Ensign	23 May 1808	p. 506
Robert Taylor, Captain	23 May 1808	p. 507
Ludwell Watts, Lieutenant	23 May 1808	p. 507
John Davis, Ensign	23 May 1808	p. 508
Dudley Peebles, Captain	23 May 1808	p. 508

Name, Rank, Unit	*Date*	*Page*
Samuel Rhodes, Lieutenant	23 May 1808	p. 509
James Fletcher, Ensign	23 May 1808	p. 509
Robert Reynolds, Captain, District 182	19 May 1808	p. 510
John A. Parks, Lieutenant, District 182	19 May 1808	p. 510
Daniel Gray, Ensign, District 182	19 May 1808	p. 511
Jacob Ammory, Lieutenant, District 85	19 May 1808	p. 511
John Welch, Captain, District 77	19 May 1808	p. 512
Thomas Newber, Captain, District 45	20 May 1808	p. 512
John Malyard, Captain, District 44	20 May 1808	p. 513
James Harrell, Lieutenant, District 44	20 May 1808	p. 513
Benjamin Wood, Ensign, District 44	20 May 1808	p. 514
John Everett, Lieutenant, District 47	20 May 1808	p. 514
Preston Wise, Ensign, District 47	20 May 1808	p. 515
James Williams, Captain, District 46	20 May 1808	p. 515
Frederick Williams, Ensign, District 46	20 May 1808	p. 516
Charles Sorrells, Lieutenant Colonel Commandant, Regiment 21	20 May 1808	p. 516
Thomas Oliver, Major, Battalion 42	20 May 1808	p. 517
Samuel Groves, Major, Battalion 43	20 May 1808	p. 517
James Ware, Captain, District 204	20 May 1808	p. 518
James Veal, Lieutenant, District 204	20 May 1808	p. 518
William Albright, Ensign, District 204	20 May 1808	p. 519
John W. Thompson, Captain, District 194	20 May 1808	p. 519
Thompson Rayland, Lieutenant, District 194	20 May 1808	p. 520
John Evans, Ensign, District 194	20 May 1808	p. 520
Neal McMullen, Captain, District 200	20 May 1808	p. 521
Martin Deadwilder, Lieutenant, District 202	20 May 1808	p. 521
Hudson Dudley, Lieutenant, District 201	20 May 1808	p. 522
Robert Ryce, Ensign, District 201	20 May 1808	p. 522
William O. Robbins, Ensign, District 203	20 May 1808	p. 523
John Wisinbaker, Captain, District 9	20 May 1808	p. 523
Philip Ulmer, Ensign, District 9	20 May 1808	p. 524
Abel G. Loper, Captain, District 10	20 May 1808	p. 524
David Hines, Lieutenant, District 10	20 May 1808	p. 525
Charles M. Golesbey, Ensign, District 10	20 May 1808	p. 525
Isareal Flerl, Captain, District 11	20 May 1808	p. 526
John Beatenback, Ensign, District 11	20 May 1808	p. 526

Georgia Military Commissions, 1798–1818

Name, Rank, Unit	Date	Page
Lewis Jenkins, Captain, District 145	20 May 1808	p. 527
Earnest C. Willick, Ensign, District 143	20 May 1808	p. 527
Dennis McClendon, Lieutenant Colonel Commandant, Regiment 19	25 May 1808	p. 528
Thomas Wootten, Major, Battalion 39	25 May 1808	p. 528
John Clements, Lieutenant, District 178	25 May 1808	p. 529
Francis Douglass, Ensign, District 178	25 May 1808	p. 529
Lewis Taliaffero, Captain, District 181	20 May 1808	p. 530
Zachariah Northam, Lieutenant, District 181	25 May 1808	p. 530
Joel H. Mallory, Ensign, District 180	25 May 1808	p. 531
William Smith, Captain, District 180	25 May 1808	p. 531
Joseph Freeman, Lieutenant, District 180	25 May 1808	p. 532
Anderson Riddle, Captain, District 179	25 May 1808	p. 532
Barnard Heard, Lieutenant, District 179	25 May 1808	p. 533
James Stallings, Ensign, District 179	25 May 1808	p. 533
Allen Thompson, Captain	25 May 1808	p. 534
William Allen, Lieutenant	26 May 1808	p. 534
John Davis, Ensign	26 May 1808	p. 535
Nathaniel Jones, Lieutenant, District 99	26 May 1808	p. 535
Allen Jones, Ensign, District 99	26 May 1808	p. 536
John Weeks, Captain	28 May 1808	p. 536
Leander Thrash, Lieutenant	28 May 1808	p. 537
George Stovall, Ensign	28 May 1808	p. 537
Henning Daniel, Lieutenant, District 139	31 May 1808	p. 538
Benjamin Meadows, Ensign, District 139	31 May 1808	p. 538
Joseph White, Captain	4 Jun 1808	p. 539
Timothy Duck, Lieutenant	4 Jun 1808	p. 539
Moses Paul, Ensign	4 Jun 1808	p. 540
Pascal Harrison, Captain	4 Jun 1808	p. 540
John P. Ryan, Lieutenant	4 Jun 1808	p. 550
Simeon Fuller, Ensign	4 Jun 1808	p. 550
Zachariah Philips, Captain	4 Jun 1808	p. 552
William Gilmore, Lieutenant	4 Jun 1808	p. 552
John McLean, Ensign	4 Jun 1808	p. 553
William Patterson, Captain, District 192	6 Jun 1808	p. 553
James Hunt, Lieutenant, District 192	6 Jun 1808	p. 554
John Patterson, Ensign, District 192	6 Jun 1808	p. 554

Name, Rank, Unit	Date	Page
John E. Dawson, Major, Battalion 22	6 Jun 1808	p. 555
William Lewis, First Lieutenant, Troop of Horse, Regiment 14	8 Jun 1808	p. 555
Vines Harwell, Second Lieutenant, Troop of Horse, Regiment 14	8 Jun 1808	p. 556
Ambrose Jones, Cornet, Troop of Horse, Regiment 14	8 Jun 1808	p. 556
David Evans, Lieutenant	10 Jun 1808	p. 557
Marcus Hemphill, Ensign	10 Jun 1808	p. 557
Benjamin Howard, Captain	10 Jun 1808	p. 558
Joseph Carter, Lieutenant Colonel Commandant	13 Jun 1808	p. 558
Daniel Pearce, Lieutenant	14 Jun 1808	p. 559
Thomas Durham, Ensign	14 Jun 1808	p. 559
Edmund Abercrombe, Lieutenant Colonel Commandant	14 Jun 1808	p. 560
Pascal Harrison, Lieutenant Colonel Commandant	15 Jun 1808	p. 560
Philip Cook, Captain, Volunteer Troop of Horse	18 Jun 1808	p. 561
Gilly Freeney, First Lieutenant, Volunteer Troop of Horse	18 Jun 1808	p. 561
Parham Buckner, Second Lieutenant, Troop of Horse	18 Jun 1808	p. 562
Thomas A. Hill, Cornet, Volunteer Troop of Horse	18 Jun 1808	p. 562
Jett Thomas, Captain, Volunteer Company of Artillery	18 Jun 1808	p. 563
Eleazer Early, First Lieutenant, Volunteer Company of Artillery	18 Jun 1808	p. 563
Thomas Rutherford, Second Lieutenant, Volunteer Company of Artillery	18 Jun 1808	p. 564
David Tool, Captain, District 116	18 May 1808	p. 564
Josiah Matthews, Lieutenant, District 116	18 Jun 1808	p. 565
William Chain, Ensign, District 116	18 Jun 1808	p. 565
Levi Horton, Ensign, District 88	20 Jun 1808	p. 566
William Jones, Lieutenant Colonel Commandant	22 Jun 1808	p. 566
William F. Luckie, Captain	24 Jun 1808	p. 567
Nelson Colly, Lieutenant	24 Jun 1808	p. 567
John Bentley, Ensign	24 Jun 1808	p. 568
William Varner, Captain	27 Jun 1808	p. 568
Aaron Smith, Lieutenant	24 Jun 1808	p. 569
William Colquet, Ensign	24 Jun 1808	p. 569
Jabez Roberts, Major	5 Jul 1808	p. 570
James S. Walker, Captain, District 120	9 Jul 1808	p. 570
Richard Wild, Lieutenant, District 120	9 Jul 1808	p. 571

Georgia Military Commissions, 1798–1818

Name, Rank, Unit	Date	Page
Uriah G. Mitchell, Major, Battalion 20	12 Jul 1808	p. 571
James McCrone, Captain, District 60	14 Jul 1808	p. 572
John Roberts, Lieutenant, District 60	14 Jul 1808	p. 572
Andrew McLean, Major, Battalion 2	14 Jul 1808	p. 573
George Pollon, Captain, District 6	14 Jul 1808	p. 573
Charles Boyd, Lieutenant, District 6	14 Jul 1808	p. 574
John Strain, Ensign, District 6	14 Jul 1808	p. 574
William Howe, Ensign, District 2	14 Jul 1808	p. 575
Harrison Young, Major	14 Jul 1808	p. 575
David White, Major	15 Jul 1808	p. 576
Lee Blacksell, Captain	18 Jul 1808	p. 576
George D. Siveet, Lieutenant	18 Jul 1808	p. 577
John Coleman, Ensign	18 Jul 1808	p. 577
Joseph Stillwell, Lieutenant, District 20	18 Jul 1808	p. 578
Walter Davis, Ensign, District 19	18 Jul 1808	p. 578
William Carathers, Captain, District 71	21 Jul 1808	p. 579
Littleberry Marsh, Lieutenant, District 71	21 Jul 1808	p. 579
George Caruthers, Ensign, District 71	21 Jul 1808	p. 580
Benajah King, Captain	21 Jul 1808	p. 580
Lewelling Williams, Captain, Volunteer Troop of Dragoons	23 Jul 1808	p. 581
Leonard M. Peek, First Lieutenant, Volunteer Troop of Dragoons	23 Jul 1808	p. 581
Nathan Powell, Second Lieutenant, Volunteer Troop of Dragoons	23 Jul 1808	p. 582
Abner McGauhey, Cornet, Volunteer Troop of Dragoons	23 Jul 1808	p. 582
Peter H. Collins, Captain, District 130	23 Jul 1808	p. 583
William Dunlap, Captain, District 190	25 Jul 1808	p. 583
Daniel McCook, Captain	30 Jul 1808	p. 584
John Rustin, Lieutenant	30 Jul 1808	p. 584
David Majors, Ensign	30 Jul 1808	p. 585
Stephen Melton, Captain	30 Jul 1808	p. 585
Lawrence Magee, Lieutenant	30 Jul 1808	p. 586
Owen Heaton, Ensign	30 Jul 1808	p. 586
William Ford, Captain	30 Jul 1808	p. 587
John Mathews, Lieutenant	30 Jul 1808	p. 587
Samuel Durham, Ensign	30 Jul 1808	p. 588

Name, Rank, Unit	*Date*	*Page*
Willis McClendon, Captain	30 Jul 1808	p. 588
John Mathews, Lieutenant	30 Jul 1808	p. 589
James Duffey, Lieutenant	30 Jul 1808	p. 589
Hader Hawthorn, Captain	1 Aug 1808	p. 590
William Ray, Lieutenant	1 Aug 1808	p. 590
Evan Thomas, Ensign	1 Aug 1808	p. 591
James Johnson, Captain	1 Aug 1808	p. 591
Samuel Carter, Lieutenant	1 Aug 1808	p. 592
Sterling Anderson, Ensign	1 Aug 1808	p. 592
Benjamin Keaton, Lieutenant	1 Aug 1808	p. 593
Jesse Gilbert, Ensign	1 Aug 1808	p. 593
Nathan Fish, Captain	6 Aug 1808	p. 594
Jacob White, Lieutenant	26 Aug 1808	p. 594
Wylie Howell, Ensign	6 Aug 1808	p. 595
James Grace, Captain	6 Aug 1808	p. 595
James Sanders, Captain	9 Aug 1808	p. 596
Avery Wheeler, Lieutenant	11 Aug 1808	p. 596
Morin Moore, Lieutenant, District 256	15 Aug 1808	p. 597
John Moore, Captain	16 Aug 1808	p. 597
William Joiner, Captain	18 Aug 1808	p. 598
Joseph Nelson, Lieutenant	18 Aug 1808	p. 598
Absalom Barrow, Ensign	18 Aug 1808	p. 599
John Mitchell, Major	24 Aug 1808	p. 599
William Page, Major, Battalion 7	24 Aug 1808	p. 600
Adam Jones, Captain	26 Aug 1808	p. 600
Thomas Albritton, Lieutenant	26 Aug 1808	p. 601
Jethro Weaver, Ensign	26 Aug 1808	p. 601
Henry Sheperd, Captain	26 Aug 1808	p. 602
Jonah Stringer, Lieutenant	26 Aug 1808	p. 602
Josiah Stringer, Ensign	26 Aug 1808	p. 603
John A. Patterson, Captain, District 175	31 Aug 1808	p. 603
Francis Smith, Major	3 Sep 1808	p. 604
Robert Walker, Captain	8 Sep 1808	p. 604
Robert Jackson, Lieutenant Colonel Commandant	8 Sep 1808	p. 605
Thomas Fulton, Major, Battalion 18	12 Sep 1808	p. 605
David Clarke, Ensign, District 82	12 Sep 1808	p. 606

Georgia Military Commissions, 1798–1818

Name, Rank, Unit	Date	Page
Lovell B. Smith, Captain, District 112	13 Sep 1808	p. 606
Abner Kelly, Lieutenant, District 112	13 Sep 1808	p. 607
Thomas Bonner, Lieutenant, District 104	13 Sep 1808	p. 607
William Davis, Captain, District 147	15 Sep 1808	p. 608
William Williams, Lieutenant, District 147	15 Sep 1808	p. 608
John Webb, Ensign, District 147	15 Sep 1808	p. 609
Hollinger Brown, Captain	17 Sep 1808	p. 609
Jeremiah Gardner, Lieutenant	17 Sep 1808	p. 610
Lewis Talbert, Ensign	17 Sep 1808	p. 610
Greene Wynn, Major	17 Sep 1808	p. 611
John Browning, Captain, District 148	20 Sep 1808	p. 611
Exum Boon, Lieutenant, District 148	20 Sep 1808	p. 612
William Jackson, Ensign, District 148	20 Sep 1808	p. 612
William Bugg, Lieutenant, District 146	20 Sep 1808	p. 613
John J. Cox, Ensign, District 146	20 Sep 1808	p. 613
Henry Devenport, Lieutenant, District 144	20 Sep 1808	p. 614
Joseph Tremble, Ensign, District 149	20 Sep 1808	p. 614
William Hall, Captain	21 Sep 1808	p. 615
Jesse Lively, Lieutenant	21 Sep 1808	p. 615
John Lungeno, Ensign	21 Sep 1808	p. 616
Henry Fulgham, Captain	21 Sep 1808	p. 616
Spier Mills, Lieutenant	21 Sep 1808	p. 617
William Taylor, Ensign	21 Sep 1808	p. 617
Benjamin Sessions, Lieutenant, Volunteer Troop of Horse, Regiment 13	5 Oct 1808	p. 618
John Williams, Second Lieutenant, Volunteer Troop of Horse, Regiment 13	5 Oct 1808	p. 618
Isaac Dennard, Cornet, Volunteer Troop of Horse, Regiment 13	5 Oct 1808	p. 619
William D. Jarrett, Captain	8 Oct 1808	p. 619
Patterson Jarrett, Lieutenant	8 Oct 1808	p. 620
William A. Cowan, Ensign	8 Oct 1808	p. 620
Hugh Hall, Captain, Volunteer Company of Riflemen	11 Oct 1808	p. 621
Allen Hodges, Lieutenant, Volunteer Company of Riflemen	11 Oct 1808	p. 621
Huston Rose, Ensign, Volunteer Company of Riflemen	11 Oct 1808	p. 622
Robert McTyre, Captain, District 122	12 Oct 1808	p. 622

Name, Rank, Unit	Date	Page
George W. Stephens, Ensign	12 Oct 1808	p. 623
Isaac Mathews, Ensign, District 143	13 Oct 1808	p. 623
William Russau, Lieutenant, District 135	13 Oct 1808	p. 624
Randolp Geiral, Ensign, District 135	13 Oct 1808	p. 624
R. L. Tait, First Lieutenant, Volunteer Troop of Horse, Regiment 21	17 Oct 1808	p. 625
Robert Hancock, Cornet, Volunteer Troop of Horse, Regiment 21	17 Oct 1808	p. 625
Ludwell Watts, Captain	21 Oct 1808	p. 626
William Ford, Lieutenant, Volunteer Company of Riflemen, Battalion 44	21 Oct 1808	p. 626
John S. Farrar, Ensign, Volunteer Company of Riflemen, Battalion 44	21 Oct 1808	p. 627
John G. Willingham, Captain, Volunteer Company of Infantry, Battalion 28	22 Oct 1808	p. 627
William Roberts, Lieutenant, Volunteer Company of Infantry, Battalion 28	22 Sep 1808	p. 628
John C. Shipp, Ensign, Volunteer Company of Infantry, Battalion 28	22 Oct 1808	p. 628
George Willingham, Ensign, District 131	22 Oct 1808	p. 629
Nathaniel Mercer, Captain	24 Oct 1808	p. 629
Joseph W. Denson, Lieutenant	24 Oct 1808	p. 630
Henry Stewart, Ensign	24 Oct 1808	p. 630
Ambrose Wright, Captain, Volunteer Company of Artillery, Regiment 9	25 Oct 1808	p. 631
John P. Harvey, First Lieutenant, Volunteer Company of Artillery, Regiment 9	25 Oct 1808	p. 631
Abraham McAfee, Major	28 Oct 1808	p. 632
Joshua Hargerly, Captain	28 Oct 1808	p. 632
Alexander Cotton, Lieutenant	28 Oct 1808	p. 633
John Bean, Ensign	28 Oct 1808	p. 633
George W. Rogers, Lieutenant	1 Nov 1808	p. 634
Reuben Aldridge, Ensign	1 Nov 1808	p. 634
Thomas A. Hill, Captain	1 Nov 1808	p. 635
Sheppard Williams, Lieutenant Colonel Commandant	7 Nov 1808	p. 635
John Everett, Major	7 Nov 1808	p. 636
Allen Wamble, Lieutenant, District 151	8 Nov 1808	p. 636

Name, Rank, Unit	Date	Page
Thaddeus Beall, Lieutenant Colonel Commandant, Regiment 11	10 Nov 1808	p. 637
William Brux, First Lieutenant, Volunteer Company of Artillery, Regiment 10	10 Nov 1808	p. 637
Andrew Harrison, Second Lieutenant, Volunteer Company of Artillery, Regiment 10	10 Nov 1808	p. 638
William Thompson, Captain, District 205	11 Nov 1808	p. 638
David Denny, Lieutenant, District 205	11 Nov 1808	p. 639
Lewis Floyd, Ensign, District 205	11 Nov 1808	p. 639
James Allison, Captain, Volunteer Company of Riflemen	12 Nov 1808	p. 640
James Knowles, Lieutenant, Volunteer Company of Riflemen	12 Nov 1808	p. 640
Thomas Merritt, Ensign, Volunteer Company of Riflemen	12 Nov 1808	p. 641
Silvanius Gibson, Captain, District 166	15 Nov 1808	p. 641
Joshua Callaway, Lieutenant, District 166	15 Nov 1808	p. 642
Kinchen Curl, Captain, District 75	16 Nov 1808	p. 642
Matthew Lowery, Lieutenant, District 75	16 Nov 1808	p. 643
Simeon Spain, Ensign, District 75	16 Nov 1808	p. 643
Hinchey Warren, Captain, District 75	16 Nov 1808	p. 644
James B. White, Lieutenant, District 75	16 Nov 1808	p. 644
James Willy, Ensign, District 75	16 Nov 1808	p. 645
George Bass, Ensign, District 73	16 Nov 1808	p. 645
Larkin Clark, Captain	16 Nov 1808	p. 646
Jeremiah Willingham, Lieutenant	16 Nov 1808	p. 646
William Penix, Ensign	16 Nov 1808	p. 647
Solomon Thompson, Major, Battalion 34	16 Nov 1808	p. 647
Mark Harden, Lieutenant, District 155	16 Nov 1808	p. 648
Daniel Furguson, Second Lieutenant, Volunteer Company of Artillery, Regiment 9	19 Nov 1808	p. 648
Joseph Paxton, Captain, Volunteer Company of Riflemen, Battalion 52	19 Nov 1808	p. 649
Giles Blalock, Lieutenant, Volunteer Company of Riflemen, Battalion 52	19 Nov 1808	p. 649
John Hobson, Captain, Volunteer Company of Riflemen, Battalion 51	19 Nov 1808	p. 650
Thomas Morris, Lieutenant, Volunteer Company of Riflemen, Battalion 51	19 Nov 1808	p. 650
John Hendricks, Major, Battalion 37	22 Nov 1808	p. 651

Name, Rank, Unit	Date	Page
Solomon Perkins, Captain, District 170	22 Nov 1808	p. 651
David A. Whatley, Lieutenant, District 170	22 Nov 1808	p. 652
Uriel Furmer, Ensign, District 170	22 Nov 1808	p. 652
James Ingram, Captain, District 78	23 Nov 1808	p. 653
Daniel Pearce, Captain	25 Nov 1808	p. 653
Thomas Durham, Lieutenant	25 Nov 1808	p. 654
John Eady, Ensign	25 Nov 1808	p. 654
Isaac Dyche, Captain, District 247	29 Nov 1808	p. 655
Thomas Dooly, Lieutenant, District 274	30 Nov 1808	p. 655
George Eberhart, Captain, District 203	30 Nov 1808	p. 656
Daniel Candlar, Captain, Volunteer Rifle Company, Battalion 67	2 Dec 1808	p. 656
John Shaw, Lieutenant, Volunteer Rifle Company, Battalion 67	2 Dec 1808	p. 657
Aron Robinson, Ensign, Volunteer Rifle Company, Battalion 67	2 Dec 1808	p. 657
Abner Durham, Captain	6 Dec 1808	p. 658
Benjamin Young, Lieutenant	6 Dec 1808	p. 658
Benjamin Ward, Ensign	6 Dec 1808	p. 659
Thomas Jackson, Captain, District 151	7 Dec 1808	p. 659
Jesse Mathews, Ensign	7 Dec 1808	p. 660
James Allison, Captain, Volunteer Company of Riflemen, Battalion 66	9 Dec 1808	p. 660
James Knowles, Lieutenant, Volunteer Company of Riflemen, Battalion 66	9 Dec 1808	p. 661
Thomas Merritt, Ensign, Volunteer Company of Riflemen, Battalion 66	9 Dec 1808	p. 661
Samuel H. Everett, Major, Battalion 58	10 Dec 1808	p. 662
John Bush, Captain, District 264	10 Dec 1808	p. 662
Joseph Hamilton, Lieutenant, District 264	10 Dec 1808	p. 663
James Jones, Ensign, District 264	10 Dec 1808	p. 663
Gabriel Jones, Captain, District 208	10 Dec 1808	p. 664
John Saunders, Lieutenant, District 208	10 Dec 1808	p. 664
Thomas Hollingsworth, Captain, District 211	10 Dec 1808	p. 665
Elijah Martin, Lieutenant, District 211	10 Dec 1808	p. 665
Thomas Cox, Captain, District 209	10 Dec 1808	p. 666
William Walraven, Lieutenant, District 209	10 Dec 1808	p. 666
Isaac Walraven, Ensign, District 209	10 Dec 1808	p. 667

Georgia Military Commissions, 1798–1818

Name, Rank, Unit	Date	Page
John Toneyhill, Ensign, District 267	10 Dec 1808	p. 667
Charles Sesseons, Lieutenant, District 265	10 Dec 1808	p. 668
Tryon Patterson, Ensign, District 215	10 Dec 1808	p. 668
James Millican, Ensign, District 262	10 Dec 1808	p. 669
Nathaniel Russell, Ensign, District 266	10 Dec 1808	p. 669
John Higginbothom, Captain, District 315	12 Dec 1808	p. 670
Nathan Pullicrew, Lieutenant, District 315	12 Dec 1808	p. 670
Nelson Bond, Ensign, District 315	12 Dec 1808	p. 671
Peter P. Butler, Ensign, District 191	12 Dec 1808	p. 671
Thompson Rayland, Captain, District 194	12 Dec 1808	p. 672
James W. Muse, Lieutenant, District 194	12 Dec 1808	p. 672
E. Evans, Ensign, District 194	12 Dec 1808	p. 673
William H. Underwood, Captain, District 199	12 Dec 1808	p. 673
Harrison Warren, Lieutenant, District 199	12 Dec 1808	p. 674
William Stone, Ensign, District 199	12 Dec 1808	p. 674
William Jones, Lieutenant, District 190	12 Dec 1808	p. 675
Solomon Towns, Ensign, District 190	12 Dec 1808	p. 675
Joshua Clark, Captain, District 193	12 Dec 1808	p. 676
Elijah Buckler, Ensign, District 193	12 Dec 1808	p. 676
Aaron Wood, Captain, District 246	13 Dec 1808	p. 677
Thompson Coker, Lieutenant, District 246	13 Dec 1808	p. 677
Richard Jones, Ensign, District 246	13 Dec 1808	p. 678
James Collins, Lieutenant, District 252	13 Dec 1808	p. 678
Samuel Willingham, Lieutenant, District 242	13 Dec 1808	p. 679
James Boggs, Ensign, District 242	13 Dec 1808	p. 679
James McCord, Lieutenant, District 254	13 Dec 1808	p. 680
Micajah Dixon, Captain, District 244	13 Dec 1808	p. 680
John Johnson, Captain, District 243	13 Dec 1808	p. 681
Robert Boren, Ensign, District 243	13 Dec 1808	p. 681
Reuben Nail, Captain, District 42	14 Dec 1808	p. 682
Benjamin Hollingsworth, Major, Battalion 58	15 Dec 1808	p. 682
Charles Burkes, Ensign, District 211	15 Dec 1808	p. 683
Leonard Rice, Ensign, District 264	15 Dec 1808	p. 683
Robert Quarterman, Lieutenant, District 14	16 Dec 1808	p. 684
Paul H. Wilkins, Lieutenant, District 16	16 Dec 1808	p. 684
Henry Rhodes, Lieutenant, District 113	16 Dec 1808	p. 685

Name, Rank, Unit	*Date*	*Page*
Davis Joblitt, Ensign, District 113	16 Dec 1808	p. 685
Benjamin Ansley, Captain, Volunteer Company of Infantry (styled the Chatham Rangers), Battalion 1	16 Dec 1808	p. 686
Charles McKenna, Lieutenant, Volunteer Company of Infantry (styled the Chatham Rangers), Battalion 1	16 Dec 1808	p. 686
John Kackler, Ensign, Volunteer Company of Infantry (styled the Chatham Rangers), Battalion 1	16 Dec 1808	p. 687
Richard Walker, Captain	19 Dec 1808	p. 687
Joseph Stafford, Lieutenant	19 Dec 1808	p. 688
Sandler Roberts, Ensign	19 Dec 1808	p. 688
Elias Fort, Lieutenant	19 Dec 1808	p. 689
Samuel Eagle, Ensign	19 Dec 1808	p. 689
William P. Burch, Captain, District 106	19 Dec 1808	p. 690
Littleberry Harris, Lieutenant, District 106	19 Dec 1808	p. 690
Mills Minton, Ensign, District 106	19 Dec 1808	p. 691
Jonathan Milner, Lieutenant, Volunteer Company of Infantry, Battalion 44	19 Dec 1808	p. 691
Benjamin Collier, Ensign, Volunteer Company of Infantry, Battalion 44	19 Dec 1808	p. 692
Samuel Hall, Captain, District 154	19 Dec 1808	p. 692
Samuel Chambless, Lieutenant, District 154	19 Dec 1808	p. 693
Cullen Dorman, Ensign, District 154	19 Dec 1808	p. 693
Jacob Robinson, Division 1, Cavalry	19 Dec 1808	p. 694
Hugh Blair, Division 2, Cavalry	19 Dec 1808	p. 694
Bedney Franklin, Division 3, Cavalry	19 Dec 1808	p. 695
Felix Gilbert, Division 4, Cavalry	19 Dec 1808	p. 695
William Tiddle, Ensign, District 155	20 Dec 1808	p. 696a
Daniel Browning, Ensign, District 42	20 Dec 1808	p. 696a
Jacob Riley, Lieutenant, District 141	6 Jan 1809	p. 696b
Zelah Pullen, Ensign, District 141	6 Jan 1809	p. 696b
David Bush, Lieutenant Colonel Commandant, Regiment 7	31 Dec 1808	p. 697a
Denwoodie R. Harrison, Captain, District 274	2 Jan 1809	p. 697a
James B. White, Major, Battalion 17	14 Jan 1809	p. 697b
Jonathan Palmer, Captain, District 121	14 Jan 1809	p. 697b
Merrett Rowland, Lieutenant, District 121	14 Jan 1809	p. 698
John R. Grigory, Captain, Volunteer Troop of Dragoons, Regiment 31	16 Jan 1809	p. 698

Georgia Military Commissions, 1798–1818

Name, Rank, Unit	Date	Page
Stephen Eiland, First Lieutenant, Volunteer Troop of Dragoons, Regiment 31	16 Jan 1809	p. 699
Solomon Beavey, Second Lieutenant, Volunteer Troop of Dragoons, Regiment 31	16 Jan 1809	p. 699
Daniel Shaw, Cornet, Volunteer Troop of Dragoons, Regiment 31	16 Jan 1809	p. 700
William Jackson, Captain	16 Jan 1809	p. 700
Jonathan Pearson, Ensign	16 Jan 1809	p. 701
William Jones, Second Lieutenant, Volunteer Troop of Horse, Regiment 10	20 Jan 1809	p. 701
Nicholas Pope, Cornet, Volunteer Troop of Horse, Regiment 10	20 Jan 1809	p. 702
John Allen, Lieutenant, District 123	20 Jan 1809	p. 702
John Grice, Ensign, District 123	20 Jan 1809	p. 703
David McKinnie, Captain, District 122	20 Jan 1809	p. 703
Abraham A. Legget, Ensign, District 120	20 Jan 1809	p. 704
Littleberry Bush, Lieutenant, District 124	20 Jan 1809	p. 704
William Strong, Lieutenant, District 221	20 Jan 1809	p. 705
James Prophet, Ensign, District 221	20 Jan 1809	p. 705
James Harden, Major, Battalion 29	24 Jan 1809	p. 706
John B. McKinney, Major	25 Jan 1809	p. 706
Willis Anderson, Major	25 Jan 1809	p. 707
Newday G. Connell, Lieutenant, District 107	25 Jan 1809	p. 707
Henry Brown, Captain	26 Jan 1809	p. 708
Donald McCoy, Lieutenant	28 Jan 1809	p. 708
Simeon Milner, Ensign	28 Jan 1809	p. 709
John Smith, Captain	28 Jan 1809	p. 709
John Gray, Lieutenant	28 Jan 1809	p. 710
John Davidson, Ensign	28 Jan 1809	p. 710
Samuel Smith, Lieutenant, Volunteer Rifle Company, Battalion 69	31 Jan 1809	p. 711
Benjamin Harvey, Ensign, Volunteer Rifle Company, Battalion 69	31 Jan 1809	p. 711
James Patton, Major	2 Feb 1809	p. 712
Drewry Williams, Captain	2 Feb 1809	p. 712
Archibald Gray, Captain, District 141	2 Feb 1809	p. 713
John Brown, Lieutenant, District 310	2 Feb 1809	p. 713
Charles Brown, Ensign, District 310	2 Feb 1809	p. 714

Name, Rank, Unit	Date	Page
Robert Ashurst, Captain	3 Feb 1809	p. 714
William Watter, Lieutenant	3 Feb 1809	p. 715
Thomas Evans, Ensign	3 Feb 1809	p. 715
William Scott, Captain, Volunteer Troop of Dragoons, Regiment 30	8 Feb 1809	p. 716
Jonathan Hagerty, First Lieutenant, Volunteer Troop of Dragoons, Regiment 30	8 Feb 1809	p. 716
Joshua Gracey, Second Lieutenant, Volunteer Troop of Dragoons, Regiment 30	8 Feb 1809	p. 717
Waymon Shopshear, Cornet, Volunteer Troop of Dragoons, Regiment 30	8 Feb 1809	p. 717
Jeremiah Willingham, Captain, District 290	8 Feb 1809	p. 718
Everett Harper, Lieutenant, District 290	8 Feb 1809	p. 718
William Phillips, Ensign, District 290	8 Feb 1809	p. 719
Jubel E. Watts, Captain, District 137	9 Feb 1809	p. 719
Samuel Hammond, Ensign, District 137	9 Feb 1809	p. 720
Walden Lewis, Lieutenant, District 286	10 Feb 1809	p. 720
Joseph Whorton, Captain, District 256	11 Feb 1809	p. 721
John Randolph, First Lieutenant, Volunteer Troop of Dragoons, Regiment 25	11 Feb 1809	p. 721
Mathew G. Parker, Cornet, Volunteer Troop of Dragoons, Regiment 25	11 Feb 1809	p. 722
William Byne, Lieutenant Colonel Commandant, Regiment 8	15 Feb 1809	p. 722
William Jackson, Lieutenant, Volunteer Company of Rangers, Battalion 1	15 Feb 1809	p. 723
John Coats, Ensign, Volunteer Company of Rangers, Battalion 1	15 Feb 1809	p. 723
John W. Mendenhall, Captain, District 273	15 Feb 1809	p. 724
Isaac Abrahams, Captain, District 26	15 Feb 1809	p. 724
James Moren, Ensign, District 26	15 Feb 1809	p. 725
Alexander Hall, Captain, District 163	17 Feb 1809	p. 725
Anderson Mize, Lieutenant, District 163	17 Feb 1809	p. 726
William Holloway, Ensign, District 163	17 Feb 1809	p. 726
Zachariah Middleton, Captain, District 280	17 Feb 1809	p. 727
William Walker, Lieutenant, District 280	17 Feb 1809	p. 727
James Malcom, Ensign, District 280	17 Feb 1809	p. 728
Edmund Welch, Ensign, District 284	17 Feb 1809	p. 728

Georgia Military Commissions, 1798–1818

Name, Rank, Unit	Date	Page
Joshua Everett, Captain, District 45	18 Feb 1809	p. 729
Benjamin Witcher, Lieutenant, District 203	18 Feb 1809	p. 729
Milborn Fulford, Captain, District 85	20 Feb 1809	p. 730
Eldrige Hargrove, Lieutenant, District 79	20 Feb 1809	p. 730
Jeremiah Warner, Ensign, District 79	20 Feb 1809	p. 731
Robert Northeat, Second Lieutenant, Volunteer Troop of Dragoons, Regiment 9	20 Feb 1809	p. 731
Able Hodge, Cornet, Volunteer Troop of Dragoons, Regiment 9	20 Feb 1809	p. 732
Russell Porter, Ensign, District 164	22 Feb 1809	p. 732
John Coats, Captain, District 164	22 Feb 1809	p. 733
Mounce Ruddle, Lieutenant, District 164	22 Feb 1809	p. 733
John Holmes, Lieutenant, District 168	22 Feb 1809	p. 734
William Brooks, Ensign, District 168	22 Feb 1809	p. 734
Eli Moffett, Captain, District 99	23 Feb 1809	p. 735
Alexander Smith, Lieutenant, District 99	23 Feb 1809	p. 735
Fearney Buck, Ensign, District 99	23 Feb 1809	p. 736
William Rogers, Lieutenant, District 136	23 Feb 1809	p. 736
James Hitchcock, Lieutenant Colonel Commandant, Regiment 24	25 Feb 1809	p. 737
John F. Cooke, Captain, District 217	25 Feb 1809	p. 737
David McCormick, Lieutenant Colonel Commandant, Regiment 6	1 Mar 1809	p. 738
James Beatty, Captain, District 50	1 Mar 1809	p. 738
Littleton Hall, Lieutenant, District 50	1 Mar 1809	p. 739
Robert Hart, Ensign, District 50	1 Mar 1809	p. 739
Isaac Hughs, Captain, Volunteer Troop of Dragoons, Regiment 29	2 Mar 1809	p. 740
Dudley Peoples, First Lieutenant, Volunteer Troop of Dragoons, Regiment 29	2 Mar 1809	p. 740
Henry D. Stone, Second Lieutenant, Volunteer Troop of Dragoons, Regiment 29	2 Mar 1809	p. 741
John B. Whatley, Cornet, Volunteer Troop of Dragoons, Regiment 29	2 Mar 1809	p. 741
David Rosser, Ensign, District 307	2 Mar 1809	p. 742
Archibald Butt, Lieutenant, District 156	4 Mar 1809	p. 742
Barnard F. Feckling, Cornet, Volunteer Troop of Dragoons, Regiment 12	4 Mar 1809	p. 743

Name, Rank, Unit	Date	Page
Daniel Stewart, Brigadier General, Cavalry	6 Mar 1809	p. 743
John Pettybone, Major, Battalion 1	8 Mar 1809	p. 744
Henry Carr, Captain, District 299	8 Mar 1809	p. 744
Crawford Downs, Lieutenant, District 299	8 Mar 1809	p. 745
Presley Barton, Captain, District 284	9 Mar 1809	p. 745
Laurence Richardson, Lieutenant, District 133	9 Mar 1809	p. 746
James Oliver, Captain, District 241	9 Mar 1809	p. 746
Gabriel Pickren, Lieutenant, District 222	9 Mar 1809	p. 747
Sterling Price, Ensign, District 222	9 Mar 1809	p. 747
Robert F. Smith, Lieutenant, District 225	9 Mar 1809	p. 748
David Day, Lieutenant, District 261	9 Mar 1809	p. 748
Nicholas Freeman, Lieutenant, District 220	9 Mar 1809	p. 749
Lennett Herring, Ensign, District 220	9 Mar 1809	p. 749
Theophilus Neal, Lieutenant, District 216	9 Mar 1809	p. 750
Samuel Bryan, Ensign, District 216	9 Mar 1809	p. 750
Alexander G. Gordan, Major, Battalion 15	15 Mar 1809	p. 751
Theophelus Hargroves, Ensign, District 129	16 Mar 1809	p. 751
Andrew Boothe, Ensign, District 131	16 Mar 1809	p. 752
John Collins, Lieutenant, District 130	16 Mar 1809	p. 752
Nathan Aldrige, Ensign, District 130	16 Mar 1809	p. 753
John Oliver, Captain, District 133	16 Mar 1809	p. 753
John Watson, Captain, District 134	16 Mar 1809	p. 754
Morgan Brown, Lieutenant, District 97	17 Mar 1809	p. 754
Thomas Waller, Ensign, District 97	17 Mar 1809	p. 755
John Jones, Lieutenant, District 313	17 Mar 1809	p. 755
John Rogers, Captain, District 258	18 Mar 1809	p. 756
John W. Pettygrew, Lieutenant, District 258	18 Mar 1809	p. 756
Peter Wallace, Ensign, District 258	18 Mar 1809	p. 757
Nehemiah Garrison, Captain	18 Mar 1809	p. 757
John Blackstocks, Lieutenant	18 Mar 1809	p. 758
John Thomason, Ensign	18 Mar 1809	p. 758
Wilson McKinney, Captain, District 248	18 Mar 1809	p. 759
Willis Jencks, Lieutenant, District 248	18 Mar 1809	p. 759
Joseph Williamson, Ensign, District 248	18 Mar 1809	p. 760
William Murdock, Captain, District 268	18 Mar 1809	p. 760
Fendley McCowen, Ensign, District 279	20 Mar 1809	p. 761

Name, Rank, Unit	Date	Page
Aaron Gozey, Lieutenant, District 79	20 Mar 1809	p. 761
John Cuningham, Captain, District 279	20 Mar 1809	p. 762
Arthur Davis, Lieutenant, District 279	20 Mar 1809	p. 762
William Tidley, Lieutenant, District 155	21 Mar 1809	p. 763
Thomas Barnes, Captain, District 102	27 Mar 1809	p. 763
Alfred Cuthbert, Captain, Volunteer Company of Infantry (styled the Republican Blues), Battalion 60	29 Mar 1809	p. 764
Charles Pope, Lieutenant, Volunteer Company of Infantry (styled the Republican Blues), Battalion 60	29 Mar 1809	p. 764
John F. Everett, Ensign, Volunteer Company of Infantry (styled the Republican Blues), Battalion 60	29 Mar 1809	p. 765
Joseph Boren, Captain, District 160	29 Mar 1809	p. 765
William Ward, Lieutenant, District 213	30 Mar 1809	p. 766
John Denman, Ensign, District 213	30 Mar 1809	p. 766
Cader Malone, Lieutenant, District 169	3 Apr 1809	p. 767
George Boswell, Ensign, District 169	3 Apr 1809	p. 767
James Hunt, Lieutenant, District 77	3 Apr 1809	p. 768
William Wylly, Lieutenant, District 6	5 Apr 1809	p. 768
Steel White, Lieutenant, Volunteer Company of Infantry (styled the Guards), Battalion 1	5 Apr 1809	p. 769
Henry N. Mounger, Ensign, Volunteer Company (styled the Guards), Battalion 1	5 Apr 1809	p. 769
William Barnard, Ensign, District 6	5 Apr 1809	p. 770
Stephen Croft, Ensign, District 1	5 Apr 1809	p. 770
John Moffett, Lieutenant, District 118	7 Apr 1809	p. 771
William Vickers, Ensign, District 118	7 Apr 1809	p. 771
Hardy Scarborough, Captain, District 80	10 Apr 1809	p. 772
John Black, Lieutenant, District 259	10 Apr 1809	p. 772
Philip Sapp, Major, Battalion 14	12 Apr 1809	p. 773
Joseph White, Captain, District 293	13 Apr 1809	p. 773
Benjamin Humphries, Lieutenant, District 293	13 Apr 1809	p. 774
Ezekiel Harris, Ensign, District 298	13 Apr 1809	p. 774
Peter Scarborough, Lieutenant, District 298	14 Apr 1809	p. 775
Plesant Williamson, Ensign, District 298	14 Apr 1809	p. 775
Major Henderson, Lieutenant Colonel, Regiment 18	14 Apr 1809	p. 776
Benjamin Hodges, Lieutenant, District 90	22 Apr 1809	p. 776
John Hambricks, Captain, District 98	22 May 1809	p. 777

Name, Rank, Unit	Date	Page
Nathan Powell, Lieutenant, District 98	22 Apr 1809	p. 777
Arrington Holt, Ensign, District 98	22 Apr 1809	p. 778
Allen Took, Captain, District 91	22 Apr 1809	p. 778
John Brown, Lieutenant, District 91	22 Apr 1809	p. 779
James Nesmith, Captain, District 38	27 Apr 1809	p. 779
John Trussell, Ensign, District 38	27 Apr 1809	p. 780
James Lockett, Captain, District 158	28 Apr 1809	p. 780
Samuel Torrance, Ensign, District 158	28 Apr 1809	p. 781
William Greson, Ensign, District 155	28 May 1809	p. 781
Nathaniel Mason, Lieutenant, District 308	2 May 1809	p. 782
Tarlton Hall, Lieutenant, District 219	6 May 1809	p. 782
Amos Ponder, Ensign, District 219	8 May 1809	p. 783
Samuel Brown, Captain, Volunteer Rifle Company, Battalion 48	8 May 1809	p. 783
Isham Hendon, Lieutenant, Volunteer Rifle Company, Battalion 48	8 May 1809	p. 784
Arnold Atkins, Ensign, Volunteer Rifle Company, Battalion 48	8 May 1809	p. 784
John Wood, Lieutenant, District 306	8 May 1809	p. 785
Harden D. Runnells, Lieutenant, Volunteer Troop of Dragoons, Regiment 30	8 May 1809	p. 785
Richard Rispiss, Captain	9 May 1809	p. 786
Robert Graham, Captain, District 324	11 May 1809	p. 786
John Hudson, Ensign, District 77	11 May 1809	p. 787
John Rudney, Captain, District 116	13 May 1809	p. 787
John Roper, Captain	15 May 1809	p. 788
Jourdan Dykes, Lieutenant	15 May 1809	p. 788
Isaac Brackin, Ensign	15 May 1809	p. 789
Archibald Lassiter, Captain	15 May 1809	p. 789
James McDonald, Captain, District 128	17 May 1809	p. 790
Robert Shaw, Ensign, District 128	17 May 1809	p. 790
Thomas Anderson, Captain, District 265	18 May 1809	p. 791
Washington Sorrels, Ensign, District 265	18 May 1809	p. 791
Samuel Harden, Captain, District 208	18 May 1809	p. 792
Thomas Ivey, Ensign, District 208	18 May 1809	p. 792
William Walraven, Captain, District 209	18 May 1809	p. 793
William Thompson, Ensign, District 244	19 May 1809	p. 793

Georgia Military Commissions, 1798–1818

Name, Rank, Unit	*Date*	*Page*
Robert E. Echols, Captain, District 244	19 May 1809	p. 794
Allen Rigsby, Lieutenant, District 244	19 May 1809	p. 794
Francis Lafiles, Ensign, District 27	19 May 1809	p. 795
Burwell Johnson, Ensign, District 224	19 May 1809	p. 795
Aaron Pease, Ensign, District 273	22 May 1809	p. 796
Eli Emanuel, Major, Battalion 16	22 May 1809	p. 796
Robert Allen, Ensign, District 74	22 May 1809	p. 797
Robert Moore, Captain, District 75	22 May 1809	p. 797
William Godbee, Lieutenant, District 68	22 May 1809	p. 798
William Williams, Captain, District 66	22 May 1809	p. 798
Abel Cain, Lieutenant, District 65	22 May 1809	p. 799
John Bell, Captain, District 62	22 May 1809	p. 799
Jesse B. Moore, Captain, District 60	22 May 1809	p. 800
Johnson Wellborn, Major, Battalion 36	25 May 1809	p. 800
Charles Ivey, Ensign, District 174	25 May 1809	p. 801
Edward Lane, Captain, District 49	25 May 1809	p. 801
Joel Hendley, Lieutenant, District 49	25 May 1809	p. 802
Willis Martin, Ensign, District 49	25 May 1809	p. 802
Henry Miller, Captain	25 May 1809	p. 803
Frederick Lanier, Lieutenant	25 May 1809	p. 803
Thomas Self, Ensign	25 May 1809	p. 804
Seaborn Denmark, Captain, District 47	25 May 1809	p. 804
Berry Jones, Lieutenant, District 44	25 May 1809	p. 805
Andrew Martin, Ensign, District 44	25 May 1809	p. 805
Edmund Godwin, Ensign, District 105	27 May 1809	p. 806
William Rowe, Captain, Volunteer Company of Infantry, Battalion 71	2 Jun 1809	p. 806
Elliot Coleman, Lieutenant, Volunteer Company of Infantry, Battalion 71	2 Jun 1809	p. 807
James Reussou, Ensign, Volunteer Company of Infantry, Battalion 71	2 Jun 1809	p. 807
Littleton Hall, Major, Battalion 12	5 Jun 1809	p. 808
James Walea, Major, Battalion 13	5 Jun 1809	p. 808
Ephraim Willis, Captain, District 53	5 Jun 1809	p. 809
Jonathan Neel, Lieutenant, District 53	5 Jun 1809	p. 809
Hezekiah Neel, Ensign, District 53	5 Jun 1809	p. 810
Nathan Miers, Captain, District 283	5 Jun 1809	p. 810

Commissions Book 1806–1809

Name, Rank, Unit	Date	Page
James Rivers, Lieutenant, District 319	5 Jun 1809	p. 811
Herbert Stevens, Ensign, District 319	5 Jun 1809	p. 811
David Rosser, Captain, District 307	6 Jun 1809	p. 812
Edward Burk, Lieutenant, District 307	6 Jun 1809	p. 812
John Golman, Lieutenant, District 317	7 Jun 1809	p. 813
Edwin S. Harris, Major, Regiment 0	10 Jun 1809	p. 813
Zachariah Williams, Major, Regiment 0	10 Jun 1809	p. 814
Isaac Jackson, Major	12 Jun 1809	p. 814
Joseph Brown, Major, Battalion 49	15 Jun 1809	p. 815
William Cook, Captain, Volunteer Rifle Company, Battalion 65	15 Jun 1809	p. 815
Jourdan Campton, Lieutenant, Volunteer Rifle Company, Battalion 65	15 Jun 1809	p. 816
Jesse Evans, Ensign, Volunteer Rifle Company, Battalion 65	15 Jun 1809	p. 816
James Nobles, Captain, District 52	20 Jun 1809	p. 817
Uriah Kinchen, Lieutenant, District 52	20 Jun 1809	p. 817
David Sears, Ensign, District 52	20 Jun 1809	p. 818
Solomon Mercer, Captain, District 58	20 Jun 1809	p. 818
Hardy Collins, Lieutenant, District 58	20 Jun 1809	p. 819
Simon Hadley Jr., Lieutenant, District 51	20 Jun 1809	p. 819
Henry Butts, Captain, Volunteer Rifle Company, Battalion 23	20 Jun 1809	p. 820
Michael Gray, Lieutenant, Volunteer Rifle Company	20 Jun 1809	p. 820
William H. Robinson, Major, Cavalry	24 Jun 1809	p. 821
John B. Wilkinson, Captain, Volunteer Troop of Dragoons	24 Jun 1809	p. 821
John M. Jones, First Lieutenant, Volunteer Troop of Dragoons	24 Jun 1809	p. 822
Solomon Salisbury, Second Lieutenant, Volunteer Troop of Dragoons	24 Jun 1809	p. 822
John Fryer, Cornet, Volunteer Troop of Dragoons	24 Jun 1809	p. 823
William H. Devine, Captain, District 310	26 Jun 1809	p. 823
Robert G. Houstoun, Captain, Volunteer Company of Infantry (styled the Georgia Foresters), Battalion 60	26 Jun 1809	p. 824
Fengal T. Fleming, Second Lieutenant, Volunteer Troop of Dragoons, Regiment 1	26 Jun 1809	p. 824
Robert Habersham, Cornet, Volunteer Troop of Dragoons, Regiment 1	26 Jun 1809	p. 825

Georgia Military Commissions, 1798–1818

Name, Rank, Unit	Date	Page
John Houghton, Major, Cavalry	27 Jun 1809	p. 825
Henry Lane, Captain, District 281	1 Jul 1809	p. 826
William Allman, Ensign, District 281	1 Jul 1809	p. 826
Lewellen Williams, Major, Cavalry	6 Jul 1809	p. 827
Isham Reece, Second Lieutenant, Volunteer Company of Cavalry	6 Jul 1809	p. 827
Thomas Wimberly, Captain, Volunteer Company of Light Dragoons	7 Jul 1809	p. 828
Henry Smith, First Lieutenant, Volunteer Company of Light Dragoons	7 Jul 1809	p. 828
John Wright, Second Lieutenant, Volunteer Company of Light Dragoons	7 Jul 1809	p. 829
Sampson Braswell, Cornet, Volunteer Company of Light Dragoons	7 Jul 1809	p. 829
Thomas Telfair, Lieutenant, Volunteer Company of Infantry (styled the Georgia Foresters), Battalion 60	8 Jul 1809	p. 830
John Malone, Ensign, Volunteer Company of Infantry (styled the Georgia Foresters), Battalion 60	8 Jul 1809	p. 830
James Welch, Captain, District 69	8 Jul 1809	p. 831
William E. Adams, Captain, District 308	10 Jul 1809	p. 831
John Kendrick, Captain	10 Jul 1809	p. 832
Elijah Cowden, Lieutenant	10 Jul 1809	p. 832
Robert Penor, Ensign	10 Jul 1809	p. 833
William Salors, Ensign, District 252	10 Jul 1809	p. 833
Austin J. Davis, Captain, District 135	10 Jul 1809	p. 834
James Oliver, Captain, District 202	13 Jul 1809	p. 834
Drewry Lesure, Lieutenant, District 202	13 Jul 1809	p. 835
Gabriel Booth, Ensign, District 202	13 Jul 1809	p. 835
Welcome Whipple, Lieutenant, District 192	13 Jul 1809	p. 836
William Fortson, Captain, District 189	13 Jul 1809	p. 836
Joshua Houghton, Lieutenant Colonel Commandant, Regiment 17	17 Jul 1809	p. 837
Clement Powers, Captain, District 10	19 Jul 1809	p. 837
Anthony Welch, Lieutenant, District 10	19 Jul 1809	p. 838
Joseph Wiggins, Ensign, District 10	19 Jul 1809	p. 838
William Ratcliff, Captain, District 301	21 Jul 1809	p. 839
David Calloway, Lieutenant, District 301	21 Jul 1809	p. 839
Jesse Ivey, Ensign, District 300	21 Jul 1809	p. 840

Name, Rank, Unit	Date	Page
Ezekiel F. Smith, Captain, District 104	21 Jul 1809	p. 840
Thornton Sandford, Lieutenant, District 104	21 Jul 1809	p. 841
Elias Fort, Major	22 Jul 1809	p. 841
Jacob Libzy, Lieutenant	22 Jul 1809	p. 842
Thomas Knight, Ensign	22 Jul 1809	p. 842
Robert Pope, Major, Battalion 45	24 Jul 1809	p. 843
Thomas Mitchell, Major, Battalion 48	24 Jul 1809	p. 843
Willis Kilgore, Ensign, District 218	24 Jul 1809	p. 844
James McDaniel, Captain, District 74	24 Jul 1809	p. 844
James Willis, Lieutenant, District 74	24 Jul 1809	p. 845
Robert Moore, Ensign, District 75	24 Jul 1809	p. 845
Archibald Graham, Ensign, District 70	24 Jul 1809	p. 846
John Ball, Captain, District 64	24 Jul 1809	p. 846
Furney May, Ensign, District 64	24 Jul 1809	p. 847
Daniel McGahey, Captain, District 65	24 Jul 1809	p. 847
William Owen, Ensign, District 65	24 Jul 1809	p. 848
Ward Taylor, Ensign, District 302	25 Jul 1809	p. 848
Lewis Hadden, Captain	26 Jul 1809	p. 849
James Stewart, Lieutenant	26 Jul 1809	p. 849
Aaron Parker, Ensign	26 Jul 1809	p. 850
William Willingham, Lieutenant, District 275	26 Jul 1809	p. 850
William Tyson, Lieutenant, District 40	26 Jul 1809	p. 851
John Whiddon, Ensign, District 40	26 Jul 1809	p. 851
Greenberry Akridge, Captain, District 54	26 Jul 1809	p. 852
Richard Levens, Lieutenant, District 54	26 Jul 1809	p. 852
William Levens, Ensign, District 54	26 Jul 1809	p. 853
James Ricks, Lieutenant, District 55	26 Jul 1809	p. 853
Samuel Hartley, Ensign, District 55	26 Jul 1809	p. 854
William McCullen, Captain, District 56	26 Jul 1809	p. 854
William Dormeny, Lieutenant, District 56	26 Jul 1809	p. 855
Christopher Messer, Ensign, District 56	26 Jul 1809	p. 855
Moses A. Roberts, Lieutenant, District 320	2 Aug 1809	p. 856
William Y. Hansell, Ensign, District 320	2 Aug 1809	p. 856
Joodison Myrick, Cornet, Volunteer Troop of Dragoons	4 Aug 1809	p. 857
Thomas Shivers, Ensign, District 115	4 Aug 1809	p. 857
Henry Harden, Captain, District 20	4 Aug 1809	p. 858

Georgia Military Commissions, 1798–1818

Name, Rank, Unit	*Date*	*Page*
John Wells, Ensign, District 20	4 Aug 1809	p. 858
Benjamin Stiles, Ensign	4 Aug 1809	p. 859
Francis Kennedy Sr., Captain, District 48	4 Aug 1809	p. 859
William Pridgen, Lieutenant, District 48	4 Aug 1809	p. 860
Henry Goodman, Ensign, District 48	4 Aug 1809	p. 860
Reding Bryan, Lieutenant, District 69	4 Aug 1809	p. 861
John Sadler, Ensign, District 69	4 Aug 1809	p. 861
David Jones, Captain, District 60	4 Aug 1809	p. 862
Berry Elsey, Lieutenant, District 270	4 Aug 1809	p. 862
Robert Braswell, Ensign, District 270	4 Aug 1809	p. 863
Thomas Rogers, Lieutenant, District 32	4 Aug 1809	p. 863
William Marcome, Ensign, District 32	4 Aug 1809	p. 864
William Clark, Ensign, District 31	4 Aug 1809	p. 864
William Mickler, Ensign, District 29	4 Aug 1809	p. 865
Stephen Brown Clark, Captain, District 1	4 Aug 1809	p. 865
Ephraim Cooper, Lieutenant, District 1	4 Aug 1809	p. 866
T. V. Gray, Lieutenant, District 3	4 Aug 1809	p. 866
William Gaston, Ensign, District 3	4 Aug 1809	p. 867
William Wyley, Ensign, District 5	4 Aug 1809	p. 867
George W. Allen, Captain, District 7	4 Aug 1809	p. 868
Richard D. Achord, Lieutenant, District 7	4 Aug 1809	p. 868
Alford Stewart, Lieutenant, District 217	4 Aug 1809	p. 869
John Bransford, Ensign, District 217	4 Aug 1809	p. 869
Gaddeal Fambrough, Lieutenant, District 223	4 Aug 1809	p. 870
Samuel Bryd, Ensign, District 223	4 Aug 1809	p. 870
John Carter, Ensign, District 218	4 Aug 1809	p. 871
Hardy Loyal, Captain, District 126	4 Aug 1809	p. 871
Caleb Hubank, Ensign, District 126	4 Aug 1809	p. 872
George Barber, Ensign, District 130	4 Aug 1809	p. 872
Peter Ryan, Captain, District 132	4 Aug 1809	p. 873
Edward Prather, Lieutenant, District 132	4 Aug 1809	p. 873
Jacob Miller, Ensign, District 133	4 Aug 1809	p. 874
John Fleming, Ensign, District 134	4 Aug 1809	p. 874
Robert Rozer, Ensign, District 135	4 Aug 1809	p. 875
Thomas Howard, Ensign, District 274	4 Aug 1809	p. 875
James Brumfield, Lieutenant, District 321	4 Aug 1809	p. 876

Name, Rank, Unit	*Date*	*Page*
Nathan Sicer, Ensign, District 321	4 Aug 1809	p. 876
Christian Treuitlen, First Lieutenant, Volunteer Troop of Dragoons	4 Aug 1809	p. 877
Samuel Fitzpatrick, Second Lieutenant, Volunteer Troop of Dragoons	4 Aug 1809	p. 877
John George Mendledorf, Lieutenant, District 11	4 Aug 1809	p. 878
William Wylly, Captain, District 12	4 Aug 1809	p. 878
Samuel Davis, Ensign, District 12	4 Aug 1809	p. 879
Jesse Scruggs, Lieutenant, District 13	4 Aug 1809	p. 879
James Long, Ensign, District 13	4 Aug 1809	p. 880
Edward King, Captain, Volunteer Troop of Dragoons	7 Aug 1809	p. 880
William Bush, First Lieutenant, Volunteer Troop of Dragoons	7 Aug 1809	p. 881
William Robbins, Second Lieutenant, Volunteer Troop of Dragoons	7 Aug 1809	p. 881
John Turk, Cornet, Volunteer Troop of Dragoons	7 Aug 1809	p. 882
John Coffee, Major, Battalion 24	14 Aug 1809	p. 882
John T. Dudley, Captain, District 201	14 Aug 1809	p. 883
John Brown, Lieutenant, District 201	14 Aug 1809	p. 883
Zuriah King, Ensign, District 199	14 Aug 1809	p. 884
Benjamin Cleveland, Captain, District 215	14 Aug 1809	p. 884
Adam Whesionhunt, Lieutenant, District 215	14 Aug 1809	p. 885
James R. Wyley, Captain, District 267	14 Aug 1809	p. 885
Groves Yarborough, Ensign, District 211	14 Aug 1809	p. 886
James Oliver, Major, Battalion 56	14 Aug 1809	p. 886
James Manghram, Ensign, District 26	14 Aug 1809	p. 887
Henry Dubignon, Ensign, District 25	14 Aug 1809	p. 887
John Hatson, Captain, District 271	14 Aug 1809	p. 888
John Brannon, Lieutenant, District 24	14 Aug 1809	p. 888
Harbard Ryals, Ensign, District 24	14 Aug 1809	p. 889
Thomas Kirk, Captain, District 23	14 Aug 1809	p. 889
Thomas Wood, Lieutenant, District 160	17 Aug 1809	p. 890
William Cook, Ensign, District 160	17 Aug 1809	p. 890
John Stillwell, Ensign, District 142	17 Aug 1809	p. 891
William Colclough, Lieutenant, District 139	17 Aug 1809	p. 891
John Bedell, Lieutenant, District 137	17 Aug 1809	p. 892
Meeks Sesson, Ensign, District 137	17 Aug 1809	p. 892

Georgia Military Commissions, 1798–1818

Name, Rank, Unit	Date	Page
Abner Wheelis, Lieutenant, District 162	17 Aug 1809	p. 893
John H. Broughton, Lieutenant, District 146	17 Aug 1809	p. 893
Thomas Wright, Ensign, District 146	17 Aug 1809	p. 894
Henry McCoy, Lieutenant, District 148	17 Aug 1809	p. 894
John Wooton, Ensign, District 148	17 Aug 1809	p. 895
Frederick Lester, Lieutenant, District 145	17 Aug 1809	p. 895
David Christopher, Ensign, District 145	17 Aug 1809	p. 896
James Nelms, Ensign, District 139	17 Aug 1809	p. 896
Henry Tripp, First Lieutenant, Volunteer Troop of Dragoons	17 Aug 1809	p. 897
Moses Wilis, Cornet, Volunteer Troop of Dragoons	17 Aug 1809	p. 897
James Hamilton, Captain, Volunteer Company of Artillery, Regiment 14	17 Aug 1809	p. 898
Peterson Thweet, First Lieutenant, Volunteer Company of Artillery, Regiment 14	17 Aug 1809	p. 898
John Turner, Second Lieutenant, Volunteer Company of Artillery, Regiment 14	17 Aug 1809	p. 899
Lard W. Harris, Captain, Volunteer Company of Light Infantry, Battalion 23	17 Aug 1809	p. 899
Henry Huff, Lieutenant, Volunteer Company of Light Infantry, Battalion 23	17 Aug 1809	p. 900
John H. Broadnax, Ensign, Volunteer Company of Light Infantry, Battalion 23	17 Aug 1809	p. 900
John T. Porter, Lieutenant, District 117	17 Aug 1809	p. 901
William Smith, Ensign, District 14	17 Aug 1809	p. 901
John Potter, Lieutenant, District 112	17 Aug 1809	p. 902
William Johnson, Ensign, District 172	17 Aug 1809	p. 902
Josiah Evans, Lieutenant, District 111	17 Aug 1809	p. 903
James Bagby, Lieutenant, District 109	17 Aug 1809	p. 903
Richard Burch, Ensign, District 106	17 Aug 1809	p. 904
Charles Hudson, Lieutenant, District 103	17 Aug 1809	p. 904
Abraham Scott, Captain, Volunteer Troop of Dragoons	22 Aug 1809	p. 905
James Montgomery, First Lieutenant, Volunteer Troop of Dragoons	22 Aug 1809	p. 905
George Roberts, Second Lieutenant, Volunteer Troop of Dragoons	22 Aug 1809	p. 906
Adam Fullerton, Cornet, Volunteer Troop of Dragoons	22 Aug 1809	p. 906
William Carrigan, Captain, District 245	22 Aug 1809	p. 907

Name, Rank, Unit	*Date*	*Page*
Richard Turner, Lieutenant, District 245	22 Aug 1809	p. 907
John Torrence, Ensign, District 245	22 Aug 1809	p. 908
David Gillispy, Lieutenant, District 250	22 Aug 1809	p. 908
Obediah Jenkins, Ensign, District 250	22 Aug 1809	p. 909
Alexander Harper, Captain, District 247	22 Aug 1809	p. 909
Richard J. Watts, Lieutenant, District 247	22 Aug 1809	p. 910
Joseph McEver, Ensign, District 247	22 Aug 1809	p. 910
Reuben Blalock, Captain, District 244	22 Aug 1809	p. 911
Burwell Camp, Lieutenant, District 244	22 Aug 1809	p. 911
Samuel King, Ensign, District 244	22 Aug 1809	p. 912
Hugh Dixon, Captain, District 251	22 Aug 1809	p. 912
William Watkins, Lieutenant, District 251	22 Aug 1809	p. 913
William Whitlock, Ensign, District 251	22 Aug 1809	p. 913
Malachie Mannel, Ensign, District 75	22 Aug 1809	p. 914
Able Hodges, Captain, Volunteer Troop of Dragoons	23 Aug 1809	p. 914
James Darby, First Lieutenant, Volunteer Troop of Dragoons	23 Aug 1809	p. 915
Isaac Harris, Captain, District 84	23 Aug 1809	p. 915
John McDonald, Lieutenant, District 84	23 Aug 1809	p. 916
William Marshall, Ensign, District 84	23 Aug 1809	p. 916
Godfrey Betsell, Captain, District 85	23 Aug 1809	p. 917
William Fleming Jr., Lieutenant, District 85	23 Aug 1809	p. 917
Harbert Smith, Ensign, District 85	23 Aug 1809	p. 918
Able Hodges, Lieutenant, District 79	23 Aug 1809	p. 918
Francis Dawkins, Ensign, District 79	23 Aug 1809	p. 919
Samuel Clark, Lieutenant, District 82	23 Aug 1809	p. 919
Benannual Bower, Ensign, District 82	23 Aug 1809	p. 920
William Foyl, Lieutenant, District 78	23 Aug 1809	p. 920
John Folks, Ensign, District 83	23 Aug 1809	p. 921
Jesse Glover, Lieutenant, District 76	23 Aug 1809	p. 921
James Pyland, Ensign, District 76	23 Aug 1809	p. 922
Philip Zimmerman, Captain, District 282	24 Aug 1809	p. 922
Thomas Pate, Ensign, District 282	24 Aug 1809	p. 923
Samuel Skidmore, Captain, District 277	24 Aug 1809	p. 923
James Davis, Lieutenant, District 277	24 Aug 1809	p. 924
Jesse Clower, Lieutenant, District 278	24 Aug 1809	p. 924
James Morrow, Ensign, District 278	24 Aug 1809	p. 925

Georgia Military Commissions, 1798–1818

Name, Rank, Unit	*Date*	*Page*
John Sparks, Lieutenant, District 284	24 Aug 1809	p. 925
Joel Ball, Ensign, District 285	24 Aug 1809	p. 926
William Randall, Lieutenant, District 287	24 Aug 1809	p. 926
Peter Barnett, Captain, District 288	24 Aug 1809	p. 927
William Hambleton, Lieutenant, District 288	24 Aug 1809	p. 927
William H. Norman, Captain, District 185	24 Aug 1809	p. 928
Thomas Pruther, Lieutenant, District 185	24 Aug 1809	p. 928
William York, Ensign, District 185	24 Aug 1809	p. 929
Samuel Jeter, Captain, District 269	24 Aug 1809	p. 929
Reuben Carpenter, Ensign, District 269	24 Aug 1809	p. 930
Jonathan Baker, Ensign, District 186	24 Aug 1809	p. 930
John Twitty, Ensign, District 187	24 Aug 1809	p. 931
Elijah Beacham, Captain, District 47	24 Aug 1809	p. 931
James Fields, Ensign, District 57	24 Aug 1809	p. 932
Jeremiah Baker, Captain, District 51	24 Aug 1809	p. 932
Jesse Warren, Captain, District 17	24 Aug 1809	p. 933
John Martin, Ensign, District 17	24 Aug 1809	p. 933
John Wallis, Lieutenant, District 23	24 Aug 1809	p. 934
Richard Purvis, Ensign, District 23	24 Aug 1809	p. 934
Timothy Freeman, Captain, District 296	24 Aug 1809	p. 935
John Price, Lieutenant, District 296	24 Aug 1809	p. 935
Peter Scarborough, Ensign, District 296	24 Aug 1809	p. 936
Marnock Glazer, Captain, District 295	24 Aug 1809	p. 936
Exum Brove, Lieutenant, District 295	24 Aug 1809	p. 937
William Hutchinson, Ensign, District 295	24 Aug 1809	p. 937
John Wilson, Lieutenant, District 311	24 Aug 1809	p. 938
George Brewer, Ensign, District 311	24 Aug 1809	p. 938
Ransom Ballard, Ensign, District 308	24 Aug 1809	p. 939
Thomas P. Hamilton, Captain	24 Aug 1809	p. 939
Isaac Williams, Lieutenant	24 Aug 1809	p. 940
John Honeycut, Ensign	24 Aug 1809	p. 940
William Philips, Lieutenant	24 Aug 1809	p. 941
Joshua Burk, Ensign	24 Aug 1809	p. 941
Able Pennington, Lieutenant, District 290	24 Aug 1809	p. 942
Samuel Baker, Ensign, District 290	24 Aug 1809	p. 942
William Smith, Captain, District 238	24 Aug 1809	p. 943

Name, Rank, Unit	Date	Page
Henry T. Moody, Lieutenant, District 238	24 Aug 1809	p. 943
William Baber, Ensign, District 238	24 Aug 1809	p. 944
Acquilla Greer, Captain, District 231	24 Aug 1809	p. 944
William McLaughlen, Ensign, District 231	24 Aug 1809	p. 945
Adam Eberhert, Ensign, District 237	24 Aug 1809	p. 945
Reuben Wade, Lieutenant, District 226	24 Aug 1809	p. 946
Henry Blake, Captain, District 227	24 Aug 1809	p. 946
Benjamin Davis, Lieutenant, District 227	24 Aug 1809	p. 947
Burwell Pope, Ensign, District 227	24 Aug 1809	p. 947
Solomon A. Stripp, Ensign, District 232	24 Aug 1809	p. 948
Samuel Walker, Ensign, District 234	24 Aug 1809	p. 948
Joshua Hagerty, Major	24 Aug 1809	p. 949
John G. Smith, Major	24 Aug 1809	p. 949
Nathaniel Moss, Captain, Volunteer Company of Riflemen, Battalion 45	24 Aug 1809	p. 950
Allen Simms, Ensign, Volunteer Company of Riflemen, Battalion 45	24 Aug 1809	p. 950
John Gresham, Second Lieutenant, Volunteer Company of Cavalry	24 Aug 1809	p. 951
John B. Barnes, Captain, Cavalry	25 Aug 1809	p. 951
Sampson Wilder, Second Lieutenant, Volunteer Troop of Dragoons	25 Aug 1809	p. 952
William Lamkin, Captain, District 123	25 Aug 1809	p. 952
Lynn McDade, Ensign, District 123	25 Aug 1809	p. 953
Jesse Stewart, Ensign, District 122	25 Aug 1809	p. 953
Gideon Seely, Lieutenant, District 124	25 Aug 1809	p. 954
Richard Wilds, Captain, District 120	25 Aug 1809	p. 954
Floyed Jarvis, Captain, District 119	25 Aug 1809	p. 955
Edward McGar, Lieutenant, District 119	25 Aug 1809	p. 955
John Moore, Ensign, District 119	25 Aug 1809	p. 956
Joel Rushing, Captain, District 154	25 Aug 1809	p. 956
Jonathan Newman, Ensign, District 154	25 Aug 1809	p. 957
Moses Williams, Ensign, District 151	25 Aug 1809	p. 957
Thomas Jones, Lieutenant, District 150	25 Aug 1809	p. 958
William Smith, Ensign, District 150	25 Aug 1809	p. 958
William Livingston, Lieutenant, District 87	25 Aug 1809	p. 959
Kinchin Hilliard, Ensign, District 87	25 Aug 1809	p. 959

Georgia Military Commissions, 1798–1818

Name, Rank, Unit	*Date*	*Page*
Robert R. Minter, Lieutenant, District 136	25 Aug 1809	p. 960
Robert Mathis, Ensign, District 136	25 Aug 1809	p. 960
Eli Rushing, Ensign, District 100	25 Aug 1809	p. 961
Archibald McWilliams, Lieutenant, District 95	25 Aug 1809	p. 961
Edmund Hopson, Captain, District 93	25 Aug 1809	p. 962
George McKigney, Lieutenant, District 86	25 Aug 1809	p. 962
Beninah McClendon, Lieutenant, District 175	25 Aug 1809	p. 963
Obadiah Flournoy, Ensign, District 175	25 Aug 1809	p. 963
Sanders Stallings, Ensign, District 79	25 Aug 1809	p. 964
Robert Wade, Ensign, District 177	25 Aug 1809	p. 964
John Horn, Lieutenant, District 171	25 Aug 1809	p. 965
John Rawles, Captain, District 37	25 Aug 1809	p. 965
Jesse Freeman, Lieutenant, District 37	25 Aug 1809	p. 966
Daniel Dorothy, Lieutenant, District 39	25 Aug 1809	p. 966
Jacob Holland, Captain, District 331	25 Aug 1809	p. 967
Robert Bowling, Captain, District 72	31 Aug 1809	p. 967
Noah Minton, Lieutenant, District 72	31 Aug 1809	p. 968
Benjamin Grubbs, Ensign, District 305	2 Sep 1809	p. 968
John Holmes, Captain, District 168	4 Sep 1809	p. 969
Richard Willis, Lieutenant, District 168	4 Sep 1809	p. 969
James Rumsey, Ensign, District 168	4 Sep 1809	p. 970
James Dunn, Lieutenant, District 134	5 Sep 1809	p. 970
Gabriel Williams, Lieutenant, District 128	5 Sep 1809	p. 971
James Pinkston, Major, Battalion 26	8 Sep 1809	p. 971
Archibald Laird, Lieutenant, District 281	9 Sep 1809	p. 972
Owen Fountain, Lieutenant, District 59	9 Sep 1809	p. 972
John Dell, Captain, District 46	14 Sep 1809	p. 973
Elijah Stanford, Lieutenant, District 46	14 Sep 1809	p. 973
James Burnett, Ensign, District 46	14 Sep 1809	p. 974
Thomas Wilcox, Captain	14 Sep 1809	p. 974
Daniel McCrarey, Lieutenant	14 Sep 1809	p. 975
William Carrell, Ensign	14 Sep 1809	p. 975
John Griggs, Lieutenant, District 102	15 Sep 1809	p. 976
Samuel Townsend, Captain, District 192	16 Sep 1809	p. 976
Bryant Rushen, Captain, District 297	16 Sep 1809	p. 977
Samuel Harvell, Lieutenant, District 192	16 Sep 1809	p. 977

Name, Rank, Unit	*Date*	*Page*
John Elliott, Captain, District 282	18 Sep 1809	p. 978
P. Bevell, Captain, District 36	19 Sep 1809	p. 978
Harrison Thurmond, Captain, Volunteer Rifle Company, Battalion 51	6 Oct 1809	p. 979
Thomas Cump, Ensign, Volunteer Rifle Company, Battalion 51	6 Oct 1809	p. 979
James Meriwether, Captain, District 241	11 Oct 1809	p. 980
William Bencon Jr., Captain, District 132	13 Oct 1809	p. 980
Isaac McNeely, Captain, District 261	11 Oct 1809	p. 981
Murdock Martin, Captain, District 216	11 Oct 1809	p. 981
David Meredith, Lieutenant, District 240	11 Oct 1809	p. 982
Simeon Bankston, Ensign, District 240	11 Oct 1809	p. 982
William Winfrey, Lieutenant, District 132	13 Oct 1809	p. 983
Thomas Ayres, Ensign, District 132	13 Oct 1809	p. 983
Frederick Dean, Ensign, District 201	14 Oct 1809	p. 984
Lemuel Pledger, Ensign, District 197	14 Oct 1809	p. 984
George Alexander, Ensign, District 195	14 Oct 1809	p. 985
Simon Henderson, Lieutenant, District 315	14 Oct 1809	p. 985
Micajah White, Ensign, District 309	14 Oct 1809	p. 986
Charles Brown, Lieutenant, District 310	14 Oct 1809	p. 986
John Wells, Ensign, District 310	14 Oct 1809	p. 987
Thomas Mullens, Lieutenant, District 312	14 Oct 1809	p. 987
Crawford West, Ensign, District 312	14 Oct 1809	p. 988
William Walker, Captain, District 280	14 Oct 1809	p. 988
Greeneberry Haynes, Ensign, District 280	14 Oct 1809	p. 989
Gilley Wooten, Captain, District 283	14 Oct 1809	p. 989
Hakins Philips, Lieutenant, District 283	14 Oct 1809	p. 990
Thomas Coleman, Captain, District 276	14 Oct 1809	p. 990
Joseph Moore, Lieutenant, District 276	14 Oct 1809	p. 991
Solomon Lasher, Ensign, District 9	14 Oct 1809	p. 991
Jacob Mitzger, Lieutenant, District 12	14 Oct 1809	p. 992
John Westbrook, Lieutenant, District 210	14 Oct 1809	p. 992
James Wilkinson, Lieutenant, District 214	14 Oct 1809	p. 993
Drewry Harrington, Ensign, District 214	14 Oct 1809	p. 993
Ansil Strickland, Captain, District 262	14 Oct 1809	p. 994
Philip Thomas, Lieutenant, District 209	14 Oct 1809	p. 994
Caleb Garrison, Ensign, District 209	14 Oct 1809	p. 995

Georgia Military Commissions, 1798–1818

Name, Rank, Unit	Date	Page
David Gafford, Lieutenant, District 302	14 Oct 1809	p. 995
William Mason, Lieutenant, District 86	14 Oct 1809	p. 996
Giles Webb, Ensign, District 86	14 Oct 1809	p. 996
Michael Peacock, Ensign, District 91	14 Oct 1809	p. 997
Ephraim Cooper, Captain, District 1	14 Oct 1809	p. 997
Thomas H. Penn, Ensign, District 124	14 Oct 1809	p. 998
Bennett, Captain	14 Oct 1809	p. 998
Dempsey Sturdevant, Lieutenant	14 Oct 1809	p. 999
Ansil Thompson, Ensign	14 Oct 1809	p. 999
Sius Taylor, Captain	14 Oct 1809	p. 1000
John Roach, Lieutenant	14 Oct 1809	p. 1000
James Tillman, Ensign	14 Oct 1809	p. 1001
Wiley Robson, Lieutenant	14 Oct 1809	p. 1001
John Dickson, Captain, District 114	14 Oct 1809	p. 1002
William Smith, Lieutenant, District 114	14 Oct 1809	p. 1002
John Gaston, Captain, District 161	14 Oct 1809	p. 1003
Alston Greene, Lieutenant, District 140	14 Oct 1809	p. 1003
Rhesa Bostwick, Ensign, District 140	14 Oct 1809	p. 1004
John Cartwright, Ensign, District 141	14 Oct 1809	p. 1004
Thomas Winston, Captain, District 237	14 Oct 1809	p. 1005
Abner Jenks, Ensign, District 226	14 Oct 1809	p. 1005
Daniel T. Blackburn, Ensign, District 41	14 Oct 1809	p. 1006
Fielding L. Thurmond, Captain, District 181	14 Oct 1809	p. 1006
Peter M. Curry, Lieutenant, District 181	14 Oct 1809	p. 1007
Guilford Cade, Ensign, District 181	14 Oct 1809	p. 1007
Samuel Brooks, Lieutenant, District 177	14 Oct 1809	p. 1008
John Poss, Ensign, District 177	14 Oct 1809	p. 1008
Daniel Coleman, Lieutenant, District 174	14 Oct 1809	p. 1009
Stephen G. Heard, Ensign, District 165	14 Oct 1809	p. 1009
John Colmonsneal, Ensign, District 164	14 Oct 1809	p. 1010
Charles Cheatham, Lieutenant, District 78	14 Oct 1809	p. 1010
William Foaks, Lieutenant, District 79	14 Oct 1809	p. 1011
Ebenezer Elliott, Ensign, District 184	14 Oct 1809	p. 1011
John Cuthbert, Lieutenant, District 16	14 Aug 1809	p. 1012
Henry Hadly, Lieutenant, District 156	14 Oct 1809	p. 1012
William McKinney, Ensign, District 156	14 Oct 1809	p. 1013

Name, Rank, Unit	Date	Page
William McGagaughey, Captain, Volunteer Troop of Dragoons	14 Oct 1809	p. 1013
Francis Lewis, Captain, Volunteer Troop of Dragoons	14 Oct 1809	p. 1014
William Childress, Ensign, Volunteer Rifle Company, Battalion 23	14 Oct 1809	p. 1014
Gustavus Gaines, Captain, Volunteer Rifle Company, Battalion 26	14 Oct 1809	p. 1015
Thomas Wingfield, Lieutenant, Volunteer Rifle Company, Battalion 36	14 Oct 1809	p. 1015
Risdon Watson, Captain, District 143	20 Oct 1809	p. 1016
John Curry, Ensign, District 143	20 Oct 1809	p. 1016
Julius Cook, Captain, District 306	23 Oct 1809	p. 1017
Jonathan Hagerty, Captain, Volunteer Troop of Dragoons	23 Oct 1809	p. 1017
George Williamson, Lieutenant, District 262	27 Oct 1809	p. 1018
William Stephens, Ensign, District 262	27 Oct 1809	p. 1018
James Little, Lieutenant, District 265	27 Oct 1809	p. 1019
Hugh Davison, Ensign, District 165	27 Oct 1809	p. 1019
Anderson Bates, Lieutenant, District 230	7 Nov 1809	p. 1020
Littleberry Kinnabrew, Ensign, District 230	7 Nov 1809	p. 1020
Benjm. F. Duyckinck, Lieutenant, Volunteer Company of Infantry (styled the Augusta Independent Blues)	7 Nov 1809	p. 1021
Charles Beach, Ensign, Volunteer Company of Infantry (styled the Augusta Independent Blues)	7 Nov 1809	p. 1021
James Smith, Captain, District 254	7 Nov 1809	p. 1022
John Anglin, Ensign, District 254	7 Nov 1809	p. 1022
William Hays, Captain, District 246	7 Nov 1809	p. 1023
John Burgess, Lieutenant, District 246	7 Nov 1809	p. 1023
David Clark, Second Lieutenant, Volunteer Company of Artillery, Regiment 9	11 Nov 1809	p. 1024
Saml. Smith, Captain, Volunteer Company of Riflemen	14 Nov 1809	p. 1024
Richd. Smith, Captain, District 323	15 Nov 1809	p. 1025
William Holley, Lieutenant, District 323	15 Nov 1809	p. 1025
William Johnson, Ensign, District 323	15 Nov 1809	p. 1026
William Haynes, Ensign, District 198	20 Nov 1809	p. 1026
Jesse Edwards, Ensign, District 189	20 Nov 1809	p. 1027
Henry Trippe, Major, Cavalry	20 Nov 1809	p. 1027
John Gibson, Captain, District 304	20 Nov 1809	p. 1028
Martin Furlow, Lieutenant, District 304	20 Nov 1809	p. 1028

Name, Rank, Unit	*Date*	*Page*
David McCoy, Captain, District 289	20 Nov 1809	p. 1029
Sanders Vann, Lieutenant, District 289	20 Nov 1809	p. 1029
Benjm. Waits, Ensign, District 289	20 Nov 1809	p. 1030
Richd. S. Easley, Captain, District 240	20 Nov 1809	p. 1030
Henry R. Sorrow, Ensign, District 237	20 Nov 1809	p. 1031
John Ridgers Jr., Lieutenant, District 195	20 Nov 1809	p. 1031
Thos. Blakey, Ensign, District 180	20 Nov 1809	p. 1032
Joseph Monroe, Ensign, District 73	20 Nov 1809	p. 1032
Darby Calhoon, Lieutenant, District 89	20 Nov 1809	p. 1033
Henry Pomele, Ensign, District 89	20 Nov 1809	p. 1033
William Woods, Lieutenant, District 43	20 Nov 1809	p. 1034
William Devenport, Captain, District 110	20 Nov 1809	p. 1034
Britton Jones, Lieutenant, District 110	20 Nov 1809	p. 1035
John Ashley, Ensign, District 110	20 Nov 1809	p. 1035
William Flemming Jr., Lieutenant, District 85	20 Nov 1809	p. 1036
Thos. King, Ensign, District 22	20 Nov 1809	p. 1036
John Collins, Lieutenant, District 21	20 Nov 1809	p. 1037
Francis Sams, Ensign, District 21	20 Nov 1809	p. 1037
Francis Kennedy, Captain, District 48	20 Nov 1809	p. 1038
Jesse Goodman, Lieutenant, District 48	20 Nov 1809	p. 1038

Georgia Military Commissions
Commissions Book 1809–1812

Name, Rank, Unit	*Date*	*Page*
Archibold Cannon, Ensign, District 48	20 Nov 1809	p. 1
Joseph Sikes, Lieutenant, District 47	20 Nov 1809	p. 1
William Williams, Ensign, District 47	20 Nov 1809	p. 2
Ralph Kitchum, Captain, District 120	20 Nov 1809	p. 2
Abraham A. Legett, Lieutenant, District 120	20 Nov 1809	p. 3
Benjm. Hale, Lieutenant, District 122	20 Nov 1809	p. 3
James McMurrey, Lieutenant, District 308	20 Nov 1809	p. 4
William C. Lawson, Ensign, District 16	20 Nov 1809	p. 4
Isaac Long, Lieutenant, District 31	22 Nov 1809	p. 5
Henry Trippe Jr., Ensign, District 102	22 Nov 1809	p. 5
John S. Porter, Lieutenant, Volunteer Company of Riflemen, Battalion 67	29 Nov 1809	p. 6
Dempsey Darrity, Captain	13 Dec 1809	p. 6
Thos. Baggett, Ensign	13 Dec 1809	p. 7
Thos. Collear, Captain	13 Dec 1809	p. 7
John Pruncey, Ensign	13 Nov 1809	p. 8
Aaron Rozar, Lieutenant	13 Dec 1809	p. 8
John McDowell, Captain, District 187	14 Dec 1809	p. 9
Jabez Langston, Ensign, District 97	15 Dec 1809	p. 9
William Gaston, Lieutenant, District 3	18 Dec 1809	p. 10
Jonathan Battelle, Ensign, District 3	18 Dec 1809	p. 10
Henry Tucker, Lieutenant, District 1	18 Dec 1809	p. 11
William Bird, Ensign, District 1	18 Dec 1809	p. 11
William Tatum, Captain, District 109	18 Dec 1809	p. 12
John Moffett, Captain, District 118	18 Dec 1809	p. 12
Tobas V. Gray, Captain, District 273	30 Dec 1809	p. 13
Ephraim Hughey, Captain, District 284	3 Jan 1810	p. 13
Aaron Parker, Lieutenant, District 280	3 Jan 1810	p. 14
James Sessions, Lieutenant, District 288	3 Jan 1810	p. 14
John Bentley, Ensign, District 288	3 Jan 1810	p. 15
Josephus Love, Major, Battalion 32	5 Jan 1810	p. 15
Ezekiel Daniel, Lieutenant, District 148	5 Jan 1810	p. 16
Daniel Henry, Ensign, District 162	5 Jan 1810	p. 16
David Parker, Ensign, District 163	5 Jan 1810	p. 17

Name, Rank, Unit	Date	Page
Solomon Towns, Lieutenant, District 190	16 Jan 1810	p. 17
William McNiece, Captain, District 244	16 Jan 1810	p. 18
Washington Dicke, Lieutenant, District 244	16 Jan 1810	p. 18
James Coil, Ensign, District 244	16 Jan 1810	p. 19
George Cornelius, Captain, District 74	16 Jan 1810	p. 19
John Davis, Lieutenant, District 64	16 Jan 1810	p. 20
George Prickett, Lieutenant, District 212	16 Jan 1810	p. 20
William Glenn, Ensign, District 212	16 Jan 1810	p. 21
William Baber, Lieutenant, District 238	16 Jan 1810	p. 21
Josiah Goodson, Lieutenant, District 20	16 Jan 1810	p. 22
Gabriel Ratcliff, Ensign, District 20	16 Jan 1810	p. 22
Josiah Devenport, Lieutenant, District 273	16 Jan 1810	p. 23
Abraham W. Scribner, Ensign, District 273	16 Jan 1810	p. 23
Jesse Mizell, Captain, District 59	16 Jan 1810	p. 24
Benjamin Cook, Ensign, District 190	16 Jan 1810	p. 24
Jesse Little, Ensign, District 307	26 Jan 1810	p. 25
Archibald Graham, Captain, District 270	1 Feb 1810	p. 25
Charles Thackston, Captain, Volunteer Company of Riflemen, Battalion 44	1 Feb 1810	p. 26
Philip Easton, Lieutenant, Volunteer Company of Riflemen, Battalion 44	1 Feb 1810	p. 26
Thomas Gay, Lieutenant, District 108	1 Feb 1810	p. 27
Joseph Walter, Ensign, District 108	1 Feb 1810	p. 27
Michael W. Huges, Ensign, Volunteer Company of Infantry styled the Republican Blues, Battalion 60	1 Feb 1810	p. 28
Joseph Sill, Lieutenant	1 Feb 1810	p. 28
Richard T. Keating, Captain	1 Feb 1810	p. 29
Abraham Aryres, Ensign, District 115	1 Feb 1810	p. 29
Clifford Woodruff, Captain, District 236	2 Feb 1810	p. 30
John Hudson, Ensign, District 72	8 Feb 1810	p. 30
Jessee Minton, Lieutenant	9 Feb 1810	p. 31
James Watts, Captain, District 91	10 Feb 1810	p. 31
William Mason, Lieutenant	10 Jan 1810	p. 32
John Sawyers, Ensign	10 Feb 1810	p. 32
Cullen Edwards, Captain	12 Feb 1810	p. 33
James Carver, Lieutenant	12 Feb 1810	p. 33
Jesse Carver, Ensign	12 Feb 1810	p. 34

Commissions Book 1809–1812

Name, Rank, Unit	Date	Page
Benjamine Moody, Ensign	12 Feb 1810	p. 34
John G. Pitman, Major, Battalion 53	15 Feb 1810	p. 35
John Lane Jr., Captain	15 Feb 1810	p. 35
William L. Ponder, Captain, District 235	15 Feb 1810	p. 36
Peterson Smith, Lieutenant, District 228	15 Feb 1810	p. 36
Thomas Britton, Ensign, District 217	15 Feb 1810	p. 37
William Horton, Lieutenant, District 103	15 Feb 1810	p. 37
Robert Horton, Ensign, District 103	15 Feb 1810	p. 38
William Marshall, Lieutenant, District 84	15 Feb 1810	p. 38
James Torrance, Captain, District 75	15 Feb 1810	p. 39
Lewis Heath, Lieutenant, District 75	15 Feb 1810	p. 39
Benjamin Shearwood, Lieutenant, District 74	15 Feb 1810	p. 40
John Harvey, Ensign, District 19	15 Feb 1810	p. 40
Elijah Powell, Captain, District 66	17 Feb 1810	p. 41
Pleasant Moore, Lieutenant, District 66	17 Feb 1810	p. 41
John Daniel, Ensign, District 66	17 Feb 1810	p. 42
Jacob Odom, Lieutenant, District 93	20 Feb 1810	p. 42
Thomas Perdue, Lieutenant, District 161	20 Feb 1810	p. 43
Manning Hill, Ensign, District 308	20 Feb 1810	p. 43
Eli Rushing, Lieutenant, District 100	22 Feb 1810	p. 44
Gibson Avers, Ensign, District 100	22 Feb 1810	p. 44
John Pray, Lieutenant Colonel, Regiment 2	22 Feb 1810	p. 45
John Bacon, Major, Battalion 4	22 Feb 1810	p. 45
William Hayles, Major, Battalion 18	22 Feb 1810	p. 46
William Perdue, Lieutenant, District 81	22 Feb 1810	p. 46
Robert Brown, Lieutenant, District 165	22 Feb 1810	p. 47
Burwell Bullock, Captain	24 Feb 1810	p. 47
Micajah Clark, Lieutenant	24 Feb 1810	p. 48
Zeus Weddington, Ensign	24 Feb 1810	p. 48
Robert Northcut, Captain, District 76	27 Feb 1810	p. 49
John Rogers, Lieutenant, District 76	27 Feb 1810	p. 49
David Lawson, Captain, District 109	27 Feb 1810	p. 50
Smith Dent, Lieutenant, District 109	27 Feb 1810	p. 50
Edwin King, Captain, District 142	27 Feb 1810	p. 51
David Jernigan, Lieutenant, District 142	27 Feb 1810	p. 51
James Hicks, Lieutenant, District 294	27 Feb 1810	p. 52

Georgia Military Commissions, 1798–1818

Name, Rank, Unit	*Date*	*Page*
Littleton Jackson, Ensign, District 294	27 Feb 1810	p. 52
John Bowden, Ensign	27 Feb 1810	p. 53
James Lambright, Second Lieutenant	27 Feb 1810	p. 53
George Barnes, Lieutenant, District 319	6 Mar 1810	p. 54
Austin Ellis, Ensign, District 319	6 Mar 1810	p. 54
Abel Pennington, Lieutenant, District 291	9 Mar 1810	p. 55
John Wood, Ensign, District 291	9 Mar 1810	p. 55
Ranson Ballard, Ensign, District 313	9 Mar 1810	p. 56
John Shepherd, Captain, District 220	9 Mar 1810	p. 56
Richard Jones, Lieutenant, District 220	9 Mar 1810	p. 57
William Price, Ensign, District 261	9 Mar 1810	p. 57
James Jones, Lieutenant, District 261	9 Mar 1810	p. 58
James Isom, Captain, District 209	9 Mar 1810	p. 58
Castleton Lyon, Lieutenant, District 211	9 Mar 1810	p. 59
John Womack, Ensign, District 264	9 Mar 1810	p. 59
William Frashier, Lieutenant, District 88	19 Mar 1810	p. 60
David Moody, Ensign, District 88	19 Mar 1810	p. 60
Richard W. Ellis, Captain, District 319	20 Mar 1810	p. 61
Allen Dixon, Lieutenant, District 45	21 Mar 1810	p. 61
Elisha Bowen, Ensign, District 45	21 Mar 1810	p. 62
John O. Baker, Ensign, District 14	21 Mar 1810	p. 62
Noble W. Glinn, Captain, District 6	21 Mar 1810	p. 63
Isham Oneal, Lieutenant, District 6	21 Mar 1810	p. 63
George Robert, Lieutenant, District 126	21 Mar 1810	p. 64
Charles McNight, Ensign, District 171	21 Mar 1810	p. 64
Benjamin Humphrey, Lieutenant, District 111	21 Mar 1810	p. 65
Thomas Jackson, Ensign, District 111	21 Mar 1810	p. 65
John Miller, Captain, District 242	21 Mar 1810	p. 66
John Ross, Ensign, District 242	21 Mar 1810	p. 66
William Griffin, Lieutenant, District 200	21 Mar 1810	p. 67
Joseph Willis, Captain, District 212	21 Mar 1810	p. 67
John B. Pendleton, Lieutenant, District 237	21 Mar 1810	p. 68
John Landrum, Captain, District 229	21 Mar 1810	p. 68
Robert Benson, Lieutenant, District 292	21 Mar 1810	p. 69
John Stewart, Lieutenant	21 Mar 1810	p. 69
John Roach, Ensign, District 304	21 Mar 1810	p. 70

Name, Rank, Unit	Date	Page
Hanley Vaughn, Lieutenant, District 310	21 Mar 1810	p. 70
Henry Miller, Captain, District 44	21 Mar 1810	p. 71
James Eason, Lieutenant, District 44	21 Mar 1810	p. 71
Stephen Rigs, Ensign, District 44	21 Mar 1810	p. 72
Nathan Bussey, Major, Battalion 56	21 Mar 1810	p. 72
John Binion, Captain, District 183	21 Mar 1810	p. 73
James Garnett, Lieutenant, District 183	21 Mar 1810	p. 73
William Gambell, Ensign, District 183	21 Mar 1810	p. 74
Jordan Liverit, Captain, District 182	21 Mar 1810	p. 74
John Carpenter, Lieutenant, District 182	21 Mar 1810	p. 75
Green Whatley, Captain	22 Mar 1810	p. 75
Joseph Morgan, Captain, District 274	22 Mar 1810	p. 76
William Stark, Ensign, District 274	22 Mar 1810	p. 76
Eli Glover, Ensign, Volunteer Company of Riflemen, Battalion 65	22 Mar 1810	p. 77
Benjamin Williamson, Lieutenant, District 312	26 Mar 1810	p. 77
Edmund Puckett, Ensign, District 312	26 Mar 1810	p. 78
Anderson Abercrombe, Captain, Volunteer Troop of Dragoons, Squadron 4, Regiment 2	30 Mar 1810	p. 78
H. F. Simmons, First Lieutenant, Volunteer Troop of Dragoons, Squadron 5, Regiment 3	30 Mar 1810	p. 79
Thomas Borem, Cornet, Volunteer Troop of Dragoons, Squadron 5, Regiment 3	30 Mar 1810	p. 79
Edom Moon, Lieutenant, District 131	3 Apr 1810	p. 80
John Hicks, Ensign, District 131	3 Apr 1810	p. 80
Walter Jones, Captain, District 129	3 Apr 1810	p. 81
Adam Hunter, Captain, District 144	3 Apr 1810	p. 81
John Cartwright, Lieutenant, District 141	3 Apr 1810	p. 82
Robert Pope, Lieutenant Colonel, Regiment 22	3 Apr 1810	p. 82
John Arnold, Captain, District 231	3 Apr 1810	p. 83
Augustin S. Clayton, Captain, District 216	3 Apr 1810	p. 83
Jesse Freeman, Lieutenant, District 216	3 Apr 1810	p. 84
Robert Trawick, Ensign, District 216	3 Apr 1810	p. 84
Winfrey Mason, Lieutenant, District 122	3 Apr 1810	p. 85
Gilbert Shearer, Ensign, District 120	3 Apr 1810	p. 85
John Hayles, Captain, District 81	3 Apr 1810	p. 86
Henry Peeples, Ensign, District 81	3 Apr 1810	p. 86

Georgia Military Commissions, 1798–1818

Name, Rank, Unit	Date	Page
William Gaston, Captain, District 3	3 Apr 1810	p. 87
James Hunter, Lieutenant, Volunteer Rangers, Battalion 1	3 Apr 1810	p. 87
William T. Williams, Ensign, Volunteer Rangers, Battalion 1	3 Apr 1810	p. 88
John Trawick, Lieutenant, District 118	3 Apr 1810	p. 88
John Heart, Captain, District 110	3 Apr 1810	p. 89
John Ashley, Lieutenant, District 110	3 Apr 1810	p. 89
James White, Ensign, District 169	3 Apr 1810	p. 90
Francis Scott, Captain, District 159	3 Apr 1810	p. 90
William F. Scott, Lieutenant, District 159	3 Apr 1810	p. 91
John Calhoon, Lieutenant, District 240	5 Apr 1810	p. 91
Danl. Taylor, Lieutenant, District 222	5 Apr 1810	p. 92
John Smith, Ensign, District 224	5 Apr 1810	p. 92
Allen Johnson, Captain, District 43	5 Apr 1810	p. 93
William Mickler, Lieutenant, District 29	5 Apr 1810	p. 93
James Hanney, Ensign, District 29	5 Apr 1810	p. 94
Charles Wright, Captain, District 329	5 Apr 1810	p. 94
Jonathan Pierson, Lieutenant, District 329	5 Apr 1810	p. 95
Edmond Hogan, Lieutenant Colonel Commandant, Regiment 36	6 Apr 1810	p. 95
William Moore, Captain, District 253	11 Apr 1810	p. 96
Thomas Stapler, Lieutenant, District 253	11 Apr 1810	p. 96
Johnson Frost, Lieutenant, District 258	11 Apr 1810	p. 97
Robert Hancock, Ensign, District 258	11 Apr 1810	p. 97
Alexander Moore, Lieutenant, District 254	11 Apr 1810	p. 98
Henry Crowell, Captain, District 98	12 Apr 1810	p. 98
Henry Achord, Ensign, District 98	12 Apr 1810	p. 99
John S. Quarterman, Captain, District 15	13 Apr 1810	p. 99
Thomas Mallard, Lieutenant, District 15	13 Apr 1810	p. 100
Benjamin Mill, Ensign, District 15	13 Apr 1810	p. 100
Samuel Torrence, Lieutenant, District 158	13 Apr 1810	p. 101
Josiah Powell, Lieutenant, District 204	13 Apr 1810	p. 101
John Myham, Lieutenant, District 279	13 Apr 1810	p. 102
Jeremiah Davis, Ensign, District 279	13 Apr 1810	p. 102
Silas Dawns, Lieutenant, District 299	13 Apr 1810	p. 103
William Barron, Ensign, District 299	13 Apr 1810	p. 103

Commissions Book 1809–1812

Name, Rank, Unit	*Date*	*Page*
Martin Goza, Lieutenant, District 99	14 Apr 1810	p. 104
Benjamin Stephens, Ensign, District 99	14 Apr 1810	p. 104
Benjm. Hollingsworth, Lieutenant Colonel, Regiment 23	16 Apr 1810	p. 105
Joseph Dickenson, Lieutenant	16 Apr 1810	p. 105
William Wofford Jr., Ensign	16 Apr 1810	p. 106
Simmons Butts, Lieutenant, District 101	17 Apr 1810	p. 106
John Hanson, Major, Battalion 52	17 Apr 1810	p. 107
Joel Flannigan, Ensign, District 276	17 Apr 1810	p. 107
Joseph McBride, Lieutenant, District 137	17 Apr 1810	p. 108
Thomas Stubbs, Lieutenant	17 Apr 1810	p. 108
Alixander Armstrong, Ensign	17 Apr 1810	p. 109
Henry Trippe, Lieutenant, District 102	17 Apr 1810	p. 109
Arnold Kelly, Captain, District 112	18 Apr 1810	p. 110
Joseph Henderson Jr., Major, Battalion 37	18 Apr 1810	p. 110
John H. Butts, Lieutenant, District 307	18 Apr 1810	p. 111
Samuel Barnett, Captain, District 257	23 Apr 1810	p. 111
James Collins, Captain, District 252	23 Apr 1810	p. 112
James Barton, Captain, District 124	23 Apr 1810	p. 112
Isaac Lou, Lieutenant, District 124	23 Apr 1810	p. 113
Smith Jones, Ensign, District 124	23 Apr 1810	p. 113
Reuben Hill, Captain, District 241	23 Apr 1810	p. 114
William Grant, Captain, District 176	23 Apr 1810	p. 114
John McGinty, Lieutenant, District 105	24 Apr 1810	p. 115
John S. Thomas, Ensign, District 105	24 Apr 1810	p. 115
James Bullock, Captain, District 205	27 Apr 1810	p. 116
Pleasant Vinson, Lieutenant, District 205	27 Apr 1810	p. 116
James Atcheson, Ensign, District 205	27 Apr 1810	p. 117
William Sweatt, Lieutenant, District 46	27 Apr 1810	p. 117
Charles Evans, Lieutenant, District 300	27 Apr 1810	p. 118
Joseph J. Moore, Major, Battalion 45	30 Apr 1810	p. 118
Andrew Ronaldson, Ensign, District 71	30 Apr 1810	p. 119
James Shelton, Ensign, District 269	30 Apr 1810	p. 119
Lindsey Thornton, Lieutenant, District 298	30 Apr 1810	p. 120
Abraham Hunter, Captain, District 35	7 May 1810	p. 120
William Kennon, Captain, Volunteer Company of Artillery, Regiment 11	8 May 1810	p. 121

Georgia Military Commissions, 1798–1818

Name, Rank, Unit	Date	Page
Archibald Hagie, Cornet, Volunteer Troop of Dragoons, Squadron 3, Regiment 2	8 May 1810	p. 121
Moses Herbert, Captain, District 4	8 May 1810	p. 122
Jonathan Battelle, Lieutenant, District 4	8 May 1810	p. 122
David Storrer, Ensign, District 4	8 May 1810	p. 123
Ignatius A. Few, Captain, District 135	8 May 1810	p. 123
Robert Rozier, Lieutenant, District 135	8 May 1810	p. 124
David Tool, Captain, District 321	8 May 1810	p. 124
Thomas E. Beall, Lieutenant, District 129	8 May 1810	p. 125
Cornelius Collins, Ensign, District 129	8 May 1810	p. 125
Reuben Easton Davis, Lieutenant, District 167	8 May 1810	p. 126
Thomas L. Malone, Lieutenant, District 3	8 May 1810	p. 126
William Rymes, Ensign, District 142	8 May 1810	p. 127
Stephen Arnold Jr., Lieutenant, District 231	8 May 1810	p. 127
Joseph H. Howard, Captain, Volunteer Company of Infantry (styled the Baldwin Independent Blues), Battalion 70	11 May 1810	p. 128
Thomas Doles, Lieutenant, Volunteer Company of Infantry (styled the Baldwin Independent Blues), Battalion 70	11 May 1810	p. 128
John T. Patterson, Ensign, Volunteer Company of Infantry (styled the Baldwin Independent Blues), Battalion 70	11 May 1810	p. 129
William H. Norman, Major, Battalion 40	14 May 1810	p. 129
James Wilson, Lieutenant, District 318	16 May 1810	p. 130
Brittain Price, Lieutenant, District 38	16 May 1810	p. 130
Isaac Dillard, Ensign, District 65	16 May 1810	p. 131
Jeremiah Lewis, Captain, District 65	16 May 1810	p. 131
John Marsh, Captain, District 70	16 May 1810	p. 132
John Seager, Lieutenant, District 70	16 May 1810	p. 132
Littleberry Allen, Ensign, District 109	16 May 1810	p. 133
Jordan Welcher, Captain, District 151	16 May 1810	p. 133
Gideon Allen, Lieutenant, District 151	16 May 1810	p. 134
Obadiah Flurnoy, Lieutenant, District 175	16 May 1810	p. 134
John Townson, Captain, District 234	16 May 1810	p. 135
Yelvinston Thaxton, Lieutenant, District 234	16 May 1810	p. 135
John Ellis, Ensign, District 234	16 May 1810	p. 136
Thomas Pugh, Captain, District 316	16 May 1810	p. 136

Name, Rank, Unit	*Date*	*Page*
Thomas Y. Gill, Lieutenant, District 316	16 May 1810	p. 137
Caleb Russell, Ensign, District 316	16 May 1810	p. 137
John H. Shaw, Lieutenant, District 286	16 May 1810	p. 138
Robert Pearman, Lieutenant, District 287	16 May 1810	p. 138
William Kelly, Ensign, District 287	16 May 1810	p. 139
Isaac Ross, Lieutenant, District 73	20 Nov 1809	p. 139
David Simpson, Lieutenant, Volunteer Troop of Dragoons, Squadron 7, Regiment 4	16 May 1810	p. 140
Richard Thomas, Cornet, Volunteer Troop of Dragoons, Squadron 7, Regiment 4	16 May 1810	p. 140
Martin Hays, Captain, District 328	17 May 1810	p. 141
Allen Ethredge, Lieutenant, District 328	17 May 1810	p. 141
Paschal Woodward, Ensign, District 318	18 May 1810	p. 142
Naughflight Howard, Ensign, District 136	18 May 1810	p. 142
Jacob Gumm, Major, Battalion 70	22 May 1810	p. 143
John Kidd, Captain, District 233	22 May 1810	p. 143
Thomas Gasaway, Ensign, District 267	22 May 1810	p. 144
Edward Major, Captain, District 119	22 May 1810	p. 144
John Skinner, Ensign, District 119	22 May 1810	p. 145
William Stafford, Captain, District 28	22 May 1810	p. 145
Thomas Moore Berrien, Captain, Volunteer Company of Infantry (styled the Homespun Foresters), Battalion 19	24 May 1810	p. 146
James Jackson, Lieutenant, Volunteer Company of Infantry (styled the Homespun Foresters), Battalion 19	24 May 1810	p. 146
Archibald Campbell, Ensign, Volunteer Company of Infantry (styled the Homespun Foresters), Battalion 19	24 May 1810	p. 147
Charles Houghton, Lieutenant, District 140	24 May 1810	p. 147
William Scott, Ensign, District 140	24 May 1810	p. 148
Richard M. Gilbert, Captain, District 277	28 May 1810	p. 148
William Hunt, Lieutenant, District 277	28 May 1810	p. 149
James Frederick, Ensign, District 277	28 May 1810	p. 149
Charles E. Haynes, Captain, District 221	28 May 1810	p. 150
Edward Bond, Lieutenant, District 221	28 May 1810	p. 150
Reubin Varner, Ensign, District 221	28 May 1810	p. 151
Philip Orr, Captain, District 166	28 May 1810	p. 151
James Josey, Lieutenant, District 166	28 May 1810	p. 152
Simeon Peteet, Ensign, District 166	28 May 1810	p. 152

Georgia Military Commissions, 1798–1818

Name, Rank, Unit	Date	Page
Isaiah T. Irwin, Captain, District 171	28 May 1810	p. 153
Micajah Bennett, Lieutenant, District 171	28 May 1810	p. 153
Daniel Coleman, Captain, District 174	28 May 1810	p. 154
Ambrose Brewer, Ensign, District 174	28 May 1810	p. 154
Roger L. Gamble, Captain, District 77	28 May 1810	p. 155
John P. Henry, Lieutenant, District 273	28 May 1810	p. 155
Jonathan Kettelle, Ensign, District 134	28 May 1810	p. 156
Jonathan Wood Jr., Ensign, District 125	28 May 1810	p. 156
Nicholas Pope, Captain, Volunteer Troop of Dragoons, Squadron 3, Regiment 2	28 May 1810	p. 157
Charles Laburan, First Lieutenant, Volunteer Troop of Dragoons, Squadron 3, Regiment 2	28 Mar 1810	p. 157
Roger Lawson, Captain, District 324	29 May 1810	p. 158
Davinport Lawson, Lieutenant, District 324	29 May 1810	p. 158
Robert Parrott, Ensign, District 324	29 May 1810	p. 159
Chester Pierce, Ensign, Volunteer Company of Infantry (styled the Milledgeville Guards), Battalion 71	31 May 1810	p. 159
Lee Blacksell, Major, Battalion 5	4 Jun 1810	p. 160
Benjamin Penn, Ensign, District 197	4 Jun 1810	p. 160
Reuben Wade, Captain, District 226	4 Jun 1810	p. 161
Thomas M. Bush, Captain, District 160	4 Jun 1810	p. 161
John Bledsoe, Lieutenant, District 229	4 Jun 1810	p. 162
Charles Dunston, Lieutenant, District 252	4 Jun 1810	p. 162
John Winters, Captain, District 255	4 Jun 1810	p. 163
Sampson Brown, Ensign, District 310	4 Jun 1810	p. 163
Joshua Ryle, Lieutenant, Volunteer Company of Riflemen, Battalion 69	4 Jun 1810	p. 164
James Smith, Ensign, Volunteer Company of Riflemen, Battalion 69	4 Jun 1810	p. 164
Siles Blalock, Captain, Volunteer Company of Riflemen, Battalion 54	11 May 1810	p. 165
Henry Justice, Lieutenant, Volunteer Company of Riflemen, Battalion 54	11 Jun 1810	p. 165
William Hodge, Ensign, Volunteer Company of Riflemen, Battalion 54	11 Jun 1810	p. 166
Jeremiah Bennett, Captain, District 99	15 Jun 1810	p. 166
Benjamin Stephens, Ensign, District 99	15 Jun 1810	p. 167
George H. Pattillo, Lieutenant, District 163	15 Jun 1810	p. 167

Name, Rank, Unit	Date	Page
Thomas Velvan, Ensign, District 163	15 Jun 1810	p. 168
William Johnston, Lieutenant, District 236	15 Jun 1810	p. 168
Ezekiel Brown, Ensign, District 236	15 Jun 1810	p. 169
William Bailey, Lieutenant, District 169	15 Jun 1810	p. 169
James Fleming, Ensign, District 138	15 Jun 1810	p. 170
Norris Lyon, Captain, Volunteer Troop of Dragoons, Squadron 6, Regiment 3	15 Jun 1810	p. 170
John Birdsong, First Lieutenant, Volunteer Troop of Dragoons, Squadron 6, Regiment 3	15 Jun 1810	p. 171
Robert Bailey, Second Lieutenant, Volunteer Troop of Dragoons, Squadron 6, Regiment 3	15 Jun 1810	p. 171
John S. Porter, Captain, Volunteer Company of Riflemen, Battalion 67	15 Jun 1810	p. 172
William Griffin, Captain	18 Jun 1810	p. 172
John W. McCall, Lieutenant	18 Jun 1810	p. 173
Nathaniel Hudson, Ensign	18 Jun 1810	p. 173
Joseph Griffin, Lieutenant, District 189	18 Jun 1810	p. 174
Elijah Cain, Lieutenant, District 110	18 Jun 1810	p. 174
John Hudwell, Ensign, District 135	18 Jun 1810	p. 175
John McGinty, Captain, District 105	18 Jun 1810	p. 175
John H. Broadnax, Captain, District 314	18 Jun 1810	p. 176
James R. Wyley, Major, Battalion 58	20 Jun 1810	p. 176
Jameson Mabry, Captain, District 177	20 Jun 1810	p. 177
Nicholas DeLaigle, Second Lieutenant, Volunteer Troop of Dragoons, Squadron 3, Regiment 2	25 Jun 1810	p. 177
Beverly Turpin, Cornet, Volunteer Troop of Dragoons, Squadron 3, Regiment 2	25 Jun 1810	p. 178
Samuel S. Steel, First Lieutenant, Volunteer Troop of Dragoons, Squadron 5, Regiment 3	25 Jun 1810	p. 178
Lovett B. Smith, Captain, District 326	25 Jun 1810	p. 179
Robert Sherrard, Lieutenant, District 326	25 Jun 1810	p. 179
John Smith, Ensign, District 326	25 Jun 1810	p. 180
James Spann, Ensign, District 325	25 Jun 1810	p. 180
Francis Lefiles, Ensign, District 9	29 Jun 1810	p. 181
Daniel Humphress, Ensign, District 74	29 Jun 1810	p. 181
Caleb Parker, Lieutenant, District 80	29 Jun 1810	p. 182
Reubin Scott, Ensign, District 179	29 Jun 1810	p. 182
Robert Harrison, Ensign, District 214	29 Jun 1810	p. 183

Georgia Military Commissions, 1798–1818

Name, Rank, Unit	*Date*	*Page*
John Torrence, Lieutenant, District 257	29 Jun 1810	p. 183
William Hollis, Ensign, District 257	29 Jun 1810	p. 184
John Chaffin, Lieutenant, District 290	29 Jun 1810	p. 184
Benjamin H. Willson, Ensign, District 290	29 Jun 1810	p. 185
Robert Middlebrooks, Ensign, District 301	29 Jun 1810	p. 185
William Gilbert, Captain, District 87	30 Jun 1810	p. 186
Wingfield Wright, Captain, District 89	30 Jun 1810	p. 186
Thomas Dawson, Captain, District 143	30 Jun 1810	p. 187
James Howard, Major, Battalion 22	5 Jul 1810	p. 187
Needham McClendon, Lieutenant, District 52	5 Jul 1810	p. 188
Edwin Harris, Lieutenant, District 73	5 Jul 1810	p. 188
John Hines Jr., Ensign, District 73	5 Jul 1810	p. 189
Jesse Pervis Jr., Ensign, District 81	5 Jul 1810	p. 189
Goode Hall, Lieutenant, District 321	5 Jul 1810	p. 190
Basdil Millen, Ensign, District 321	5 Jul 1810	p. 190
Joseph Sill, Captain, District 333	5 Jul 1810	p. 191
David Clark, Lieutenant	5 Jul 1810	p. 191
Thomas Barton Harden, Lieutenant, District 7	17 Jul 1810	p. 192
Francis Hopkins, Lieutenant, District 21	17 Jul 1810	p. 192
William Sams, Ensign, District 21	17 Jul 1810	p. 193
Edward Jourdan, Lieutenant, District 164	17 Jul 1810	p. 193
James Wright, Lieutenant, District 274	17 Jun 1810	p. 194
Thomas Lamar, Lieutenant, District 305	17 Jul 1810	p. 194
Lary Lary, Ensign, District 305	17 Jul 1810	p. 195
William Huckeby, Captain, District 299	17 Jul 1810	p. 195
Benjamin Babb, Ensign, District 306	17 Jul 1810	p. 196
John S. Thomas, Lieutenant, District 105	17 Jul 1810	p. 196
Daniel Stewart, Cavalry	6 Mar 1809	p. 197
Garah Davis, Ensign, Volunteer Company of Riflemen, Battalion 29	17 Jul 1810	p. 198
Wilson Collins, Ensign	17 Jul 1810	p. 198
Vines Harwell, First Lieutenant, Volunteer Troop of Dragoons, Squadron 4, Regiment 3	17 Jul 1810	p. 199
William Hall, Major, Battalion 79	20 Jul 1810	p. 199
William Kelly, Lieutenant	20 Jul 1810	p. 200
William Smith, Ensign	20 Jul 1810	p. 200
Benjamin Faircloth, Lieutenant	20 Jul 1810	p. 201

Name, Rank, Unit	Date	Page
Isaac Dennard, Lieutenant, District 325	20 Jul 1810	p. 201
Whereat Lewis, Captain	20 Jul 1810	p. 202
Jehabud Scarborough, Lieutenant, District 330	20 Jul 1810	p. 202
Exum Webb, Ensign, District 330	20 Jul 1810	p. 203
Benjamine Keeton, Captain	20 Jul 1810	p. 203
James Taylor, Lieutenant	20 Jul 1810	p. 204
John Ard, Ensign	20 Jul 1810	p. 204
Gabriel Gunn, Captain, District 292	20 Jul 1810	p. 205
Lemuel Wilson, Lieutenant, District 292	20 Jul 1810	p. 205
Jesse Townsend, Ensign, District 292	20 Jul 1810	p. 206
John Campton, First Lieutenant, Volunteer Troop of Dragoons, Squadron 5, Regiment 3	20 Jul 1810	p. 206
Fields Wilson, Cornet, Volunteer Troop of Dragoons, Squadron 5, Regiment 3	20 Jul 1810	p. 207
John Willis, Captain	21 Jul 1810	p. 207
Elisha Hubbard, Lieutenant	21 Jul 1810	p. 208
Michael Muckelroy, Ensign	21 Jul 1810	p. 208
Whitmill Hill, Lieutenant, District 293	27 Jul 1810	p. 209
James Hall, Ensign, District 293	27 Jul 1810	p. 209
Robert Owens, Captain	27 Jul 1810	p. 210
John McMichael, Lieutenant	27 Jul 1810	p. 210
Jesse Hays, Ensign	27 Jul 1810	p. 211
Samuel Chambles, Captain, District 154	31 Jul 1810	p. 211
Richard Flowers, Lieutenant, District 154	31 Jul 1810	p. 212
John McDaniel, Ensign, District 154	31 Jul 1810	p. 212
William H. Durkee, Captain, District 5	31 Jul 1810	p. 213
James Speer, Lieutenant, District 10	31 Jul 1810	p. 213
Jesse Harris, Ensign, District 10	31 Jul 1810	p. 214
John C. Cramer, Ensign, District 11	31 Jul 1810	p. 214
Robert Mathews, Ensign, District 117	31 Jul 1810	p. 215
Jacob Metzger, Captain, District 12	31 Jul 1810	p. 215
Benjamine Gnenn, Ensign, District 12	31 Jul 1810	p. 216
Jacob Reed, Ensign, District 13	31 Jul 1810	p. 216
David Nichols, Lieutenant, District 63	31 Jul 1810	p. 217
Jesse Carpenter, Ensign, District 63	31 Jul 1810	p. 217
John Bryant, Ensign, District 118	31 Jul 1810	p. 218
Henry Hawsey, Lieutenant, District 255	31 Jul 1810	p. 218

Georgia Military Commissions, 1798–1818

Name, Rank, Unit	Date	Page
John Bennett, Ensign, District 255	30 Jul 1810	p. 219
John Durham, Captain, District 225	31 Jul 1810	p. 219
Jonathan Knights, Captain	31 Jul 1810	p. 220
Abraham Knights, Ensign	31 Jul 1810	p. 220
William Ford, Captain, Volunteer Company of Riflemen, Battalion 45	31 Jul 1810	p. 221
Henry L. Edwards, Ensign, Volunteer Company of Riflemen, Battalion 45	31 Jul 1810	p. 221
William Ashton, Lieutenant, District 142	7 Aug 1810	p. 222
R. M. Williamson Jr., Captain, District 37	7 Aug 1810	p. 222
R. M. Williamson Sr., Lieutenant, District 37	7 Aug 1810	p. 223
James Rush, Ensign, District 102	7 Aug 1810	p. 223
Samuel Moore, Ensign, District 160	7 Aug 1810	p. 224
John C. Smith, Captain, District 242	7 Aug 1810	p. 224
Solmon Chandler, Lieutenant, District 242	7 Aug 1810	p. 225
John Finch, Ensign, District 242	7 Aug 1810	p. 225
Brinkley Boice, Lieutenant, District 281	7 Aug 1810	p. 226
William Mainor, Ensign, District 281	7 Aug 1810	p. 226
James Pugh, Ensign, District 329	7 Aug 1810	p. 227
Charles Mathews, Lieutenant, District 77	9 Aug 1810	p. 227
Siloe Arrington, Ensign, District 77	9 Aug 1810	p. 228
William S. Shearley, Ensign, District 84	9 Aug 1810	p. 228
Augustus Kennedy, Lieutenant, District 119	9 Aug 1810	p. 229
Ralph Kilgore, Lieutenant, District 187	9 Aug 1810	p. 229
David Frazor, Ensign, District 187	9 Aug 1810	p. 230
Ashley Wood, Captain	9 Aug 1810	p. 230
Daniel Pines, Lieutenant	9 Aug 1810	p. 231
Thomas Underwood, Ensign	9 Aug 1810	p. 231
Thomas Long, Lieutenant, District 203	14 Aug 1810	p. 232
Stephen Coleman, Lieutenant, District 174	15 Aug 1810	p. 232
William Bryan, Ensign, District 180	15 Aug 1810	p. 233
Augustin Cooper, Ensign, District 175	15 Aug 1810	p. 233
James Sharp, Lieutenant, District 278	15 Aug 1810	p. 234
Elias Crockett, Captain, District 278	15 Aug 1810	p. 234
Francis Foster, Ensign, District 278	15 Aug 1810	p. 235
Robert Moore, Captain, District 74	15 Aug 1810	p. 235
Job Herrington, Lieutenant, District 260	15 Aug 1810	p. 236

Name, Rank, Unit	Date	Page
William Hand, Ensign, District 260	15 Aug 1810	p. 236
William Anderson, Cornet, Volunteer Troop of Dragoons, Squadron 1, Regiment 1	15 Aug 1810	p. 237
Benjamin Hawthorn, Captain, Volunteer Company of Riflemen, Battalion 53	15 Aug 1810	p. 237
George D. Lester, Lieutenant, Volunteer Company of Riflemen, Battalion 53	15 Aug 1810	p. 238
Shelton Magruder, Ensign, Volunteer Company of Riflemen, Battalion 53	15 Aug 1810	p. 238
George A. Gordon, Lieutenant, District 226	16 Aug 1810	p. 239
David White, Lieutenant Colonel Commandant, Regiment 30	23 Aug 1810	p. 239
John Stroud, Captain, District 249	23 Aug 1810	p. 240
Evan Lewis, Lieutenant, District 60	23 Aug 1810	p. 240
Arthur Bowers, Ensign, District 60	23 Aug 1810	p. 241
Wilie Sutten, Lieutenant, District 83	23 Aug 1810	p. 241
Lewis Howell, Ensign, District 83	23 Aug 1810	p. 242
James Logan, Lieutenant, District 50	23 Aug 1810	p. 242
Thomas G. Leigh, Ensign, District 133	23 Aug 1810	p. 243
James D. Cole, Captain, Volunteer Troop of Dragoons, Squadron 6, Regiment 3	23 Aug 1810	p. 243
George W. Moore, First Lieutenant, Volunteer Troop of Dragoons, Squadron 6, Regiment 3	23 Aug 1810	p. 244
William Beel, Second Lieutenant, Volunteer Troop of Dragoons, Squadron 6, Regiment 3	23 Aug 1810	p. 244
Thomas Moore, Cornet, Volunteer Troop of Dragoons, Squadron 6, Regiment 3	23 Aug 1810	p. 245
Edmond Corley, Lieutenant, Volunteer Company of Riflemen, Battalion 67	23 Aug 1810	p. 245
Eli Bryant, Major, Battalion 57	27 Aug 1810	p. 246
Amos Ponder, Captain, District 219	27 Aug 1810	p. 246
John L. Ponder, Lieutenant, District 219	27 Aug 1810	p. 247
Benjamine Pleister, Lieutenant, District 210	27 Aug 1810	p. 247
Delona Williamson, Lieutenant, District 209	27 Aug 1810	p. 248
Christian Allbright, Ensign, District 207	27 Aug 1810	p. 248
Thomas Pulliam, Ensign, District 206	27 Aug 1810	p. 249
Samuel Trippe, Second Lieutenant, Volunteer Troop of Dragoons, Squadron 4, Regiment 2	27 Aug 1810	p. 249
William Morgan, Captain	3 Sep 1810	p. 250

Name, Rank, Unit	*Date*	*Page*
James Jones, Lieutenant	3 Sep 1810	p. 250
Hezekiah D. D. L. Williams, Ensign	3 Sep 1810	p. 251
Levin Greer, Lieutenant, District 98	4 Sep 1810	p. 251
Marshall Smith, Captain	7 Sep 1810	p. 252
Jonathan Benton, Lieutenant	7 Sep 1810	p. 252
Jesse Benton, Ensign	7 Sep 1810	p. 253
James S. Tyson, Ensign, District 320	7 Sep 1810	p. 253
Wyatt Brown, Captain	7 Sep 1810	p. 254
Richard Schockly, Lieutenant	7 Sep 1810	p. 254
Squire Markum, Ensign	7 Sep 1810	p. 255
William Glascock, Lieutenant, District 123	7 Sep 1810	p. 255
Robert Watkins, Ensign, District 123	7 Sep 1810	p. 256
Jeremiah Dobbs, Lieutenant, District 312	7 Sep 1810	p. 256
Blassingham Paulett, Lieutenant, District 61	7 Sep 1810	p. 257
Golphin Harvey, Ensign, District 61	7 Sep 1810	p. 257
Thomas Gordon, Captain	10 Sep 1810	p. 258
Daniel D. Mobley, Lieutenant	10 Sep 1810	p. 258
John Moore, Ensign, District 105	10 Sep 1810	p. 259
Ezekiel Wimberly, Major, Battalion 80	12 Sep 1810	p. 259
Ebenezer Torrence, Lieutenant, District 143	12 Sep 1810	p. 260
William Lea, Captain	13 Sep 1810	p. 260
John Gillion, Lieutenant	13 Sep 1810	p. 261
Meredith Landrum, Ensign	13 Sep 1810	p. 261
Littleberry Clanton, Lieutenant, District 125	13 Sep 1810	p. 262
Arthur Foster, Ensign, District 125	13 Sep 1810	p. 262
Charles Howard, Lieutenant, District 91	13 Sep 1810	p. 263
Etheldread Faircloth, Ensign, District 80	13 Sep 1810	p. 263
Asa Allen, Lieutenant Colonel, Regiment 27	17 Sep 1810	p. 264
Royal Bryant Bryant, Captain, District 206	17 Sep 1810	p. 264
William B. Bryant, Lieutenant, District 206	17 Sep 1810	p. 265
Newdy G. Connel, Captain, District 107	17 Sep 1810	p. 265
Selby Vinson, Lieutenant, District 107	17 Sep 1810	p. 266
Edmond Gilbert, Ensign, District 107	17 Sep 1810	p. 266
Joseph Cleaveland, Ensign, District 208	17 Sep 1810	p. 267
William Starling, Lieutenant, District 235	17 Sep 1810	p. 267
James Davis, Captain, Volunteer Company of Riflemen, Battalion 66	20 Sep 1810	p. 268

Commissions Book 1809–1812

Name, Rank, Unit	Date	Page
William Gammonon, Lieutenant, Volunteer Company of Riflemen, Battalion 66	20 Sep 1810	p. 268
Henry Tompson, Ensign, Volunteer Company of Riflemen, Battalion 66	20 Sep 1810	p. 269
Gideon Mayo, Lieutenant	20 Sep 1810	p. 269
Jesse Baker, Ensign, District 113	20 Sep 1810	p. 270
Jesse Gilbert, Lieutenant, District 332	24 Sep 1810	p. 270
John Domminy, Ensign, District 332	24 Sep 1810	p. 271
John Johnson, Lieutenant, District 43	28 Sep 1810	p. 271
Daniel Johnson, Ensign, District 43	28 Sep 1810	p. 272
William Stevens, Ensign, District 57	28 Sep 1810	p. 272
John Gray, Captain, District 67	28 Sep 1810	p. 273
William Hamilton, Captain, District 86	28 Sep 1810	p. 273
James Blanchart, Captain, District 126	28 Sep 1810	p. 274
Edmond Raimey, Ensign, District 217	28 Sep 1810	p. 274
Joel Flanagin, Lieutenant, District 276	28 Sep 1810	p. 275
Tandy W. King, Captain	28 Sep 1810	p. 275
Thomas White, Captain	28 Sep 1810	p. 276
John Long, Lieutenant	28 Sep 1810	p. 276
John Sanders, Ensign	28 Sep 1810	p. 277
William Reid, Captain	28 Sep 1810	p. 277
Levy Martin, Lieutenant	28 Sep 1810	p. 278
William Woodley, Ensign	28 Sep 1810	p. 278
Gethro B. Spivey, Major, Battalion 81	5 Oct 1810	p. 279
Stephen Canady, Lieutenant, District 19	5 Oct 1810	p. 279
Robert Lester, Lieutenant, District 238	5 Oct 1810	p. 280
Turner Hamner Jr., Ensign, District 238	5 Oct 1810	p. 280
Cyrus Billingsby, Captain, District 285	5 Oct 1810	p. 281
James Runnells, Ensign	5 Oct 1810	p. 281
William Cauly, Major, Battalion 73	8 Oct 1810	p. 282
Jesse Janson, Ensign	10 Oct 1810	p. 282
Thomas P. Hamilton, Major, Battalion 64	10 Oct 1810	p. 283
John M. Dooly, Lieutenant Colonel Commandant, Regiment 20	15 Oct 1810	p. 283
Isaac Furman, Captain, District 186	15 Oct 1810	p. 284
Jeremiah Tompson, Lieutenant, District 186	15 Oct 1810	p. 284
James Kinney, Ensign, District 186	15 Oct 1810	p. 285

Georgia Military Commissions, 1798–1818

Name, Rank, Unit	Date	Page
David Carter, Captain, District 39	15 Oct 1810	p. 285
John Strikeland, Lieutenant, District 39	15 Oct 1810	p. 286
William Todd, Lieutenant, District 18	15 Oct 1810	p. 286
James Moody, Ensign, District 18	15 Oct 1810	p. 287
Jesse Wilks, Lieutenant, Volunteer Company of Riflemen, Battalion 45	15 Oct 1810	p. 287
William Ward, Captain, District 213	15 Oct 1810	p. 288
Jeremiah Ray, Lieutenant, District 303	15 Oct 1810	p. 288
John H. Triplett, Ensign, District 303	15 Oct 1810	p. 289
Jacob Furgerson, First Lieutenant, Volunteer Troop of Dragoons, Squadron 5, Regiment 3	15 Oct 1810	p. 289
James K. Garrett, Second Lieutenant, Volunteer Troop of Dragoons, Squadron 5, Regiment 3	15 Oct 1810	p. 290
James Robertson, Cornet, Volunteer Troop of Dragoons, Squadron 5, Regiment 3	15 Oct 1810	p. 290
John Arnold, Major, Battalion 76	26 Oct 1810	p. 291
John Gallman, Captain, District 317	26 Oct 1810	p. 291
Lewellin Spain, Lieutenant, District 75	26 Oct 1810	p. 292
John Webb, Ensign, District 202	26 Oct 1810	p. 292
William Bagby, Ensign, District 304	26 Oct 1810	p. 293
Angus McCurry, Captain, District 198	26 Oct 1810	p. 293
Clement Dollar, Lieutenant, District 198	26 Oct 1810	p. 294
William Tyler, Ensign, District 198	26 Oct 1810	p. 294
William Mitchell, Ensign, District 219	26 Nov 1810	p. 295
White Rossiter, Captain, District 239	30 Oct 1810	p. 295
Charles S. Lloyd, Lieutenant, District 239	30 Oct 1810	p. 296
William W. Brinton, Ensign, District 239	30 Oct 1810	p. 296
Dudley Jones, Major, Battalion 46	9 Nov 1810	p. 297
Hardy Scarborough, Major, Battalion 9	9 Nov 1810	p. 297
Alixander Hall, Major, Battalion 35	9 Nov 1810	p. 298
Job Tison, Captain, District 27	9 Nov 1810	p. 298
Samuel Akins, Lieutenant, District 27	9 Nov 1810	p. 299
Zackarius Timmons, Ensign, District 27	9 Nov 1810	p. 299
Josiah Sikes, Captain	9 Nov 1810	p. 300
Arthur Sikes, Lieutenant	9 Nov 1810	p. 300
William Sapp, Ensign	9 Nov 1810	p. 301
John P. Blackmon, Captain, District 42	9 Nov 1810	p. 301

Name, Rank, Unit	Date	Page
Stephen W. Blunt, Captain, District 60	9 Nov 1810	p. 302
Leonard Sims, Captain, District 185	9 Nov 1810	p. 302
Shimee Mann, Captain, District 231	9 Nov 1810	p. 303
Jesse F. Heard, Lieutenant, District 165	9 Nov 1810	p. 303
Seth Batson, Lieutenant, District 304	9 Nov 1810	p. 304
George Dilworth, Ensign, District 33	9 Nov 1810	p. 304
John Jones, Ensign, District 165	9 Nov 1810	p. 305
Michael Gill, Ensign, District 220	9 Nov 1810	p. 305
Able Usher, Ensign, District 259	9 Nov 1810	p. 306
Joel Slaughter, Captain	10 Nov 1810	p. 306
William Hickey, Lieutenant	10 Nov 1810	p. 307
William Bailey, Ensign	10 Nov 1810	p. 307
Needham Parker, Captain	10 Nov 1810	p. 308
William Evans, Lieutenant	10 Nov 1810	p. 308
Sampson Harvill, Ensign	10 Nov 1810	p. 309
William Byne, Brigadier General, Brigade 2, Division 1	12 Nov 1810	p. 309
Valentine Walker, Brigadier General, Brigade 1, Division 2	12 Nov 1810	p. 310
Eppis Brown, Brigadier General, Brigade 2, Division 2	12 Nov 1810	p. 310
Frederick Beall, Brigadier General, Brigade 2, Division 4	12 Nov 1810	p. 311
Jesse Gilbert, Captain, District 332	13 Nov 1810	p. 311
Joel Butler, Lieutenant, District 332	13 Nov 1810	p. 312
Elijah Watson, Ensign, District 89	13 Nov 1810	p. 312
Thomas Gilbert, Captain	13 Nov 1810	p. 313
Isaac Childs, Lieutenant	13 Nov 1810	p. 313
James Ard, Ensign	13 Nov 1810	p. 314
John T. Reeves, Cornet, Squadron 4, Regiment 2	16 Nov 1810	p. 314
Moses A. Roberts, Captain, District 320	26 Nov 1810	p. 315
Lewis Brantly, Captain, District 283	26 Nov 1810	p. 315
William Lemans, Ensign, District 283	26 Nov 1810	p. 316
William Coleman, Ensign, District 276	26 Nov 1810	p. 316
Johnson Wellborn, Lieutenant Colonel Commandant, Regiment 4	27 Nov 1810	p. 317
Martin Kobb, Captain, District 300	4 Dec 1810	p. 317
Edmond Wheelis, Lieutenant, District 300	4 Dec 1810	p. 318
Ezekiel Perkins, Lieutenant, District 145	4 Dec 1810	p. 318
Guilford Floyd, Ensign, District 145	4 Dec 1810	p. 319

Georgia Military Commissions, 1798–1818

Name, Rank, Unit	Date	Page
John Darnell, Ensign, District 321	4 Dec 1810	p. 319
Bleakley Edens, Lieutenant	7 Dec 1810	p. 320
Evan Thomas, Ensign	7 Dec 1810	p. 320
Thomas Stewart, Captain, District 36	8 Dec 1810	p. 321
Peter Donalson, Lieutenant, District 122	10 Dec 1810	p. 321
David Horseman, Ensign, District 65	10 Dec 1810	p. 322
Thomas Barnes, Captain, District 167	10 Dec 1810	p. 322
Churchwell Gibson, Captain, District 155	10 Dec 1810	p. 323
Alixander Williamson, Captain, District 263	10 Dec 1810	p. 323
Horrell Mangum, Ensign, District 264	10 Dec 1810	p. 324
Seth Strange, Captain, District 264	10 Dec 1810	p. 324
Ignatius Pursell, Captain, District 267	10 Dec 1810	p. 325
Jeptha Holcombe, Lieutenant, District 267	10 Dec 1810	p. 325
Thomas Townsend, Ensign, District 267	10 Dec 1810	p. 326
Gilbert Longstreet, Lieutenant, Volunteer Company of Rangers, Regiment 10	10 Dec 1810	p. 326
Augustine Slaughter, Ensign, Volunteer Company of Rangers, Regiment 10	10 Dec 1810	p. 327
Samuel Woods, Ensign, District 141	10 Dec 1810	p. 327
John Miles, Captain, District 275	10 Dec 1810	p. 328
Charles Beach, Lieutenant, Augusta Independent Blues, Regiment 10	12 Dec 1810	p. 328
William Godfry, Captain, District 44	12 Dec 1810	p. 329
James Rhodes, Lieutenant, District 204	1 Jan 1811	p. 329
William Caile, Captain, District 80	1 Jan 1811	p. 330
James S. Tison, Lieutenant, District 320	1 Jan 1811	p. 330
Thomas Stewart, Captain, District 232	1 Jan 1811	p. 331
Jonathan Glaze, Lieutenant, District 232	1 Jan 1811	p. 331
William Braint, Ensign, District 232	1 Jan 1811	p. 332
Thomas Mangham, Lieutenant	1 Jan 1811	p. 332
John P. Stewart, Captain	1 Jan 1811	p. 333
Joseph Dickerson, Captain	1 Jan 1811	p. 333
Frederick Freeman, Second Lieutenant, Volunteer Troop of Dragoons, Squadron 5, Regiment 3	11 Jan 1811	p. 334
William Carter, Lieutenant, District 41	14 Jan 1811	p. 334
Ephraim Deloach, Ensign, District 41	14 Jan 1811	p. 335
Henry Fletcher, Lieutenant, District 48	14 Jan 1811	p. 335

Commissions Book 1809–1812

Name, Rank, Unit	*Date*	*Page*
John Grimer, Ensign, District 48	14 Jan 1811	p. 336
John Brantley, Lieutenant, District 102	14 Jan 1811	p. 336
Jesse Griggs, Ensign, District 102	14 Jan 1811	p. 337
Lemuel Swanson, Captain, District 138	14 Jan 1811	p. 337
James Fleming, Lieutenant, District 138	14 Jan 1811	p. 338
Charles M. Heard, Captain, District 178	14 Jan 1811	p. 338
Marcus Mitcham, Lieutenant, District 178	14 Jan 1811	p. 339
William Duke, Ensign, District 105	14 Jan 1811	p. 339
William Arnold, Ensign, District 261	14 Jan 1811	p. 340
William Patrick, Ensign, District 287	14 Jan 1811	p. 340
William Willis, Ensign, Volunteer Company of Riflemen, Battalion 66	14 Jan 1811	p. 341
Lewis Lee, Captain	14 Jan 1811	p. 341
Pascal Hammock, Lieutenant	14 Jan 1811	p. 342
John Smedley, Ensign	14 Jan 1811	p. 342
Reddick Howard, Ensign, District 320	14 Jan 1811	p. 343
Philip Cook, Major, Cavalry, Squadron 5, Regiment 3	28 Jan 1811	p. 343
Morgan Malone, Captain, District 156	24 Jan 1811	p. 344
James Prevatt, Lieutenant	24 Jan 1811	p. 344
Gruf Chieves, Captain, District 163	24 Jan 1811	p. 345
John McKenny, Lieutenant Colonel Commandant, Regiment 10	25 Jan 1811	p. 345
Joseph Boyle Chambers, Lieutenant Colonel, Regiment 14	26 Jan 1811	p. 346
Daniel McRainie, Captain	28 Jan 1811	p. 346
James Smith, Lieutenant	28 Jan 1811	p. 347
John Fletcher, Ensign	28 Jan 1811	p. 347
Thomas Colquitt, Captain, District 109	28 Jan 1811	p. 348
George Nelson, Lieutenant, District 109	28 Jan 1811	p. 348
John Pucket, Ensign, District 109	28 Jan 1811	p. 349
Robert Harvey, Lieutenant, District 8	1 Feb 1811	p. 349
Charles Clark, Lieutenant, District 65	1 Feb 1811	p. 350
Peter Lyon, Ensign, District 65	1 Feb 1811	p. 350
John White, Captain, District 309	1 Feb 1811	p. 351
Garlington Puliam, Lieutenant, District 309	1 Feb 1811	p. 351
Charles Wood, Ensign, District 309	1 Feb 1811	p. 352

Georgia Military Commissions, 1798–1818

Name, Rank, Unit	Date	Page
Michael W. Hughes, Lieutenant, Volunteer Company (styled Republican Blues), Battalion 60	1 Feb 1811	p. 352
John Ash, Ensign, Volunteer Company (styled the Republican Blues), Battalion 60	1 Feb 1811	p. 353
Ezekiel Daniel Jr., Lieutenant, District 89	2 Feb 1811	p. 353
Frederick S. Fell, Ensign, Savannah Volunteer Guards, Battalion 1	9 Feb 1811	p. 354
John Jeter, Lieutenant, District 307	9 Feb 1811	p. 354
John Moore, Ensign	9 Feb 1811	p. 355
Archibald Little, Lieutenant, District 155	9 Feb 1811	p. 355
James Wilder, Ensign, District 155	9 Feb 1811	p. 356
Benjamine Hill, Captain, District 280	9 Feb 1811	p. 356
William Jones, Lieutenant, District 280	9 Feb 1811	p. 357
George Grimes, Ensign, District 280	9 Feb 1811	p. 357
Richard G. Brown, Captain, District 115	12 Feb 1811	p. 358
Benjamin Hodges, Captain, District 90	12 Feb 1811	p. 358
James C. Watson, Captain, District 318	13 Feb 1811	p. 359
Thomas White, Major, Battalion 66	18 Feb 1811	p. 359
Thomas Watkins, Major, Battalion 27	18 Feb 1811	p. 360
James Boyet, Lieutenant, District 80	18 Feb 1811	p. 360
Reuben Brown, Captain, District 162	18 Feb 1811	p. 361
Lazarus Atkinson, Lieutenant, District 162	18 Feb 1811	p. 361
George King, Captain	18 Feb 1811	p. 362
Alfred Thompson, Ensign	18 Feb 1811	p. 362
Eli Emanuel, Lieutenant Colonel Commandant, Regiment 8	27 Feb 1811	p. 363
Joel Smith, Captain, District 360	27 Feb 1811	p. 363
Charles Evans, Captain, District 301	27 Feb 1811	p. 364
Gideon Hays, Lieutenant, District 59	27 Feb 1811	p. 364
James Chason, Ensign, District 59	27 Feb 1811	p. 365
Joseph Wilson, Lieutenant, District 69	27 Feb 1811	p. 365
Richard M. Stiles, Captain, Volunteer Company of Artillery, Regiment 1	27 Feb 1811	p. 366
James Barton, Captain, District 284	4 Mar 1811	p. 366
William Manor, Lieutenant, District 284	4 Mar 1811	p. 367
James A. Goodwin, Captain, District 288	4 Mar 1811	p. 367
Howell Vaughn, Lieutenant, District 288	4 Mar 1811	p. 368

Name, Rank, Unit	Date	Page
George Price, Ensign, District 288	4 Mar 1811	p. 368
Reubin Rasbury, Lieutenant, District 242	4 Mar 1811	p. 369
George Stovall, Captain, District 210	7 Mar 1811	p. 369
William H. Wafford, Lieutenant, District 371	7 Mar 1811	p. 370
William White, Ensign, District 213	7 Mar 1811	p. 370
Henry Wheeler, Ensign, District 212	7 Mar 1811	p. 371
John F. Myrick, Lieutenant, District 318	7 Mar 1811	p. 371
Larkin Wright, Ensign, District 318	7 Mar 1811	p. 372
James Sanders, Captain, District 67	13 Mar 1811	p. 372
Francis Ross, Lieutenant, District 368	13 Mar 1811	p. 373
Joel Newsome, Captain, District 108	13 Mar 1811	p. 373
William Dooly, Captain, District 200	13 Mar 1811	p. 374
John Cobb, Lieutenant, District 306	13 Mar 1811	p. 374
Samuel Willingham, Captain, District 252	13 Mar 1811	p. 375
Littleberry Harris, Captain, District 106	13 Mar 1811	p. 375
Richard C. Burch, Lieutenant, District 106	13 Mar 1811	p. 376
Green E. Lamb, Ensign, District 106	13 Mar 1811	p. 376
Wade Hampton, Captain, District 32	13 Mar 1811	p. 377
William Daniel, Lieutenant, District 32	13 Mar 1811	p. 377
William Vince, Ensign, District 32	13 Mar 1811	p. 378
Daniel A. Whatley, Captain, District 170	13 Mar 1811	p. 378
Samuel Miller, Lieutenant, District 170	13 Mar 1811	p. 379
Julius Daniel, Ensign, District 170	13 Mar 1811	p. 379
John W. Thomas, Captain, District 219	13 Mar 1811	p. 380
Robert Mitchell, Lieutenant, District 219	13 Mar 1811	p. 380
William Trasher, Lieutenant, District 136	13 Mar 1811	p. 381
James Brown, Ensign, District 136	13 Mar 1811	p. 381
Moses D. White, Lieutenant, District 362	18 Mar 1811	p. 382
Josiah Yarborough, Ensign, District 362	18 Mar 1811	p. 382
Samuel Paschal, Lieutenant, District 177	20 Jun 1810	p. 383
John Shearer, Ensign, District 177	20 Jun 1810	p. 383
Mickerness Goode, Captain, District 99	20 Mar 1811	p. 384
William Connell, Lieutenant, District 107	20 Mar 1811	p. 384
Peter Stovall, Major, District 36	20 Mar 1811	p. 385
John Humphries, Major, Battalion 67	20 Mar 1811	p. 385
William Miles, Ensign, District 115	20 Mar 1811	p. 386a

Georgia Military Commissions, 1798–1818

Name, Rank, Unit	*Date*	*Page*
Benjamin Merritt, Lieutenant, District 140	20 Mar 1811	p. 386a
Payton Pinkard, Lieutenant, District 366	20 Mar 1811	p. 386b
Richard Taliaferro, Lieutenant, District 115	20 Mar 1811	p. 386b
Thomas Llysle, Ensign, District 366	20 Mar 1811	p. 388
Pleasant Towns, Captain, District 286	20 Mar 1811	p. 388
Frederic Johnson, Lieutenant, District 279	20 Mar 1811	p. 389
Richard Mitcham, Ensign, District 286	20 Mar 1811	p. 389
Jordan Morell, Ensign, District 279	20 Mar 1811	p. 390
Samuel Lark, Major, Battalion 75	20 Mar 1811	p. 390
James Jones, Lieutenant, District 190	20 Mar 1811	p. 391
Robert Dixon, Captain, District 114	20 Mar 1811	p. 391
Robert Bowling, Major, Battalion 16	27 Mar 1811	p. 392
Joshua Clark, Major, Battalion 59	27 Mar 1811	p. 392
Blassengame Paulett, Captain, District 61	27 Mar 1811	p. 393
James Patten, Captain, District 255	27 Mar 1811	p. 393
Andrew Boyd, Captain, District 245	27 Mar 1811	p. 394
John Baily, Ensign, District 245	27 Mar 1811	p. 394
Keneth Irvine, Ensign, District 16	27 Mar 1811	p. 395
Henry Fenncy, Lieutenant, District 358	27 Mar 1811	p. 395
James Spear, Lieutenant, District 86	27 Mar 1811	p. 396
Jetho Kellund, Ensign, District 86	27 Mar 1811	p. 396
Chappell Sledge, Major, Battalion 23	28 Mar 1811	p. 397
Thomas Hudson, Major, Battalion 24	2 Apr 1811	p. 397
James Durham, Captain, District 372	2 Apr 1811	p. 398
Jesse F. Heard, Captain, District 165	2 Apr 1811	p. 398
Joseph Hubbard, Captain, District 233	2 Apr 1811	p. 399
Edward Traylor, Lieutenant, District 233	2 Apr 1811	p. 399
Benjamin S. Lanier, Captain, District 259	2 Apr 1811	p. 400
Jeremiah W. Ray, Captain, District 303	8 Apr 1811	p. 400
Peter H. Collins, Major, Battalion 28	8 Apr 1811	p. 401
Peter Donaldson, Captain, District 122	8 Apr 1811	p. 401
Isham Fuller, Captain, District 131	8 Apr 1811	p. 402
Robert Shaw, Lieutenant, District 128	8 Apr 1811	p. 402
John Roney, Ensign, District 128	8 Apr 1811	p. 403
Gilbert Shearer, Lieutenant, District 120	8 Apr 1811	p. 403
William Teddlie, Captain, District 158	13 Apr 1811	p. 404

Name, Rank, Unit	*Date*	*Page*
George Poulin, Captain, District 6	13 Apr 1811	p. 404
George Penny, Ensign, District 6	13 Apr 1811	p. 405
James Bentley, Ensign, District 201	13 Apr 1811	p. 405
Obediah Morris, Ensign, District 133	13 Apr 1811	p. 406
Noah Minton, Captain, District 72	13 Apr 1811	p. 406
Samuel Hughster, Lieutenant, District 72	13 Apr 1811	p. 407
Jesse Hanley, Ensign, District 72	13 Apr 1811	p. 407
Henry Tucker, Captain, District 1	18 Apr 1811	p. 408
Jeremiah Griffin, Lieutenant, Volunteer Company of Riflemen, Battalion 29	18 Apr 1811	p. 408
James Jackson, Captain, Volunteer Company of Infantry (styled the Homespun Foresters), Battalion 19	18 Apr 1811	p. 409
Archibald Campbell, Lieutenant, Volunteer Company of Infantry (styled the Homespun Foresters), Battalion 19	18 Apr 1811	p. 409
Samuel Trippe, Captain, Volunteer Troop of Dragoons, Squadron 4, Regiment 3	18 Apr 1811	p. 410
Joseph Morton, Second Lieutenant, Volunteer Troop of Dragoons, Squadron 6, Regiment 3	18 Apr 1811	p. 410
Drury Stovall, Lieutenant, District 167	18 Apr 1811	p. 411
John Burdine, Ensign, District 167	18 Apr 1811	p. 411
Samuel Clarke, Captain, District 82	18 Apr 1811	p. 412
Shadrick Rawles, Ensign, District 82	18 Apr 1811	p. 412
Francis M. Thompson, Lieutenant, District 231	18 Apr 1811	p. 413
Mathew Rainey, Ensign, District 231	18 Apr 1811	p. 413
Christian Albright, Captain, District 207	18 Apr 1811	p. 414
John Albright, Lieutenant, District 207	18 Apr 1811	p. 414
Isaac Gilbert, Ensign, District 207	18 Apr 1811	p. 415
Clemuel Joines, Ensign, District 142	18 Apr 1811	p. 415
Thomas Gay, Captain, District 111	18 Apr 1811	p. 416
Abner Welborn, Captain, District 177	18 Apr 1811	p. 416
Mason Harwell, Captain, District 102	22 Apr 1811	p. 417
John Cason, Lieutenant, District 73	24 Apr 1811	p. 417
William McCullers, Captain, District 74	24 Apr 1811	p. 418
Archibald Lessley, Captain, District 323	24 Apr 1811	p. 418
John Hill, Major, Battalion 69	24 Apr 1811	p. 419
John Bishop, Ensign, District 108	24 Apr 1811	p. 419
Thomas Mock, Ensign, District 12	24 Apr 1811	p. 420

Georgia Military Commissions, 1798–1818

Name, Rank, Unit	*Date*	*Page*
James Fletcher, Captain, District 277	24 Apr 1811	p. 420
Humphry Gilmore, Lieutenant, District 277	24 Apr 1811	p. 421
Elijah Lee, Ensign, District 277	24 Apr 1811	p. 421
Norman McLeod, First Lieutenant, Volunteer Company of Artillery, Regiment 1	24 Apr 1811	p. 422
Gardner Tufts, Second Lieutenant, Volunteer Company of Artillery, Regiment 1	24 Apr 1811	p. 422
Arington F. Smith, Major, Battalion 25	30 Apr 1811	p. 423
John Hudson, Ensign, District 69	2 May 1811	p. 423
Benjamin Bruton, Lieutenant, District 122	2 May 1811	p. 424
Wilie Hilleard, Lieutenant, District 112	2 May 1811	p. 424
William Goodbee, Captain, District 68	2 May 1811	p. 425
Hardy Hay, Lieutenant, District 68	2 May 1811	p. 425
Abraham Heath, Ensign, District 68	2 May 1811	p. 426
James Hathhorn, Lieutenant, District 70	2 May 1811	p. 426
Norval Roberts, Ensign, District 70	2 May 1811	p. 427
Enoch Farmer, Captain, District 77	2 May 1811	p. 427
John Sandiford, Lieutenant, District 75	2 May 1811	p. 428
Howell Hines, Captain, District 10	2 May 1811	p. 428
Edward Morgan, Lieutenant, District 184	2 May 1811	p. 429
Archibald Davis, Ensign, District 93	2 May 1811	p. 429
Uriah Amason, Captain, District 96	4 May 1811	p. 430
Benjamine Amason, Lieutenant, District 96	4 May 1811	p. 430
Cullin Cato, Ensign, District 96	4 May 1811	p. 431
Jacob Lensey, Captain, District 312	6 May 1811	p. 431
West Whitaker, Captain, District 369	6 May 1811	p. 432
James B. McCready, Lieutenant, District 320	7 May 1811	p. 432
John P. Harvey, Captain, Volunteer Troop of Dragoons, Squadron 2, Regiment 1	9 May 1811	p. 433
Joseph Boren, Captain, District 103	11 May 1811	p. 433
Robert Horton, Lieutenant, District 103	11 May 1811	p. 434
John P. Carey, Lieutenant, District 216	13 May 1811	p. 434
Cary Wood, Ensign, District 216	13 May 1811	p. 435
Isaac Daniel, Lieutenant, District 221	13 May 1811	p. 435
James L. Oliver, Ensign, District 120	13 May 1811	p. 436
James Dabney, Lieutenant, District 363	13 May 1811	p. 436
William P. Beall, Captain, District 130	13 May 1811	p. 437

Name, Rank, Unit	*Date*	*Page*
Thomas Pace, Lieutenant, District 130	13 May 1811	p. 437
Dread Pace, Ensign, District 130	13 May 1811	p. 438
Edward Williams, Captain, District 249	13 May 1811	p. 438
William Wallace, Lieutenant, District 249	13 May 1811	p. 439
Fuller Milsaps, Ensign, District 249	13 May 1811	p. 439
Robert Montgomery, Captain, District 247	13 May 1811	p. 440
James Wardlaw, Lieutenant, District 247	13 May 1811	p. 440
Robert Barnwell, Ensign, District 247	13 May 1811	p. 441
Frederick Bryan, Captain, District 28	13 May 1811	p. 441
Thornton Sandford, Captain, District 104	20 May 1811	p. 442
Elijah Evans, Lieutenant, District 139	20 May 1811	p. 442
Spencer Thomas, Ensign, District 139	20 May 1811	p. 443
William Patrick, Captain, District 287	20 May 1811	p. 443
James McClorough, Lieutenant, District 232	20 May 1811	p. 444
William Arnold, Lieutenant, District 261	20 May 1811	p. 444
L. H. Marks, Captain, District 85	20 May 1811	p. 445
Thomas L. Malone, Captain, District 3	20 May 1811	p. 445
Henry Jones, Ensign, District 157	20 May 1811	p. 446
Reubin Walker, Captain, District 121	20 May 1811	p. 446
Aaron Davis, Lieutenant, District 121	20 May 1811	p. 447
Peter Legueax, Lieutenant, District 135	20 May 1811	p. 447
James Young, Ensign, District 135	20 May 1811	p. 448
John Reed, Lieutenant, District 132	20 May 1811	p. 448
Peter Rynn, Ensign, District 132	20 May 1811	p. 449
Graves Swanson, Captain, District 138	20 May 1811	p. 449
Thomas Harvey, Lieutenant, District 341	20 May 1811	p. 450
Amos Forehand, Ensign, District 341	20 May 1811	p. 450
Frederick Carter, Captain, District 56	22 May 1811	p. 451
Samuel Swilly, Lieutenant, District 56	22 May 1811	p. 451
Samuel Jackson, Lieutenant Colonel, Regiment 24	22 May 1811	p. 452
Henry Hailford, Captain, District 272	22 May 1811	p. 452
Elijah Alcorn, Captain, District 268	22 May 1811	p. 453
Thomas Brooks, Lieutenant, District 268	22 May 1811	p. 453
Charles Hardman, Ensign, District 237	22 May 1811	p. 454
Jacob H. Bosser, Ensign, District 8	22 May 1811	p. 454
Garland T. Watkins, Captain, District 194	22 May 1811	p. 455

Georgia Military Commissions, 1798–1818

Name, Rank, Unit	Date	Page
John McConnell, Lieutenant, District 256	22 May 1811	p. 455
Robert Watkins, Captain, District 123	22 May 1811	p. 456
George Muny, Lieutenant, District 123	22 May 1811	p. 456
Edward Sims, Captain, District 315	22 May 1811	p. 457
Jacob Higginbottam, Ensign, District 315	22 May 1811	p. 457
David Clark, First Lieutenant, Volunteer Company of Artillery, Regiment 9	23 May 1811	p. 458
Thomas W. Shivers, First Lieutenant, Volunteer Troop of Dragoons, Squadron 3, Regiment 2	3 Jun 1811	p. 458
John Puckett, Lieutenant	3 Jun 1811	p. 459
Elisha Padgett, Captain, District 91	3 Jun 1811	p. 459
Jemsey Raly, Ensign, District 91	3 Jun 1811	p. 460
Alexander G. Raiford, Ensign, District 92	3 Jun 1811	p. 460
William Mase, Lieutenant, District 264	3 Jun 1811	p. 461
Joel Leverett, Captain, District 109	3 Jun 1811	p. 461
Merret Rowland, Ensign, District 79	3 Jun 1811	p. 462
James W. Crews, Lieutenant, District 7	3 Jun 1811	p. 462
Henry Goodman, Lieutenant, District 87	3 Jun 1811	p. 463
Henry Butts, Captain, Volunteer Company of Riflemen, Battalion 68	6 Jun 1811	p. 463
Charles Hudson, Lieutenant, Volunteer Company of Riflemen, Battalion 68	6 Jun 1811	p. 464
John Cooper, Ensign, Volunteer Company of Riflemen, Battalion 68	6 Jun 1811	p. 464
Pliny Dobbins, Captain, District 193	6 Jun 1811	p. 465
George Spencer, Ensign, District 193	6 Jun 1811	p. 465
James Morrison, Major, Battalion 41	6 Jun 1811	p. 466
Adam Watkins, Lieutenant, District 129	6 Jun 1811	p. 466
Zachariah Young, Ensign, District 129	6 Jun 1811	p. 467
Jonathan Parish, Captain, District 303	6 Jun 1811	p. 467
Joseph Cook, Lieutenant, District 303	6 Jun 1811	p. 468
Henry Spratling, Captain, District 166	6 Jun 1811	p. 468
John Johnson, Lieutenant, District 166	6 Jun 1811	p. 469
Matin Douglass, Ensign, District 166	6 Jun 1811	p. 469
Ezekiel F. Smith, Captain, District 300	6 Jun 1811	p. 470
Mathew Wilkins, Ensign, District 300	6 Jun 1811	p. 470
John W. Jones, Captain, District 313	6 Jun 1811	p. 471

Name, Rank, Unit	Date	Page
Andrew Borders, Lieutenant, District 255	8 Jun 1811	p. 471
Preston Hardy, Ensign, District 255	8 Jun 1811	p. 472
Alixander Meriwether, Second Lieutenant, Volunteer Company of Artillery, Regiment 9	10 Jun 1811	p. 472
Moses Ivy, First Lieutenant, Volunteer Company of Artillery, Regiment 11	10 Jun 1811	p. 473
William Darsey, Second Lieutenant, Volunteer Company of Artillery, Regiment 11	10 Jun 1811	p. 473
Henry Bell, Lieutenant, District 137	10 Jun 1811	p. 474
John Hackney, Ensign, District 137	10 Jun 1811	p. 474
Joseph Jamison, Captain, District 326	10 Jun 1811	p. 475
Joseph Neilson, Lieutenant, District 326	10 Jun 1811	p. 475
Joseph Glisson, Captain, District 44	10 Jun 1811	p. 476
James C. Lewis, Ensign, District 44	10 Jun 1811	p. 476
William Bryant, Ensign, District 179	10 Jun 1811	p. 477
Josiah Terrell, Ensign, District 17	10 Jun 1811	p. 477
John Carrell, Ensign, District 168	10 Jun 1811	p. 478
Wyat Parish, Ensign, District 337	10 Jun 1811	p. 478
John Adams, Ensign, District 108	10 Jun 1811	p. 479
William Avery, Ensign, District 310	15 Jun 1811	p. 479
Joel Waiscoat, Ensign, District 9	17 Jun 1811	p. 480
Samuel G. Burch, Lieutenant, District 5	17 Jun 1811	p. 480
Stephen Butler, Captain, District 38	17 Jun 1811	p. 481
Lemuel Gresham, Lieutenant, District 161	17 Jun 1811	p. 481
John Thompson, Ensign, District 161	17 Jun 1811	p. 482
Noah Scarborough, Lieutenant, District 372	17 Jun 1811	p. 482
Littleberry Bostwick, Ensign, District 372	17 Jun 1811	p. 483
Richard Smith, Ensign, District 287	17 Jun 1811	p. 483
Frederick Freeman, Captain, Volunteer Troop of Dragoons, Squadron 5, Regiment 3	18 Jun 1811	p. 484
Ashley Wood, Major, Battalion 80	18 Jun 1811	p. 484
Allen Took, Captain, District 347	22 Jun 1811	p. 485
James Johnson, Lieutenant, District 347	22 Jun 1811	p. 485
John Blackburn, Ensign, District 347	22 Jun 1811	p. 486
William Lee, Captain, District 146	22 Jun 1811	p. 486
Thomas Castelo, Lieutenant, District 146	22 Jun 1811	p. 487
Moses T. Hopkins, Ensign, District 146	22 Jun 1811	p. 487

Georgia Military Commissions, 1798–1818

Name, Rank, Unit	Date	Page
William Bailey Jr., Captain, District 238	22 Jun 1811	p. 488
Asa Holliway, Ensign, District 233	22 Jun 1811	p. 488
James Parker, Lieutenant, District 104	22 Jun 1811	p. 489
John Brooks, Ensign, District 104	22 Jun 1811	p. 489
Shadrack Rawls, Lieutenant, District 82	22 Jun 1811	p. 490
John Speight, Captain, District 353	22 Jun 1811	p. 490
William Barefield, Ensign, District 353	22 Jun 1811	p. 491
Castleton Lyon, Captain, District 211	22 Jun 1811	p. 491
Charles Williamson, Lieutenant, District 211	22 Jun 1811	p. 492
John Thornton Jr., Captain, Volunteer Company of Riflemen, Battalion 38	22 Jun 1811	p. 492
John Burdett, Lieutenant, Volunteer Company of Riflemen, Battalion 38	22 Jun 1811	p. 493
Benjamin Gresham, Ensign, Volunteer Company of Riflemen, Battalion 38	22 Jun 1811	p. 493
James B. Landrum, Captain, Volunteer Company of Riflemen, Battalion 44	22 Jun 1811	p. 494
David Simpson, Captain, Volunteer Troop of Dragoons, Squadron 7, Regiment 4	22 Jun 1811	p. 494
Robert Allison Jr., Second Lieutenant, Volunteer Troop of Dragoons, Squadron 6, Regiment 3	24 Jun 1811	p. 495
Nicholas Howard, Lieutenant, District 163	25 Jun 1811	p. 495
Benjamin Futrell, Ensign, District 163	25 Jun 1811	p. 496
William DeWolf, Captain, District 62	25 Jun 1811	p. 496
Charles Dix, Lieutenant, District 62	25 Jun 1811	p. 497
John Lamb, Ensign, District 62	25 Jun 1811	p. 497
Joseph Drew Jr., Ensign, District 57	25 Jun 1811	p. 498
Gilbert Longstreet, Captain, Volunteer Company of Infantry (styled the Augusta Volunteer Rangers), Battalion 75	28 Jun 1811	p. 498
Augustine Slaughter, Lieutenant, Volunteer Company of Infantry (styled the Augusta Volunteer Rangers), Battalion 75	28 Jun 1811	p. 499
Moses Rodgers, Ensign, Volunteer Company of Infantry (styled the Augusta Volunteer Rangers), Battalion 75	28 Jun 1811	p. 499
Jonathan Kimbrough, Lieutenant, District 179	1 Jul 1811	p. 500
Littleberry Marsh, Captain, District 71	1 Jul 1811	p. 500
William Haddock, Lieutenant, District 90	1 Jul 1811	p. 501
Frederick G. Horton, Ensign, District 90	1 Jul 1811	p. 501

Name, Rank, Unit	Date	Page
Peter F. Mehone, Lieutenant, District 313	1 Jul 1811	p. 502
Josiah Rodgers, Ensign, District 313	1 Jul 1811	p. 502
Lewis Lester, Ensign, District 226	1 Jul 1811	p. 503
Burwell Greene, Lieutenant, District 301	1 Jul 1811	p. 503
James Savage, Ensign, District 307	1 Jul 1811	p. 504
John Young, Captain, District 35	1 Jul 1811	p. 504
John Locke, Lieutenant, District 156	1 Jul 1811	p. 505
Jesse Robinson, Second Lieutenant, Squadron 2, Regiment 1	1 Jul 1811	p. 505
John Paul Jr., Cornet, Squadron 2, Regiment 1	1 Jul 1811	p. 506
Joseph Collins, Lieutenant, District 322	2 Jul 1811	p. 506
Fielding Ellice, Ensign, District 322	2 Jul 1811	p. 507
Andrew Dill, Lieutenant, Company of Infantry (styled the Augusta Independent Blues), Battalion 75	6 Jul 1811	p. 507
Gabriel Clarke, Ensign, Company of Infantry (styled the Augusta Independent Blues), Battalion 75	6 Jul 1811	p. 508
William Starnes, Captain, District 218	6 Jul 1811	p. 508
Benniel McClendon, Lieutenant, District 285	6 Jul 1811	p. 509
John Boling, Ensign, District 285	6 Jul 1811	p. 509
William Wooten, Captain, District 373	6 Jul 1811	p. 510
John Moore, Lieutenant, District 373	6 Jul 1811	p. 510
Littleberry Kennebrew, Captain, District 230	6 Jul 1811	p. 511
William McAlpin, Lieutenant, District 367	6 Jul 1811	p. 511
Grunbruy Allen, Ensign, District 367	6 Jul 1811	p. 512
John B. Simmons, Captain, Volunteer Company of Riflemen, Battalion 23	6 Jul 1811	p. 512
Samuel Pullen, Lieutenant, District 126	8 Jul 1811	p. 513
William Oliver, Ensign, District 126	8 Jul 1811	p. 513
John McDonald, Captain, District 335	8 Jul 1811	p. 514
Jonas Driggars, Lieutenant, District 335	8 Jul 1811	p. 514
Simon Driggars, Ensign, District 335	8 Jul 1811	p. 515
Joseph Sutton, Captain, District 306	8 Jul 1811	p. 515
Jourdin Mabry, Ensign, District 176	8 Jul 1811	p. 516
George Dilworth, Lieutenant, District 33	8 Jul 1811	p. 516
Arthur Burney, Captain, District 352	9 Jul 1811	p. 517
William K. Hall, Lieutenant, District 352	9 Jul 1811	p. 517
Asa Hooks, Ensign, District 352	9 Jul 1811	p. 518

Georgia Military Commissions, 1798–1818

Name, Rank, Unit	*Date*	*Page*
William Cowart, Captain, District 83	9 Jul 1811	p. 518
William Harrison, Major, Battalion 2	12 Jul 1811	p. 519
William Cates, Captain, District 250	12 Jul 1811	p. 519
James Harvill, Lieutenant, District 250	12 Jul 1811	p. 520
Robert Kelly, Ensign, District 250	12 Jul 1811	p. 520
Elisha Hubbard, Lieutenant, District 276	12 Jul 1811	p. 521
Robert Polley, Ensign, District 276	12 Jul 1811	p. 521
Robert Oglesby, Lieutenant, District 202	12 Jul 1811	p. 522
David Moore, Ensign, District 202	12 Jul 1811	p. 522
Charles Rhiney, Lieutenant, District 60	12 Jul 1811	p. 523
Horatio J. Goss, Lieutenant, District 193	12 Jul 1811	p. 523
Samuel Slaton, First Lieutenant, Volunteer Troop of Dragoons, Squadron 7, Regiment 4	12 Jul 1811	p. 524
Timothy King, Captain, Volunteer Company of Infantry, Battalion 9	12 Jul 1811	p. 524
Edward Pitcher, Lieutenant, Volunteer Company of Infantry, Battalion 9	12 Jul 1811	p. 525
William Hill, Ensign, Volunteer Company of Infantry, Battalion 9	12 Jul 1811	p. 525
Edmund Nunn, Captain, Volunteer Company of Infantry (styled the Marion Rangers), Battalion 80	12 Jul 1811	p. 526
Thomas H. Penn, Lieutenant, Volunteer Company of Infantry (styled the Marion Rangers), Battalion 80	12 Jul 1811	p. 526
James Spann, Ensign, Volunteer Company of Infantry (styled the Marion Rangers), Battalion 80	12 Jul 1811	p. 527
Isaac Mallet, Captain, District 304	12 Jul 1811	p. 527
Jonathan Battelle, Captain, District 4	12 Jul 1811	p. 528
Young Beckham, Captain, District 93	16 Jul 1811	p. 528
Harrison Young, Lieutenant Colonel Commandant, Regiment 30	18 Jul 1811	p. 529
Willis Roberts, Lieutenant, District 127	18 Jul 1811	p. 529
Absalom Howard, Ensign, District 127	18 Jul 1811	p. 530
James Watkins, Lieutenant, District 220	18 Jul 1811	p. 530
Bolling Whitton, Ensign, District 220	18 Jul 1811	p. 531
William Cumming, Captain, Volunteer Company of Infantry (styled the Augusta Volunteer Blues), Battalion 75	18 Jul 1811	p. 531
Edward L. Thomas, Captain, District 209	18 Jul 1811	p. 532

Name, Rank, Unit	Date	Page
Michael Box, Lieutenant, District 209	18 Jul 1811	p. 532
Solomon Everett, Ensign, District 209	18 Jul 1811	p. 533
Joseph Hamilton, Captain, District 374	18 Jul 1811	p. 533
William Smith, Lieutenant, District 374	18 Jul 1811	p. 534
Jeremiah Milner, Lieutenant, District 214	18 Jul 1811	p. 534
David Read, Ensign, District 214	18 Jul 1811	p. 535
Thomas Gasway, Lieutenant, District 267	18 Jul 1811	p. 535
Joseph Jones, Ensign, District 267	18 Jul 1811	p. 536
Edward Stovy, Captain, District 264	18 Jul 1811	p. 536
Joseph Dickerson Jr., Ensign, District 371	18 Jul 1811	p. 537
Thomas Maberry, Ensign, District 282	29 Jul 1811	p. 537
Amos Baker, Captain, District 191	29 Jul 1811	p. 538
John Hubbard, Lieutenant, District 191	29 Jul 1811	p. 538
Solomon Towns, Ensign, District 191	29 Jul 1811	p. 539
William A. Bugg, Captain, District 124	29 Jul 1811	p. 539
David E. Twiggs, Lieutenant, District 124	29 Jul 1811	p. 540
Jonathan Lyons, Ensign, District 124	29 Jul 1811	p. 540
Joseph Durham, Ensign, District 225	29 Jul 1811	p. 541
Rederick Little, Lieutenant, District 78	29 Jul 1811	p. 541
Samuel Piles, Lieutenant, District 27	29 Jul 1811	p. 542
Solomon Moody, Ensign, District 27	29 Jul 1811	p. 542
Nehemiah Garrison, Captain, District 227	29 Jul 1811	p. 543
Young Setters, Lieutenant, District 227	29 Jul 1811	p. 543
Hugh Willson, Ensign, District 227	29 Jul 1811	p. 544
Samuel Findley, Ensign, District 281	29 Jul 1811	p. 544
Francis Foster, Lieutenant, District 278	29 Jul 1811	p. 545
John Oakes, Ensign, District 229	29 Jul 1811	p. 545
Ambrose Ray, Ensign, District 100	30 Jul 1811	p. 546
William Cooper, Ensign, District 311	2 Aug 1811	p. 546
Benjamine Henry, Lieutenant, District 287	2 Aug 1811	p. 547
James W. Ledbetter, Lieutenant, District 111	2 Aug 1811	p. 547
Jacob Driscoll, Ensign, District 111	2 Aug 1811	p. 548
Thomas Bowen, Captain, District 251	2 Aug 1811	p. 548
Robert Oban, Lieutenant, District 251	2 Aug 1811	p. 549
Willis Smith, Ensign, District 251	2 Aug 1811	p. 549
John Nall, Ensign, District 364	2 Aug 1811	p. 550

Georgia Military Commissions, 1798–1818

Name, Rank, Unit	*Date*	*Page*
Lewis Wynn, Captain, District 298	2 Aug 1811	p. 550
William R. Wilson, Lieutenant, District 55	7 Aug 1811	p. 551
Benjamin Webb, Ensign, District 55	7 Aug 1811	p. 551
Joseph Capter, Ensign, District 334	7 Aug 1811	p. 552
Robert Douglass, Lieutenant, District 259	7 Aug 1811	p. 552
Charles Cain, Ensign, District 110	7 Aug 1811	p. 553
Moses Mulkey, Major, Battalion 15	7 Aug 1811	p. 553
Galphin Harvey, Lieutenant, District 61	7 Aug 1811	p. 554
James Shaffer, Ensign, District 130	7 Aug 1811	p. 554
Edward Flowers, Lieutenant, District 289	7 Aug 1811	p. 555
Thomas Monk, Ensign, District 289	7 Aug 1811	p. 555
Jonathan Palmer, Captain, District 121	7 Aug 1811	p. 556
Eli Anderson, Lieutenant, District 121	7 Aug 1811	p. 556
John Todd, Lieutenant, District 369	7 Aug 1811	p. 557
Francis Hobson, Captain, District 242	7 Aug 1811	p. 557
Robert Brodnax, Captain, District 374	12 Aug 1811	p. 558
Justice Lake, Lieutenant, District 374	12 Aug 1811	p. 558
John Smith, Ensign, District 374	12 Aug 1811	p. 559
Joshua Willis, Captain, District 172	14 Aug 1811	p. 559
George Gibson, Lieutenant, District 172	14 Aug 1811	p. 560
Thomas Wooten, Lieutenant Colonel, Regiment 19	15 Aug 1811	p. 560
Robert Bowman, Captain, District 8	15 Aug 1811	p. 561
Isaac Thrash, Lieutenant, District 368	15 Aug 1811	p. 561
John Weeks, Ensign, District 368	15 Aug 1811	p. 562
Royalbud Philips, Captain, District 54	20 Aug 1811	p. 562
Asa Fulwood, Lieutenant, District 54	20 Aug 1811	p. 563
William C. Philips, Ensign, District 54	20 Aug 1811	p. 563
Jeremiah Lamar, Captain, District 305	21 Aug 1811	p. 564
Thomas Prather, Lieutenant, District 175	22 Aug 1811	p. 564
Aaron W. Greer, Lieutenant, District 158	22 Aug 1811	p. 565
William Mulkey, Captain, District 67	22 Aug 1811	p. 565
William Gunn, Lieutenant, District 67	22 Aug 1811	p. 566
Dennis Allen, Ensign, District 67	22 Aug 1811	p. 566
William Smith, Captain, District 354	22 Aug 1811	p. 567
Archibald Thompson, Ensign, District 354	22 Aug 1811	p. 567
Josiah D. Cothran, Major, Battalion 82	28 Aug 1811	p. 568

Name, Rank, Unit	*Date*	*Page*
John Shelman, Major, Battalion 50	28 Aug 1811	p. 568
Arthur Sheffield, Captain, District 349	28 Aug 1811	p. 569
William Hand, Lieutenant, District 349	28 Aug 1811	p. 569
Zackariah Davis, Ensign, District 349	28 Aug 1811	p. 570
Nathaniel Nicholson, Captain, District 375	28 Aug 1811	p. 570
Josiah Favours, Lieutenant, District 375	28 Aug 1811	p. 571
William Evans, Lieutenant, District 308	28 Aug 1811	p. 571
William Isler, Lieutenant	28 Aug 1811	p. 572
James Howell, Ensign, District 134	28 Aug 1811	p. 572
John Vass, Ensign, District 346	28 Aug 1811	p. 573
Ebenezer S. Rees, Ensign, District 5	6 Sep 1811	p. 573
Jacob Campbell, Ensign, District 33	6 Sep 1811	p. 574
Thomas King, Captain, District 22	6 Sep 1811	p. 574
Thomas Gould, Lieutenant, District 22	6 Sep 1811	p. 575
William McElvey, Captain, District 351	6 Sep 1811	p. 575
Edmond P. Wester, Lieutenant, District 42	6 Sep 1811	p. 576
Elisha Slaton, Major, Cavalry, Squadron 7, Regiment 4	6 Sep 1811	p. 576
William W. Smith, Captain, Volunteer Troop of Dragoons, Squadron 7, Regiment 4	6 Sep 1811	p. 577
Vincent B. Lowe, First Lieutenant, Volunteer Troop of Dragoons, Squadron 7, Regiment 4	6 Sep 1811	p. 577
John Harris, Second Lieutenant, Volunteer Troop of Dragoons, Squadron 7, Regiment 4	6 Sep 1811	p. 578
John K. M. Charleton, Cornet, Volunteer Troop of Dragoons, Squadron 7, Regiment 4	6 Sep 1811	p. 578
John Rabun, Ensign, District 278	6 Sep 1811	p. 579
John Hamilton, Ensign, District 286	6 Sep 1811	p. 579
Thomas Hadley, Captain, District 291	6 Sep 1811	p. 580
Chesley Arnold, Lieutenant, District 236	6 Sep 1811	p. 580
John Colquet, Ensign, District 236	6 Sep 1811	p. 581
William Nunnelie, Lieutenant, District 194	6 Sep 1811	p. 581
Joseph Ellison, Ensign, District 208	6 Sep 1811	p. 582
Archibald Nelson, Captain, Volunteer Company of Riflemen, Battalion 51	12 Sep 1811	p. 582
Joshua Bunkley, Captain, District 159	12 Sep 1811	p. 583
John Willson, Lieutenant, District 159	12 Sep 1811	p. 583
Benjamin Segar, Lieutenant, District 71	12 Sep 1811	p. 584

Georgia Military Commissions, 1798–1818

Name, Rank, Unit	*Date*	*Page*
Cadar Wiat, Ensign, District 71	12 Sep 1811	p. 584
Nathaniel Tatum, Captain, District 356	12 Sep 1811	p. 585
William Joiner, Lieutenant, District 356	12 Sep 1811	p. 585
John Noales, Ensign, District 169	12 Sep 1811	p. 586
Robert Owens, Major, Battalion 65	17 Sep 1811	p. 586
John W. Brutchfield, Lieutenant, District 231	17 Sep 1811	p. 587
Joseph Shewmake, Ensign, District 68	17 Sep 1811	p. 587
Allen Waites, Ensign, District 373	12 Sep 1811	p. 588
Josiah Griffin, Captain, District 189	19 Sep 1811	p. 588
Jesse Edwards, Lieutenant, District 189	19 Sep 1811	p. 589
Richard Brown, Ensign, District 189	19 Sep 1811	p. 589
Seth Hearon, Captain, District 367	19 Sep 1811	p. 590
John Felton, Lieutenant, District 226	19 Sep 1811	p. 590
William Nothern, Ensign, District 170	19 Sep 1811	p. 591
Thomas Forth, Captain, Volunteer Company of Infantry (styled the Independent Blues), Battalion 14	26 Sep 1811	p. 591
Stephen W. Blunt, Lieutenant, Volunteer Company of Infantry (styled the Independent Blues), Battalion 14	26 Sep 1811	p. 592
Beverly Randolph, Ensign, Volunteer Company of Infantry (styled the Independent Blues), Battalion 14	26 Sep 1811	p. 592
Abel L. Hatin, Captain, District 275	30 Sep 1811	p. 593
Peter Merrell, Lieutenant, District 275	30 Sep 1811	p. 593
Josiah Cason, Ensign, District 275	30 Sep 1811	p. 594
Edmond Garrey, Lieutenant, District 39	30 Sep 1811	p. 594
Alexander Gorden, Ensign, District 39	30 Sep 1811	p. 595
John C. Spinks, Lieutenant, District 303	30 Sep 1811	p. 595
James Humphries, Ensign, District 303	30 Sep 1811	p. 596
James Park, Lieutenant, District 309	30 Sep 1811	p. 596
Thomas Hightower, Ensign, District 309	30 Sep 1811	p. 597
Thomas Wagnon, Lieutenant, District 160	30 Sep 1811	p. 597
Nothey Gilmore, Ensign, District 160	30 Sep 1811	p. 598
Thomas Covington, Captain, District 133	30 Sep 1811	p. 598
William Norton, Lieutenant, Volunteer Company of Riflemen, Battalion 44	30 Sep 1811	p. 599
Joseph James, Ensign, Volunteer Company of Riflemen, Battalion 44	30 Sep 1811	p. 599
John Harvey, Lieutenant, District 19	4 Oct 1811	p. 600

Commissions Book 1809–1812

Name, Rank, Unit	Date	Page
Nathan Nolley, Lieutenant, District 113	4 Oct 1811	p. 600
John McDaniel, Ensign, District 118	4 Oct 1811	p. 601
John Trussell, Lieutenant, District 38	4 Oct 1811	p. 601
James Nesmith, Ensign, District 38	4 Oct 1811	p. 602
Robert Williamson, Captain, District 365	4 Oct 1811	p. 602
Edmond Sutherlin, Lieutenant, District 234	4 Oct 1811	p. 603
Joseph Bentley, Ensign, District 234	4 Oct 1811	p. 603
Nauflet Howard, Lieutenant, District 95	11 Oct 1811	p. 604
James Howard, Ensign, District 95	11 Oct 1811	p. 604
Kendred Braswell, Captain, District 57	11 Oct 1811	p. 605
Hosa W. Sullivan, Captain, District 60	11 Oct 1811	p. 605
Archibald Ritcher, Ensign, District 264	11 Oct 1811	p. 606
John Patridge, Ensign, District 168	11 Oct 1811	p. 606
James Potter, Captain, District 112	11 Oct 1811	p. 607
William Floyd, Lieutenant, District 238	11 Oct 1811	p. 607
Thomas Stephens, Ensign, District 238	11 Oct 1811	p. 608
Greenberry Haynes, Lieutenant, District 282	11 Oct 1811	p. 608
Lemuel Gresham, Captain, District 161	11 Oct 1811	p. 609
David Anderson, Lieutenant, District 218	11 Oct 1811	p. 609
Robert Martin, Captain, District 222	11 Oct 1811	p. 610
Reubin Stewart, Lieutenant, District 222	11 Oct 1811	p. 610
David Wright, Ensign, District 222	11 Oct 1811	p. 611
Thomas Payne, Captain, District 212	12 Oct 1811	p. 611
William H. Dewly, Captain, District 209	12 Oct 1811	p. 612
William Smith, Major, Battalion 39	12 Oct 1811	p. 612
Archibald Huggie, First Lieutenant, Volunteer Troop of Horse, Squadron 3, Regiment 2	12 Oct 1811	p. 613
Paul Keller, Lieutenant, District 8	12 Oct 1811	p. 613
James Bigham, Lieutenant, District 76	15 Oct 1811	p. 614
Bush Deafnell, Ensign, District 76	15 Oct 1811	p. 614
John S. Thomas, Captain, District 105	15 Oct 1811	p. 615
Thomas Simmons, Captain, Volunteer Company of Riflemen, Battalion 67	15 Oct 1811	p. 615
Peter Coulter, Lieutenant, Volunteer Company of Riflemen, Battalion 67	19 Oct 1811	p. 616
William Brown, Ensign, Volunteer Company of Riflemen, Battalion 67	19 Oct 1811	p. 616

Georgia Military Commissions, 1798–1818

Name, Rank, Unit	Date	Page
William Mullikan, Ensign, Volunteer Company of Riflemen, Battalion 38	19 Oct 1811	p. 617
Thomas Bonner, Captain, District 282	19 Oct 1811	p. 617
Ralph Blackwell, Ensign, District 196	19 Oct 1811	p. 618
John Ross, Lieutenant, District 237	19 Oct 1811	p. 618
William Justice, Ensign, District 257	19 Oct 1811	p. 619
Exom Boon, Captain, District 295	7 Nov 1811	p. 619
Isaac Moore Jr., Ensign, District 295	19 Nov 1811	p. 620
Andrew Smith, Lieutenant, District 236	19 Nov 1811	p. 620
John Johnston, Captain, District 328	19 Nov 1811	p. 621
Benjamin Lancaster, Lieutenant, District 328	19 Nov 1811	p. 621
Samuel Jackson, Ensign, District 328	19 Nov 1811	p. 622
Tandy Glaze, Lieutenant, District 185	19 Nov 1811	p. 622
Mordica M. Sheftall, Ensign, District 2	19 Nov 1811	p. 623
John H. Patterson, Major, Battalion 38	19 Nov 1811	p. 623
John W. Pendleton, Captain, District 237	19 Nov 1811	p. 624
Alfred Steward, Captain, District 217	19 Nov 1811	p. 624
Eli Glover, Captain, Volunteer Company of Riflemen, Battalion 65	19 Nov 1811	p. 625
John Hardman, Captain, Volunteer Company of Riflemen, Battalion 62	19 Nov 1811	p. 625
James Heard, Lieutenant, Volunteer Company of Riflemen, Battalion 62	19 Nov 1811	p. 626
Baker Man, Ensign, Volunteer Company of Riflemen, Battalion 62	19 Nov 1811	p. 626
William Mulkey, Captain, District 67	28 Nov 1811	p. 627
William Gunn, Lieutenant, District 67	28 Nov 1811	p. 627
Dennis Allen, Ensign, District 67	28 Nov 1811	p. 628
Samuel W. Hutchens, Captain, District 221	28 Nov 1811	p. 628
Thomas Dicken, Ensign, District 221	28 Nov 1811	p. 629
Peter M. Curry, Captain, District 181	28 Nov 1811	p. 629
Benjamin Harvey, Lieutenant, District 314	28 Nov 1811	p. 630
Hezekiah Hudman, Ensign, District 314	28 Nov 1811	p. 630
Benjamin Witcher, Captain, District 205	2 Dec 1811	p. 631
Robert Orr, Ensign, District 205	2 Dec 1811	p. 631
Henry Jennings, Ensign, District 230	2 Dec 1811	p. 632
Joshua Graham, Lieutenant, District 359	2 Dec 1811	p. 632

Name, Rank, Unit	Date	Page
Simon Woodson, Ensign, District 359	2 Dec 1811	p. 633
Noah Ryus, Ensign, District 298	2 Dec 1811	p. 633
William Smith, Captain, District 114	2 Dec 1811	p. 634
Manning H. Gore, Captain, District 59	2 Dec 1811	p. 634
Thomas Gribbon, Lieutenant, District 1	2 Dec 1811	p. 635
William J. Sims, Ensign, District 1	2 Dec 1811	p. 635
Samuel Trippe, First Lieutenant, Volunteer Troop of Dragoons, Squadron 4, Regiment 2	2 Dec 1811	p. 636
Archibald Thompson, Lieutenant, District 354	4 Dec 1811	p. 636
Levi T. Taylor, Lieutenant, District 209	9 Dec 1811	p. 637
Charles Baker, Ensign, District 209	9 Dec 1811	p. 637
Neal Cleaveland, Ensign, District 213	9 Dec 1811	p. 638
Baley Conner, Major, Battalion 57	9 Dec 1811	p. 638
Reuben N. Hargrove, Lieutenant, District 342	9 Dec 1811	p. 639
Davis Gross, Lieutenant, District 292	9 Dec 1811	p. 639
Isaac Hammons, Ensign, District 292	9 Dec 1811	p. 640
John Jeffers, Ensign, District 80	9 Dec 1811	p. 640
Henry Fillinger, Ensign, District 140	16 Dec 1811	p. 641
Britton Bucker, Lieutenant, District 295	16 Dec 1811	p. 641
Simon Henderson, Lieutenant, District 171	16 Dec 1811	p. 642
James M. Reynolds, Ensign, District 171	16 Dec 1811	p. 642
Foster Smith, Captain, District 225	16 Dec 1811	p. 643
Joseph W. Dennis, Captain, District 354	16 Dec 1811	p. 643
James E. White, Ensign, District 195	16 Dec 1811	p. 644
Silas Madows, Lieutenant, District 299	16 Dec 1811	p. 644
Thomas Gaddis, Ensign, District 199	16 Dec 1811	p. 645
Silas Downes, Captain, District 377	16 Dec 1811	p. 645
William Kelly, Lieutenant, District 377	16 Dec 1811	p. 646
William Strouder, Ensign, District 377	16 Dec 1811	p. 646
James Hunter, Captain, Volunteer Company of Infantry (styled the Chatham Rangers), Battalion 1	21 Dec 1811	p. 647
George Heard, Ensign, District 224	21 Dec 1811	p. 647
James Wimberly, Lieutenant, District 304	21 Dec 1811	p. 648
William Amos, Ensign, District 304	21 Dec 1811	p. 648
John Anglin, Ensign, District 356	21 Dec 1811	p. 649
William Russel, Captain	21 Dec 1811	p. 649
John Williams, Captain, District 378	24 Dec 1811	p. 650

Georgia Military Commissions, 1798–1818

Name, Rank, Unit	*Date*	*Page*
Alexander Bryan, Lieutenant, District 378	24 Dec 1811	p. 650
Samuel M. Wilson, Lieutenant, District 156	6 Jan 1812	p. 651
William McKinney, Ensign, District 156	6 Jan 1812	p. 651
Ansel Walker, Lieutenant, District 28	6 Jan 1812	p. 652
Stephen Browning, Ensign, District 28	6 Jan 1812	p. 652
David Smith, Captain, District 364	6 Jan 1812	p. 653
Jehu Arnold, Lieutenant, District 116	6 Jan 1812	p. 653
Thomas Cloyd, Ensign, District 116	6 Jan 1812	p. 654
James Robertson, Lieutenant, District 217	6 Jan 1812	p. 654
Samuel Robertson, Ensign, District 217	6 Jan 1812	p. 655
William Jones, Captain, District 280	6 Jan 1812	p. 655
George Grimes, Lieutenant, District 280	6 Jan 1812	p. 656
William Gill, Captain, District 180	6 Jan 1812	p. 656
Solomon Willson, Lieutenant, District 61	6 Jan 1812	p. 657
Gipson Gray, Ensign, District 61	6 Jan 1812	p. 657
Daniel Dupree, Captain, District 94	6 Jan 1812	p. 658
Isham Laurence, Lieutenant, District 94	6 Jan 1812	p. 658
Thomas Jones, Ensign, District 94	6 Jan 1812	p. 659
John Hilton, Captain, District 79	6 Jan 1812	p. 659
Peter Fontain, Lieutenant, District 79	6 Jan 1812	p. 660
Jesse Robertson, First Lieutenant, Volunteer Troop of Dragoons, Squadron 2, Regiment 1	6 Jan 1812	p. 660
Lindzey Coleman, Captain, Fire Company in the City of Augusta	6 Jan 1812	p. 661
John Cashin, First Lieutenant, Fire Company in the City of Augusta	6 Jan 1812	p. 661
Bathazer Bouyer, Second Lieutenant, Fire Company in the City of Augusta	6 Jan 1812	p. 662
John Campbell, Ensign, Fire Company in the City of Augusta	6 Jan 1812	p. 662
Edward Sikes, Ensign, District 19	16 Jan 1812	p. 663
William Williams, Ensign, District 108	16 Jan 1812	p. 663
James Hampton, Captain, District 255	16 Jan 1812	p. 664
Washington Allen, Captain, District 263	16 Jan 1812	p. 664
Lewis C. Holland, Captain, District 289	16 Jan 1812	p. 665
Benjamin Digby, Ensign, District 231	16 Jan 1812	p. 665
William Barnes, Lieutenant, District 355	16 Jan 1812	p. 666

Name, Rank, Unit	Date	Page
Gaines Thompson, Lieutenant, District 180	18 Jan 1812	p. 666
William Dobbs, Ensign, District 212	18 Jan 1812	p. 667
Robert J. Cabell, Captain, District 220	18 Jan 1812	p. 667
Samuel Harvell, Captain, District 379	18 Jan 1812	p. 668
William Powell, Lieutenant, District 379	18 Jan 1812	p. 668
Joseph Crawford, Ensign, District 379	18 Jan 1812	p. 669
Lansford Long, Captain, District 319	20 Jan 1812	p. 669
Tomlinson Fort, Captain, Volunteer Company of Infantry (styled the Baldwin Volunteers), Battalion 71	22 Jan 1812	p. 670
Fleming Grantland, Lieutenant, Volunteer Company of Infantry (styled the Baldwin Volunteers), Battalion 71	22 Jan 1812	p. 670
Mark Harden, Captain, District 372	28 Jan 1812	p. 671
Greenberry Thomas, Lieutenant, District 372	28 Jan 1812	p. 671
William R. Jones, Ensign, District 372	28 Jan 1812	p. 672
James Shaffer, Lieutenant, District 130	31 Jan 1812	p. 672
John Dawson, Captain, District 141	31 Jan 1812	p. 673
John Hollingsworth, Captain, District 211	31 Jan 1812	p. 673
David Gallaspay, Captain, District 250	31 Jan 1812	p. 674
Francis Smith, Lieutenant, District 250	31 Jan 1812	p. 674
Silas Brooks, Ensign, District 250	31 Jan 1812	p. 675
William Posey, Captain, District 339	31 Jan 1812	p. 675
Andrew Posey, Ensign, District 339	31 Jan 1812	p. 676
Mossman Houston, Captain, Volunteer Troop of Dragoons styled the Chatham Hussars, Squadron 1, Regiment 1	31 Jan 1812	p. 676
Richard F. Williams, First Lieutenant, Volunteer Troop of Dragoons styled the Chatham Hussars, Squadron 1, Regiment 1	31 Jan 1812	p. 677
George W. McAllister, Second Lieutenant, Volunteer Troop of Dragoons styled the Chatham Hussars, Squadron 1, Regiment 1	31 Jan 1812	p. 677
George L. Pope, Cornet, Volunteer Troop of Dragoons styled the Chatham Hussars, Squadron 1, Regiment 1	31 Jan 1812	p. 678
Michael Long, Lieutenant, District 8		p. 678
Robert V. Marye, Ensign, Volunteer Company of Infantry (styled the Baldwin Volunteers), Battalion 71	4 Feb 1812	p. 679
William Arnold, Captain, District 261	11 Feb 1812	p. 679
Joshua Welch, Lieutenant, District 261	11 Feb 1812	p. 680
Samuel Welch, Ensign, District 261	11 Feb 1812	p. 680

Name, Rank, Unit	Date	Page
Solomon Terrell, Captain, District 160	11 Feb 1812	p. 681
James Kilgore, Captain, District 175	11 Feb 1812	p. 681
John Hathway, Lieutenant, District 4	11 Feb 1812	p. 682
James England, Ensign, District 4	11 Feb 1812	p. 682
Patrick McGrath, Lieutenant, District 122	11 Feb 1812	p. 683
Abel Penington, Captain, District 380	11 Feb 1812	p. 683
John Philips, Lieutenant, District 380	11 Feb 1812	p. 684
James Butterman, Ensign, District 380	11 Feb 1812	p. 684
Archibald Thomas, Second Lieutenant, Volunteer Company of Artillery, Regiment 14	11 Feb 1812	p. 685
Nicholas Connelly, Second Lieutenant, Volunteer Troop of Dragoons, Squadron 2, Regiment 1	11 Feb 1812	p. 685
Nicholas Stiles, Lieutenant, District 268	11 Feb 1812	p. 686
John House, Ensign, District 268	11 Feb 1812	p. 686
Enoch Rogers, Captain, District 258	11 Feb 1812	p. 687
Peter Wallice, Lieutenant, District 258	11 Feb 1812	p. 687
Robert Boyle, Ensign, District 258	11 Feb 1812	p. 688
John Beasley, Major, Battalion 44	14 Feb 1812	p. 688
Lemuel Buchanan, Ensign, District 115	14 Feb 1812	p. 689
Reese Pilchin, Ensign, District 151	14 Feb 1812	p. 689
John C. Wright, Lieutenant, District 218	14 Feb 1812	p. 690
William Flippin, Ensign, District 218	14 Feb 1812	p. 690
Elijah Miers, Lieutenant, District 281	14 Feb 1812	p. 691
William Harris, Ensign, District 281	14 Feb 1812	p. 691
John Wood, Ensign, District 318	14 Feb 1812	p. 692
John Kittles, Captain, District 330	14 Feb 1812	p. 692
Richard Satter, Ensign, District 330	14 Feb 1812	p. 693
Joseph Rain, Captain, District 381	22 Feb 1812	p. 693
Samuel Naly, Lieutenant, District 381	22 Feb 1812	p. 694
William Beasley, Ensign, District 381	22 Feb 1812	p. 694
John F. Lason, Lieutenant, District 161	22 Feb 1812	p. 695
Joseph Cleavland, Lieutenant, District 208	22 Feb 1812	p. 695
Samuel B. Hardman, Captain, District 237	22 Feb 1812	p. 696
Wesley Glazier, Ensign, District 295	22 Feb 1812	p. 696
Benjamin Hurbert, Captain, Volunteer Company of Artillery, Regiment 31	24 Feb 1812	p. 697

Name, Rank, Unit	Date	Page
Kinchen Curl, First Lieutenant, Volunteer Company of Artillery, Regiment 31	24 Feb 1812	p. 697
Green Hill, Second Lieutenant, Volunteer Company of Artillery, Regiment 31	24 Feb 1812	p. 698
Elisha Gates, Lieutenant, District 320	24 Feb 1812	p. 698
Josiah Gilbert, Ensign, District 320	24 Feb 1812	p. 699
Francis Hopkins, Major, Battalion 6	28 Feb 1812	p. 699
John Price, Captain, District 296	28 Feb 1812	p. 700
Frizel M. Edrington, Ensign, District 183	28 Feb 1812	p. 700
Joshua Porter, Lieutenant, District 331	29 Feb 1812	p. 701
Peter McArthur, Ensign, District 329	29 Feb 1812	p. 701
Blake Morgan, Ensign, District 252	9 Mar 1812	p. 702
John Hatheway, Captain, District 4	13 Mar 1812	p. 702
Henry S. Cutter, Lieutenant, District 4	13 Feb 1812	p. 703
Warren Green, Lieutenant, District 74	13 Mar 1812	p. 703
Henry Hilliard, Ensign, District 74	13 Mar 1812	p. 704
Thomas Kendall, Captain, District 154	13 Mar 1812	p. 704
Elijah Jones, Lieutenant, District 134	13 Mar 1812	p. 705
Samuel McCurry, Ensign, District 154	13 Mar 1812	p. 705
Anthony Lewis, Captain, District 260	13 Mar 1812	p. 706
Burwell Williams, Lieutenant, District 260	13 Mar 1812	p. 706
William McCarthy, Ensign, District 260	13 Mar 1812	p. 707
Jacob Phinizy, Captain, District 228	16 Mar 1812	p. 707
Kinchen Little, Captain, District 317	17 Mar 1812	p. 708
John L. Alford, Second Lieutenant, Squadron 4, Regiment 2	17 Mar 1812	p. 708
Lewis Atkinson, Cornet, Squadron 4, Regiment 2	17 Mar 1812	p. 709
Thomas Hyde, Major, Battalion 52	24 Mar 1812	p. 709
John C. Patrick, Major, Battalion 84	24 Mar 1812	p. 710
Peter Cone, Lieutenant, District 47	24 Mar 1812	p. 710
Jesse Moran, Lieutenant, District 105	24 Mar 1812	p. 711
John Jeter, Lieutenant, District 279	24 Mar 1812	p. 711
John Mayes, Ensign, District 279	24 Mar 1812	p. 712
Jesse Roberts, Ensign, District 276	24 Mar 1812	p. 712
Elias Rad, Captain, District 291	24 Mar 1812	p. 713
Joel Bailey, Lieutenant, District 291	24 Mar 1812	p. 713
Fleming Dodson, Ensign, District 291	24 Mar 1812	p. 714

Georgia Military Commissions, 1798–1818

Name, Rank, Unit	Date	Page
William Hamilton, Captain, District 86	30 Mar 1812	p. 714
Frederick Carter, Lieutenant, District 86	30 Mar 1812	p. 715
Thomas Benson, Ensign, District 86	30 Mar 1812	p. 715
Charles A. Hill, Captain, District 87	30 Mar 1812	p. 716
Moses Pullen, Lieutenant, District 87	30 Mar 1812	p. 716
William B. Hill, Ensign, District 87	30 Mar 1812	p. 717
Robert R. Cox, Lieutenant, District 263	30 Mar 1812	p. 717
James Hanney, Lieutenant, District 29	30 Mar 1812	p. 718
Joseph Bashtott, Ensign, District 29	30 Mar 1812	p. 718
Thomas Burke, Major, Battalion 1	30 Mar 1812	p. 719
Samuel Moore, Lieutenant, District 160	30 Mar 1812	p. 719
Samuel G. Snow, Ensign, District 160	3 Apr 1812	p. 720
Lewis Galloway, Ensign, District 81	6 Apr 1812	p. 720
Peter Strozier, Lieutenant, District 171	6 Apr 1812	p. 721
Guilford Cade, Lieutenant, District 181	6 Apr 1812	p. 721
Sterling Barrett, Ensign, District 181	6 Apr 1812	p. 722
Rice Tate, Lieutenant, District 190	6 Apr 1812	p. 722
Richard Parks, Captain, District 269	6 Apr 1812	p. 723
George Lucas, Lieutenant, District 361	6 Apr 1812	p. 723
Myrick Weatherby, Ensign, District 361	6 Apr 1812	p. 724
John Hickman, Lieutenant, District 366	6 Apr 1812	p. 724
William Brown, Ensign, District 366	6 Apr 1812	p. 725
Moses Manly, Ensign, District 370	6 Apr 1812	p. 725
Charles A. Dennis, Captain, Volunteer Company of Riflemen, Battalion 68	9 Apr 1812	p. 726
Moses D. White, Captain, District 362	9 Apr 1812	p. 726
John Vest, Ensign, District 362	9 Apr 1812	p. 727
Edward Lane, Lieutenant, District 306	9 Apr 1812	p. 727
Moses Stamps, Captain, District 243	9 Apr 1812	p. 728
Lamkin Vandimer, Ensign, District 243	9 Apr 1812	p. 728
John C. Smith, Captain, District 242	9 Apr 1812	p. 729
Isaac Brewer, Ensign, District 242	9 Apr 1812	p. 729
Richard M. Gilbert Sr., Captain, District 288	9 Apr 1812	p. 730
Burwell Britton, Lieutenant, District 288	9 Apr 1812	p. 730
William Green, Ensign, District 288	9 Apr 1812	p. 731
Robert W. Russel, Ensign, District 248	9 Apr 1812	p. 731
Moses Moore, Lieutenant, District 91	9 Apr 1812	p. 732

Name, Rank, Unit	Date	Page
Jessee Peacock, Ensign, District 91	9 Apr 1812	p. 732
William Smith, Captain, District 254	9 Apr 1812	p. 733
William Spurgin, Captain, District 249	9 Apr 1812	p. 733
William Orine, Captain, District 234	9 Apr 1812	p. 734
Mason Jones, Captain, District 236	9 Apr 1812	p. 734
Samuel Marlow, Lieutenant, District 180	9 Apr 1812	p. 735
Joseph Smith, Ensign, District 180	9 Apr 1812	p. 735
Martin Dasher, Ensign, District 11	9 Apr 1812	p. 736
William L. Wemms, Ensign, District 166	9 Apr 1812	p. 736
John N. Dunn, Ensign, District 228	9 Apr 1812	p. 737
William Cawley, Lieutenant Colonel, Regiment 34	13 Apr 1812	p. 737
Joseph Blackshear, Captain, District 344	13 Apr 1812	p. 738
James Barlow, Lieutenant, District 344	13 Apr 1812	p. 738
Elias Cassels, Captain, District 17	13 Apr 1812	p. 739
Alexander Martin, Lieutenant, District 17	13 Apr 1812	p. 739
Thomas Bassett, Lieutenant, District 21	13 Apr 1812	p. 740
Moses Young, Ensign, District 21	13 Apr 1812	p. 740
Thomas Huff, Ensign, District 103	16 Apr 1812	p. 741
Reuben Walker, Captain, District 121	16 Apr 1812	p. 741
James Caswell, Lieutenant, District 121	16 Apr 1812	p. 742
Robert McMannis, Ensign, District 121	16 Apr 1812	p. 742
John Willis, Lieutenant, District 176	16 Apr 1812	p. 743
William Royal, Ensign, District 190	16 Apr 1812	p. 743
William A. Slaughter, Ensign, District 369	16 Apr 1812	p. 744
Richard Shackleford, Cornet, Volunteer Troop of Dragoons of Columbia County, Squadron 3, Regiment 2	16 Apr 1812	p. 744
Francis Williams, Captain, District 313	18 Apr 1812	p. 745
Thomas Curry, Ensign, District 313	18 Apr 1812	p. 745
John Keener, Captain, District 323	20 Apr 1812	p. 746
Enos Young, Ensign, District 142	20 Apr 1812	p. 746
Lovett B. Smith, Captain, District 376	20 Apr 1812	p. 747
Simon Bateman, Lieutenant, District 376	20 Apr 1812	p. 747
Daniel Taylor, Captain	20 Apr 1812	p. 748
Gideon Watson, Lieutenant	20 Apr 1812	p. 748
Hugh Polk, Ensign	20 Apr 1812	p. 749
William Mironey, Captain	20 Apr 1812	p. 749
Richard R. Simms, Lieutenant	20 Apr 1812	p. 750

Georgia Military Commissions, 1798–1818

Name, Rank, Unit	Date	Page
John Strawder, Ensign	20 Apr 1812	p. 750
Robert Robey, Lieutenant, Volunteer Company of Riflemen, Battalion 65	20 Apr 1812	p. 751
Timothy Duck, Ensign, Volunteer Company of Riflemen, Battalion 65	20 Apr 1812	p. 751
Jonathan Lyon, Lieutenant, District 124	21 Apr 1812	p. 752
David Kelly, Ensign, District 124	21 Apr 1812	p. 752
Betan Blount, Lieutenant, District 301	21 Apr 1812	p. 753
Abel Arrington, Ensign, District 301	21 Apr 1812	p. 753
Samuel Buchainon, Ensign, District 319	25 Apr 1812	p. 754
John J. Shly, Ensign, District 9	27 Apr 1812	p. 754
Benjamin Burton, Captain, District 20	27 Apr 1812	p. 755
Benjamin Waldron, Lieutenant, District 20	27 Apr 1812	p. 755
James Beaty Jr., Ensign, District 72	27 Apr 1812	p. 756
Joseph W. Oneall, Captain, District 271	27 Apr 1812	p. 756
William Legg, Lieutenant, District 255	27 Apr 1812	p. 757
Thomas Doherty, Lieutenant, District 283	27 Apr 1812	p. 757
William Cook, Ensign, District 283	27 Apr 1812	p. 758
Jesse Thomas, Lieutenant, District 286	27 Apr 1812	p. 758
John Akins, Lieutenant, District 312	27 Apr 1812	p. 759
William Reese, Lieutenant, District 374	27 Apr 1812	p. 759
Charles Brown, Ensign, District 374	27 Apr 1812	p. 760
Isaac Knowles, Ensign, District 308	27 Apr 1812	p. 760
John Thomas, Captain, District 343	27 Apr 1812	p. 761
John G. Jones, Lieutenant, District 343	27 Apr 1812	p. 761
Richard Taylor, Ensign, District 343	27 Apr 1812	p. 762
Archibald Campbell, Captain, Volunteer Company of Infantry (styled the Homespun Foresters), Battalion 19	27 Apr 1812	p. 762
John Schley, Ensign, Volunteer Company of Infantry (styled the Homespun Foresters), Battalion 19	27 Apr 1812	p. 763
Michael Long, Lieutenant, District 8	1 May 1812	p. 763
Samuel Jeter, Captain, District 182	1 May 1812	p. 764
Sylvanus Kindrick, Lieutenant, District 182	1 May 1812	p. 764
Thomas Kindrick, Ensign, District 182	1 May 1812	p. 765
Andrew G. Mays, Captain, District 186	1 May 1812	p. 765
John Hemphill, Captain, District 245	1 May 1812	p. 766
Samuel Hemphill, Lieutenant, District 245	1 May 1812	p. 766

Name, Rank, Unit	Date	Page
John Williams, Lieutenant, District 257	1 May 1812	p. 767
Micheal Boisclean, Second Lieutenant, Volunteer Troop of Dragoons, Squadron 3, Regiment 2	1 May 1812	p. 767
John H. Montgomery, Cornet, Volunteer Troop of Dragoons, Squadron 3, Regiment 2	1 May 1812	p. 768
John Cartledge, First Lieutenant, Volunteer Company of Artillery, Regiment 11	2 May 1812	p. 768
Kinchen P. Thiscatt, Captain, District 102	4 May 1812	p. 769
Ezekiel Wimberly, Captain, District 136	4 May 1812	p. 769
John Micars, Lieutenant, District 136	4 May 1812	p. 770
William Wadkins, Ensign, District 136	4 May 1812	p. 770
Harris Allen, Second Lieutenant, Volunteer Troop of Dragoons, Squadron 5, Regiment 3	4 May 1812	p. 771
Eli Lester, Lieutenant, District 317	5 May 1812	p. 771
David Baker, Ensign, District 317	5 May 1812	p. 772
Joshua Hagerty, Lieutenant Colonel Commandant, Regiment 38	6 May 1812	p. 772
Pleasant Towns, Major, Battalion 61	6 May 1812	p. 773
Francis Tufts, Captain, District 7	6 May 1812	p. 773
James Boyl, Captain, District 219	6 May 1812	p. 774
Richard Laurece, Lieutenant, District 219	6 May 1812	p. 774
James Talbot, Ensign, District 219	6 May 1812	p. 775
Francis Tramel, Lieutenant, District 225	6 May 1812	p. 775
Stephen Mobley, Captain, District 365	6 May 1812	p. 776
James Kinman, Lieutenant, District 365	6 May 1812	p. 776

Georgia Military Commissions
Commissions Book 1812–1815

Name, Rank, Unit	Date	Page
William Kinman, Ensign, District 365	6 May 1812	p. 1
John Meeks, Ensign, District 208	6 May 1812	p. 1
Etheldred Fountain, Ensign, District 84	11 May 1812	p. 2
Jesse Yeates, Lieutenant, District 341	11 May 1812	p. 2
James Fowler, Captain, District 23	11 May 1812	p. 3
John M. P. McGuire, Lieutenant, District 23	11 May 1812	p. 3
John Pruster, Ensign, District 23	11 May 1812	p. 4
Jessee Scruggs, Captain, District 13	14 May 1812	p. 4
Richard Shipp, Ensign, District 131	14 May 1812	p. 5
John Reeves, Ensign, District 133	14 May 1812	p. 5
John Mercer, Lieutenant, District 170	14 May 1812	p. 6
Daniel Williams, Ensign, District 170	14 May 1812	p. 6
Myal Green, Ensign, District 232	14 May 1812	p. 7
Zachariah Smith, Captain, District 195	14 May 1812	p. 7
Reubin C. Beck, Lieutenant, District 195	14 May 1812	p. 8
Horatio Goss, Captain, District 193	14 May 1812	p. 8
Stephen Dennis, Lieutenant, District 193	14 May 1812	p. 9
Henry P. White, Ensign, District 193	14 May 1812	p. 9
Robert Hancock, Lieutenant, District 258	14 May 1812	p. 10
James Pettyjohn, Ensign, District 258	14 May 1812	p. 10
Larkin Cleveland, First Lieutenant, Volunteer Troop of Dragoons, Squadron 5, Regiment 3	14 May 1812	p. 11
Edward Butler, Second Lieutenant, Volunteer Troop of Dragoons, Squadron 5, Regiment 3	14 May 1812	p. 11
John Webb, Lieutenant, District 202	19 May 1812	p. 12
Stephen Cowart, Captain, District 83	19 May 1812	p. 12
Hampton Ingrum, Lieutenant, District 93	19 May 1812	p. 13
Seth Fountain, Ensign, District 83	19 May 1812	p. 13
Benjamin J. Randle, Ensign, District 163	19 May 1812	p. 14
Elijah Fields, Ensign, District 348	19 May 1812	p. 14
Philip McKinzie, Captain, Volunteer Company of Riflemen, Battalion 72	19 May 1812	p. 15
Lawrence Magee, Lieutenant, Volunteer Company of Riflemen, Battalion 72	19 May 1812	p. 15

Georgia Military Commissions, 1798–1818

Name, Rank, Unit	Date	Page
William Permenter, Ensign, Volunteer Company of Riflemen, Battalion 72	19 May 1812	p. 16
George Jones, Captain, District 69	28 May 1812	p. 16
Talliver Dillard, Lieutenant, District 69	23 May 1812	p. 17
John Ballenger, Ensign, District 69	23 May 1812	p. 17
Stephen White, Lieutenant, District 310	23 May 1812	p. 18
David Frazier, Lieutenant, District 187	23 May 1812	p. 18
David P. Hillhouse, Lieutenant, District 164	23 May 1812	p. 19
Lewis Brown, Ensign, District 164	23 May 1812	p. 19
Eli Champion, Ensign, District 108	23 May 1812	p. 20
Marriner Culpepper, Ensign, District 156	23 May 1812	p. 20
Red Benjamin Smith, Ensign, District 364	23 May 1812	p. 21
John Foster, Ensign, Volunteer Company of Riflemen, Battalion 51	23 May 1812	p. 21
James Hogan, Captain, District 52	25 May 1812	p. 22
Uriah Kinchen, Lieutenant, District 52	25 May 1812	p. 22
Elijah Furn, Ensign, District 52	25 May 1812	p. 23
Milben Fulford, Captain, District 85	25 May 1812	p. 23
Thomas Dupree, Lieutenant, District 85	25 May 1812	p. 24
Herbert Smith Jr., Ensign, District 85	25 May 1812	p. 24
John Love, Captain, District 341	25 May 1812	p. 25
Silas Watson, Lieutenant, District 341	25 May 1812	p. 25
Samuel Pinkum, Ensign, District 341	25 May 1812	p. 26
David Hews, Ensign, District 138	25 May 1812	p. 26
Stewart Anderson, Captain, Volunteer Troop of Dragoons, Squadron 6, Regiment 3	25 May 1812	p. 27
Mathew D. Thompson, Ensign, District 204	8 Jun 1812	p. 27
Arthur Foster, Captain, District 125	10 Jun 1812	p. 28
Allen Took, Lieutenant Colonel Commandant, Regiment 36	16 Jun 1812	p. 28
Jonathan Benton, Captain, District 357	20 Jun 1812	p. 29
Jessee Benton, Lieutenant, District 357	20 Jun 1812	p. 29
Isham Gresham, Ensign, District 357	20 Jun 1812	p. 30
Thomas Theifs, Ensign, District 8	20 Jun 1812	p. 30
Clem Powers, Captain, District 10	20 Jun 1812	p. 31
Charles Roberts, Captain, District 70	20 Jun 1812	p. 31
Benjamin Madray, Ensign, District 70	20 Jun 1812	p. 32

Name, Rank, Unit	Date	Page
John Hodge, Lieutenant, District 119	20 Jun 1812	p. 32
George Pearson, Ensign, District 119	20 Jun 1812	p. 33
George Cornelius, Captain, District 74	20 Jun 1812	p. 33
George Kennedy, Lieutenant, Volunteer Company of Infantry (styled the Augusta Independent Blues), Battalion 75	20 Jun 1812	p. 34
Charles Dame, Ensign, Volunteer Company of Infantry (styled the Augusta Independent Blues), Battalion 75	20 Jun 1812	p. 34
James Blackson, Lieutenant, District 130	20 Jun 1812	p. 35
William Crawford, Ensign, District 130	20 Jun 1812	p. 35
Joseph Tankersly, Lieutenant, District 127	20 Jun 1812	p. 36
Thomas Lyon, Ensign, District 126	20 Jun 1812	p. 36
Philip Stud, Lieutenant, District 135	20 Jun 1812	p. 37
Wiley Roberts, Ensign, District 135	20 Jun 1812	p. 37
Willis Roberts, Ensign, District 274	20 Jun 1812	p. 38
Shackfield Walker, Lieutenant, District 175	20 Jun 1812	p. 38
William C. Boring, Captain, District 174	20 Jun 1812	p. 39
James Woodruff, Lieutenant, District 174	20 Jun 1812	p. 39
John Combs, Ensign, District 174	20 Jun 1812	p. 40
Stephen G. Heard, Lieutenant, District 165	20 Jun 1812	p. 40
Joshua Kelly, Ensign, District 165	20 Jun 1812	p. 41
Samuel Gilmore, Lieutenant, District 186	20 Jun 1812	p. 41
Peyton Bibb, Lieutenant Colonel Commandant, Regiment 28	20 Jun 1812	p. 42
Henry Suddith, Lieutenant, District 184	20 Jul 1812	p. 42
James Gober, Lieutenant, District 210	20 Jun 1812	p. 43
Thomas Bell, Ensign, District 210	20 Jun 1812	p. 43
Henry Bryan, Ensign, District 206	20 Jun 1812	p. 44
Isaac Brooks, Lieutenant, District 243	20 Jun 1812	p. 44
Meredith Adams, Ensign, District 243	20 Jun 1812	p. 45
Henry Stoneham, Lieutenant, District 254	20 Jun 1812	p. 45
Pinket Dean, Ensign, District 254	20 Jun 1812	p. 46
William Perkins, Captain, District 145	20 Jun 1812	p. 46
Hardy Crawford, Lieutenant, District 145	20 Jun 1812	p. 47
John Johnson, Ensign, District 145	20 Jun 1812	p. 47
John McBride, Lieutenant, District 146	20 Jun 1812	p. 48
Vincent Watts, Ensign, District 146	20 Jun 1812	p. 48

Georgia Military Commissions, 1798–1818

Name, Rank, Unit	Date	Page
Frederick H. Williams, Ensign, District 137	20 Jun 1812	p. 49
Greene Andrews, Captain, District 112	20 Jun 1812	p. 49
Willis Shivers, Captain, District 111	20 Jun 1812	p. 50
Ezekiel Veazey, Ensign, District 110	20 Jun 1812	p. 50
Archibald R. S. Hunter, Ensign, District 106	20 Jun 1812	p. 51
John B. Flournoy, Lieutenant, District 104	20 Jun 1812	p. 51
Austin Ford, Ensign, District 104	20 Jun 1812	p. 52
Samuel Webb, Ensign, District 89	20 Jun 1812	p. 52
Shadrick Adkins, Captain, District 346	20 Jun 1812	p. 53
Elisha Hanks, Lieutenant, District 346	20 Jun 1812	p. 53
William Taylor, Ensign, District 346	20 Jun 1812	p. 54
Silas Wood, Captain, District 354	20 Jun 1812	p. 54
Samuel Duly, Lieutenant, District 354	20 Jun 1812	p. 55
Daniel Stringer, Ensign, District 354	20 Jun 1812	p. 55
Whitmill Curry, Ensign, District 324	20 Jun 1812	p. 56
Timothy Brenin, Lieutenant, District 372	20 Jun 1812	p. 56
John Collier, Captain, District 345	20 Jun 1812	p. 57
Elisha Calloway, Lieutenant, District 345	20 Jun 1812	p. 57
Gilbert Chancelor, Ensign, District 345	20 Jun 1812	p. 58
James Rousseau, Lieutenant, District 115	20 Jun 1812	p. 58
Abraham B. Fannin, Ensign, Volunteer Company of Infantry (styled the Baldwin Volunteers), Battalion 71	20 Jun 1812	p. 59
James Moss, First Lieutenant, Volunteer Company of Artillery, Regiment 33	20 Jun 1812	p. 59
Joseph Stovall, Second Lieutenant, Volunteer Company of Artillery, Regiment 33	20 Jun 1812	p. 60
Elijah Presly, Ensign, District 309	20 Jun 1812	p. 60
Peter Thomas, Captain, District 302	20 Jun 1812	p. 61
Jessee Thomas, Captain, District 286	20 Jun 1812	p. 61
Zachariah Eates, Lieutenant, District 294	20 Jun 1812	p. 62
William Cook, Ensign, District 294	20 Jun 1812	p. 62
Henry W. Evans, Captain, Volunteer Company of Riflemen, Battalion 77	20 Jun 1812	p. 63
David Evans, Lieutenant, Volunteer Company of Riflemen, Battalion 77	20 Jun 1812	p. 63
Henry G. Ramsay, Ensign, Volunteer Company of Riflemen, Battalion 77	20 Jun 1812	p. 64
Bryant Rushing, Major, Battalion 77	20 Jun 1812	p. 64

Name, Rank, Unit	Date	Page
Duncan Thompson, Captain, District 51	20 Jun 1812	p. 65
Drury Alston, Lieutenant, District 51	20 Jun 1812	p. 65
Brinkly Gandy, Ensign, District 51	20 Jun 1812	p. 66
Reubin King, Ensign, District 271	20 Jun 1812	p. 66
James Littleton, Ensign, District 158	20 Jun 1812	p. 67
Duke Hamilton, Captain, Volunteer Troop of Dragoons, Squadron 4, Regiment 2	20 Jun 1812	p. 67
Robert B. Glenn, Second Lieutenant, Volunteer Troop of Dragoons, Squadron 4, Regiment 2	20 Jun 1812	p. 68
John W. Compton, Captain, Volunteer Troop of Dragoons, Squadron 5, Regiment 3	20 Jun 1812	p. 68
Thomas A. Banks, Major, Battalion 59	26 Jun 1812	p. 69
Francis Thomas, Lieutenant, District 109	26 Jun 1812	p. 69
Francis Lawson, Ensign, District 109	26 Jun 1812	p. 70
Gideon Kellam, Captain, District 350	26 Jun 1812	p. 70
Daniel W. Shim, Lieutenant, District 350	20 Jun 1812	p. 71
Thomas Cole, Ensign, District 350	26 Jun 1812	p. 71
Dennis Posey, Lieutenant, District 339	26 Jun 1812	p. 72
Benajah McClendon, Captain, District 285	26 Jun 1812	p. 72
John Willson, Captain, Volunteer Company of Riflemen, Battalion 84	26 Jun 1812	p. 73
William C. H. Findley, Lieutenant, Volunteer Company of Riflemen, Battalion 84	29 Jun 1812	p. 73
Benjamin Scott, Ensign, Volunteer Company of Riflemen, Battalion 84	20 Jun 1812	p. 74
Andrew Smith, Captain, District 326	1 Jul 1812	p. 74
James N. Sutton, Ensign, District 326	1 Jul 1812	p. 75
James Rowsey, Ensign, District 315	2 Jul 1812	p. 75
Ambrose Wright, Major, Battalion 19	13 Jul 1812	p. 76
David Elliott, Ensign, District 284	13 Jul 1812	p. 76
James Dimond, Lieutenant, District 296	13 Jul 1812	p. 77
Sterling Price, Ensign, District 296	13 Jul 1812	p. 77
Benjamin Jones, Lieutenant, District 7	13 Jul 1812	p. 78
John Sanderlin, Ensign, District 7	13 Jul 1812	p. 78
Henry Feen, Ensign, District 79	13 Jul 1812	p. 79
Robert Willis, Lieutenant, District 82	13 Jul 1812	p. 79
Joshua Child, Ensign, District 82	13 Jul 1812	p. 80
Shadrick Rogers, Ensign, District 100	13 Jul 1812	p. 80

Georgia Military Commissions, 1798–1818

Name, Rank, Unit	Date	Page
Wooden Driskell, Ensign, District 111	13 Jul 1812	p. 81
John Jones, Ensign, District 159	13 Jul 1812	p. 81
Willie Fletcher, Lieutenant, District 277	13 Jul 1812	p. 82
John Cohorn, Ensign, District 277	13 Jul 1812	p. 82
Robert Martin, Ensign, District 287	13 Jul 1812	p. 83
Richard W. Ellis, Ensign, District 305	13 Jul 1812	p. 83
Benjamin Muborn, Captain, District 347	13 Jul 1812	p. 84
Ezekiel Slaughter, Ensign, District 377	13 Jul 1812	p. 84
Nicholas Connelly, First Lieutenant, Volunteer Troop of Light Dragoons, Squadron 2, Regiment 1	13 Jul 1812	p. 85
Alexander McDaniel, Ensign, District 356	20 Jul 1812	p. 85
John Terrell, Ensign, District 17	23 Jul 1812	p. 86
George Dudley, Captain, District 37	23 Jul 1812	p. 86
William Sowell, Lieutenant, District 37	23 Jul 1812	p. 87
Richard Sharbrew, Ensign, District 37	23 Jul 1812	p. 87
Henry Marshall, Ensign, District 71	23 Jul 1812	p. 88
Samuel Heisler, Captain, District 72	23 Jul 1812	p. 88
Ephraim Night, Ensign, District 162	23 Jul 1812	p. 89
Joshua S. Callaway, Lieutenant, District 168	23 Jul 1812	p. 89
Joseph Frost, Ensign, District 169	23 Jul 1812	p. 90
John Burshell, Ensign, District 179	23 Jul 1812	p. 90
Matthew J. Williams, Lieutenant, District 191	23 Jul 1812	p. 91
John Gunter, Ensign, District 191	23 Jul 1812	p. 91
Thomas D. Jordan, Lieutenant, District 214	23 Jul 1812	p. 92
James Cowen, Captain, District 250	23 Jul 1812	p. 92
Joel Lockhart Jr., Ensign, District 269	23 Jul 1812	p. 93
Edward Williams, Captain, District 281	23 Jul 1812	p. 93
James Allen, Lieutenant, District 281	23 Jul 1812	p. 94
Hardy Williams, Ensign, District 281	23 Jul 1812	p. 94
Ephraim Heard, Captain, District 290	23 Jul 1812	p. 95
Charles Heard, Lieutenant, District 290	23 Jul 1812	p. 95
Caleb Bailey, Ensign, District 290	23 Jul 1812	p. 96
Jessee Wammack, Lieutenant, District 358	23 Jul 1812	p. 96
Lemuel Dossey, Ensign, District 358	23 Jul 1812	p. 97
James H. Bull, Lieutenant, District 373	23 Jul 1812	p. 97
David Sanders, Ensign, District 373	23 Jul 1812	p. 98
James Clark, Captain, District 384	23 Jul 1812	p. 98

Name, Rank, Unit	Date	Page
Daniel Cornwall, Lieutenant, District 384	23 Jul 1812	p. 99
Jonnis Cardin, Ensign, District 384	23 Jul 1812	p. 99
Thomas A. Hill, Major, Battalion 79	23 Jul 1812	p. 100
Nathaniel McCall, Lieutenant, District 48	23 Jul 1812	p. 100
Edwin Sturdivant, First Lieutenant, Volunteer Troop of Light Dragoons, Squadron 5, Regiment 3	23 Jul 1812	p. 101
William Robertson, Second Lieutenant, Volunteer Troop of Light Dragoons, Squadron 5, Regiment 3	23 Jul 1812	p. 101
Thomas Elkins, Captain, District 6	6 Aug 1812	p. 102
William John King, Ensign, District 22	6 Aug 1812	p. 102
Jonathan Neel, Captain, District 53	23 Aug 1812	p. 103
Sampson Dillard, Lieutenant, District 53	6 Aug 1812	p. 103
Ephraim Willis, Ensign, District 53	6 Aug 1812	p. 104
William McLeod, Captain, District 54	6 Aug 1812	p. 104
Joseph Brooker, Ensign, District 54	6 Aug 1812	p. 105
Thomas E. Ward, Captain, District 56	6 Aug 1812	p. 105
William Snell, Lieutenant, District 56	6 Aug 1812	p. 106
Standley Hall, Ensign, District 56	6 Aug 1812	p. 106
James Willey, Lieutenant, District 57	6 Aug 1812	p. 107
Matthew Dunn, Ensign, District 64	6 Aug 1812	p. 107
John McCroan, Lieutenant, District 72	6 Aug 1812	p. 108
Thomas Clifton, Lieutenant, District 80	6 Aug 1812	p. 108
Henry Clifton, Ensign, District 80	6 Aug 1812	p. 109
John Briscoe Jr., Lieutenant, District 129	6 Aug 1812	p. 109
Henry Bell, Lieutenant, District 137	6 Aug 1812	p. 110
William Beasley, Lieutenant, District 139	6 Aug 1812	p. 110
Jessee Asberry, Ensign, District 139	6 Aug 1812	p. 111
Thomas Simmons, Ensign, District 187	6 Aug 1812	p. 111
Thomas Akins, Ensign, District 212	6 Aug 1812	p. 112
John Farmbrough, Lieutenant, District 223	6 Aug 1812	p. 112
James Harkness, Lieutenant, District 286	6 Aug 1812	p. 113
James Hoy, Ensign, District 304	6 Aug 1812	p. 113
Jonathan Pearson, Captain, District 329	6 Aug 1812	p. 114
Nathaniel G. Waller, Lieutenant, District 359	6 Aug 1812	p. 114
Rhode L. Smith, Ensign, District 359	6 Aug 1812	p. 115
William J. Minton, Captain, District 368	6 Aug 1812	p. 115
David Thrash, Lieutenant, District 368	6 Aug 1812	p. 116

Georgia Military Commissions, 1798–1818

Name, Rank, Unit	Date	Page
Archibald Pitche, Lieutenant, District 374	6 Aug 1812	p. 116
Thomas Johnson, Captain, District 386	6 Aug 1812	p. 117
Etheldred Howell, Lieutenant, District 386	6 Aug 1812	p. 117
James Dykes, Captain, District 387	6 Aug 1812	p. 118
John Rucker Jr., First Lieutenant, Volunteer Troop of Light Dragoons, Squadron 7, Regiment 4	6 Aug 1812	p. 118
John Willis, Second Lieutenant, Volunteer Troop of Light Dragoons, Squadron 7, Regiment 4	6 Aug 1812	p. 119
James Fortson, Cornet, Volunteer Troop of Light Dragoons, Squadron 7, Regiment 4	6 Aug 1812	p. 119
John Green Bostwick, Second Lieutenant, Volunteer Troop of Light Dragoons, Squadron 2, Regiment 1	6 Aug 1812	p. 120
Ephraim Pharr, Ensign, Volunteer Company of Riflemen, Battalion 45	6 Aug 1812	p. 120
John Shley, First Lieutenant, Volunteer Company of Homespun Foresters, Battalion 19	6 Aug 1812	p. 121
James Saffold, Captain, Volunteer Company of Artillery, Regiment 31	6 Aug 1812	p. 121
David Clark, Captain, Volunteer Company of Artillery, Regiment 9	6 Aug 1812	p. 122
Ephraim Tiner, Lieutenant, District 13	12 Aug 1812	p. 122
Anderson Williams, Ensign, District 13	12 Aug 1812	p. 123
John Rudisill, Ensign, District 107	12 Aug 1812	p. 123
John Lary, Ensign, District 112	12 Aug 1812	p. 124
David P. Hillhouse, Captain, District 164	12 Aug 1812	p. 124
Abner Tatum, Lieutenant, District 188	12 Aug 1812	p. 125
Edward Rambart, Ensign, District 188	12 Aug 1812	p. 125
Heflin Rhodes, Lieutenant, District 230	12 Aug 1812	p. 126
Reuben Payne, Lieutenant, District 266	12 Aug 1812	p. 126
Samuel Tucker, Ensign, District 266	12 Aug 1812	p. 127
Joel Ball, Lieutenant, District 285	12 Aug 1812	p. 127
James B. Morgan, Ensign, District 285	12 Aug 1812	p. 128
James Stanley, Captain, District 297	12 Aug 1812	p. 128
John Bean, Lieutenant, District 297	12 Aug 1812	p. 129
George Thompson, Ensign, District 297	12 Aug 1812	p. 129
Marrel Collier, Lieutenant, District 316	12 Aug 1812	p. 130
James Irwin, Lieutenant, District 321	12 Aug 1812	p. 130
Edward Bryant, Lieutenant, District 346	12 Aug 1812	p. 131

Name, Rank, Unit	*Date*	*Page*
Alexander Merriwether, First Lieutenant, Volunteer Company of Artillery, Regiment 9	12 Aug 1812	p. 131
Hosea Webster, Ensign, Volunteer Company of Homespun Foresters, Battalion 19	12 Aug 1812	p. 132
William Fannin, Ensign, District 287	19 Aug 1812	p. 132
James Chappel, Ensign, District 360	19 Aug 1812	p. 133
John Love, Ensign, District 376	19 Aug 1812	p. 133
Obadiah Dumas, Ensign, District 378	19 Aug 1812	p. 134
Willie B. Ector, Ensign, District 386	12 Aug 1812	p. 134
William Hoge, Ensign, District 134	19 Aug 1812	p. 135
Reuben Dawson, Ensign, District 143	19 Aug 1812	p. 135
Thomas Maddox, Lieutenant, District 153	19 Aug 1812	p. 136
Daniel Bell, Captain, District 275	27 Aug 1812	p. 136
Thomas L. Hall, Lieutenant, District 275	27 Aug 1812	p. 137
Willson Conner, Captain, Volunteer Company of Mounted Riflemen, Battalion 10	27 Aug 1812	p. 137
Stephen Mitlock, Lieutenant, Volunteer Company of Mounted Riflemen, Battalion 10	27 Aug 1812	p. 138
Joseph Richardson, Ensign, Volunteer Company of Mounted Riflemen, Battalion 10	27 Aug 1812	p. 138
Uriah Jenkins, Ensign, District 91	31 Aug 1812	p. 139
James Allen, Captain, District 94	31 Aug 1812	p. 139
John Curry, Ensign, District 94	31 Aug 1812	p. 140
Asa Jourdan, Lieutenant, District 96	31 Aug 1812	p. 140
John Linton, Ensign, District 96	31 Aug 1812	p. 141
Isaac Downs, Ensign, District 125	31 Aug 1812	p. 141
Zachariah Gholston, Captain, District 205	31 Aug 1812	p. 142
William Edwards, Lieutenant, District 205	31 Aug 1812	p. 142
Stephen McCurdy, Ensign, District 205	31 Aug 1812	p. 143
David Nowlin, Ensign, District 242	31 Aug 1812	p. 143
Samuel Williamson, Ensign, District 263	31 Aug 1812	p. 144
Joseph Vardeman, Ensign, District 278	31 Aug 1812	p. 144
William Weeks, Lieutenant, District 307	31 Aug 1812	p. 145
Nobles Porter, Captain, District 352	31 Aug 1812	p. 145
John Gilbert, Lieutenant, District 352	31 Aug 1812	p. 146
James Collins, Ensign, District 331	31 Aug 1812	p. 146
Leon H. Marks, Second Lieutenant, Volunteer Company of Artillery, Regiment 9	31 Aug 1812	p. 147

Georgia Military Commissions, 1798–1818

Name, Rank, Unit	Date	Page
William Varner, Captain, Volunteer Troop of Light Dragoons, Squadron 5, Regiment 3	31 Aug 1812	p. 147
Gabriel Richardson, First Lieutenant, Volunteer Troop of Light Dragoons, Squadron 5, Regiment 3	31 Aug 1812	p. 148
Tapley Holt, Second Lieutenant, Volunteer Troop of Light Dragoons, Squadron 5, Regiment 3	31 Aug 1812	p. 148
Robert Duke, Cornet, Volunteer Troop of Light Dragoons, Squadron 5, Regiment 3	31 Aug 1812	p. 149
Archibald Clark, Captain, Volunteer Troop of Light Dragoons, Squadron 1, Regiment 1	31 Aug 1812	p. 149
John Boog, First Lieutenant, Volunteer Troop of Light Dragoons, Squadron 1, Regiment 1	31 Aug 1812	p. 150
Francis Young, Second Lieutenant, Volunteer Troop of Light Dragoons, Squadron 1, Regiment 1	31 Aug 1812	p. 150
Lewis Levy, Cornet, Volunteer Troop of Light Dragoons, Squadron 1, Regiment 1	31 Aug 1812	p. 151
Richard F. Williams, Captain, Volunteer Troop of Light Dragoons, Squadron 1, Regiment 1	31 Aug 1812	p. 151
G. W. McAlister, First Lieutenant, Volunteer Troop of Light Dragoons, Squadron 1, Regiment 1	31 Aug 1812	p. 152
George L. Cope, Second Lieutenant, Volunteer Troop of Light Dragoons, Squadron 1, Regiment 1	31 Aug 1812	p. 152
Joseph Habersham Jr., Cornet, Volunteer Troop of Light Dragoons, Squadron 1, Regiment 1	31 Aug 1812	p. 153
Samuel King, Lieutenant, District 16	4 Sep 1812	p. 153
Lewis S. Brown, Lieutenant, District 164	4 Sep 1812	p. 154
Ballard McDermont, Ensign, District 240	4 Sep 1812	p. 154
William H. Miles, Captain, District 291	4 Sep 1812	p. 155
John A. Williams, Lieutenant, District 347	4 Sep 1812	p. 155
Charles Bush, Ensign, District 347	4 Sep 1812	p. 156
John Wynn, Captain, Volunteer Company of Light Infantry, Battalion 4	10 Sep 1812	p. 156
William Flemming, Lieutenant, Volunteer Company of Light Infantry, Battalion 4	10 Sep 1812	p. 157
John Cuthbert, Ensign, Volunteer Company of Light Infantry, Battalion 4	10 Sep 1812	p. 157
Jack F. Cock, Captain, Volunteer Company of Riflemen, Battalion 48	10 Sep 1812	p. 158
James Kinny, Lieutenant, Volunteer Company of Riflemen, Battalion 48	10 Sep 1812	p. 158

Name, Rank, Unit	Date	Page
Christopher Garlington, Ensign, Volunteer Company of Riflemen, Battalion 48	10 Sep 1812	p. 159
Henry Lane, Captain, Volunteer Company of Light Infantry, Battalion 62	10 Sep 1812	p. 159
Archibald Land, Lieutenant, Volunteer Company of Light Infantry, Battalion 62	10 Sep 1812	p. 160
Britain Nicholson, Ensign, Volunteer Company of Light Infantry, Battalion 62	10 Sep 1812	p. 160
William Maxwell, Captain, District 5	10 Sep 1812	p. 161
John Boston, Lieutenant, District 12	10 Sep 1812	p. 161
James Reizer, Ensign, District 12	10 Sep 1812	p. 162
Thomas Thaaton, Ensign, District 234	10 Sep 1812	p. 162
Thomas McLendon, Lieutenant, District 362	10 Sep 1812	p. 163
Josiah G. Telfair, Captain, Volunteer Troop of Light Dragoons, Squadron 3, Regiment 2	12 Sep 1812	p. 163
William F. Jackson, First Lieutenant, Volunteer Troop of Light Dragoons, Squadron 3, Regiment 2	12 Sep 1812	p. 164
James C. Walker, Second Lieutenant, Volunteer Troop of Light Dragoons, Squadron 3, Regiment 2	12 Sep 1812	p. 164
Charles Beall, Cornet, Volunteer Troop of Light Dragoons, Squadron 3, Regiment 2	12 Sep 1812	p. 165
Joel Porter, Major, Battalion 73	12 Sep 1812	p. 165
Charles Wright, Major, Battalion 85	12 Sep 1812	p. 166
John Murphy, Ensign, District 72	12 Sep 1812	p. 166
Seth Watson, Ensign, District 77	12 Sep 1812	p. 167
Ephraim Philips, Captain, District 348	12 Sep 1812	p. 167
David Pipkin, Lieutenant, District 348	12 Sep 1812	p. 168
David Pipkin, Ensign, District 348	12 Sep 1812	p. 168
Daniel Windham, Ensign, District 355	12 Sep 1812	p. 169
Ignatius A. Few, Captain, Volunteer Troop of Dragoons, Squadron 3, Regiment 2	15 Sep 1812	p. 169
Warner L. Kennon, First Lieutenant, Volunteer Troop of Dragoons, Squadron 3, Regiment 2	15 Sep 1812	p. 170
Mark A. Candler, Second Lieutenant, Volunteer Company of Dragoons, Squadron 3, Regiment 2	15 Sep 1812	p. 170
Jesse Roberts, Cornet, Volunteer Troop of Dragoons, Squadron 3, Regiment 2	15 Sep 1812	p. 171
Samuel Owing, Captain, District 24	15 Sep 1812	p. 171

Georgia Military Commissions, 1798–1818

Name, Rank, Unit	Date	Page
John Cumming, Captain, Volunteer Company of Infantry (denominated the Savannah Fencibles), Battalion 1	22 Sep 1812	p. 172
George Anderson, Lieutenant, Volunteer Company of Infantry (denominated the Savannah Fencibles), Battalion 1	22 Sep 1812	p. 172
John P. Williamson, Ensign, Volunteer Company of Infantry (denominated the Savannah Fencibles), Battalion 1	22 Sep 1812	p. 173
Robert J. Houston, Captain, Volunteer Company of Infantry (styled the Georgia Foresters), Battalion 60	22 Sep 1812	p. 173
George Whitfield, Lieutenant, Volunteer Company of Infantry (styled the Georgia Foresters), Battalion 60	22 Sep 1812	p. 174
Henry W. Oakman, Ensign, Volunteer Company of Infantry (styled the Georgia Foresters), Battalion 60	22 Sep 1812	p. 174
William Whiddon, Lieutenant, District 40	22 Sep 1812	p. 175
Jesse McAlphens, Ensign, District 40	22 Sep 1812	p. 175
Williamson Boswell, Ensign, District 367	22 Sep 1812	p. 176
Benjamin Starritt, Ensign, District 215	22 Sep 1812	p. 176
Jacob Patton, Ensign, District 167	22 Sep 1812	p. 177
Henry P. White, Lieutenant, District 193	22 Sep 1812	p. 177
William Wiley, Captain, District 132	22 Sep 1812	p. 178
Nathan Truitt, Cornet, Volunteer Troop of Dragoons, Squadron 7, Regiment 4	22 Sep 1812	p. 178
Frederick Freeman, Major, Cavalry, Squadron 5, Regiment 3	22 Sep 1812	p. 179
William B. Bulloch, Captain, Volunteer Company of Militia (styled the Savannah Heavy Artillery), Regiment 1	22 Sep 1812	p. 179
George V. Procter, First Lieutenant, Volunteer Company of Militia (styled the Savannah Heavy Artillery), Regiment 1	22 Sep 1812	p. 180
William Gaston, Second Lieutenant, Volunteer Company of Militia (styled the Savannah Heavy Artillery), Regiment 1	22 Sep 1812	p. 180
Thomas W. Harris, Captain, Volunteer Troop of Light Dragoons, Squadron 4, Regiment 3	24 Sep 1812	p. 181
William Hemphill, First Lieutenant, Volunteer Troop of Light Dragoons, Squadron 4, Regiment 3	24 Sep 1812	p. 181
William Davis, Cornet, Volunteer Troop of Light Dragoons, Squadron 4, Regiment 3	24 Sep 1812	p. 182

Name, Rank, Unit	Date	Page
Thomas Giles, Ensign, District 161	25 Sep 1812	p. 182
John C. Payne, Ensign, District 214	25 Sep 1812	p. 183
Richard Walker, Captain, District 335	25 Sep 1812	p. 183
Evan Jones, Ensign, District 335	25 Sep 1812	p. 184
Abram Lucas, Captain, Volunteer Troop of Light Dragoons, Squadron 4, Regiment 3	25 Sep 1812	p. 184
David Hicks, First Lieutenant, Volunteer Troop of Light Dragoons, Squadron 4, Regiment 3	25 Sep 1812	p. 185
Henry W. Raley, Second Lieutenant, Volunteer Troop of Light Dragoons, Squadron 4, Regiment 3	25 Sep 1812	p. 185
Reddick Bell, Cornet, Volunteer Troop of Light Dragoons, Squadron 4, Regiment 3	25 Sep 1812	p. 186
John Sturdivant, Captain, Volunteer Company of Riflemen, Battalion 78	26 Sep 1812	p. 186
David Averitt, Lieutenant, Volunteer Company of Riflemen, Battalion 78	26 Sep 1812	p. 187
James Birdsong, Ensign, Volunteer Company of Riflemen, Battalion 78	26 Sep 1812	p. 187
Alexander Bonner, Second Lieutenant, Volunteer Company of Artillery, Regiment 14	30 Sep 1812	p. 188
Greene Wallace, Lieutenant, District 326	30 Sep 1812	p. 188
John Williams, Lieutenant, District 222	30 Sep 1812	p. 189
William Wright, Ensign, District 222	30 Sep 1812	p. 189
John Smith, Ensign, District 164	30 Sep 1812	p. 190
Andrew Russel, Lieutenant, District 62	30 Sep 1812	p. 190
Richard Sharp, Captain, District 144	7 Oct 1812	p. 191
Elijah Jordan, Lieutenant, District 144	7 Oct 1812	p. 191
Abner Simonton, Ensign, District 144	8 Oct 1812	p. 192
John Sudor, Ensign, District 122	10 Oct 1812	p. 192
Thomas Lawrence, Captain, District 366	19 Oct 1812	p. 193
George B. McIntosh, Lieutenant, District 3	19 Oct 1812	p. 193
John B. Habersham, Ensign, District 3	19 Oct 1812	p. 194
Thomas Davis, Lieutenant, District 272	19 Oct 1812	p. 194
A. B. McAlister, Ensign, District 272	19 Oct 1812	p. 195
Henry Harbock, Ensign, District 6	19 Oct 1812	p. 195
Levi Smith, Ensign, District 20	19 Oct 1812	p. 196
Henry Gignilliat, Captain, District 23	19 Oct 1812	p. 196
John Fetchat, Ensign, District 31	19 Oct 1812	p. 197

Name, Rank, Unit	Date	Page
John Peacock, Ensign, District 44	19 Oct 1812	p. 197
Phinias Oliver, Lieutenant, District 88	19 Oct 1812	p. 198
Collier Foster, Ensign, District 119	19 Oct 1812	p. 198
Dempsey Powell, Ensign, District 221	19 Oct 1812	p. 199
Peachy R. Gilmore, Ensign, District 231	19 Oct 1812	p. 199
Drury Goolsby, Ensign, District 238	19 Oct 1812	p. 200
Joseph Norman, Captain, District 252	19 Oct 1812	p. 200
John Wommack, Captain, District 267	19 Oct 1812	p. 201
Joseph Nolley, Lieutenant, District 267	19 Oct 1812	p. 201
Robert Chambers, Ensign, District 301	19 Oct 1812	p. 202
John Singletary, Lieutenant, District 329	19 Oct 1812	p. 202
Amos Barnes, Ensign, District 329	19 Oct 1812	p. 203
Thomas Pridgen, Captain, District 340	19 Oct 1812	p. 203
Lewey Smith, Ensign, District 340	19 Oct 1812	p. 204
Richard Shackleford, Second Lieutenant, Volunteer Troop of Light Dragoons, Squadron 3, Regiment 2	19 Oct 1812	p. 204
Emanuel Bennett, Lieutenant, District 49	5 Sep 1812	p. 205
Daniel Boatwright, Ensign, District 49	5 Nov 1812	p. 205
Richard Strother, Lieutenant, District 111	5 Sep 1812	p. 206
Thomas Carr, Captain, District 135	5 Nov 1812	p. 206
James Mapping, Lieutenant, District 135	5 Nov 1812	p. 207
Richard J. Willis, Captain, District 168	5 Nov 1812	p. 207
John H. Milner, Ensign, District 168	5 Nov 1812	p. 208
James Allen, Captain, District 207	5 Nov 1812	p. 208
John Newton, Ensign, District 207	5 Nov 1812	p. 209
James Stewart, Lieutenant, District 232	5 Nov 1812	p. 209
Isaac Thrash, Lieutenant, District 261	5 Nov 1812	p. 210
James Simms, Ensign, District 261	5 Nov 1812	p. 210
Zachariah Eates, Captain, District 294	5 Nov 1812	p. 211
Henry Stovall, Lieutenant, District 294	5 Nov 1812	p. 211
Israel Gragg, Lieutenant, District 325	5 Nov 1812	p. 212
John Corcker, Ensign, District 325	5 Nov 1812	p. 212
William Simms, Captain, District 355	5 Nov 1812	p. 213
Nimrod Buzbee, Lieutenant, District 355	5 Nov 1812	p. 213
John Thomas, Ensign, District 375	5 Nov 1812	p. 214
Stephen Justus, Lieutenant, Volunteer Company of Riflemen, Battalion 53	5 Nov 1812	p. 214

Name, Rank, Unit	Date	Page
Joseph McCutching, Ensign, Volunteer Company of Riflemen, Battalion 53	5 Nov 1812	p. 215
Moses Herbert, Ensign, Volunteer Company of Heavy Artillery, Regiment 1	5 Nov 1812	p. 215
Samuel S. Steele, Captain, Volunteer Troop of Light Dragoons, Squadron 5, Regiment 3	5 Nov 1812	p. 216
Henry Williams, First Lieutenant, Volunteer Troop of Light Dragoons, Squadron 3, Regiment 2	5 Nov 1812	p. 216
Nathaniel Pearrie, Cornet, Volunteer Troop of Light Dragoons, Squadron 3, Regiment 2	5 Nov 1812	p. 217
James Dilworth, Ensign, District 33	10 Nov 1812	p. 217
Andrew Townsend, Captain, District 280	10 Nov 1812	p. 218
Anderson Holt, Captain, District 320	10 Nov 1812	p. 218
John Hardie, Lieutenant, District 328	10 Nov 1812	p. 219
Micajah Dickson, Ensign, District 328	10 Nov 1812	p. 219
Hardy Anderson, Lieutenant, District 59	20 Nov 1812	p. 220
Jesse Lewis, Ensign, District 59	20 Nov 1812	p. 220
Job Gresham, Ensign, District 69	20 Nov 1812	p. 221
John W. Ray, Lieutenant, District 147	20 Nov 1812	p. 221
John Walton, Lieutenant, District 183	20 Nov 1812	p. 222
Levi Walker, Ensign, District 183	20 Nov 1812	p. 222
Gibson Blalock, Ensign, District 186	20 Nov 1812	p. 223
John Walters, Captain, District 214	20 Nov 1812	p. 223
John P. Carey, Captain, District 216	20 Nov 1812	p. 224
John Fambrough, Lieutenant, District 223	20 Nov 1812	p. 224
David Willoby, Ensign, District 223	20 Nov 1812	p. 225
Miles Hardy, Captain, District 297	20 Nov 1812	p. 225
Joseph Middlebrook, Lieutenant, District 298	20 Nov 1812	p. 226
John Lucas, Lieutenant, District 322	20 Nov 1812	p. 226
William Wemberly, Jr., Ensign, District 322	20 Nov 1812	p. 227
William Dorsey, Second Lieutenant, Volunteer Company of Artillery	20 Nov 1812	p. 227
Edmund Hopson, Captain, Volunteer Company of Light Infantry, Battalion 21	20 Nov 1812	p. 228
William Hopson, Lieutenant, Volunteer Company of Light Infantry, Battalion 21	20 Nov 1812	p. 228
Archibald McNeil, Ensign, Volunteer Company of Light Infantry, Battalion 21	20 Nov 1812	p. 229

Georgia Military Commissions, 1798–1818

Name, Rank, Unit	Date	Page
Richard H. Thomas, Captain, Volunteer Troop of Light Dragoons, Squadron 4, Regiment 2	20 Nov 1812	p. 229
James L. Perry, First Lieutenant, Volunteer Troop of Light Dragoons, Squadron 4, Regiment 2	20 Nov 1812	p. 230
Lewis Holland, Second Lieutenant, Volunteer Troop of Light Dragoons, Squadron 4, Regiment 2	20 Nov 1812	p. 230
Theophilus Sutton, Cornet, Volunteer Troop of Light Dragoons, Squadron 4, Regiment 2	20 Nov 1812	p. 231
Samuel Passmore, Second Lieutenant, Volunteer Troop of Light Dragoons, Squadron 4, Regiment 2	20 Nov 1812	p. 231
Joseph Blackshear, Lieutenant Colonel, Regiment 39	20 Nov 1812	p. 232
William Brown, Captain, Volunteer Company of Riflemen, Battalion 63	23 Nov 1812	p. 232
John Milligan, Lieutenant, Volunteer Company of Riflemen, Battalion 63	23 Nov 1812	p. 233
Nathan Hackney, Ensign, Volunteer Company of Riflemen, Battalion 63	20 Nov 1812	p. 233
Michael Buckhalter, Ensign, District 259	23 Nov 1812	p. 234
Jesse Gunn, Lieutenant, District 279	23 Nov 1812	p. 234
Matthew Watson, Ensign, Volunteer Company of Infantry (entitled the Independent Blues), Battalion 70	23 Nov 1812	p. 235
James M. Gilmore, Captain, Volunteer Company of Riflemen, Battalion 22	27 Nov 1812	p. 235
Green H. Jordan, Lieutenant, Volunteer Company of Riflemen, Battalion 22	27 Nov 1812	p. 236
John H. Gilmore, Ensign, Volunteer Company of Riflemen, Battalion 22	27 Nov 1812	p. 236
Benjamin J. Sanderlin, Ensign, District 1	2 Dec 1812	p. 237
James Vincent, Ensign, District 29	2 Dec 1812	p. 237
David Wilson, Lieutenant, District 41	2 Dec 1812	p. 238
Daniel J. Blackburn, Ensign, District 41	2 Dec 1812	p. 238
William Roussoan, Ensign, District 115	2 Dec 1812	p. 239
Elias Wilson, Lieutenant, District 134	2 Dec 1812	p. 239
John Grimes, Ensign, District 134	2 Dec 1812	p. 240
Robert Tucker, Ensign, District 146	2 Dec 1812	p. 240
Jesse Booles, Lieutenant, District 148	2 Dec 1812	p. 241
David Muncrief, Lieutenant, District 160	2 Dec 1812	p. 241
David Scarborough, Lieutenant, District 341	2 Dec 1812	p. 242
John Maddox, Ensign, District 379	2 Dec 1812	p. 242

Commissions Book 1812–1815

Name, Rank, Unit	Date	Page
Edward McGehee, Captain, District 364	2 Dec 1812	p. 243
James McGehee, Ensign, District 364	2 Dec 1812	p. 243
John Lasseter, Captain, Volunteer Company of Riflemen, Battalion 65	2 Dec 1812	p. 244
Benjamin Smith, Lieutenant, Volunteer Company of Riflemen, Battalion 65	2 Dec 1812	p. 244
Obed Sadawhite, Ensign, Volunteer Company of Riflemen, Battalion 65	2 Dec 1812	p. 245
John H. Ashe, First Lieutenant, Volunteer Company of Infantry (called the Republican Blues), Battalion 60	2 Dec 1812	p. 245
Francis M. Stone, Second Lieutenant, Volunteer Company of Infantry (called the Republican Blues), Battalion 60	2 Dec 1812	p. 246
Samuel Rhan, Ensign, Volunteer Company of the Militia called the Republican Blues, Battalion 60	2 Dec 1812	p. 246
Allen Daniel, Major General, Division 4	3 Dec 1812	p. 247
Jeptha V. Harris, Brigadier General, Brigade 1, Division 4	3 Dec 1812	p. 247
David Adams, Major General, Division 5	9 Dec 1812	p. 248
William Lee, Brigadier General, Brigade 1, Division 5	9 Dec 1812	p. 248
David Blackshear, Brigadier General, Brigade 2, Division 5	9 Dec 1812	p. 249
Abraham Bessent, Captain, Volunteer Company of Guards, Battalion 8	11 Dec 1812	p. 249
John Ross, Lieutenant, Volunteer Company of Guards, Battalion 8	11 Dec 1812	p. 250
John Blair, Ensign, Volunteer Company of Guards, Battalion 8	11 Dec 1812	p. 250
John G. Lumsdan, First Lieutenant, Volunteer Troop of Light Dragoons, Squadron 6, Regiment 3	15 Dec 1812	p. 251
Peter J. Williams, Cornet, Volunteer Troop of Light Dragoons, Squadron 6, Regiment 3	15 Dec 1812	p. 251
Shubal Starnes Welborn, Lieutenant, District 177	15 Dec 1812	p. 252
John Moreman, Ensign, District 177	15 Dec 1812	p. 252
William Davies, Second Lieutenant, Volunteer Company of Artillery in Savannah, Regiment 1	15 Dec 1812	p. 253
Nathaniel Waller, Lieutenant, District 319	16 Dec 1812	p. 253
Philip Ulmer, Ensign, District 9	18 Dec 1812	p. 254
Francis Jones, Captain, District 35	18 Dec 1812	p. 254
Middleton Pool, Ensign, District 100	18 Dec 1812	p. 255
David Reeves, Ensign, District 300	18 Dec 1812	p. 255

Georgia Military Commissions, 1798–1818

Name, Rank, Unit	Date	Page
Isaac Carter, Lieutenant, District 357	18 Dec 1812	p. 256
John Benton, Ensign, District 357	18 Dec 1812	p. 256
John Smith, Captain, District 381	18 Dec 1812	p. 257
James Jackson, Captain, Volunteer Troop of Light Dragoons, Squadron 2, Regiment 1	24 Dec 1812	p. 257
Henry W. Cobb, First Lieutenant, Volunteer Troop of Light Dragoons, Squadron 2, Regiment 1	24 Dec 1812	p. 258
Benjamin Bryan, Second Lieutenant, Volunteer Troop of Light Dragoons, Squadron 2, Regiment 1	24 Dec 1812	p. 258
Elisha Moreland, Cornet, Volunteer Troop of Light Dragoons, Squadron 2, Regiment 1	24 Dec 1812	p. 259
William Mickler, Captain, District 29	30 Dec 1812	p. 259
Hezekiah Lewis, Lieutenant, District 60	30 Dec 1812	p. 260
Jesse Attaway, Ensign, District 60	30 Dec 1812	p. 260
Richard Gordon, Ensign, District 95	30 Dec 1812	p. 261
Isaac Ray, Captain, District 147	30 Dec 1812	p. 261
Allen S. Johnson, Ensign, District 147	30 Dec 1812	p. 262
James Fannin, Captain, District 160	30 Dec 1812	p. 262
Coleman Reynolds, Ensign, District 225	30 Dec 1812	p. 263
Benjamin Collier, Captain, District 228	30 Dec 1812	p. 263
Moses Yarborough, Lieutenant, District 251	30 Dec 1812	p. 264
John Jones, Ensign, District 317	30 Dec 1812	p. 264
Duncan McRae, Lieutenant, District 337	30 Dec 1812	p. 265
Richard Wooten, Ensign, District 337	30 Dec 1812	p. 265
Samuel S. Law, Major, Cavalry, Squadron 1, Regiment 1	30 Dec 1812	p. 266
Goodwin Myrick, First Lieutenant, Baldwin Troop of Light Dragoons, Squadron 5, Regiment 3	30 Dec 1812	p. 266
Andrew Maybank, Major, Battalion 4	30 Dec 1812	p. 267
Tandy W. Key, Major, Battalion 84	30 Dec 1812	p. 267
John Holmes, Lieutenant, Volunteer Company of Riflemen, Battalion 45	30 Dec 1812	p. 268
George Waters, Ensign, Volunteer Company of Riflemen, Battalion 45	30 Dec 1812	p. 268
John B. Barnes, Cavalry	19 Jan 1813	p. 269
Jethro Barnes, Lieutenant, District 105	28 Jan 1813	p. 269
Benjamin Marshall, Ensign, District 105	28 Jan 1813	p. 270
Bryan Welch, Ensign, District 19	28 Jan 1813	p. 270

Name, Rank, Unit	Date	Page
Robert Mackay, First Lieutenant, Volunteer Company of Artillery in Savannah, Regiment 1	28 Jan 1813	p. 271
David Adams, Ensign, District 5	28 Jan 1813	p. 271
David Kenney, Lieutenant, District 216	28 Jan 1813	p. 272
Miles Smith, Ensign, District 216	28 Jan 1813	p. 272
John Neidlinger, Captain, District 11	28 Jan 1813	p. 273
Jesse Arrowood, Ensign, District 208	28 Jan 1813	p. 273
William Garner, Captain, District 161	28 Jan 1813	p. 274
Mathew Gaston, Lieutenant, District 161	28 Jan 1813	p. 274
Lodwick Alford, Captain, District 149	28 Jan 1813	p. 275
Abram. Wallace, Ensign, District 104	28 Dec 1813	p. 275
James Avery, Lieutenant, District 379	28 Jan 1813	p. 276
Leonard Wilson, Captain, District 363	28 Jan 1813	p. 276
Isaac Moore Jr., Lieutenant, District 290	28 Jan 1813	p. 277
James Tatum, Captain, District 188	28 Jan 1813	p. 277
Joseph Jones, Captain, Volunteer Company of Militia (styled the Liberty Light Infantry)	28 Jan 1813	p. 278
John Elliott, First Lieutenant, Volunteer Company of Militia (styled the Liberty County Light Infantry)	28 Jan 1813	p. 278
James McMurray, Captain, District 389	28 Jan 1813	p. 279
Robert Bourks, Ensign, District 389	28 Jan 1813	p. 279
James Wright, Lieutenant, District 312	28 Jan 1813	p. 280
Nicholas W. Wells, Ensign, District 312	28 Jan 1813	p. 280
John Murphy, Ensign, District 388	28 Jan 1813	p. 281
Joseph B. Bryant, Major, Battalion 86	28 Jan 1813	p. 281
Elijah Barker, Ensign, District 350	28 Jan 1813	p. 282
Evan Thomas, Ensign, District 387	28 Jan 1813	p. 282
Thomas Hill, Ensign, District 121	28 Jan 1813	p. 283
Moses Fort, Captain, District 372	28 Jan 1813	p. 283
Henry Raines, Lieutenant, District 167	28 Jan 1813	p. 284
Nathan Tanter, Lieutenant, District 328	28 Jan 1813	p. 284
John Deloach, Ensign, District 328	28 Jan 1813	p. 285
Thomas Guess, Ensign, District 170	28 Jan 1813	p. 285
Sampson Wilder, Captain, Volunteer Troop of Light Dragoons, Squadron 3, Regiment 2	28 Jan 1813	p. 286
Elijah Blackshear, Major, Battalion 87	30 Jan 1813	p. 286
Isaac R. Youngblood, Lieutenant, District 117	30 Jan 1813	p. 287

Georgia Military Commissions, 1798–1818

Name, Rank, Unit	*Date*	*Page*
Garland Pearson, Captain, District 176	22 Feb 1813	p. 287
Stephen Reed, Captain, Volunteer Troop of Light Dragoons, Squadron 8, Regiment 4	26 Feb 1813	p. 288
James Scism, First Lieutenant, Volunteer Company of Light Dragoons, Squadron 8, Regiment 4	26 Feb 1813	p. 288
Michael Dixon, Second Lieutenant, Volunteer Troop of Light Dragoons, Squadron 8, Regiment 4	26 Feb 1813	p. 289
Thomas Obarr, Cornet, Volunteer Troop of Light Dragoons, Squadron 8, Regiment 4	26 Feb 1813	p. 289
Jonathan Gaulding, Ensign, District 17	26 Feb 1813	p. 290
William Hill, Ensign, District 20	26 Feb 1813	p. 290
James Royal, Ensign, District 190	26 Feb 1813	p. 291
James Epps, Ensign, District 276	26 Feb 1813	p. 291
Benjamin Stowers, Lieutenant, District 200	26 Feb 1813	p. 292
Richard Ward, Ensign, District 200	26 Feb 1813	p. 292
Jared Harper, Lieutenant, District 187	26 Feb 1813	p. 293
Joshua S. Calloway, Captain, District 168	26 Feb 1813	p. 293
Henry Fenn, Lieutenant, District 94	26 Feb 1813	p. 294
Joel Simonton, Lieutenant, District 141	26 Feb 1813	p. 294
Fancis Boykin, Lieutenant, District 163	26 Feb 1813	p. 295
Moses Credill, Ensign, District 163	26 Feb 1813	p. 295
John McCravy, Lieutenant, District 321	26 Feb 1813	p. 296
Ashly Cawthon, Captain, District 344	26 Feb 1813	p. 296
John Stringer, Ensign, District 344	26 Feb 1813	p. 297
John Reeves, Lieutenant, District 133	26 Feb 1813	p. 297
Jessee Grigg, Lieutenant, District 102	26 Feb 1813	p. 298
Joseph L. Hill, Captain, District 357	26 Feb 1813	p. 298
Jeremiah Bridges, Ensign, District 357	26 Feb 1813	p. 299
Richard E. Spann, Lieutenant, District 325	26 Feb 1813	p. 299
Sion Fireash, Ensign, District 42	26 Feb 1813	p. 300
William Carter, Captain, District 42	26 Feb 1813	p. 300
James Williams, Lieutenant, District 5	26 Feb 1813	p. 301
Joseph Tillman, Ensign, District 5	26 Feb 1813	p. 301
Dugal McBride, Ensign	26 Feb 1813	p. 302
Benjamin Story, Lieutenant, District 150	26 Feb 1813	p. 302
John Atkins, Ensign, District 150	26 Feb 1813	p. 303
David F. Adams, Captain, District 55	26 Feb 1813	p. 303

Name, Rank, Unit	Date	Page
Absalom Crestler, Ensign, District 255	26 Feb 1813	p. 304
Isham Frowhawk, Lieutenant, District 346	26 Feb 1813	p. 304
John Allen, Cornet, Volunteer Troop of Dragoons, Squadron 5, Regiment 3	26 Feb 1813	p. 305
John Peeples, Cornet, Volunteer Troop of Dragoons, Squadron 5, Regiment 3	26 Feb 1813	p. 305
Peter Bennock, First Lieutenant, Volunteer Company of Artillery in the City of Augusta, Regiment 10	26 Feb 1813	p. 306
George W. Moore, Captain, Volunteer Troop of Dragoons, Squadron 6, Regiment 3	26 Feb 1813	p. 306
Robert Mackay, Captain, Volunteer Company of Artillery in the City of Augusta, Regiment 1	26 Feb 1813	p. 307
John P. Williamson, Lieutenant, Volunteer Company of Infantry (styled the Savannah Fencibles), Battalion 1	26 Feb 1813	p. 307
Benjamin Boroughs, Ensign, Volunteer Company of Infantry (styled the Savannah Fencibles), Battalion 1	26 Feb 1813	p. 308
James Meriwether, Captain, Volunteer Company of Riflemen, Battalion 49	26 Feb 1813	p. 308
John G. Meriwether, Lieutenant, Volunteer Company of Riflemen, Battalion 49	26 Feb 1813	p. 309
Lewis M. Poulett, Ensign, Volunteer Company of Riflemen, Battalion 49	26 Feb 1813	p. 309
George Reed, Captain, Volunteer Troop of Light Dragoons, Squadron 8, Regiment 4	26 Feb 1813	p. 310
Robert Boren, First Lieutenant, Volunteer Troop of Dragoons, Squadron 8, Regiment 4	26 Feb 1813	p. 310
Sylvester Nelson, Second Lieutenant, Volunteer Troop of Dragoons, Squadron 8, Regiment 4	26 Feb 1813	p. 311
Mathew G. Barker, Cornet, Volunteer Troop of Dragoons, Squadron 8, Regiment 4	26 Feb 1813	p. 311
Isaac Jackson, Lieutenant Colonel Commandant, Regiment 40	26 Feb 1813	p. 312
Lewis Easters, Captain, District 305	5 Mar 1813	p. 312
Jones Kendrick, Captain, District 174	5 Mar 1813	p. 313
William J. Sims, Captain, District 8	5 Mar 1813	p. 313
James W. Crews, Lieutenant, District 8	9 Mar 1813	p. 314
Simon Parker, Ensign, District 77	9 Mar 1813	p. 314
John Lyon, Ensign, District 79	9 Mar 1813	p. 315
Henry Gibson, Captain, District 134	9 Mar 1813	p. 315

Georgia Military Commissions, 1798–1818

Name, Rank, Unit	Date	Page
James Martin, Ensign, District 157	9 Mar 1813	p. 316
Martin Jones, Lieutenant, District 267	9 Mar 1813	p. 316
James Harris, Ensign, District 302	9 Mar 1813	p. 317
William Davies, First Lieutenant, Chatham Artillery Company, Regiment 1	9 Mar 1813	p. 317
James Gould, Second Lieutenant, Chatham Artillery Company, Regiment 1	9 Mar 1813	p. 318
Charles H. Stephens, Ensign, Volunteer Company (styled the Chatham Rangers), Battalion 1	9 Mar 1813	p. 318
John Lamkin, Captain, Troop of Light Dragoons in Lincoln County, Squadron 7, Regiment 4	15 Mar 1813	p. 319
Thomas Lamar, First Lieutenant, Troop of Light Dragoons in Lincoln County, Squadron 7, Regiment 4	15 Mar 1813	p. 319
James Wadsworth, Second Lieutenant, Troop of Light Dragoons in Lincoln County, Squadron 7, Regiment 4	15 Mar 1813	p. 320
Charles Jennings, Cornet, Troop of Light Dragoons in Lincoln County, Squadron 7, Regiment 4	15 Mar 1813	p. 320
William Tuggle, Ensign, District 138	19 Mar 1813	p. 321
James Bullard, Ensign, District 293	19 Mar 1813	p. 321
Samuel W. Langston, Ensign, District 300	19 Mar 1813	p. 322
Richard Ratcliff, Captain, District 360	19 Mar 1813	p. 322
Joshua Smith, Lieutenant, District 376	19 Mar 1813	p. 323
Benjamin Lasseter, Lieutenant, Volunteer Company of Riflemen, Battalion 65	19 Mar 1813	p. 323
Alexander McKenzie, Lieutenant, Volunteer Company of Artillery, Regiment 10	19 Mar 1813	p. 324
William S. Mitchell, Captain, Volunteer Company of Riflemen, Battalion 71	22 Mar 1813	p. 324
John Hass, Lieutenant, Volunteer Company of Riflemen, Battalion 71	22 Mar 1813	p. 325
John Bozeman, Ensign, Volunteer Company of Riflemen, Battalion 71	22 Mar 1813	p. 325
Benjamin Harvey, Major, Battalion 88	29 Mar 1813	p. 326
Thomas Howell, Ensign, District 110	29 Mar 1813	p. 326
Michael Boisclair, Captain, Volunteer Troop of Dragoons, Squadron 3, Regiment 2	29 Mar 1813	p. 327
John Watkins, Lieutenant, District 78	29 Mar 1813	p. 327
Cofield Knight, Ensign, District 78	29 Mar 1813	p. 328
Allen Lanier, Captain, District 46	29 Mar 1813	p. 328

Name, Rank, Unit	*Date*	*Page*
Hustis Studstill, Lieutenant, District 46	29 Mar 1813	p. 329
John Beasley, Ensign, District 46	29 Mar 1813	p. 329
Isham S. Fannin, Major, Battalion 63	6 Apr 1813	p. 330
James Meriwether, Captain, District 223	6 Apr 1813	p. 330
John Johnston, Lieutenant, District 28	8 Apr 1813	p. 331
William R. Webster, Lieutenant, District 122	8 Apr 1813	p. 331
Daniel Hannah, Ensign, District 122	8 Apr 1813	p. 332
Barnett Goolesby, Ensign, District 165	8 Apr 1813	p. 332
Joel Hood, Lieutenant, District 168	8 Apr 1813	p. 333
Hiram Williams, Captain, District 172	8 Apr 1813	p. 333
James Cohron, Ensign, District 172	8 Apr 1813	p. 334
Samuel Prewitt Jr., Lieutenant, District 208	8 Apr 1813	p. 334
Zebulon Savage, Ensign, District 203	8 Apr 1813	p. 335
John E. Irvin, Captain, District 233	8 Apr 1813	p. 335
Charles Christian, Lieutenant, District 248	8 Apr 1813	p. 336
Tilmon Hemphill, Ensign, District 279	8 Apr 1813	p. 336
Stephen Wisters, Ensign, District 341	8 Apr 1813	p. 337
Marcus Varner, Ensign, District 368	8 Apr 1813	p. 337
Aron B. Puckett, Ensign, District 369	8 Apr 1813	p. 338
Henry Kendall Jr., Second Lieutenant, Volunteer Troop of Light Dragoons, Squadron 3, Regiment 2	8 Apr 1813	p. 338
Henry Dawson, Captain, Troop of Light Dragoons, Squadron 7, Regiment 4	8 Apr 1813	p. 339
Allen Martin, First Lieutenant, Troop of Light Dragoons, Squadron 7, Regiment 4	8 Apr 1813	p. 339
George H. Hughes, Second Lieutenant, Troop of Light Dragoons, Squadron 7, Regiment 4	8 Apr 1813	p. 340
Thompson Ware, First Lieutenant, Troop of Light Dragoons, Squadron 3, Regiment 2	8 Apr 1813	p. 340
Wm. P. Dearmont, Second Lieutenant, Troop of Light Dragoons, Squadron 3, Regiment 2	8 Apr 1813	p. 341
Smith Jones, Cornet, Troop of Light Dragoons, Squadron 3, Regiment 2	8 Apr 1813	p. 341
Willoughby Barton, Captain, Volunteer Company of Rangers, Battalion 75	8 Apr 1813	p. 342
Loveberry McCombs, Lieutenant, Volunteer Company of Rangers, Battalion 75	8 Apr 1813	p. 342

Georgia Military Commissions, 1798–1818

Name, Rank, Unit	Date	Page
Hendly Varner, Ensign, Volunteer Company of Rangers, Battalion 75	8 Apr 1813	p. 343
Nathaniel Nicholson, Major, Battalion 89	19 Apr 1813	p. 343
John Adams, Ensign, District 243	19 Apr 1813	p. 344
William P. Sissom, Ensign, District 13	19 Apr 1813	p. 344
Henry Roads, Ensign, District 102	19 Apr 1813	p. 345
Collin Foster, Lieutenant, District 119	19 Apr 1813	p. 345
James D. Willis, Ensign, District 168	19 Apr 1813	p. 346
Fancis Arnold, Captain, District 261	19 Apr 1813	p. 346
Joshua Rees, Lieutenant, District 274	19 Apr 1813	p. 347
Fleming Bates, Lieutenant, District 306	19 Apr 1813	p. 347
William McAlpin, Captain, District 290	19 Apr 1813	p. 348
Elisha Ellis, Ensign, District 290	19 Apr 1813	p. 348
William Buck, Captain, District 99	19 Apr 1813	p. 349
Jesse Prosser, Ensign, District 99	19 Apr 1813	p. 349
Stiring Wallace, Ensign, District 61	21 Apr 1813	p. 350
William R. Caldwell, Captain, District 62	21 Apr 1813	p. 350
Nathan Bradford, Ensign, District 181	21 Apr 1813	p. 351
Dennis Duncan, Lieutenant, District 209	21 Apr 1813	p. 351
Thomas Ivy, Ensign, District 209	21 Apr 1813	p. 352
Obadiah Formby, Ensign, District 288	21 Apr 1813	p. 352
Joshua Hawthorn, Captain, District 353	21 Apr 1813	p. 353
John Davis, Lieutenant, District 353	21 Apr 1813	p. 353
Timothy Seas, Ensign, District 353	21 Apr 1813	p. 354
George Powell, Lieutenant, District 366	21 Apr 1813	p. 354
Mark Smith, Second Lieutenant, Volunteer Troop of Dragoons in Oglethorpe County, Squadron 6, Regiment 3	21 Apr 1813	p. 355
Alexander Johnston, Lieutenant, District 326	26 Apr 1813	p. 355
John F. Lloyd, Captain, District 6	29 Apr 1813	p. 356
Edward Poythress, Ensign, District 72	29 Apr 1813	p. 356
John Culbreath, Ensign, District 126	29 Apr 1813	p. 357
Benjamin Wallace, Ensign, District 169	29 Apr 1813	p. 357
Stephen White, Lieutenant, District 182	29 Apr 1813	p. 358
Hincher Thomas, Ensign, District 182	29 Apr 1813	p. 358
Osborn Childers, Captain, District 325	29 Apr 1813	p. 359
Jacob Chaneker, Ensign, District 341	29 Apr 1813	p. 359

Name, Rank, Unit	Date	Page
John Hutson, Lieutenant, District 364	29 Apr 1813	p. 360
Peter Donaldson, Major, Battalion 75	29 Apr 1813	p. 360
William G. Allen, Ensign, Volunteer Company of Riflemen, Battalion 67	29 Apr 1813	p. 361
Edgeworth Pugh, Ensign, District 329	30 Apr 1813	p. 361
Hosea Webster, Captain, Volunteer Company of Infantry (styled the Homespun Foresters), Battalion 19	4 May 1813	p. 362
Roger L. Gamble, Lieutenant, Volunteer Company of Infantry (styled the Homespun Foresters), Battalion 19	4 May 1813	p. 362
John Calder, Ensign, District 21	6 May 1813	p. 363
James Rachels, Lieutenant, District 114	6 May 1813	p. 363
Jeremiah Duckworth, Ensign, District 114	6 May 1813	p. 364
Woody Dozier, Lieutenant, District 115	6 May 1813	p. 364
John Clark, Lieutenant, District 215	6 May 1813	p. 365
Joseph Dobson, Ensign, District 215	6 May 1813	p. 365
Isaac Funderberg, Captain, District 224	6 May 1813	p. 366
John A. Cockburn, Lieutenant, District 224	6 May 1813	p. 366
Garrett Craft, Ensign, District 224	6 May 1813	p. 367
Matthew J. Pass, Lieutenant, District 237	6 May 1813	p. 367
Harris Trammel, Lieutenant, District 239	6 May 1813	p. 368
Elijah Lovin, Ensign, District 239	6 May 1813	p. 368
William Millsap, Lieutenant, District 249	6 May 1813	p. 369
Turner Moreland, Captain, District 375	6 May 1813	p. 369
Wyatt Singleton, Ensign, District 377	6 May 1813	p. 370
Thomas Moore, First Lieutenant, Volunteer Troop of Light Dragoons, Squadron 6, Regiment 3	6 May 1813	p. 370
Nathan Isler, Lieutenant, District 332	12 May 1813	p. 371
Willis Conner, Ensign, District 332	12 May 1813	p. 371
Neidham McLendon, Captain, District 52	14 May 1813	p. 372
John Rhodes, Ensign, District 119	14 May 1813	p. 372
Hezekiah Davis, Lieutenant, District 134	14 May 1813	p. 373
William C. Umphries, Lieutenant, District 138	14 May 1813	p. 373
Casper Howell, Ensign, District 162	14 May 1813	p. 374
Amos McLendon, Lieutenant, District 178	14 May 1813	p. 374
Andrew Porder, Ensign, District 178	14 May 1813	p. 375
Wistley Mayfield, Lieutenant, District 210	14 May 1813	p. 375
James Smith, Ensign, District 210	14 May 1813	p. 376

Georgia Military Commissions, 1798–1818

Name, Rank, Unit	Date	Page
Willie Ross, Ensign, District 242	14 May 1813	p. 376
William Chalmers, Captain, District 265	14 May 1813	p. 377
William Brock, Lieutenant, District 265	14 May 1813	p. 377
Robert S. Bailey, Ensign, District 265	14 May 1813	p. 378
Joel Lockhart Jr., Lieutenant, District 269	14 May 1813	p. 378
George H. Johnson, Ensign, District 274	14 May 1813	p. 379
Benjamin Selman, Lieutenant, District 288	14 May 1813	p. 379
Samuel W. Langston, Lieutenant, District 300	14 May 1813	p. 380
Henry Pitts, Captain, District 342	14 May 1813	p. 380
Arthur Fort, Lieutenant, District 372	14 May 1813	p. 381
John Danner, Ensign, District 372	14 May 1813	p. 381
Golphin Harvey, Second Lieutenant, Volunteer Troop of Light Dragoons, Squadron 2, Regiment 1	14 May 1813	p. 382
Robert R. Reid, Captain, District 120	14 May 1813	p. 382
James McLaws, Lieutenant, District 120	14 May 1813	p. 383
Thomas Glascock, Captain, District 122	14 May 1813	p. 383
James Glenn, Lieutenant, District 190	21 May 1813	p. 384
Angus Calhoon, Captain, District 275	21 May 1813	p. 384
William Twilley, Ensign, District 315	21 May 1813	p. 385
Harvey Kindrick, Lieutenant, District 314	21 May 1813	p. 385
William Wimberly, Lieutenant, District 322	21 May 1813	p. 386
James Berry, Lieutenant, District 367	21 May 1813	p. 386
George Kinnedy, Captain, Volunteer Company of Infantry (styled the Augusta Independent Blues), Battalion 75	21 May 1813	p. 387
George Heard, First Lieutenant, Volunteer Troop of Light Dragoons, Squadron 6, Regiment 3	21 May 1813	p. 387
Shadrack Atkinson, Major, Battalion 79	27 May 1813	p. 388
Charles Dame, Lieutenant, Volunteer Company (styled the Augusta Independent Blues), Battalion 75	27 May 1813	p. 388
John Powers, Ensign, Volunteer Company (styled the Augusta Independent Blues), Battalion 75	27 May 1813	p. 389
Richard Rowell, Captain, District 7	21 May 1813	p. 389
Joseph Wiggins, Lieutenant, District 7	27 May 1813	p. 390
William Colson, Captain, District 67	27 May 1813	p. 390
Edward Tabb, Ensign, District 67	27 May 1813	p. 391
Thomas Booth, Captain, District 221	27 May 1813	p. 391
James Hartsfield, Lieutenant, District 235	27 May 1813	p. 392

Name, Rank, Unit	Date	Page
Elijah Woodruff, Ensign, District 236	27 May 1813	p. 392
Levi Miller, Lieutenant, District 343	27 May 1813	p. 393
Ernst William Geyer, Lieutenant, District 64	27 May 1813	p. 393
John Knight, Lieutenant, District 65	4 Jun 1813	p. 394
Josiah Scutchings, Lieutenant, District 73	27 Jun 1813	p. 394
Gideon Willis, Lieutenant, District 79	4 Jun 1813	p. 395
John Rudisill, Ensign, District 107	4 Jun 1813	p. 395
Henry Fruman, Lieutenant, District 245	4 Jun 1813	p. 396
John Carlisle, Ensign, District 245	4 Jun 1813	p. 396
Binaniul Bower, Ensign, Volunteer Company (styled the Homespun Foresters), Battalion 19	4 Jun 1813	p. 397
Steele White, Major, Battalion 1	14 Jun 1813	p. 397
John P. Oates, Captain, District 2	14 Jun 1813	p. 398
John Filchett, Lieutenant, District 31	14 Jun 1813	p. 398
Samuel C. Daniel, Lieutenant, District 137	14 Jun 1813	p. 399
James Murphy, Lieutenant, District 299	14 Jun 1813	p. 399
William Bayne, Ensign, District 299	14 Jun 1813	p. 400
James Cloud, Ensign, District 323	14 Jun 1813	p. 400
Shadrack W. Gibson, Second Lieutenant, Volunteer Company of Artillery, Regiment 11	14 Jun 1813	p. 401
James Clayton, Ensign, Volunteer Company of Riflemen, Battalion 23	17 Jun 1813	p. 401
Richard Caldwell, Ensign, Volunteer Guards, Battalion 8	21 Jun 1813	p. 402
Jacob Frederick, Lieutenant, District 122	21 Jun 1813	p. 402
Stephen Granberry, Captain, District 154	21 Jun 1813	p. 403
William Wood, Ensign, District 266	21 Jun 1813	p. 403
William Walker, Captain, District 282	21 Jun 1813	p. 404
John G. Towers, Captain, Volunteer Company of Riflemen, Battalion 61	21 Jun 1813	p. 404
Reuben Bishop, Lieutenant, Volunteer Company of Riflemen, Battalion 61	21 Jun 1813	p. 405
Benjamin Thomas, Ensign, Volunteer Company of Riflemen, Battalion 61	21 Jun 1813	p. 405
M. M. Sheftal, Lieutenant, District 2	21 Jun 1813	p. 406
David M. Crawford, Ensign, District 130	21 Jun 1813	p. 406
Bailey Bell, Captain, District 300	6 Jul 1813	p. 407
Richard Harris, Ensign, District 358	6 Jul 1813	p. 407
James Hendirikin, Lieutenant, District 379	6 Jul 1813	p. 408

Georgia Military Commissions, 1798–1818

Name, Rank, Unit	*Date*	*Page*
Thomas Connell, Ensign, District 81	10 Jul 1813	p. 408
Moses Harris, Ensign, District 136	10 Jul 1813	p. 409
Jesse Oslin, Ensign, District 161	10 Jul 1813	p. 409
Joel Holcomb, Lieutenant, District 241	10 Jul 1813	p. 410
Daniel Simmers, Ensign, District 241	10 Jul 1813	p. 410
Gilbert Smith, Lieutenant, District 283	10 Jul 1813	p. 411
M. L. Hatton, Captain, District 338	10 Jul 1813	p. 411
William Cooksey, Ensign, District 338	10 Jul 1813	p. 412
Armstead Richardson, Second Lieutenant, Volunteer Troop of Dragoons, Squadron 5, Regiment 3	10 Jul 1813	p. 412
Greenberry Gaither, Cornet, Volunteer Troop of Dragoons, Squadron 5, Regiment 3	10 Jul 1813	p. 413
Henry Butts, Captain, Volunteer Company of Riflemen, Battalion 69	12 Jul 1813	p. 413
James W. Shropshire, Lieutenant, Volunteer Company of Riflemen, Battalion 69	12 Jul 1813	p. 414
Philip Graybill, Ensign, Volunteer Company of Riflemen, Battalion 69	12 Jul 1813	p. 414
Thomas W. Shivers, Cornet, Volunteer Troop of Light Dragoons, Squadron 3, Regiment 2	16 Jul 1813	p. 415
Thomas McKegney, Ensign, District 76	16 Jul 1813	p. 415
Isaac N. Johnston, Ensign, District 226	16 Jul 1813	p. 416
Christopher Hand, Ensign, District 229	16 Jul 1813	p. 416
James McEwen, Ensign, District 250	16 Jul 1813	p. 417
Wood Moreland, Lieutenant, District 390	16 Jul 1813	p. 417
John Alston, Lieutenant, District 51	20 Jul 1813	p. 418
Jacob Raulerson, Lieutenant, District 335	20 Jul 1813	p. 418
William Lester, Captain, District 346	20 Jul 1813	p. 419
Allen Greene, Lieutenant, District 301	21 Jul 1813	p. 419
Jonathan Miller, Ensign, District 118	22 Jul 1813	p. 420
David Danney, Ensign, District 201	22 Jul 1813	p. 420
John Johnson, Captain, District 217	22 Jul 1813	p. 421
Josiph Ewing, Lieutenant, District 217	22 Jul 1813	p. 421
Jacob Burn, Lieutenant, District 220	22 Jul 1813	p. 422
John Fletcher, Ensign, District 220	22 Jul 1813	p. 422
Perriman Moody, Lieutenant, District 260	22 Jul 1813	p. 423
Harrison Hand, Ensign, District 260	22 Jul 1813	p. 423
John Sanders, Ensign, District 269	22 Jul 1813	p. 424

Name, Rank, Unit	Date	Page
Benjamin McGuoirk, Ensign, District 288	22 Jul 1813	p. 424
Garland Hagler, Ensign, District 290	22 Jul 1813	p. 425
John Sullivan, Ensign, District 322	22 Jul 1813	p. 425
Reuben Warren, Captain, District 374	22 Jul 1813	p. 426
Thomas Jackson, Lieutenant, District 374	22 Jul 1813	p. 426
William Gaston, First Lieutenant, Savannah Heavy Artillery Company, Regiment 1	22 Jul 1813	p. 427
Moses Herbert, Second Lieutenant, Savannah Heavy Artillery Company, Regiment 1	22 Jul 1813	p. 427
Lazarus Raney, Lieutenant, District 6	28 Jun 1813	p. 428
William Lavinder, Ensign, District 6	28 Jun 1813	p. 428
Silas Taturn, Lieutenant, District 186	28 Jun 1813	p. 429
Charles McKinney Jr., Ensign, District 251	28 Jun 1813	p. 429
Josiah Ellington, Lieutenant, District 254	28 Jun 1813	p. 430
Zachariah Wortham, Lieutenant, District 341	28 Jun 1813	p. 430
Nathaniel Smith, Lieutenant, District 354	28 Jun 1813	p. 431
William Spears, Ensign, District 354	28 Jun 1813	p. 431
Frederick S. Fell, Lieutenant, Volunteer Guards, Battalion 1	28 Jun 1813	p. 432
John J. Roberts, Ensign, Volunteer Guards, Battalion 1	28 Jun 1813	p. 432
Andrew Gamble, Captain, District 77	3 Aug 1813	p. 433
Simon Parker, Lieutenant, District 77	3 Aug 1813	p. 433
James Powers, Ensign, District 122	3 Aug 1813	p. 434
Haleot Alford, Ensign, District 149	3 Aug 1813	p. 434
Samuel Hall, Captain, District 163	3 Aug 1813	p. 435
James Halley, Ensign, District 199	3 Aug 1813	p. 435
Thomas Owens, Lieutenant, District 240	3 Aug 1813	p. 436
Claiborn Maddox, Ensign, District 248	3 Aug 1813	p. 436
Theodore Guerry, Ensign, District 331	3 Aug 1813	p. 437
William L. Griggs, Ensign, District 378	3 Aug 1813	p. 437
John M. Berrien, Captain, Volunteer Troop of Dragoons, Squadron 1, Regiment 1	3 Aug 1813	p. 438
James M. Wayne, First Lieutenant, Volunteer Troop of Dragoons, Squadron 1, Regiment 1	3 Aug 1813	p. 438
Robert Newell, Second Lieutenant, Volunteer Troop of Dragoons, Squadron 1, Regiment 1	3 Aug 1813	p. 439
George Glenn, Cornet, Volunteer Troop of Dragoons, Squadron 1, Regiment 1	3 Mar 1813	p. 439

Georgia Military Commissions, 1798–1818

Name, Rank, Unit	Date	Page
Archibald M. C. Harriet, Ensign, District 302	4 Aug 1813	p. 440
Alexander Meriwether, Captain, District 82	9 Aug 1813	p. 440
James Elders, Ensign, District 7	11 Aug 1813	p. 441
Reubin Underwood, Ensign, District 89	11 Mar 1813	p. 441
John Tippett, Captain, District 345	11 Aug 1813	p. 442
Vinson Harrelson, Ensign, District 148	11 Aug 1813	p. 442
John W. Torrence, Ensign, District 158	11 Aug 1813	p. 443
Brice McEven, Lieutenant, District 227	11 Aug 1813	p. 443
Robert Kirkham, Ensign, District 326	11 Aug 1813	p. 444
Robert C. Trawick, Ensign, Volunteer Company of Riflemen, Battalion 84	11 Aug 1813	p. 444
Frederick Davis, Lieutenant, Volunteer Company of Riflemen, Battalion 51	11 Aug 1813	p. 445
Thomas Wadsworth, Ensign, Volunteer Company of Riflemen, Battalion 51	11 Aug 1813	p. 445
Nicholas Childers, Captain, District 320	14 Aug 1813	p. 446
Harvey Herrington, Lieutenant, Volunteer Company of Infantry (styled the Baldwin Independent Blues), Battalion 70	18 Aug 1813	p. 446
Joseph D. Fannin, Captain, Volunteer Troop of Dragoons, Squadron 5, Regiment 3	23 Aug 1813	p. 447
Benjamin Lane, Lieutenant, Volunteer Troop of Dragoons, Squadron 5, Regiment 3	23 Aug 1813	p. 447
Edmund Butts, Second Lieutenant, Volunteer Troop of Dragoons, Squadron 5, Regiment 3	23 Aug 1813	p. 448
Richard Manly, Cornet, Volunteer Troop of Dragoons, Squadron 5, Regiment 3	23 Aug 1813	p. 448
Henley Varner, Lieutenant, Volunteer Company of Infantry (styled the Augusta Volunteer Rangers), Battalion 75	25 Aug 1813	p. 449
James G. Blunt, Ensign, Volunteer Company of Infantry (styled the Augusta Volunteer Rangers), Battalion 75	25 Aug 1813	p. 449
Robert Burton, Lieutenant, District 262	27 Aug 1813	p. 450
Edward L. Christian, Ensign, District 262	27 Aug 1813	p. 450
William Loftin, Ensign, District 306	27 Aug 1813	p. 451
John Thomas, Lieutenant, District 213	27 Aug 1813	p. 451
Shadrack Vining, Ensign, District 208	27 Aug 1813	p. 452
William Reynolds, Ensign, District 133	27 Aug 1813	p. 452
Niedham Masse, Captain, District 304	27 Aug 1813	p. 453

Name, Rank, Unit	Date	Page
James Barnard, Captain, District 5	27 Aug 1813	p. 453
Richard W. Ellis, Ensign, District 319	27 Aug 1813	p. 454
John Rawls, Lieutenant, District 36	27 Aug 1813	p. 454
Ephram Hunter, Ensign, District 36	27 Aug 1813	p. 455
William T. Hansell, Captain, District 245	27 Aug 1813	p. 455
William Bailie, Ensign, District 245	27 Aug 1813	p. 456
James Williams, Captain, District 336	27 Aug 1813	p. 456
William King, Lieutenant, District 336	27 Aug 1813	p. 457
Solomon Brannen, Ensign, District 336	27 Aug 1813	p. 457
Pleasant Bonner, Second Lieutenant, Volunteer Company of Artillery, Regiment 4	27 Aug 1813	p. 458
John Joice, Captain, District 340	27 Aug 1813	p. 458
Benjamin G. Cray, Captain, District 337	27 Aug 1813	p. 459
James Tippet, Lieutenant, District 337	27 Aug 1813	p. 459
Calvin Quinn, Ensign, District 337	27 Aug 1813	p. 460
Joseph Dorsett, Captain, District 392	27 Aug 1813	p. 460
Josiah Stewart, Lieutenant, District 392	27 Aug 1813	p. 461
John Mullins, Ensign, District 392	27 Aug 1813	p. 461
Henry W. Williams, Captain, Volunteer Company of Riflemen in the City of Savannah, Battalion 1	27 Aug 1813	p. 462
James Morrison, Lieutenant, Volunteer Company of Riflemen in the City of Savannah, Battalion 1	27 Aug 1813	p. 462
John Lewis, Ensign, Volunteer Company of Riflemen in the City of Savannah, Battalion 1	27 Aug 1813	p. 463
Arnelius Torrence, Ensign, District 357	27 Aug 1813	p. 463
Thomas Wright, Ensign, District 312	27 Aug 1813	p. 464
Kinchen Jowell, Ensign, District 56	7 Sep 1813	p. 464
Zadock Satter, Ensign, District 85	7 Sep 1813	p. 465
Peter Cone, Captain, District 45	7 Sep 1813	p. 465
Henry Melton, Lieutenant, District 45	7 Sep 1813	p. 466
Reuben King, Captain, District 271	7 Sep 1813	p. 466
Preserved Alger, Captain, District 259	7 Sep 1813	p. 467
Hillory Cason, Ensign, District 259	7 Sep 1813	p. 467
William Beall, Captain, District 263	7 Sep 1813	p. 468
John Reid, Ensign, District 361	7 Sep 1813	p. 468
Robert Hutcherson, Ensign, District 101	7 Sep 1813	p. 469
Alexander T. Ash, Lieutenant, District 263	7 Sep 1813	p. 469

Georgia Military Commissions, 1798–1818

Name, Rank, Unit	*Date*	*Page*
David S. Lowry, Ensign, District 263	7 Sep 1813	p. 470
Peter Donaldson, Lieutenant Colonel, Regiment 10	14 Sep 1813	p. 470
Edwin Baker, Captain, District 158	14 Sep 1813	p. 471
John Hardie, Major, Battalion 8	14 Sep 1813	p. 471
Wm. L. Fokes, Captain, District 82	14 Sep 1813	p. 472
Malichiah Bussey, Ensign, District 183	14 Sep 1813	p. 472
Benjamin Bryant, Captain, Volunteer Troop of Dragoons styled the Jefferson Hussars, Squadron 2, Regiment 1	14 Sep 1813	p. 473
John Sherrod Thomas, First Lieutenant, Volunteer Company of Artillery, Regiment 33	21 Sep 1813	p. 473
Ebenezer Bothwell, Ensign, District 77	26 Sep 1813	p. 474
David Robinson, Ensign, District 217	26 Sep 1813	p. 474
Robert R. Minter, Lieutenant, District 293	26 Sep 1813	p. 475
Josiah Gilbert, Lieutenant, District 320	26 Sep 1813	p. 475
Thomas P. Hamilton, Lieutenant Colonel Commandant, Regiment 30	26 Sep 1813	p. 476
Thomas Lamar, Major, Battalion 40	26 Sep 1813	p. 476
Grief Chieves, Captain, District 306	22 Oct 1813	p. 477
Joseph Stinson, Captain, District 187	22 Oct 1813	p. 477
Jesse Burch, Lieutenant, District 124	22 Oct 1813	p. 478
John Carter, Lieutenant, District 159	22 Oct 1813	p. 478
James Mapp, Lieutenant, District 109	22 Oct 1813	p. 479
Harrel H. Carrell, Ensign, District 362	22 Oct 1813	p. 479
May Mullins, Ensign, District 385	22 Oct 1813	p. 480
Francis Straughn, Ensign, District 221	22 Oct 1813	p. 480
Eli Cornett, Ensign, District 71	22 Oct 1813	p. 481
Thomas B. Grantland, Ensign, District 320	22 Oct 1813	p. 481
John Jones, Lieutenant, District 35	22 Oct 1813	p. 482
Robert Dixon, Ensign, District 35	22 Oct 1813	p. 482
Thomas Atkinson, Ensign, Volunteer Company of Light Artillery, Battalion 62	22 Oct 1813	p. 483
Thomas Henley, Lieutenant, Volunteer Company of Infantry (styled the Augusta Independent Blues), Battalion 75	22 Oct 1813	p. 483
Abram Sheftal, Lieutenant, District 4	22 Oct 1813	p. 484
John Brooks, Ensign, District 154	10 Nov 1813	p. 484
Henry Rose, Ensign, District 179	10 Nov 1813	p. 485
Nathan Dixon, Ensign, District 375	10 Nov 1813	p. 485

Name, Rank, Unit	Date	Page
William Ansley, Lieutenant, District 146	10 Nov 1813	p. 486
Edmund Welch, Lieutenant, District 283	10 Nov 1813	p. 486
Jesse George, Lieutenant, District 295	10 Nov 1813	p. 487
Robert Boyle, Lieutenant, District 258	10 Nov 1813	p. 487
Jacob Rogers, Ensign, District 258	10 Nov 1813	p. 488
William Larrisee, Lieutenant, District 34	10 Nov 1813	p. 488
John Seever, Ensign, District 34	10 Nov 1813	p. 489
Elkanah Powell, Lieutenant, District 330	10 Nov 1813	p. 489
Eli Collins, Ensign, District 330	10 Nov 1813	p. 490
David Girtman, Captain, District 386	10 Nov 1813	p. 490
Zelah Pullin, Lieutenant, District 386	10 Nov 1813	p. 491
John Atkinson, Captain, District 33	10 Nov 1813	p. 491
George Penticost, Major, Battalion 52	10 Nov 1813	p. 492
John W. Powers, Major, Battalion 75	10 Nov 1813	p. 492
David Wimberly, Ensign, Volunteer Company of Infantry in Washington County, Battalion 21	10 Nov 1813	p. 493
John Lamar, Captain, Volunteer Troop of Light Dragoons, Squadron 3, Regiment 2	10 Nov 1813	p. 493
Jonathan Robinson, Captain, Volunteer Troop of Light Dragoons, Squadron 2, Regiment 1	10 Nov 1813	p. 494
Henry Dutton, First Lieutenant, Volunteer Troop of Light Dragoons, Squadron 2, Regiment 1	10 Nov 1813	p. 494
John Mathews, Second Lieutenant, Volunteer Troop of Light Dragoons, Squadron 2, Regiment 1	10 Nov 1813	p. 495
Christopher F. Bunce, Cornet, Volunteer Troop of Light Dragoons, Squadron 2, Regiment 1	10 Nov 1813	p. 495
James G. Reynolds, Lieutenant, District 340	10 Nov 1813	p. 496
Hugh McCall, Ensign, District 340	10 Nov 1813	p. 496
Clement Bryant, Captain, Volunteer Company of Mounted Riflemen, Battalion 12	12 Nov 1813	p. 497
Simon Hadley, Lieutenant, Volunteer Company of Mounted Riflemen, Battalion 12	12 Nov 1813	p. 497
Moses Daniel, Ensign, Volunteer Company of Mounted Riflemen, Battalion 12	12 Nov 1813	p. 498
Jarrel Beasley, Major, Battalion 64	20 Nov 1813	p. 498
William Livingston, Captain, District 87	20 Nov 1813	p. 499
Hugh Thomas, Captain, District 391	20 Nov 1813	p. 499

Georgia Military Commissions, 1798–1818

Name, Rank, Unit	Date	Page
Thomas W. Baxter, First Lieutenant, Volunteer Company of Artillery in Hancock County, Regiment 4	20 Nov 1813	p. 500
John Collins, Captain, Volunteer Company of Riflemen, Battalion 29	20 Nov 1813	p. 500
Roger Harkins, Lieutenant, Volunteer Company of Riflemen, Battalion 29	20 Nov 1813	p. 501
William Hardin, Ensign, Volunteer Company of Riflemen, Battalion 29	20 Nov 1813	p. 501
Thomas Freeman, Ensign, District 174	27 Nov 1813	p. 502
Andrew Baxter, Lieutenant, District 103	27 Nov 1813	p. 502
Robert Burt, Ensign, District 103	27 Nov 1813	p. 503
Stephen Daniel, Ensign, District 378	27 Nov 1813	p. 503
Jesse Astin, Ensign, District 161	27 Nov 1813	p. 504
Green McMichal, Ensign, District 295	27 Nov 1813	p. 504
Samuel Williamson, Ensign, District 263	27 Nov 1813	p. 505
John Rice, Lieutenant, District 169	27 Nov 1813	p. 505
Francis Smith, Lieutenant Colonel Commandant, Regiment 33	27 Nov 1813	p. 506
John S. Walker, Ensign, Volunteer Company of Infantry (styled the Augusta Independent Blues), Battalion 75	27 Nov 1813	p. 506
John Bostie, Lieutenant, Volunteer Troop of Light Dragoons, Squadron 2, Regiment 1	27 Nov 1813	p. 507
Charles Cheatham, Cornet, Volunteer Troop of Light Dragoons, Squadron 2, Regiment 1	27 Nov 1813	p. 507
William Hurt, Captain, District 156	4 Dec 1813	p. 508
Robert Hill, Lieutenant, District 104	8 Dec 1813	p. 508
James A. Curry, Lieutenant, District 112	8 Dec 1813	p. 509
Thomas Humphrey, Ensign, District 112	8 Dec 1813	p. 509
William P. Easley, Captain, District 240	8 Dec 1813	p. 510
William Stapler, Lieutenant, District 252	8 Dec 1813	p. 510
Robert Fullerton, Ensign, District 252	8 Dec 1813	p. 511
Nathan Bond, Ensign, District 263	8 Dec 1813	p. 511
Allen McClendon, Captain, District 295	8 Dec 1813	p. 512
James B. Stewart, Lieutenant, District 334	8 Dec 1813	p. 512
James Buland, Lieutenant, District 363	8 Dec 1813	p. 513
Lewis J. Dupree, Captain, Volunteer Company of Riflemen, Battalion 53	8 Nov 1813	p. 513

Name, Rank, Unit	Date	Page
Hezekiah Embrey, Lieutenant, Volunteer Company of Riflemen, Battalion 53	8 Dec 1813	p. 514
Elisha Laye, Ensign, Volunteer Company of Riflemen, Battalion 53	8 Dec 1813	p. 514
Benjamin Stovall, First Lieutenant, Volunteer Troop of Light Dragoons, Squadron 7, Regiment 4	8 Dec 1813	p. 515
Stephen Day, Ensign, District 128	23 Dec 1813	p. 515
Isham T. Hogan, Ensign, District 203	23 Dec 1813	p. 516
John Charles, Ensign, District 358	23 Dec 1813	p. 516
Bartlett McCrary, Ensign, District 321	23 Dec 1813	p. 517
Ephraim Strickland, Ensign, District 204	23 Dec 1813	p. 517
Lewis Floyd, Ensign, District 205	23 Dec 1813	p. 518
Elisha Reid, Lieutenant, District 389	23 Dec 1813	p. 518
James Howard, Lieutenant, District 329	23 Dec 1813	p. 519
Augustin Hulett, Lieutenant, District 60	23 Dec 1813	p. 519
John T. Forth, Ensign, District 60	23 Dec 1813	p. 520
Charles Dewitt, Lieutenant, District 271	23 Dec 1813	p. 520
Hugh W. Proudfoot, Ensign, District 271	23 Dec 1813	p. 521
Absolam Adams, Captain, District 212	23 Dec 1813	p. 521
Thomas Dobbs, Ensign, District 212	23 Dec 1813	p. 522
Marshall, Captain, District 120	23 Dec 1813	p. 522
Dreadril Pace, Lieutenant, District 120	23 Dec 1813	p. 523
John H. Lamar, Ensign, District 120	23 Dec 1813	p. 523
Joseph Bagby, Captain, District 246	23 Dec 1813	p. 524
James McRight, Captain, District 251	23 Dec 1813	p. 524
John Boyle, Captain, District 241	23 Dec 1813	p. 525
John G. Colbert, Captain, District 139	23 Dec 1813	p. 525
Roger Lawson Gamble, Captain, Volunteer Company of Infantry (styled the Homespun Foresters), Battalion 19	23 Dec 1813	p. 526
Joeday Newsom, Lieutenant Colonel Commandant, Regiment 12	28 Jan 1814	p. 526
Henry Cox, Major, Battalion 71	28 Jan 1814	p. 527
John Carter, Captain, District 159	28 Jan 1814	p. 527
Isaac J. Barret, Captain, District 266	28 Jan 1814	p. 528
John Dell, Captain, District 336	28 Jan 1814	p. 528
Hendley Nalley, Lieutenant, District 269	28 Jan 1814	p. 529
Hermon Mercer, Lieutenant, District 170	28 Jan 1814	p. 529

Name, Rank, Unit *Date* *Page*

Joshua Willis, Lieutenant, District 176	28 Jan 1814	p. 530
James Murphey, Lieutenant, District 304	28 Jan 1814	p. 530
Simon Henderson, Captain, District 315	28 Jan 1814	p. 531
Edmund Gilbert, Ensign, District 304	28 Jan 1814	p. 531
Jeremiah Maxwell, Lieutenant, District 315	28 Jan 1814	p. 532
Samuel Meredith, Ensign, District 329	28 Jan 1814	p. 532
Martain Kidd, Ensign, District 198	28 Jan 1814	p. 533
John Knox, Ensign, District 183	28 Jan 1814	p. 533
Farr H. Trammell, Captain, District 239	9 Feb 1814	p. 534
Parkes Middleton, Lieutenant, District 239	9 Feb 1814	p. 534
William Marshall, Captain, District 84	9 Feb 1814	p. 535
Robert Fillinger, Captain, District 355	9 Feb 1814	p. 535
Josias W. Shaw, Captain, District 226	9 Feb 1814	p. 536
John Cobb, Captain, District 283	9 Feb 1814	p. 536
John L. Wright, Captain, District 278	9 Feb 1814	p. 537
John G. Mayno, Lieutenant, District 217	9 Feb 1814	p. 537
Pleasant Hulsey, Ensign, District 209	9 Feb 1814	p. 538
Aaron Jones Jr., Ensign, District 154	9 Feb 1814	p. 538
Ebenezer Miles, Ensign, District 359	9 Feb 1814	p. 539
John Weathers, Ensign, District 161	9 Feb 1814	p. 539
John H. Gilmore, Captain, Volunteer Company of Riflemen, Battalion 22	9 Feb 1814	p. 540
John Willson, Captain, Volunteer Troop of Light Dragoons, Squadron 9, Regiment 5	9 Feb 1814	p. 540
James Glass, First Lieutenant, Volunteer Troop of Light Dragoons, Squadron 9, Regiment 5	9 Feb 1814	p. 541
Robert Benson, Second Lieutenant, Volunteer Troop of Light Dragoons, Squadron 9, Regiment 5	9 Feb 1814	p. 541
James Prophitt, Cornet, Volunteer Troop of Light Dragoons, Squadron 9, Regiment 5	9 Feb 1814	p. 542
Douglass Watson, Lieutenant Colonel Commandant, Regiment 16	18 Feb 1814	p. 542
Presley Christian, Captain, District 202	18 Feb 1814	p. 543
Sackfield N. Walker, Captain, District 175	18 Feb 1814	p. 543
Thomas Prather, Lieutenant, District 175	18 Feb 1814	p. 544
Israel Weitman, Lieutenant, District 11	18 Feb 1814	p. 544
Samuel Dasher, Ensign, District 11	18 Feb 1814	p. 545
John Rawls, Lieutenant, District 36	18 Feb 1814	p. 545

Name, Rank, Unit	Date	Page
Moses Harris, Lieutenant, District 136	18 Feb 1814	p. 546
Obediah Chappel, Lieutenant, District 187	18 Feb 1814	p. 546
John Dawson, Ensign, District 8	18 Feb 1814	p. 547
John B. Neal, Ensign, District 127	18 Feb 1814	p. 547
Athael Pullin, Ensign, District 386	18 Feb 1814	p. 548
Benaniel Bower, Lieutenant, Volunteer Company of Infantry (styled the Homespun Foresters), Battalion 19	18 Feb 1814	p. 548
Mathew Huff, Ensign, District 198	9 Mar 1814	p. 549
Thomas Gray, Ensign, District 20	9 Mar 1814	p. 549
James Bone, Ensign, District 283	9 Mar 1814	p. 550
Lewis D. Hobzinback, Lieutenant, District 214	9 Mar 1814	p. 550
James H. Campbell, Lieutenant, District 277	9 Mar 1814	p. 551
Jacob Gimble, Captain, District 368	9 Mar 1814	p. 551
Turner Parsons, Ensign, District 368	9 Mar 1814	p. 552
David Hollin, Lieutenant, District 351	9 Mar 1814	p. 552
Jesse Collins, Ensign, District 351	9 Mar 1814	p. 553
James Alston, Major, Battalion 89	9 Mar 1814	p. 553
Stephen W. Blount, Captain, Volunteer Company of Infantry (styled the Independent Blues), Battalion 16	9 Mar 1814	p. 554
John Cone, Ensign, Volunteer Company of Riflemen, Battalion 27	9 Mar 1814	p. 554
David Hodge, Ensign, District 290	11 Mar 1814	p. 555
Robert Hill, Captain, District 104	11 Mar 1814	p. 555
John Purifoy, Ensign, District 104	11 Mar 1814	p. 556
Michael Bourke, Ensign, Volunteer Company of Infantry (styled the Homespun Foresters), Battalion 19	11 Mar 1814	p. 556
Peter Shick, Second Lieutenant, Volunteer Company of Cavalry styled the Chatham Troop of Light Dragoons, Squadron 1, Regiment 1	11 Mar 1814	p. 557
John Bostick, First Lieutenant, Volunteer Company of Cavalry styled the Chatham Troop of Light Dragoons, Squadron 1, Regiment 1	11 Mar 1814	p. 557
William Hayles, Lieutenant Colonel Commandant, Regiment 9	17 Mar 1814	p. 558
James Reisser, Lieutenant, District 12	17 Mar 1814	p. 558
Henry H. Hand, Lieutenant, District 38	17 Mar 1814	p. 559
Falton Kemp, Ensign, District 38	17 Mar 1814	p. 559
Francis Scott, Lieutenant, District 159	17 Mar 1814	p. 560

Georgia Military Commissions, 1798–1818

Name, Rank, Unit	Date	Page
Henry Alford, Ensign, District 160	17 Mar 1814	p. 560
John Conner, Ensign, District 240	17 Mar 1814	p. 561
Richard Dozier, Lieutenant, District 224	17 Mar 1814	p. 561
Lewis Lee, Captain, District 332	17 Mar 1814	p. 562
Jordan Abbott, Major, Battalion 33	23 Mar 1814	p. 562
John McDaniel, Ensign, District 99	24 Mar 1814	p. 563
William Wallace, Ensign, District 27	29 Mar 1814	p. 563
Edmund Gray, Captain, District 62	29 Mar 1814	p. 564
James Powers, Lieutenant, District 122	29 Mar 1814	p. 564
Archabald Martin, Captain, District 211	29 Mar 1814	p. 565
Thompson Terrell, Lieutenant, District 211	29 Mar 1814	p. 565
Tapley Bullard, Lieutenant, District 360	29 Mar 1814	p. 566
Fort Alford, Captain, District 347	29 Mar 1814	p. 566
John Cheely, Captain, District 114	8 Apr 1814	p. 567
Thomas Walton, Lieutenant, District 120	8 Apr 1814	p. 567
William Sayre Jr., Ensign, District 120	8 Apr 1814	p. 568
Henry Jones, Lieutenant, District 157	8 Apr 1814	p. 568
James Wheeler, Ensign, District 157	8 Apr 1814	p. 569
James Stewart, Ensign, District 221	8 Apr 1814	p. 569
Francis Straughn, Captain, District 241	8 Apr 1814	p. 570
Nathan Gan, Lieutenant, District 241	8 Apr 1814	p. 570
Sherwood Harper, Ensign, District 241	8 Apr 1814	p. 571
Elisha Wade, Ensign, District 260	8 Apr 1814	p. 571
William Moon, Lieutenant, District 345	8 Apr 1814	p. 572
John Smith, Ensign, District 345	8 Apr 1814	p. 572
John Barton, Lieutenant, District 392	8 Apr 1814	p. 573
James Marshall, Second Lieutenant, Volunteer Troop of Horse (styled the Jefferson Hussars)	8 Apr 1814	p. 573
Ulysses Duperis, Lieutenant, District 6	18 Apr 1814	p. 574
John Gould Butler, Ensign	18 Apr 1814	p. 574
William W. Hazzard, Captain, District 31	18 Apr 1814	p. 575
George Stapleton, Ensign, District 81	18 Apr 1814	p. 575
Peter Albritton, Captain, District 98	18 Apr 1814	p. 576
James Armstron, Lieutenant, District 98	18 Apr 1814	p. 576
Isaac Law, Captain, District 124	18 Apr 1814	p. 577
Hazlewood Wilkinson, Ensign, District 145	18 Apr 1814	p. 577
Thomas Neal, Captain, District 150	18 Apr 1814	p. 578

Name, Rank, Unit	*Date*	*Page*
James Hobbs, Lieutenant, District 150	18 Apr 1814	p. 578
Edmund Parham, Captain, District 155	18 Apr 1814	p. 579
Jacob Smith, Ensign, District 180	18 Apr 1814	p. 579
James A. Tait, Captain, District 192	18 Apr 1814	p. 580
Temri Tait, Lieutenant, District 192	18 Apr 1814	p. 580
Isham Morgan, Ensign, District 192	18 Apr 1814	p. 581
Richard Jones, Captain, District 288	18 Apr 1814	p. 581
Amos F. Byington, Captain, District 320	18 Apr 1814	p. 582
Jacob Lasseter, Lieutenant, District 327	18 Apr 1814	p. 582
Aaron Rease, Ensign, District 327	18 Apr 1814	p. 583
Thomas Mitchell, Lieutenant, District 395	18 Apr 1814	p. 583
David T. Smith, Ensign, District 395	18 Apr 1814	p. 584
Frederick Scott, First Lieutenant, Hancock Troop of Dragoons, Squadron 4, Regiment 3	18 Apr 1814	p. 584
Andrew Gamble, Major, Battalion 15	18 Apr 1814	p. 585
George R. Brown, Captain, District 79	21 Apr 1814	p. 585
Asa Welch, Ensign, District 79	21 Apr 1814	p. 586
Thomas Fason, Captain, District 118	21 Apr 1814	p. 586
Joseph Brown, Lieutenant, District 118	21 Apr 1814	p. 587
John McDonald, Ensign, District 128	21 Apr 1814	p. 587
John C. Hall, Captain, District 234	21 Apr 1814	p. 588
William Smith, Captain, District 238	21 Apr 1814	p. 588
William Redding, Lieutenant, District 317	21 Apr 1814	p. 589
John Redding, Ensign, District 317	21 Apr 1814	p. 589
Joel Chivers, Captain, District 322	21 Apr 1814	p. 590
Nicholas Johnston, Ensign, District 373	21 Apr 1814	p. 590
Benjamin Burroughs, Lieutenant, Volunteer Company of Infantry (styled the Savannah Fencibles), Battalion 1	21 Apr 1814	p. 591
Thomas Jones, Ensign, Volunteer Company of Infantry (styled the Savannah Fencibles), Battalion 1	21 Apr 1814	p. 591
Andrew Frazer, Captain, District 17	27 Apr 1814	p. 592
Baxter Smith, Ensign, District 17	27 Apr 1814	p. 592
William Stafford, Captain, District 28	27 Apr 1814	p. 593
Orin Horn, Lieutenant, District 58	27 Apr 1814	p. 593
David Griffin, Ensign, District 58	27 Apr 1814	p. 594
Henry Oneal, Ensign, District 87	27 Apr 1814	p. 594
Samuel Edmunson, Lieutenant, District 140	27 Apr 1814	p. 595

Georgia Military Commissions, 1798–1818

Name, Rank, Unit	*Date*	*Page*
Henry Gibbons, Lieutenant, District 117	27 Apr 1814	p. 595
Thomas Waters, Ensign, District 217	27 Apr 1814	p. 596
Jonathan Benton, Ensign, District 296	27 Apr 1814	p. 596
Ebenezer S. Rees, Captain, Independent Company of Riflemen, Battalion 1	28 Apr 1814	p. 597
Etheldred Fountain, Lieutenant, District 84	28 Apr 1814	p. 597
Lewelling Robinson, Ensign, District 90	28 Apr 1814	p. 598
John Porter, Lieutenant, District 147	28 Apr 1814	p. 598
Sherwood B. Johnson, Ensign, District 147	28 Apr 1814	p. 599
Richard Colton, Ensign, District 171	28 Apr 1814	p. 599
John K. M. Charlton, Captain, District 179	28 Apr 1814	p. 600
Collin Sledge, Ensign, District 307	28 Apr 1814	p. 600
Thomas Glasscock, Captain, Volunteer Company of Infantry (styled the Augusta Volunteer Infantry), Battalion 76	5 May 1814	p. 601
James Miles, Lieutenant, Volunteer Company of Infantry (styled the Augusta Volunteer Infantry), Battalion 75	5 May 1814	p. 601
John T. Graves, Ensign, Volunteer Company of Infantry (styled the Augusta Volunteer Infantry), Battalion 75	5 May 1814	p. 602
Isaac Birdson, Lieutenant Colonel Commandant, Regiment 8	12 May 1814	p. 602
Evans Myrick, Major, Battalion 30	12 May 1814	p. 603
Joseph Wiggins, Captain, District 7	12 May 1814	p. 603
Henry Taylor, Captain, District 8	12 May 1814	p. 604
Lemuel Tippings, Captain, District 44	12 May 1814	p. 604
Stephen Riggs, Lieutenant, District 44	12 May 1814	p. 605
Joseph Underhill, Ensign, District 44	12 May 1814	p. 605
James Bigham, Captain, District 76	12 May 1814	p. 606
Ebenezer Bothwell, Captain, District 77	12 May 1814	p. 606
John McCondichie, Lieutenant, District 93	12 May 1814	p. 607
William Hubert, Lieutenant, District 104	12 May 1814	p. 607
John McAllister, Ensign, District 116	12 May 1814	p. 608
John F. Barnett, Lieutenant, District 218	12 May 1814	p. 608
David Harris, Ensign, District 218	12 May 1814	p. 609
John Varner, Ensign, District 234	12 May 1814	p. 609
William Harkins, Ensign, District 276	12 May 1814	p. 610
Mabry Harrigin, Ensign, District 320	12 May 1814	p. 610
Moses Johnston, Lieutenant, District 384	12 May 1814	p. 611

Name, Rank, Unit	Date	Page
John Sparrow, Ensign, District 384	12 May 1814	p. 611
Hardy Perry, Lieutenant, Volunteer Company of Infantry (styled the Independent Blues), Battalion 14	12 May 1814	p. 612
John McPherson Berrien, Cavalry, Regiment 1	18 May 1814	p. 612
John McDowell, Major, Battalion 40	18 May 1814	p. 613
Christian Albright, Captain, District 262	18 May 1814	p. 613
John B. Cade, Ensign, District 281	18 May 1814	p. 614
Benjamin Penn, Lieutenant, District 197	18 May 1814	p. 614
Samuel Paxton, Ensign, District 197	18 May 1814	p. 615
Christian F. Triebner, Ensign, District 12	24 May 1814	p. 615
John Lamp, Lieutenant, District 62	24 May 1814	p. 616
Britain Mays, Lieutenant, District 83	24 May 1814	p. 616
Bennet Mafford, Ensign, District 85	24 May 1814	p. 617
John Figg, Ensign, District 94	24 May 1814	p. 617
George Hamilton, Ensign, District 175	24 May 1814	p. 618
Mathew Parr, Captain, District 267	24 May 1814	p. 618
William Brown, Ensign, District 313	24 May 1814	p. 619
Michael Rodolph, Ensign, Volunteer Company of Riflemen, Battalion 36	24 May 1814	p. 619
Bartholomew Latuzan, Captain, Troop of Cavalry, Squadron 3, Regiment 2	24 May 1814	p. 620
Galphin Harvey, First Lieutenant, Volunteer Troop of Cavalry, Squadron 3, Regiment 2	24 May 1814	p. 620
James G. Blount, Lieutenant, Augusta Volunteer Rangers, Battalion 75	28 May 1814	p. 621
Warren Greene, Captain, District 74	28 May 1814	p. 621
David Fitzgerald, Ensign, District 74	28 May 1814	p. 622
Lee Reeves, Lieutenant, District 99	28 May 1814	p. 622
Thomas Hardison, Ensign, District 136	28 May 1814	p. 623
David Smith, Captain, District 364	28 May 1814	p. 623
Benjamin Ward, Lieutenant, District 364	28 May 1814	p. 624
William Rimes, Ensign, District 364	28 May 1814	p. 624
Willie Philips, Lieutenant, District 379	28 May 1814	p. 625
Robert Mills, Lieutenant, District 134	4 Jun 1814	p. 625
Lewis Knight, Ensign, District 134	4 Jun 1814	p. 626
John Perry, Ensign, District 155	4 Jun 1814	p. 626
Westley Mayfield, Captain, District 210	4 Jun 1814	p. 627

Georgia Military Commissions, 1798–1818

Name, Rank, Unit	Date	Page
Benjamin M. Griffin, Captain, District 339	4 Jun 1814	p. 627
Ebenezer Moore, Captain, District 358	4 Jun 1814	p. 628
Farquhard McRae Jr., Lieutenant, District 340	8 Jun 1814	p. 628
Tandy Key, Lieutenant Colonel Commandant, Regiment 25	8 Jun 1814	p. 629
James Dilworth, Lieutenant, District 35	8 Jun 1814	p. 629
Thomas M. Kigney, Lieutenant, District 76	8 Jun 1814	p. 630
Robert Wade, Ensign, District 132	8 Jun 1814	p. 630
John Bentley, Captain, District 193	8 Jun 1814	p. 631
John Brown, Lieutenant, District 193	8 Jun 1814	p. 631
Isaac Hendrick, Ensign, District 193	8 Jun 1814	p. 632
John Colly, Captain, District 203	8 Jun 1814	p. 632
Stephen Hubert, Lieutenant, District 337	8 Jun 1814	p. 633
Edmund B. Glasscock, Ensign, Augusta Volunteer Rangers, Battalion 75	8 Jun 1814	p. 633
Turner F. Gatlin, Second Lieutenant, Volunteer Troop of Cavalry, Squadron 10, Regiment 5	8 Jun 1814	p. 634
Thomas W. Shivers, Captain, Volunteer Troop of Cavalry, Squadron 3, Regiment 2	8 Jun 1814	p. 634
John Fountain, First Lieutenant, Volunteer Troop of Cavalry, Squadron 3, Regiment 2	8 Jun 1814	p. 635
John G. Butler, Ensign, District 7	15 Jun 1814	p. 635
James H. Scruggs, Lieutenant, District 13	15 Jun 1814	p. 636
Elihu Wilson, Ensign, District 13	15 Jun 1814	p. 636
Paul H. Wilkins, Captain, District 14	15 Jun 1814	p. 637
Alexander Martin, Lieutenant, District 14	15 Jun 1814	p. 637
Daniel Buchannon, Ensign, District 14	15 Jun 1814	p. 638
John Cannady, Ensign, District 19	15 Jun 1814	p. 638
Andrew Dorsey, Ensign, District 212	15 Jun 1814	p. 639
Sherod Rowland, Lieutenant, District 231	15 Jun 1814	p. 639
Joseph Arnold, Ensign, District 231	15 Jun 1814	p. 640
David McGuirt, Lieutenant, District 292	15 Jun 1814	p. 640
William Banks, First Lieutenant, Volunteer Troop of Dragoons, Squadron 7, Regiment 4	15 Jun 1814	p. 641
John G. Pitman, Lieutenant Colonel Commandant, Regiment 26	23 Jun 1814	p. 641
Osborn Wiggins, Lieutenant, Volunteer Company (styled the Baldwin Indpendent Blues), Battalion 70	23 Jun 1814	p. 642

Name, Rank, Unit	Date	Page
Wiliam Hendry, Lieutenant, District 17	23 Jun 1814	p. 642
John McTerrell, Ensign, District 17	23 Jun 1814	p. 643
John Lane, Lieutenant, District 49	23 Jun 1814	p. 643
William Holliday, Ensign, District 49	23 Jun 1814	p. 644
Zebulon Cox, Lieutenant, District 57	23 Jun 1814	p. 644
Robert Knight, Ensign, District 57	23 Jun 1814	p. 645
Phares Goare, Ensign, District 109	23 Jun 1814	p. 645
James Powers, Captain, District 122	23 Jun 1814	p. 646
William C. Dillon, Lieutenant, District 122	23 Jun 1814	p. 646
Isaac Blount, Ensign, District 122	23 Jun 1814	p. 647
Thomas Moseley, Captain, District 148	23 Jun 1814	p. 647
Levoy Wilkins, Captain, District 167	23 Jun 1814	p. 648
Joseph Hall, Ensign, District 82	23 Jun 1814	p. 648
David Willson, Captain, District 152	23 Jun 1814	p. 649
Isaiah Wilson, Lieutenant, District 152	23 Jun 1814	p. 649
Joseph Blackwell, Captain, District 190	23 Jun 1814	p. 650
Hardy Everett, Captain, District 259	23 Jun 1814	p. 650
Harrison Jones, Lieutenant, District 288	23 Jun 1814	p. 651
Avington Phelps, Ensign, District 299	23 Jun 1814	p. 651
Simeon Woodson, Ensign, District 330	23 Jun 1814	p. 652
Edward Pilcher, Ensign, District 334	23 Jun 1814	p. 652
Bartley C. Williams, Ensign, District 350	23 Jun 1814	p. 653
John Reid, Lieutenant, District 365	23 Jun 1814	p. 653
John M. Duke, Ensign, District 365	23 Jun 1814	p. 654
Jacob Pierce, Ensign, District 372	23 Jun 1814	p. 654
Constantine Church, Cornet, Volunteer Troop of Cavalry, Squadron 7, Regiment 4	23 Jun 1814	p. 655
William P. Dearmond, First Lieutenant, Volunteer Troop of Cavalry, Squadron 3, Regiment 2	23 Jun 1814	p. 655
Smith Jones, Second Lieutenant, Volunteer Troop of Cavalry, Squadron 3, Regiment 2	23 Jun 1814	p. 656
John Turpin, Cornet, Volunteer Troop of Cavalry, Squadron 3, Regiment 2	23 Jun 1814	p. 656
William Permenter, Captain, Volunteer Company of Riflemen, Battalion 72	25 Jun 1814	p. 657
James Wright, Captain, District 312	27 Jun 1814	p. 657
John T. Waller, Lieutenant, District 312	27 Jun 1814	p. 658

Georgia Military Commissions, 1798–1818

Name, Rank, Unit	Date	Page
James C. Watson, Major, Battalion 70	28 Jun 1814	p. 658
Richard I. Willis, Major, Battalion 36	28 Jun 1814	p. 659
John G. Kugley, Ensign, District 7	28 Jun 1814	p. 659
Reuben C. Beck, Captain, District 195	28 Jun 1814	p. 660
James Swanson, Captain, District 232	28 Jun 1814	p. 660
William R. Russel, Ensign, District 232	28 Jun 1814	p. 661
Daniel Buckner, Ensign, District 314	28 Jun 1814	p. 661
Samuel Crocket, Ensign, District 295	28 Jun 1814	p. 662
Noah Scarborough, Lieutenant, District 356	28 Jun 1814	p. 662
William L. Gary, Second Lieutenant, Volunteer Company of Artillery, Regiment 14	30 Jun 1814	p. 663
Nathan Morris, Lieutenant, District 111	6 Jul 1814	p. 663
James Blackmon, Lieutenant Colonel, Regiment 4	13 Jul 1814	p. 664
Henry Harbock, Ensign, District 6	13 Jul 1814	p. 664
John Rawls, Captain, District 36	13 Jul 1814	p. 665
John Tarnall, Lieutenant, District 74	13 Jul 1814	p. 665
Henry Latimer, Captain, District 112	13 Jul 1814	p. 666
Daniel Hair, Ensign, District 117	13 Jul 1814	p. 666
Holcut Alford, Lieutenant, District 149	13 Jul 1814	p. 667
Robert Hackett, Captain, District 213	13 Jul 1814	p. 667
John Fletcher, Lieutenant, District 220	13 Jul 1814	p. 668
James Smith, Ensign, District 225	13 Jul 1814	p. 668
Simeon White, Captain, District 258	13 Jul 1814	p. 669
Robert Samuel, Lieutenant, District 320	13 Jul 1814	p. 669
Henry B. Hill, Lieutenant, District 328	13 Jul 1814	p. 670
Thomas Hawkins, Ensign, District 328	13 Jul 1814	p. 670
David Pipkin, Captain, District 348	13 Jul 1814	p. 671
Thomas Wright, Ensign, District 367	13 Jul 1814	p. 671
Moses Daniel, Captain, District 393	13 Jul 1814	p. 672
James M. Wayne, Captain, Volunteer Troop of Cavalry styled the Chatham Light Dragoons, Squadron 1, Regiment 1	13 Jul 1814	p. 672
James Scott, Ensign, District 33	19 Jul 1814	p. 673
Reuben Neil, Lieutenant, District 59	19 Jul 1814	p. 673
Charles Bonwell, Lieutenant, District 64	19 Jul 1814	p. 674
Thomas Mayfield, Lieutenant, District 210	19 Jul 1814	p. 674
Kinchen P. Tyson, Ensign, District 298	19 Jul 1814	p. 675

Name, Rank, Unit	Date	Page
John Wood, Captain, District 318	19 Jul 1814	p. 675
Matthias H. Beard, Lieutenant, District 349	19 Jul 1814	p. 676
Hozias Davis, Ensign, District 349	13 Jul 1814	p. 676
James Mason, Lieutenant, District 358	19 Jul 1814	p. 677
Thomas Cates, Ensign, District 60	19 Jul 1814	p. 677
James Gaines, Captain, District 92	26 Jul 1814	p. 678
James E. White, Lieutenant, District 195	26 Jul 1814	p. 678
William White, Ensign, District 195	26 Jul 1814	p. 679
Martin Deadwilder, Ensign, District 202	26 Jul 1814	p. 679
Robert Huff, Lieutenant, District 237	26 Jul 1814	p. 680
John B. Cooper, Ensign, District 342	26 Jul 1814	p. 680
Peter Herstin, Ensign, District 375	26 Jul 1814	p. 681
Wilson McKinney, Major, Battalion 51	4 Aug 1814	p. 681
Joseph M. Oneal, Captain, District 22	4 Aug 1814	p. 682
Samuel Bigham, Ensign, District 76	4 Jul 1814	p. 682
Thomas Clements, Ensign, District 84	4 Nov 1814	p. 683
Charles Atchison, Ensign, District 159	4 Feb 1814	p. 683
Samuel Bentley, Ensign, District 261	4 Nov 1814	p. 684
William Dudley, Ensign, District 201	4 Nov 1814	p. 684
Jacob Eberhart, Lieutenant, District 203	4 Nov 1814	p. 685
William Cunningham, Ensign, District 203	4 Nov 1814	p. 685
Robert Billups, Captain, District 219	4 Aug 1814	p. 686
Horatio Nunnelley, Lieutenant, District 139	4 Aug 1814	p. 686
Joseph Williams, Ensign, District 292	4 Aug 1814	p. 687
Benjamin Allen, Lieutenant, District 204	4 Aug 1814	p. 687
William A. Underwood, Ensign, District 343	4 Aug 1814	p. 688
James G. Blount, Captain, Volunteer Company (styled the Augusta Vol Rangers), Battalion 75	4 Aug 1814	p. 688
William Glasscock, First Lieutenant, Volunteer Artillery Company of Augusta, Regiment 10	4 Aug 1814	p. 689
Isaac Anthony, Second Lieutenant, Volunteer Company of Artillery of Augusta, Regiment 10	4 Aug 1814	p. 689
William Fillingim, Ensign, District 355	4 Aug 1814	p. 690
Francis Woodward, Cornet, Troop of Cavalry, Squadron 3, Regiment 2	4 Nov 1814	p. 690
Daniel Johnson, Major, Battalion 53	6 Nov 1814	p. 691
John McConnell, Major, District 54	9 Aug 1814	p. 691

Georgia Military Commissions, 1798–1818

Name, Rank, Unit	Date	Page
Benjamin Sanderlin, Captain, District 1	11 Aug 1814	p. 692
Doctor Bunch, Lieutenant, District 123	11 Aug 1814	p. 692
William Call, Ensign, District 149	11 Aug 1814	p. 693
Joseph Rucker, Lieutenant, District 196	11 Aug 1814	p. 693
Charles Walden, Lieutenant, District 296	11 Aug 1814	p. 694
Robert G. Crittenden, Lieutenant, District 318	11 Aug 1814	p. 694
Wilson Collins, Ensign, District 318	11 Aug 1814	p. 695
Ephraim Phair, Ensign, District 390	11 Aug 1814	p. 695
Littleton Spivey, Captain, District 73	18 Aug 1814	p. 696
John Hines, Lieutenant, District 73	18 Aug 1814	p. 696
Jourdan Baker, Ensign, District 73	18 Aug 1814	p. 697
Amos McLendon, Captain, District 178	18 Aug 1814	p. 697
David Taliaferro, Lieutenant, District 181	18 Aug 1814	p. 698
Jacob Brasellon, Captain, District 248	18 Aug 1814	p. 698
Dempsey Bobo, Ensign, District 266	18 Aug 1814	p. 699
Jordan Compton, Second Lieutenant, Volunteer Troop of Cavalry, Squadron 9, Regiment 5		p. 699
Nathaniel Smith Jr., Cornet, Troop of Cavalry, Squadron 6, Regiment 3	18 Aug 1814	p. 700
Needham Avena, Ensign, District 306	23 Aug 1814	p. 700
Dolby Wooten, Ensign, District 160	7 Sep 1814	p. 701
Benjamin Gates, Ensign, District 354	7 Sep 1814	p. 701
Rigdon Norris, Lieutenant, District 294	7 Sep 1814	p. 702
James Park, Captain, District 139	7 Sep 1814	p. 702
Charles Austin, Lieutenant, District 250	7 Sep 1814	p. 703
William H. Walker, Ensign, District 250	7 Sep 1814	p. 703
Joseph J. Scott, Captain, District 257	7 Sep 1814	p. 704
Nathaniel Jarrett, Lieutenant, District 257	7 Sep 1814	p. 704
Littleberry House, Ensign, District 257	7 Sep 1814	p. 705
Edmund Glascock, Lieutenant, Augusta Volunteer Rangers, Battalion 75	7 Sep 1814	p. 705
John Holliday, Captain, Volunteer Company of Riflemen, Battalion 36	7 Sep 1814	p. 706
David Culbertson, Ensign, District 148	29 Aug 1814	p. 706
Elisha Strong, Captain, Volunteer Company of Riflemen, Battalion 45	7 Sep 1814	p. 707
George Waters, Lieutenant, Volunteer Company of Riflemen, Battalion 45	7 Sep 1814	p. 707

Name, Rank, Unit	Date	Page
Benjamin Martin, Captain, Volunteer Company of Riflemen, Battalion 28	7 Sep 1814	p. 708
James Cary, Lieutenant, Volunteer Company of Riflemen, Battalion 28	7 Sep 1814	p. 708
Charles A. Crawford, Ensign, Volunteer Company of Riflemen, Battalion 28	7 Sep 1814	p. 709
Allen Lovelace, Cornet, Volunteer Troop of Light Dragoons, Squadron 3, Regiment 2	7 Sep 1814	p. 709
Zachariah Williams, Lieutenant Colonel, Cavalry, Regiment 2	7 Sep 1814	p. 710
James Scisson, Captain, Volunteer Troop of Light Dragoons, Squadron 8, Regiment 4	7 Sep 1814	p. 710
James Leddell, First Lieutenant, Volunteer Troop of Light Dragoons, Squadron 8, Regiment 4	7 Sep 1814	p. 711
Nathaniel C. Jarrett, Second Lieutenant, Volunteer Troop of Light Dragoons, Squadron 8, Regiment 4	7 Sep 1814	p. 711
Charles Hemphill, Cornet, Volunteer Troop of Light Dragoons, Squadron 8, Regiment 4	17 Sep 1814	p. 712
John Davis, Captain, Volunteer Troop of Light Dragoons, Squadron 2, Regiment 1	7 Sep 1814	p. 712
William B. White, First Lieutenant, Volunteer Troop of Light Dragoons, Squadron 2, Regiment 1	7 Sep 1814	p. 713
Peter J. Golding, Second Lieutenant, Volunteer Troop of Light Dragoons, Squadron 2, Regiment 1	7 Sep 1814	p. 713
Zachariah L. Tomlin, Cornet, Volunteer Troop of Light Dragoons, Squadron 2, Regiment 1	7 Sep 1814	p. 714
William W. Williamson, Captain, Volunteer Troop of Cavalry, Squadron 7, Regiment 4	26 Sep 1814	p. 714
David Simpson, First Lieutenant, Volunteer Troop of Cavalry, Squadron 7, Regiment 4	26 Sep 1814	p. 715
Irvin Lawson, Second Lieutenant, Volunteer Troop of Cavalry, Squadron 7, Regiment 4	26 Sep 1814	p. 715
Jesse J. Roan, Cornet, Volunteer Troop of Cavalry, Squadron 7, Regiment 4	26 Sep 1814	p. 716
Henry Reid, Cornet, Volunteer Troop of Cavalry, Squadron 8, Regiment 4	26 Sep 1814	p. 716
Daniel Brinson, Lieutenant Colonel Commandant, Regiment 6	26 Sep 1814	p. 717
William C. Ware, Ensign, Volunteer Company of Infantry (styled the Augusta Volunteer Rangers), Battalion 75	26 Sep 1814	p. 717

Georgia Military Commissions, 1798–1818

Name, Rank, Unit	*Date*	*Page*
Edmund P. Wester, Captain, District 42	26 Sep 1814	p. 718
Thomas Wells, Ensign, District 77	26 Sep 1814	p. 718
John M. Candichia, Captain, District 93	26 Sep 1814	p. 719
Stith Barkesdale, Lieutenant, District 178	26 Sep 1814	p. 719
Thomas Evans, Lieutenant, District 179	26 Sep 1814	p. 720
Jeremiah Pace, Ensign, District 220	26 Sep 1814	p. 720
William H. Dickson, Captain, District 251	26 Sep 1814	p. 721
James Locket Sr., Captain, District 300	26 Sep 1814	p. 721
James Humphris, Lieutenant, District 303	26 Sep 1814	p. 722
James Chappel, Captain, District 360	26 Sep 1814	p. 722
John Grimsley, Captain, District 298	13 Oct 1814	p. 723
John Rieves, Captain, District 133	13 Oct 1814	p. 723
Thomas Clifton, Captain, District 80	13 Oct 1814	p. 724
Enoch Everitt, Captain, District 17	13 Oct 1814	p. 724
Joseph M. Post, Captain, District 290	13 Oct 1814	p. 725
Jesse Morris, Lieutenant, District 18	13 Oct 1814	p. 725
James Clarke, Lieutenant, District 195	13 Oct 1814	p. 726
James Stone, Lieutenant, District 78	13 Oct 1814	p. 726
James W. Cooper, Lieutenant, District 161	13 Oct 1814	p. 727
Jason Bryant, Ensign, District 92	13 Oct 1814	p. 727
Milas Young, Ensign, District 142	13 Oct 1814	p. 728
Jonathan Mulkey, Lieutenant, District 360	13 Oct 1814	p. 728
Joel Renfroe, Ensign, District 360	13 Oct 1814	p. 729
Zachariah Fields, Ensign, District 303	13 Oct 1814	p. 729
Abram Card, Ensign, Volunteer Company of Riflemen, Battalion 66	13 Oct 1814	p. 730
Eleathan Bark, Ensign, Volunteer Company of Riflemen, Battalion 72	13 Oct 1814	p. 730
James Hunter, Captain, Volunteer Company of Infantry (styled the Savannah Fencibles), Battalion 1	13 Oct 1814	p. 731
Harris, Ensign, District 227	28 Oct 1814	p. 731
Vincent Lee, Ensign, District 48	28 Oct 1814	p. 732
John Beasley, Ensign, District 46	28 Oct 1814	p. 732
James G. Randle, Ensign, District 146	28 Oct 1814	p. 733
John Broughton, Ensign, District 14	28 Oct 1814	p. 733
George Lucas, Captain, District 361	28 Oct 1814	p. 734
William T. Rencau, Captain, District 231	28 Oct 1814	p. 734

Name, Rank, Unit	Date	Page
William Borland, Captain, District 115	28 Oct 1814	p. 735
Barnabus Pace, Captain, District 306	28 Oct 1814	p. 735
William A. Dunham, Captain, District 4	28 Oct 1814	p. 736
Robert R. Harden, Lieutenant, District 4	28 Oct 1814	p. 736
James S. Bullock, Ensign, District 4	28 Oct 1814	p. 737
Joseph Willson, Captain, Volunteer Company of Riflemen, Battalion 4	28 Oct 1814	p. 737
Robert Quarterman, Lieutenant, Volunteer Company of Riflemen, Battalion 4	28 Oct 1814	p. 738
John Dunwoody, Ensign, Volunteer Company of Riflemen, Battalion 4	28 Oct 1814	p. 738
Josiah Rancey, Ensign, Volunteer Company of Riflemen, Battalion 45	28 Oct 1814	p. 739
Thomas K. Gold, Captain, Volunteer Company of Infantry (styled the Republican Blues), Battalion 6	28 Oct 1814	p. 739
William King, Lieutenant, Volunteer Company of Infantry (styled the Republican Blues), Battalion 6	28 Oct 1814	p. 740
Edward E. Baker, Ensign, Volunteer Company of Infantry (styled the Republican Blues), Battalion 6	28 Oct 1814	p. 740
William Augustus Fennell, Quartermaster General	10 Nov 1814	p. 741
Elias Beall, Brigadier General, Brigade 2, Division 3	10 Nov 1814	p. 741
Henry Buford, Captain, Volunteer Company of Riflemen, Battalion 55	16 Nov 1814	p. 742
John Price, Lieutenant, Volunteer Company of Riflemen, Battalion 55	16 Nov 1814	p. 742
John Buford, Ensign, Volunteer Company of Riflemen, Battalion 55	16 Nov 1814	p. 743
William M. Kelly, Ensign, District 1	16 Nov 1814	p. 743
John Harris, Ensign, District 178	16 Nov 1814	p. 744
Paul Furr, Ensign, District 374	16 Nov 1814	p. 744
William Ford, Lieutenant, District 348	16 Nov 1814	p. 745
Ephraim Strickland, Lieutenant, District 204	16 Nov 1814	p. 745
Robert Millican, Lieutenant, District 262	16 Nov 1814	p. 746
Isaac Huddleston, Lieutenant, District 302	16 Nov 1814	p. 746
John B. Jacobs, Lieutenant, District 335	16 Nov 1814	p. 747
Stephen Drane, Lieutenant, District 133	16 Nov 1814	p. 747
James Hemphill, Lieutenant, District 256	16 Nov 1814	p. 748
Cornelius Wright, Ensign, District 256	16 Nov 1814	p. 748

Georgia Military Commissions, 1798–1818

Name, Rank, Unit	*Date*	*Page*
William Whidden, Captain, District 40	16 Nov 1814	p. 749
Devorax Jarrett, Captain, District 215	16 Nov 1814	p. 749
Pleasant Compton, Captain, District 233	16 Nov 1814	p. 750
John Ross, Captain, Volunteer Company of Infantry (styled the Volunteer Guards of St. Marys), Battalion 8	16 Nov 1814	p. 750
Joseph Bachlott, Lieutenant, Volunteer Company of Infantry (styled the Volunteer Guards of St. Marys), Battalion 8	16 Nov 1814	p. 751
Benjamin Davis, Major, Battalion 45	16 Nov 1814	p. 751
Nathaniel Wofford, Major, Battalion 47	16 Nov 1814	p. 752
Charles W. Christian, Major, Battalion 42	16 Nov 1814	p. 752
Charles Carter, Lieutenant Colonel Commandant, Regiment 28	16 Nov 1814	p. 753
Henry Williamson, Ensign, District 311	17 Nov 1814	p. 753
Quinea Oneall, Ensign, District 109	21 Dec 1814	p. 754
Christopher Bowen, Lieutenant, District 227	21 Dec 1814	p. 754
Moses Ayres, Ensign, District 212	21 Dec 1814	p. 755
Lewis Conner, Lieutenant, District 36	21 Dec 1814	p. 755
William Flinn, Lieutenant, District 361	21 Dec 1814	p. 756
Matin M. Dye, Captain, District 65	21 Dec 1814	p. 756
Joseph Maddox, Captain, District 254	21 Dec 1814	p. 757
William Bailey, Captain, District 381	21 Dec 1814	p. 757
John W. Mayfield, Lieutenant, District 268	21 Dec 1814	p. 758
Benjamin Griffitt, Ensign, District 268	21 Dec 1814	p. 758
David Sears, Captain, District 52	21 Dec 1814	p. 759
Ezekiel McClendon, Ensign, District 52	21 Dec 1814	p. 759
Andrew Maulden, Captain, District 208	21 Dec 1814	p. 760
Joseph Cleveland, Lieutenant, District 208	21 Dec 1814	p. 760
Amos Williams, Ensign, District 208	21 Dec 1814	p. 761
Samuel Calhoun, Cornet, Captain Gregon's Troop of Light Dragoons in Jones County, Squadron 9, Regiment 5	21 Dec 1814	p. 761
William Cowart, Second Lieutenant, Captain Harveys Troop of Light Dragoons in Jefferson County, Squadron 2, Regiment 1	21 Dec 1814	p. 762
John C. Smith, Captain, Volunteer Troop of Light Dragoons in Hancock County, Squadron 4, Regiment 2	21 Dec 1814	p. 762
Samuel Hale, Captain, Volunteer Troop of Light Dragoons in Richmond County, Squadron 3, Regiment 2	21 Dec 1814	p. 763

Name, Rank, Unit	Date	Page
William P. Triplett, Third Lieutenant, Volunteer Troop of Light Dragoons in Oglethorpe County, Squadron 3, Regiment 6	21 Dec 1814	p. 763
Joshua Tillery, Cornet, Volunteer Troop of Light Dragoons in Oglethorpe County, Squadron 6, Regiment 3	21 Dec 1814	p. 764
Nathaniel Waller, Captain, District 319	9 Jan 1815	p. 764
Soloman Robinson, Ensign, District 115	16 Jan 1815	p. 765
James Piles, Ensign, District 27	16 Jan 1815	p. 765
Robert Dodd, Ensign, District 83	16 Jan 1815	p. 766
John Burnett, Lieutenant, District 26	16 Jan 1815	p. 766
Thomas Holliday, Lieutenant, District 75	16 Jan 1815	p. 767
Jesse Wall, Lieutenant, District 93	16 Jan 1815	p. 767
Thomas Shelton, Ensign, District 93	16 Jan 1815	p. 768
Duncan McRae, Lieutenant, District 340	16 Jan 1815	p. 768
Luke Mann, Captain, District 20	16 Jan 1815	p. 769
John Wells, Lieutenant, District 20	16 Jan 1815	p. 769
Hiram Peek, Captain, District 110	16 Jan 1815	p. 770
John Parker, Captain, District 241	16 Jan 1815	p. 770
James Wardlaw, Captain, District 247	16 Jan 1815	p. 771
James S. Fleming, Captain, District 264	16 Jan 1815	p. 771
Edward Flowers, Captain, District 289	16 Jan 1815	p. 772
John R. Golding, Captain, Volunteer Company of Infantry (styled the Franklin Colledge Volunteers), Battalion 48	16 Jan 1815	p. 772
John M. Erwin, Lieutenant, Volunteer Company of Infantry (styled the Franklin Colledge Volunteers), Battalion 48	16 Jan 1815	p. 773
Richard H. Randolph, Ensign, Volunteer Company of Infantry (styled the Franklin Colledge Volunteers), Battalion 48	16 Jan 1815	p. 773
Edward Strong, Major, Battalion 45	16 Jan 1815	p. 774
Goodwin Myrick, Captain, Volunteer Troop of Light Dragoons, Squadron 5, Regiment 3	16 Jan 1815	p. 774
James Beaty, Captain, District 72	30 Jan 1815	p. 775
Franklin Keall, Lieutenant, District 6	30 Jan 1815	p. 775
Allen Denmark, Ensign, District 6	30 Jan 1815	p. 776
Henry Weston, Lieutenant, District 62	30 Jan 1815	p. 776
Solomon Ward, Lieutenant, District 330	30 Jan 1815	p. 777

Georgia Military Commissions, 1798–1818

Name, Rank, Unit	Date	Page
Dawson Webb, Ensign, District 330	30 Jan 1815	p. 777
Jepthe Q. Williford, Ensign, District 204	30 Jan 1815	p. 778
Robert Quarterman, Captain, Volunteer Company of Riflemen, Battalion 4	30 Jan 1815	p. 778
Thomas Lovett, Cornet, Volunteer Company of Cavalry, Squadron 2, Regiment 1	30 Jan 1815	p. 779
John Ricks, Captain, District 395	3 Feb 1815	p. 779
Samuel Gregory, Lieutenant, District 395	3 Feb 1815	p. 780
Daniel Ricks, Ensign, District 395	3 Feb 1815	p. 780
Joel W. Leftwick, Captain, District 138	2 Feb 1815	p. 781
Thomas Pleasants, Second Lieutenant, Light Dragoons in Jones County, Squadron 9, Regiment 5	6 Feb 1815	p. 781
John Bucks, Captain, District 249	8 Feb 1815	p. 782
Richard Farrer, Captain, District 172	8 Feb 1815	p. 782
Harvy Harrington, Lieutenant, District 319	8 Feb 1815	p. 783
Wylie Clowdes, Ensign, District 233	8 Feb 1815	p. 783
Josiah Lawrens, Lieutenant, Volunteer Company of Riflemen in Chatham County, Battalion 1	8 Feb 1815	p. 784
William Everitt, Ensign, Volunteer Company of Riflemen in Chatham County, Battalion 1	8 Feb 1815	p. 784
Ralph May, Lieutenant, Volunteer Company in Chatham County (styled the Savannah Fencibles), Battalion 1	8 Feb 1815	p. 785
William S. Kempton, Ensign, Volunteer Company in Chatham County (styled the Savannah Fencibles), Battalion 1	8 Feb 1815	p. 785
John Allen, First Lieutenant, Company of Cavalry in Baldwin County, Squadron 5, Regiment 3	8 Feb 1815	p. 786
William T. Williams, Third Lieutenant, Volunteer Company (styled the Volunteer Light Artillery in Chatham County), Regiment 1	21 Feb 1815	p. 786
Abner Willborn, Major, Battalion 38	21 Feb 1815	p. 787
Zadock Satter, Captain, District 85	21 Feb 1815	p. 787
Edward Sims, Captain, District 189	21 Feb 1815	p. 788
Benjamin Penn, Captain, District 197	21 Feb 1815	p. 788
John Dunwoodie, Lieutenant, Volunteer Company (styled the Volunteer Riflemen), Battalion 45	21 Feb 1815	p. 789
Benjamin Mell, Ensign, Volunteer Company (styled the Volunteer Riflemen), Battalion 45	21 Feb 1815	p. 789
Silas Overstreet, Lieutenant, District 40	21 Feb 1815	p. 790

Name, Rank, Unit	Date	Page
Samuel Carter, Ensign, District 40	21 Feb 1815	p. 790
James Carter, Lieutenant, District 108	21 Feb 1815	p. 791
Nicholas Carter, Ensign, District 7	21 Feb 1815	p. 791
George Low, Ensign, District 103	21 Feb 1815	p. 792
Menoah Bolton, Ensign, District 167	21 Feb 1815	p. 792
Thomas W. Harris, Ensign, District 387	21 Feb 1815	p. 793
William M. Scruggs, Captain, District 62	13 Mar 1815	p. 793
Solomon Perkins, Captain, District 173	13 Mar 1815	p. 794
Peter Randal, Lieutenant, District 107	13 Mar 1815	p. 794
Cable Higgenbotham, Lieutenant, District 197	13 Mar 1815	p. 795
Thomas Mehaffey, Lieutenant, District 247	13 Mar 1815	p. 795
William Harris, Lieutenant, District 338	13 Mar 1815	p. 796
James A. Rogers, Ensign, District 338	13 Mar 1815	p. 796
John Winter, Ensign, District 9	13 Mar 1815	p. 797
Roban Parham, Ensign, District 136	13 Mar 1815	p. 797
Richard Collars, Ensign, District 185	13 Mar 1815	p. 798
John Buckhannon, Cornet, Volunteer Troop of Light Dragoons, Squadron 5, Regiment 3	6 Apr 1815	p. 798
Turner Young, Ensign, District 357	6 Apr 1815	p. 799
John Smith, Ensign, District 227	6 Apr 1815	p. 799
William Cunningham, Lieutenant, District 203	6 Apr 1815	p. 800
Josiah Prewitt, Lieutenant, District 248	6 Apr 1815	p. 800
Dooby Wooten, Captain, District 160	6 Apr 1815	p. 801
Breton Mayo, Captain, District 83	6 Apr 1815	p. 801
Charles Harris, Captain, District 227	6 Apr 1815	p. 802
John Lile, Captain, District 255	6 Apr 1815	p. 802
Andrew Hendrix, Captain, District 255	6 Apr 1815	p. 803
Jesse Wall, Captain, District 356	6 Apr 1815	p. 803
Enick Blackshear, Lieutenant, District 356	6 Apr 1815	p. 804
Richard J. Holliday, Captain, District 177	6 Apr 1815	p. 804
Isaiah Paschall, Lieutenant, District 177	6 Apr 1815	p. 805
Plenny Sheffield, Captain, District 334	6 Apr 1815	p. 805
James Barden, Lieutenant, District 334	6 Apr 1815	p. 806
Bartholomew Osteen, Ensign, District 334	6 Apr 1815	p. 806
John Walker, Captain, Company of Cavalry in Jasper County, Squadron 9, Regiment 5	17 Apr 1815	p. 807
James Claiborn, Ensign, District 113	17 Apr 1815	p. 807

Georgia Military Commissions, 1798–1818

Name, Rank, Unit	*Date*	*Page*
John Wright, Lieutenant, District 62	17 Apr 1815	p. 808
Joseph Shoemake, Lieutenant, District 68	17 Apr 1815	p. 808
Samuel Edmunson, Captain, District 140	17 Apr 1815	p. 809
James Morris, Captain, District 267	17 Apr 1815	p. 809
Adam P. Vandiver, Lieutenant, District 267	17 Apr 1815	p. 810
James Beatey Jr., Major, Battalion 16	17 Apr 1815	p. 810
John P. Blackmon, Lieutenant Colonel Commandant, Regiment 6	17 Apr 1815	p. 811
Levi Ellis, Lieutenant, Volunteer Company of Riflemen, Battalion 65	28 Apr 1815	p. 811
William Fitch, Ensign, District 19	28 Apr 1815	p. 812
Laird B. Fleming, Ensign, District 85	28 Apr 1815	p. 812
John Nay, Ensign, District 288	18 Apr 1815	p. 813
Nicholas Howard, Captain, District 143	28 Apr 1815	p. 813
Josiah Rogers, Lieutenant, District 143	28 Apr 1815	p. 814
James Clark, Ensign, District 143	28 Apr 1815	p. 814
Paul Saterwhite, Captain, District 221	28 Apr 1815	p. 815
Isaac Hill, Lieutenant, District 221	28 Apr 1815	p. 815
Martin Crow, Ensign, District 221	28 Apr 1815	p. 816
William Edmondson, Captain, District 232	28 Apr 1815	p. 816
Johnson Hendon, Captain, District 235	28 Apr 1815	p. 817
Littleberry G. Glenn, Captain, District 377	28 Apr 1815	p. 817
Edwin D. King, Lieutenant Colonel, Regiment 17	1 May 1815	p. 818
Nicholas Thompkins, Captain, District 309	2 May 1815	p. 818
Mareo Phinizy, Captain, District 222	8 May 1815	p. 819
Drury Cooper, Ensign, District 222	8 May 1815	p. 819
Parker Middleton, Captain, District 239	8 May 1815	p. 820
Ballard McDurmont, Lieutenant, District 239	8 May 1815	p. 820
Hardy C. Willis, Captain, District 139	8 May 1815	p. 821
Harrison Oneal, Lieutenant, District 139	8 May 1815	p. 821
Lee Jeffries, Captain, District 380	8 May 1815	p. 822
John Mann, Captain, District 118	8 May 1815	p. 822
Thomas W. Benson, Captain, District 86	8 May 1815	p. 823
Moses Fort, Major, Battalion 72	8 May 1815	p. 823
Armsted Richardson, Captain, Volunteer Troop of Cavalry, Squadron 5, Regiment 3	8 May 1815	p. 824
William Hill, Ensign, District 68	16 Aug 1815	p. 824

Name, Rank, Unit	Date	Page
John M. Devenport, Lieutenant, District 120	16 May 1815	p. 825
Samuel G. Starr, Ensign, District 120	16 May 1815	p. 825
Adam Shaws, Lieutenant, District 355	16 May 1815	p. 826
Benjamin Lassetter, Lieutenant, District 364	16 May 1815	p. 826
James G. Randale, Captain, District 146	16 May 1815	p. 827
Henry Hogan, Captain, District 384	16 May 1815	p. 827
Benjamin Gates, Captain, District 354	16 May 1815	p. 828
Samuel Ellis, Lieutenant, District 354	16 May 1815	p. 828
Alexander Watson, Captain, District 378	16 May 1815	p. 829
Henry F. Mercier, Lieutenant, District 318	16 May 1815	p. 829
William Wood, Ensign, District 318	16 May 1815	p. 830
John Young, Major, Battalion 9	16 May 1815	p. 830
William Gaston, Captain, Volunteer Company (styled the Heavy Artillery), Regiment 1	24 May 1815	p. 831
Moses Herbert, First Lieutenant, Volunteer Company, Regiment 1	24 May 1815	p. 831
Joseph Cumming, Second Lieutenant, Volunteer Company, Regiment 1	24 May 1815	p. 832
Thomas Hosey, Captain, Volunteer Company of Artillery, Regiment 40	24 May 1815	p. 832
John Hudson, First Lieutenant, Volunteer Company of Artillery, Regiment 40	24 May 1815	p. 833
Jesse Bledsoe, Second Lieutenant, Volunteer Company of Artillery, Regiment 40	24 May 1815	p. 833
William W. Oliver, Captain, District 38	24 May 1815	p. 834
Resdon Oliver, Lieutenant, District 38	24 May 1815	p. 834
Moses Oliver, Ensign, District 38	24 May 1815	p. 835
Richard Burch, Captain, District 106	24 May 1815	p. 835
Samuel Pulling, Captain, District 126	24 May 1815	p. 836
Cornelius Collins, Captain, District 129	24 May 1815	p. 836
Leonard B. Sims, Captain, District 130	24 May 1815	p. 837
William Hammond, Captain, District 162	24 May 1815	p. 837
Joseph Stephens, Captain, District 372	24 May 1815	p. 838
William Griggs, Ensign, District 65	24 May 1815	p. 838
William Alford, Ensign, District 160	24 May 1815	p. 839
John Barkston, Ensign, District 294	31 May 1815	p. 839
Thomas Brown, Ensign, District 201	31 May 1815	p. 840
James Sarford, Ensign, District 139	31 May 1815	p. 840

Georgia Military Commissions, 1798–1818

Name, Rank, Unit	Date	Page
Isaac Curry, Ensign, District 112	31 May 1815	p. 841
James Bertram, Lieutenant, District 380	31 May 1815	p. 841
William H. Easternod, Ensign, District 380	31 May 1815	p. 842
William G. Andens, Lieutenant, District 236	31 May 1815	p. 842
James O. Smith, Ensign, District 236	31 May 1815	p. 843
William Wright, Lieutenant, District 222	31 May 1815	p. 843
Christian F. Huck, Lieutenant, District 7	31 May 1815	p. 844
James Wimberly, Captain, District 325	31 May 1815	p. 844
Theopholus S. Lane, Captain, District 229	31 May 1815	p. 845
Lewis S. Brown, Captain, District 164	31 May 1815	p. 845
John Porter, Captain, District 147	31 May 1815	p. 846
Uriah Richards, Captain, District 142	31 May 1815	p. 846
Reubin Stillwell, Lieutenant, District 142	31 May 1815	p. 847
Simmons Butts, Captain, District 101	31 May 1815	p. 847
Benanuel Bower, Captain, Volunteer Company of Infantry (styled the Homespun Foresters), Battalion 19	31 May 1815	p. 848
Alexander McDonnell, Major, Battalion 48	31 May 1815	p. 848
Alexander W. Alpin, Major, Battalion 31	31 May 1815	p. 849
James Beaty, Captain, District 72	7 Jun 1815	p. 849
Charles Bennel, Captain, District 64	7 Jun 1815	p. 850
Anthony Mills, Ensign, District 64	7 Jun 1814	p. 850
Mathew Fain, Captain, District 337	7 Jun 1815	p. 851
John Edwards, Lieutenant, District 337	7 Jun 1815	p. 851
Yancy Sanders, Major, Cavalry, Squadron 3, Regiment 2	12 Jun 1815	p. 852
Mathew Haughton, Second Lieutenant, Volunteer Troop of Cavalry, Squadron 6, Regiment 3	28 Jun 1815	p. 852
Irbane Leonard, Cornet, Volunteer Troop of Cavalry, Squadron 6, Regiment 3	28 Jun 1815	p. 853
John Chambers, Lieutenant, Volunteer Company (styled the Homespun Forresters), Battalion 19	28 Jun 1815	p. 853
Tandy Jones, Ensign, Volunteer Company of Infantry, Battalion 19	28 Jun 1815	p. 854
Thomas Glascock, Captain, Volunteer Company (styled the Independent Blues), Battalion 75	28 Jun 1815	p. 854
Kinchen McKinney, Ensign, District 153	28 Jun 1815	p. 855
James Norris, Ensign, District 301	28 Jun 1815	p. 855
Benjamin Mercey, Ensign, District 309	28 Jun 1815	p. 856
Elijah Brockman, Ensign, District 232	28 Jun 1815	p. 856

Name, Rank, Unit	*Date*	*Page*
David B. Driskel, Ensign, District 392	28 Jun 1815	p. 857
Daniel Humphrey, Lieutenant, District 74	28 Jun 1815	p. 857
Thompson English, Lieutenant, District 95	28 Jun 1815	p. 858
Edmond Jourdan, Lieutenant, District 110	28 Jun 1815	p. 858
Jeremiah P. Ransom, Ensign, District 110	28 Jun 1815	p. 859
Jeremiah Winter, Lieutenant, District 124	28 Jun 1815	p. 859
John W. Walton, Lieutenant, District 130	28 Jun 1815	p. 860
Hezekiah Grubles, Ensign, District 130	28 Jun 1815	p. 860
Mark Ship, Lieutenant, District 131	28 Jun 1815	p. 861
Jesse Clay, Ensign, District 131	28 Jun 1815	p. 861
Robin McNeely, Lieutenant, District 138	28 Jun 1815	p. 862
Rhesa Bostick, Lieutenant, District 140	28 Jun 1815	p. 862
Philemon Edmondson, Ensign, District 140	28 Jun 1815	p. 863
Benjamin Wallace, Lieutenant, District 169	28 Jun 1815	p. 863
Edmund Ogletree, Ensign, District 169	28 Jun 1815	p. 864
Christopher Pearson, Lieutenant, District 288	28 Jun 1815	p. 864
Richard Manly, Lieutenant, District 307	28 Jun 1815	p. 865
John Robinson, Lieutenant, District 313	28 Jun 1815	p. 865
Sidney Anderson, Lieutenant, District 382	28 Jun 1815	p. 866
Maxwell Anderson, Ensign, District 382	28 Jun 1815	p. 866
James H. P. Scruggs, Captain, District 13	28 Jun 1815	p. 867
Samuel Eigle, Captain, District 24	28 Jun 1815	p. 867
Thomas Oneel, Captain, District 28	28 Jun 1815	p. 868
William Oneel, Lieutenant, District 28	28 Jun 1815	p. 868
Lewellen M. Robinson, Captain, District 90	28 Jun 1815	p. 869
Joel Dean, Lieutenant, District 90	28 Jun 1815	p. 869
John Kiss, Captain, District 102	28 Jun 1815	p. 870
John McCallister, Captain, District 116	28 Jun 1815	p. 870
Hardy Crawford, Captain, District 145	28 Jun 1815	p. 871
Gilford Floid, Ensign, District 145	28 Jun 1815	p. 871
John H. Watts, Captain, District 146	28 Jun 1815	p. 872
Josiah Watts, Ensign, District 146	28 Jun 1815	p. 872
William Eubank, Captain, District 183	28 Jun 1815	p. 873
Heslin Roades, Captain, District 230	28 Jun 1815	p. 873
Henry Jennings, Lieutenant, District 230	28 Jun 1815	p. 874
Anderson Hatley, Ensign, District 230	28 Jun 1815	p. 874

Georgia Military Commissions, 1798–1818

Name, Rank, Unit	Date	Page
David Rogers, Captain, District 242	28 Jun 1815	p. 875
Joseph Vardiman, Captain, District 278	28 Jun 1815	p. 875
William H. Henry, Captain, District 287	28 Jun 1815	p. 876
Daniel Kelly, Lieutenant, District 287	28 Jun 1815	p. 876
George Greene, Ensign, District 287	28 Jun 1815	p. 877
William H. Morrow, Captain, District 292	28 Jun 1815	p. 877
Washington Kise, Captain, District 311	28 Jun 1815	p. 878
John Kendrick, Lieutenant, District 311	28 Jun 1815	p. 878
Holeman Stevens, Captain, District 326	28 Jun 1815	p. 879
Martin G. Mims, Captain, District 327	28 Jun 1815	p. 879
Francis J. Ross, Captain, District 345	28 Jun 1815	p. 880
Isaac Smith, Ensign, District 345	28 Jun 1815	p. 880
Joab Tison, Captain, District 353	28 Jun 1815	p. 881
John S. Davis, Lieutenant, District 358	28 Jun 1815	p. 881
Jacob Early, Captain, District 363	28 Jun 1815	p. 882
Devenport Graves, Captain, District 379	28 Jun 1815	p. 882
William L. Gary, Major, Battalion 26	28 Jun 1815	p. 883
Churchwell Gibson, Major, Battalion 34	28 Jun 1815	p. 883
Henry Early, Major, Battalion 44	28 Jun 1815	p. 884
Farr Trammell, Major, Battalion 49	28 Jun 1815	p. 884
William W. Olliver, Major, Battalion 55	28 Jun 1815	p. 885
Greene B. Marshall, Major, Battalion 75	28 Jun 1815	p. 885
James Marshall, Lieutenant Colonel, Regiment 1	28 Jun 1815	p. 886
William Wilkins, Lieutenant Colonel, Regiment 1	28 Jun 1815	p. 886
William Lucas, Captain, Volunteer Company (styled the Volunteer Riflemen), Battalion 1	5 Jul 1815	p. 887
Ephraim Keefer, Ensign, District 12	5 Jul 1815	p. 887
Joshua Sim, Ensign, District 129	5 Jul 1815	p. 888
James Shows, Ensign, District 355	5 Jul 1815	p. 888
Jonathan Burgess, Lieutenant, District 147	5 Jul 1815	p. 889
John Boles, Ensign, District 147	5 Jul 1815	p. 889
James Sterling, Lieutenant, District 235	5 Jul 1815	p. 890
William Montgomery, Captain, District 120	5 Jul 1815	p. 890
Robert Brice, Captain, District 214	5 Jul 1815	p. 891
John A. Williams, Captain, District 347	5 Jul 1815	p. 891
David Bergen, Captain, District 246	5 Jun 1815	p. 892
Elisha Burson, Lieutenant, District 246	5 Jul 1815	p. 892

Name, Rank, Unit	Date	Page
Marvel Milsaps, Ensign, District 246	5 Jul 1815	p. 893
Hezekiah L. Embrey, Captain, District 252	5 Jul 1815	p. 893
Ellis Swenney, Lieutenant, District 252	5 Jul 1815	p. 894
Jesse Perrey, Ensign, District 252	5 Jul 1815	p. 894
James Blair, Lieutenant Colonel, Regiment 23	5 Jul 1815	p. 895
Martin Wood, Cornet, Volunteer Troop of Cavalry, Squadron 10, Regiment 5	12 Jul 1815	p. 895
Robert Standfield, Ensign, District 226	12 Jul 1815	p. 896
James Smith, Ensign, District 299	12 Jul 1815	p. 896
Gideon Willis, Captain, District 79	12 Jul 1815	p. 897
Eli Walden, Ensign, District 79	12 Jul 1815	p. 897
James Daniel, Captain, District 107	12 Jul 1815	p. 898
John Ashley, Ensign, District 107	12 Jul 1815	p. 898
John A. Evans, Captain, District 111	12 Jul 1815	p. 899
Moses Stamps, Captain, District 243	12 Jul 1815	p. 899
Wayde Hill, Captain, District 368	12 Jul 1815	p. 900
John White, Ensign, District 193	26 Jun 1815	p. 900
John Griffith, Ensign, District 377	26 Jul 1815	p. 901
George Flynt, Ensign, District 176	26 Jul 1815	p. 901
William Forsyth, Ensign, District 320	26 Jul 1815	p. 902
John Bailey, Ensign, District 203	26 Jul 1815	p. 902
Lewis Hunt, Lieutenant, District 376	26 Jul 1815	p. 903
Robert Wadd, Lieutenant, District 83	26 Jul 1815	p. 903
John K. Charlton, Lieutenant, District 164	26 Jul 1815	p. 904
James Pearrea (Pearrce?), Lieutenant, District 126	26 Jul 1815	p. 904
John Bates, Lieutenant, District 142	26 Jul 1815	p. 905
David Christopher, Lieutenant, District 234	26 Jul 1815	p. 905
Christopher Hand, Lieutenant, District 229	26 Jul 1815	p. 906
Peter Bailey, Ensign, District 229	26 Jul 1815	p. 906
Lewis Wileman, Lieutenant, District 9	26 Jul 1815	p. 907
Charles Wisenbaker, Ensign, District 9	26 Jul 1815	p. 907
Godfrey Lee, Captain, District 352	26 Jul 1815	p. 908
Andrew Sheppard, Captain, District 352	26 Jul 1815	p. 908
Robert Jenkins, Captain, District 314	26 Jul 1815	p. 909
William Robinson, Lieutenant, District 314	26 Jul 1815	p. 909
Asa Wright, Captain, District 236	26 Jul 1815	p. 910
James Humphrees, Captain, District 303	26 Jul 1815	p. 910

Georgia Military Commissions, 1798–1818

Name, Rank, Unit	Date	Page
Dabny Berry, Captain, District 121	26 Jul 1815	p. 911
Edmund Bugg, Captain, District 123	26 Jul 1815	p. 911
Thomas H. Kendall, Captain, District 112	26 Jul 1815	p. 912
Thomas Theess, Captain, District 8	26 Jul 1815	p. 912
Tolliver Dillard, Captain, District 69	26 Jul 1815	p. 913
Raymond Demere, Captain, District 21	26 Jul 1815	p. 913
George Stapleton, Captain, District 81	26 Jul 1815	p. 914
John Willis, Captain, District 20	26 Jul 1815	p. 914
Zadock Smith, Captain, District 179	26 Jul 1815	p. 915
G. Shurholster, Captain, District 328	26 Jul 1815	p. 915
John Hawkins, Lieutenant, District 328	26 Jul 1815	p. 916
Wm. Underwood, Ensign, District 328	26 Jul 1815	p. 916
Thomas Reeves, Captain, District 180	26 Jul 1815	p. 917
Jesse Stallings, Lieutenant, District 180	26 Jul 1815	p. 917
James Flemester, Ensign, District 180	26 Jul 1815	p. 918
Elijah Jordan, Captain, District 144	26 Jul 1815	p. 918
John N. Stewart, Lieutenant, District 144	26 Jul 1815	p. 919
Charlton Stephens, Ensign, District 144	24 Jul 1815	p. 919
John Nunnelie, Major, Battalion 41	26 Jul 1815	p. 920
William L. Walker, Major, Battalion 68	26 Jul 1815	p. 920
George Osburne, Second Lieutenant, Troop of Cavalry, Squadron 5, Regiment 3	26 Jul 1815	p. 921
Marke K. Wood, Captain, Troop of Cavalry, Squadron 10, Regiment 5	26 Jul 1815	p. 921
Davis Smith, First Lieutenant, Troop of Cavalry, Squadron 10, Regiment 5	26 Jul 1815	p. 922
Ransom L. Dean, Second Lieutenant, Volunteer Troop of Cavalry, Squadron 10, Regiment 5	26 Jul 1815	p. 922
John Smith, Cornet, Troop of Cavalry, Squadron 10, Regiment 5	26 Jul 1815	p. 923
John Whitaker, Captain, District 171	5 Aug 1815	p. 923
John W. Bates, Lieutenant, District 177	5 Aug 1815	p. 924
Daniel Greene, Ensign, District 44	5 Aug 1815	p. 924
Elijah Callum, Ensign, District 235	5 Aug 1815	p. 925
Elisha Hubbard, Captain, District 276	5 Aug 1815	p. 925
Andrew Harris, Lieutenant, District 76	5 Aug 1815	p. 926
Lewis Maddox, Ensign, District 86	5 Aug 1815	p. 926

Name, Rank, Unit	Date	Page
Benjamin Coleman, Captain, District 299	5 Aug 1815	p. 927
Elisha Hightower, Lieutenant, District 160	5 Aug 1815	p. 927
Abner Stringer, Lieutenant, District 61	5 Aug 1815	p. 928
Thomas Kicklighton, Ensign, District 7	5 Aug 1815	p. 928
John Irwin, Lieutenant Colonel, Regiment 13	5 Aug 1815	p. 929
Richard T. Willis, Lieutenant Colonel, Regiment 18	5 Aug 1815	p. 929
Frederick S. Fell, Captain, Volunteer Company (styled the Savannah Volunteer Guards), Battalion 1	5 Aug 1815	p. 930
John T. Roberts, Lieutenant, Volunteer company of Infantry, Battalion 1	5 Aug 1815	p. 930
John Pondar, Ensign, Volunteer Company of Infantry (styled the Savannah Volunteer Guards), Battalion 1	5 Aug 1815	p. 931
James E. White, Major, Battalion 59	22 Aug 1815	p. 931
John B. Norris, Major, Battalion 60	22 Aug 1815	p. 932
Henry Lane, Major, Battalion 62	22 Aug 1815	p. 932
George M. Weatherby, Captain, District 302	22 Aug 1815	p. 933
George D. Taylor, Captain, District 181	22 Aug 1815	p. 933
Josiah Newton, Captain, District 216	22 Aug 1815	p. 934
James Roland, Captain, District 152	22 Aug 1815	p. 934
Ange Delapiriere, Captain, District 219	22 Aug 1815	p. 935
Samuel Taver, Ensign, District 65	22 Aug 1815	p. 935
Walker Perkins, Lieutenant, District 145	22 Aug 1815	p. 936
Tuttle Moreland, Lieutenant, District 347	22 Aug 1815	p. 936
Bartholomew Johnson, Ensign, District 278	22 Aug 1815	p. 937
Robert Mullins, Ensign, District 284	22 Aug 1815	p. 937
Isaiah Wafford, Ensign, District 128	22 Aug 1815	p. 938
William M. Ward, Ensign, District 367	22 Aug 1815	p. 938
Benjamin Orear, Ensign, District 142	22 Aug 1815	p. 939
William Deakle, Ensign, District 59	22 Aug 1815	p. 939
John Lary, Ensign, District 114	22 Aug 1815	p. 940
William Scott, Lieutenant, District 31	22 Aug 1815	p. 940
Herron Herring, Ensign, District 31	22 Aug 1815	p. 941
Thomas Stapleton, Lieutenant, District 81	22 Aug 1815	p. 941
Jacob Young, Ensign, District 81	22 Aug 1815	p. 942
John B. Cade, Lieutenant, District 181	22 Aug 1815	p. 942
Gibson C. Walton, Ensign, District 181	22 Aug 1815	p. 943
Jordan Allen, Lieutenant, District 14	22 Aug 1815	p. 943

Georgia Military Commissions, 1798–1818

Name, Rank, Unit	Date	Page
John Weeks, Ensign, District 368	22 Aug 1815	p. 944
John Webb, Captain, District 14	22 Aug 1815	p. 944
John B. Broughton, Lieutenant, District 14	22 Aug 1815	p. 945
James C. Phelps, Ensign, District 14	22 Aug 1815	p. 945
John Parks, Ensign, Volunteer Company of Riflemen, Battalion 29	22 Aug 1815	p. 946
Greene Hill, First Lieutenant, Volunteer Company of Artillery, Regiment 31	22 Aug 1815	p. 946
Henry Pickard, Second Lieutenant, Volunteer Company of Artillery, Regiment 31	22 Aug 1815	p. 947
David Godward, Lieutenant, District 378	22 Aug 1815	p. 947
Jesse Conner, Ensign, District 378	22 Aug 1815	p. 948
William Bennett, First Lieutenant, Volunteer Company of Cavalry, Squadron 7, Regiment 4	22 Aug 1815	p. 948
Jesse J. Roan, Second Lieutenant, Volunteer Troop of Light Dragoons, Squadron 7, Regiment 4	22 Aug 1815	p. 949
William Lee, Cornet, Volunteer Troop of Cavalry, Squadron 7, Regiment 4	22 Aug 1815	p. 949
James Harden, Ensign, District 90	1 Sep 1815	p. 950
Moses Guest, Lieutenant, District 211	1 Sep 1815	p. 950
Wade White, Lieutenant, District 239	1 Sep 1815	p. 951
James Dickson, Ensign, District 239	1 Sep 1815	p. 951
Zachariah Fields, Lieutenant, District 303	1 Sep 1815	p. 952
William D. Algiers, Lieutenant, District 342	1 Sep 1815	p. 952
Leroy Sale, Captain, District 165	1 Aug 1815	p. 953
Burwell Pope, Lieutenant Colonel, Regiment 22	1 Sep 1815	p. 953
Daniel Jackson, Ensign, District 286	16 Sep 1815	p. 954
Arthur Cruse, Ensign, District 304	16 Sep 1815	p. 954
John Brooks, Ensign, District 312	16 Sep 1815	p. 955
Josiah Goodson, Lieutenant, District 20	16 Sep 1815	p. 955
B. Jordan, Lieutenant, District 92	16 Sep 1815	p. 956
William Ray, Lieutenant, District 100	16 Sep 1815	p. 956
Gray Andrews, Ensign, District 100	16 Sep 1815	p. 957
Henry Pope, Lieutenant, District 167	16 Sep 1815	p. 957
William Little, Lieutenant, District 173	16 Sep 1815	p. 958
James Sanford, Ensign, District 173	16 Sep 1815	p. 958
William Twitty, Lieutenant, District 305	16 Sep 1815	p. 959
James W. Alston, Captain, District 51	16 Sep 1815	p. 959

Name, Rank, Unit	Date	Page
Jeremiah Gilly, Lieutenant, District 51	16 Sep 1815	p. 960
Wyley Hayes, Ensign, District 51	16 Sep 1815	p. 960
Jacob Oliver, Captain, District 38	16 Sep 1815	p. 961
John Oliver, Ensign, District 38	16 Sep 1815	p. 961
Daniel Humphrey, Captain, District 74	16 Sep 1815	p. 962
Richard Gordan, Captain, District 95	16 Sep 1815	p. 962
Stephen Deare, Captain, District 133	16 Sep 1815	p. 963
Manning Richard, Captain, District 136	16 Sep 1815	p. 963
James West, Captain, District 137	16 Sep 1815	p. 964
John Hackney, Lieutenant, District 137	16 Sep 1815	p. 964

Georgia Military Commissions
Commissions Book 1815–1818

Name, Unit, Rank	*Date*	*Page*
James W. Cooper, Captain, District 161	16 Sep 1815	p. 1
Samuel Overstreet, Captain, District 188	16 Sep 1815	p. 1
Martin Willis, Lieutenant, District 188	16 Sep 1815	p. 2
John Sanders, Ensign, District 188	16 Sep 1815	p. 2
Archibald Drake, Captain, District 228	16 Sep 1815	p. 3
Tilman Hemphill, Captain, District 279	16 Sep 1815	p. 3
Hezekiah Dodwell, Captain, District 306	16 Sep 1815	p. 4
Isaac Avered, Lieutenant, District 306	16 Sep 1815	p. 4
Nathan Philips, Ensign, District 106	16 Sep 1815	p. 5
Fred'k Johnson, Captain, District 308	16 Sep 1815	p. 5
John Wilson, Ensign, District 318	16 Sep 1815	p. 6
Henry May, Captain, District 389	16 Sep 1815	p. 6
Elijah Powell, Major, Battalion 15	16 Sep 1815	p. 7
Dennis Dent, Major, Battalion 28	30 Sep 1815	p. 7
Gabriel Gunn, Major, Battalion 77	30 Sep 1815	p. 8
Randol Johnson, Captain, District 39	30 Sep 1815	p. 8
Chadore Handcock, Lieutenant, District 39	30 Sep 1815	p. 9
John Hubbert, Captain, District 157	30 Sep 1815	p. 9
Simeon Walker, Captain, District 168	30 Sep 1815	p. 10
Thomas J. Gregory, Captain, District 189	30 Sep 1815	p. 10
Clabourn Haws, Captain, District 357	30 Sep 1815	p. 11
Richard Shockley, Captain, District 370	30 Sep 1815	p. 11
Thomas King, Lieutenant, District 370	30 Sep 1815	p. 12
William Lawrance, Captain, District 373	30 Sep 1815	p. 12
John Overstreet, Lieutenant, District 57	30 Sep 1815	p. 13
Edward Rick, Ensign, District 57	30 Sep 1815	p. 13
James W. Josey, Lieutenant, District 85	30 Sep 1815	p. 14
Edmond Jeter, Lieutenant, District 101	30 Sep 1815	p. 14
James Richardson, Ensign, District 101	30 Sep 1815	p. 15
Benjamin James, Lieutenant, District 121	30 Sep 1815	p. 15
Thoma Gin, Ensign, District 121	30 Sep 1815	p. 16
Cordial Wellborn, Lieutenant, District 139	30 Sep 1815	p. 16
Joseph Akin, Lieutenant, District 148	30 Sep 1815	p. 17
John Southerland, Ensign, District 148	30 Sep 1815	p. 17

Georgia Military Commissions, 1798–1818

Name, Unit, Rank	Date	Page
William Cole, Lieutenant, District 149	30 Sep 1815	p. 18
Hamilton Watts, Ensign, District 149	30 Sep 1815	p. 18
William Jackson, Lieutenant, District 179	30 Sep 1815	p. 19
George Carter, Lieutenant, District 197	30 Sep 1815	p. 19
Newton Bramblet, Lieutenant, District 212	30 Sep 1815	p. 20
Joseph Waters, Lieutenant, District 227	30 Sep 1815	p. 20
Robert Wiseman, Ensign, District 274	30 Sep 1815	p. 21
Jacob Watts, Captain, Volunteer Corps of Riflemen	6 Oct 1815	p. 21
Constantine Church, Captain, Company of Cavalry, Squadron 7, Regiment 4	6 Oct 1815	p. 22
Reichard Shackleford, Captain, Company of Cavalry, Squadron 5, Regiment 2	6 Oct 1815	p. 22
Thomas Hollida, Ensign, District 354	6 Oct 1815	p. 23
Ruben Woodruff, Ensign, District 236	6 Oct 1815	p. 23
Deal Mills, Ensign, District 212	6 Oct 1815	p. 24
Jesse Moran, Lieutenant, District 319	6 Oct 1815	p. 24
Jesse Harper, Lieutenant, District 284	6 Oct 1815	p. 25
John G. Walker, Lieutenant, District 279	6 Oct 1815	p. 25
John Herrage, Ensign, District 279	6 Oct 1815	p. 26
Michael Welch, Lieutenant, District 69	6 Oct 1815	p. 26
Thomas Lewis, Ensign, District 69	6 Oct 1815	p. 27
Daniel W. Shire, Captain, District 350	6 Oct 1815	p. 27
James W. Shire, Lieutenant, District 350	6 Oct 1815	p. 28
Morgan Prevatt, Captain, District 335	6 Oct 1815	p. 28
John Jeter, Captain, District 317	6 Oct 1815	p. 29
James Nobles, Captain, District 275	6 Oct 1815	p. 29
Sanders Nobles, Lieutenant, District 275	6 Oct 1815	p. 30
Joseph Ryals, Ensign, District 275	6 Oct 1815	p. 30
Martin Holliday, Captain, District 245	6 Oct 1815	p. 31
Bartley Montgomery, Lieutenant, District 245	6 Oct 1815	p. 31
Medad McClendon, Ensign, District 178	6 Oct 1815	p. 32
John Gresham, Captain, District 170	6 Oct 1815	p. 32
Gilbert Kent, Ensign, District 170	6 Oct 1815	p. 33
Urial Farmer, Lieutenant, District 170	6 Oct 1815	p. 33
John Watkins, Captain, District 163	6 Oct 1815	p. 34
John Brown, Lieutenant, District 163	6 Oct 1815	p. 34
John Pattille, Ensign, District 163	6 Oct 1815	p. 35

Commissions Book 1815–1818

Name, Unit, Rank	**Date**	**Page**
Josiah Rogers, Captain, District 143	6 Oct 1815	p. 35
Roger Lawson, Major, Battalion 80	6 Oct 1815	p. 36
Benjamin Henry, Major, Battalion 61	6 Oct 1815	p. 36
Jesse Theard, Major, Battalion 36	6 Oct 1815	p. 37
Nicholas Howard, Major, Battalion 32	6 Oct 1815	p. 37
John Mercer, Major, Battalion 30	6 Oct 1815	p. 38
Daniel M. Hall, Ensign, District 115	12 Oct 1815	p. 38
Jame Mathews, Lieutenant, District 242	12 Oct 1815	p. 39
Peter Anglin, Ensign, District 242	12 Oct 1815	p. 39
Edward Butler, Captain, Company of Cavalry, Squadron 5, Regiment 3	12 Oct 1815	p. 40
Daniel M. Hall, Ensign, District 303	19 Oct 1815	p. 40
Elihu Wilson, Lieutenant, District 13	19 Oct 1815	p. 41
Furnifold Willis, Lieutenant, District 79	19 Oct 1815	p. 41
Harmon Howard, Lieutenant, District 97	19 Oct 1815	p. 42
Silas Floyd, Ensign, District 97	19 Oct 1815	p. 42
Daniel Kelly, Lieutenant, District 161	19 Oct 1815	p. 43
David A. Newsom, Captain, District 138	19 Oct 1815	p. 43
James Wynne, Captain, District 159	19 Oct 1815	p. 44
Robert Robuck, Captain, District 196	19 Oct 1815	p. 44
John Hansard, Ensign, District 196	19 Oct 1815	p. 45
Lewis Parkes, Captain, District 269	19 Oct 1815	p. 45
Hezekiah F. Goss, Captain, District 277	19 Oct 1815	p. 46
Allen Harper, Ensign, District 277	19 Oct 1815	p. 46
Batson Bulloch, Captain, District 355	19 Oct 1815	p. 47
John Harvy, Captain, District 19	25 Oct 1815	p. 47
John Burnett Jr., Captain, District 26	25 Oct 1815	p. 48
John Daniel, Captain, District 66	25 Oct 1815	p. 48
Silas Elliott, Lieutenant, District 66	25 Oct 1815	p. 49
Abner Moore, Ensign, District 66	25 Oct 1815	p. 49
Joseph Duke, Captain, District 282	25 Oct 1815	p. 50
John Robinson, Captain, District 313	25 Oct 1815	p. 50
William Brown, Lieutenant, District 313	25 Oct 1815	p. 51
Jehu Williams, Ensign, District 373	25 Oct 1815	p. 51
Mathew Hodge, Captain, District 324	25 Oct 1815	p. 52
William Mason, Captain, District 390	25 Oct 1815	p. 52
Emanuel Cox, Ensign, District 390	25 Oct 1815	p. 53

Georgia Military Commissions, 1798–1818

Name, Unit, Rank	*Date*	*Page*
James McLeroy, Lieutenant, District 240	25 Oct 1815	p. 53
William Clifton, Ensign, District 240	25 Oct 1815	p. 54
James Cox, Ensign, District 360	25 Oct 1815	p. 54
Jared Dennard, Captain, Regiment 0	30 Oct 1815	p. 55
Robert Hodges, First Lieutenant, Regiment 0	30 Oct 1815	p. 55
Shadrack Wall, Second Lieutenant, Regiment 0	30 Oct 1815	p. 56
Joab Pinson, Major, Battalion 22	2 Nov 1815	p. 57
Hezekiah D. Adams, Lieutenant, District 223	6 Nov 1815	p. 57
Thomas Hart, Lieutenant, Troop of Cavalry, Squadron 6, Regiment 3	11 Nov 1815	p. 58
John W. Crutchfield, Cornet, Troop of Cavalry, Squadron 6, Regiment 3	11 Nov 1815	p. 58
Abram Card, Captain, Volunteer Corps of Riflemen, Battalion 66	11 Nov 1815	p. 59
John Carter, Lieutenant, Volunteer Corps of Riflemen, Battalion 38	11 Nov 1815	p. 59
Abram Brooks, Ensign, Volunteer Rifle Corps, Battalion 38	11 Nov 1815	p. 60
Ellis Cheek, Ensign, District 370	11 Nov 1815	p. 60
James Bigham, Ensign, District 76	11 Nov 1815	p. 61
Oliver Waldron, Ensign, District 19	11 Nov 1815	p. 61
George Epperson, Lieutenant, District 264	11 Nov 1815	p. 62
Richard Baker, Ensign, District 264	11 Nov 1815	p. 62
Obadiah Hooper, Lieutenant, District 263	11 Nov 1815	p. 63
Joseph Henderson, Lieutenant, District 196	11 Nov 1815	p. 63
Joshua David, Lieutenant, District 168	11 Nov 1815	p. 64
Caleb Sappington, Ensign, District 168	11 Nov 1815	p. 64
Noah Callaway, Lieutenant, District 165	11 Nov 1815	p. 65
Francis Jett, Lieutenant, District 143	11 Nov 1815	p. 65
Morris Malpass, Lieutenant, District 136	11 Nov 1815	p. 66
James Casey, Lieutenant, District 58	11 Nov 1815	p. 66
James Whellon, Lieutenant, District 45	11 Nov 1815	p. 67
Isaac H. Horn, Captain, District 386	11 Nov 1815	p. 67
James Kirkland, Ensign, District 386	11 Nov 1815	p. 68
John Wiley, Captain, District 383	11 Nov 1815	p. 68
John A. Ragland, Captain, District 379	11 Nov 1815	p. 69
Robert Wright, Captain, District 367	11 Nov 1815	p. 69

Name, Unit, Rank	Date	Page
William M. Ward, Lieutenant, District 367	11 Nov 1815	p. 70
Abner Bartlet, Captain, District 366	11 Nov 1815	p. 70
Joseph Hickman, Lieutenant, District 366	11 Nov 1815	p. 71
Alexander Cimpson [Simpson], Ensign, District 348	11 Nov 1815	p. 71
Harvey Hardinson, Captain, District 348	11 Nov 1815	p. 72
Robert Johnson, Captain, District 327	11 Nov 1815	p. 72
Aron Reeve, Ensign, District 327	11 Nov 1815	p. 73
Joseph Middlebrook, Captain, District 298	11 Nov 1815	p. 73
Sharod Roland, Captain, District 231	11 Nov 1815	p. 74
Obadiah M. B. Fielder, Captain, District 286	11 Nov 1815	p. 74
James Royland, Captain, District 190	11 Nov 1815	p. 75
William Davis, Lieutenant, District 190	11 Nov 1815	p. 75
John Johnson, Captain, District 166	11 Nov 1815	p. 76
Preston Brook, Lieutenant, District 166	11 Nov 1815	p. 76
John Carvill, Ensign, District 166	11 Nov 1815	p. 77
John Wise, Captain, District 48	11 Nov 1815	p. 77
Berry Jones, Captain, District 44	11 Nov 1815	p. 78
Joseph Underhill, Lieutenant, District 44	11 Nov 1815	p. 78
Soleman Walker, Captain, District 32	11 Nov 1815	p. 79
Neely Dobson, Major, Battalion 58	11 Nov 1815	p. 79
Isaiah T. Irwin, Major, Battalion 37	11 Nov 1815	p. 80
Richard Gordan, Major, Battalion 21	11 Nov 1815	p. 80
William Bailey, Major, Battalion 8	11 Nov 1815	p. 81
Samuel Piles, Major, Battalion 7	11 Nov 1815	p. 81
Gaines Thompson, Lieutenant Colonel, Regiment 28	11 Nov 1815	p. 82
John Floyd, Major General, Division 1	24 Nov 1815	p. 82
Thomas P. Hamilton, Brigadier General, Brigade 1, Division 5	24 Nov 1815	p. 83
Francis Hopkins, Brigadier General, Brigade 1, Division 1	24 Nov 1815	p. 83
James Bandy, First Lieutenant, Troop of Cavalry, Squadron 5, Regiment 3	24 Nov 1815	p. 84
John Means, Second Lieutenant, Troop of Cavalry, Squadron 5, Regiment 3	25 Nov 1815	p. 84
Jacob Best, Ensign, District 35	25 Nov 1815	p. 85
Littleton Mapp, Lieutenant, District 109	25 Nov 1815	p. 85
Nathaniel Dent, Ensign, District 109	25 Nov 1815	p. 86
George G. Higginbotham, Lieutenant, District 189	25 Nov 1815	p. 86

Georgia Military Commissions, 1798–1818

Name, Unit, Rank	Date	Page
Leroy Upshear, Ensign, District 189	25 Nov 1815	p. 87
William Allum, Lieutenant, District 369	25 Nov 1815	p. 87
Grumberry Baker, Lieutenant, District 206	25 Nov 1815	p. 88
Richard Chandler, Ensign, District 206	25 Nov 1815	p. 88
Joseph Arnold, Lieutenant, District 231	25 Nov 1815	p. 89
John Simmons, Ensign, District 231	25 Nov 1815	p. 89
Samuel Howard, Lieutenant, District 352	25 Nov 1815	p. 90
Nathaniel Bostick, Captain, District 76	25 Nov 1815	p. 90
Michael L. Shockley, Captain, District 109	25 Nov 1815	p. 91
Jeremiah Ragan, Captain, District 147	25 Nov 1815	p. 91
Wily G. Tatem, Captain, District 187	25 Nov 1815	p. 92
Gabriel A. Moffett, Captain, District 217	25 Nov 1815	p. 92
Gerry Smith Jr., Captain, District 280	25 Nov 1815	p. 93
Seaborn Jones, Lieutenant, District 280	25 Nov 1815	p. 93
Ezekiel Gilbert, Ensign, District 280	25 Nov 1815	p. 94
Edmund Welch, Captain, District 283	25 Nov 1815	p. 94
Joshua Knight, Lieutenant, District 283	25 Nov 1815	p. 95
William Beltcher, Ensign, District 283	25 Nov 1815	p. 95
Richard W. Ellis, Captain, District 319	25 Nov 1815	p. 96
Stephen Mobley, Major, Battalion 65	25 Nov 1815	p. 96
Joel McClendon, Captain, District 362	28 Nov 1815	p. 97
Thomas Harvey, Lieutenant, District 362	28 Nov 1815	p. 97
Benjamin Sessions, Captain, Troop of Cavalry, Squadron 4, Regiment 2	2 Dec 1815	p. 98
George Sessions, First Lieutenant, Troop of Cavalry, Squadron 4, Regiment 2	2 Dec 1815	p. 98
William Pace, Second Lieutenant, Troop of Cavalry, Squadron 4, Regiment 2	2 Dec 1815	p. 99
Josiah Jones, Cornet, Troop of Cavalry, Squadron 4, Regiment 2	2 Dec 1815	p. 99
Daniel M. Hall, Captain, District 115	2 Dec 1815	p. 100
John Brown, Captain, District 122	2 Dec 1815	p. 100
Charles Spear, Lieutenant, District 122	2 Dec 1815	p. 101
Samuel Liverman, Ensign, District 122	2 Dec 1815	p. 101
Jacob Riley, Captain, District 141	2 Dec 1815	p. 102
Thomas Johnson, Ensign, District 141	2 Dec 1815	p. 102
Henry Rose, Lieutenant, District 179	2 Dec 1815	p. 103

Name, Unit, Rank	*Date*	*Page*
Wilie Gilbert, Lieutenant, District 332	2 Dec 1815	p. 103
Thomas Pierce, Ensign, District 332	2 Dec 1815	p. 104
James Smith, Ensign, District 379	13 Dec 1815	p. 104
William Williams, Lieutenant, District 19	13 Dec 1815	p. 105
Greene D. Brantley, Lieutenant, District 113	13 Dec 1815	p. 105
James Flemister, Lieutenant, District 180	13 Dec 1815	p. 106
Samuel Tucker, Lieutenant, District 266	13 Dec 1815	p. 106
Telmon Oxford, Lieutenant, District 305	13 Dec 1815	p. 107
John Tudor, Ensign, District 305	13 Dec 1815	p. 107
Robert Doad, Captain, District 83	13 Dec 1815	p. 108
John T. Neal, Captain, District 213	13 Dec 1815	p. 108
Zachariah Fears, Captain, District 286	13 Dec 1815	p. 109
Willis Hawkins, Lieutenant, District 286	13 Dec 1815	p. 109
Thomas Woodward, Captain, District 318	13 Dec 1815	p. 110
William Joiner, Captain, District 356	13 Dec 1815	p. 110
Horwell Marble, Lieutenant, District 287	13 Dec 1815	p. 111
William Durmmond, Captain, District 381	13 Dec 1815	p. 111
Zachariah Roberts, Ensign, District 381	13 Dec 1815	p. 112
James M. Bates, First Lieutenant, Troop of Cavalry, Squadron 3, Regiment 2	2 Jan 1816	p. 112
Martin Towns, First Lieutenant, Troop of Cavalry, Squadron 9, Regiment 5	2 Jan 1816	p. 113
Joseph Cumming, Captain, Volunteer Company of Artillery, Regiment 1	2 Jan 1816	p. 113
William E. Adams, Lieutenant Colonel, Regiment 32	2 Jan 1816	p. 114
Thomas Stapleton, Captain, District 81	2 Jan 1816	p. 114
David Lewis, Captain, District 82	2 Jan 1816	p. 115
Rufus Christian, Captain, District 202	2 Jan 1816	p. 115
John Marr, Captain, District 283	2 Jan 1816	p. 116
Thomas Coram, Lieutenant, District 152	2 Jan 1816	p. 116
Hincher Thomas, Lieutenant, District 182	2 Jan 1816	p. 117
Thomas Ashley, Ensign, District 182	2 Jan 1816	p. 117
Hawkins Howard, Lieutenant, District 389	2 Jan 1816	p. 118
Thomas Ray, Ensign, District 294	2 Jan 1816	p. 118
John Irwin, Brigadier General, Brigade 2, Division 2	17 Jan 1816	p. 119
William Hammond, Major, Battalion 35	17 Jan 1816	p. 119
Thomas Spencer, Captain, District 299	17 Jan 1816	p. 120

Georgia Military Commissions, 1798–1818

Name, Unit, Rank	*Date*	*Page*
James Stewart, Captain, District 221	17 Jan 1816	p. 120
John Pittman, Captain, District 127	17 Jan 1815	p. 121
Roff Huff, Captain, District 103	17 Jan 1816	p. 121
Sylatus Williams, Captain, District 97	17 Jan 1816	p. 122
Nathan Breed, Lieutenant, District 155	17 Jan 1816	p. 122
James Giles, Lieutenant, District 309	17 Jan 1816	p. 123
William Hunter, Ensign, District 259	17 Jan 1816	p. 123
Reason Watson, Captain, District 391	17 Jan 1816	p. 124
Wm E. Dean, Lieutenant, District 391	17 Jan 1816	p. 124
William Williams, Captain, District 361	17 Jan 1816	p. 125
Robert Henderson, Lieutenant, District 361	17 Jan 1816	p. 125
John Curry, Captain, District 95	17 Jan 1816	p. 126
James G. Griffin, Ensign, District 95	17 Jan 1816	p. 126
Barnard W. Fickling, Lieutenant, District 153	17 Jan 1816	p. 127
Henry Hinton, Ensign, District 153	17 Jan 1816	p. 127
William F. Williams, Second Lieutenant, Volunteer Company of Artillery, Regiment 1	17 Jan 1816	p. 128
William Maxwell, Captain, Troop of Cavalry, Squadron 1, Regiment 1	17 Jan 1816	p. 128
Robert C. McConnell, First Lieutenant, Troop of Cavalry, Squadron 1, Regiment 1	17 Jan 1816	p. 129
Allen Wiggins, Captain, District 317	22 Jan 1816	p. 129
William Evans, Captain, District 308	9 Feb 1816	p. 130
Elisha Brooks, Lieutenant, District 308	9 Feb 1816	p. 130
Nathan Jones, Lieutenant, Volunteer Company of Riflemen, Battalion 66	21 Feb 1816	p. 131
Jeremiah Smith, Ensign, Volunteer Troop of Riflemen, Battalion 66	21 Feb 1816	p. 131
William Weeks, Major, Battalion 68	21 Feb 1816	p. 132
Christian F. Hunk, Captain, District 7	21 Feb 1816	p. 132
John Gray, Captain, District 67	21 Feb 1816	p. 133
William Rachels, Lieutenant, District 67	21 Feb 1816	p. 133
Edward Harris, Captain, District 150	21 Feb 1816	p. 134
Mathew McCrarey, Captain, District 154	21 Feb 1816	p. 134
Jonathan Cooper, Lieutenant, District 154	21 Feb 1816	p. 135
John A. Cotton, Captain, District 304	21 Feb 1816	p. 135
Richard Barkesdale, Lieutenant, District 304	21 Feb 1816	p. 136

Commissions Book 1815–1818

Name, Unit, Rank	Date	Page
Henry Boyd, Ensign, District 304	21 Feb 1816	p. 136
Bartley Wood, Lieutenant, District 62	21 Feb 1816	p. 137
Jesse Connel, Lieutenant, District 81	21 Feb 1816	p. 137
Henry Whitehead, Ensign, District 81	21 Feb 1816	p. 138
Thomas Johnson, Lieutenant, District 141	21 Feb 1816	p. 138
William Pittard, Lieutenant, District 235	21 Feb 1816	p. 139
Jonathan Rush, Lieutenant, District 267	21 Feb 1816	p. 139
Benjamin Buckner, Lieutenant, District 310	21 Feb 1816	p. 140
Lauchlin McCrary, Lieutenant, District 315	21 Feb 1816	p. 140
John Swan, Ensign, District 137	21 Feb 1816	p. 141
Thomas Childers, Ensign, District 190	21 Feb 1816	p. 141
Wiley Jones, Ensign, District 367	21 Feb 1816	p. 142
Churchill Allen, Ensign, District 374	21 Feb 1816	p. 142
James McCurdy, Lieutenant, District 205	21 Feb 1816	p. 143
John Mead, Ensign, District 205	21 Feb 1816	p. 143
James White, Cornet, Troop of Cavalry, Squadron 5, Regiment 3	21 Feb 1816	p. 144
Isaac Hudgings, Ensign, District 362	21 Feb 1816	p. 144
Daniel Luke, Ensign, District 366	21 Feb 1816	p. 145
Jesse George, Captain, District 295	29 Feb 1816	p. 145
Timothy Rogers, First Lieutenant, Troop of Cavalry, Squadron 9, Regiment 5	14 Mar 1816	p. 146
James Lewis, Major, Cavalry, Squadron 4, Regiment 2	14 Mar 1816	p. 146
Henry Dawson, Major, Battalion of Cavalry, Squadron 7, Regiment 4	14 Mar 1816	p. 147
Thomas Price, Ensign, District 3	14 Mar 1816	p. 147
Henry Walker Jr., Ensign, District 85	14 Mar 1816	p. 148
David A. Perryman, Ensign, District 134	14 Mar 1816	p. 148
Major W. May, Ensign, District 140	14 Mar 1816	p. 149
Peyton Wade, Ensign, District 141	14 Mar 1816	p. 149
Richard Sale, Ensign, District 167	14 Mar 1816	p. 150
Anguish Clubreath, Ensign, District 203	14 Mar 1816	p. 150
William Wadsworth, Ensign, District 247	14 Mar 1816	p. 151
William F. Mapp, Ensign, District 276	14 Mar 1816	p. 151
Edmund Dodson, Ensign, District 282	14 Mar 1816	p. 152
William Blalock, Ensign, District 300	14 Mar 1816	p. 152
Fielding Strangler, Ensign, District 319	14 Mar 1816	p. 153

Georgia Military Commissions, 1798–1818

Name, Unit, Rank	Date	Page
Henry Vincent, Ensign, District 359	14 Mar 1816	p. 153
Charles C. Hayward, Lieutenant, District 74	14 Mar 1816	p. 154
George W. Watkins, Lieutenant, District 123	14 Mar 1816	p. 154
Terral Riley, Lieutenant, District 133	14 Mar 1816	p. 155
William Geer, Lieutenant, District 147	14 Mar 1816	p. 155
Young D. Allen, Ensign, District 147	14 Mar 1816	p. 156
John Kimborough, Lieutenant, District 160	14 Mar 1816	p. 156
William Jones, Lieutenant, District 195	14 Mar 1816	p. 157
Samuel Hanson, Lieutenant, District 242	14 Mar 1816	p. 157
Blake Morgan, Lieutenant, District 252	14 Mar 1816	p. 158
Joseph McLeroy, Ensign, District 252	14 Mar 1816	p. 158
William Wallace, Lieutenant, District 322	14 Mar 1816	p. 159
Charles Beal, Captain, District 119	14 Mar 1816	p. 159
John Travis, Captain, District 151	14 Mar 1816	p. 160
John Tarver Jr., Captain, District 171	14 Mar 1816	p. 160
William D. Orm, Lieutenant, District 171	14 Mar 1816	p. 161
Samuel Bentley Jr., Captain, District 201	14 Mar 1816	p. 161
Jesse Pierce, Captain, District 332	14 Mar 1816	p. 162
Thomas Williams, Captain, District 337	14 Mar 1816	p. 162
Morgan Brown, Lieutenant Colonel, Regiment 13	14 Mar 1816	p. 163
Thomas Kicklighter, Lieutenant, District 7	14 Mar 1816	p. 163
Henley Varner, Ensign, Volunteer Company of Infantry, Battalion 75	14 Mar 1816	p. 164
Harmon Mercer, Captain, Troop of Cavalry, Squadron 7, Regiment 4	21 Mar 1816	p. 164
Jesse Blackley, Ensign, District 164	21 Mar 1816	p. 165
John S. Cobb, Ensign, District 122	21 Mar 1816	p. 165
David Appason, Lieutenant, District 288	21 Mar 1816	p. 166
William Mitchell, Ensign, District 288	21 Mar 1816	p. 166
Abel Barge, Captain, District 88	21 Mar 1816	p. 167
Samuel Whitaker, Lieutenant, District 88	21 Mar 1816	p. 167
Charles Martin, Ensign, District 88	21 Mar 1816	p. 168
Edmund Dillard, Captain, District 90	21 Mar 1816	p. 168
Whitfield Sledge, Captain, District 133	21 Mar 1816	p. 169
Lazarus Atkinson, Captain, District 162	21 Mar 1816	p. 169
Thomas King, Captain, District 370	21 Mar 1816	p. 170
Robert Belcher, Captain, District 372	21 Mar 1816	p. 170

Name, Unit, Rank	*Date*	*Page*
Andrew Gordon, Major, Battalion 67	21 Mar 1816	p. 171
Nathan Bussey, Lieutenant Colonel, Regiment 20	21 Mar 1816	p. 171
John M. Stewart, Second Lieutenant, Troop of Cavalry, Squadron 1, Regiment 1	2 Apr 1816	p. 172
Daniel Hicks, Lieutenant, District 115	2 Apr 1816	p. 172
Thomas Loyd, Lieutenant, District 166	2 Apr 1816	p. 173
Charles Word, Lieutenant, District 213	2 Apr 1816	p. 173
William Norwon, Lieutenant, District 187	2 Apr 1816	p. 174
James Smith, Lieutenant, District 289	2 Apr 1816	p. 174
James Weldon, Lieutenant, District 365	2 Apr 1816	p. 175
Bedford Shorter, Ensign, District 365	2 Apr 1816	p. 175
William C. Gibson, Lieutenant, District 373	2 Apr 1816	p. 176
William Bridges, Ensign, District 373	2 Apr 1816	p. 176
Silas Hollis, Captain, District 2	2 Apr 1816	p. 177
James H. Lawrence, Lieutenant, District 2	2 Apr 1816	p. 177
Thomas Crapon, Ensign, District 2	2 Apr 1816	p. 178
Henry H. Hand, Captain, District 64	2 Apr 1816	p. 178
Aron Thompson, Lieutenant, District 64	2 Apr 1816	p. 179
Archibald Davis, Captain, District 94	2 Apr 1816	p. 179
William T. Williams, First Lieutenant, Corps of Light Artillery, Regiment 1	12 Apr 1816	p. 180
Donald McLeod, Second Lieutenant, Corps of Light Artillery, Regiment 1	12 Apr 1816	p. 180
Eli Campbell, Ensign, District 24	12 Apr 1816	p. 181
Benjamin Brown, Ensign, District 142	12 Apr 1816	p. 181
Robert Venable, Ensign, District 145	12 Apr 1816	p. 182
Josiah Chatham, Ensign, District 165	12 Apr 1816	p. 182
David Moore, Ensign, District 286	12 Apr 1816	p. 183
William Smith, Ensign, District 376	12 Apr 1816	p. 183
John Edwards, Lieutenant, District 299	12 Apr 1816	p. 184
William Porter, Lieutenant, District 330	12 Apr 1816	p. 184
David Smith, Captain, District 87	12 Apr 1816	p. 185
Mathew Smith, Lieutenant, District 87	12 Apr 1816	p. 185
William Greer, Captain, District 98	12 Apr 1816	p. 186
William Arman, Captain, District 161	12 Apr 1816	p. 186
David Patterson, Captain, District 172	12 Apr 1816	p. 187
William Hilliard, Lieutenant, District 172	12 Apr 1816	p. 187

Georgia Military Commissions, 1798–1818

Name, Unit, Rank	*Date*	*Page*
Thomas Davis, Ensign, District 172	12 Apr 1816	p. 188
George Fliynt, Captain, District 176	12 Apr 1816	p. 188
Thomas P. Boroughs, Captain, District 206	12 Apr 1816	p. 189
Thomas Akins, Captain, District 212	12 Apr 1816	p. 189
Shemei Mann, Captain, District 233	12 Apr 1816	p. 190
Samuel Ellis, Captain, District 354	12 Apr 1816	p. 190
William A. Slaughter, Captain, District 369	12 Apr 1816	p. 191
Clement Powers, Major, Battalion 3	12 Apr 1816	p. 191
John H. Brodnax, Major, Battalion 88	12 Apr 1816	p. 192
Joham S. Fannin, Lieutenant Colonel, Regiment 29	16 Apr 1816	p. 192
Asia White, First Lieutenant, Troop of Cavalry, Squadron 7, Regiment 4	22 Apr 1816	p. 193
Samuel Sturges, Ensign, District 120	22 Apr 1816	p. 193
John Cunningham, Ensign, District 308	22 Apr 1816	p. 194
James C. Mangham, Lieutenant, District 26	22 Apr 1816	p. 194
John B. Pritchard, Ensign, District 26	22 Apr 1816	p. 195
Morris Walden, Lieutenant, District 79	22 Apr 1816	p. 195
James Parker, Lieutenant, District 156	22 Apr 1816	p. 196
John Johnston, Lieutenant, District 190	22 Apr 1816	p. 196
Bennett Dooly, Lieutenant, District 198	22 Apr 1816	p. 197
Joshua Holmes, Ensign, District 198	22 Apr 1816	p. 197
Simeon Seales, Lieutenant, District 200	22 Apr 1816	p. 198
James Highsmith, Ensign, District 200	22 Apr 1816	p. 198
James A. Cooper, Lieutenant, District 274	22 Apr 1816	p. 199
Daniel Roberts, Lieutenant, District 342	22 Apr 1816	p. 199
George W. Nelson, Captain, District 108	22 Apr 1816	p. 200
Eppy White, Captain, District 193	22 Apr 1816	p. 200
William H. Parker, Ensign, District 193	22 Apr 1816	p. 201
Robert Jones, Captain, District 229	22 Apr 1816	p. 201
Edward Sturdevin, Captain, District 363	22 Apr 1816	p. 202
William Dowsing, Major, Battalion 56	22 Apr 1816	p. 202
John Seborn, Lieutenant Colonel, Regiment 24	22 Apr 1816	p. 203
James S. Weeks, Lieutenant, District 295	22 Apr 1816	p. 203
Wenloch C. Pearson, Ensign, District 329	1 May 1816	p. 204
Joseph W. Robinson, Cornet, Troop of Cavalry, Squadron 7, Regiment 4	5 Feb 1816	p. 204

Name, Unit, Rank	*Date*	*Page*
John Patterson, Captain, Troop of Cavalry styled the Jefferson Hussars, Squadron 2, Regiment 1	5 Feb 1816	p. 205
John P. Snow, Ensign, District 162	5 Feb 1816	p. 205
Allen R. Wootten, Ensign, District 180	5 Feb 1816	p. 206
George W. Wheeler, Lieutenant, District 82	5 Feb 1816	p. 206
Hardy Sutton, Ensign, District 82	5 Feb 1816	p. 207
Benjamin Orean, Lieutenant, District 142	5 Feb 1816	p. 207
Benjamin Hill, Lieutenant, District 158	5 Feb 1816	p. 208
Arnold Seal, Lieutenant, District 298	5 Feb 1816	p. 208
James Cadenhead, Ensign, District 298	5 Feb 1816	p. 209
Bailey Bell, Lieutenant, District 300	5 Feb 1816	p. 209
Mathew F. Hamilton, Lieutenant, District 316	5 Feb 1816	p. 210
David Hutchins, Ensign, District 316	5 Feb 1816	p. 210
Thomas Buckhanon, Lieutenant, District 321	5 Feb 1816	p. 211
Bartlett Sheffield, Ensign, District 321	5 Feb 1816	p. 211
Jeremiah Bell, Lieutenant, District 324	5 Feb 1816	p. 212
Littleton Tyson, Lieutenant, District 345	5 Feb 1816	p. 212
Elijah Dean, Captain, District 86	5 Feb 1816	p. 213
William Edmonds, Captain, District 178	5 Feb 1816	p. 213
Timothy Smith, Captain, District 187	5 Feb 1816	p. 214
Francis B. Smart, Captain, District 293	5 Feb 1816	p. 214
Lewis Stephens, Captain, District 322	5 Feb 1816	p. 215
John Reid, Captain, District 365	5 Feb 1816	p. 215
John Griffith, Captain, District 377	5 Feb 1816	p. 216
George M. Waters, Major, Battalion 5	5 Feb 1816	p. 216
Jesse Harrison, Major, Battalion 6	5 Feb 1816	p. 217
Henry P. Jones, Major, Battalion 17	5 Feb 1816	p. 217
George G. Nowland, Lieutenant Colonel, Regiment 35	5 Feb 1816	p. 218
Robert Bryan, Captain, District 375	10 May 1816	p. 218
James T. Underwood, Lieutenant, District 375	10 May 1816	p. 219
Thomas Leveritt, Ensign, District 375	10 May 1816	p. 219
Benjamin Wallace, Captain, District 169	10 May 1816	p. 220
Edmund Ogletree, Lieutenant, District 169	10 May 1816	p. 220
Leonard Coffin, Ensign, District 169	10 May 1816	p. 221
James Richards, Captain, District 291	10 May 1816	p. 221
Aristarcus Newton, Lieutenant, District 291	10 May 1816	p. 222
Thomas Harris, Ensign, District 291	10 May 1816	p. 222

Georgia Military Commissions, 1798–1818

Name, Unit, Rank	Date	Page
James Fleming, Captain, District 78	10 May 1816	p. 223
Richard Flectin, Lieutenant, District 78	10 May 1816	p. 223
Thomas Mountain, Ensign, District 78	10 May 1816	p. 224
James Glass, Captain, District 396	10 May 1816	p. 224
Benjamin Fulsom, Ensign, District 396	10 May 1816	p. 225
John Oliver, Captain, District 224	10 May 1816	p. 225
James Curreten, Lieutenant, District 224	10 May 1816	p. 226
Elisha Hood, Ensign, District 224	10 May 1816	p. 226
Delaware Lacy, Ensign, District 123	10 May 1816	p. 227
Thomas Rhoads, Ensign, District 305	10 May 1816	p. 227
John C. Baker, Ensign, District 368	10 May 1816	p. 228
William Harrison, Ensign, District 369	10 May 1816	p. 228
George T. Bond, Ensign, District 213	10 May 1816	p. 229
David Ravins, Ensign, District 232	10 May 1816	p. 229
Hiram M. Derican, Ensign, District 115	10 May 1816	p. 230
William Spierr, Lieutenant, District 383	10 May 1816	p. 230
Lewis McLeroy, Ensign, District 383	10 May 1816	p. 231
Robert Shuler, Lieutenant, District 386	10 May 1816	p. 231
Samuel Ford, Ensign, District 386	10 May 1816	p. 232
Jordan Anderson, Lieutenant, District 350	10 May 1816	p. 232
James J. Davis, Ensign, District 350	10 May 1816	p. 233
Elijah Calloway, Lieutenant, District 357	10 May 1816	p. 233
Uriah Parker, Ensign, District 357	10 May 1816	p. 234
Thomas Henderson, Captain, District 316	10 May 1816	p. 234
Mark Williams, Ensign, District 316	10 May 1816	p. 235
Seth Eason, Captain, District 84	10 May 1816	p. 235
Lewis Marshall, Ensign, District 84	10 May 1816	p. 236
Jesse Little, Captain, District 307	10 May 1816	p. 236
William Moseley, Ensign, District 307	10 May 1816	p. 237
Duncan McMillon, Captain, District 393	10 May 1816	p. 237
Neel McCrarey, Lieutenant, District 393	10 May 1816	p. 238
Charles McQueen, Captain, District 260	10 May 1816	p. 238
Peter Anders, Lieutenant, District 260	10 May 1816	p. 239
William Yarborough, Lieutenant, District 384	10 May 1816	p. 239
Christopher Baker, Lieutenant, District 370	10 May 1816	p. 240
Anderson Ward, Lieutenant, District 314	10 May 1816	p. 240

Name, Unit, Rank	*Date*	Page
James Burtan, Captain, District 380	10 May 1816	p. 241
James Wright, Captain, District 222	10 May 1816	p. 241
Aaron W. Grier, Captain, District 158	10 May 1816	p. 242
Elias Wilson, Captain, District 134	10 May 1816	p. 242
Uriah Kinchen, Captain, District 52	10 May 1816	p. 243
Fowler F. Adrian, Major, Battalion 46	10 May 1816	p. 243
Robert Owen, Lieutenant Colonel, Regiment 30	10 May 1816	p. 244
John Chambers, Cornet, Troop of Cavalry, Squadron 2, Regiment 1	10 May 1816	p. 244
Allen Lovlace, First Lieutenant, Troop of Cavalry, Squadron 3, Regiment 2	30 May 1816	p. 245
Thomas W. Murrell, Second Lieutenant, Troop of Cavalry, Squadron 3, Regiment 2	30 May 1816	p. 245
Aaron Aldridge, Cornet, Troop of Cavalry, Squadron 3, Regiment 2	30 May 1816	p. 246
Joseph Bachlott, Captain, Volunteer Corps (styled the Guards), Battalion 8	30 May 1816	p. 246
John Bashlott, Ensign, Volunteer Company, Battalion 8	30 May 1816	p. 247
John Dunwoody, Captain, Volunteer Company, Battalion 4	30 May 1816	p. 247
Benjamin Mill, Lieutenant, Volunteer Company, Battalion 4	30 May 1816	p. 248
John Mill, Ensign, Volunteer Company, Battalion 4	30 May 1816	p. 248
James Barton, Major, Battalion 63	30 May 1816	p. 249
William R. McIntosh, Captain, District 22	30 May 1816	p. 249
David G. Jones, Captain, District 29	30 May 1816	p. 250
Charles Howell, Lieutenant, District 29	30 May 1816	p. 250
Daniel D. Copp, Ensign, District 29	30 May 1816	p. 251
Moses McCall, Captain, District 36	30 May 1816	p. 251
Ivey Thompson, Lieutenant, District 36	30 May 1816	p. 252
Wiley Dowdey, Ensign, District 36	30 May 1816	p. 252
Joseph Durrence, Captain, District 41	30 May 1816	p. 253
Terrel Higdon, Captain, District 57	30 May 1816	p. 253
Robert Fleming, Captain, District 82	30 May 1816	p. 254
Jeremiah Winters, Captain, District 124	30 May 1816	p. 254
James Rucker Jr., Captain, District 195	30 May 1816	p. 255
Alexander Fash, Captain, District 207	30 May 1816	p. 255
John Hollingsworth, Captain, District 211	13 May 1816	p. 256

Georgia Military Commissions, 1798–1818

Name, Unit, Rank	*Date*	*Page*
James Hemphill, Captain, District 256	30 May 1816	p. 256
Benjamin Higginbotham, Captain, District 315	30 May 1816	p. 257
Henry Hunt, Lieutenant, District 315	30 May 1816	p. 257
David Bozeman, Captain, District 326	30 May 1816	p. 258
Samuel Stevens, Lieutenant, District 326	30 May 1816	p. 258
Absalom Holcomb, Captain, District 374	30 May 1816	p. 259
Charles Ritchell, Lieutenant, District 374	30 May 1816	p. 259
William Adare, Captain, District 382	30 May 1816	p. 260
Eli Tanner, Captain, District 392	30 May 1816	p. 260
Cade D. Strickland, Captain, District 397	30 May 1816	p. 261
Jonathan Moore, Lieutenant, District 397	30 May 1816	p. 261
Wylie H. Whatley, Ensign, District 397	30 May 1816	p. 262
James Blunt, Lieutenant, District 72	30 May 1816	p. 262
Jesse Johns, Ensign, District 72	30 May 1816	p. 263
Richmond Colbert, Lieutenant, District 106	30 May 1816	p. 263
John P. Snow, Lieutenant, District 162	30 May 1816	p. 264
Micajah Alane, Lieutenant, District 179	30 May 1816	p. 264
Barkesdale B. Neely, Ensign, District 179	30 May 1816	p. 265
Samuel Higginbotham, Lieutenant, District 204	30 May 1816	p. 265
John Griffith, Ensign, District 204	30 May 1816	p. 266
Reubin Oakes, Ensign, District 229	30 May 1816	p. 266
Hurry Britain, Ensign, District 229	30 May 1816	p. 267
Alexander Hudson, Lieutenant, District 268	30 May 1816	p. 267
Aquilla Hardy, Lieutenant, District 269	30 May 1816	p. 268
Marris McGill, Ensign, District 269	30 May 1816	p. 268
Jesse Conner, Lieutenant, District 378	30 May 1816	p. 269
Samuel M. Sleigh, Ensign, District 19	30 May 1816	p. 269
Levi Spurlin, Ensign, District 154	30 May 1816	p. 270
James J. Wilson, Ensign, District 235	30 May 1816	p. 270
Elial Mosely, Ensign, District 358	30 May 1816	p. 271
Francis J. Rudulph, Lieutenant, St. Marys Volunteer Guards, Battalion 8	17 Jun 1816	p. 271
Elisha Strong, Major, Battalion 44	17 Jun 1816	p. 272
John Lowe, Major, Battalion 50	17 Jun 1816	p. 272
Jacob P. Brooks, Major, Battalion 51	17 Jun 1816	p. 273
John Thomas, Major, Battalion 81	17 Jun 1816	p. 273
Solomon Moody, Captain, District 27	17 Jun 1816	p. 274

Name, Unit, Rank	*Date*	*Page*
Mathew Carter, Lieutenant, District 27	17 Jun 1816	p. 274
Joseph Manning, Ensign, District 27	17 Jun 1816	p. 275
William Long, Captain, District 31	17 Jun 1816	p. 275
James Scott, Lieutenant, District 31	17 Jun 1816	p. 276
Isaac Bailey, Ensign, District 31	17 Jun 1816	p. 276
James Roberts, Captain, District 37	17 Jun 1816	p. 277
William Burnes, Lieutenant, District 37	17 Jun 1816	p. 277
Thomas Pengree, Ensign, District 37	17 Jun 1816	p. 278
William Roswood, Captain, District 75	17 Jun 1816	p. 278
John Wilson, Captain, Volunteer Company of Riflemen, Battalion 88	17 Jun 1816	p. 279
Ephraim Phare, Lieutenant, Volunteer Company of Riflemen, Battalion 88	17 Jun 1816	p. 279
David D. Smith, Ensign, Volunteer Company of Riflemen, Battalion 88	17 Jun 1816	p. 280
William F. Jackson, Captain, District 129	17 Jun 1816	p. 280
George Jarrell, Captain, District 205	17 Jun 1816	p. 281
Harris Toney, Captain, District 264	17 Jun 1816	p. 281
Nathaniel Bell, Lieutenant, District 23	17 Jun 1816	p. 282
William Gerrald, Ensign, District 23	17 Jun 1816	p. 282
Nathaniel W. Renfroe, Lieutenant, District 95	17 Jun 1816	p. 283
William Johnston, Lieutenant, District 110	17 Jun 1816	p. 283
John A. Lightfoot, Ensign, District 110	17 Jun 1816	p. 284
Charles Atchisson, Lieutenant, District 159	17 Jun 1816	p. 284
Lindsay Johnson, Lieutenant, District 202	17 Jun 1816	p. 285
William C. Willis, Lieutenant, District 339	17 Jun 1816	p. 285
William Esterwood, Lieutenant, District 380	17 Jun 1816	p. 286
John Monk, Ensign, District 133	17 Jun 1816	p. 286
Moses Cockran, Ensign, District 283	17 Jun 1816	p. 287
James Vest, Ensign, District 289	17 Jun 1816	p. 287
David Reaves, Ensign, District 377	17 Jun 1816	p. 288
Jacob Smith, Second Lieutenant, Troop of Cavalry, Squadron 8, Regiment 4	21 Jun 1816	p. 288
James Acooper, Captain, District 274	21 Jun 1816	p. 289
Zachariah Dickinson, Ensign, District 239	21 Jun 1816	p. 289
Richard Magers, Lieutenant, District 256	21 Jun 1816	p. 290
John Lacy, Lieutenant, District 233	21 Jun 1816	p. 290

Georgia Military Commissions, 1798–1818

Name, Unit, Rank	Date	Page
Edward Bryan, Captain, District 346	21 Jun 1816	p. 291
Thomas Prather, Captain, District 175	21 Jun 1816	p. 291
Zachariah Thigby, Lieutenant, District 175	21 Jun 1816	p. 292
Andrew Page, Ensign, District 175	21 Jun 1816	p. 292
Joshua Davis, Lieutenant, District 168	21 Jun 1816	p. 293
Parker Eason, Ensign, District 168	21 Jun 1816	p. 293
David Lewis, Lieutenant, District 69	21 Jun 1816	p. 294
John Ballenger, Ensign, District 69	21 Jun 1816	p. 294
William McCrarey, Lieutenant, District 331	25 Jun 1816	p. 295
William Brock, Ensign, District 331	25 Jun 1816	p. 295
George Parker, Ensign, District 380	27 Jun 1816	p. 296
David Walker, Captain, District 184	27 Jun 1816	p. 296
Jameson Maby, Lieutenant, District 184	27 Jun 1816	p. 297
Arnold Zelner, Ensign, District 184	27 Jun 1816	p. 297
John L. McIntosh, Lieutenant, District 21	27 Jun 1816	p. 298
John McDonald, Ensign, District 21	27 Jun 1816	p. 298
Elisha Cain, Lieutenant, District 348	27 Jun 1816	p. 299
Archibald Harris, Captain, District 302	28 Jun 1816	p. 299
Jonathan Benton, Major, Battalion 77	10 Jul 1816	p. 300
Richard Kilpatrick, Lieutenant, District 8	10 Jul 1816	p. 300
Elisha S. Walker, Captain, District 128	10 Jul 1816	p. 301
Soloman Fudge, Lieutenant, District 128	10 Jul 1816	p. 301
Hiram Day, Ensign, District 128	10 Jul 1816	p. 302
Matthews Huff, Captain, District 139	10 Jul 1816	p. 302
Elijah Buckley, Lieutenant, District 193	10 Jul 1816	p. 303
John Dilliard, Ensign, District 193	10 Jul 1816	p. 303
James M. Roache, Ensign, District 391	10 Jul 1816	p. 304
Edward Smith, Lieutenant, District 228	10 Jul 1816	p. 304
Overton Phelps, Ensign, District 228	10 Jul 1816	p. 305
Edward Collier, Ensign, Augusta Blues, Battalion 75	10 Jul 1816	p. 305
Patrick J. Barnett, Captain, District 174	10 Jul 1816	p. 306
David Frazier, Lieutenant, District 96	10 Jul 1816	p. 306
Stephen Garner, Ensign, District 96	10 Jul 1816	p. 307
William Smith, Lieutenant Colonel, Regiment 18	10 Jul 1816	p. 307
Williard Roberts, Lieutenant, District 70	16 Jul 1816	p. 308
Charles Baxter White, Ensign, District 70	16 Jul 1816	p. 308

Name, Unit, Rank	*Date*	*Page*
Fielding Macknowel, Captain, District 66	16 Jul 1816	p. 309
William Scott Jr., Captain, District 33	16 Jul 1816	p. 309
James S. Bulloch, Captain, District 3	16 Jul 1816	p. 310
William Gilliland, Lieutenant, District 3	16 Jul 1816	p. 310
Kincheon Jewell, Lieutenant, District 55	16 Jul 1816	p. 311
Reuben Runnells, Ensign, District 55	16 Jul 1816	p. 311
Littleton Long, Ensign, District 360	16 Jul 1816	p. 312
Francis Moreland, Lieutenant, District 347	16 Jul 1816	p. 312
James A. Tippings, Major, Battalion 10	16 Jul 1816	p. 313
Joseph Crews, Captain, District 334	16 Jul 1816	p. 313
Jobin Giddens, Lieutenant, District 334	16 Jul 1816	p. 314
Reuben Turner, Ensign, District 334	16 Jul 1816	p. 314
Shadrach Jacobs, Captain, District 335	16 Jul 1816	p. 315
John McDaniel, Captain, District 99	16 Jul 1816	p. 315
John Hardy, Lieutenant, District 99	16 Jul 1816	p. 316
Zadock McDaniel, Ensign, District 99	16 Jul 1816	p. 316
Benjamin Leggett, Lieutenant, District 74	25 Jul 1816	p. 317
Johna Spence, Ensign, District 74	25 Jul 1816	p. 317
Thomas Wortham, Lieutenant, District 219	25 Jul 1816	p. 318
Thomas Dabney Carr, Major, Battalion 29	25 Jul 1816	p. 318
Charles Porter, Lieutenant, District 274	25 Jul 1816	p. 319
Joseph W. Carmichael, First Lieutenant, Troop of Cavalry, Squadron 3, Regiment 2	25 Jul 1816	p. 319
Samuel Shelly, Second Lieutenant, Troop of Cavalry, Squadron 3, Regiment 2	25 Jul 1816	p. 320
C. H. Dasher, Captain, District 9	25 Jul 1816	p. 320
Joseph Taylor, Lieutenant, District 9	25 Jul 1816	p. 321
Thomas Brown, Lieutenant, District 201	25 Jul 1816	p. 321
Benjamin Burton, Captain, District 10	25 Jul 1816	p. 322
James Burton, Ensign, District 10	25 Jul 1816	p. 322
William H. Barnhill, Ensign, District 212	25 Jul 1816	p. 323
William Rachel, Captain, District 114	25 Jul 1816	p. 323
Britain Smith, Lieutenant, District 114	25 Jul 1816	p. 324
Peyton Hattaway, Ensign, District 114	25 Jul 1816	p. 324
James W. Armstrong, Captain, District 113	25 Jul 1816	p. 325
Thomas Login, Lieutenant, District 113	25 Jul 1816	p. 325
Thomas Tilman, Ensign, District 113	25 Jul 1816	p. 326

Georgia Military Commissions, 1798–1818

Name, Unit, Rank	Date	Page
William Wilson, Ensign, District 255	25 Jul 1816	p. 326
Henry George, Ensign, District 246	25 Jul 1816	p. 327
John Hughey, Captain, District 284	25 Jul 1816	p. 327
Thillis C. Bridge, Captain, District 230	25 Jul 1816	p. 328
Benjamin Harvey, Lieutenant Colonel, Regiment 40	25 Jul 1816	p. 328
Shadrach Rogers, Lieutenant, District 99	25 Jul 1816	p. 329
Anthony Cromby, Ensign, District 98	25 Jul 1816	p. 329
Richard Alday, Ensign, District 63	3 Aug 1816	p. 330
William Hightower, Captain, District 225	3 Aug 1816	p. 330
Mark Ship, Captain, District 131	3 Aug 1816	p. 331
William Richardson, Lieutenant, District 131	3 Aug 1816	p. 331
William Page, Ensign, District 131	3 Aug 1816	p. 332
Benjamin Williams, Captain, District 239	3 Aug 1816	p. 332
Elisha Loving, Ensign, District 239	3 Aug 1816	p. 333
James Legon, Captain, District 223	3 Aug 1816	p. 333
Robert Moore, Captain, District 139	3 Aug 1816	p. 334
Frederich Jolly, Ensign, District 302	3 Aug 1816	p. 334
Seaborne Maddox, Captain, District 248	3 Aug 1816	p. 335
Reuben McClung, Ensign, District 248	3 Aug 1816	p. 335
Andrew F. Fraser, Captain, District 17	3 Aug 1816	p. 336
Alexander Martin, Lieutenant, District 17	3 Aug 1816	p. 336
John Roberts, Captain, District 53	3 Aug 1816	p. 337
John Love, Captain, District 337	3 Aug 1816	p. 337
Alexander McDade, Captain, District 100	3 Aug 1816	p. 338
Alexander McDonald, Captain, District 155	3 Aug 1816	p. 338
Dennis McDonald, Lieutenant, District 332	3 Aug 1816	p. 339
Martin Brown, Second Lieutenant, Troop of Cavalry, Squadron 2, Regiment 1	13 Aug 1816	p. 339
Archibald Campbell, First Lieutenant, Troop of Cavalry, Squadron 2, Regiment 1	13 Aug 1816	p. 340
Richard Garner, Lieutenant, District 387	13 Aug 1816	p. 340
John Orren, Ensign, District 65	13 Aug 1816	p. 341
John Kemp, Lieutenant, District 222	13 Aug 1816	p. 341
James Stephen, Ensign, District 222	13 Aug 1816	p. 342
Robert T. Gains, Captain, District 199	13 Aug 1816	p. 342
John Huff, Ensign, District 162	13 Aug 1816	p. 343
Jesse Barnes, Ensign, District 108	13 Aug 1816	p. 343

Commissions Book 1815–1818

Name, Unit, Rank	Date	Page
Richard T. Loyd, Captain, District 296	13 Aug 1816	p. 344
Samuel McClendon, Ensign, District 285	13 Aug 1816	p. 344
Alford Johnson, Ensign, District 227	13 Aug 1816	p. 345
Richard Manly, Major, Battalion 69	13 Aug 1816	p. 345
Andrew Posey, Lieutenant, District 346	13 Aug 1816	p. 346
Thomas Rogers, Ensign, District 346	13 Aug 1816	p. 346
John Berry, Lieutenant, District 23	13 Aug 1816	p. 347
Aris Cox, Lieutenant, District 151	13 Aug 1816	p. 347
William Price, Lieutenant, District 73	17 Aug 1816	p. 348
Henry Linch, Ensign, District 73	17 Aug 1816	p. 348
Abraham Nally, Lieutenant, District 265	17 Aug 1816	p. 349
Alexander Murphey, Ensign, District 265	17 Aug 1816	p. 349
Matthew T. Hamilton, Captain, District 316	17 Aug 1816	p. 350
Albert Winters, Captain, District 253	17 Aug 1816	p. 350
Robert Samuel, Captain, District 320	23 Aug 1816	p. 351
William Porr, Captain, District 220	23 Aug 1816	p. 351
Thomas Flanagun, Captain, District 371	23 Aug 1816	p. 352
Charles Crawford, Lieutenant, District 371	23 Aug 1816	p. 352
George Dickerson, Ensign, District 143	23 Aug 1816	p. 353
George Dawson, Captain, District 143	23 Aug 1816	p. 353
Thomas L. Edward, Captain, District 101	23 Aug 1816	p. 354
Robert Kelly, Lieutenant, District 316	23 Aug 1816	p. 354
Norrell Roberts, Lieutenant, District 52	23 Aug 1816	p. 355
Elias Branch, Ensign, District 52	23 Aug 1816	p. 355
Josias Boswell, Ensign, District 309	23 Aug 1816	p. 356
Sion Smith, Captain, District 343	23 Aug 1816	p. 356
John G. Underwood, Lieutenant, District 343	23 Aug 1816	p. 357
Tomas Rigins, Ensign, District 350	23 Aug 1816	p. 357
William Mayo, Captain, District 350	23 Aug 1816	p. 358
Francis Jones, Major, Battalion 9	23 Aug 1816	p. 358
Samuel Hall, Lieutenant, District 328	23 Aug 1816	p. 359
Jesse Ruston, Ensign, District 328	23 Aug 1816	p. 359
William Starnes, Captain, District 218	6 Sep 1816	p. 360
William Jerkins, Ensign, District 7	6 Sep 1816	p. 360
David Griffin, Captain, District 58	6 Sep 1816	p. 361
Moses Warren, Lieutenant, District 58	6 Sep 1816	p. 361

Name, Unit, Rank	*Date*	*Page*
John Edenfield, Ensign, District 58	6 Sep 1816	p. 362
James Hartsfield, Lieutenant, District 236	6 Sep 1816	p. 362
Jeter Hogg, Lieutenant, District 109	6 Sep 1816	p. 363
Joseph Blake, Captain, District 364	6 Sep 1816	p. 363
Edmund Dodson, Lieutenant, District 282	6 Sep 1816	p. 364
Thomas Wright, Major, Battalion 78	6 Sep 1816	p. 364
Samuel Liverman, Ensign, District 120	6 Sep 1816	p. 365
Augustin B. Longstreet, Captain, District 398	6 Sep 1816	p. 365
Samuel Miller, Lieutenant, District 398	6 Sep 1816	p. 366
Moses Rogers, Ensign, District 398	6 Sep 1816	p. 366
Giles Easter, Ensign, District 42	6 Sep 1816	p. 367
William Bivin, Lieutenant, District 320	17 Sep 1816	p. 367
Gabriel Wright, Ensign, District 199	17 Sep 1816	p. 368
Elijah Christian, Ensign, District 201	17 Sep 1816	p. 368
David Kennedy, Lieutenant, District 392	17 Sep 1816	p. 369
Tandy Glaze, Captain, District 185	17 Sep 1816	p. 369
Solomon York, Lieutenant, District 185	17 Sep 1816	p. 370
Richard Prather, Ensign, District 185	17 Sep 1816	p. 370
William Mosley, Lieutenant, District 307	17 Sep 1816	p. 371
Joseph Smith, Major, Battalion 39	17 Sep 1816	p. 371
Austin Martin, Lieutenant, District 174	17 Sep 1816	p. 372
Martin Webster, Ensign, District 174	17 Sep 1816	p. 372
Robert B. Glenn, Captain, Squadron 4, Regiment 2, Hancock County	17 Sep 1816	p. 373
Joseph Lyon, Ensign, District 223	26 Sep 1816	p. 373
Henry Dollar, Ensign, District 198	26 Sep 1816	p. 374
Rice Garnett, Ensign, District 126	26 Sep 1816	p. 374
John Parks, Captain, Volunteer Rifle Company, Battalion 29	26 Sep 1816	p. 375
Joseph Stewart, Lieutenant, District 363	26 Sep 1816	p. 375
John Hodnet, Captain, Volunteer Rifle Company, Battalion 77	26 Sep 1816	p. 376
Ellis Swing, Lieutenant, Volunteer Rifle Company, Battalion 77	26 Sep 1816	p. 376
Dudley Millum, Ensign, Volunteer Rifle Company, Battalion 77	26 Sep 1816	p. 377
Edwin Sturdivant, Major, Battalion 84	26 Sep 1816	p. 377

Name, Unit, Rank	*Date*	*Page*
Jordan Allen, Captain, District 368	26 Sep 1816	p. 378
Jonathan Lyon, Lieutenant, District 121	26 Sep 1816	p. 378
Thomas Grace, Ensign, District 121	26 Sep 1816	p. 379
Medad McLendon, Lieutenant, District 179	26 Sep 1816	p. 379
John W. Mays, Ensign, District 179	26 Sep 1816	p. 380
John McDowell, Ensign, District 95	26 Sep 1816	p. 380
Joseph M. Robinson, First Lieutenant, Cavalry, Squadron 7, Regiment 4	26 Sep 1816	p. 381
James Mappin, Captain, District 135	5 Oct 1816	p. 381
Randolph Gerald, Lieutenant, District 135	5 Oct 1816	p. 382
Early Gerald, Ensign, District 135	5 Oct 1816	p. 382
Henry Hateley, Lieutenant, District 296	5 Oct 1816	p. 383
Torman Walthall, Ensign, District 296	5 Oct 1816	p. 383
Stephen Leul, Ensign, District 251	5 Oct 1816	p. 384
Henry Freeman, Captain, District 245	5 Oct 1816	p. 384
Thomas Twitty, Lieutenant, District 249	5 Oct 1816	p. 385
Seth Fountain, Lieutenant, District 83	5 Oct 1816	p. 385
Isaac Land, Ensign, District 83	5 Oct 1816	p. 386
Uriah Jinkins, Captain, District 91	5 Oct 1816	p. 386
William Peacock, Lieutenant, District 91	5 Oct 1816	p. 387
Edden Holt, Lieutenant, District 90	5 Oct 1816	p. 387
Isaac T. Moreland, Ensign, District 390	5 Oct 1816	p. 388
Samuel A. Jones, First Lieutenant	14 Oct 1816	p. 388
William C. H. Findley, Second Lieutenant	14 Oct 1816	p. 389
William Bence, Cornet, Troop of Dragoons, Squadron 9, Regiment 5	14 Oct 1816	p. 389
James Rhew, Lieutenant, District 317	15 Oct 1816	p. 390
Simeon Roberts, Captain, District 70	15 Oct 1816	p. 390
Samuel Moose, Lieutenant, District 145	15 Oct 1816	p. 391
William M. Simpkins, Ensign, District 145	15 Oct 1816	p. 391
William H. Dickson, Major, Battalion 54	15 Oct 1816	p. 392
Thomas McKigney, Captain, District 76	15 Oct 1816	p. 392
Benjamin Witcher, Major, Battalion 43	15 Oct 1816	p. 393
James Reid, Lieutenant, District 307	15 Oct 1816	p. 393
William Pridgeon, Lieutenant, District 41	15 Oct 1816	p. 394
Robert Brewer, Ensign, District 41	15 Oct 1816	p. 394

Georgia Military Commissions, 1798–1818

Name, Unit, Rank	Date	Page
Benjamin B. Norris, Captain, Cavalry, Squadron 2, Regiment 1	15 Oct 1816	p. 395
Deonyshus Oliver, Captain, District 191	15 Oct 1816	p. 395
John B. Simmons, Lieutenant, District 101	21 Oct 1816	p. 396
Lewis Parker, Ensign, District 101	21 Oct 1816	p. 396
Gabriel Priest, Captain, District 32	22 Oct 1816	p. 397
Emerald Brigham, Lieutenant, District 32	22 Oct 1816	p. 397
James Harris, Ensign, District 32	22 Oct 1816	p. 398
William Flippin, Lieutenant, District 218	22 Oct 1816	p. 398
Moses Bledsoe, Ensign, District 218	22 Oct 1816	p. 399
Jonas Brand, Ensign, District 220	22 Oct 1816	p. 399
John Barton, Lieutenant, District 267	22 Oct 1816	p. 400
William Sparks, Ensign, District 267	22 Oct 1816	p. 400
John Cawthow, Ensign, District 370	22 Oct 1816	p. 401
John Kimborough, Lieutenant, District 379	22 Oct 1816	p. 401
John Hays, Captain, District 363	22 Oct 1816	p. 402
Bevins Brook, Captain, District 250	22 Oct 1816	p. 402
Isaac Smith, Lieutenant, District 345	22 Oct 1816	p. 403
Jared Johnson, Ensign, District 89	22 Oct 1816	p. 403
Thomas D. Gordon, Lieutenant, District 164	22 Oct 1816	p. 404
Asa Dearing, Ensign, District 164	22 Oct 1816	p. 404
George Chandler, Ensign, District 66	26 Oct 1816	p. 405
Adam Cox, Lieutenant, District 283	26 Oct 1816	p. 405
John C. Barker, Lieutenant, District 368	26 Oct 1816	p. 406
John T. Brooks, Lieutenant, District 312	26 Oct 1816	p. 406
John Beckham, Ensign, District 312	26 Oct 1816	p. 407
Tisse Smith, Captain, District 327	26 Oct 1816	p. 407
Samuel Simmons, Captain, Volunteer Rifle Company	26 Oct 1816	p. 408
William Simmons, Lieutenant, Volunteer Rifle Company	26 Oct 1816	p. 408
Jeremiah Barnett, Ensign, District 62	26 Oct 1816	p. 409
Jeremiah Smith, Captain, District 85	26 Oct 1816	p. 409
James Sparks, Lieutenant, District 139	5 Nov 1816	p. 410
Radsom Meadows, Ensign, District 139	5 Nov 1816	p. 410
Jehu Marsh, Captain, District 84	5 Nov 1816	p. 411
James Barnett, Lieutenant, District 271	5 Nov 1816	p. 411
Edmund Abbot, Ensign, District 271	5 Nov 1816	p. 412
Alexander Vaugham, Lieutenant, District 158	5 Nov 1816	p. 412

Name, Unit, Rank	*Date*	*Page*
William Wagman, Ensign, District 158	5 Nov 1816	p. 413
Joshua Dobson, Ensign, District 282	8 Nov 1816	p. 413
Joshua Grace, Lieutenant, District 380	8 Nov 1816	p. 414
John Haynes, Captain, District 208	8 Nov 1816	p. 414
Amos Williams, Lieutenant, District 208	8 Nov 1816	p. 415
Mark Meeks, Ensign, District 208	8 Nov 1816	p. 415
Joseph H. Mead, Lieutenant, District 245	8 Nov 1816	p. 416
Charles R. Waller, Captain, District 312	8 Nov 1816	p. 416
Joseph Tilman, Lieutenant, District 49	8 Nov 1816	p. 417
Valentine Walker, Major General, Division 2	9 Nov 1816	p. 417
Jett Thomas, Major General, Division 3	9 Nov 1816	p. 418
William Waller Jr., Captain, District 97	15 Nov 1816	p. 418
Silas Floyd, Lieutenant, District 97	15 Nov 1816	p. 419
Julius Martin, Ensign, District 97	15 Nov 1816	p. 419
Arnold Seal, Captain, District 298	15 Nov 1816	p. 420
William Fail, Ensign, District 313	15 Nov 1816	p. 420
Samuel Higginbotham, Captain, District 204	15 Nov 1816	p. 421
Alexander Meriwether, Captain, Volunteer Artillery Company	21 Nov 1816	p. 421
Leon H. Marks, First Lieutenant, Regiment 9	21 Nov 1816	p. 422
Charles B. Lee, Captain, District 236	21 Nov 1816	p. 422
John Berry, Ensign, District 236	21 Nov 1816	p. 423
John Andress, Lieutenant, District 80	21 Nov 1816	p. 423
Stephen Boyt, Ensign, District 80	21 Nov 1816	p. 424
Gideon Brantly, Ensign, District 91	21 Nov 1816	p. 424
Hardy Collins, Lieutenant, District 351	21 Nov 1816	p. 425
Benjamin Milton, Ensign, District 351	21 Nov 1816	p. 425
Van Leonard, Captain, District 278	21 Nov 1816	p. 426
Benjamin Russell, Captain, District 181	21 Nov 1816	p. 426
Ellis Graves, Captain, District 183	3 Dec 1816	p. 427
Jonathan Hall, Lieutenant, District 33	3 Dec 1816	p. 427
Lewis Thigpin, Ensign, District 33	3 Dec 1816	p. 428
Mathew H. Leggett, Ensign, District 314	3 Dec 1816	p. 428
Isham Thompson, Lieutenant, District 122	3 Dec 1816	p. 429
Lewis Dewett, Ensign, District 384	3 Dec 1816	p. 429
James Langston, Lieutenant, District 255	3 Dec 1816	p. 430
James Gore, Ensign, District 255	3 Dec 1816	p. 430

Georgia Military Commissions, 1798–1818

Name, Unit, Rank	Date	Page
James Smith, Captain, District 261	3 Dec 1816	p. 431
William Anderson, Lieutenant, District 261	3 Dec 1816	p. 431
Nathan Nawley, Lieutenant, District 375	3 Dec 1816	p. 432
James Lamberth, Ensign, District 375	3 Dec 1816	p. 432
James B. Stewart, Major, Battalion 74	3 Dec 1816	p. 433
Blasingame Bulett, Captain, District 61	27 Mar 1811	p. 433
Abner Stringer, Lieutenant, District 61	5 Aug 1815	p. 434
Daniel Humphrey, Captain, District 74	16 Sep 1815	p. 434
William T. Williams, Captain, Company of Light Artillery, Regiment 1	10 Dec 1816	p. 435
Donald McLeod, First Lieutenant, Company of Light Artillery, Regiment 1	10 Dec 1816	p. 435
John Drysdal, Second Lieutenant, Company of Light Artillery, Regiment 1	10 Dec 1816	p. 436
William Tuggle, Captain, District 138	10 Dec 1816	p. 436
William G. Hunter, Lieutenant, District 259	10 Dec 1816	p. 437
William Bird, Captain, District 11	10 Dec 1816	p. 437
Asberry Wheeler, Lieutenant, District 318	10 Dec 1816	p. 438
William Wiggins, Lieutenant, District 124	10 Dec 1816	p. 438
David Kelly, Ensign, District 124	10 Dec 1816	p. 439
Daniel Jorden, Ensign, District 60	10 Dec 1816	p. 439
John P. Harvey, Major, Cavalry, Squadron 2, Regiment 1	10 Dec 1816	p. 440
Joseph W. Cooper, Cornet, Cavalry, Squadron 7, Regiment 4	10 Dec 1816	p. 440
Josiah Newton, Major, Battalion 48	24 Jan 1817	p. 441
Jordan Welcher, Captain, District 79	6 Jan 1817	p. 441
Theophilus Hardy, Ensign, District 136	6 Jan 1817	p. 442
Frederick Jolly, Lieutenant, District 302	6 Jan 1817	p. 442
William Fleming, Captain, Volunteer Company of Light Infantry, Battalion 4	6 Jan 1817	p. 443
John A. Culthbert, Lieutenant, Volunteer Company of Light Infantry, Battalion 4	6 Jan 1817	p. 443
Oliver Stevens, Ensign, Volunteer Company of Light Infantry, Battalion 4	6 Jan 1817	p. 444
Moses Edleman, Ensign, District 397	6 Jan 1817	p. 444
Hiram Powel, Lieutenant, District 355	6 Jan 1817	p. 445
Hardy Griffin, Captain, District 344	6 Jan 1817	p. 445
Bennet Whitehead, Lieutenant, District 344	6 Jan 1817	p. 446

Name, Unit, Rank	*Date*	*Page*
William R. Smith, Ensign, District 344	6 Jan 1817	p. 446
Charles Cheatham, Captain, District 82	6 Jan 1817	p. 447
James Pelot, Captain, Volunteer Company of Light Infantry, Battalion 6	6 Jan 1817	p. 447
John Bergamy, Ensign, District 165	6 Jan 1817	p. 448
William McRary, Captain, District 331	6 Jan 1817	p. 448
Talton F. Keith, Lieutenant, District 125	6 Jan 1817	p. 449
Gabriel Avery, Ensign, District 125	6 Jan 1817	p. 449
John Stathings, Lieutenant, District 304	6 Jan 1817	p. 450
Joseph Loughren, Ensign, District 304	6 Jan 1817	p. 450
Greene B. Talbot, Captain, District 400	6 Jan 1817	p. 451
George Pattilloe, Lieutenant, District 400	6 Jan 1817	p. 451
Daniel Barber, Ensign, District 400	6 Jan 1817	p. 452
Wilie Belcher, Captain, District 323	6 Jan 1817	p. 452
Elijah Sheaver, Ensign, District 177	6 Jan 1817	p. 453
Thomas Handly, Captain, Augusta Independent Blues, Battalion 75	6 Jan 1817	p. 453
James A. Black, Lieutenant, Augusta Independent Blues, Battalion 75	6 Jan 1817	p. 454
James Stewart, Ensign, Augusta Independent Blues, Battalion 75	6 Jan 1817	p. 454
James Kinchen, Lieutenant, District 52	6 Jan 1817	p. 455
John Parre, Ensign, District 52	6 Jan 1817	p. 455
William Brook, Captain, District 166	6 Jan 1817	p. 456
Enoch Callaway, Lieutenant, District 166	6 Jan 1817	p. 456
Charles Dawson, Ensign, District 166	6 Jan 1817	p. 457
James Torrence, Captain, District 75	6 Jan 1817	p. 457
Isaac Waters, Captain, District 35	6 Jan 1817	p. 458
William Wright, Captain, District 399	6 Jan 1817	p. 458
John Sparks, Lieutenant, District 399	6 Jan 1817	p. 459
Benjamin Smith, Ensign, District 399	6 Jan 1817	p. 459
Oliver Lavender, Ensign, District 260	6 Jan 1817	p. 460
John Mathis, Second Lieutenant, Cavalry, Squadron 4, Regiment 2	6 Jan 1817	p. 460
John Needlenger, Captain, Volunteer Company of Infantry, Battalion 3	6 Jan 1817	p. 461
Israel Witeman, Lieutenant, Volunteer Company of Infantry, Battalion 3	6 Jan 1817	p. 461

Georgia Military Commissions, 1798–1818

Name, Unit, Rank	*Date*	*Page*
John J. Mitzger, Ensign, Volunteer Company of Infantry, Battalion 3	6 Jan 1817	p. 462
Jame Clark, Second Lieutenant, Volunteer Company of Artillery, Regiment 9	6 Jan 1817	p. 462
Robert Brodnax, Major, Battalion 69	15 Feb 1817	p. 463
Matthew Orr, Captain, District 205	15 Feb 1817	p. 463
Pleasant Hightower, Captain, District 105	15 Feb 1817	p. 464
Reuben Oakes, Lieutenant, District 227	15 Feb 1817	p. 464
Benjamin Vaughn, Lieutenant, District 211	15 Feb 1817	p. 465
Littleberry Bagwell, Lieutenant, District 156	15 Feb 1817	p. 465
Michael Cody, Ensign, District 156	15 Feb 1817	p. 466
William Montgomery, Ensign, District 122	15 Feb 1817	p. 466
Alexander Murray, Captain, District 234	15 Feb 1817	p. 467
Fleminon Holebrooks, Lieutenant, District 193	15 Feb 1817	p. 467
Joshua Evans, Captain, District 379	15 Feb 1817	p. 468
Josiah Avant, Lieutenant, District 98	15 Feb 1817	p. 468
William King, Ensign, District 369	15 Feb 1817	p. 469
Abner Bradley, Captain, District 241	15 Feb 1817	p. 469
John Hodges, Lieutenant, District 241	15 Feb 1817	p. 470
Humphrey Edwards, Ensign, District 241	15 Feb 1817	p. 470
Joseph Walters, Captain, District 227	15 Feb 1817	p. 471
John Dean, Captain, District 217	15 Feb 1817	p. 471
William W. Oslin, Ensign, District 368	15 Feb 1817	p. 472
John E. McCall, Ensign, District 45	15 Feb 1817	p. 472
Rigdon Brown, Lieutenant, District 266	15 Feb 1817	p. 473
James Neal, Captain, District 153	15 Feb 1817	p. 473
Thomas Ivy, Lieutenant, District 153	15 Feb 1817	p. 474
James Thomas, Ensign, District 153	15 Feb 1817	p. 474
Allen Dykes, Lieutenant, District 331	15 Feb 1817	p. 475
George R. Davis, Ensign, District 373	15 Feb 1817	p. 475
Ebenezer Miles, Captain, District 297	15 Feb 1817	p. 476
Francis Hobby, Lieutenant, District 346	15 Feb 1817	p. 476
Enoch McClendon, Lieutenant, District 362	15 Feb 1817	p. 477
Jeptha George, Ensign, District 362	15 Feb 1817	p. 477
John Sutherland, Lieutenant, District 148	15 Feb 1817	p. 478
George G. Higginbotham, Captain, District 189	15 Feb 1817	p. 478
Wiley Wimberly, Lieutenant, District 67	15 Feb 1817	p. 479

Name, Unit, Rank	*Date*	*Page*
James Norris, Captain, District 301	15 Feb 1817	p. 479
John F. Pope, Lieutenant, District 301	15 Feb 1817	p. 480
James M. Roach, Lieutenant, District 391	15 Feb 1817	p. 480
Elias Taylor, Ensign, District 302	15 Feb 1817	p. 481
Samuel Hamilton, Captain, District 271	15 Feb 1817	p. 481
Edward D. Malone, Captain, District 287	15 Feb 1817	p. 482
Thomas Gresham, Captain, District 169	15 Feb 1817	p. 482
William Lee, Lieutenant, District 169	15 Feb 1817	p. 483
David Wimberly, Captain, District 93	15 Feb 1817	p. 483
Thomas U. Morrell, Captain, District 4	15 Feb 1817	p. 484
John Morrell, Lieutenant, District 4	15 Feb 1817	p. 484
Jamas McClish, Ensign, District 4	15 Feb 1817	p. 485
James McGehee, Lieutenant, District 319	15 Feb 1817	p. 485
James Jolly, Ensign, District 319	15 Feb 1817	p. 486
Joshua Culwell, Lieutenant, District 144	15 Feb 1817	p. 486
David S. Jernagan, Ensign, District 144	15 Feb 1817	p. 487
Moses Wylie, Second Lieutenant, Cavalry, Squadron 4, Regiment 2	18 Feb 1817	p. 487
Thomas M. Berrian, Captain, Troop of Cavalry, Squadron 2, Regiment 1	18 Feb 1817	p. 488
John Seay, Ensign, Volunteer Rifle Company, Battalion 39	18 Feb 1817	p. 488
John Hardin, Lieutenant, District 308	18 Feb 1817	p. 489
Jonathan Pearson, Major, Battalion 85	18 Feb 1817	p. 489
Bane Boyd, Lieutenant, District 41	18 Feb 1817	p. 490
James Baird, Lieutenant, District 181	18 Feb 1817	p. 490
Elijah Boid, Captain, District 396	18 Feb 1817	p. 491
Isaac Cain, Captain, District 110	18 Feb 1817	p. 491
Nathan Bowen, Captain, District 332	18 Feb 1817	p. 492
Joshua Morgan, Ensign, District 220	18 Feb 1817	p. 492
John Duncan, Lieutenant, District 209	18 Feb 1817	p. 493
Martin Thomas, Ensign, District 209	18 Feb 1817	p. 493
George Lokey, Lieutenant, District 204	18 Feb 1817	p. 494
Blake Baggett, Lieutenant, District 278	18 Feb 1817	p. 494
James Dubery, Ensign, District 380	18 Feb 1817	p. 495
Littleton Wynn, Ensign, District 307	18 Feb 1817	p. 495
Andrew Russel, Captain, District 63	18 Feb 1817	p. 496
John Rogers, Captain, District 159	18 Feb 1817	p. 496

Georgia Military Commissions, 1798–1818

Name, Unit, Rank	Date	Page
James Swiret, Ensign, District 118	18 Feb 1817	p. 497
Lewis Lamp, Captain, District 76	18 Feb 1817	p. 497
James Martin, Lieutenant, District 76	18 Feb 1817	p. 498
William McCorkle, Lieutenant Colonel, Regiment 38	18 Feb 1817	p. 498
John Dregors, Ensign, District 17	18 Feb 1817	p. 499
Harvy Kindrick, Captain, District 314	18 Feb 1817	p. 499
Carrinton Robertson, Ensign, District 169	18 Feb 1817	p. 500
Robert Sallet, Captain, District 21	18 Feb 1817	p. 500
David Dobbs, Captain, District 198	18 Feb 1817	p. 501
John Edenfield, Ensign, District 58	18 Feb 1817	p. 501
Samuel Piles, Lieutenant Colonel, Regiment 3	19 Feb 1817	p. 502
Robert Bruce, Major, Battalion 57	19 Feb 1817	p. 502
James Nephew Jr., Lieutenant, Darien Guards, Battalion 6	19 Feb 1817	p. 503
Hugh W. Proudfoot, Ensign, Darien Guards, Battalion 6	19 Feb 1817	p. 503
Clayton Thomas, Captain, District 188	19 Feb 1817	p. 504
John Scott, Major General, Division 3	3 Mar 1817	p. 504
John H. Fannin, Pay Master General	3 Mar 1817	p. 505
David Lowe, Lieutenant, District 274	22 Mar 1817	p. 505
John Cosby, Ensign, District 274	22 Mar 1817	p. 506
Michael Griffin, Captain, District 131	22 Mar 1817	p. 506
John Reaves, Lieutenant, District 131	22 Mar 1817	p. 507
Andrew Booth, Ensign, District 131	22 Mar 1817	p. 507
Benjamin Burroughs, Captain, District 125	22 Mar 1817	p. 508
John Briscor, Lieutenant, District 127	22 Mar 1817	p. 508
Berry Oliver, Captain, District 129	22 Mar 1817	p. 509
Charles Mathews, Lieutenant, District 129	22 Mar 1817	p. 509
Charles Pulin, Ensign, District 129	22 Mar 1817	p. 510
David Kinney, Captain, District 216	22 Mar 1817	p. 510
Thomas Childers, Captain, District 190	22 Mar 1817	p. 511
John Laidler, Lieutenant, District 69	22 Mar 1817	p. 511
Noel Lester, Ensign, District 61	22 Mar 1817	p. 512
Jacob Linder, Captain, District 20	22 Mar 1817	p. 512
Charnel Hightower, Ensign, District 218	22 Mar 1817	p. 513
William Cone, Captain, District 270	22 Mar 1817	p. 513
Basil Lowe, Lieutenant, District 270	22 Mar 1817	p. 514
George Lowe, Ensign, District 270	22 Mar 1817	p. 514

Name, Unit, Rank	*Date*	*Page*
Nicholas Howard, Lieutenant Colonel, Regiment 17	26 Mar 1817	p. 515
Barnard C. Heard, Captain, Troop of Cavalry, Squadron 7, Regiment 4	26 Mar 1817	p. 515
William Harrison, Lieutenant Colonel, Regiment 35	26 Mar 1817	p. 516
Christian H. Dasher, Major, Battalion 3	26 Mar 1817	p. 516
William Mimms, Lieutenant, District 357	26 Mar 1817	p. 517
John Gay, Ensign, District 357	26 Mar 1817	p. 517
Robert Turman, Lieutenant, District 191	26 Mar 1817	p. 518
William Bullard, Ensign, District 191	26 Mar 1817	p. 518
Lindsay Johnson, Captain, District 202	26 Mar 1817	p. 519
Larken Carleton, Lieutenant, District 146	26 Mar 1817	p. 519
Allen Bowells, Ensign, District 146	26 Mar 1817	p. 520
James Sparks, Captain, District 139	26 Mar 1817	p. 520
Elias Champion, Lieutenant, District 108	26 Mar 1817	p. 521
Mark E. Moore, Ensign, District 108	26 Mar 1817	p. 521
Joseph Cooper, Captain, District 108	26 Mar 1817	p. 522
Thomas Coleman, Ensign, District 111	26 Mar 1817	p. 522
Thomas Goore, Ensign, District 103	26 Mar 1817	p. 523
Jephthah George, Lieutenant, District 362	26 Mar 1817	p. 523
Henry Moore, Lieutenant, District 294	26 Mar 1817	p. 524
George Tucker, Ensign, District 294	26 Mar 1817	p. 524
Wiley Dean, Ensign, District 364	26 Mar 1817	p. 525
Solomon Chapman, Ensign, District 378	26 Mar 1817	p. 525
Edmund Walton, Captain, Company of Artillery, Regiment 31	26 Mar 1817	p. 526
Seth S. Langston, Captain, District 83	26 Mar 1817	p. 526
David M. Burns, Captain, District 251	26 Mar 1817	p. 527
Absalom Kincy, Ensign, District 391	26 Mar 1817	p. 527
Andrew C. Townsend, Captain, District 284	26 Mar 1817	p. 528
Posey Johnston, Lieutenant, District 284	26 Mar 1817	p. 528
John Ware, Ensign, District 284	26 Mar 1817	p. 529
William Meador, Lieutenant, District 279	26 Mar 1817	p. 529
Sion Hudson, Lieutenant, District 278	26 Mar 1817	p. 530
Joshua S. Wells, Ensign, District 278	26 Mar 1817	p. 530
William C. Parker, Captain, District 280	26 Mar 1817	p. 531
James Wiley, Lieutenant, District 229	26 Mar 1817	p. 531
Thomas Varner, Lieutenant, District 230	26 Mar 1817	p. 532

Name, Unit, Rank	Date	Page
James Riley, Ensign, District 230	26 Mar 1817	p. 532
James Hale, Lieutenant, District 235	26 Mar 1817	p. 533
Robert Myrick, Captain, District 232	26 Mar 1817	p. 533
Isham Brooks, Captain, District 375	26 Mar 1817	p. 534
Theodore Montford, First Lieutenant, Company of Artillery, Regiment 40	26 Mar 1817	p. 534
Otho Beall, Captain, District 310	26 Mar 1817	p. 535
Charles Linch, Lieutenant, District 310	26 Mar 1817	p. 535
William Colson, Captain, District 36	26 Mar 1817	p. 536
George F. McCall, Lieutenant, District 36	26 Mar 1817	p. 536
Joseph Anderson, Ensign, District 36	26 Mar 1817	p. 537
John A. Tally, Captain, District 340	26 Mar 1817	p. 537
Thomas Pitts, Ensign, District 340	26 Mar 1817	p. 538
Aaron Davis, Lieutenant, District 330	26 Mar 1817	p. 538
Sterlig Gray, Ensign, District 330	26 Mar 1817	p. 539
Ezekiel Daniel Jr., Captain, District 89	26 Mar 1817	p. 539
John Fleming, Ensign, District 158	26 Mar 1817	p. 540
Lemuel D. Buchannan, Captain, District 115	31 Mar 1817	p. 540
Sampson D. Jinkins, Ensign, District 133	31 Mar 1817	p. 541
John Richards, Ensign, District 291	31 Mar 1817	p. 541
Elijah Roberts, Captain, District 385	31 Mar 1817	p. 542
John Gaseway, Lieutenant, District 385	31 Mar 1817	p. 542
Daniel Short, Ensign, District 385	31 Mar 1817	p. 543
John M. Shirey, Lieutenant, District 90	31 Mar 1817	p. 543
Wiley Jordan, Ensign, District 90	31 Mar 1817	p. 544
John Robertson, Captain, District 313	31 Mar 1817	p. 544
John W. Parker, Lieutenant, District 313	31 Mar 1817	p. 545
Asbury Cowles, Ensign, District 375	31 Mar 1817	p. 545
Peter Baugh, Captain, District 388	31 Mar 1817	p. 546
James Lake, Lieutenant, District 388	31 Mar 1817	p. 546
Samuel Johnson, Ensign, District 231	31 Mar 1817	p. 547
Absalom Hix, Ensign, District 210	7 Apr 1817	p. 547
John Dupree, Lieutenant, District 143	7 Apr 1817	p. 548
John Moody, Ensign, District 143	7 Apr 1817	p. 548
Samuel Moore, Captain, District 145	7 Apr 1817	p. 549
Collin Alexander, Captain, District 300	7 Apr 1817	p. 549
Dolphin Flyd, Lieutenant, District 300	7 Apr 1817	p. 550

Name, Unit, Rank	Date	Page
John Hart, Ensign, District 300	7 Apr 1817	p. 550
James Sterling, Captain, District 254	7 Apr 1817	p. 551
Joseph H. Mead, Captain, District 245	7 Apr 1817	p. 551
William W. Strokes, Captain, District 187	7 Apr 1817	p. 552
Richard Prather, Lieutenant, District 187	7 Apr 1817	p. 552
Thomas Davis, Ensign, District 154	7 Apr 1817	p. 553
Benjamin Legett, Captain, District 74	7 Apr 1817	p. 553
Thomas Taylor, Captain, District 141	14 Apr 1817	p. 554
Daniel Rankin, Ensign, District 141	14 Apr 1817	p. 554
Allen Glenn, Ensign, District 238	14 Apr 1817	p. 555
Hartwell H. Tarver, Captain, District 172	14 Apr 1817	p. 555
Mulkey Cohron, Ensign, District 172	14 Apr 1817	p. 556
Joseph Morgan, Captain, Volunteer Company (styled the Marion Independent Blues), Battalion 72	14 Apr 1817	p. 556
Robert Fleming, Lieutenant, Volunteer Company (styled the Marion Indpendent Blues), Battalion 72	14 Apr 1817	p. 557
John M. Shelman, Ensign, Volunteer Company (styled the Marion Independent Blues), Battalion 72	14 Apr 1817	p. 557
Lunsford C. Pitts, Captain, Troop of Cavalry, Squadron 10, Regiment 6	14 Apr 1817	p. 558
Samuel W. Way, First Lieutenant, Troop of Cavalry, Squadron 10, Regiment 6	14 Apr 1817	p. 558
John J. Underwood, Second Lieutenant, Troop of Cavalry, Squadron 10, Regiment 6	14 Apr 1817	p. 559
Lewis Joiner, Cornet, Troop of Cavalry, Squadron 10, Regiment 6	14 Apr 1817	p. 559
Richard Cotton, Lieutenant, District 171	16 Apr 1817	p. 560
Seth Brown, Ensign, District 171	16 Apr 1817	p. 560
Furney F. Gatling, Captain, Company of Cavalry, Squadron 10, Regiment 5	18 Apr 1817	p. 561
John Beurdeng, Captain, District 225	18 Apr 1817	p. 561
James Ritchey, Lieutenant, District 225	18 Apr 1817	p. 562
Charles G. Moore, Ensign, District 225	18 Apr 1817	p. 562
James C. Walker, Captain, District 130	18 Apr 1817	p. 563
Robert Dens, Captain, District 1	18 Apr 1817	p. 563
Samuel Roe, Lieutenant, District 1	18 Apr 1817	p. 564
Henry Senterfett, Captain, District 386	18 Apr 1817	p. 564
John Heardy, Lieutenant, District 386	18 Apr 1817	p. 565

Georgia Military Commissions, 1798–1818

Name, Unit, Rank	Date	Page
John Powell, Ensign, District 386	18 Apr 1817	p. 565
Greene Henderson, Lieutenant, District 280	18 Apr 1817	p. 566
Hyram Sharp, Ensign, District 280	18 Apr 1817	p. 566
George W. Watkins, Captain, District 123	18 Apr 1817	p. 567
Theophilus Williams, Lieutenant, District 35	18 Apr 1817	p. 567
James Howard, Captain, District 329	18 Apr 1817	p. 568
William Tate, Lieutenant, District 329	18 Apr 1817	p. 568
Daniel McMillian, Ensign, District 329	18 Apr 1817	p. 569
Churchill Gibson, Lieutenant Colonel, Regiment 12	18 Apr 1817	p. 569
Thomas Hudson, Lieutenant Colonel, Regiment 14	30 Apr 1817	p. 570
Jesse Dunford, Ensign, District 75	10 May 1817	p. 570
Simeon A. Fraser, Second Lieutenant, Troop of Cavalry, Squadron 1, Regiment 1	10 May 1817	p. 571
Samuel F. Prescot, Captain, District 68	10 May 1817	p. 571
Isaac D. Lyon, Ensign, Savannah Volunteer Guards, Battalion 1	10 May 1817	p. 572
Benjamin Tait, Ensign, District 190	10 May 1817	p. 572
Tillman Powel, Captain, District 215	10 May 1817	p. 573
Joseph Dobson, Lieutenant, District 215	10 May 1817	p. 573
Richard Smith, Ensign, District 215	10 May 1817	p. 574
William Harrill, Ensign, District 148	10 May 1817	p. 574
Joseph Riley, Major, Battalion 32	10 May 1817	p. 575
Chesley Mims, Lieutenant, District 112	10 May 1817	p. 575
William W. Abbett, Lieutenant, District 82	10 May 1817	p. 576
Sylvanus Ripley, Ensign, District 82	10 May 1817	p. 576
David Smith, Lieutenant, District 77	10 May 1817	p. 577
James O. Abbott, Ensign, District 84	10 May 1817	p. 577
Zachariah Cowart, Ensign, District 83	10 May 1817	p. 578
Daniel Rosser, First Lieutenant, Volunteer Company of Artillery, Regiment 31	10 May 1817	p. 578
John Talbot, Second Lieutenant, Volunteer Company of Artillery, Regiment 31	10 May 1817	p. 579
Henry Thompson, Lieutenant, District 361	10 May 1817	p. 579
Wm. A. Brown, Ensign, District 361	10 May 1817	p. 580
James Sattawhite, Lieutenant, District 364	10 May 1817	p. 580
Jesse New, Captain, District 252	10 May 1817	p. 581
Seth Cason, Lieutenant, District 182	10 May 1817	p. 581

Name, Unit, Rank	*Date*	*Page*
Hiram Brown, Ensign, District 182	10 May 1812	p. 582
Samuel Landers, Lieutenant, District 183	10 May 1817	p. 582
George E. Matthews, Captain, District 229	10 May 1817	p. 583
Matthew Newgin, Lieutenant, District 312	10 May 1817	p. 583
William Pace, Captain, District 387	10 May 1817	p. 584
James Gorman, Ensign, District 323	10 May 1817	p. 584
Micajah Wilkinson, Lieutenant, District 326	10 May 1817	p. 585
John Smith, Ensign, District 326	10 May 1817	p. 585
John Jefferson, Captain, District 356	10 May 1817	p. 586
Elias Hays, Lieutenant, District 356	10 May 1817	p. 586
Fielding Rucker, Lieutenant, District 179	10 May 1817	p. 587
Suddoth Tole, Ensign, District 179	10 May 1817	p. 587
William Cummins, Captain, District 96	10 May 1817	p. 588
John S. Brown, Cornet, Troop of Light Dragoons, Squadron 4, Regiment 2	15 Jul 1817	p. 588
Moses Thompson, Ensign, District 64	15 May 1817	p. 589
Edward Courier, Captain, District 224	15 May 1817	p. 589
Jacob Treadwell, Lieutenant, District 224	15 May 1817	p. 590
Ambrose Hill, Ensign, District 224	15 May 1817	p. 590
Eppy White, Captain, District 192	15 May 1817	p. 591
Leroy Burton, Ensign, District 192	15 May 1817	p. 591
William Wheeler, Captain, District 162	15 May 1817	p. 592
James Smith, Captain, District 289	15 May 1817	p. 592
George Hornbuckle, Ensign, District 289	15 May 1817	p. 593
Dennis Allen, Lieutenant, District 366	15 May 1817	p. 593
John Nichols, Ensign, District 316	15 May 1817	p. 594
Robert Venable, Lieutenant, District 245	15 May 1817	p. 594
Charles O'Kelly, Captain, District 230	15 May 1817	p. 595
James Berry, Captain, District 369	15 May 1817	p. 595
Wiley Jones, Lieutenant, District 367	15 May 1817	p. 596
John Skinner, Ensign, District 367	15 May 1817	p. 596
Thomas Busten, Ensign, District 388	15 May 1817	p. 597
John Freeman, Captain, District 38	15 May 1817	p. 597
John T. Sharp, Captain, District 43	15 May 1817	p. 598
Daniel Gray, Lieutenant, District 43	15 May 1817	p. 598
Robert D. Cannon, Ensign, District 43	15 May 1817	p. 599
William Cunyers, Captain, District 42	15 May 1817	p. 599

Georgia Military Commissions, 1798–1818

Name, Unit, Rank	*Date*	*Page*
John Grace, Lieutenant, District 42	15 May 1817	p. 600
Brascella Slaton, Ensign, District 42	15 May 1817	p. 600
Simon Bateman, Ensign, District 376	15 May 1817	p. 601
Martin S. Walker, Lieutenant, District 165	15 May 1817	p. 601
William P. Triplett, Captain, Volunteer Troop of Light Dragoons, Squadron 6, Regiment 3	15 May 1817	p. 602
John Mann, Major, Battalion 26	28 May 1817	p. 602
David Simpson, Captain, Volunteer Troop of Light Dragoons, Squadron 7, Regiment 4	29 May 1817	p. 603
John Peteat, First Lieutenant, Volunteer Troop of Light Dragoons, Squadron 7, Regiment 4	29 May 1817	p. 603
Nathaniel Truitt, Second Lieutenant, Volunteer Troop of Light Dragoons, Squadron 7, Regiment 4	29 May 1817	p. 604
Joseph Quarterman, Ensign, District 15	29 May 1817	p. 604
Benjamin Harriss, Lieutenant, District 188	29 May 1817	p. 605
Jarrard Suddoth, Ensign, District 188	29 May 1817	p. 605
James Flemister, Captain, District 180	29 May 1817	p. 606
Claborn Freeman, Lieutenant, District 180	29 May 1817	p. 606
William Frum, Ensign, District 180	29 May 1817	p. 607
Thomas Smith, Ensign, District 328	29 May 1817	p. 607
Samuel Shelly, Lieutenant, District 154	29 May 1817	p. 608
Ferdinand Gresham, Ensign, District 301	29 May 1817	p. 608
Thomas Jones, First Lieutenant, Volunteer Company of Heavy Artillery, Regiment 1	29 May 1817	p. 609
James Laurence, Captain, District 2	29 May 1817	p. 609
Charles Jauers, Lieutenant, District 2	29 May 1817	p. 610
Moses Herbert, Captain, Volunteer Company of Heavy Artillery, Regiment 1	29 May 1817	p. 610
Perryman Moody, Captain, District 260	29 May 1817	p. 611
John Pickren, Lieutenant, District 260	29 May 1817	p. 611
Austin Buch, Lieutenant, District 138	29 May 1817	p. 612
Willis Forester, Ensign, District 138	29 May 1817	p. 612
Samuel Butler, Lieutenant, District 99	29 May 1817	p. 613
Henry Stockman, Ensign, District 99	29 May 1817	p. 613
Elijah Sherrer, Lieutenant, District 176	29 May 1817	p. 614
Thomas Marter, Ensign, District 176	29 May 1817	p. 614
Isaac Justice, Captain, District 117	29 May 1817	p. 615
John Webb, Lieutenant, District 117	29 May 1817	p. 615

Name, Unit, Rank	Date	Page
Charles Ennis, Ensign, District 117	29 May 1817	p. 616
Arcibald Cain, Ensign, District 348	29 May 1817	p. 616
David Sillivan, Captain, District 392	29 May 1817	p. 617
Philemon R. Wilhight, Lieutenant, District 202	29 May 1817	p. 617
James Morris, Ensign, District 202	29 May 1817	p. 618
Nathaniel C. Jarratt, Captain, District 257	29 May 1817	p. 618
William R. Anderson, Lieutenant, District 257	29 May 1817	p. 619
Allen Justice, Ensign, District 257	29 May 1817	p. 619
John Hubert, Major, Battalion 34	29 May 1817	p. 620
Jonathan Roach, Captain, District 113	29 May 1817	p. 620
James H. Ravins, Lieutenant, District 232	29 May 1817	p. 621
Henry P. White, Lieutenant, District 205	29 May 1817	p. 621
Daniel M. Crane, Lieutenant, District 8	29 May 1817	p. 622
William Burkes, Major, Battalion 39	29 May 1817	p. 622
James Harrison, Captain, Volunteer Troop of Light Dragoons, Squadron 10, Regiment 5	29 May 1817	p. 623
James Brown, First Lieutenant, Volunteer Troop of Light Dragoons, Squadron 10, Regiment 5	29 May 1817	p. 623
David Graham, Second Lieutenant, Volunteer Troop of Light Dragoons, Squadron 10, Regiment 5	29 May 1817	p. 624
Thomas Harvey, Cornet, Volunteer Troop of Light Dragoons, Squadron 10, Regiment 5	29 May 1817	p. 624
Sterling Acre, Lieutenant, District 139	29 May 1817	p. 625
William Rhoades, Ensign, District 139	29 May 1817	p. 625
Francis Miller, Lieutenant, District 261	9 Jun 1817	p. 626
Micajah Williamson, Ensign, District 261	29 Jun 1817	p. 626
Simon Bunce, Captain, District 9	9 Jun 1817	p. 627
Jacob Rogers, Captain, District 258	9 Jun 1817	p. 627
Michael Dickson, Captain, District 268	9 Jun 1817	p. 628
George Hanford, Captain, District 305	9 Jun 1817	p. 628
William Jones, Captain, Volunteer Company (styled the Independent Blues), Battalion 75	9 Jun 1817	p. 629
David Curry, Major, Battalion 21	9 Jun 1817	p. 629
James Burnett, Lieutenant, Darien Volunteer Guards, Battalion 6	12 Jun 1817	p. 630
Henry Milton, Captain, District 48	12 Jun 1817	p. 630
John Goodman, Ensign, District 48	12 Jun 1817	p. 631
David Akridge, Lieutenant, District 222	12 Jun 1817	p. 631

Name, Unit, Rank	Date	Page
Elijah Creel, Ensign, District 222	12 Jun 1817	p. 632
David James, Lieutenant, District 189	12 Jun 1817	p. 632
James Murray, Ensign, District 189	12 Jun 1817	p. 633
Perter Brown, Captain, District 214	12 Jun 1817	p. 633
Gilbert Cleveland, Lieutenant, District 214	12 Jun 1817	p. 634
Daniel McNabb, Lieutenant, District 39	12 Jun 1817	p. 634
John Bates, Captain, District 142	12 Jun 1817	p. 635
John Orear, Lieutenant, District 142	12 Jun 1817	p. 635
James Campbell, Ensign, District 142	12 Jun 1817	p. 636
Samuel Crockett, Lieutenant, District 295	12 Jun 1817	p. 636
Zachariah McMichael, Lieutenant, District 365	12 Jun 1817	p. 637
Samuel H. Davis, Ensign, District 362	12 Jun 1817	p. 637
Allison Kent, Ensign, District 279	12 Jun 1817	p. 638
Andrew Harris, Lieutenant, District 276	12 Jun 1817	p. 638
William Mapp, Ensign, District 276	12 Jun 1817	p. 639
John Briant, Ensign, District 232	12 Jun 1817	p. 639
William H. Avery, Captain, District 306	12 Jun 1817	p. 640
Laurens Manning, Lieutenant, District 337	12 Jun 1817	p. 640
Daniel Malry, Ensign, District 177	12 Jun 1817	p. 641
Terry Reynolds, Captain, District 171	12 Jun 1817	p. 641
Daniel Horne, Lieutenant, District 167	12 Jun 1817	p. 642
Isaac Harvey, Ensign, District 19	26 Jun 1817	p. 642
Asa Powell, Ensign, District 217	26 Jun 1817	p. 643
Joseph Wiggins, Major, Battalion 2	26 Jun 1817	p. 643
Thomas E. Hardee, Ensign, District 33	26 Jun 1817	p. 644
Bartley Higginbotham, Lieutenant, District 196	26 Jun 1817	p. 644
Leroy Burton, Lieutenant, District 192	26 Jun 1817	p. 645
Thomas Coleman, Captain, District 111	26 Jun 1817	p. 645
Thomas H. Kendall, Major, Battalion 25	26 Jun 1817	p. 646
Obadiah P. Cheatham, Ensign, District 78	26 Jun 1817	p. 646
Mark McCutchin, Ensign, District 385	26 Jun 1817	p. 647
William Payner, Ensign, District 256	26 Jun 1817	p. 647
Henry Hatley, Captain, District 296	26 Jun 1817	p. 648
Michael Deason, Ensign, District 296	26 Jun 1817	p. 648
Joseph T. Matthews, Ensign, District 187	26 Jun 1817	p. 649
Jacob W. Moreland, Lieutenant, District 345	26 Jun 1817	p. 649

Name, Unit, Rank	**Date**	**Page**
Thomas Irwin, Ensign, District 345	26 Jun 1817	p. 650
Jesse Lee, Lieutenant, District 86	26 Jun 1817	p. 650
Simion Christian, Ensign, District 262	26 Jun 1817	p. 651
William Jenkins, Captain, District 277	26 Jun 1817	p. 651
George T. Wing, Ensign, District 271	26 Jun 1817	p. 652
Henry Jordan, Ensign, District 226	26 Jun 1817	p. 652
Greene Johnson, Ensign, District 237	26 Jun 1817	p. 653
William Hunter, Captain, District 259	26 Jun 1817	p. 653
Stephen Martin, Ensign, District 259	26 Jun 1817	p. 654
Gilbert Kent, Lieutenant, District 170	26 Jun 1817	p. 654
Howard Portwood, Ensign, District 170	26 Jun 1817	p. 655
Josiah Avant, Captain, District 98	26 Jun 1817	p. 655
Wm. L. Hardeson, Ensign, District 98	26 Jun 1817	p. 656
William C. Morgan, First Lieutenant, Troop of Light Dragoons, Squadron 7, Regiment 4	26 Jun 1817	p. 656
Archibald Pittman, Cornet, Volunteer Troop of Light Dragoons, Squadron 7, Regiment 4	26 Jun 1817	p. 657
Medad McLendon, Captain, District 179	10 Jul 1817	p. 657
John W. Mays, Lieutenant, District 179	10 Jul 1817	p. 658
William Buttrill, Ensign, District 155	10 Jul 1817	p. 658
Seaborn J. Harrison, Ensign, District 152	10 Jul 1817	p. 659
Isaiah Chain, Lieutenant, District 372	10 Jul 1817	p. 659
James Conner, Ensign, District 309	10 Jul 1817	p. 660
Martin Russel, Lieutenant, District 105	10 Jul 1817	p. 660
John Russel, Ensign, District 105	10 Jul 1817	p. 661
Farler Adams, Lieutenant, District 134	10 Jul 1817	p. 661
Philip Stenchcomb, Ensign, District 197	10 Jul 1817	p. 662
John Henry, Lieutenant, District 201	10 Jul 1817	p. 662
William Akins, Lieutenant, District 212	10 Jul 1817	p. 663
Arther Foster, Lieutenant, District 145	10 Jul 1817	p. 663
William M. Simkins, Ensign, District 145	10 Jul 1817	p. 664
James C. Mangham, Major, Battalion 7	10 Jul 1817	p. 664
Charles Youngblood, Ensign, District 116	10 Jul 1817	p. 665
William Miller, Captain, District 118	10 Jul 1817	p. 665
Francis Thomas, Major, Battalion 24	10 Jul 1817	p. 666
John Bransford, Lieutenant, District 289	10 Jul 1817	p. 666
Leroy G. Harris, Captain, District 342	10 Jul 1817	p. 667

Georgia Military Commissions, 1798–1818

Name, Unit, Rank	Date	Page
Sterling Finnie, Captain, District 279	10 Jul 1817	p. 667
Charles S. Gyton, First Lieutenant, Troop of Cavalry, Squadron 10, Regiment 5	10 Jul 1817	p. 668
Henry W. Raleigh, Captain, Troop of Cavalry, Squadron 10, Regiment 5	14 Jul 1817	p. 668
Jesse Denard, First Lieutenant, Troop of Cavalry, Squadron 10, Regiment 5	14 Jul 1817	p. 669
Burnett Purvis, Cornet, Troop of Cavalry, Squadron 10, Regiment 5	14 Jul 1817	p. 669
Lemuel Laseter, Ensign, District 67	16 Jul 1817	p. 670
Israel Weitman, Lieutenant, District 11	16 Jul 1817	p. 670
Nathaniel Zittrover, Ensign, District 11	16 Jul 1817	p. 671
Michael Garrason, Captain, District 10	16 Jul 1817	p. 671
Neely Dobson, Lieutenant Colonel, Regiment 23	16 Jul 1817	p. 672
Charles Templing, Ensign, District 111	16 Jul 1817	p. 672
James Dabney, Ensign, District 79	16 Jul 1817	p. 673
Robert Bailey, Ensign, District 81	16 Jul 1817	p. 673
James Burrow, Lieutenant, District 297	16 Jul 1817	p. 674
Abner J. Dearing, Ensign, District 380	16 Jul 1817	p. 674
Anguish Culbreath, Captain, District 203	16 Jul 1817	p. 675
William Fannin, Captain, District 282	16 Jul 1817	p. 675
Daniel Duncan, Lieutenant, District 282	16 Jul 1817	p. 676
Ornan Whatley, Ensign, District 282	16 Jul 1817	p. 676
James C. Harrold, Lieutenant, District 271	16 Jul 1817	p. 677
Hannan R. Hubbard, Captain, District 157	16 Jul 1817	p. 677
Zachariah Hopson, Lieutenant, District 157	16 Jul 1817	p. 678
Andrew N. Johnson, Captain, District 28	16 Jul 1817	p. 678
James Strickling, Lieutenant, District 28	16 Jul 1817	p. 679
William Munden, Ensign, District 28	16 Jul 1817	p. 679
Jarad Johnson, Lieutenant, District 89	16 Jul 1817	p. 680
Robert Traywick, First Lieutenant, Troop of Cavalry, Squadron 9, Regiment 5	17 Jul 1817	p. 680
Charles Cates, Second Lieutenant, Troop of Cavalry, Squadron 9, Regiment 5	17 Jul 1817	p. 681
Jacob Watson, Second Lieutenant, Volunteer Troop of Light Dragoons, Squadron 10, Regiment 5	22 Jul 1817	p. 681
John R. Gregory, Lieutenant Colonel, Cavalry, Regiment 5	24 Jul 1817	p. 682

Name, Unit, Rank	*Date*	*Page*
John Houghton, Lieutenant Colonel, Cavalry, Regiment 3	2 Aug 1817	p. 682
William Hillis, Lieutenant, District 68	1 Aug 1817	p. 683
John Hillis, Ensign, District 68	1 Aug 1817	p. 683
John B. Barker, Lieutenant, District 130	1 Aug 1817	p. 684
John Tinsly, Ensign, District 130	1 Aug 1817	p. 684
Joseph Tillman, Captain, District 49	1 Aug 1817	p. 685
Bryant Jones, Ensign, District 49	1 Aug 1817	p. 685
William J. Dudley, Captain, District 12	1 Aug 1817	p. 686
William Barker, Ensign, District 137	1 Aug 1817	p. 686
Matthew T. Hameltion, Major, Battalion 51	1 Aug 1817	p. 687
Absalom Glover, Ensign, District 76	1 Aug 1817	p. 687
Bailey Bell, Captain, District 300	1 Aug 1817	p. 688
William Waggoner, Lieutenant, District 305	1 Aug 1817	p. 688
Joseph Bert, Ensign, District 305	1 Aug 1817	p. 689
Thomas Jefferson, Captain, District 358	1 Aug 1817	p. 689
David Frazer, Lieutenant, District 185	1 Aug 1817	p. 690
Samuel Glaze, Ensign, District 185	1 Aug 1817	p. 690
Robert Brown, Ensign, District 306	1 Aug 1817	p. 691
John Hayles, Lieutenant, Augusta Fire Company, Battalion 75	1 Aug 1817	p. 691
Alexander Mackinzie, Ensign, Augusta Fire Company, Battalion 75	1 Aug 1817	p. 692
Henry Wilson, Captain, District 338	1 Aug 1817	p. 692
George Greer, Lieutenant, District 98	1 Aug 1817	p. 693
Thomas Taylor, Ensign, District 168	1 Aug 1817	p. 693
Lemuel Thigpen, Ensign, District 151	1 Aug 1817	p. 694
William H. Blount, Captain, District 156	1 Aug 1817	p. 694
Elias Wilson, Major, Battalion 29	5 Aug 1817	p. 695
James Sanderlin, Captain, District 7	11 Aug 1817	p. 695
Arden Powell, Second Lieutenant, Troop of Cavalry, Squadron 2, Regiment 1	11 Aug 1817	p. 696
Thomas Seay, Lieutenant, Rifle Company, Battalion 29	11 Aug 1817	p. 696
David Rankin, Captain, District 141	11 Aug 1817	p. 697
John Weathers, Lieutenant, District 161	11 Aug 1817	p. 697
Joseph Manning, Lieutenant, District 27	11 Aug 1817	p. 698
Wilson Pope, Ensign, District 358	11 Aug 1817	p. 699
James Reynolds, Lieutenant, District 378	11 Aug 1817	p. 699

Georgia Military Commissions, 1798–1818

Name, Unit, Rank	Date	Page
John Lucas, Major, Battalion 90	11 Aug 1817	p. 700
William Moore, Lieutenant, District 341	11 Aug 1817	p. 700
John Rowland, Ensign, District 341	11 Aug 1817	p. 701
Silas Overstreet, Captain, District 40	11 Aug 1817	p. 701
William Drawdy, Lieutenant, District 40	11 Aug 1817	p. 702
Matthew M. Dees, Ensign, District 40	11 Aug 1817	p. 702
William Deloatch, Captain, District 401	11 Aug 1817	p. 703
William Davis, Lieutenant, District 401	11 Aug 1817	p. 703
John Baxter, Ensign, District 401	11 Aug 1817	p. 704
Milton Pouton, Ensign, District 167	11 Aug 1817	p. 704
William Iverson, Lieutenant, District 66	16 Aug 1817	p. 705
George B. Mires, Ensign, District 198	16 Aug 1817	p. 705
Ridgdon Brown, Captain, District 266	16 Aug 1817	p. 706
Samuel W. Miller, Lieutenant, District 298	16 Aug 1817	p. 706
Joseph C. Clemm, Ensign, District 298	16 Aug 1817	p. 707
Ebemelik Pate, Ensign, District 355	16 Aug 1817	p. 707
Timothy L. Rogers, Captain, Troop of Light Dragoons, Squadron 9, Regiment 5	18 Aug 1817	p. 708
Jeremiah Matthews, Lieutenant, District 220	20 Aug 1817	p. 708
James S. Bulloch, Major, Battalion 60	20 Aug 1817	p. 709
Grantham Rose, Lieutenant, District 193	20 Aug 1817	p. 709
Isaac Allman, Ensign, District 193	20 Aug 1817	p. 710
John Clark, Major, Battalion 58	20 Aug 1817	p. 710
Frederick Freeman, Ensign, District 245	20 Aug 1817	p. 711
John Davis, Lieutenant, District 379	20 Aug 1817	p. 711
Dolphin D. Floyd, Captain, District 300	20 Aug 1817	p. 712
George Wyche, Major, Battalion 89	20 Aug 1817	p. 712
Martin Swearingen, Lieutenant, District 343	20 Aug 1817	p. 713
William Bower, Ensign, District 343	20 Aug 1817	p. 713
William B. Holt, Lieutenant, District 123	20 Aug 1817	p. 714
Jesse Johnson, Ensign, District 123	20 Aug 1817	p. 714
Lewis L. Griffin, Ensign, Marion Independent Blues, Battalion 72	20 Aug 1817	p. 715
Henry C. Dawson, Lieutenant Colonel, Regiment 4	20 Aug 1817	p. 715
Barnard C. Heard, Major, Cavalry, Squadron 7, Regiment 4	20 Aug 1817	p. 716

Name, Unit, Rank	*Date*	*Page*
John W. Compton, Major, Cavalry, Squadron 9, Regiment 5	2 Sep 1817	p. 716
Samuel Calhoon, First Lieutenant, Troop of Light Dragoons, Squadron 9, Regiment 5	13 Sep 1817	p. 717
Harmon B. Hargrove, Ensign, District 342	13 Sep 1817	p. 717
Henry Williams, Captain, District 152	13 Sep 1817	p. 718
Charles Sebert, Ensign, District 386	13 Sep 1817	p. 718
Thomas C. Kindrick, Captain, District 128	13 Sep 1817	p. 719
Daniel Galbreath, Lieutenant, District 144	13 Sep 1817	p. 719
John B. Cromwell, Ensign, District 144	13 Sep 1817	p. 720
Joseph Dubignon, Captain, District 25	13 Sep 1817	p. 720
Josiah Lyon, Lieutenant, District 171	13 Sep 1817	p. 721
Jonathan G. Mann, Second Lieutenant, Volunteer Company of Light Artillery, Regiment 40	17 Sep 1817	p. 721
Luke Partrick, Cornet, Troop of Light Dragoons, Squadron 8, Regiment 4	17 Sep 1817	p. 722
Josiah Horton, Lieutenant, District 300	17 Sep 1817	p. 722
Jacob King, Ensign, District 300	17 Sep 1817	p. 723
John Griffin, Ensign, District 331	17 Sep 1817	p. 723
John Hodges, Ensign, District 87	17 Sep 1817	p. 724
Jesse Howell, Ensign, District 242	17 Sep 1817	p. 724
Wm. Levingston, Cornet, Cavalry, Squadron 2, Regiment 1	19 Sep 1817	p. 725
John Permento, Captain, Volunteer Company of Riflemen, Battalion 72	19 Sep 1817	p. 726
Herbert Robinson, Lieutenant, Volunteer Company of Riflemen, Battalion 72	19 Sep 1817	p. 726
John Knight, Ensign, Volunteer Company of Riflemen, Battalion 72	19 Sep 1817	p. 727
Lunsford C. Pitts, Major, Cavalry, Squadron 10, Regiment 5	22 Sep 1817	p. 727
William Herbert, Captain, District 104	22 Sep 1817	p. 728
James Meriwether, Major, Battalion 49	23 Sep 1817	p. 728
James Desmukes, Lieutenant, District 125	23 Sep 1817	p. 729
Joseph Overton, Ensign, District 125	19 Sep 1817	p. 729
Simon Batemin, Lieutenant, District 376	23 Sep 1817	p. 730
David Kean, Captain, District 351	29 Sep 1817	p. 730
David Lang, Lieutenant, District 259	29 Sep 1817	p. 731

Georgia Military Commissions, 1798–1818

Name, Unit, Rank	*Date*	*Page*
Benjamin Pully, Ensign, District 115	29 Sep 1817	p. 731
Collin Dillard, Ensign, District 89	29 Sep 1817	p. 732
Alexander McCalpin, Lieutenant Colonel, Regiment 16	30 Sep 1817	p. 732
John Jennings, Lieutenant, District 190	30 Sep 1817	p. 733
Solomon Jones, Ensign, District 190	30 Sep 1817	p. 733
Shadrick Vining, Lieutenant, District 308	30 Sep 1817	p. 734
Nephtaline Martin, Ensign, District 382	30 Sep 1817	p. 734
Burwell Cannon, Lieutenant, District 112	30 Sep 1817	p. 735
Jesse S. Brown, Ensign, District 112	30 Sep 1817	p. 735
Isaac Mooning, Lieutenant, District 397	30 Sep 1817	p. 736
Francis E. Bailey, Ensign, District 397	30 Sep 1817	p. 736
Elias Champion, Captain, District 108	30 Sep 1817	p. 737
John S. Lace, Captain, District 109	30 Sep 1817	p. 737
Bartholomew Johnson, Ensign, District 279	30 Sep 1817	p. 738
Battle Mayfield, Ensign, District 268	30 Sep 1817	p. 738
James Byrns, Lieutenant, District 362	3 Sep 1817	p. 739
Claborn Beville, Captain, District 36	3 Sep 1817	p. 739
Wiley Dowdy, Lieutenant, District 36	3 Sep 1817	p. 740
Benjamin S. Moore, Captain, District 281	3 Sep 1817	p. 740
Britain Nicholson, Lieutenant, District 281	3 Sep 1817	p. 741
George Harris, Ensign, District 281	3 Sep 1817	p. 741
James Akin, Lieutenant, District 216	3 Sep 1817	p. 742
John Rogers, Lieutenant, District 258	3 Sep 1817	p. 742
Michael Whitmer, Ensign, District 258	3 Sep 1817	p. 743
John McGill, Lieutenant, District 269	3 Sep 1817	p. 743
Henry Hardy, Ensign, District 269	3 Sep 1817	p. 744
Allen Chandler, Ensign, District 207	3 Sep 1817	p. 744
Chesley B. Mimms, Captain, District 112	3 Sep 1817	p. 745
James Bankhead, Lieutenant, District 389	3 Sep 1817	p. 745
Thomas Wadsworth, Captain, District 247	3 Sep 1817	p. 746
Walter T. Colquitt, Lieutenant, District 107	3 Sep 1817	p. 746
John H. Colquitt, Ensign, District 107	3 Sep 1817	p. 747
Isham Ready, Lieutenant, District 321	3 Sep 1817	p. 747
Nathan T. Sandeford, Lieutenant, District 74	3 Sep 1817	p. 748
Amos Bullard, Ensign, District 74	3 Sep 1817	p. 748
William Wyatt, Captain, District 292	3 Sep 1817	p. 749

Commissions Book 1815–1818

Name, Unit, Rank	Date	Page
John Bentley, Captain, District 297	3 Sep 1817	p. 749
James Millener, Ensign, District 297	3 Sep 1817	p. 750
Kinchin Dawson, Lieutenant, District 384	3 Sep 1817	p. 750
James M. Tayor, Ensign, District 384	3 Sep 1817	p. 751
John Lane, Captain, District 49	3 Sep 1817	p. 751
James Kirkland, Lieutenant, District 49	3 Sep 1817	p. 752
Daniel Kirkland, Ensign, District 49	3 Sep 1817	p. 752
Samuel Pearman, Lieutenant Colonel, Regiment 29	3 Sep 1817	p. 753
George Powell, Second Lieutenant, Volunteer Troop of Dragoons, Squadron 9, Regiment 5	13 Oct 1817	p. 753
Isaac Walsh, Cornet, Volunteer Troop of Dragoons, Squadron 9, Regiment 5	13 Oct 1817	p. 754
James White, First Lieutenant, Volunteer Troop of Dragoons, Squadron 5, Regiment 3	13 Oct 1817	p. 754
Thomas Barton, Second Lieutenant, Volunteer Troop of Dragoons, Squadron 5, Regiment 3	13 Oct 1817	p. 755
John Worsham, First Lieutenant, Volunteer Troop of Dragoons, Squadron 5, Regiment 3	13 Oct 1817	p. 755
William Daniel, Cornet, Volunteer Troop of Dragoons, Squadron 5, Regiment 3	13 Oct 1817	p. 756
Martin Towns, Captain, Volunteer Troop of Dragoons, Squadron 9, Regiment 5	13 Oct 1817	p. 756
Thomas Willingham, Ensign, District 131	13 Oct 1817	p. 757
William Casaty, Ensign, District 299	13 Oct 1817	p. 757
Lewis Johnson, Lieutenant, District 360	13 Oct 1817	p. 758
James Bone, Captain, District 383	13 Oct 1817	p. 758
William W. Abbott, Captain, District 82	13 Oct 1817	p. 759
Morris Walden, Captain, District 79	13 Oct 1817	p. 759
Josiah B. Harper, Lieutenant, District 277	13 Oct 1817	p. 760
Thomas Chatham, Ensign, District 400	13 Oct 1817	p. 760
George W. Elliot, Lieutenant, District 141	13 Oct 1817	p. 761
Thomas Myres, Ensign, District 141	13 Oct 1817	p. 761
Thomas Copeland, Ensign, District 160	13 Oct 1817	p. 762
Elijah England, Captain, District 265	13 Oct 1817	p. 762
Hamilton Sanford, Ensign, District 173	13 Oct 1817	p. 763
Joseph Walker, Ensign, District 95	13 Oct 1817	p. 763
John Jackson, Captain, District 94	13 Oct 1817	p. 764
Loyd Riddle, Ensign, District 92	13 Oct 1817	p. 764

Georgia Military Commissions, 1798–1818

Name, Unit, Rank	Date	Page
Thaddeus G. Holt, Captain, Volunteer Company of Artillery, Regiment 33	22 Oct 1817	p. 765
Thomas M. Bush, First Lieutenant, Volunteer Company of Artillery, Regiment 33	22 Oct 1817	p. 765
Daniel Newnan, Major General, Division 3	10 Nov 1817	p. 766
Edmund Shackelford, Brigadier General, Brigade 1, Division 3	10 Nov 1817	p. 766
John C. Easter, Lieutenant Colonel (Adjutant General)	13 Nov 1817	p. 767
Wm. G. Macon, Captain, District 163	27 Nov 1817	p. 767
Joel Freeman, Lieutenant, District 262	27 Nov 1817	p. 768
Bithal Morgan, Ensign, District 262	27 Nov 1817	p. 768
Isaac Daniel, Ensign, District 41	27 Nov 1817	p. 769
Thomas Moseley, Major, Battalion 31	27 Nov 1817	p. 769
Samuel Hamilton, Captain, District 316	27 Nov 1817	p. 770
John Johnson, Captain, District 245	27 Nov 1817	p. 770
Henry L. Britain, Captain, District 229	27 Nov 1817	p. 771
Henry Lunsford, Lieutenant, District 229	27 Nov 1817	p. 771
Matthew Averett, Ensign, District 231	27 Nov 1817	p. 772
Coleman Tarpely, Lieutenant, District 234	27 Nov 1817	p. 772
Hardiman Owens, Ensign, District 234	27 Nov 1817	p. 773
John G. Bowles, Captain, District 230	27 Nov 1817	p. 773
Heram C. Harriss, Captain, District 247	27 Nov 1817	p. 774
Wm H. Barnett, Captain, District 226	27 Nov 1817	p. 774
George Davis, Lieutenant, District 226	27 Nov 1817	p. 775
Ephraim Keifer, Lieutenant, District 12	27 Nov 1817	p. 775
Aaron Lovett, Ensign, District 12	27 Nov 1817	p. 776
Wm H. Gilliland, Captain, District 3	27 Nov 1817	p. 776
David Chiles, Captain, District 353	27 Nov 1817	p. 777
John Brown, Lieutenant, District 328	27 Nov 1817	p. 777
Bredgor Webb, Captain, District 201	27 Nov 1817	p. 778
George B. Myers, Lieutenant, District 198	27 Nov 1817	p. 778
Joel Winfield, Lieutenant, District 221	27 Nov 1817	p. 779
James Straughn, Ensign, District 221	27 Nov 1817	p. 779
James Meriwether, Captain, District 223	27 Nov 1817	p. 780
Benjamin Watson, Captain, District 134	27 Nov 1817	p. 780
Peter B. Short, Lieutenant, District 135	27 Nov 1817	p. 781
Whitmill Travis, Captain, District 151	27 Nov 1817	p. 781

Name, Unit, Rank	Date	Page
John Horn, Lieutenant, District 151	27 Nov 1817	p. 782
Michael L. Dent, Captain, District 165	27 Nov 1817	p. 782
Wm Upshaw, Lieutenant, District 165	27 Nov 1817	p. 783
Job Hammond, Captain, District 263	27 Nov 1817	p. 783
David Ramsey, Lieutenant, District 263	27 Nov 1817	p. 784
Richard H. Thomas, Lieutenant Colonel, Regiment 36	28 Nov 1817	p. 784
John B. Simmons, Major, Battalion 23	28 Nov 1817	p. 785
Aristarchuse Newton, Major, Battalion 84	28 Nov 1817	p. 785
John Binion, Second Lieutenant, Volunteer Troop of Light Dragoons, Squadron 4, Regiment 2	29 Nov 1817	p. 786
Armstead Richardson, Major, Cavalry, Squadron 5, Regiment 3	9 Dec 1817	p. 786
Stewart Anderson, Major, Cavalry, Squadron 4, Regiment 3	9 Dec 1817	p. 787
Jacob Robinson, Captain, Cavalry, Squadron 10, Regiment 5	9 Dec 1817	p. 787
Reuben Hicklin, Second Lieutenant, Troop of Light Dragoons, Squadron 4, Regiment 2	9 Dec 1817	p. 788
Benjamin Tarver, Cornet, Troop of Light Dragoons, Squadron 4, Regiment 2	9 Dec 1817	p. 788
Wiley Thompson, Major General, Division 4	12 Dec 1817	p. 789
William C. Morgan, Captain, Volunteer Troop of Light Dragoons, Squadron 7, Regiment 5	1 Jan 1818	p. 789
R. H. Long, Second Lieutenant, Volunteer Troop of Light Dragoons, Squadron 7, Regiment 5	1 Jan 1817	p. 790
Joseph Hughey, Cornet, Volunteer Troop of Light Dragoons, Squadron 5, Regiment 3	1 Jan 1818	p. 790
John Clements, Cornet, Volunteer Troop of Light Dragoons, Squadron 2, Regiment 1	1 Jan 1818	p. 791
John Sparks, First Lieutenant, Volunteer Troop of Light Dragoons, Squadron 9, Regiment 5	1 Jan 1818	p. 791
Thomas Hunt, Second Lieutenant, Volunteer Troop of Light Dragoons, Squadron 9, Regiment 5	1 Jan 1818	p. 792
Larkin Carlton, Captain, District 146	5 Jan 1818	p. 792
Bird Lee, Ensign, District 93	5 Jan 1818	p. 793
Josias Boswell, Lieutenant, District 309	5 Jan 1818	p. 793
Hardiman Willingham, Lieutenant, District 290	5 Jan 1818	p. 794
Thomas Smith, Ensign, District 290	5 Jan 1817	p. 794

Georgia Military Commissions, 1798–1818

Name, Unit, Rank	Date	Page
Henry T. Hall, Ensign, Volunteer Company of Infantry, Battalion 6	5 Jan 1818	p. 795
Nathaniel G. Waller, Captain, District 359	5 Jan 1818	p. 795
William Smarr, Captain, District 85	5 Jan 1818	p. 796
Kinchin Curl, Captain, District 361	5 Jan 1818	p. 796
Dennis McClendon, Ensign, District 361	5 Jan 1818	p. 797
Bailey Chandler, Captain, District 243	5 Jan 1818	p. 797
William Watts, Lieutenant, District 243	5 Jan 1818	p. 798
Robert Chandler, Ensign, District 243	5 Jan 1818	p. 798
Stephen P. Scott, Ensign, District 390	5 Jan 1818	p. 799
Eli Buckner, Captain, District 310	5 Jan 1818	p. 799
Theodorick Montfort, Captain, Volunteer Company of Artillery, Battalion 40	5 Jan 1818	p. 800
Edward Dudley, First Lieutenant, Volunteer Company of Artillery, Battalion 40	5 Jan 1818	p. 800
William Harvill, Captain, District 148	5 Jan 1818	p. 801
James Woodham, Ensign, District 161	5 Jan 1818	p. 801
Matthew McMichael, Lieutenant, District 295	5 Jan 1818	p. 802
James B. Watters, Ensign, District 295	5 Jan 1818	p. 802
Daniel Oneal, Ensign, District 52	5 Jan 1818	p. 803
William H. Morrow, Lieutenant Colonel, Regiment 41	5 Jan 1818	p. 803
Alexander Northcut, Ensign, District 296	5 Jan 1818	p. 804
Andrew Partrick, Lieutenant, District 237	5 Jan 1818	p. 804
John Mason, Lieutenant, District 57	5 Jan 1818	p. 805
James Oats, Captain, District 222	5 Jan 1818	p. 805
Greene Cousins, Captain, District 318	5 Jan 1818	p. 806
Isaac Bailey, Lieutenant, District 31	5 Jan 1818	p. 806
David H. Hampton, Lieutenant, District 382	5 Jan 1818	p. 807
Gallip Dasher, Lieutenant, District 9	5 Jan 1818	p. 807
Edward Alexander, Ensign, District 198	5 Jan 1818	p. 808
Simon W. Nichols, Ensign, District 2	5 Jan 1818	p. 808
Thomas B. Price, Lieutenant, District 3	5 Jan 1818	p. 809
Robert Raiford, Ensign, District 3	5 Jan 1818	p. 809
Samuel Clay, Captain, District 295	5 Jan 1818	p. 810
John Foster, Ensign, District 396	5 Jan 1818	p. 810
James Wilder, Lieutenant, District 155	5 Jan 1818	p. 811
David Cummins, Lieutenant, District 96	5 Jan 1818	p. 811

Name, Unit, Rank	*Date*	*Page*
John G. Robinson, Captain, District 90	5 Jan 1818	p. 812
Jesse Blackeley, Lieutenant, District 104	5 Jan 1818	p. 812
Juprey Desmukes, Ensign, District 104	5 Jan 1818	p. 813
Thomas Goore, Lieutenant, District 103	5 Jan 1818	p. 813
Moses Fillingin, Lieutenant, District 355	5 Jan 1818	p. 814
Richard Whitaker, Ensign, District 97	5 Jan 1818	p. 814
Willis Burney, Captain, District 92	5 Jan 1818	p. 815
Jeremiah Missick, Lieutenant, District 88	5 Jan 1818	p. 815
John W. Harper, Ensign, District 241	5 Jan 1818	p. 816
Morris Smith, Captain, District 38	5 Jan 1818	p. 816
Thomas White, Second Lieutenant, Volunteer Company of Artillery, Regiment 33	16 Jan 1818	p. 817
Carter B. Harrison, Lieutenant Colonel, Regiment 31	3 Mar 1818	p. 817
John W. Hanson, Lieutenant, District 400	5 Mar 1818	p. 818
Morgan Bellar, Ensign, District 400	5 Mar 1818	p. 818
Thomas H. Evans, Lieutenant, District 308	5 Mar 1818	p. 819
Allen Greene, Captain, District 378	5 Mar 1818	p. 819
John Edward, Lieutenant, District 306	5 Mar 1818	p. 820
Thomas Bennett, Lieutenant, District 255	5 Mar 1818	p. 820
Robert Tuttle, Lieutenant, District 67	5 Mar 1818	p. 821
Henry McNorrill, Ensign, District 67	5 Mar 1818	p. 821
John G. Colbert, Major, Battalion 61	5 Mar 1818	p. 822
Martin Brooks, Captain, District 94	5 Mar 1818	p. 822
James Fletcher, Captain, District 277	5 Mar 1818	p. 823
Jesse Pitman, Lieutenant, District 324	5 Mar 1818	p. 823
James Smyney, Lieutenant, District 316	5 Mar 1818	p. 824
Samuel Stephens, Ensign, District 376	5 Mar 1818	p. 824
John Taylor, Ensign, District 391	5 Mar 1818	p. 825
William Harris, Captain, District 13	5 Mar 1818	p. 825
Dingley Lokey, Ensign, District 152	5 Mar 1818	p. 826
William Davis, Lieutenant, District 79	5 Mar 1818	p. 826
Isham Thompson, Major, Battalion 75	5 Mar 1818	p. 827
Henry Josey, Captain, District 167	5 Mar 1818	p. 827
Thomas Bustin, Captain, District 374	5 Mar 1818	p. 828
Willis Alexander, Lieutenant, District 195	5 Mar 1818	p. 828
Jacob M. Cleveland, Ensign, District 195	5 Mar 1818	p. 829
James Wilson, Lieutenant, District 200	5 Mar 1818	p. 829

Georgia Military Commissions, 1798–1818

Name, Unit, Rank	Date	Page
Alexander Hudson, Ensign, District 200	5 Mar 1818	p. 830
Hugh Ector, Captain, District 312	5 Mar 1818	p. 830
John Bryant, Lieutenant, District 312	5 Mar 1818	p. 831
John W. Scott, Captain, District 113	5 Mar 1818	p. 831
William Meshon, Lieutenant, District 113	5 Mar 1818	p. 832
John Brantley, Captain, District 102	5 Mar 1818	p. 832
William W. Oslin, Captain, District 368	5 Mar 1818	p. 833
Yelventon Thaxton, Ensign, District 234	5 Mar 1818	p. 833
Larkin Colbert, Lieutenant, District 235	5 Mar 1818	p. 834
Joel Whitehead, Ensign, District 235	5 Mar 1818	p. 834
John Phinizy, Captain, District 228	5 Mar 1818	p. 835
George Stephens, Lieutenant, District 209	5 Mar 1818	p. 835
John B. Hawkins, Ensign, District 209	5 Mar 1818	p. 836
Hugh McDonald, Lieutenant, District 265	5 Mar 1818	p. 836
Joseph Hodges, Ensign, District 265	5 Mar 1818	p. 837
Thomas Clayton, Lieutenant, District 101	5 Mar 1818	p. 837
James Clubb, Lieutenant, District 25	5 Mar 1818	p. 838
Luke Blount, Ensign, District 25	5 Mar 1818	p. 838
Daniel Morgan, Ensign, District 230	5 Mar 1818	p. 839
Henry H. Lumpkin, Lieutenant, District 231	5 Mar 1818	p. 839
William Rowland, Lieutenant, District 163	5 Mar 1818	p. 840
Archibald Tapley, Ensign, District 163	5 Mar 1818	p. 840
James Ransom, Lieutenant, District 162	5 Mar 1818	p. 841
William Mallory, Ensign, District 162	5 Mar 1818	p. 841
James Dunn, Lieutenant, District 141	5 Mar 1818	p. 842
Jonathan Burges, Lieutenant, District 146	5 Mar 1818	p. 842
James Bledsoe, Ensign, District 146	5 Mar 1818	p. 843
Timothy Hopkins, Ensign, District 31	5 Mar 1818	p. 843
James Pritchard, Lieutenant, District 26	5 Mar 1818	p. 844
Gee Dupree, Ensign, District 26	5 Mar 1818	p. 844
Aaron Everitt, Captain, District 48	5 Mar 1818	p. 845
Joseph Hagin, Lieutenant, District 48	5 Mar 1818	p. 845
Joshua Knight, Captain, District 283	5 Mar 1818	p. 846
John C. Adamson, Ensign, District 283	5 Mar 1818	p. 846
Edmund Ogletree, Captain, District 169	5 Mar 1818	p. 847
Garland Rice, Lieutenant, District 169	5 Mar 1818	p. 847

Name, Unit, Rank	*Date*	*Page*
James Rice, Ensign, District 169	5 Mar 1818	p. 848
John Willis, Captain, District 176	5 Mar 1818	p. 848
Robert Carter, Lieutenant, District 176	5 Mar 1818	p. 849
William C. Humphries, Lieutenant, District 277	5 Mar 1818	p. 849
James Cawthorn, Ensign, District 277	5 Mar 1818	p. 850
Silas Tatum, Captain, District 186	5 Mar 1818	p. 850
Robert B. Smiley, Lieutenant, District 186	5 Mar 1818	p. 851
Benjamin S. Lanier, Captain, District 349	5 Mar 1818	p. 851
John Tinderson, Lieutenant, District 349	5 Mar 1818	p. 852
James J. Moore, Captain, District 329	5 Mar 1818	p. 852
Alexander Moore, Lieutenant, District 329	5 Mar 1818	p. 853
Jesse Kinney, Ensign, District 329	5 Mar 1818	p. 853
Nathan Maddox, Captain, District 348	5 Mar 1818	p. 854
Benjamin Steagall, Ensign, District 348	5 Mar 1818	p. 854
Etheldred Fountain, Captain, District 84	5 Mar 1818	p. 855
William G. Dekle, Captain, District 59	5 Mar 1818	p. 855
Thomas Bell, Captain, District 62	5 Mar 1818	p. 856
Elias Redfield, Ensign, District 62	5 Mar 1818	p. 856
William Bottey, Lieutenant, District 82	5 Mar 1818	p. 857
George Granbury, Ensign, District 82	5 Mar 1818	p. 857
Joel Bailey, Captain, District 291	5 Mar 1818	p. 858
Laurence Smith, Lieutenant, District 291	5 Mar 1818	p. 858
Benjamin Herrage, Ensign, District 291	5 Mar 1818	p. 859
Stephen H. Gilmore, Captain, Volunteer Troop of Light Dragoons, Squadron 5, Regiment 3	6 Mar 1818	p. 859
Cary Wood, First Lieutenant, Volunteer Troop of Light Dragoons, Squadron 5, Regiment 3	6 Mar 1818	p. 860
John Thurmond, Second Lieutenant, Volunteer Troop of Light Dragoons, Squadron 5, Regiment 3	6 Mar 1818	p. 860
Benjamin Purcy, Cornet, Volunteer Troop of Light Dragoons, Squadron 5, Regiment 3	6 Mar 1818	p. 861
Peter Alexander, First Lieutenant, Volunteer Troop of Light Dragoons, Squadron 5, Regiment 3	6 Mar 1818	p. 861
John Portson, Second Lieutenant, Volunteer Troop of Light Dragoons, Squadron 7, Regiment 4	6 Mar 1818	p. 862
George Osborn, Captain, Volunteer Troop of Light Dragoons, Squadron 5, Regiment 3	6 Mar 1818	p. 862

Georgia Military Commissions, 1798–1818

Name, Unit, Rank	*Date*	*Page*
Lewis Daniel, First Lieutenant, Volunteer Troop of Light Dragoons, Squadron 5, Regiment 3	6 Mar 1818	p. 863
William W. Baker, Cornet, Volunteer Troop of Light Dragoons, Squadron 1, Regiment 1	6 Mar 1818	p. 863
Thomas W. Shivers, Captain, Volunteer Troop of Light Dragoons, Squadron 3, Regiment 2	23 Mar 1818	p. 864
William Lowe, First Lieutenant, Volunteer Troop of Light Dragoons, Squadron 3, Regiment 2	23 Mar 1818	p. 864
Joshua Jordan, Second Lieutenant, Volunteer Troop of Light Dragoons, Squadron 3, Regiment 2	23 Mar 1818	p. 865
Zepheniah Hicks, Cornet, Volunteer Troop of Light Dragoons, Squadron 3, Regiment 2	6 Mar 1818	p. 865
Yelventon P. King, Captain, Volunteer Troop of Light Dragoons, Squadron 6, Regiment 3	14 Apr 1818	p. 866
Charles H. Nelson, Major, Battalion 37	24 Feb 1818	p. 866
Richard Colbert, Major, Battalion 24	24 Feb 1818	p. 867
Martin Russell, Captain, District 105	13 Mar 1818	p. 867
Rowell Reese, Ensign, District 387	13 Mar 1818	p. 868
George Johnson, Captain, District 306	13 Mar 1818	p. 868
Stephen Hackney, Captain, District 286	13 Mar 1818	p. 869
Peter Hamilton, Lieutenant, District 286	13 Mar 1818	p. 869
Lemuel Chapman, Ensign, District 286	13 Mar 1818	p. 870
James Johns, Lieutenant, District 292	13 Mar 1818	p. 870
Robert Douglass, Captain, District 36	13 Mar 1818	p. 871
Thomas Maddox, Ensign, District 36	13 Mar 1818	p. 871
William E. Brodnax, Lieutenant, District 107	13 Mar 1818	p. 872
Charles Phillips, Captain, District 361	13 Mar 1818	p. 872
John Courson, Lieutenant, District 361	13 Mar 1818	p. 873
Spencer Owens, Ensign, District 361	13 Mar 1818	p. 873
James Russell, Ensign, District 27	13 Mar 1818	p. 874
James Huckaby, Ensign, District 172	13 Mar 1818	p. 874
Robert Rakstraw, Ensign, District 229	13 Mar 1818	p. 875
Baley Bledsoe, Ensign, District 148	13 Mar 1818	p. 875
David Sherrell, Lieutenant, District 140	13 Mar 1818	p. 876
Greene Andrews, Lieutenant, District 100	13 Mar 1818	p. 876
Jones Buckhalter, Captain, District 299	13 Mar 1818	p. 877
Greene B. Jack, Lieutenant, District 223	13 Mar 1818	p. 877
Richard Maxwell, Ensign, District 223	13 Mar 1818	p. 879

Name, Unit, Rank	Date	Page
Daniel Kohely, Lieutenant, District 248	13 Mar 1818	p. 879
Burwell Cook, Ensign, District 248	13 Mar 1818	p. 880
Wooten Daeskill, Ensign, District 108	13 Mar 1818	p. 880
Thomas Willingham, Captain, District 131	13 Mar 1818	p. 881
Rolly Willingham, Lieutenant, District 131	13 Mar 1818	p. 881
Jesse Holder, Ensign, District 131	13 Mar 1818	p. 882
George McKinny, Ensign, District 174	13 Mar 1818	p. 882
William S. Howard, Lieutenant, District 181	13 Mar 1818	p. 883
M. B. Ward, Captain, District 63	13 Mar 1818	p. 883
Josiah Alday, Lieutenant, District 63	13 Mar 1818	p. 884
James Young, Lieutenant, District 129	13 Mar 1818	p. 884
Thomas E. Beall, Ensign, District 129	13 Mar 1818	p. 885
John Kimbro, Captain, District 160	13 Mar 1818	p. 885
Lewis Powell, Lieutenant, District 66	13 Mar 1818	p. 886
Simeon Davis, Ensign, District 66	13 Mar 1818	p. 886
Benjamin Penn, Captain, District 197	13 Mar 1818	p. 887
Wyatt Hicks, Lieutenant, District 197	13 Mar 1818	p. 887
Jesse Brown, Ensign, District 197	13 Mar 1818	p. 888
Joseph Sentell, Captain, District 373	13 Mar 1818	p. 888
William Nelmes, Lieutenant, District 193	13 Mar 1818	p. 889
Joseph Attaway, Captain, District 370	13 Mar 1818	p. 889
James Couch, Lieutenant, District 370	13 Mar 1818	p. 890
Josiah Goolsby, Ensign, District 370	13 Mar 1818	p. 890
Samuel Nelms, Captain, District 139	13 Mar 1818	p. 891
William Moon, Lieutenant, District 139	13 Mar 1818	p. 891
H. Oneal, Ensign, District 139	13 Mar 1818	p. 892
Amelius Torrance, Lieutenant, District 322	13 Mar 1818	p. 892
John Miller, Captain, District 265	13 Mar 1818	p. 893
Hiram Beasley, Lieutenant, District 222	13 Mar 1818	p. 893
Reuben Stewart, Ensign, District 222	13 Mar 1818	p. 894
Isaac Thrash, Ensign, District 368	13 Mar 1818	p. 894
James H. Speer, Ensign, District 287	13 Mar 1818	p. 895
Archibald Bilbo, Ensign, District 217	13 Mar 1818	p. 895
Turner Duke, Ensign, District 70	13 Mar 1818	p. 896
John R. Russell, Lieutenant, District 366	13 Mar 1818	p. 896
David S. Murray, Major, Battalion 40	13 Mar 1818	p. 897

Georgia Military Commissions, 1798–1818

Name, Unit, Rank	Date	Page
William H. Avery, Major, Battalion 68	13 Mar 1818	p. 897
John White, Ensign, District 193	13 Mar 1818	p. 898
Archibald Sheets, Lieutenant, District 166	13 Mar 1818	p. 898
John H. Biurdon, Lieutenant, District 375	13 Mar 1818	p. 899
John Hargrove, Lieutenant, District 102	13 Mar 1818	p. 899

Name Index

A

Abbett
William W. 298
Abbot
Edmund................ 288
Abbott
James O. 298
Jordan 238
Jorden 20
Jordon 107
William W. 309
Abercrombe
Anderson 157
Edmund................ 123
Abercrombie
Andrew 99
Leonard 25
Abney
Isaac 29, 42
Abott
Loveless.................. 65
Abrahams
Abraham 8, 41
Isaac 133
Achinson
Barton 69
Achord
Henry 158
Richard D. 142
Acock
Reddick 41
Acooper
James 281
Acre
Sterling 301
Acridge
John........................ 46

Adair
Jacob 54
Robert 52
Adams
Abraham 120
Absolam 235
David............ 217, 219
David F. 220
Edmund 101
Farler 303
Hezekiah D...........268
James....................102
John 89, 181, 224
Meredith 203
Thomas 60
William E..... 140, 271
Adamson
Greenbury...............71
John C...................314
Adare
William 280
Adkins
Bartlet.............. 29, 42
Shadrick................204
Adrian
Fowler F................279
Akin
James....................308
Joseph 265
Akins
John 198
Samuel..................170
Thomas 207, 276
William 303
Akridge
David....................301
Greenberry 141
Alane
Micajah 280

Alberton
Mathew................... 57
Albright
Christian 177, 241
John 177
William 121
Albriton
Manly..................... 70
Albritton
Peter 238
Thomas 125
Alcorn
Elijah 179
Alday
Josiah 317
Richard 284
Alders
John 31
Aldridge
Aaron 279
Reuben.................. 127
Aldrige
Nathan 135
Alexander
Collin 296
Edward 312
Elias.................. 14, 27
Ezekiel.................... 56
George 149
James...................... 53
Peter 315
William 106
Willis 313
Alford
Fort 238
Haleot 229
Henry.................... 238
Holcut 244
Jacob 42

Alford, cont.
John 50
John L. 195
Lodwick 219
William 255
William Jr. 5

Alger
Preserved 231

Algiers
William D. 262

Allbright
Christian 167

Allen
Asa 71, 85, 103, 168
Benjamin 49, 245
Churchill............... 273
Clem 72
Dennis ... 186, 190, 299
George 61
George W. 142
Gideon 160
Grunbruy 183
Harris 199
Howard 73
James 70, 206, 209, 214
John 68, 111, 132, 221, 252
John T. 96
Jordan 261, 287
Littleberry 160
Moses 15
Robert 84, 138
Waddle 58
Washington 192
William 25, 58, 122
William G. 225
Young D. 274

Allison
Alexander H. 79
James 128, 129

Allison, cont.
Robert Jr. 182
William 65

Allman
Isaac 306
Samuel 119
William 140

Allum
William 270

Almon
John 37

Alpin
Alexander W. 256

Alston
Drury 205
James 34, 73, 237
James W. 262
John 228

Amason
Benjamine 178
Uriah 178

Ammory
Jacob 121

Amos
William 191

Andens
William G. 256

Anders
John 56
Peter 278

Anderson
Abraham 48
David 189
Eli 186
George 212
Hardy 215
Jesse 51
John S. 98
Jordan 278
Joseph 296
Maxwell 257

Anderson, cont.
Robert 63
Sidney 257
Sindney 98
Sterling 125
Stewart 202, 311
Thomas 137
William ... 82, 86, 115, 167, 290
William R. 301
Willis 132

Andress
John 289

Andrews
Alexander 45
Gray 262
Greene 204, 316
John 2

Anglin
John 151, 191
Peter 267

Angling
Henry 94
John Jr. 69

Ansley
Benjamin 34, 105, 131
William 233

Anthony
Henry T. 52
Isaac 245

Appason
David 274

Appleby
John 29, 42

Appling
Thomas 82

Ard
James 171
John 165

Arman
William 275

Name Index

Armer
Joseph 96
Armore
John...................... 48
Armour
James 66
William................... 43
Armstead
John...................... 41
Armstong
Jonathan 58
Armstron
James 238
Armstrong
Alixander 159
James W.............. 283
John...................... 44
Thomas.................. 92
Arnett
Edward.................. 41
William................... 78
Arnold
Champness 93
Chesley................ 187
Fancis 224
Jehu..................... 192
John.. 75, 93, 157, 170
Joseph 25, 242, 270
Stephen Jr. 160
William. 173, 179, 193
Aron
Peter......................... 4
Arrant
Peter................. 24, 45
Arrington
Abel 198
Siloe 166
Arrowood
Jesse 219
Aryres
Abraham 154

Asberry
Jessee....................207
Ash
Alexander T. 231
John 174
Ashe
John H. 217
Ashley
John 152, 158, 259
Thomas 271
Ashly
James.....................98
William 68
Ashton
William 166
Ashurst
Robert 133
Askew
William 74, 107
Astin
Jesse.....................234
Atcherson
Barton 97
Atcheson
James....................159
Atchison
Barton 110
Charles...................245
Atchisson
Charles...................281
Atkins
Arnold 137
Asa 93
John 220
Atkinson
John 105, 233
Lazarus 174, 274
Lewis............ 115, 195
Shadrack..............226
Thomas 232

Attaway
Jesse 218
Joseph...................317
Austin
Charles 246
Henry................31, 91
Joseph...................54
Autrey
Alexander 34
Avant
Josiah 292, 303
Avena
Needham 246
Avered
Isaac 265
Averett
Matthew 310
Averitt
David 213
Avers
Gibson...................155
Avery
Gabriel..................291
Harbert...................92
James....................219
William 181
William H. 302, 318
Avird
Needam 58
Ayres
Gadwill 42
Garland 103
John 20
Moses............103, 250
Thomas 149

B

Babb
Benjamin 164

Baber
  Thomas 119
  William 147, 154
Bachlott
  Joseph 250, 279
Backler
  Garten.....................48
Bacon
  Edmund 105
  John 28, 80, 155
  John B. 101
  William Hobson 74
Bagby
  Abner 99
  James....................144
  Joseph 235
  William 170
Baggett
  Blake 293
  Thos. 153
Bagwell
  Littleberry 118, 292
Bailey
  Caleb 206
  Christopher 11
  Francis E. 308
  Isaac.............281, 312
  Joel 195, 315
  John 14, 68, 259
  Peter 259
  Robert 163, 304
  Robert S. 226
  William ..79, 163, 171, 250, 269
  William Jr. 182
Bailie
  William 231
Baily
  John 176
Baird
  James....................293

Baker
  Amos 95, 185
  Bright 67, 107
  Calvin 105
  Charles 191
  Christopher 278
  David 199
  Edward E. 249
  Edwin 69, 232
  Elijah 95
  Grumberry 270
  Jeremiah 146
  Jesse 169
  John A. 11
  John C. 278
  John O. 156
  Jonathan 83, 146
  Jourdan 246
  Richard 268
  Samuel 146
  Stephen 111
  William 115
  William W. 316
  Zachariah 95
Baldwin
  Augustus 6, 112
  Ebenezer 12
Ball
  Joel 22, 146, 208
  John......................141
  Sampson...........67, 90
Ballard
  Levin......................92
  Ransom.................146
  Ranson..................156
  Silas........................85
Ballenger
  John..............202, 282
Bandy
  James 269

Bankhead
  James 308
Banks
  Thomas A. 205
  William 242
Bankston
  Reuben 51
  Simeon 149
Banner
  Henry 64
Barber
  Daniel...................291
  George 142
  Israel 13
Barbree
  John.........................3
Barden
  James 253
Barefield
  William 182
Barge
  Abel 274
Bark
  Eleathan 248
Barker
  Elijah....................219
  John B. 305
  John C. 288
  Mathew G. 221
  William 305
Barkesdale
  Richard 272
  Stith 248
Barks
  Henry 24
Barksdale
  Jeffery 21
Barkston
  John.....................255
Barlow
  James 197

Barnand
    John 105
Barnard
    James 105, 231
    John W. 116
    Timothy 15
    William 136
Barnes
    Amos 214
    George 156
    Jesse 284
    Jethro 218
    John B. . 109, 147, 218
    Thomas... 36, 136, 172
    William 27, 69, 110, 192
Barnett
    James 288
    Jeremiah 288
    John 18
    John F. 240
    Nathan 92
    Patrick J. 282
    Peter 146
    Samuel 111, 159
    William 76
    Wm H. 310
Barnette
    Nathan 55
Barnhill
    William H. 283
Barnwell
    Robert 179
Barret
    Isaac J. 235
Barrett
    Sterling 196
    Thomas 49, 100
Barron
    Samuel 1, 39
    Silas 62

Barron, cont.
    Thomas 61
    William 158
Barrott
    Isaac I. 100
    Thomas 46
Barrow
    Absalom 42, 125
    James 74
Bartlet
    Abner 269
Barton
    Archur 113
    Atchison 56
    James 92, 105, 159, 174, 279
    John 238, 288
    Presley 24, 135
    Thomas 309
    Willoughby 223
Bash
    John 9
Bashlott
    John 279
Bashtott
    Joseph 196
Bass
    Alexander 76
    Drury 113
    Ephram 110
    George 128
    Nathan 59
Bassett
    John 91
    Thomas 197
    William 52
Bastie
    John 72
Bateman
    Simon 197, 300

Batemin
    Simon 307
Bates
    Anderson 151
    Fleming 224
    James M. 271
    John 259, 302
    John W. 260
    Randolph 120
Batson
    Seth 71, 171
Battelle
    Jonathan 153, 160, 184
Baugh
    Peter 296
Baxter
    Andrew 234
    Jeremiah 78, 95
    John 306
    Thomas W. ... 117, 234
Bayne
    William 227
Beach
    Charles 151, 172
Beacham
    Elijah 68, 146
Beal
    Charles 274
    Frederick 102
    James 98
    William P. 36
Beale
    Josiah 11
    Robert 57
Beall
    Charles 211
    Elias 93, 249
    Frederick 47, 171
    Hezekiah 40
    Howell 77

Beall, cont.
  James 92
  John 18
  Josiah 21
  Otho 296
  Thaddeus 77, 128
  Thadeus 58
  Thomas E. 160, 317
  William 94, 231
  William P. 178
Bealle
  William Jr. 21
Bean
  Abraham 103
  John 127, 208
Beard
  John 71
  Matthias H. 245
Bearden
  Arthur 40, 102
Beasley
  Hiram 317
  Jareal 106
  Jareld 28
  Jarrel 233
  John 15, 194, 223, 248
  Robert 45
  William ... 15, 194, 207
Beasly
  John 60
Beatenback
  John 121
Beatey
  James Jr. 254
Beatty
  James 134
Beaty
  James 15, 251, 256
  James Jr. 198
Beavey
  Solomon 132

Beck
  Reuben C. 244
  Reubin C. 201
Beckham
  John 288
  Solomon 56
  Young 184
Beddingfield
  Allen 72
Bedell
  John 143
Beel
  William 167
Beggs
  David 112
Belcher
  Robert 274
  Wilie 291
Bell
  Bailey ... 227, 277, 305
  Daniel 209
  Eleazer 37
  Henry 181, 207
  Jeremiah 277
  John 113, 138
  Mayfield 43
  Nathaniel 281
  Reddick 213
  Samuel 104
  Thomas ... 65, 203, 315
Bellamy
  Alexander 31
Bellar
  Morgan 313
Beltcher
  William 270
Bence
  William 287
Bencon
  William Jr. 149

Bender
  John 114
Benge
  Micajah 86
Bennel
  Charles 256
  Peter 59
Bennett
  Emanuel 214
  Jeremiah 162
  John 166
  Micajah 162
  Peter 105
  Richard 39
  Thomas 313
  William 262
  Winston 77, 94
Bennett: 150
Benning
  John 116
Bennock
  Peter 221
Benson
  Robert 156, 236
  Thomas 196
  Thomas W. 254
Bentley
  James 177
  John 123, 153, 242, 309
  Joseph 189
  Samuel 245
  Samuel Jr. 274
Bently
  Isaac 72
Benton
  Jesse 168
  Jessee 202
  John 218
  Jonathan 168, 202, 240, 282

Benton, cont.
  Levi 88
Berckum
  Alen 65
Berdles
  William 88
Bergamy
  John 291
Bergen
  David 258
Bernard
  Robert 91
Berrian
  Thomas M. 293
Berrien
  John M. 229
  John McPherson .. 241
  Thomas Moore 161
Berry
  Dabny 260
  James 226, 299
  Jesse 58
  John 285, 289
Bert
  Joseph 305
Bertram
  James 256
Bessent
  Abraham 217
Best
  Jacob 269
Bethune
  John 8
  Lathland 74
Betsell
  Godfrey 145
Bettice
  Wyott 27
Bettis
  John 10

Beurdeng
  John 297
Bevell
  P. 149
Bevill
  James 14
Beville
  Claborn 308
Bibb
  Peyton 118, 203
Biddle
  Abner 74
Bigham
  James ... 189, 240, 268
  Samuel 245
Bilbo
  Archibald 317
Billingsbea
  John 55
Billingsby
  Cyrus 169
Billingslea
  Cerous 2
Billups
  Robert 245
Binion
  John 119, 157, 311
Binning
  Joseph 103
Binns
  William 47
Bird
  Andrew 22
  James 13, 71
  Jesse 9, 36
  Samuel 12
  William 153, 290
Birdson
  Isaac 240
Birdsong
  Isaac 90

Birdsong, cont.
  Isac 55
  James 213
  John 163
Birk
  Charles 78
Bishop
  Charles 15
  John 177
  Reuben 227
Biurdon
  John H. 318
Bivin
  William 286
Bivins
  Shadrick 1
Black
  James A. 291
  John 136
  Thomas 60, 102
Blackburn
  Daniel J. 216
  Daniel T. 150
  John 181
Blackeley
  Jesse 313
Blackley
  Jesse 274
  William 86
Blackmon
  James 244
  John P. 170, 254
Blacksell
  Lee 105, 124, 162
Blackshear
  David 217
  Elijah 219
  Enick 253
  Joseph 25, 197, 216
Blackson
  James 203

Blackstocks
   John 135
Blackwell
   Dunstar 53
   Joseph 243
   Ralph 190
Blair
   Hugh 131
   James 259
   John 217
Blake
   Henry 147
   John 27
   Joseph 286
   William 35, 48
Blakey
   Thos. 152
Blalock
   Gibson 215
   Giles 128
   Reuben 145
   Siles 162
   William 96, 273
Blanchard
   Benjamin 7
Blanchart
   James 169
Bland
   Stephen 86
Bledsoe
   Baley 316
   James 314
   Jesse 255
   John 162
   Moses 288
Blount
   Betan 198
   Isaac 243
   James G. 241, 245
   Luke 314
   Stephen 24

Blount, cont.
   Stephen W. 89, 237
   Thomas 81
   William H. 305
Blunt
   James 280
   James G. 230
   Stephen W. 171, 188
Boatwright
   Daniel 214
Bobo
   Dempsey 246
Bogan
   Shadrack 97
Boggs
   Aron 56
   James 130
Bohannon
   James 48
Boice
   Brinkley 166
Boid
   Elijah 293
Boisclair
   Michael 222
Boisclean
   Micheal 199
Boles
   Henry 107
   Job J. 48
   John 258
Boling
   John 183
Bolles
   Job F. 109
Bolton
   Menoah 253
Bond
   Edward 161
   George T. 278
   John 44, 85

Bond, cont.
   Nathan 234
   Nelson 130
   Richard 113
   Robert 85
Bone
   James 237, 309
Bonner
   Alexander 213
   Henry 96
   Jeremiah 39
   Pleasant 231
   Thomas 119, 126, 190
   Zadock 112
Bonwell
   Charles 244
Boog
   John 105, 210
Booker
   Richardson 23, 103
Booles
   Jesse 55, 216
Boon
   Benjamin 112
   Exom 190
   Exum 126
   Martin 99
Booth
   Andrew 294
   Gabriel 140
   Thomas 226
   Zachariah 20
Boothe
   Andrew 135
Borders
   Andrew 181
Boreland
   Abraham 38
Borem
   Thomas 157

Boren
    Joseph 136, 178
    Robert 130, 221
Boring
    William C. 203
Borland
    William 249
Boroughs
    Benjamin 221
    Thomas P. 276
Bosser
    Jacob H. 179
Bostick
    John 237
    Nathan 104
    Nathaniel 270
    Rhesa 257
Bostie
    John 234
Boston
    John 82, 211
Bostwick
    Chesley 63
    John 58, 67, 92
    John Green 208
    Little B. 66
    Littleberry 181
    Rhesa 150
Boswell
    George 136
    Josias 285, 311
    Williamson 212
Bothwell
    Ebenezer 232, 240
Bottey
    William 315
Bourguin
    John 48
Bourguoin
    John Jacob 28

Bourke
    Michael 237
Bourks
    Robert 219
Bouyer
    Bathazer 192
Bowden
    John 156
Bowdre
    Edward 40
Bowells
    Allen 295
Bowen
    Christopher 250
    Elisha 156
    Nathan 293
    Thomas 185
Bower
    Benaniel 237
    Benannual 145
    Benanuel 256
    Binaniul 227
    William 306
Bowers
    Arthur 167
Bowler
    James C. 84
Bowles
    Jesse 78
    John G. 310
    William 48
Bowling
    Robert 81, 148, 176
    Thomas 87
Bowman
    Robert 186
Box
    Michael 185
Boyakin
    John 74

Boyd
    Andrew 176
    Bane 293
    Charles 124
    Henry 273
    John 12
Boyet
    James 174
Boykin
    Fancis 220
    Lodowick 117
Boyl
    James 199
Boyle
    John 235
    Robert 194, 233
Boyt
    Stephen 289
Bozeman
    David 280
    John 222
Brach
    Nathaniel P. 49
Brack
    Benjamin 8
    William 98
Brackenridge
    Richard 81
Brackin
    Isaac 137
Bradford
    Nathan 224
Bradley
    Abner 292
    Micajah 4
Bradshaw
    Henry 16
    Thomas 16
Brady
    Samuel 29

Braint
  William 172
Brake
  Matthew 89
Bramblet
  Newton 266
Branch
  Elias 285
Brand
  Jonas 288
Brannen
  Solomon 231
Brannon
  John 143
Bransford
  John 142, 303
Brantley
  Amos 2
  Greene D..............271
  John 173, 314
  Joseph..............82, 91
Brantly
  Gideon...................289
  Lewis....................171
Brasellon
  Jacob 246
Brasswell
  Allen........................68
  Kindred Jr. 89
  Robert 62
Braswell
  Kendred 189
  Robert 142
  Sampson 140
  Samuel 46
Bratcher
  Henry......................40
Braughton
  John 66
Brazill
  Allen.........................2

Breed
  John 38
  Nathan 272
Brenin
  Timothy 204
Brewer
  Ambrose 162
  Barrett....................28
  David 39
  Drewry...................39
  George 146
  Isaac 196
  Joseph..................107
  Robert...................287
Briant
  John 302
Brice
  John 69
  Robert...................258
Bridge
  Thillis C.................284
Bridger
  Joseph Laurence 84
Bridges
  Jeremiah 220
  Thomas...................88
  William 275
Bridgewater
  Samuel 68
Briers
  Lawrence................34
Briggs
  Elkanah............23, 57
  James 53
  Samuel 20
Brigham
  Emerald................288
Brindley
  Fraser 58
Brinkley
  J. 100

Brinson
  Daniel....................247
Brinton
  William W............ 170
Briscoe
  John..................... 119
  John Jr. 207
Briscor
  John..................... 294
Britain
  Henry L. 310
  Hurry 280
Britton
  Burwell 196
  Thomas 155
Brixey
  Thomas 53
Broadnax
  John H. 144, 163
Brock
  William 226, 282
Brockman
  Elijah.................... 256
Brodnax
  John H. 276
  Robert........... 186, 292
  William E............. 316
Brook
  Bevins 288
  Preston................. 269
  William 291
Brooker
  Joseph 207
Brooks
  Abram 268
  Christopher.......... 103
  Elisha 272
  George 101
  Isaac 203
  Isham 296
  Jacob P. 280

Brooks, cont.
- James 118
- Job 107
- John 182, 232, 262
- John T. 288
- Jonathan 43
- Lodowick 58
- Martin 313
- Michajah 98
- Robert 115
- Samuel 103, 150
- Silas 193
- Thomas 179
- William 134

Broome
- John 16, 46

Broughton
- Charles 74
- John 248
- John B. 262
- John H. 144
- William 47

Brove
- Exum 146

Brown
- Benjamin 275
- Charles . 132, 149, 198
- David 97
- Eppis 171
- Epps 66
- Ezekiel 95, 163
- Francis 34
- George R. 239
- Henry 71, 80, 132
- Hiram 299
- Hollinger 107, 114, 126
- James 12, 175, 301
- Jeremiah 54
- Jesse 317
- Jesse S. 308

Brown, cont.
- John .. 7, 38, 132, 137, 143, 242, 266, 270, 310
- John S. 299
- Joseph 139, 239
- Lewis 202
- Lewis S. 210, 256
- Martin 284
- Morgan 135, 274
- Perter 302
- Reuben 174
- Richard 188
- Richard G. 174
- Ridgdon 306
- Rigdon 292
- Robert 98, 155, 305
- Sampson 162
- Samuel 87, 137
- Seth 297
- Thomas 255, 283
- William 54, 70, 87, 189, 196, 216, 241, 267
- Wm. A. 298
- Wyatt 168

Browning
- Benjamin 32
- Daniel 131
- John 126
- Stephen 192
- William 106

Broxton
- Hezekiah 77

Bruce
- Robert 294

Brumfield
- James 142

Brunson
- Whitehouse 23

Brutchfield
- John W. 188

Bruton
- Benjamin 9, 178

Brux
- William 128

Bryan
- Alexander 192
- Benjamin 48, 218
- Edward 28, 282
- Frederick 179
- Henry 203
- James 63
- John 83
- Needham 73
- Reding 142
- Robert 99, 277
- Samuel 135
- William 1, 166

Bryant
- Benjamin 232
- Clement 233
- Edward 208
- Eli 85, 167
- Jason 248
- John 101, 165, 314
- Joseph B. 219
- Nathan 23
- Royal Bryant 168
- Samuel 107
- William 181
- William B. 168

Bryd
- Samuel 142

Buch
- Austin 300

Buchainon
- Samuel 198

Buchanan
- Lemuel 194

Buchannan
    Lemuel D. 296
Buchannon
    Daniel 242
Buck
    Fearney................134
    William 224
Buckannon
    James.....................56
Bucker
    Britton 191
Buckhalter
    Jones....................316
    Michael 216
Buckhaman
    Patrick C................65
Buckhannon
    John 253
    Thomas 71
Buckhanon
    Thomas 277
Buckholts
    Peter 71
    William 65
Buckler
    Elijah 130
Buckley
    Elijah 282
Buckner
    Benjamin 273
    Daniel 244
    Eli..........................312
    Parham 123
Bucks
    John 252
    William 93
Budges
    Merrell 75
Buford
    Henry 249
    John 249

Bugg
    Edmund...............260
    Samuel 20
    William 126
    William A. 185
Buggs
    Aron.......................60
Buison
    Hezekiah 72
Buland
    James 234
Bulett
    Blasingame 290
Bulger
    Thomas..................93
Bull
    James H. 206
    John.......................71
    Thomas...............119
Bullard
    Amos...................308
    James 222
    Tapley..................238
    William 295
Bulloch
    Batson 267
    Burrel 94
    Hawkins 19
    James S. 283, 306
    William B. 212
Bullock
    Batson 63, 72
    Burrell 12
    Burwell.................155
    James 159
    James S. 249
Bulman
    Thomas..................75
Bunce
    Christopher F.......233
    Simon 301

Bunch
    Doctor..................246
    Frederick...............91
Bunkley
    Jesse......................31
    Joshua.................187
Bunn
    Moses 88
Bunyard
    Ephraim 104
Burch
    Charles..................26
    Jesse....................232
    Joseph 26
    Richard 144, 255
    Richard C. 175
    Samuel G. 181
    William P. 80, 131
Burden
    Joseph 11
Burdett
    John.....................182
Burdine
    John.....................177
Burgay
    John.....................114
Burges
    Jonathan..............314
Burgess
    John.....................151
    Jonathan..............258
Burham
    Charles..................87
Burk
    Edward................139
    Joshua.................146
    Michael 53
Burke
    David.....................67
    Michael 31, 74

Name Index

Burke, cont.
    Thomas.... 35, 98, 106, 196
Burkes
    Charles 130
    William 301
Burn
    Jacob 228
Burnes
    William 281
Burnett
    James 148, 301
    John 251
    John Jr. 267
    Samuel 120
Burney
    Arthur 79, 183
    Willis 10, 72, 313
Burns
    David M................ 295
    William 87
Burroughs
    Benjamin...... 239, 294
Burrow
    James 304
Burrows
    James 108
Bursay
    Nathan 76
Burshell
    John 206
Burson
    Elisha 258
Burt
    Robert 234
Burtan
    James 279
Burton
    Benjamin...... 198, 283
    James 283
    John 55

Burton, cont.
    Leroy 299, 302
    Robert 230
Bush
    Charles.................210
    David............. 62, 131
    John 129
    Levi 27
    Littleberry 132
    Sanders 14
    Thomas M.... 162, 310
    William 143
Bussey
    Malichiah..............232
    Nathan... 83, 157, 275
Busten
    Thomas 299
Bustin
    Thomas 313
Butler
    Aaron 94
    Edmund 112
    Edward .. 94, 201, 267
    Joel 171
    John 13, 77, 86
    John G...................242
    John Gould 238
    John W..................120
    Peter P. 130
    Samuel.................300
    Stephen................181
    William 44, 108
    Zachariah..............119
Butt
    Archibald 134
Butter
    Reuben...................22
Butterman
    James....................194
Buttrill
    Thomas 9

Buttrill, cont.
    William 303
Butts
    Anthony 115
    Edmund...............230
    Henry....139, 180, 228
    John H. 159
    Simmons.......159, 256
Buzbee
    Nimrod 214
Byford
    William 95
Byington
    Amos F..................239
Byne
    William ..77, 102, 133, 171
Byrns
    James....................308

C

C*
    Peter 18
Cabaness
    Harrison 118
Cabell
    Robert J................193
Caboness
    Henry......................28
Caboniss
    George 43
    Henry B. 43
Cade
    Guilford 150, 196
    John B. 241, 261
Cadenhead
    James....................277
Caile
    William 172

Cain
  Abel 36, 94, 138
  Arcibald 301
  Charles 186
  Elijah 163
  Elisha 282
  Isaac 293
  William 8
Cairey
  Robert 110
Cairy
  William 114
Calder
  John 225
Caldwell
  Henry G. 50
  John 22
  Richard 227
  William R. 224
Calhoon
  Angus 226
  Darby 152
  John 158
  Micajah 19
  Samuel 307
Calhoun
  Josiah 115
  Samuel 250
Call
  William 246
Callaghan
  Thomas 25
Callahan
  John 49
Callaway
  David 118
  Enoch 291
  Joshua 128
  Joshua S. 206
  Noah 268

Calloway
  David 140
  Elijah 278
  Elisha 204
  Joshua S. 220
Callum
  Elijah 260
Camp
  Andrew 62
  Burwell 145
  Cial 87
  Hosea 111
  William 38, 62
Campbell
  Archibald. 31, 45, 161, 177, 198, 284
  Eli 275
  Jacob 187
  James 302
  James H. 237
  Jesse 67, 107
  John 7, 62, 192
Campton
  John 165
  Jourdan 139
Canady
  Stephen 169
Candichia
  John M. 248
Candlar
  Daniel 129
Candler
  Daniel 85
  Hezekiah 49
  Jeremiah 96
  Mark A. 211
  Sterling 85
  Zachariah 75
Canlor
  Daniel 65

Cannady
  John 242
Cannon
  Archibold 153
  Burwell 308
  Caleb 48
  James 110
  Robert D. 299
  Samuel 5
Cantelore
  Thomas 111
Capter
  Joseph 186
Carathers
  Aaron 37
  William 124
Card
  Abram 248, 268
Cardin
  Jonnis 207
Carel
  William 60
Carey
  John P. 178, 215
Carleton
  Henry Jr. 83
  Larken 295
  Thomas 44
Carlisle
  John 227
Carlton
  Henry Jr. 89
  Larkin 311
Carmichael
  John 5
  Joseph W. 283
Carnes
  Peter Johnston 17
  Thomas Petters 10
Carpenter
  George 101

Name Index

Carpenter, cont.
    Jesse 165
    John 157
    Joshua 95
    Reuben 146

Carr
    Benjamin 110
    Henry 135
    James ... 5, 15, 45, 114
    Thomas 214
    Thomas Dabney ... 283

Carrell
    Harrel H. 232
    John 181
    William 148

Carrigan
    William 144

Carrol
    Sterling 108

Carson
    John E. 103
    Joseph 32

Carswell
    Alexander 50
    John 35

Carter
    Baynes 38
    Charles 118, 250
    Charles R. 93
    David 117, 170
    Frederick 179, 196
    George 266
    Isaac 218
    James 253
    John 60, 142, 232, 235, 268
    Joseph 2, 18, 123
    Littleton 27
    Mathew 281
    Michael 114
    Moore 82

Carter, cont.
    Nicholas 253
    Richard D. 114
    Robert 315
    Samuel ... 94, 125, 253
    Solomon 38
    Thomas 34, 82, 106
    William 172, 220

Cartledge
    John 199

Cartwright
    John 150, 157

Caruthers
    George 124
    James 119

Carver
    James 154
    Jesse 154

Carvill
    John 269

Carwell
    James 75

Cary
    James 247

Casaty
    William 309

Casey
    James 103, 268
    John 114
    Thomas 22

Cash
    James 72

Cashin
    John 192

Casly
    Warham 60

Cason
    Hillory 231
    John 177
    Josiah 188
    Seth 298

Cassels
    Elias 90, 197

Castelo
    Thomas 181

Casten
    Patrick 11

Caswell
    Alexander 10, 13
    James 84, 197
    John 1, 11
    Martin 18

Catchen
    Meredith 120

Catching
    Benjamin 12

Cates
    Charles 304
    Thomas 245
    William 184

Cathrell
    Joshua 106

Cato
    Cullin 178
    Wyche 50

Cauly
    William 169

Cavanah
    William 21

Cavenah
    William 49

Cawley
    William 197

Cawsly
    William 66

Cawthon
    Ashly 220

Cawthorn
    James 315
    William 21

Cawthow
    John 288

Chaffin
  John 105, 164
  Nathan....................37
Chain
  Isaiah 303
  William 123
Chalmers
  William 226
Chambers
  John 256, 279
  Joseph B. 27
  Joseph Boyle.........173
  Robert 214
Chambles
  Samuel..................165
Chambless
  Samuel..................131
Champ
  William 101
Champion
  Eli..........................202
  Elias 295, 308
Chance
  Vincent 18
Chancelor
  Gilbert...................204
Chandler
  Allen......................308
  Bailey....................312
  George...................288
  Richard 270
  Robert 312
  Solmon 166
Chaneker
  Jacob 224
Channel
  Matthew 97
Chapman
  Lemuel..................316
  Solomon 295

Chappel
  James ...113, 209, 248
  Obediah 237
Charles
  John......................235
Charleton
  John K. M. 187
  Thomas..................25
Charlton
  John K. 259
  John K. M. 240
  Thomas W. P. 52
Chason
  James 174
Chatham
  Josiah 275
  Thomas.................309
Cheatham
  Charles .150, 234, 291
  Obadiah P. 302
  William 13
Cheek
  Ellis 268
Cheely
  John......................238
Chieves
  Grief......................232
  Gruf 173
Child
  Joshua 205
Childers
  Nicholas........107, 230
  Osborn 224
  Thomas.........273, 294
Childress
  William..................151
Childs
  Isaac 171
Chiles
  David 310

Chinault
  John....................... 13
Chinken
  John....................... 64
Chisolm
  Edmund Burke 92
  John....................... 64
  William 113
Chivers
  Joel 98, 239
  Willis 46
Christian
  Abda 53
  Charles................. 223
  Charles W. 250
  Edward L. 230
  Elijah.................... 286
  James 54, 66, 67
  Presley 95, 236
  Rufus.................... 271
  Simion 303
  William 4, 103
Christie
  Elijah..................... 37
Christopher
  Benjamin 50
  David............ 144, 259
Church
  Constantine . 243, 266
Cimpson [Simpson]
  Alexander............. 269
Claiborn
  James 253
Clanton
  Littleberry 168
Clark
  Archibald 80, 210
  Charles................. 173
  David... 151, 164, 180, 208
  Jame..................... 292

Clark, cont.
    James 206, 254
    John 225, 306
    Joshua 130, 176
    Larken Jr. 95
    Larkin 128
    Micajah 155
    Robert.................... 29
    Samuel 145
    Stephen B......... 84, 91
    Stephen Brown 142
    William 60, 68, 142
    Zachariah 1

Clarke
    Archibald.............. 101
    David 125
    Gabriel 183
    James 118, 248
    Johnson 19
    Joseph Hill 109
    Joshua 73
    Samuel 177

Clarkson
    Joseph 68

Clay
    Jesse 257
    Samuel 64, 312

Clayton
    Augustin S. 157
    George R... 57, 74, 108
    George Rootes 67
    James 227
    Thomas................. 314

Cleaveland
    Joseph 168
    Neal 191

Cleavland
    Joseph 194

Cleghorn
    William 95

Clements
    Andrew 84
    Gabriel 76
    Jacob 109
    John 122, 311
    Thomas 245
    William 104

Clemm
    Joseph C. 306

Cleveland
    Benjamin 143
    Gilbert..................302
    Jacob M.................313
    Joseph 250
    Larkin 201

Clifton
    Henry 207
    Thomas 207, 248
    William 268

Cloud
    James...................227

Clouds
    Wylly 93

Clowdes
    Wylie 252

Clowdis
    Wylie 106

Clower
    Jesse....................145
    Morgan.................102

Cloyd
    Thomas 192

Clubb
    James...................314

Clubreath
    Anguish.................273

Coarsey
    John 51

Coates
    William 28

Coats
    John 78, 133, 134
    William 20

Cobb
    Benjamin..............114
    Henry W. 218
    John 175, 236
    John A. 110
    John S...................274

Cobbs
    John 67

Cock
    Caleb.........................3
    Jack F. 210
    Needham 42

Cockburn
    John A. 225

Cocke
    Caleb......................22

Cockran
    Jacob......................76
    James...........2, 28, 52
    John 12
    Moses...................281

Cocks
    James.....................41

Cody
    Jacob......................59
    Michael 292

Coffee
    John 99, 143

Coffin
    Leonard 277

Cogle
    Roger 56

Cohoon
    Ephraim 47

Cohorn
    John 206
    Robert....................29

Cohron
   James 223
   Mulkey 297
Coil
   James 154
Coker
   Philip 42
   Thompson 130
Cokron
   Job 18
Colbert
   John 62
   John G. 235, 313
   Larkin 314
   Nicholas 46
   Philip 46, 75
   Richard 316
   Richmond 280
   William 14
Colclough
   William 143
Coldwell
   James 116
Cole
   James D. 167
   Robert 66
   Thomas 83, 205
   William 266
Coleman
   Benjamin 261
   Daniel 150, 162
   Elliot 138
   Isaac 80
   James 11
   John 124
   Jonathan 50
   Lindzey 192
   Samuel 31
   Stephen 166
   Thomas 120, 149, 295, 302

Coleman, cont.
   Thompson 25
   William 171
Colins
   Jesse 66
Collars
   Richard 253
Collear
   Thos. 153
Collier
   Benjamin 131, 218
   Edward 282
   Isac 60
   John 204
   Marrel 208
   William 4, 20
   Williamson 40
Collin
   Jesse 85
Collins
   Cornelius 160, 255
   Eli 233
   George 48
   Hardy 139, 289
   James ... 130, 159, 209
   Jesse 237
   John ... 64, 66, 89, 115, 135, 152, 234
   Joseph 183
   Josiah 85
   Lewis 50, 105
   Peter H. .. 96, 115, 124, 176
   William 116
   Wilson 164, 246
Colly
   John 242
   Nelson 123
Colmonsneal
   John 150

Colquet
   John 187
   William 123
Colquit
   Robert 45
Colquitt
   John H. 308
   Robert 18
   Thomas 173
   Walter T. 308
Colson
   Abraham 28
   Dennis 13, 84
   Henry 84
   William 226, 296
Colton
   Richard 240
Combs
   John 203
Comean
   John 100
Compton
   John W. 205, 307
   Jordan 246
   Pleasant . 79, 105, 250
Conard
   Jonathan 75
Cone
   John 237
   Peter 195, 231
   William 36, 294
   William Jr. 118
Coney
   Aquilla 75
   Jeremiah 50, 75
Connel
   Jesse 58, 273
   Newdy G. 168
Connell
   Newday G. 132
   Thomas 228

Connell, cont.
William 175
Connelly
Nicholas 194, 206
Conner
Baley 191
Boley 85
Frederick 22
George 32
James 303
Jesse 262, 280
John 16, 238
Lewis 250
Willis 225
Willson 209
Cook
Benjamin 154
Burwell 317
John 4, 17
Joseph 180
Julius 116, 151
Philip 123, 173
William 33, 82, 139, 143, 198, 204
Zadock 35, 87
Cooke
John F. 134
Cooksey
William 228
Cooper
Arthur 41
Augustin 166
Cornelius 34
Drury 254
Ephraim 112, 142, 150
James A. 276
James W. 248, 265
John 51, 82, 98, 99, 180
John B. 245
John W. 112

Cooper, cont.
Jonathan 88, 272
Joseph 53, 295
Joseph Jr. 99
Joseph W. 290
Philip 51
Thomas 6
William 185
Cope
Adam 17
Charles 101
George L. 210
Copeland
John 83
Thomas 309
Coplin
John 50
Copp
Daniel D. 279
Coram
Thomas 271
Corcker
John 214
Cork
Elijah 91
Corker
Jesse 120
Philip 29
Corley
Benjamin 115
Edmond 167
Edmund 70
Cormick
John 34
Cornelius
George 154, 203
Rowland 24
Cornett
Eli 232
Josiah 53

Cornwall
Daniel 207
Cosby
Garland 25
John 294
Cothran
Josiah D. 186
Cottins
Joseph 11
Cottle
John J. 115
Cotton
Alexander 127
John A. 272
Richard 297
Smith 15
Couch
James 317
Coulter
Ford 116
Peter 189
William 68
Courier
Edward 299
Coursey
Absalom 52
Absalam 46
Courson
James 34
John 316
Courter
Harmon 110
Cousins
Greene 312
Covington
Thomas 188
Cowan
William A. 126
Cowart
John 19
Stephen 201

Cowart, cont.
   William .109, 184, 250
   Zachariah 298
Cowden
   Elijah 140
Cowen
   James....................206
Cowles
   Asbury 296
Cowley
   William 94
Cowling
   Slauter 40, 51
Cox
   Adam....................288
   Aris 285
   Asa 43, 115
   Cary 44
   Edward 63, 116
   Emanuel 267
   Ephraim..................78
   Henry...........114, 235
   James....................268
   John 2, 50
   John J. 126
   Matthew 5
   Moses 78
   Robert R...............196
   Thomas 129
   Zebulon 243
Crabtree
   John 94
Crafford
   Archibald 51
Craft
   Garrett..................225
Cragg
   Henry 31
Craircather
   William 85

Cramer
   John C. 165
Crane
   Daniel M................301
Crapon
   Thomas.................275
Crawford
   Charles 285
   Charles A. 247
   David M.................227
   Elisha 89
   Hardy 203, 257
   Joel 100
   Joseph...................193
   Robert...................104
   Solomon..................63
   William.................203
Crawley
   Archibald................16
Cray
   Benjamin G. 231
Credill
   Moses....................220
Creel
   Elijah....................302
Creny
   Isaac 68
Crestler
   Absalom................221
Crews
   David 24
   Isaac 101
   James W........180, 221
   Joseph...................283
   Thomas...................10
Crittenden
   Robert G. 246
Crittenger
   Henry P. 66
Crittinger
   Pryor......................66

Crocket
   Samuel 244
Crockett
   Elias 166
   Samuel 302
Croft
   Stephen................136
Cromby
   Anthony 284
Cromwell
   John B. 307
Crosier
   John.......................59
Cross
   Stephen.................. 22
Crouder
   James 91
Crow
   Martin 254
Crowder
   James 41
Crowell
   Henry 113, 158
Crozier
   John....................... 13
Cruise
   Isham 10
Cruse
   Arthur 262
Crutchfield
   John W. 268
Culbertson
   David 246
Culbreath
   Anguish................304
   John......................224
Culpepper
   John....................... 32
   Marriner 202
Culthbert
   John A. 290

Culwell
Joshua 293
Cumming
John........ 52, 105, 212
JohnSr..................... 21
Joseph 255, 271
William.................. 184
Cummingham
Samuel 89
Cummins
David 312
William................. 299
Cump
Thomas................. 149
Cuningham
John...................... 136
Cunningham
Andrew 45
Drurry 103
George 46
James 28, 41, 44
John............... 54, 276
Samuel 43
William........ 245, 253
Cunyers
William................. 299
Cupp
John....................... 73
Curl
Kinchen .. 98, 128, 195
Kinchin................. 312
Curll
Kinchen 81
Curreten
James 278
Curry
David 301
Isaac 256
James A................. 234
John...... 151, 209, 272
Joseph 28

Curry, cont.
Nicholas 5
Peter M. 150, 190
Quinny 93
Thomas 197
Whitmill................204
William 70
Cuthbert
Alfred 136
John 150, 210
Louis B....................63
Cutter
Henry S................195

D

Dabney
James........... 178, 304
Daeskill
Wooten 317
Dale
Samuel 15
Dame
Charles......... 203, 226
Dancy
Francis 71
Danely
Thomas 22
Daniel
Allen.......... 34, 61, 217
Curtice 77
Enoch 51
Ezekiel 153
Ezekiel Jr..... 174, 296
Henning 122
Isaac............. 178, 310
James..... 92, 108, 259
James K. 58
Jepthat....................57
John 155, 267
Julius 175

Daniel, cont.
Lewis 316
Moses 25, 233, 244
Samuel C. 227
Septhah 44
Stephen 69, 234
William ... 32, 175, 309
Danner
John 226
Danney
David 228
Darben
William 99
Darby
James............ 104, 145
Jeremiah 69
Dardin
John 70
Darnell
John 172
Darrity
Dempsey 153
Darsey
James..................... 20
William 181
Dasher
Benjamin 2
C. H...................... 283
Christian 82
Christian H. 295
Gallip 312
Martin 197
Samuel................. 236
Davenport
Jack Smith 18
William 82
David
Joshua 268
Davidson
George H. 63
John 132

Davies
  William 217, 222
Davis
  Aaron 179, 296
  Abner 37
  Abram 118
  Archibald 178, 275
  Arthur 136
  Austin J. 140
  Benjamin .19, 93, 147, 250
  Edward Lloyed 47
  Elnothan 115
  Frederick 230
  Garah 164
  George 39, 310
  George R. 292
  Henry 104
  Hezekiah 225
  Hozias 245
  Ishmeal 115
  James 145, 168
  James J. 278
  Jeremiah 158
  John 16, 120, 122, 154, 224, 247, 306
  John S. 258
  Jonathan 47, 98
  Joseph 19
  Joshua 282
  Reuben Easton 160
  Samuel 27, 51, 143
  Samuel H. 302
  Simeon 317
  Thomas 5, 37, 213, 276, 297
  Walter 104, 124
  William ..98, 126, 212, 269, 306, 313
  Zackariah 187

Davison
  Hugh 151
Dawkins
  Francis 145
Dawns
  Silas 158
Dawson
  Charles 291
  George 285
  Henry 223, 273
  Henry C. 306
  John 193, 237
  John E. 81, 123
  Kinchin 309
  Reuben 209
  Riger 55
  Robert 108
  Thomas 49, 58, 164
Day
  Ambrose 104
  David 135
  Hiram 282
  Stephen 235
De Montmollen
  John Sam'l 8
Deadwilder
  Martin 121, 245
Deafnell
  Bush 189
Deakle
  William 261
Dean
  Elijah 277
  Frederick 149
  Joel 257
  John 81, 292
  Pinket 203
  Ransom L. 260
  Wiley 295
  Wm E. 272

Deare
  Stephen 263
Dearing
  Abner J. 304
  Asa 288
Dearmond
  William P. 243
Dearmont
  Wm. P. 223
Deason
  Michael 302
Deering
  John B. 72
Dees
  James 71
  Matthew M. 306
Dekle
  Charles 44
  William G. 315
DeLaigle
  Nicholas 163
Delapiriere
  Ange 261
Dell
  John 148, 235
Deloach
  Ephraim 172
  John 219
Deloatch
  William 306
Deloath
  Abraham 96
Demere
  Raymond 12, 260
  Raymond Jr. 91
Demire
  Raymond Jr. 113
DeMontmollin
  John S. 105
Demott
  Garrett 118

Name Index

Denard
    Jesse 304
Denman
    James 85
    John 136
Denmark
    Allen 251
    Seaborn 71, 138
    Stephen 6, 19
Dennard
    Bird 94
    Isaac 126, 165
    Jared 268
    John 94
Dennis
    Charles A. 196
    Daniel 38, 48, 49
    Joseph W. 191
    Peter 18
    Richard 23, 25, 50
    Stephen 201
Denny
    David 128
Dens
    Robert 297
Densler
    Philip 61
Denson
    Cally 84
    Joseph 75
    Joseph W. 127
Dent
    Dennis 265
    Michael L. 311
    Nathaniel 269
    Smith 155
    Thomas 43
Derby
    James 41
Derican
    Hiram M. 278

Desmukes
    James 307
    Juprey 313
Devall
    Alexander 73
Deveaux
    Charles H. 80
Devenport
    Henry 126
    John M. 255
    Josiah 154
    William 152
Devereux
    Samuel 38
Devine
    William H. 139
Dewett
    Lewis 289
Dewitt
    Charles 235
Dewly
    William H. 189
DeWolf
    William 182
Dexter
    Payne 71
Dial
    Larkin 87
Diamond
    Robert 16
Dicke
    Washington 154
Dicken
    Thomas 87, 190
Dickenson
    Joseph 159
Dickerson
    George 285
    John 63
    Joseph 172
    Joseph Jr. 185

Dickinson
    Zachariah 281
Dickson
    David 46
    James 262
    John 150
    Micajah 215
    Michael 301
    Thomas 23, 82
    William H. 248, 287
Digby
    Benjamin 192
Dill
    Andrew 183
    John 82
Dillard
    Collin 308
    Edmund 274
    George W. 77, 114
    Isaac 160
    Sampson 207
    Talliver 202
    Tolliver 260
Dillen
    Thomas 13
Dilliard
    John 282
Dillon
    John 102
    William C. 243
Dilworth
    George 171, 183
    James 215, 242
Dimond
    James 205
Dinkins
    William 96
Divine
    William 89
Dix
    Charles 182

Dixon
  Allen 156
  Ephraim 85
  Hugh 145
  Micajah 130
  Michael 220
  Nathan 232
  Robert 176, 232
  Tillman S. 38
  Tilman S. 106, 116
  Windsor 67
Dixson
  Robert 76
Doad
  Robert 271
Dobbins
  Pliny 180
Dobbs
  David 294
  Jeremiah 168
  Josiah 58
  Thomas 235
  William 193
Dobson
  Joseph 225, 298
  Joshua 289
  Neely .65, 70, 269, 304
Dodd
  Robert 251
Dodridge
  Elisha 99
  Noah 114
Dodson
  Edmund 273, 286
  Fleming 195
  Joshua 40, 87
Dodwell
  Hezekiah 265
Doherty
  Thomas 198

Doles
  Thomas 33, 50, 160
Dollar
  Clement 170
  Henry 286
Dolly
  Daniel 59
Dolvin
  William 65, 104
Domminy
  John 169
Donaldson
  Peter 176, 225, 232
Donalson
  Peter 172
Dooly
  Bennett 276
  John M. 58, 169
  Thomas 129
  William 175
Dopson
  Joseph 9
Dorman
  Cullen 131
Dormeny
  William 141
Dorothy
  Daniel 148
Dorsett
  Joseph 231
Dorsey
  Andrew 242
  William 215
Dossey
  Lemuel 206
Dougherty
  Charles 32
  Dempsey 73
  George 107
Douglass
  David 85

Douglass, cont.
  Francis 122
  Isaac 111
  Jones 115
  Matin 180
  Robert 63, 186, 316
Dowdey
  Wiley 279
Dowdy
  Wiley 308
Downer
  John 57
Downes
  Silas 191
Downs
  Crawford 135
  Isaac 209
  Silas 36
Dowsing
  William 276
Doyle
  Francis 79
Dozier
  James 63, 113
  John 31
  Richard 238
  Woody 225
Drake
  Archibald 79, 265
  Elias 64
  Shamme 83
Drane
  Shemel 69
  Stephen 249
Drawdy
  William 306
Dregors
  John 294
Drew
  Joseph Jr 182
  Josiah 53

Name Index

Driggars
  Jonas 183
  Simon 183
Driscoll
  Jacob 185
Driskel
  David B. 257
Driskell
  Wooden 206
Drysdal
  John 290
Dubery
  James 293
Dubignon
  Henry 143
  Joseph 91, 113, 307
Duck
  Timothy 122, 198
Duckworth
  Jeremiah 225
Dudley
  Edward 312
  George 206
  Hudson 121
  John 7, 27
  John T. 143
  William 245
  William J. 305
Duffey
  James 125
Duglass
  Robert 14
  Wright 19
Duke
  Epps 23
  Greene R. 64
  John 92, 96
  John M. 243
  Joseph 267
  Robert 210
  Turner 317

Duke, cont.
  William 173
Dukes
  Epps 45
  Jesse 99
  Stephen 114
  Thomas 1
Duly
  Samuel 204
Dumas
  Obadiah 209
Dunaven
  Harbert 69
Duncan
  Aaron 35, 113
  Daniel 304
  Dennis 224
  John 293
  Mathew 45
  William 35
Dunefant
  Burrell 32
Dunevant
  Herbert 81
Duneway
  William 86
Dunford
  Jesse 298
Dunham
  William 77
  William A. 67, 249
Dunlap
  William 124
Dunn
  Ephiam 60
  James 148, 314
  John N. 197
  Matthew 207
  William 62
Dunston
  Charles 162

Dunwody
  John 68
Dunwoodie
  John 252
Dunwoody
  John 249, 279
Duperis
  Ulysses 238
Dupree
  Daniel 192
  Gee 314
  John 296
  Lewis J. 234
  Reed 69
  Thomas 202
Duprey
  Reid 40
Dupuis
  William 8
Durden
  William 110
Durdens
  William 44, 73
Durham
  Abner 117, 129
  George 8
  Isac 55
  James 29, 176
  John 166
  Joseph 185
  Samuel 124
  Thomas 123, 129
Durkee
  Wiliam 116
  William 79
  William H. 57, 165
Durmmond
  William 271
Durrance
  Joseph 71

Durrence
  Joseph 279
Dutton
  Henry 233
Duychinche
  Benjamin 112
Duyckinck
  Benjm. F. 151
Dyall
  George 72
Dyche
  Isaac 129
Dye
  Becham 54
  Hopkins 37
  Matin M. 250
Dykes
  Allen 292
  George 69
  James 208
  Jourdan 137

E

Eads
  Randal 75
Eady
  John 129
Eagle
  Samuel 131
Early
  Eleazer 123
  Henry 258
  Jacob 258
  Jeremiah 114
Earp
  Pullen 14
Easley
  John 4
  Richard 33
  Richd. S. 152

Easley, cont.
  Roderick 32
  William P. 234
Easly
  John 47, 85
  Warham 66
Eason
  James 157
  Parker 282
  Seth 278
Easter
  Giles 286
  John C. 310
Easternod
  William H. 256
Easters
  Lewis 221
Easton
  Philip 154
Eates
  Zachariah 204, 214
Eatman
  William 109
Eaton
  John 7
Eberhart
  David 32
  George 129
  Jacob 245
Eberhert
  Adam 147
Echols
  Robert E. 138
Ector
  Hugh 314
  Joseph 104
  William 119
  Willie B. 209
Edenfield
  John 286, 294

Edens
  Bleakley 172
Edge
  James 103
Edleman
  Moses 290
Edmonds
  John 5, 83
  Signor 93
  William 277
Edmondson
  Philemon 257
  Thomas 31
  William 254
Edmundson
  Crawford 104
  William 112
Edmunson
  Samuel 239, 254
Edrington
  Frizel M. 195
Edward
  John 313
  Thomas L. 285
  William 81, 116
Edwards
  Asa 52
  Augustine 103
  Benjamin 23
  Cullen 53, 154
  Henry L. 166
  Humphrey 292
  Jesse 151, 188
  John 256, 275
  Reuben Edward 88
  Robert 75
  Thomas 81
  William 15, 209
Eigle
  Samuel 257

Name Index

Eiland
Stephen 132
Elders
James 230
Elkins
Thomas 207
Ellen
Archilaus F. 24
Ellerbee
Edward 22
Ellice
Fielding 183
Ellington
Josiah 229
Rice 70
Elliot
George W 309
Elliott
David 205
Ebenezer 150
John 60, 149, 219
Silas 267
Ellis
Austin 156
Elisha 224
Isaac 21
John 160
Levi 63, 80, 254
Radford 20
Richard W. ... 156, 206, 231, 270
Samuel 255, 276
Thomas 90
William 31, 74
Ellison
Joseph 187
Elmore
James 71
Elsey
Berry 118, 142

Emanuel
Eli 81, 138, 174
Embree
Jess 37
Embrey
Hezekiah 235
Hezekiah L. 259
England
Elijah 309
James 194
Engle
John 96
English
James 51
Perminus 41
Thompson 257
Ennis
Charles 301
Nathaniel 97
Epperson
George 268
Epps
James 220
Erwin
Christopher 2
John M. 251
Espey
James 31
Esterwood
William 281
Ethredge
Allen 161
Eubank
William 257
Eubanks
George 80
Eubant
George 112
Evans
Charles 159, 174
David 45, 123, 204

Evans, cont.
E. 130
Edward 116
Elijah 59, 179
George M. 62
George W. 97
Henry 69
Henry W. 204
Jesse 32, 139
John 121
John A. 259
Joshua 292
Josiah 144
Mordicai 6
Thomas 133, 248
Thomas H. 313
William .171, 187, 272
Everett
Enoch 13
Hardy 117, 243
John 121, 127
John F. 136
Joshua 134
Samuel 85
Samuel H. 129
Solomon 185
Everitt
Aaron 314
Enoch 48, 248
William 252
Everte
John 71
Ewing
James 40
Josiph 228
Ezell
Hartwell 80

F

Fail
William 289
Fain
David 75
Mathew 256
Faircloth
Benjamin 164
Etheldread 168
Fambrough
Gaddeal 142
John 215
Fann
William 112
Fannin
Abraham B. 204
Isham S. 70, 223
James 218
Joham S. 276
John H. 294
Joseph D. 230
William 209, 304
Fanning
Middleton 37
William 48
Farley
Gates F. 96
James 14
Farmborough
Gadial 94
Farmbrough
John 207
Farmer
Enoch 178
Isaac 5
Mills 92
Urial 266
Farrar
John S. 127

Farrer
Barrett 79
Richard 252
Fash
Alexander 279
Fason
Thomas 239
Faulkner
William 100
Fausett
Abraham 92
Favours
Josiah 187
Fears
Zachariah 271
Feckling
Barnard F 134
Fee
Samuel 75
Feen
Henry 205
Fell
Frederick S.. 174, 229, 261
Felton
John 188
Fenn
Henry 220
Fenncy
Henry 176
Fennel
Etheldred 69
Fennell
William Augustus 249
Ferrell
Archilous 1
Byrd 14
Ferrels
Samuel 54
Fetchat
John 213

Few
Ignatius A. 160, 211
Joseph 82
Fickling
Barnard W. 272
Barnet 81
Fielder
Obadiah M. B. 269
Fields
Elijah 201
James 146
Seth 80
Zachariah 248, 262
Figg
John 241
Filchett
John 227
Fillinger
Henry 191
Robert 236
Fillingim
William 245
Fillingin
Moses 313
Finch
James 108
John 166
William 108
Findley
Samuel 185
William C. H. 205, 287
Finnie
Sterling 304
Fireash
Sion 220
Fish
Nathan 117, 125
Fitch
William 254
Fitchell
Charles 101

Fitzgerald
David 241
Fitzjarrel
David 22
Fitzpatrick
Samuel 143
Flake
Thomas................. 57
William 84
Flanagin
Joel 169
Flanagun
Thomas................ 285
Flanigan
Vincent 102
Flanneken
David 17
Flannigan
Joel 159
Flectin
Richard................ 278
Flemester
James 260
Fleming
Fengal T. 139
James ... 163, 173, 278
James S. 251
John 142, 296
Laird B. 254
Robert...... 32, 55, 279, 297
Samuel 114
William............ 80, 290
William Jr. 145
Flemister
James 271, 300
Flemming
John....................... 76
William............ 28, 210
William Jr. 152

Flerl
Isareal...................121
Fletcher
Henry 172
James... 121, 178, 313
John 12, 173, 228, 244
Willie....................206
Flinn
William 250
Flippin
William 194, 288
Fliynt
George...................276
Floid
Gilford...................257
Flournoy
Francis...................45
Gibson....................92
John B. 79, 204
Obadiah 148
Robert 33, 57
Flowers
Edward 186, 251
Richard 165
Floyd
Dolphin D. 306
Guilford.................171
John 3, 10, 44, 68, 97, 101, 269
Lewis............ 128, 235
Silas 267, 289
Uz............................68
William 189
Flurnoy
Obadiah 160
Flyd
Dolphin 296
Flynt
George...................259
Foaks
William 150

Fokes
Wm. L. 232
Folks
John 145
Folsom
Laurence................80
Lawrence............... 12
Fontain
Peter 192
Ford
Austin 204
Samuel.................278
William ..11, 124, 127, 166, 249
Fore
Jonathan 49
Forehand
Amos.....................179
Foreman
Isaac 84
Forester
Willis 300
Formby
Obadiah.................224
Forrest
John 84
Forson
Thomas...................92
Forsyth
William 259
Fort
Arthur....................226
Elias............131, 141
John 119
Moses............219, 254
Tomlinson.............193
Forth
Henry......................27
John T...................235
Thomas 14, 35, 188

Fortson
  James 208
  William 34, 140
Foster
  Arther 303
  Arthur ... 111, 168, 202
  Collier 214
  Collin 224
  Francis 166, 185
  George W. 43
  Hardy 79
  James 111
  John 38, 202, 312
Fountain
  Etheldred 201, 240, 315
  John 242
  Owen 148
  Seth 201, 287
  William 104
Fowler
  James 201
  John 80
Fox
  James 88
  Nicholas 57, 79
Foxwell
  William 5
Foyl
  William 145
Frammell
  Daniel 82
Franklin
  Bedney 34, 131
  Easom 98
  Thomas 28
Fraser
  Andrew F. 284
  Simeon A. 298
Frashier
  William 156

Frazer
  Andrew 239
  David 305
Frazier
  David 202, 282
Frazor
  David 166
Frederick
  Jacob 227
  James 161
Freeman
  Claborn 300
  Frederick 172, 181, 212, 306
  Henry 287
  James 12
  Jesse 148, 157
  Joel 310
  John 101, 299
  Joseph 59, 99, 122
  Nicholas 135
  Noah 117
  Thomas 234
  Timothy 146
Freeney
  Gilly 123
Friar
  John 24
Frost
  Johnson 158
  Joseph 206
Frowhawk
  Isham 221
Frum
  William 300
Fruman
  Henry 227
  Hugh 21
Fryer
  John 139

Fudge
  Benjamin 89
  Soloman 282
Fulcher
  Armstead 97
Fulford
  Milben 202
  Milborn 134
Fulgham
  Henry 126
  Jesse 71
Fuller
  Isaac 27
  Isham 69, 176
  Simeon 122
  Uriah 96
Fullerlove
  John 46
Fullerton
  Adam 144
  Robert 234
Fullilove
  John 55
Fulsom
  Benjamin 278
Fulton
  Samuel 10
  Thomas 53, 125
Fulwood
  Asa 186
Funderberg
  Isaac 225
Funderburg
  Isaac 112
Funderburgh
  Isaac 87
Furgerson
  Jacob 170
Furguson
  Daniel 128

Name Index

Furlow
  Martin 151
Furman
  Isaac 169
Furmer
  Uriel 129
Furn
  Elijah 202
Furr
  Paul 249
Fussell
  William 3
Futch
  Thomas 10
Futrell
  Benjamin 182

G

Gaddis
  John 69
  Thomas 191
Gaddy
  David 1
  James 35, 98
Gafford
  David 150
Gaines
  Gustavus 151
  James 245
Gains
  George G. 5
  Robert T. 284
Gaither
  Greenberry 228
Galbreath
  Daniel 307
Gallaspay
  David 193

Gallman
  John 170
Galloway
  Lewis 196
Gambell
  William 157
Gamble
  Andrew 229, 239
  Roger L. 162, 225
  Roger Lawson 235
Gammonon
  William 169
Gan
  Nathan 238
Gandey
  Brinkley 73
Gandy
  Brinkly 205
Gardner
  Jeremiah 126
  Robert A. 28
  William 44, 69
Garlington
  Christopher 211
Garlman
  David 46
Garner
  Pressley 54
  Richard 284
  Stephen 282
  William 219
Garnett
  James 157
  Rice 286
Garrason
  Michael 304
Garret
  Obediah 51
Garrett
  James K. 170
  John 60

Garrett, cont.
  Samuel 35, 101
Garrey
  Edmond 188
Garrison
  Caleb 149
  Darius 2
  John 85
  Nehemiah 135, 185
Garthright
  William 111
Gartrell
  William 37
Gartrill
  Jeremiah 79
Gary
  Richard 76
  William L. 244, 258
Gasaway
  Thomas 161
Gaseway
  John 296
Gaslin
  John 66
Gaston
  John 150
  Mathew 219
  William 142, 153, 158,
    212, 229, 255
Gasway
  Thomas 185
Gates
  Benjamin 246, 255
  Elisha 195
  Hezekiah 110
  Horatio 74
  Silas 41
  Volantine 50
Gather
  Churchwell 108

Gathright
  Miles 71
Gatlen
  Stephen....................52
Gatlin
  Stephen....................59
  Turner F. 242
Gatling
  Furney F..............297
Gauden
  Jonathan.................65
Gaulding
  Dempsey 17
  Jonathan...............220
Gay
  Gilbert...............45, 66
  Joel........................106
  John 295
  Thomas .102, 154, 177
Geer
  William 274
Geiral
  Randolp.................127
Gen
  Nathan....................55
George
  Henry.....................284
  Jephthah...............295
  Jeptha 292
  Jesse 233, 273
  Reubin 72
Gerald
  Early 287
  Randolph 287
Gerardeau
  John B....................10
Germany
  John 80
  Samuel....................37
  Washington 87

Gerrald
  William.................281
Gerrard
  William...................23
Gertman
  David......................97
Geyer
  Ernst William 227
Gholston
  Zachariah 209
Gibbons
  Henry....................240
Gibbs
  Thomas...............9, 22
Gibson
  Chruchwell...........113
  Churchill 298
  Churchwell...172, 258
  George 186
  Henry....................221
  John............113, 151
  Robert...............41, 74
  Shadrack W..........227
  Silvanius 128
  William..................13
  William C. 275
Giddens
  Jobin 283
Gignilliat
  Henry....................213
Gilbert
  Bird.......................108
  Drury......................55
  Edmond 168
  Edmund.................236
  Ezekiel..................270
  Felix......................131
  Isaac 177
  Jesse 125, 169, 171
  John............4, 94, 209
  Josiah 195, 232

Gilbert, cont.
  Richard M. 161
  Richard M.Sr. 196
  Thomas 171
  Wilie 271
  William 164
Giles
  James 272
  Thomas 213
Gill
  David..................... 114
  John...................... 107
  Michael 171
  Thomas Y. 161
  William 192
Gillashie
  Daniel..................... 27
Gillespie
  Daniel..................... 86
Gilliam
  Miles...................... 92
Gilliland
  William 283
  Wm H. 310
Gillion
  John...................... 168
Gillispy
  David..................... 145
Gilly
  Jeremiah 263
Gilmore
  Humphry 178
  James 106
  James M. 216
  John.................. 92, 94
  John H. 216, 236
  Nothey 188
  Peachy R. 214
  Samuel 203
  Stephen................ 106
  Stephen H. 315

Name Index

Gilmore, cont.
William 122
Gilstrap
Henry 16
Gimble
Jacob 237
Gin
Thoma 265
Girtman
David 233
Glascock
Edmund 246
Thomas 226, 256
William 168
Glass
James 236, 278
Glasscock
Edmund B. 242
Thomas 240
William 245
Glaze
Jonathan 172
Patrick 78
Samuel 305
Tandy 190, 286
Glazer
Hiram 108
Marnock 146
Glazier
Hiram 114
Wesley 194
Glen
Noble 109
Glenn
Allen 297
George 229
James 226
Littleberry G. 254
Robert B. 205, 286
Samuel 4, 47
William 154

Glinn
Noble W. 156
Glisson
Joseph 181
Glover
Absalom 305
Eli 157, 190
Jesse 145
Gnann
Solomon 4
Gnenn
Benjamine 165
Goare
Phares 243
Gober
James 203
Gobert
Benjamin Jr. 31
Godbee
William 138
Godfrey
Francis 82
Godfry
William 172
Godward
David 262
Godwin
Alexander 61
Edmund 138
Goember
Augustus 116
Goffard
Thomas 64
Gold
Thomas K. 249
Golding
John R. 251
Peter J. 247
Goldwire
James 8

Golesbey
Charles M. 121
Golman
John 139
Good
William 23
Goodbee
William 178
Goodbread
Philip 7
Goode
Mickerness 175
William 99
Goodgame
Alexander 42
Goodman
Henry 142, 180
Jesse 152
John 301
Goodson
Josiah 154, 262
Goodwin
James A. 174
John 92
Goolesby
Barnett 223
Goolsby
Drury 214
Josiah 317
Goore
Thomas 295, 313
Gordan
Alexander G. 135
Richard 263, 269
Gorden
Alexander 188
Ambrose 6
Gordon
Alexander 55
Alexander G. 74
Andrew 275

351

Gordon, cont.
George A. 167
Joseph 44
Richard 218
Thomas 168
Thomas D. 288
Gordy
Thomas 98
Gore
Elisha 3
James 289
Manning H. 191
Gorman
James 299
Goss
Hezekiah F. 267
Horatio 201
Horatio J. 184
Isom 43
Gould
James 222
Thomas 187
Goza
Martin 159
Gozey
Aaron 136
Grace
James 125
John 300
Joshua 289
Josiah 56
Thomas 287
Gracey
Joshua 133
Gragg
Israel 214
Graham
Archibald 141, 154
David 301
Joshua 190
Robert 137

Graham, cont.
Thomas 65
Granberry
Leammis 115
Stephen 227
Granbury
George 315
Grandy
Brinkley 90
Grant
William 159
Grantham
Ignatius 91, 104
Grantland
Fleming 193
Thomas B. 232
Grass
Mund 50
Graves
Devenport 258
Divenport 108
Ellis 289
John T. 240
Robert 69
Gray
Absalom 6
Archibald 49, 132
Daniel 121, 299
Edmund 238
Gipson 192
John ... 32, 39, 96, 132, 169, 272
John J. 61
Michael 139
Richard 35
Sterlig 296
T. V. 142
Thomas 237
Tobas V. 153
William 109
William W. 111

Graybill
Henry 60, 69
Philip 228
Green
Edward 38
Myal 201
Sutton 28
Thomas 93
Warren 195
William 196
Greene
Allen 228, 313
Alston 150
Aquilla 69
Burwell 183
Daniel 260
George 258
John 117
Nathaniel R. ... 51, 105
Warren 241
Greenlaw
David 49
Greenwood
Henry 97
Greer
Aaron W. 186
Abraham 55, 63
Acquilla 147
George 305
Henry 45
Levin 168
William 275
Greeson
Abraham 33
Gregg
John 99
Gregory
John R. 304
Samuel 252
Thomas J. 265
William G. 111

352

Name Index

Gresham
- Benjamin 182
- Ferdinand 300
- George 23
- Isham 202
- Job 215
- John .. 63, 83, 147, 266
- Lemuel 181, 189
- Thomas 24, 293
- Young 81

Greson
- William 137

Gribbon
- Thomas 191

Grice
- John 132

Grier
- Aaron W. 279

Griffin
- Aventon 53
- Benjamin M. 242
- David 93, 239, 285
- Hardy 290
- James G. 272
- Jeremiah 177
- John 307
- Joseph 41, 54, 163
- Josiah 188
- Lewis L. 306
- Michael 294
- Noah 59
- Snoden 76
- Thomas 96
- William 156, 163

Griffith
- Cabel 70
- John 259, 277, 280
- Morgan 45

Griffitt
- Benjamin 250

Grigg
- Jessee 220

Griggs
- Jesse 173
- John 148
- William 255
- William L. 229

Grigory
- John R. 131

Grimball
- Paul 25

Grimer
- John 173

Grimerly
- Joseph 73

Grimes
- George 174, 192
- John 216
- Sterling 21, 120
- William 29, 42

Grimsley
- John 248
- Joseph 69

Grines
- Thomas 52

Grissom
- Edmond 38

Grooms
- Elijah 27

Groover
- David 6

Gross
- Davis 191

Grovenstine
- John 4, 62

Groves
- Samuel 76, 121

Grubbs
- Benjamin 148

Grubles
- Hezekiah 257

Guerry
- Theodore 229

Guess
- Thomas 219

Guest
- Moses 262

Gumm
- Jacob 161

Gummage
- William 63

Gunn
- Gabriel 165, 265
- Jacob 100, 118
- James 68
- Jesse 216
- William 186, 190

Gunter
- John 206

Gypson
- Benjamin 44

Gyton
- Charles S. 304

H

Habersham
- John B. 213
- Joseph Jr. 210
- Robert 139

Hackett
- Robert 244

Hackney
- John 181, 263
- Nathan 216
- Stephen 316

Hadden
- Lewis 141

Haddlesey
- William 46

Haddock
- William 182

353

Haden
    Samuel 78
Hadley
    Frederick 85
    Henry 40, 103
    Simon 233
    Simon Jr. 139
    Thomas 187
Hadly
    Henry 150
Hagerty
    Jonathan 133, 151
    Joshua 147, 199
Haggard
    James 60
Hagie
    Archibald 160
Hagin
    Joseph 314
Hagler
    Garland 229
Hail
    Joshua 64
Hailford
    Henry 179
Haines
    Richard 4
Hair
    Daniel 244
Hale
    Benjm 153
    James 296
    Joshua 52
    Samuel 250
Hales
    William 23
Hall
    Alexander 133
    Alixander 170
    Benjamin 13
    Daniel M. 267, 270

Hall, cont.
    Goode 164
    Henry T. 312
    Hugh 126
    James 100, 165
    James M. 84
    John 47, 90
    John C. 239
    Jonathan 289
    Joseph 243
    Lewis 9
    Littleton 134, 138
    Nathaniel 107
    Samuel . 131, 229, 285
    Standley 207
    Tarlton 137
    Thomas L. 209
    William .. 5, 14, 36, 84,
        102, 126, 164
    William K. 183
Halley
    James 229
    Nathaniel 27
Hally
    Nathaniel 4
Hambleton
    William 146
Hambricks
    John 136
Hameltion
    Matthew T. 305
Hamelton
    James 83
Hamett
    John 27
Hamilton
    Andrew 16, 64
    Arthur 5
    Duke 205
    George 241
    James 38, 144

Hamilton, cont.
    John 187
    Joseph 185
    Joseph 129
    Mathew F. 277
    Matthew T. 285
    Peter 316
    Samuel 293, 310
    Thomas P. ... 146, 169,
        232, 269
    William 169, 196
Hammet
    John 73
Hammilton
    Duke 76
    George 116
    Thomas P. 116
Hammock
    Jesse 59
    John 20
    Pascal 173
Hammond
    Abner 57
    Job 311
    Samuel 133
    William 255, 271
Hammons
    Isaac 191
Hamner
    Turner Jr. 169
Hampton
    David H. 312
    James 192
    John 32
    Joseph 111
    Wade 175
Hancock
    James 4
    Robert ... 127, 158, 201
    William 45

Name Index

Hand
- Christopher .. 228, 259
- Harrison 228
- Henry H. 237, 275
- William 167, 187

Handcock
- Chadore 265

Handle
- James G. 55

Handley
- Thomas 55

Handly
- Thomas 291

Hanford
- George 301

Hanks
- Elisha 204

Hanley
- Jesse 177

Hannah
- Daniel 223

Hanner
- William 38

Hanney
- James 158, 196

Hansard
- John 267

Hansell
- William T. 231
- William Y. 141

Hanson
- John 159
- John W. 313
- Samuel 274

Harbock
- Henry 213, 244

Hardee
- Allen 113
- Thomas E. 302

Harden
- Edward 63, 89, 106

Harden, cont.
- Henry 141
- James ... 119, 132, 262
- Jehu E. 107
- John 115
- Mark 128, 193
- Martin 106
- Robert R. 249
- Samuel 137
- Thomas Barton 164

Hardeson
- Wm. L. 303

Hardie
- John 215, 232

Hardiman
- John 15, 45

Hardin
- John 293
- Martin 42
- William 234

Harding
- Ebenezer 56

Hardinson
- Harvey 269

Hardison
- Thomas 241

Hardman
- Charles 179
- John 190
- Samuel B. 194

Hardwich
- Garland 92

Hardy
- Aquilla 280
- Henry 308
- John . 68, 69, 102, 283
- Miles 58, 215
- Preston 181
- Theophilus 290

Hargerly
- Joshua 127

Hargrove
- Eldrige 64, 134
- Harmon B. 307
- John 318
- Pleasant 115
- Reuben N. 191

Hargroves
- Theophelus 135

Harkins
- Roger 234
- William 240

Harkness
- James 207

Harly
- William 92

Harper
- Alexander 145
- Allen 267
- Averet 29
- Benjamin J. 37, 110
- Everett 94, 133
- Haywood 95
- Jared 220
- Jesse 266
- John 37
- John W. 313
- Josiah 119
- Josiah B. 309
- Sherwood 238
- Thomas 35

Harrel
- Thomas 82

Harrell
- Hardy 20
- Isaac 67
- James 108, 121
- John C. 104, 119

Harrelson
- Bradley 119
- Vinson 230

355

Harriet
  Archibald M. C. 230
Harrigin
  Mabry 240
Harrill
  William 1, 298
Harrilson
  Elisha.....................63
Harrington
  Drewry..................149
  Harrey 85
  Harvy 252
Harris
  Andrew 260, 302
  Archibald 282
  Buckner 32
  Charles 253
  David 240
  Edward 114, 272
  Edwin....................164
  Edwin S. 139
  Ezekiel 136
  Gedion...........107, 118
  George..................308
  Gresham 82
  Isaac......................145
  James............222, 288
  Jeptha V. 217
  Jesse 44, 165
  John 34, 111, 187, 249
  Laird M. 102
  Lard W. 144
  Leroy G. 303
  Littleberry 131, 175
  Morris 39
  Moses 228, 237
  Richard 227
  Terry 63
  Thomas 277
  Thomas McCall 81
  Thomas W.....212, 253

Harris, cont.
  Walton 42, 67
  William.... 16, 59, 194,
    253, 313
Harris:......................248
Harrison
  Andrew 128
  Carter B. 313
  Cater B. 117
  Denwoodie R. 131
  James 301
  Jesse 277
  Jesse H. 67
  John 51
  Pascal 122, 123
  Richard 74
  Robert............85, 163
  Samuel 36
  Seaborn J. 303
  Terrell Cook 74
  William..84, 106, 184,
    278, 295
Harriss
  Benjamin..............300
  Heram C. 310
Harrold
  James C................304
Hart
  David 80
  Hardy 51
  John 297
  Robert...................134
  Thomas.................268
Hartley
  Samuel 141
Hartsfield
  Allen 57
  Henry......................77
  James 226, 286
Harvel
  James 23

Harvell
  Samuel 148, 193
Harvey
  Benjamin 94, 132,
    190, 222, 284
  Charles................ 4, 11
  Galphin 186, 241
  Golphin 168, 226
  Isaac 302
  James 38
  John........ 47, 155, 188
  John P. . 127, 178, 290
  Nehemiah 47
  Robert................... 173
  Thomas 179, 270, 301
Harvill
  James 184
  Sampson 171
  William 312
Harvy
  John...................... 267
Harwell
  Mason................... 177
  Vines 123, 164
Hass
  John...................... 222
Hastley
  James 100
Hatcher
  Archibald 35
  John................. 27, 55
Hatchett
  William 52
Hateley
  Henry 287
Hatheway
  John...................... 195
Hathhorn
  James 178
Hathway
  John...................... 194

356

Hatin
    Abel L. 188
Hatley
    Anderson 257
    Henry 302
Hatson
    John...................... 143
Hattaway
    Peyton 283
Hatton
    M. L. 228
Haughton
    Mathew 256
Hawkins
    John...................... 260
    John B. 314
    Mathew 20
    Pinkethman 116
    Solomon................... 49
    Thomas.................. 244
    William................. 117
    Willis 271
Haws
    Clabourn 265
Hawsey
    Henry 165
Hawthorn
    Benjamin...... 102, 167
    Hader 125
    Joshua 224
    Peter 76
    William 76
Hay
    Hardy 178
    William 43
Hayes
    Etheldred 82
    Mark 86
    Wyley................... 263
Hayles
    John.............. 157, 305

Hayles, cont.
    William 110, 155, 237
Haynes
    Charles E. 161
    Greenberry 189
    Greeneberry..........149
    John 289
    Thomas 23, 44, 64
    Thomas Jr...............96
    William 151
Hays
    Curtis 79
    Elias 299
    Gideon...................174
    Jesse 165
    John 288
    Martin...................161
    William 151
Hayward
    Charles C. 274
Hazzard
    William W.............238
Heard
    Alexander 119
    Barnard 122
    Barnard C.... 295, 306
    Charles..................206
    Charles M. 173
    Ephraim................206
    George.......... 191, 226
    James....................190
    Jesse........................86
    Jesse F. 171, 176
    John 37, 59, 93
    Stephen G. ... 150, 203
Heardy
    John 297
Hearn
    Tabard 73
    William 117

Hearon
    Seth.......................188
Heart
    John 158
Heath
    Abraham...............178
    Adam 87
    Lewis 155
Heaton
    Owen.....................124
Heifner
    Jacob 75
Heisler
    Samuel..................206
Helms
    James......................82
Hemphill
    Charles 247
    James...........249, 280
    John 198
    Marcus..................123
    Samuel..................198
    Tilman 265
    Tilmon 223
    William 212
Henderson
    Daniel 35
    Greene 298
    John 21
    Joseph............91, 268
    Joseph Jr. 85, 159
    Major 53, 136
    Robert 272
    Samuel....................57
    Simon....149, 191, 236
    Thomas 278
    William 115
Hendirikin
    James....................227
Hendley
    Joel 138

Hendley, cont.
   Samuel 89
   William 86, 89
Hendon
   Isham 137
   Johnson 254
Hendrick
   Isaac 242
   John 60
Hendricks
   James 29
   John 128
Hendrix
   Andrew 253
   James 42
Hendry
   Wiliam 243
   William 110
Henley
   Thomas 232
Henly
   More 62
Henry
   Benjamin 267
   Benjamine 185
   Benson 85
   Daniel 91, 153
   John 71, 80, 303
   John P. 162
   William H. 258
Henson
   John 54
Henton
   Jacob 34
Herb
   George 74, 91
Herbert
   Benjamin 60
   Moses ... 160, 215, 229, 255, 300
   William 307

Herndon
   Walker 77
Herrage
   Benjamin 315
   John 266
Herren
   Thomas 4
Herring
   Herron 261
   Lennett 135
Herrington
   Harvey 5, 230
   Job 166
Herstin
   Peter 245
Hewell
   William 73
Hewett
   William 112
Hews
   David 202
Hickey
   William 171
Hicklin
   Reuben 311
Hickling
   Hugh 93
Hickman
   John 196
   Joseph 269
Hicks
   Abner 116
   Daniel 275
   David 213
   James 155
   John 157
   Wyatt 317
   Zepheniah 316
Higden
   Burrell 7
   Terrill 7

Higdon
   Burrel 75
   Charles 53
   Terrel 279
Higgenbotham
   Cable 253
Higginbotham
   Bartley 302
   Benjamin 280
   Benjmain 70
   George G. 269, 292
   Nelson 58
   Samuel 280, 289
Higginbothom
   Benjamin G. 118
   John 130
Higginbottam
   Jacob 180
Highsmith
   James 276
Hightower
   Charnel 294
   Daniel 45
   Elisha 261
   Jacob D. 111
   Pleasant 292
   Thomas 188
   William 284
Hill
   Ambrose 299
   Benjamin 59, 277
   Benjamine 174
   Charles A. 196
   Green 195
   Greene 262
   Henry B. 244
   Isaac 117, 254
   James 44
   Jesse 73
   Joel 35
   John 64, 115, 177

Hill, cont.
  Joseph L. 220
  Manning 155
  Mountain 81
  Reuben 159
  Robert 234, 237
  Thomas 219
  Thomas A. ... 123, 127, 207
  Wayde 259
  Whitmill 165
  William . 184, 220, 254
  William B. 196

Hillard
  Francis 21, 39
  Kinchen 78
  William 93

Hilleard
  John 108
  Kinchin 68
  Wilie 178

Hillger
  Shaler 24

Hillhouse
  David 16
  David P. 202, 208

Hilliard
  Francis 77
  Henry 195
  Kinchin 147
  Willey 50
  William 275

Hillis
  John 305
  William 305

Hilton
  John 192
  Peter 72

Hilyer
  Shaler 50

Hines
  David 121
  Howell 178
  John 80, 246
  John Jr. 164
  Joseph 113

Hinsley
  Thomas 54

Hinson
  John 99
  Philip 90

Hinton
  Henry 272

Hitchcock
  James 66, 134
  William 100

Hix
  Absalom 296

Hobbs
  James 239

Hobby
  Francis 292

Hobkins
  Richard 118

Hobson
  Francis 186
  Hardy 53
  John 2, 12, 128

Hobzinback
  Lewis D. 237

Hodge
  Able 134
  Allen 115
  Benjamin 113
  David 237
  Eliot 22
  John 203
  Mathew 267
  Stephen 111
  William 19, 162

Hodges
  Able 145
  Allen 126
  Benjamin 136, 174
  Elias 41
  John 292, 307
  Joseph 314
  Robert 268
  Samuel 69

Hodnet
  John 286

Hogan
  Edmond 158
  Henry 255
  Isham T. 235
  James 202
  John 9, 28

Hoge
  Jonathan 58
  Stephen 45
  William 209

Hogg
  Jeter 286
  Thomas 119

Holcomb
  Absalom 280
  Joel 228

Holcombe
  Jeptha 172

Holder
  Jesse 317
  John 54

Holebrooks
  Fleminon 292

Holiday
  Furney 29

Holland
  Jacob 148
  John 10
  Lewis 76, 216

Holland, cont.
    Lewis C. 192
    Thomas 25
    William 93
Holley
    Hazel......................14
    William 151
Hollida
    Thomas 266
Holliday
    Abner 59
    Benjamin W............85
    Furney 35
    John 246
    Martin...................266
    Owen......................59
    Richard J. 253
    Thomas 251
    William 243
Hollin
    David 237
Hollingsworth
    Benjamin 101, 130
    Benjm....................159
    Jesse 38
    John 193, 279
    Thomas 129
Hollingswoth
    Jesse 39
    Samuel....................42
    Vaul 33
Hollis
    Silas 275
    William 164
Holliway
    Asa 182
Holloway
    William 71, 133
Holly
    Hazel........................3

Holmes
    John 134, 148, 218
    Joshua 276
    William J..............101
Holt
    Anderson 215
    Arrington..............137
    Edden 287
    Simon 83
    Singleton 63
    Tapley.....97, 104, 210
    Thaddeus 81, 114, 118
    Thaddeus G. 310
    William 116
    William B. 306
Holton
    John 46
    Mark 29
Holvel
    Nathaniel 66
Holzendorf
    John L. R. 52
Honeycut
    John 146
Hood
    Elisha 278
    Joel 223
Hooks
    Asa 183
    Thomas 60
Hooper
    John 38
    Obadiah................268
    Richard.............53, 78
Hopkins
    Francis .164, 195, 269
    John 94, 112
    Moses T. 181
    Timothy 314
    Wiliam 87
    William 4

Hopson
    Brigs.......................54
    Edmund 148, 215
    William 215
    Zachariah.............304
Horn
    Isaac 16
    Isaac H. 268
    John..............148, 311
    Jordon 94
    Josiah 42
    Orin 239
    Richard 51
    Thomas B. 70
Hornbuckle
    George 299
Horne
    Daniel...................302
Horseman
    David....................172
Horton
    Frederick G...........182
    John..........................1
    Josiah 307
    Levi 123
    Robert...........155, 178
    William 155
Hosea
    Thomas 48
Hosey
    Thomas 255
Houghtan
    John........................77
Houghton
    Charles..................161
    John..............140, 305
    Joshua 49, 62, 140
House
    John......................194
    Littleberry 246
    Nimrod 1

Houston
  Mossman 105, 193
  Robert J. 120, 212
Houstoun
  Robert G. 139
Howard
  Absalom 184
  Benjamin 123
  Charles 168
  Harmon 267
  Hawkins 271
  James 69, 164, 189, 235, 298
  John 16, 35
  Joseph H. 160
  Lemuel 93
  Nauflet 189
  Naughflight.......... 161
  Nicholas 182, 254, 267, 295
  Reddick 173
  Samuel 270
  Thomas................. 142
  Vaughflile............. 102
  William S. 317
Howe
  William................. 124
Howell
  Casper 225
  Charles 279
  Etheldred 208
  Hezekiah 23, 50
  James 187
  Jesse 307
  John...................... 23
  Lewis 167
  McKinne................ 99
  Nathaniel 74
  Thomas........... 99, 222
  Wylie 125

Hoy
  James....................207
Hubank
  Caleb 142
Hubbard
  Elisha... 165, 184, 260
  Hannan R. 304
  John 185
  Joseph 176
Hubbert
  John 265
Hubert
  Hyram 52
  John 301
  Stephen................242
  William 240
Huck
  Christian F. 256
Huckaby
  James....................316
Huckeby
  William 164
Huddlecy
  Charles...................34
Huddleston
  Isaac......................249
Hudgings
  Isaac......................273
Hudgins
  Robert 32
Hudman
  Hezekiah...............190
Hudson
  Alexander 280, 314
  Charles......... 144, 180
  Garrett....................73
  Irby........................102
  John 137, 154, 178, 255
  Nathaniel...............163
  Rouland..................63

Hudson, cont.
  Samuel....................59
  Sion 295
  Thomas....54, 77, 102, 176, 298
  William 32, 70
Hudspeth
  Richard 86
Hudwell
  John 163
Huff
  Henry...............69, 144
  John 284
  Mathew.................237
  Matthews 282
  Robert 245
  Roff 272
  Thomas 197
Huges
  Michael W. 154
Huggie
  Archibald 189
Hughes
  George H. 223
  Michael W. 174
Hughey
  Ephraim 153
  John 284
  Joseph..................311
Hughs
  Isaac 134
  John 96, 103
Hughster
  Samuel..................177
Hulett
  Augustin...............235
Hulsey
  Pleasant................236
Hulsy
  John 68

Hummock
  Thomas 22
Humphrees
  James 259
Humphress
  Daniel 163
Humphrey
  Benjamin 89, 156
  Daniel ... 257, 263, 290
  Thomas 234
Humphries
  Benjamin 136
  George 29, 42
  James 2, 47, 188
  John 47, 175
  William C. 315
Humphris
  James 248
Humphry
  Jesse 57
Hunk
  Christian F. 272
Hunnells
  Peter 102
Hunt
  Henry 280
  James 122, 136
  Joel 77
  Lewis 259
  Richardson 10
  Thomas 311
  William 161
Hunter
  Abner 13
  Abraham 24, 159
  Adam 157
  Archibald R. S. 204
  Ephram 231
  Hardy 58
  James ... 116, 158, 191, 248

Hunter, cont.
  William ... 17, 272, 303
  William G. 290
Hurbert
  Benjamin 194
  Benjmain 69
Hurt
  Benjamin 78
  William 234
Husler
  George 82
Hutchens
  Samuel W. 190
Hutcherson
  Robert 231
Hutchins
  Barrel 64
  David 277
  John 81
Hutchinson
  Jesse 9
  Lewis 84
  William 146
Hutson
  John 225
Hyde
  Thomas 195

I

Ingram
  James 129
Ingrum
  Hampton 201
Innis
  Nathaniel 43
  Nicholas 31
Irvin
  John E. 223
Irvine
  Keneth 176

Irwin
  David 70
  Isaiah T. 162, 269
  James 208
  John .. 40, 81, 261, 271
  Thomas 303
Isler
  Nathan 225
  William 187
Isom
  James 156
Ive
  Anderson 95
Iverson
  William 306
Ivery
  Bennet 86
Ivey
  Bennet 56
  Charles 138
  Jesse 140
  Moses 103
  Samson 21
  Thomas 137
Ivy
  Moses 181
  Thomas 224, 292

J

Jack
  Greene B. 316
  Patrick 72
Jackson
  Abraham 6, 97
  Abram 73
  Benjamin 42
  Daniel 262
  Ebenezer 17
  Frederick 9
  Greene 44

Name Index

Jackson
Henry 20
Isaac 96, 115, 139, 221
James 31, 161, 177, 218
John 309
Josiah 34
Littleton 156
Robert 23, 125
Samuel ... 45, 179, 190
Thomas. 129, 156, 229
William.. 79, 126, 132, 133, 266
William F. 211, 281

Jacob
Mordecai 20

Jacobs
John B. 249
Shadrach 283

James
Benjamin.............. 265
David 302
Enoch 54
Joseph 188
Samuel 62

Jamison
John 118
Joseph 181

Jansan
William 55

Janson
Jesse 169

Jarratt
Deverux 110
Nathaniel C. 301

Jarrell
George 281

Jarrett
Archilus 32
Devorax 250
Jacob 95

Jarrett, cont.
Nathaniel 246
Nathaniel C. 247
Patterson 126
William D. 126

Jarves
Jacob 59

Jarvis
Floyed 147

Jauers
Charles 300

Jay
James 46

Jeffers
John 191
Osborne 15

Jefferson
John 299
Thomas 305

Jeffries
Lee 254

Jencks
Willis 135

Jenkins
Allen 24
Charles Cavenah 35
James 77, 83
James Robert 108
John 8
Lewis 81, 122
Littleberry 9, 45
Obediah 145
Robert 259
Royal 12
Uriah 209
William 303

Jenks
Abner 150

Jennings
Charles 222
Henry 190, 257

Jennings, cont.
John 308

Jerkins
William 285

Jernagan
David S. 293

Jernegan
Jesse 13

Jernigan
David 155

Jerrels
Charles 63

Jeter
Edmond 265
John 83, 174, 195, 266
Samuel 146, 198

Jett
Francis 268

Jewell
Kincheon 283

Jinkins
Sampson D. 296
Uriah 287

Jirkins
Zachariah 26

Joblitt
Davis 131

Johns
James 316
Jesse 280

Johnson
Aaron 28
Alford 285
Allen 158
Allen S. 218
Andrew N. 304
Bartholomew 261, 308
Burwell 138
Daniel 33, 72, 84, 169, 245
Edward 81

363

Johnson, cont.
    Frederic 176
    Fred'k....................265
    George...................316
    George H...............226
    Greene 303
    James......70, 125, 181
    James Jr. 104
    Jarad.....................304
    Jared 288
    Jesse 306
    John 67, 130, 169, 180, 203, 228, 269, 310
    John J. 61
    Lewis.....................309
    Lindsay 281, 295
    Malcom 95
    Peter 53
    Randol...................265
    Robert 108, 269
    Samuel..................296
    Sherwood B. 240
    Thomas ..85, 208, 270, 273
    Thomas De Mattos.25
    William 24, 40, 111, 144, 151

Johnston
    Alexander 224
    Allen..........................9
    Daniel 26, 107
    George H...............103
    Isaac N..................228
    James..................8, 32
    John 190, 223, 276
    Moses 240
    Nicholas 239
    Posey 295
    William 163, 281

Joice
    John 231
    Richard 92

Joiner
    Jacob......................75
    Joseph......................4
    Lewis 297
    Roderick 109
    William.125, 188, 271

Joines
    Clemuel 177

Jolly
    Frederich..............284
    Frederick..............290
    James 293
    Michael...................32

Jones
    Aaron Jr. 236
    Adam 61, 80, 125
    Allen 122
    Ambrose 123
    Benjamin..............205
    Berry............138, 269
    Britton 19, 152
    Bryant 305
    David 142
    David D. 110
    David G. 279
    Drury Jr. 68, 82
    Dudley 170
    Elijah 195
    Evan 213
    Ezra 104
    Francis 217, 285
    Gabriel..................129
    George 202
    Harrison...............243
    Henry......59, 179, 238
    Henry P. 277

Jones, cont.
    James.. 47, 57, 67, 81, 101, 129, 156, 168, 176
    Jesse 89
    John. 22, 95, 106, 118, 135, 171, 206, 218, 232
    John G. 198
    John L. 98
    John M. 139
    John W. 180
    Joseph 48, 185, 219
    Josiah 270
    Martin 222
    Mason............ 77, 197
    Moses 32, 59
    Nathan 272
    Nathaniel............. 122
    Nimrod 26, 103
    Noble 51
    Philip 97
    Randle 115
    Richard 130, 156, 239
    Rissle 56
    Robert................... 276
    Russell Jr. 111
    Samuel 48
    Samuel A. 287
    Seaborn 270
    Simson 73
    Smith.... 159, 223, 243
    Solomon 308
    Tandy 256
    Thomas 2, 98, 147, 192, 239, 300
    Walter 96, 157
    Wiley 273, 299
    William . 6, 51, 65, 73, 101, 109, 123, 130

Jones, cont.
   William 132, 174, 192, 274, 301
   William R. 193
   William Sr. 65
   Wylee 38
   Zachariah 3, 50

Jordan
   B. 262
   Burrell 6
   Burwell 71
   Elijah 213, 260
   Green H. 216
   Henry 36, 303
   Joshua 316
   Thomas D. 206
   Wiley 296

Jorden
   Daniel 290

Jordon
   James 7

Josey
   Henry 313
   James 161
   James W. 265

Jourdan
   Asa 209
   Edmond 257
   Edward 164

Jowell
   Kinchen 231

Jurdine
   Leonard 74

Justice
   Allen 301
   Dempsey 16, 53
   Henry 162
   Isaac 300
   William 190

Justus
   Stephen 214

K

Kackler
   John 131

Keall
   Franklin 251

Kean
   David 307

Keating
   Richard T. 91, 154

Keaton
   Benjamin 125
   Jesse 55

Keefer
   Ephraim 258

Keeling
   Leonard 70

Keener
   John 197

Keeth
   Asa 17

Keeton
   Benjamine 165

Keifer
   Ephraim 310

Keith
   George 74
   Talton F. 291

Kellam
   Gideon 205

Kellebrew
   William 46

Keller
   Paul 189

Kellet
   James 46

Kellough
   Thomas 39

Kellund
   Jetho 176

Kelly
   Abner 111, 126
   Arnold 159
   Daniel 258, 267
   David 198, 290
   Giles 115
   Joshua 203
   Patrick 92
   Robert 184, 285
   William . 161, 164, 191
   William F. 118
   William M. 249

Kemon
   William W. 89

Kemp
   Falton 237
   John 284

Kempton
   William S. 252

Kenan
   Thomas H. 70

Kendall
   Henry 43, 56
   Henry Jr. 223
   Thomas 195
   Thomas H. 260, 302

Kendrick
   Barnel 9
   John 140, 258
   Jones 38, 221
   William 2

Kenman
   William 38

Kennebrew
   Littleberry 183

Kennedey
   William 27

Kennedy
   Augustus 166
   David 286
   Eli 96

Kennedy, cont.
    Francis 152
    Francis Sr. 142
    George 203
    Joshua 31
    Robert 27
    William 5

Kenney
    David 219

Kennion
    Charles 114

Kennon
    Warner L. 211
    William 159

Kent
    Allison 302
    Gilbert 266, 303
    Peter 33

Kerksy
    Isaac 84

Kettelle
    Jonathan 162

Key
    Kenedy 110
    Tandy 242
    Tandy W. 218

Kicklighter
    Thomas 274

Kicklighton
    Thomas 261

Kidd
    John 33, 88, 161
    Martain 236

Kigney
    Thomas M. 242

Kilgore
    James 194
    John 29, 42
    Ralph 166
    Willis 141

Kilpatrick
    Richard 282

Kimborough
    John 274, 288

Kimbro
    John 73, 317

Kimbrough
    Jonathan 182
    Thomas 45

Kinan
    Owen H. 114

Kinchen
    James 291
    John 56
    Uriah 139, 202, 279

Kincy
    Absalom 295

Kindall
    Henry 113

Kindrick
    Harvey 226
    Harvy 294
    Sylvanus 198
    Thomas 198
    Thomas C. 307

King
    Benajah 124
    Edward 143
    Edwin 155
    Edwin D. 254
    George 174
    Jacob 307
    James 35
    John 8, 67, 109
    John Jr. 7
    L. 100
    Lambert 58
    Reuben 231
    Reubin 205
    Samuel ... 72, 145, 210
    Tandy W. 169

King, cont.
    Thomas . 10, 187, 265, 274
    Thomas Jr. 92
    Thos. 152
    Timothy 184
    William 44, 63, 65, 104, 231, 249, 292
    William John 207
    Yelventon P. 316
    Zuriah 143

Kinman
    James 199
    William 201

Kinnabrew
    Littleberry 151

Kinnedy
    George 226

Kinney
    David 294
    James 169
    Jesse 315

Kinny
    James 210

Kirk
    Thomas 72, 143

Kirkham
    Robert 230

Kirkland
    Daniel 309
    James 268, 309
    Richard 11

Kirkpatrick
    John 44
    Samuel 53

Kirlin
    William 113

Kise
    Washington 258

Kiss
    John 257

Kitchum
  Ralph 153
Kittles
  John 194
Knight
  Allen 70
  Cofield 222
  John 227, 307
  Joshua 270, 314
  Lewis 241
  Robert 243
  Thomas 141
  William 105
  Woodward 105
Knights
  Abraham 166
  Jonathan 166
Knowles
  Isaac 198
  James 128, 129
Knox
  John 236
Kobb
  Martin 171
Kogler
  John 2
Kohely
  Daniel 317
Kubler
  Joshua 14
Kugley
  John G. 244

L

Laburan
  Charles 162
Lace
  John S. 308
Lacey
  Isaac 16

Lacy
  Delaware 278
  John 281
Lafiles
  Francis 138
Laidler
  John 294
Laird
  Archibald 148
Lake
  James 296
  Justice 186
Lamar
  Charles 81
  Jeremiah 46, 186
  John 233
  John H. 235
  Thomas 164, 222, 232
Lamaster
  Joseph 46
Lamb
  Abraham 50
  Green E. 175
  John 182
Lambert
  Ezekiel 50
Lamberth
  James 290
Lambright
  James 101, 156
Lamkin
  John 39, 222
  William 53, 147
Lamp
  John 241
  Lewis 294
Lamsdin
  Elijah 65
Lancaster
  Benjamin 190

Land
  Archibald 211
  Isaac 287
Landeford
  Benjamin 13
Landers
  Samuel 299
Landrum
  James B. 182
  John 88, 156
  Meredith 168
  Thomas B. 119
Lane
  Benjamin 230
  Charles 75
  Edward .111, 138, 196
  Henry 140, 211, 261
  John 6, 243, 309
  John Jr. 155
  Simeon 79
  Theopholus S. 256
  William D. 52
Lanear
  William 114
Lang
  David 307
  Isaac 118
Langdon
  Isaac 17
Langford
  John 72
Langston
  Benjamin 40
  David 13, 31, 86
  Jabez 153
  James 289
  Samuel W. 222, 226
  Seth S. 80, 295
Lanier
  Allen 222
  Benjamin S. ..176, 315

Lanier
  Clement 84, 101
  Frederick 138
  Lewis.......................53
Lansdown
  John 111
Largent
  John 24
Lark
  Samuel..................176
Larrisee
  William 233
Lary
  John 80, 208, 261
  Lary 164
Laseter
  Lemuel..................304
Lasher
  Solomon 149
Lason
  John F...................194
Lasseter
  Benjamin 222
  Jacob 239
  John 217
Lassetter
  Benjamin 255
Lassiter
  Archibald 137
  Jesse 55
Lastinger
  Andrew 48
Lathrop
  Asa 82
Latimer
  Henry....................244
  John 23
Latuzan
  Bartholomew 241
Laurance
  Richard 66

Laurece
  Richard.................199
Laurence
  Isham....................192
  James 300
  William...................55
Lavender
  Oliver....................291
  William.................109
Lavinder
  William.................229
Law
  Isaac 238
  Joseph Jr. 27
  Samuel 59
  Samuel S. 218
Lawrance
  William.................265
Lawrence
  James H. 275
  Thomas.................213
Lawrens
  Josiah 252
Lawson
  David 155
  Davinport 162
  Francis 205
  Irvin......................247
  John 8, 31
  Roger 62, 162, 267
  William C. 153
Laye
  Elisha 235
Lazenby
  Robert.....................87
Lea
  William 168
Leach
  Robert...................120
Ledbetter
  Isaac 9

Ledbetter, cont.
  James W. 185
  Samuel 61
  William 86
Leddell
  James 247
Lee
  Bird 311
  Charles B. 289
  Elijah................... 178
  Godfrey 259
  Jesse 46, 303
  John....................... 37
  Lewis.... 110, 173, 238
  Saymer 2
  Vincent................ 248
  William 181, 217, 262, 293
  William Jr............. 62
Lefiles
  Francis 163
Leftwick
  Joel W. 252
Legett
  Abraham A. 153
  Benjamin 297
Legg
  William 198
Legget
  Abraham A. 132
Leggett
  Benjamin 33, 283
  Mathew H. 289
Legon
  James 284
Legueax
  Peter.................... 179
Leigh
  Thomas G............. 167
Lemans
  William 171

368

Lemar
  Bird 56
Lemle
  Daniel 110
Lensey
  Jacob 178
Leonard
  Irbane 256
  Van 289
Lessley
  Archibald 177
Lester
  Eli 199
  Frederick 144
  George 88
  George D. 167
  Joshua 66
  Lewis 183
  Noel 294
  Robert 169
  William 228
Lesure
  Drewry 140
Leul
  Stephen 287
Levens
  Richard 141
  William 141
Leverett
  Joel 105, 180
  Robert Jr. 89
Leveritt
  Thomas 277
Levingston
  William 114
  Wm. 307
Levy
  Lewis 210
Lewis
  Anthony 195
  David 271, 282

Lewis, cont.
  Eleazer 21, 39
  Evan 97, 167
  Exum 100
  Francis 151
  Hezekiah 218
  James 75, 273
  James C. 181
  Jeremiah 160
  Jesse 215
  John ... 32, 43, 50, 231
  John D. 109
  Jonathan 51
  Richard 95
  Thomas 266
  Walden 133
  Whereat 165
  William 89, 123
Libzy
  Jacob 141
Lightfoot
  John A. 281
Lile
  John 253
Liles
  Sherod 61
Linch
  Charles 296
  Henry 285
Linder
  Jacob 294
Lindsay
  Abraham 40
  James 11
  John 58
Lindsey
  Jonah 72
Lindsy
  Dennis 34
Linsay
  Jacob 62

Linton
  John 209
Little
  Abram 114
  Archibald 174
  Frederick 3
  James .. 64, 85, 96, 151
  Jesse 154, 278
  Kinchen 195
  Littleberry 64
  Littleburry 8
  Rederick 185
  William 80, 262
Littlejohns
  Silas 96
Littleton
  James 205
Lively
  Jesse 126
Liverit
  Jordan 157
Liverman
  Samuel 270, 286
Livingston
  William 147, 233
Lloyd
  Charles S. 170
  John 45
  John F. 224
  Thomas 34
  William 37
Llysle
  Thomas 176
Lock
  Samuel 97
Locke
  John 183
Locket
  James Sr. 248
Lockett
  James 137

Lockett, cont.
    Reuben 79
    Thomas 110
    Winfrey 72

Lockhart
    Jesse 115
    Joel Jr. 206, 226
    Samuel 17, 68, 89

Lofftley
    Jesse 28

Lofley
    Wright 107

Loflin
    Elijah 56

Loften
    Elkanah 46
    John 1

Lofthy
    Jesse 77

Loftin
    William 230

Loftlin
    John 83

Logan
    James 167

Login
    Thomas 283

Lokey
    Dingley 313
    George 293

Long
    Drury 113
    Isaac 153
    James 65, 113, 143
    John 169
    Lansford 193
    Littleton 283
    Michael 193, 198
    R. H. 311
    Richard 113
    Thomas 166

Long, cont.
    William 281

Longstreet
    Augustin B. 286
    Gilbert .. 109, 172, 182

Loper
    Abel 2, 31
    Abel G. 121

Lord
    Hezekiah 35

Lott
    Arthur Jr. 119
    Jesse 26
    John Jr. 2
    Robert 84
    William 2

Lou
    Isaac 159

Loughren
    Joseph 291

Love
    James 78
    John 202, 209, 284
    Josephus 83, 153

Lovelace
    Allen 247

Loven
    Adam 93

Lovett
    Aaron 310
    John F. 120
    John P. 55
    Thomas 90, 252

Lovin
    Elijah 225

Loving
    Elisha 284

Lovlace
    Allen 279

Low
    George 10, 253

Low, cont.
    Lunsford 98
    Saumel S. 10

Lowe
    Aquilla 74
    Basil 294
    David 294
    Edmond 17
    George 294
    John 280
    Vincent B. 187
    William 316

Lowery
    Matthew 128

Lowry
    Benjamin 95
    David S. 232

Lowther
    Charles 40

Loyal
    Hardy 142

Loyd
    Elijah 94
    George 94
    Moses 55
    Richard T. 285
    Thomas 275
    William 95

Lucas
    Abram 213
    George 196, 248
    John 215, 306
    Robert 117
    William 117, 258

Luckie
    William F. 123

Luke
    Daniel 273
    James 31
    Reuben 45

Lumpkin
- Henry H. 314
- William 20

Lumsdan
- John G. 217

Lungeno
- John 126

Lunsford
- Henry 310

Lyle
- Daniel 28

Lynum
- William 72

Lyon
- Castleton 156, 182
- Isaac D. 298
- John 221
- Jonathan 198, 287
- Joseph 286
- Josiah 307
- Norris 163
- Peter 173
- Thomas 203

Lyons
- Jonathan 185

M

Maberry
- Thomas 185

Mabrey
- Walter 119

Mabry
- Jameson 163
- Jourdin 183

Maby
- Jameson 282

Machey
- William 22

Machin
- Charles 116

Machin, cont.
- Joseph 52

Mackay
- Robert 219, 221

Mackinzie
- Alexander 305

Macknowel
- Fielding 283

Macon
- Wm. G. 310

Maddox
- Andrew 77
- Claiborn 229
- John 216
- Joseph 87, 250
- Lewis 260
- Nathan 315
- Notley 99
- Seaborne 284
- Thomas 103, 209, 316
- William 12
- William Jr. 27

Madows
- Silas 191

Madray
- Benjamin 202

Madry
- Joseph 83

Mafford
- Bennet 241

Magee
- James 101
- Lawrence 124, 201
- William 106, 107

Magers
- Richard 281

Magruder
- Shelton 167

Maguier
- William 62

Mahaffey
- William 18

Mahone
- John K. 83
- Rowland 94

Mahony
- James 70

Mainor
- William 166

Major
- Edward 161

Majors
- David 124
- James 63

Malcom
- James 133

Mallard
- Thomas 158

Mallet
- Isaac 184

Mallett
- Isaac 31, 37

Mallory
- Joel H. 122
- William 314

Malone
- Cader 136
- Edward D. 293
- John 78, 140
- Morgan 173
- Sherod 99
- Thomas L. 160, 179

Malpass
- Morris 268

Malry
- Daniel 302

Malyard
- John 121

Man
- Baker 190

Mangham
James C. 276, 303
Thomas 77, 172
Manghram
James...................143
Mangum
Horrell 172
Maning
John 102
Manley
Green 3
Manly
Moses 196
Richard .230, 257, 285
Mann
Baker 119
David 36
Hardy.....................51
John 254, 300
Jonathan G. 307
Luke 251
Shemei 276
Shimee 171
Thomas 31
Mannel
Malachie 145
Manning
Joseph 281, 305
Laurens.................302
Manor
William 22, 174
Manson
James.....................13
Mapp
James...................232
Jeremiah.................70
Littleton................269
William 302
William F..............273
Mappin
James...................287

Mapping
James 214
Marble
Horwell.................271
Marcey
John S...................106
Marchman
Stephen 100
Marchnan
Stephen 52
Marcome
William 142
Mare
George W................64
Marks
L. H......................179
Leon H...67, 104, 110,
209, 289
Markum
Squire 168
Marlow
Samuel 197
Marr
John......................271
Mars
John B. ...89, 105, 112
Marsh
Jehu 288
John 25, 160
Littleberry....124, 182
Marshall
Benjamin..............218
Greene B. 258
Henry....................206
James 52, 106, 238, 258
John 7
Joseph.............27, 35
Lewis 278
Solomon..................55
Stephen 24

Marshall, cont.
William 145, 155, 236
Marshall 235
Marter
Thomas 300
Martin
Alexander.... 197, 242, 284
Allen 27, 223
Andrew................. 138
Archabald 238
Austin................... 286
Benjamin 247
Charles................. 274
Cornelius................ 79
David..................... 21
Elijah.. 2, 37, 117, 129
George 73
Jacob 76
James 1, 2, 16, 46, 105, 222, 294
John.. 3, 7, 18, 37, 146
Julius 289
Levy............. 117, 169
Murdock 149
Nephtaline 308
Robert.. 104, 118, 189, 206
Samuel 69
Stephen 303
William 68
Willis 37, 138
Zadock 48
Martindale
John....................... 94
Marye
Robert V. 193
Mase
William 180
Mason
Cullin L. 106

Name Index

Mason, cont.
    James 245
    John 312
    John C. 19
    Nathaniel 137
    William 113, 150, 154, 267
    Winfrey 157

Masse
    Niedham 230

Massey
    John S. 88

Massie
    Peter 107

Mathews
    Benjamin 107
    Charles 166, 294
    George 45
    Isaac 127
    Jame 267
    Jesse 129
    John. 12, 93, 124, 125, 233
    Masheck 110
    Peter 101
    Robert 165
    Timothy 43, 56
    William 5

Mathis
    John 291
    Robert 148

Matthews
    Elisha 24
    George 10
    George E. 299
    Jeremiah 306
    John 1
    Joseph T. 302
    Josiah 123
    William 90

Mattison
    James 64

Mattocks
    John 97

Maulden
    Andrew 250

Maund
    Daniel 61

Maxwell
    Jeremiah 236
    John 120
    Richard 316
    Richard M. 80
    Simmons 3
    William ... 49, 75, 211, 272
    William Jr. 49

May
    Furney 141
    Henry 265
    James 80
    John 68
    Major W. 273
    Ralph 252

Maybank
    Andrew 28, 218

Mayes
    John 195

Mayfield
    Battle 308
    John W. 250
    Thomas 244
    Westley 241
    Wistley 225

Mayno
    John G. 236

Mayo
    Breton 253
    Gideon 36, 169
    William 285

Mays
    Andrew G. 198
    Britain 241
    John 102
    John W. 287, 303
    William 103

McAfee
    Abraham 127
    Green 120

McAlister
    A. B. 213
    G. W. 210

McAllister
    George W. 193
    John 240

McAlphens
    Jesse 212

McAlpin
    William 183, 224

McAnnally
    John 98

McArthur
    Peter 195

McBride
    Dugal 220
    John 203
    Joseph 159

McCain
    Alexander 70

McCall
    George F. 296
    Hugh 233
    James 23
    John E. 292
    John W. 163
    Moses 279
    Nathaniel 207
    Robert 48
    Thomas 51
    William 71, 91

McCallister
  John 257
McCalpin
  Alexander 308
McCarthy
  William 195
McCarty
  Cornelius 19
  Roger 61
McCash
  Robert 23
McClaine
  Allen 18
McClendon
  Allen 234
  Benajah 205
  Beninah 148
  Benniel 183
  Dennis 122, 312
  Enoch 292
  Ezekiel 250
  Francis 78
  Ishen 61
  Joel 94, 270
  Medad 266
  Needham 164
  Samuel 285
  Stephen 73
  Willis 125
McCleroy
  Jacob 24
McClester
  Joseph 72
McClindon
  Jacob 86
McClish
  Jamas 293
McClorough
  James 179
McClung
  Reuben 284

McCluskey
  David H. 111
McClusky
  Benjamin 65
McCombs
  Loveberry 223
  Robert 62, 91
McCondichie
  John 240
McConnell
  John 16, 180, 245
  Joseph 54
  Robert C. 272
McCook
  Daniel 124
McCord
  James .49, 54, 83, 130
McCorkle
  William 294
McCormick
  David 57, 134
McCowen
  Fendley 135
McCoy
  Archibald 83
  David 152
  Donald 132
  Everett 95
  Henry 144
  Leroy 119
  Stephen 48
  William 31
McCrarey
  Daniel 148
  Mathew 272
  Neel 278
  William 282
McCrary
  Bartlett 235
  Ezekiel 111
  Lauchlin 273

McCravy
  Isaac 73
  John 220
  Stuard 46
McCray
  Isaac 48
McCready
  James B. 178
McCroan
  John 207
McCrone
  James 124
McCullen
  William 141
McCullers
  William 177
McCullough
  Joseph 56
McCurdy
  David 19
  James 273
  John 52
  Stephen 209
McCurry
  Angus 170
  Samuel 195
McCutchin
  Mark 302
McCutching
  Joseph 215
McDade
  Alexander 284
  Lynn 147
  William 114
McDaniel
  Alexander 206
  James 86, 141
  Jeremiah 97
  John 97, 104, 165,
      189, 238, 283
  Zadock 283

Name Index

McDermont
  Ballard 210
  Edward 99
McDonald
  Alexander 24, 284
  David 76
  Dennis 284
  Donald 31
  Hugh 314
  James 103, 137
  John 2, 37, 53, 145, 183, 239, 282
  Norman 11
  William 72, 75
McDonnell
  Alexander 256
McDorman
  John 84
McDougall
  Robert 38
McDowel
  James 95
McDowell
  James 92
  John 153, 241, 287
  William 95
McDurmont
  Ballard 254
McElvey
  William 187
McEven
  Brice 230
McEver
  Joseph 145
McEwen
  James 228
McFalls
  Thomas 60
McFarlin
  William 4

McGagaughey
  William 151
McGahey
  Daniel 141
McGar
  Edward 147
McGarlan
  William 73
McGarrity
  Abner 58
McGauhey
  Abner 124
McGee
  John 2
McGehe
  Samuel 29
McGehee
  Edward 217
  James 217, 293
McGenty
  John 73
McGill
  John 308
  Marris 280
McGillis
  Randolph 7
McGinthy
  Robert 83
McGinty
  John 159, 163
McGrady
  Silas 34
McGrath
  Patrick 194
McGriff
  William 42
McGuire
  John M. P. 201
McGuirt
  David 242

McGuoirk
  Benjamin 229
McIntosh
  David 33
  George B. 213
  John L. 282
  William R. 279
McIver
  Andrew 47
  Donald 112
McKee
  John 77
McKeever
  Robert 29, 42
McKegney
  Thomas 228
McKenna
  Charles 105, 131
McKenne
  Barna 49
McKenney
  John 37
McKenny
  Caleb 26
  John 173
McKenzie
  Alexander 222
  William 28, 53
McKigney
  George 148
  Thomas 287
McKigny
  Beattie 56
McKinne
  John 22
  Roger 120
McKinney
  Charles Jr. 229
  John B. 132
  Kinchen 256
  William 150, 192

375

McKinney, cont.
   Wilson 135, 245
McKinnie
   David 132
McKinny
   George 317
McKinzee
   Alen 62
McKinzie
   John 47
   Philip 201
   William 41
McKissack
   Archibald 77
McKleroy
   William 59
McKnight
   Robert 23
McKorkle
   William 87
McLaughlen
   William 147
McLaws
   James 226
McLean
   Andrew 124
   John 122
McLendon
   Amos 225, 246
   Benniah 106
   Medad 287, 303
   Neidham 225
   Thomas 211
McLeod
   Donald 275, 290
   Murdock 91
   Norman 178
   William 207
McLeroy
   James 268
   Joseph 274

McLeroy, cont.
   Lewis 278
McMannis
   Robert 197
McMichael
   John 19, 165
   Matthew 312
   Shadrich 76
   Zachariah 302
McMichal
   Green 234
McMight
   Mathew 46
McMillan
   Alexander 69
McMillian
   Daniel 298
McMillon
   Duncan 278
McMullen
   Jeremiah 100
   Neal 121
McMurphy
   John 119
McMurray
   James 219
McMurrey
   James 153
McNabb
   Daniel 302
McNair
   Duncan 64, 111
   Samuel 43
McNeely
   Isaac 149
   John 81
   Robin 257
McNeil
   Archibald 215
McNiece
   William 154

McNiel
   Daniel 9
McNight
   Charles 156
McNorel
   Mackry 88
McNorrill
   Henry 313
McQueen
   Charles 278
McRae
   Duncan 218, 251
   Farquhard Jr. 242
   John 108
McRainie
   Daniel 173
McRary
   William 291
McRight
   James 235
McTerrell
   John 243
McTier
   Holland 1
McTyeire
   Holland 17
   Robert 17
   William 18
McTyre
   Robert 126
McTyree
   William 97
McWilliams
   Archibald 148
Mead
   Cowles 49
   John 273
   Joseph H. 289, 297
   Miner 13
Meador
   Isaac 75

Name Index

Meador, cont.
William 295
Meadows
Benjamin 122
Radsom 288
Means
John 269
Meeks
John 101, 201
Mark 289
Mehaffey
Thomas 253
Meham
Alexander 87
Mehoffy
William 44
Mehone
Peter F. 183
Meikum
James 21
Mekell
George 13
Mell
Benjamin 252
Melson
Daniel 20
Melton
Elijah 52
Henry 231
Stephen 124
Mendenhall
John W. 111, 133
Mendledorf
John George 143
Mercer
Harmon 274
Herman 60
Hermon 235
John 201, 267
Nathaniel 19, 127
Solomon 139

Mercey
Benjamin 256
Mercier
Henry F. 255
Meredith
David 149
Samuel 236
Meriwether
Alexander 230, 289
Alixander 181
James .. 149, 221, 223, 307, 310
John G. 221
Nicholas 43
Valentine 10
Merrell
Peter 188
Merritt
Benjamin 176
Thomas 128, 129
Merriwether
Alexander 209
Mersson
James 56
Meshon
William 314
Messer
Christopher 141
Metzger
Jacob 165
Mezill
David 38
Micars
John 199
Micham
Thomas 104
Mickell
George 48
Mickler
Jacob 7
William 142, 158, 218

Middlebrook
Joseph 215, 269
Robert 74
Middlebrooks
Robert 164
Middleton
James 22
Parker 254
Parkes 236
Zachariah 133
Zackriah 56
Miers
Elijah 194
Nathan 138
Mikell
Charles 71, 96
James 58
Thomas 71
Miles
David 17
Ebenezer 236, 292
James 240
John 172
Thomas 112
William 175
William H. 210
Mill
Benjamin 158, 279
John 279
Millen
Basdil 164
Millener
James 309
Miller
Charles 77, 100
Francis 52, 301
Henry 138, 157
Jacob 142
John 156, 317
Jonathan 228
Joseph 12

377

Miller, cont.
   Levi 227
   Richard 120
   Samuel 175, 286
   Samuel W. 306
   Thomas H. 105, 118
   William 5, 303

Millican
   James 130
   Robert 249

Milligan
   John 216

Mills
   Anthony 256
   Deal 266
   Robert 241
   Spier 126
   William 5

Millsap
   William 225

Millum
   Dudley 286

Milner
   Jeremiah 185
   John H. 214
   Jonathan 131
   Pitman 86
   Simeon 132
   Smith 49

Milsaps
   Fuller 179
   Marvel 259

Milton
   Benjamin 289
   Henry 301
   Homer V. 88, 102

Milzger
   David 91

Mimms
   Chesley B. 308
   William 295

Mims
   Chesley 298
   Martin G. 258

Miner
   John B. 71

Minis
   Abraham 23

Minter
   Robert R. 148, 232

Minton
   Jessee 154
   Mills 131
   Noah 148, 177
   William J. 207

Mirell
   Benjamin 84

Mires
   George B. 306
   Nathaniel 60

Mironey
   William 197

Missick
   Jeremiah 313

Mitcham
   Marcus 173
   Richard 176

Mitchel
   Thomas 87

Mitchell
   David Bradie 48
   David Brydie 97
   John 18, 125
   Robert 175
   Thomas 141, 239
   Uriah G. 124
   William 170, 274
   William S. 222

Mitlock
   Stephen 209

Mitzger
   Jacob 149

Mitger
   John J. 292

Mitzker
   David 37

Mixon
   William 11

Mize
   Anderson 133

Mizell
   David 111
   Jesse 154

Mobley
   Daniel D. 168
   James M. 118
   Stephen .. 47, 199, 270
   William 53, 92

Mock
   Jacob 51
   Thomas 177

Modishead
   Brooks 34

Moffett
   Eli 102, 134
   Gabriel A. 270
   John 136, 153

Molton
   Elijah 66

Monfort
   James 22

Mongomery
   Samuel 62

Monk
   John 281
   Myal 71
   Thomas 186

Monroe
   Joseph 152

Montford
   Theodore 296

Montfort
   James 27

Montfort, cont.
   Theodorick 312
   Theophilus 91

Montgomery
   Bartley 266
   David 116
   Jacob 14
   James 144
   James M. C. 114
   John 14
   John H. 199
   Marthew Scott 87
   Robert 179
   Samuel 23, 70, 84
   Washington 99
   William ... 44, 258, 292

Montmollin
   T. L. D. 34

Moody
   Benjamine 155
   David 156
   Henry T. 147
   James 170
   John 296
   Perriman 228
   Perryman 300
   Solomon 185, 280

Moon
   Bowler 40
   Edom 157
   Robert 65
   William ... 91, 238, 317

Mooning
   Isaac 308

Moor
   Samuel 38

Moore
   Abner 267
   Alexander 158, 315
   Andrew 118
   Anthony 73

Moore, cont.
   Benjamin S. 308
   Charles 52
   Charles G. 297
   David 184, 275
   Ebenezer 39, 242
   Edward 2, 68
   George 19
   George W. 6, 167, 221
   Henry 295
   Isaac Jr. 190, 219
   Jacob 10, 120
   James .. 27, 29, 39, 42, 48, 82, 120
   James J. 315
   Jesse 40
   Jesse B. ... 97, 102, 138
   Joel 111
   John 125, 147, 168, 174, 183
   Jonathan 280
   Joseph 149
   Joseph J. 98, 159
   Luke 32, 44
   Mark E. 295
   Morin 125
   Moses 196
   Pleasant 85, 155
   Robert 22, 68, 95, 109, 138, 141, 166, 284
   Samuel . 166, 196, 296
   Thomas 167, 225
   Thomas Jr. 87
   William . 17, 120, 158, 306
   William A. 61, 90
   Williscie 87
   Youg 100

Moose
   Samuel 287

Morable
   Robert 87

Moran
   Jesse 195, 266

More
   Jacob 84

Morehead
   John 112

Morel
   Benjamin 8
   John H. 32, 47

Moreland
   Elisha 85, 218
   Francis 283
   George 41
   Howel 106
   Howell 109
   Isaac T. 287
   Jacob W. 302
   Turner 225
   Tuttle 261
   Wood 228

Morell
   Jordan 176

Moreman
   John 217

Moren
   James 133

Morgan
   Bithal 310
   Blake 195, 274
   Daniel 314
   Edward 178
   George 117
   Isham 239
   James 112
   James B. 208
   Joseph 157, 297
   Joshua 293
   Stephen 43
   Stokeley 1

Morgan, cont.
   William ...99, 116, 167
   William C. 303, 311
Moriarty
   Dennis......................18
Morrell
   John 293
   Thomas U. 293
Morris
   Chesley 86
   James............254, 301
   James M. 109
   Jesse 248
   John 106
   Joseph......................38
   Nathan...................244
   Obediah 177
   Shadrick 78
   Thomas 100, 128
Morrison
   James......95, 180, 231
   Norman...................29
Morrow
   James....................145
   Joseph......................21
   William H. 258, 312
Morton
   James......................35
   Joseph.....88, 104, 177
Moseley
   Lewis.......................41
   Thomas 243, 310
   William 278
Mosely
   Benjamin 82
   Elial 280
Mosley
   William 286
Moss
   James....................204
   Nathaniel..............147

Mott
   Isaac 26
Moulder
   Lewis.......................93
Mound
   Daniel............80, 106
   Malichi 106
Mounger
   Edwin 71
   Henry N................136
   Thomas...................79
Mountain
   Robert...................104
   Thomas.................278
Moxley
   Daniel.....................33
Muborn
   Benjamin..............206
Muckelroy
   Michael.................165
Muckleroy
   James 87
Mulkey
   Jonathan 248
   Moses............76, 186
   William .110, 186, 190
Mullens
   Thomas.................149
Mullikan
   William 190
Mullins
   Hardy 118
   John 231
   May.......................232
   Robert...................261
   Thomas...................69
   William 119
Muncrief
   David 216
Munday
   Stephen 28

Munden
   William 304
Munroe
   Neil....................85, 90
Muny
   George 180
Murdock
   Jeremiah 68
   William 135
Murkeson
   John........................48
Murphey
   Alexander.............285
   Cornelius................35
   James 236
Murphie
   Mills 3
Murphree
   Mills 35
Murphy
   James 227
   John............. 211, 219
Murray
   Alexander.............292
   David 103
   David S. 317
   James 302
Murrell
   Thomas W. 279
Murrey
   James 112
Murrow
   Ransom 95
Muse
   James W. 130
Musgrove
   Robert H. 95, 110
Myers
   George B. 310
Myham
   John......................158

Myres
    Thomas 309
Myrick
    Evans 240
    Goodwin 218, 251
    John 106
    John F. 175
    Joodison 141
    Robert 296

N

Nail
    Reuben 130
Nall
    John 185
Nalley
    Hendley 235
Nally
    Abraham 285
Naly
    Samuel 194
Napier
    Thomas 111
Nawley
    Nathan 290
Nay
    John 254
Neal
    James 292
    John B. 237
    John T. 271
    Theophilus 135
    Thomas 238
Neblack
    Thomas 60
Needlenger
    John 291
Neel
    Hezekiah 138
    Jonathan 138, 207

Neely
    Barkesdale B. 280
Neidlinger
    John 219
Neil
    Reuben 244
    Reubin 90
    Stephen 60
Neilson
    John 92
    Joseph 181
Nelmes
    William 317
Nelmns
    Thomas 8
Nelms
    James 144
    James R. 100
    Samuel 317
    Thomas 31
Nelson
    Archbalid 86
    Archibald 187
    Charles H. 316
    George 77, 173
    George W. 276
    John 34
    Joseph 125
    Sylvester 221
Nephew
    James Jr. 294
Nesmith
    James 137, 189
New
    Jesse 298
Newber
    Thomas 121
Newbern
    Thomas 13, 26
Newell
    Robert 229

Newgin
    Matthew 299
Newman
    Jonathan 147
    Thomas 36
Newnan
    Daniel 310
Newsom
    David A. 267
    Jody 20
    Joeday 235
    Joedy 103
    Robert 115
Newsome
    Joel 175
Newton
    Aristarchuse 311
    Aristarcus 277
    John 214
    Josiah 261, 290
Neyland
    Gilbert 68, 107
Neyle
    Samson 60
Nicholas
    David 75
Nichols
    David 165
    John 299
    Simon W. 312
Nicholson
    Britain 211, 308
    James H. 83
    Nathaniel 187, 224
    Samuel 114
Night
    Ephraim 206
Nix
    John 119
    William 78

Nixon
    Joseph 117
Noales
    John 188
Nobles
    Dennis 3
    James 139, 266
    Robert 32
    Sanders 266
    William 90
Nolley
    Joseph 214
    Nathan 189
Norman
    George 14
    Joseph 214
    Lewis 76, 85
    William 83
    William H. 146, 160
Norris
    Benjamin B. 288
    James 256, 293
    John B. 261
    Rigdon 246
Northam
    Zachariah 122
Northcut
    Alexander 117, 312
    Robert 155
Northeat
    Robert 134
Northern
    Samuel 116
Norton
    William 188
Norwon
    William 275
Nothern
    William 188
Nowlan
    George Galphin 73

Nowland
    George 107, 117
    George G. 277
Nowlin
    David 209
    George G. 110
Nunn
    Edmund 184
Nunnelie
    John 260
    William 187
Nunnelley
    Horatio 245

O

Oakes
    John 185
    Reuben 292
    Reubin 280
Oakman
    Henry W. 212
Oates
    John P. 227
    John Peter 7, 107
    William 110
Oats
    James 312
Oban
    Robert 185
Obarr
    Thomas 220
O'Berry
    James 22
Odom
    Jacob 155
Ogle
    William 62
Oglesby
    Robert 184

Ogletree
    Edmund 257, 277, 314
    William 23
O'Kelly
    Charles 299
Oldfields
    William 87
Oliver
    Berry 294
    Daniel 110
    Deonyshus 288
    Jacob 263
    James 31, 135, 140, 143
    James L. 178
    John 135, 263, 278
    Moses 255
    Phinias 214
    Resdon 255
    Risden 101, 107
    Robert 57
    Thomas 95, 121
    William 183
    William W. 255
Olliver
    William W. 258
Oneal
    Daniel 312
    H. 317
    Harrison 254
    Henry 239
    Isham 156
    John 109
    Joseph M. 245
O'Neal
    James 39
Oneall
    Joseph W. 198
    Quinea 250
Oneel
    Thomas 257

Oneel, cont.
William 257
Oniel
Daniel H. 108
Orean
Benjamin 277
Orear
Benjamin 261
John 302
Orine
William 197
Orm
William D. 274
Orr
Matthew 292
Philip 161
Robert 190
Orren
John 284
Osborn
George 315
Osborne
George 81
Osburne
George 260
Osgood
John Jr. 25
Oslin
Jesse 228
William W. ... 292, 314
Osteen
Bartholomew 253
Ounsell
Daniel 6
Overa
Needom 46
Overstreet
John 265
Samuel 265
Silas 252, 306

Overton
Joseph 307
Owen
John 68
Robert 279
William 93, 141
Owens
Elijah 58
George 24
Hardiman 310
John 88
Robert 165, 188
Samuel 74
Spencer 316
Thomas 229
Owing
Samuel 211
Oxford
Jonathan 8, 25
Telmon 271

P

Pace
Barnabus 249
Dread 179
Dreadril 235
Isaac 39
James 39
Jeremiah 248
Nathaniel 23
Nathaniel Jr. 4
Thomas 22, 81, 179
William 270, 299
Padget
Elijah 42
Padgett
Elisha 102, 180
Page
Allen 19
Andrew 282

Page, cont.
James 47
William 125, 284
Paget
William 51
Palmer
Jonathan 104, 131, 186
Parham
Edmund 239
Roban 253
Robert 15
Paris
John 68
Parish
Harris 108
Jonathan 107, 180
Josiah 100
Wyat 181
Park
James 188, 246
William 86
Parker
Aaron 141, 153
Caleb 82, 163
David 98, 153
George 282
James 182, 276
John 251
John W. 296
Lewis 288
Mathew 111
Mathew G. 133
Needham 171
Simon 221, 229
Uriah 278
William C. 295
William H. 276
Parkes
Lewis 267
William 93

Parks
    John ..15, 47, 262, 286
    John A. 121
    John B. 86
    Richard 196
    William 20
Parlin
    Charles 26
Parmore
    Thomas 80
Parr
    Mathew 241
Parramore
    Noah 15
Parre
    John 291
Parrott
    Robert 162
Parsons
    Turner 237
    William 10
Partrick
    Andrew 312
    Luke 307
Paschal
    Samuel 175
Paschall
    Isaiah 253
Pass
    Matthew J. 225
Passmore
    Samuel 216
Pate
    Ebemelik 306
    Thomas 45, 145
Patman
    William 15
Patrick
    John C. 195
    Luke 34
    William 173, 179

Patrick, cont.
    William C. 117
Patridge
    Jarrett 99
    John 189
Patten
    James 176
Patterson
    David 275
    James 23, 72
    John 122, 277
    John A. 125
    John H. 190
    John T. 160
    Tryon 130
    William ... 33, 120, 122
Pattille
    John 266
Pattillo
    George H. 162
Pattilloe
    George 291
Patton
    Jacob 212
    James 52, 132
    Samuel 15
Paul
    John Jr. 183
    Moses 122
Paulett
    Blassengame 176
    Blassingham 168
    John 107
    William 18
Paxton
    John 13
    Joseph 65, 128
    Robert 111
    Samuel 241
Payne
    Daniel 61

Payne, cont.
    Elijah 41
    Fleming 20
    John C. 213
    Nathaniel 47
    Reuben 208
    Thomas 119, 189
    William 46, 84, 106
    Zachariah 41
Payner
    William 302
Peabler
    Thomas 16
Peace
    John 33
Peacock
    Eli 55
    Jessee 197
    John 214
    Michael 150
    William 287
Pearce
    Abraham 5
    Daniel 123, 129
Pearman
    Robert 161
    Samuel 309
Pearre
    William 114
Pearrea (Pearrce?)
    James 259
Pearrie
    Nathaniel 215
Pearson
    Christopher 257
    Garland 220
    George 55, 203
    Henry 9
    John 93
    Jonathan 132, 207, 293

Pearson, cont.
 Leonard 45
 Wenloch C. 276
 William................... 32
Peary
 Burrel 55
Pease
 Aaron.................... 138
Peavy
 Archibald................ 87
Peebles
 Dudley 120
 Henry 43
Peek
 Hiram 251
 Leonard M............ 124
Peeke
 Henry 37
Peeples
 Dudley 78
 Henry 157
 John...................... 221
Peevy
 Abraham 98
Pelot
 James 89, 113, 291
Pemberton
 Atton 84
Pendleton
 John B. 156
 John W. 190
Pendral
 Ralph 59
Pengree
 Thomas................. 281
Penington
 Abel 194
Penix
 William................. 128
Penman
 Robert.................... 86

Penn
 Benjamin 162, 241, 252, 317
 Thomas H. ... 150, 184
Pennington
 Abel 156
 Able 146
 John 60
 William 63, 91
Penny
 George...................177
Penor
 Robert 140
Penticost
 George...................233
Peoples
 Dudley...................134
 Jesse......................105
Perdue
 Thomas 155
 William 155
Perkins
 Constantine 81
 Ezekiel 171
 Newton....................79
 Richard 117
 Solomon . 60, 129, 253
 Walker 261
 William 203
Permenter
 William 202, 243
Permento
 John 307
Perrey
 Jesse......................259
Perry
 Hardy 241
 James L. 216
 John 241
 Michael 93
 Nicholas 108

Perryman
 David A................273
Pervis
 Jesse Jr.................164
Peteat
 John 300
Peteet
 Simeon..................161
Pettibone
 John 79
Pettilane
 John 61
Pettybone
 John 135
Pettygrew
 John W. 135
Pettyjohn
 James....................201
Phair
 Ephraim 246
Phare
 Ephraim 281
Pharoah
 Frances 91
Pharr
 Ephraim 208
Phelps
 Avington...............243
 James C...............262
 Overton.................282
Philips
 Dempsey.................35
 Ephraim 211
 Hakins 149
 John 194
 Matthew 119
 Nathan 265
 Royalbud 186
 William 146
 William C. 186
 Willie 241

Philips, cont.
    Zachariah 122
Phillips
    Charles 316
    Isaac 34
    James 38
    William 133
Phinizy
    Jacob 195
    John 314
    Mareo 254
Pickard
    Henry 262
    Micajah 108
Pickering
    William 84
Pickett
    Francis 18
Pickren
    Gabriel 135
    John 300
Pickron
    William 77
Pierce
    Chester 162
    Jacob 243
    Jesse 274
    Thomas 271
Pierson
    Jonathan 158
Pigot
    John Jr. 24
Pilcher
    Edward 243
    Stephen 1
Pilchin
    Reese 194
Piles
    James 251
    Samuel . 120, 185, 269, 294

Pines
    Daniel 166
Pinkard
    Payton 176
Pinkham
    Samuel 26
Pinkston
    James 92, 148
Pinkum
    Samuel 202
Pinson
    Jacob 108
    Joab 268
Pipkin
    David 211, 244
Pitche
    Archibald 208
Pitcher
    Edward 184
Pitman
    Icabod 77
    Jesse 313
    John G. 155, 242
    Philip 94
Pittard
    William 273
Pittman
    Archibald 303
    John 32, 272
    John G. 87
Pitts
    Henry 226
    Lunsford C. .. 297, 307
    Thomas 296
Pleasants
    Thomas 252
Pledger
    Lemuel 149
Pleister
    Benjamine 167

Pointer
    John 63
Polhill
    Thomas 6
    Thomas Jr. 91
Polk
    Hugh 197
Polley
    Robert 184
Pollon
    George 124
Pomele
    Henry 152
Pondar
    John 261
Ponder
    Abner 59
    Amos 137, 167
    James H. 100
    John L. 167
    William L. 155
Pool
    Middleton 217
Pope
    Burwell 147, 262
    Charles 136
    George L. 193
    Henry 262
    John F. 293
    Leroy 11
    Nicholas . 33, 132, 162
    Robert 98, 141, 157
    Wiley 104
    Wilson 305
Porder
    Andrew 225
Porr
    William 285
Porter
    Charles 283
    Joel 211

Name Index

Porter, cont.
- John 240, 256
- John S. 153, 163
- John T. 144
- Johnston 78
- Joshua 195
- Nobles 209
- Oliver 26
- Robert 107
- Russell 134
- William 275

Portson
- John 315

Portwood
- Howard 303

Posey
- Andrew 193, 285
- Benjamin 3
- Dennis 205
- William 193

Poss
- John 150
- William 50

Post
- Joseph M. 248

Potter
- James 189
- John 144

Poulett
- Lewis M. 221

Poulin
- George 177

Poullen
- John 61

Poullin
- John 107

Pouton
- Milton 306

Powel
- Hiram 290
- John 60

Powel, cont.
- Josiah 58
- Thomas 9
- Tillman 298

Powell
- Abraham T. 43
- Allen B. 52, 109
- Arden 305
- Asa 302
- Dempsey 214
- Elijah 74, 155, 265
- Elkanah 233
- George 224, 309
- James 46, 84
- John . 78, 89, 103, 298
- Josiah 158
- Lewis 317
- Nathan 124, 137
- William 56, 65, 87, 193

Powers
- Clem 202
- Clement 140, 276
- James ... 229, 238, 243
- John 226
- John W. 233

Poythress
- Edward 224
- William 96

Prather
- Edward 142
- Richard 286, 297
- Thomas 186, 236, 282

Pratt
- Hillery 117

Pray
- John 37, 155

Prescot
- Samuel F. 298

Presly
- Elijah 204

Presswood
- Thomas J. 26

Prevatt
- James 173
- Morgan 266

Prewitt
- Josiah 253
- Samuel Jr. 223

Price
- Brittain 160
- George 175
- James 74
- John 146, 195, 249
- Sterling 135, 205
- Thomas 273
- Thomas B. 312
- William 156, 285

Prichard
- Richard 45

Prickett
- George 154

Pridgen
- Thomas 214
- William 142

Pridgeon
- William 287

Priest
- Gabriel 288

Prince
- George 35
- Oliver 28

Pritchard
- James 314
- John B. 276

Procter
- George V. 212

Proctor
- Jonas 39, 98

Prophet
- James 132

Prophitt
James 236
Prosser
Jesse 224
Proudfoot
Hugh W 235, 294
Provost
William 74
Pruncey
John 153
Prussell
John 78
Pruster
John 201
Pruther
Thomas 146
Pucket
John 173
Puckett
Aron B 223
Edmund 157
John 180
Pugh
Edgeworth 225
James 33, 166
Thomas 160
William 39
Puliam
Garlington 173
Pulin
Charles 294
Pullen
Moses 196
Samuel 183
Zelah 131
Pulliam
Thomas 167
Pullicrew
Nathan 130
Pullin
Athael 237

Pullin, cont.
Zelah 233
Pulling
Samuel 255
Pully
Benjamin 308
Purcy
Benjamin 315
Purifoy
John 237
Pursell
Ignatius 172
Pursil
Ignatius 11
Purvis
Burnett 304
Richard 146
Pyland
James 145
Pyle
John 119

Q

Quarterman
John S 120, 158
Joseph 300
Robert ... 130, 249, 252
Quinn
Calvin 231

R

Rabun
John 187
Rachel
William 283
Rachels
George 90
James 225
William 272

Rad
Elias 195
Radcliff
Richard 118
Rae
John 71
Raes
Jacob 6
Ragan
Jeremiah 270
Ragland
John A. 268
John R. 49
Raiford
Alexander G. 180
Robert 312
Raimey
Edmond 169
Rain
Joseph 194
Raines
Cadwallader 20
Henry 219
Joseph 68
Rainey
Mathew 177
Rakstraw
Robert 316
Raleigh
Henry W. 304
Raley
Henry W. 213
Raly
Jemsey 180
Rambart
Edward 208
Ramey
Noah 64
Ramsay
Henry G. 204

Ramsey
   David 311
   George 71
   James 31, 111
   John 96
   Noah 37
Rancey
   Josiah 249
Randal
   Peter 253
Randale
   James G. 255
Randall
   William 146
Randle
   Benjamin J. 201
   James G. 248
Randolph
   Beverly 188
   George F. 108
   John 133
   Richard H. 251
Raney
   Isham 66
   Joseph 20
   Lazarus 229
Rankin
   Daniel 297
   David 305
Rannolds
   Preston 16
Ransom
   James 314
   Jeremiah P. 257
Rasbury
   Reubin 175
Ratcliff
   Gabriel 154
   Richard 222
   William 140

Ratliff
   John 54
Raulerson
   Jacob 228
Ravins
   David 278
   James H. 301
Rawles
   John 148
   Shadrick 177
Rawls
   John 231, 236, 244
   Shadrack 182
Ray
   Ambrose 185
   Charles 39, 63
   David 115
   Isaac 218
   Jeremiah 170
   Jeremiah W. 176
   John W. 215
   Robert 50
   Thomas 271
   William 125, 262
Raygan
   Asa 88, 100
Rayland
   Thompson 121, 130
Rayston
   Robert 23
Read
   Charles 104
   David 185
   George Padden 5
   Robert 66
Ready
   Isham 308
   Peter 5
Rease
   Aaron 239
   John 69

Reaves
   David 281
   John 294
Reddick
   James 118
Redding
   John 239
   William 239
Reddock
   David 51
Redfield
   Elias 315
Reece
   Isham 140
Reed
   Alexander 27, 46
   George 221
   Jacob 165
   John 179
   Robert 45, 46
   Stephen 109, 220
Rees
   Ebenezer S. .. 187, 240
   Joshua 224
Reese
   Drury 89
   Littleton 89
   Rowell 316
   Sittleton 25
   William 198
Reeve
   Aron 269
Reeves
   David 217
   John 201, 220
   John T. 171
   Lee 241
   Thomas 260
Reid
   Alexander 69
   Elisha 235

Reid, cont.
   George 60
   Henry 247
   James 287
   John 33, 231, 243, 277
   Joseph 85
   Robert R. 226
   Stephen 99
   William 169

Reisser
   James 237

Reizer
   James 211

Rencau
   William T. 248

Render
   James 27, 37
   Joshua Jr. 93

Renders
   Joshua 116

Renfro
   Stephen 102
   William 101

Renfroe
   Elisha 31
   Joel 248
   Nathaniel 102
   Nathaniel W. 281

Rentfro
   Stephen 73
   William 73

Resher
   Francis 96

Reussou
   James 138

Revear
   Henry L. 112

Reveir
   John R. 45

Reynolds
   Coleman 218

Reynolds, cont.
   Hezekiah 106
   James 305
   James G. 233
   James M. 191
   Reubin 40
   Robert 121
   Terry 302
   William ... 96, 115, 230

Rhan
   Samuel 217

Rhew
   James 287

Rhiney
   Charles 184

Rhoades
   William 301

Rhoads
   Thomas 278

Rhodes
   Aaron 68
   Heflin 208
   Henry 130
   James 172
   John 225
   Samuel 121
   Thomas 6

Rice
   Garland 314
   James 315
   Jesse 29, 42
   John 234
   Leonard 130

Richard
   Manning 263

Richards
   James 277
   John 296
   Uriah 256

Richardson
   Amos 95

Richardson, cont.
   Armstead 228, 311
   Armsted 254
   Gabriel 18, 210
   James 265
   Jonathan 34
   Joseph 209
   Laurence 135
   Schuyter 109
   Thomas 14
   William 284

Rick
   Edward 265

Ricks
   Daniel 252
   James 141
   John 252

Riddle
   Anderson 122
   Loyd 309
   Thomas 41

Ridgers
   John Jr. 152

Ridgeway
   David 16
   Drury 76

Rieves
   John 248

Rigby
   Thomas R. 90

Riggs
   Stephen 240
   William 84

Rigins
   Tomas 285

Rigs
   Stephen 157

Rigsby
   Allen 138

Riley
   Jacob 131, 270

Name Index

Riley, cont.
    James 296
    Joseph 298
    Terral 274
    Thomas 115

Rimes
    William 241

Ringold
    Richard 57

Ripley
    Sylvanus 298

Rispiss
    Richard 137

Ritchell
    Charles 280

Ritcher
    Archibald 189

Ritchey
    James 297

Rivers
    James 139
    Robert 20

Roach
    James M. 293
    John 150, 156
    Jonathan 301

Roache
    James M. 282

Roades
    Heslin 257

Roads
    Henry 224

Roan
    Jesse J. 247, 262

Robbins
    Josiah 92
    William 143
    William O. 121

Roberds
    John 52

Roberson
    Edward 19
    Isac 59

Robert
    George 156

Roberts
    Abram 33
    Charles 202
    Daniel 21, 276
    Elijah 296
    George 96, 144
    Isham 13
    Jabez 114, 123
    James 281
    Jesse 52, 195, 211
    John 98, 124, 284
    John J. 229
    John T. 261
    Moses A. 141, 171
    Norrell 285
    Norval 178
    Richard 31
    Rowland 82
    Sandler 131
    Simeon 287
    Wiley 203
    William 109, 127
    Williard 282
    Willis 184, 203
    Zachariah 271

Robertson
    Abednego 95
    Carrinton 294
    Edmund 68
    James 170, 192
    Jesse 192
    John 296
    Noel 45
    Samuel 192
    Thomas 7, 53
    Tryer 94

Robertson, cont.
    William 46, 207

Robey
    Robert 198
    William 33

Robins
    Pheny 96
    Phiney 49

Robinson
    Aron 129
    David 232
    Herbert 307
    Isaac 40
    Jacob 25, 131, 311
    James 67, 74
    Jesse 112, 183
    John 257, 267
    John G. 313
    Jonathan 233
    Joseph M. 287
    Joseph W. 276
    Lewellen M. 257
    Lewelling 240
    Samuel 4
    Soloman 251
    William 259
    William H. 109, 139

Robson
    Wiley 150

Robuck
    Robert 267

Rockmore
    Thomas 94

Rodgers
    Enoch 41
    Josiah 183
    Moses 182

Rodny
    John 83

Rodolph
    Michael 241

Roe
  Samuel 297
  Shadrach 29
Roebuck
  George 100
Rogers
  David 258
  Drury 41
  Enoch 194
  Frederick 50
  George W. 127
  Jacob 233, 301
  James A. 253
  John 135, 155, 293, 308
  Josiah 254, 267
  Moses 286
  Peleg 87
  Poley 40
  Shadrach 284
  Shadrick 205
  Thomas 142, 285
  Timothy 273
  Timothy L. 306
  William 47, 134
Roland
  James 261
  Reubin 36
  Reves 19
  Sharod 269
Ronaldson
  Andrew 159
Roney
  John 176
Roper
  John 137
Roric
  John 71
Rorie
  John 99

Rose
  Grantham 306
  Henry 232, 270
  Huston 126
  Stephen 118
Ross
  Etheldred 99, 112
  Francis 175
  Francis J. 258
  Isaac 161
  Isham 89
  James 58
  John 156, 190, 217, 250
  Reubin 78
  William 86
  Willie 226
  Wyley 112
Rosser
  Daniel 298
  David 134, 139
  Elijah 116
Rossiter
  White 170
Roswood
  William 281
Roundtree
  George 73
Rousseau
  James 204
Roussoan
  William 216
Rowden
  Laban 99
Rowe
  William 138
Rowell
  Randolph 49
  Richard 226
Rowland
  James 74

Rowland, cont.
  John 306
  Merret 180
  Merrett 131
  Sherod 242
  William 314
Rowsey
  James 205
Rowton
  Richard 86
Royal
  James 220
  William 197
Royland
  James 269
Rozar
  Aaron 153
Rozer
  Robert 142
Rozier
  Robert 160
Rucker
  Azmon 113
  Barton 118
  Fielding 299
  James Jr. 279
  John Jr. 208
  Joseph 246
Ruddell
  Abraham 99
Ruddle
  Mounce 134
Rudisill
  John 208, 227
Rudney
  John 137
Rudolph
  Robert 68
Rudulph
  Francis J. 280

Name Index

Rumsey
James 148
Runnalds
Thomas.................. 20
Runnells
Harden D. 137
James 169
Reuben 283
Runsly
James 62
Rush
James 166
Jonathan 273
Rushen
Bryant 148
John....................... 46
Rushing
Bryant 204
Eli 148, 155
Joel 147
John........................ 1
Mathew 44
Russau
William................. 127
Russel
Andrew......... 213, 293
James 70
John..................... 303
Martin 303
Robert W. 196
William................. 191
William R. 244
Russell
Benjamin.............. 289
Caleb 161
James 316
John R. 317
Martin 316
Nathaniel 130
Ruster
David 71

Rustin
John 124
Ruston
Jesse......................285
Rutherford
John 10
John B.....................40
Thomas 123
Rutledge
James......................58
Thomas 5, 54
Ryals
Harbard 143
Joseph 266
Ryan
John P. 122
Peter......................142
Ryant
James 117
Ryce
Robert 121
Ryle
Joshua...................162
Rymes
William 160
Rynn
Peter......................179
Ryus
Noah......................191

S

Sadawhite
Obed......................217
Sadler
John 142
Saffold
James....................208
Sage
Francis..................109

Sale
Leroy.....................262
Richard 273
Salisbury
Solomon 139
Sallet
Robert 294
Salors
William 140
Salsbury
John 88
Salters
Robert 34
Sams
Francis..................152
William 164
Samuel
Benjamin 88
Robert 244, 285
Sandeford
James......................18
Nathan T. 308
Sanderford
John 37
Sanderlin
Benjamin 246
Benjamin J. 216
James....................305
John 205
Sanders
David 206
Edward 64
James............125, 175
Jeremiah 115
John 85, 169, 228, 265
Mark 15
Phillip....................64
Richard 49
William 92
Yancy 256

393

Sandford
  Robert 18
  Thornton 141, 179
Sandiford
  James 25
  John 178
Sanford
  Hamilton 309
  James 262
Sansom
  Robert 58
  William 94
Sapp
  John 50
  Lill 11
  Philip 136
  William 170
Sappington
  Caleb 268
Sarford
  James 255
Sargeant
  John 12
Saterwhite
  Paul 254
Sattawhite
  James 298
Satter
  Richard 194
  Zadock 231, 252
Saunders
  John 129
  Richard 54
  William 7
Savage
  James 43, 100, 183
  Zebulon 223
Savedge
  Solomon 91
Savidge
  John 111

Sawyer
  John 112
Sawyers
  John 154
Saxon
  Wiley 63
Sayre
  William Jr. 238
Scarber
  Jonathan 72
Scarboroug
  Ichabud 64
  Jonathan 110
Scarborough
  David 216
  Hardy 136, 170
  Jehabud 165
  Moses 75
  Noah 181, 244
  Peter 136, 146
  Shadrach 12
  Shadrick 39
Scarlett
  Francis 107
Schley
  John 198
  Michael 25
  William 113
Schockly
  Richard 168
Schweighoffer
  Abiel 39
Scism
  James 220
Scisson
  James 247
Scott
  Abraham 56, 144
  Andrew 99
  Benjamin 205
  Francis 158, 237

Scott, cont.
  Frederick 100, 239
  James 79, 244, 281
  John 294
  John W. 314
  Joseph A. 64
  Joseph J. 246
  Reubin 163
  Stephen P. 312
  Thomas 32, 33, 84, 93
  Thomas W. 75
  William . 4, 16, 35, 62,
    133, 161, 261
  William F. 158
  William Jr. 283
Scribner
  Abraham W. 154
Scriven
  John 62, 67
Scrivener
  Jesse 104
Scroggin
  Chatham D. 3
  Chatten 98
Scrogin
  Nehemah 66
Scruggs
  Gross 76
  James H. 242
  James H. P. 257
  Jesse 143
  Jessee 201
  William M. 253
Scurlock
  Joshua 29, 42
  Presley 4
Scutchings
  Josiah 227
Seager
  John 160

Name Index

Seagrove
James 110
Seal
Arnold 277, 289
Seale
John 24
Seales
Simeon 276
Thomas 12
Sealey
Gedion 112
Sears
David 139, 250
Seas
Timothy 224
Seay
John 293
Thomas 305
Sebert
Charles 307
Seborn
John 276
Seely
Ezekiel 99
Gideon 147
Seever
John 233
Segar
Benjamin 187
Segraves
Jacob 28
Self
Thomas 138
William 87
Selman
Benjamin 226
John 44, 82
Semonton
Abner 58
Sentell
Joseph 317

Senterfett
Henry 297
Sepp
John 76
Sesseons
Charles 130
Sessions
Benjamin 79, 126, 270
George 270
James 153
Sesson
Meeks 143
Richard M. 100
Setters
Young 185
Sexton
William 102
Shackelford
Edmund 310
Shackleford
John W. 86
Reichard 266
Richard 197, 214
Shad
Solomon 65
Shafer
Henry 113
Shaffer
James 186, 193
Shap
Grove 119
Sharbrew
Richard 206
Shark
John 19
Sharp
Bardle 61
Daniel 65
Hyram 298
James 166
John T. 299

Sharp, cont.
Richard 213
Wiley 51, 65
Sharpe
Basdel 24
Shaw
Daniel 132
Henry 36
John 129
John H. 161
Josias W. 236
Robert 137, 176
Shaws
Adam 255
Sheales
William 63
Shearer
Gilbert 157, 176
John 175
Shearhouse
John 82
Shearley
William S. 166
Shearwood
Benjamin 155
Sheaver
Elijah 291
Sheets
Archibald 318
Nicholas 61
Tarlton 104
Sheffield
Arthur 187
Bartlett 277
John 22
Plenny 253
Sheftal
Abram 232
M. M. 227
Sheftall
Mordica M. 190

395

Shellman
John 57
Shelly
Samuel 283, 300
Shelman
John 75, 187
John M. 297
Michael 106
Michall 67
Shelton
James 159
Thomas 251
Sheperd
Henry 125
Shepherd
John 156
William 92
Sheppard
Andrew 259
Henry 70
Simon 117
Thomas 27
Sherley
Moses 75
Sherrard
Robert 163
Sherrell
David 316
Sherrer
Elijah 300
Sherwood
Robert 91
Sheuman
John 17
Shewmake
Joseph 188
Shick
Peter 61, 237
Shields
James 45, 78
John 16

Shim
Daniel W. 205
Ship
Mark 257, 284
Shipp
John C. 127
Richard 201
Shire
Daniel W. 266
James W. 266
Shirey
John M. 296
Shivers
Thomas 141
Thomas W. ... 180, 228, 242, 316
Willis 89, 204
Shley
John 208
Shly
John J. 198
Shockley
Michael L. 270
Richard 265
Shoemake
Joseph 254
Shopshear
Waymon 133
Shores
David 50
Short
Daniel 296
Edward 115
Peter B. 310
Shorter
Bedford 275
Shouders
John 62
Shows
James 258

Shrift
Robert 76
Shropshire
James W. 228
Shuler
Robert 278
Shurholster
G. 260
Sicer
Nathan 143
Sickington
Christopher 107
Sidwell
David 85
Siegler
Emanuel 82
Sikes
Arthur 170
Edward 192
Joseph 153
Josiah 170
Sill
Joseph 154, 164
Sillivan
David 301
Silman
John 88, 95
Sim
Joshua 258
Simkins
William M. 303
Simmers
Daniel 228
Simmonds
Joseph 32
Simmons
Benjamin 77
H. F. 157
Henry 101
James 17
John 2, 71, 270

Name Index

Simmons, cont.
    John B. .. 183, 288, 311
    Samuel 288
    Thomas 189, 207
    William 288

Simms
    Allen 147
    Bartlett 69
    James 214
    John 41
    Julius 120
    Richard 107
    Richard R. 197
    William 214
    Zachariah 100

Simonton
    Abner 213
    Joel 220

Simpkins
    William M. 287

Simpson
    David ... 161, 182, 247, 300
    William 86

Sims
    Edward 180, 252
    John H. 101
    Leonard 171
    Leonard B. 255
    Robert 48
    William J. 191, 221

Singletary
    John 214

Singleton
    Wyatt 225

Sinquefield
    Zachriah 63

Sissom
    William P. 224

Sister
    Alexander 43

Siveet
    George D. 124

Skidmore
    Samuel 145

Skimmer
    William 55

Skinner
    John 161, 299

Slair
    Elijah 53

Slanton
    John B. 93

Slater
    Abner 107
    Jesse 75
    William 75

Slaton
    Brascella 300
    Elisha 187
    James 66
    Jesse 66
    Samuel 184

Slaughter
    Augustine 172, 182
    Ezekiel 206
    Joel 171
    Reuben 41
    Samson 39
    William 50
    William A. 197, 276

Sledge
    Chappel 80, 117
    Chappell 176
    Collin 240
    Whitfield 274

Sleigh
    Samuel M. 280

Slocumb
    John C. 79

Slubblefield
    Peter 79

Sludstill
    Hustus 13

Smally
    Michael 118

Smarr
    William 312

Smart
    Francis B. 277
    James 96

Smedley
    John 173

Smiley
    Robert B. 315

Smith
    Aaron 123
    Alexander 102, 134
    Andrew 190, 205
    Arington F. 178
    Baxter 117, 239
    Benjamin 217, 291
    Britain 283
    Burrel 22
    Burrill 17
    Cuthbert 88, 100
    Daniel 34
    David ... 192, 241, 275, 298
    David D. 281
    David T. 239
    Davis 260
    Ebenezer 5
    Edward 282
    Ezekiel 83, 99
    Ezekiel F. 141, 180
    Foster 191
    Francis 7, 107, 114, 125, 193, 234
    Gerry Jr. 270
    Gilbert 228
    Harbert 145
    Henry 61, 140

Smith, cont.
   Herbert Jr. 202
   Isaac 258, 288
   Jacob 239, 281
   James ... 50, 67, 70, 82, 86, 151, 162, 173, 225, 244, 259, 271, 275, 290, 299
   James O. 256
   Jeremiah 272, 288
   Joel 102, 174
   John 20, 36, 60, 70, 79, 104, 132, 158, 163, 186, 213, 218, 238, 253, 260, 299
   John C. ... 166, 196, 250
   John G. 147
   Joseph ... 103, 197, 286
   Joshua 222
   Laurence 315
   Levi 213
   Lewey 214
   Lewis 102
   Lovell B. 126
   Lovett B. 163, 197
   Lovit 102
   Mark 224
   Marshall 168
   Mathew 275
   Miles 219
   Morris 107, 313
   Nathaniel 100, 229
   Nathaniel Jr. 246
   Nehemiah 23
   Peter 58
   Peterson 72, 155
   Red Benjamin 202
   Rhode L. 207
   Richard 181, 298
   Richd. 151
   Robert F. 135

Smith, cont.
   Rowland 76
   Saml. 151
   Samuel 107, 132
   Shadrach 86
   Sion 285
   Thomas .. 64, 120, 300, 311
   Timothy 277
   Tisse 288
   Voluntine 70
   William 5, 7, 8, 29, 38, 52, 59, 78, 85, 94, 108, 120, 122, 144, 146, 147, 150, 164, 185, 186, 189, 191, 197, 239, 275, 282
   William Jr. 81
   William R. 291
   William W. 187
   Willis 185
   Zachariah 201
   Zadock 260
Smyney
   James 313
Smyth
   Samuel M. 81
Snead
   John G. 51, 84
Snell
   Christopher 50
   William 207
Snow
   John P. 277, 280
   Mark 99
   Moses 55
   Samuel G. 196
Solomon
   James 81
   Willis 49

Son
   William 75
Sorrells
   Charles 48, 121
Sorrels
   Washington 137
Sorrow
   Henry R. 152
   William 64
Southerland
   John 265
Sowell
   William 206
Spain
   Drewey 17
   Drury 79
   Lewellin 170
   Simeon 128
Spalding
   Thomas 12
Spank
   Francis 41
Spann
   James 163, 184
   John 114
   Richard E. 220
Sparks
   Hardy 82
   James 44, 288, 295
   John 146, 291, 311
   Millington 113
   Thomas 64
   William 288
Sparrow
   John 241
Spear
   Charles 270
   James 176
   John 99
Spears
   John 41

Name Index

Spears, cont.
   William 229
   Willis 13
Speer
   James 165
   James H. 317
Speight
   John 182
Spell
   Joseph 21, 36
Spence
   Johna 283
   Tharpe 33
Spencer
   George 180
   Samuel 28
   Thomas 111, 271
Spierr
   William 278
Spinks
   Baker 79
   John 56, 110
   John C. 188
Spivey
   Gethro B. 169
   Littleton 246
Spraddling
   William 117
Spratling
   Henry 180
Springfield
   Aaron 72
Sprylaw
   Samuel 25
Spurgin
   William 197
Spurlin
   John 80
   Levi 280
Spurlock
   Allen 94

Stackhouse
   Samuel Hastings 28
Stafford
   Ezekiel 97
   Joseph 131
   William .. 93, 161, 239
Staley
   Timothy 55
Stallings
   James 122
   Jesse 260
   John 73, 114
   Moses 64
   Pallasiah 44
   Sanders 148
Staly
   Timothy 14
Stamps
   Moses 196, 259
   Thomas 88
Standfield
   Robert 259
Standifer
   Jesse 78
Standley
   Dempsey 71
Stanford
   David 11, 116
   Elijah 148
Stanley
   James 208
Stansile
   John 75
Stapler
   Thomas 158
   William 234
Stapleton
   George 238, 260
   Thomas 261, 271
Stark
   William 157

Starling
   William 168
Starnes
   William 183, 285
Starr
   Samuel G. 255
Starritt
   Benjamin 212
Stathings
   John 291
Steagall
   Benjamin 315
Steel
   Samuel S. 163
Steele
   Sampson T. 15
   Samuel S. 215
Stenchcomb
   Philip 303
Stinchcomb
   Levi 95
Stenson
   Micajah 66
Stephen
   James 284
Stephens
   Benjamin 159, 162
   Caleb 5
   Charles H. 222
   Charlton 260
   George 314
   George W. 127
   Isaac 94
   Joseph 255
   Lewis 277
   Samuel 313
   Solomon 95
   Thomas 94, 189
   William 14, 74, 151
Stephenson
   John 104

Sterling
   James............258, 297
Stern
   William 92
Stevens
   Herbert 139
   Holeman 258
   Oliver 290
   Samuel..................280
   William 169
Steward
   Alfred 190
Stewart
   Alford 142
   Allen........................15
   Daniel 135, 164
   George.....................39
   Henry.....................127
   James.......73, 95, 141,
      214, 238, 272, 291
   James B. 234, 290
   Jesse 147
   John 43, 156
   John M..................275
   John N. 260
   John P....................172
   Joseph...................286
   Josiah....................231
   Reuben..................317
   Reubin 189
   Richard 64, 76
   Thomas .109, 113, 172
   Thomas R. 104
   William 34
Stiles
   Benjamin 142
   Nicholas................194
   Richard M.......43, 174
Stillwell
   John 143
   Joseph...........105, 124

Stillwell, cont.
   Reubin 256
Stinson
   Joseph...................232
Stirk
   Benjamin................ 10
Stith
   John................35, 117
Stivers
   Joshua 55
Stobo
   William 76
Stockman
   Henry.....................300
Stohl
   Charles 68
Stokes
   Richard.......52, 65, 72
Stoncham
   George 87
Stone
   Francis M. 217
   Henry D..........62, 134
   James 248
   Ransom.................102
   William...........14, 130
Stoneham
   Henry....................203
Storey
   Edward 22
Storrer
   David 160
Storry
   Anthony..................67
   Edward...................66
Story
   Benjamin...............220
   Edward.................113
Stoval
   Peter 57

Stovall
   Benjamin 235
   Drury..................... 177
   George .. 100, 122, 175
   Henry 214
   Joseph 204
   Peter............... 38, 175
Stovy
   Edward................. 185
Stowart
   John........................ 76
Stowers
   Benjamin 220
Straham
   John........................ 43
Strain
   John...................... 124
Strange
   Seth 172
Strangler
   Fielding................. 273
Straughn
   Francis 232, 238
   James 310
Strawder
   John...................... 198
Strickland
   Ansil 149
   Cade D. 280
   Drury...................... 16
   Ephraim 235, 249
   Hardy 99
   Sion 16
Strickling
   James 304
Strikeland
   John...................... 170
Stringer
   Abner............ 261, 290
   Alexander............... 75
   Daniel................... 204

Name Index

String, cont.
    John 220
    Jonah 125
    Josiah 125
    Smith 102

Stringfellow
    Henry 45

Stripp
    Solomon A. 147

Strokes
    William W. 297

Strong
    Edward 251
    Elijah 69
    Elisha 246, 280
    William 132

Strother
    George 48
    Richard 214

Stroud
    Isaac 112
    John 167

Strouder
    William 191

Strozier
    Peter 196

Strudlie
    Frederick 21

Stuart
    Archibald 98
    James 77

Stubblefield
    Peter 108

Stubbs
    Thomas 159

Stud
    Philip 203

Studevant
    John 116

Studstill
    Hustis 223

Sturdevant
    Dempsey 150

Sturdevin
    Edward 276

Sturdivant
    Edwin 207, 286
    John 213

Sturges
    Oliver 33, 46
    Samuel 276
    William 81

Suddith
    Henry 203

Suddoth
    Jarrard 300

Sudor
    John 213

Sullivan
    Hosa W. 189
    John 229

Sullon
    Abemilick 94

Sumford
    Richard 50

Surrey
    William 45

Sutherland
    John 292

Sutherlin
    Edmond 189

Sutten
    Wilie 167

Suttle
    Jesse 32

Sutton
    Benjamin 43
    Hardy 277
    James N. 205
    Joseph 183
    Theophilus 216

Swain
    Sherod 42
    Sherod G. 82

Swan
    John 273

Swanson
    Graves 179
    James 244
    Lemuel 173

Swearingame
    Bolin 74

Swearingen
    Bolen 91
    Martin 306

Swearingham
    John 36
    Samuel 36

Sweatt
    William 159

Swenney
    Ellis 259

Swilly
    Rizen 120
    Samuel 179

Swing
    Ellis 286

Swiret
    James 294

Sykes
    Joseph 50, 97
    Thomas 35

T

Tabb
    Edward 226
    Thomas 110

Tait
    Benjamin 298
    James A. 239
    R. L. 127

Tait, cont.
    Temri 239
    William 54
Talbert
    Lewis 126
    Thomas 47
Talbot
    Greene B. 291
    James 199
    John 298
Taliaferro
    Benjamin 12, 70
    David 246
    Lewis B. 76, 93
    Richard 176
Taliaffero
    Lewis 122
Tallaws
    Rodham 53
Talley
    William 7
Tally
    Abraham 69
    John A. 296
    Obediah 119
Talman
    Benjamin 65
Tankersley
    John 103
Tankersly
    Joseph 203
Tanner
    Eli 280
Tanter
    Nathan 219
Tapley
    Archibald 314
    Ephraim 91
Tarnall
    John 244

Tarpely
    Coleman 310
Tarver
    Benjamin 311
    Hartwell H. 297
    John Jr. 274
Tate
    Henry 57
    Rice 196
    Robert L. 43
    William 298
Tatem
    Wily G. 270
Tatom
    Abner 70
    James 70
Tattnall
    Josiah Jr. 43
Tatum
    Abner 208
    James 219
    Nathaniel 188
    Silas 315
    William 153
Taturn
    Silas 229
Taver
    Samuel 261
Taylor
    Arthur 5
    Charles 11
    Daniel 197
    Danl. 158
    David Jr. 116
    Elias 293
    Francis 97
    George D. 261
    Henry 240
    James 18, 83, 165
    John 41, 61, 313
    Jordan 74

Taylor, cont.
    Joseph 72, 283
    Levi T. 191
    Moses 116
    Reubin 62
    Reubin G. 67
    Richard 198
    Robert 120
    Sius 150
    Thomas 297, 305
    Ward 141
    William .. 98, 126, 204
    Woody 93
Tayor
    James M. 309
Teakle
    Charles 18
Teddlie
    William 176
Telfair
    Josiah G. 211
    Thomas 120, 140
Tellman
    John 71
Templing
    Charles 304
Tennel
    Joseph 65
Terrell
    Charles 81
    John 206
    Josiah 181
    Philemon 120
    Richmond 79
    Solomon 194
    Thompson 238
Terry
    David 16
Thaaton
    Thomas 211

Name Index

Thackston
    Charles 154
Thadford
    William 78
Tharp
    Charles 5
Thaxton
    Yelventon 314
    Yelvinston 160
Theard
    Jesse 267
Theess
    Thomas 260
Theifs
    Thomas 202
Thigby
    Zachariah 282
Thigpen
    Lemuel 305
Thigpin
    Lewis 289
Thiscatt
    Kinchen P 199
Thomas
    Archibald 194
    Benjamin 227
    Blassingame ... 44, 59, 89
    Clayton 294
    Darius 41
    David 23, 97
    Edward L. 184
    Evan 125, 172, 219
    Francis 205, 303
    Greenberry 193
    Hincher 224, 271
    Hugh..................... 233
    James 26, 292
    James Fillet 82
    James T. 110
    Jesse 198

Thomas, cont.
    Jessee 204
    Jett 123, 289
    John 43, 198, 214, 230, 280
    John S . . 159, 164, 189
    John Sherrod 232
    John W. 175
    Lott 15
    Martin 293
    Nicholas 98
    Peter 36, 204
    Philip 42, 149
    Richard 161
    Richard H. ... 216, 311
    Spencer 179
    Thephulas 101
    Thomas 65
    Ticey 90
    William 67
Thomason
    Edmond 37
    John 44, 87, 135
    Thomas 48
Thompkins
    Donald 74
    John 118
    Nicholas 254
Thompson
    Alfred 174
    Allen 122
    Allen C. 101
    Ansil 150
    Archibald 85, 186, 191
    Aron 275
    B. William 66
    Benjamin 93
    Duncan 36, 205
    Farley 103
    Francis M. 177
    Gaines 193, 269

Thompson, cont.
    George 208
    Henry 298
    Ichabud 108
    Isham 289, 313
    Ivey 279
    James 1, 21, 94
    John 3, 48, 66, 84, 117, 181
    John W. 121
    Leonard 3
    Mathew D. 202
    Moses 299
    Reuben 11
    Samuel 83
    Solomon 40, 128
    Thomas 28
    Wiley 95, 311
    William 60, 76, 95, 128, 137
    Wylly 34
Thomson
    Robert 60
    Runtin 61
    Samuel 65
    William 54
Thorn
    James 93
Thornton
    John Jr. 182
    Jordan 106
    Lindsey ... 70, 115, 159
    Robert 2
    Solomon 15, 23
    Thomas 71
Thrash
    David 207
    George 116
    Isaac 186, 214, 317
    Leander 122

Thurman
  Fielding L. 35
Thurmond
  Fielding...................19
  Fielding L. 150
  Harrison 149
  John 315
Thursby
  Thomas B. 105
Thweat
  John 108
  Peterson..................83
Thweet
  Peterson................144
Tiddle
  William 131
Tidley
  William 136
Tillery
  Henry.......................41
  Joshua...................251
Tillman
  James....................150
  Joseph...........220, 305
Tilly
  James......................89
Tilman
  Joseph...................289
  Thomas 283
Timmons
  Zackarius..............170
Tinar
  Joshua.....................65
Tinderson
  John 315
Tiner
  Ephraim.................208
Tinsly
  John 305
Tippet
  James....................231

Tippett
  John 230
Tippings
  James A................283
  Lemuel..................240
Tipton
  Thomas................... 11
Tison
  James S. 172
  Joab 258
  Job 78, 170
Todd
  John 20, 51, 186
  Robert.....................70
  William.................170
Tole
  Suddoth 299
Tolsome
  Ebenezer 20
Tomlin
  Zachariah L..........247
Tommy
  Joseph.................... 37
Tompson
  Henry....................169
  Jeremiah 169
Toney
  Harris 281
Toneyhill
  John 130
Took
  Allen 113, 137, 181, 202
Tool
  David 123, 160
Toossing
  Paul 37
Torrance
  Amelius 317
  James 98, 155
  Samuel 137

Torrence
  Arnelius 231
  Ebenezer 168
  James 291
  John.............145, 164
  John W. 230
  Samuel 158
Touhand
  Amos 101
Tower
  Bird 81
Towers
  John G..................227
Towns
  John W. 110
  Martin 271, 309
  Pleasant 176, 199
  Solomon 130, 154, 185
Townsend
  Andrew..................215
  Andrew C. 295
  Eli 28
  Jesse.....................165
  Samuel 148
  Thomas 172
Townson
  John......................160
Towson
  Meshac 12
Tramel
  Francis 199
Trammel
  Harris...................225
Trammell
  Daniel..................... 94
  Farr 258
  Farr H. 236
Trantham
  Absalom 95
Trasher
  William 175

Name Index

Travis
    John 274
    Whitmill 310
Trawick
    John 158
    Robert 157
    Robert C. 230
Traylor
    Archibald 37
    Edward 176
    Randolph 33
Traywick
    John 52
    Robert 304
Treadwell
    Jacob 299
Tredwell
    John 86
Treeney
    Peter 100
Tremble
    Joseph 126
Treuitlen
    Christian 143
Trice
    James 51
Triebner
    Christian F. 241
Triplett
    John H. 93, 170
    William P. 251, 300
Tripp
    Henry 58, 144
Trippe
    Henry 31, 151, 159
    Henry Jr. 153
    Samuel . 167, 177, 191
Triptell
    William 61
Trotte
    Francis 57

Troup
    George M. 23
Truitt
    Nathan 212
    Nathaniel 300
Truman
    William 63
Trussell
    John 137, 189
Trutlin
    Christian 62
Tucker
    Allen 43
    Andrew 38
    Frederick 41
    George 295
    Henry 153, 177
    Jesse 9, 19
    Robert 89, 216
    Samuel 208, 271
    Thomas 118
Tudor
    John 271
Tufts
    Francis 109, 199
    Gardner 178
Tuggle
    George 28
    William 222, 290
Tulloss
    Joshua 84
    Rodham 108
Tunnel
    John 93
Turk
    John 143
Turman
    George 70
    Robert 295
Turnell
    William B. 56

Turner
    Absalom 83
    Benjamin 68
    James 35, 103
    John 102, 111, 144
    Reuben 283
    Richard 145
    Thomas 83
Turpin
    Beverly 163
    John 243
Tuttle
    David 87
    James 87
    Robert 313
Twiggs
    David E. 185
Twilley
    William 226
Twitty
    John 146
    Thomas 287
    William 262
Tye
    James 87
Tyler
    William 170
Tynes
    Flyming 90
Tyson
    James S. 168
    Job 88
    Kinchen P. 244
    Littleton 277
    William 141
Tyus
    William 108

U

Ulmer
Charles 6
Philip 121, 217
Ulmor
Charles 39
Umphries
Isaac.........................87
William C. 225
Underhill
Joseph 240, 269
Underwood
James T. 277
John 54
John G. 285
John J. 297
Reubin 230
Thomas 166
William A. 245
William H. 130
Wm. 260
Upshaw
Wm........................311
Upshear
Leroy 270
Usher
Able 171

V

Valley
George 36
Van Brackle
John 3
Vandimer
Lamkin 196
Vandiver
Adam P. 254
Vann
Sanders..................152

Vardeman
Joseph....................209
Vardiman
Joseph....................258
Varner
Hendly 224
Henley 230, 274
John.......................240
Marcus 223
Reubin 161
Thomas 295
William 123, 210
Vass
John.......................187
Vaugham
Alexander 288
Vaughan
Benjamin.................21
William 34
Vaughn
Benjamin...............292
Hanley 157
Howell 174
Vaughters
John.......................100
Veal
James 121
Veasy
Caleb.....................106
Veazey
Ezekiel...................204
Velvan
Thomas 163
Venable
Abraham 44
Robert...........275, 299
Ventress
Stephen 118
Vest
James 281
John.......................196

Vevrell
Lancelot 109
Vickers
William 136
Vince
William 175
Vincent
Henry 274
James 216
Vining
John........................80
Shadrack 230
Shadrick 308
Vinson
George 26
Pleasant 159
Selby.....................168
Vivion
Thacker 45
Thacker Jr. 4, 67

W

Wadd
Robert....................259
Wade
Elisha 238
Jesse.....................119
Moses 15
Peyton 273
Reuben 147, 162
Robert...........148, 242
Wadkins
Joseph P. 63
William 199
Wadsworth
James 222
Thomas 230, 308
William 273
Wafford
Isaiah 261

Wafford, cont.
William H. 175
Waggoner
William 305
Wagman
William 289
Wagnon
Daniel 65
Thomas 188
Wailes
Levin 42
Waiscoat
Joel 181
Waites
Allen 188
Waits
Benjm. 152
Walden
Charles 14, 246
Eli 259
Morris 276, 309
Waldhour
John 14
Waldron
Benjamin 198
Oliver 268
Walea
James 138
Walker
Ansel 192
David 282
Elisha S. 282
Freeman 24
George 57
Henry Jr. 273
Horatio 39
Isaac 17, 38
James 50, 54
James C. 211, 297
James Jr. 34
James S. 123

Walker, cont.
James Y. 116
Jeremiah 49, 83
Joel 10
John 98, 253
John G. 266
John S. 234
Joseph 309
Levi 215
Londy 119
Martin S. 300
Reuben 197
Reubin 179
Richard . 78, 104, 131, 213
Robert 66, 125
Sackfield N. 236
Samuel 147
Shackfield 203
Simeon 265
Soleman 269
Valentine .. 55, 88, 93, 171, 289
William 116, 133, 149, 227
William H. 246
William L. 260
Wall
Henry 77
Jesse 251, 253
Shadrach 34
Shadrack 268
Wallace
Abraham 79
Abram. 219
Benjamin 224, 257, 277
Greene 213
James 56, 84
Peter 135
Robert 115

Wallace, cont.
Stiring 224
William . 179, 238, 274
Waller
Charles R. 289
James 80
John T. 243
Nathaniel 217, 251
Nathaniel G.. 207, 312
Nathaniel Jr. 80
Thomas 135
William Jr. 289
Wallice
Peter 194
Wallis
John 146
Walraven
Isaac 129
William 129, 137
Walsh
Isaac 309
Walter
Burrel 59
Joseph 154
Walters
John 215
Joseph 103, 292
Walthall
Torman 287
Walton
Augustine G. 72
Averton 58
Edmund 295
Gibson C. 261
John 1, 215
John W. 257
Overton 24, 46
Resdon 89
Risden 108
Thomas 238

Wamble
  Allen 127
  Drury 6
Wammack
  Jessee 206
Ward
  Anderson 278
  Benjamin 129, 241
  Elisha 49, 54
  John 111
  M. B. 317
  Richard 220
  Solomon 251
  Thomas E. 207
  William ...63, 136, 170
  William M. 261, 269
Wardlaw
  James 179, 251
Ware
  Edward 26
  Francis W. 69
  James 101, 121
  John 295
  Joseph 97, 109
  Nicholas 21
  Thomas 115
  Thompson 223
  William C. 247
Warner
  Elijah 89
  Jeremiah 134
Warren
  Harrison 130
  Hinchey 128
  Hinchin 109
  Jeremiah 115
  Jesse 24, 146
  Moses 285
  Reuben 229
  Richard 6, 37

Washington
  George 65
Waterman
  Flavius 92
Waters
  George 218, 246
  George M. 277
  Isaac 117, 291
  Joseph 43, 46, 266
  Thomas 240
Wates
  Archibald 65
Watkin
  William 109
Watkins
  Adam 180
  Garland T. 88, 179
  George W. 274, 298
  James 184
  John 222, 266
  Joseph R. 54
  Matthew 117
  Robert 168, 180
  Thomas 174
  William 145
Watley
  John H. 94
Watson
  Alexander 255
  Benjamin 310
  Douglass .96, 105, 236
  Duglas 19
  Elijah 171
  Frederick 55
  Gideon 197
  Jacob 304
  James C. 174, 244
  James P. 110
  John 51, 135
  Matthew 216
  Reason 272

Watson, cont.
  Reddich 24
  Risdon 151
  Seth 211
  Silas 202
  William 118
Watter
  George 88
  William 133
Watters
  James B. 312
  Peter 21
Watts
  Archibald 74
  Hamilton 266
  Jacob 266
  Jacobus 19, 44
  James 154
  John H. 89, 257
  Josiah ... 105, 108, 257
  Jubel E. 133
  Ludwell 120, 127
  Richard J. 145
  Thomas 33, 53, 89
  Vincent 203
  William 29, 312
Way
  Samuel W. 297
Wayne
  James M. 229, 244
  William 33, 70
Weatherby
  Benjamin 96
  George M. 261
  Myrick 196
Weathers
  John 236, 305
  William 33
Weaver
  Jethro 125
  Reuben 88

Name Index

Webb
- Benjamin 186
- Bredgor 310
- Dawson 252
- Exum 165
- Giles 150
- John 126, 170, 201, 262, 300
- Samuel 204

Webster
- Hosea 209, 225
- Martin 286
- William R. 223

Weddington
- Zeus 155

Weeks
- James S. 276
- John. 40, 80, 122, 186, 262
- Thomas 113
- William 209, 272

Weitman
- Israel 236, 304

Welborn
- Abner 177
- Shubal Starnes 217

Welch
- Anthony 140
- Asa 239
- Bryan 218
- Edmund 133, 233, 270
- James 75, 101, 140
- John 86, 121
- Joshua 193
- Michael 266
- Samuel 193
- William 106

Welcher
- Jordan 160, 290

Weldon
- James 275

Wellborn
- Cordial 265
- Johnson 138, 171

Wells
- Abner 116
- James 70
- John 142, 149, 251
- Joshua S. 295
- Nicholas W. 219
- Thomas 248

Wemberly, Jr.
- William 215

Wemms
- William L. 197

Wenthers
- William 92

West
- Charles 29
- Crawford 149
- Henry 24
- James 263
- Warren 19

Westbrook
- John 149

Wester
- Edmond P. 187
- Edmund P. 248

Weston
- Henry 251

Whatley
- Daniel A. 175
- David 99
- David A. 129
- Elisha 70
- Green 157
- John B. 134
- Ornan 304
- Pheneas 97
- Wylie H. 280

Wheatley
- Richard 103

Wheeler
- Asberry 290
- Avery 92, 125
- Benjamin 42
- Charles 109
- George W. 277
- Henry 175
- James 238
- William 299

Wheelis
- Abner 144
- Edmond 171

Whelley
- Micajah 49

Whellon
- James 268

Whesionhunt
- Adam 143

Whidden
- William 250

Whiddon
- Eli 73
- John 141
- William 212

Whight
- James 72

Whipple
- Welcome 140

Whitaker
- John 260
- Richard 105, 313
- Samuel 274
- West 178

Whitcumbe
- Notley 11

White
- Alexander 20
- Asia 276
- Charles Baxter 282
- David 117, 124, 167
- Eppy 276, 299

409

White, cont.
   George 29, 42
   Henry P. 201, 212, 301
   Jacob 117, 125
   James ... 119, 158, 273, 309
   James B. 128, 131
   James E. 191, 245, 261
   Jno Y. 64
   John 106, 173, 259, 318
   Joseph 122, 136
   Micajah 149
   Moses D. 175, 196
   Robert 6, 69
   Simeon 244
   Steel 136
   Steele 112, 227
   Stephen 202, 224
   Thomas . 169, 174, 313
   Wade 262
   William 6, 95, 175, 245
   William B. 247
Whitecomb
   William 116
Whitefield
   Robert 69
Whitehead
   Benjamin 76
   Bennet 290
   Henry 273
   Joel 314
Whiteman
   Matthew 2
Whitfield
   George 212
Whitley
   Richard 96

Whitlock
   William 145
Whitmer
   Michael 308
Whitten
   Elias 51
   Robert 51
Whittenton
   Calvin 64
Whitton
   Bolling 184
   George 76
Whorton
   Joseph 71, 133
Wiat
   Cadar 188
Wigfall
   Samuel 81
Wiggins
   Allen 272
   Jesse 68
   Joseph .. 140, 226, 240, 302
   Osborn 242
   William 66, 290
Wilborn
   Curtis 13
   Samuel 26
Wilbourn
   Isaac 10
Wilcox
   Moses 86
   Thomas 148
   William 34
Wild
   Richard 123
Wilder
   James 174, 312
   Sampson 147, 219
   Simeon 72
   Thomas 13, 58

Wilder, cont.
   William 59
Wilds
   Richard 147
Wileman
   Lewis 259
Wiley
   James 295
   John 268
   William 212
Wilhight
   Philemon R. 301
Wilis
   Moses 144
Wilkerson
   Dempsey 53
Wilkins
   Jabez 86
   Levoy 243
   Mathew 180
   Paul H. 130, 242
   William 58, 258
Wilkinson
   Baily 74
   Dempsey 75
   Hazlewood 238
   James 149
   John B. 139
   Micajah 299
   William 1
Wilks
   Jesse 170
Willborn
   Abner 252
Willey
   James 207
William
   Owen 82
Williams
   Amos 250, 289
   Anderson 208

Name Index

Williams, cont.
- Bartley C. 243
- Benjamin 72, 284
- Bryant 60
- Burrell 32
- Burwell 195
- Daniel 201
- Drewry 132
- Duke 64
- Edward 179, 206
- Francis 197
- Frederick 121
- Frederick H. 204
- Gabriel 148
- Hardy 206
- Henry 215, 307
- Henry W. 47, 231
- Hezekiah D. D. L. 168
- Hiram 223
- Isaac 146
- Isac 60
- James ... 121, 220, 231
- Jehu 267
- Jesse 84
- John 126, 191, 199, 213
- John A. 210, 258
- Joseph 245
- Joshua 59
- Lewellen 140
- Lewelling 124
- Mark 278
- Matthew J. 206
- Moses 147
- Paul 44, 68
- Peter J. 217
- Richard F. 193, 210
- Rowland 3, 9
- Sheppard .. 37, 76, 127
- Simon 36, 50
- Stafford 118

Williams, cont.
- Sylatus 272
- Theophilus 298
- Thomas 103, 274
- William 19, 27, 35, 68, 72, 126, 138, 153, 192, 271, 272
- William F. 272
- William T. 158, 252, 275, 290
- Zachariah.. 22, 57, 79, 109, 139, 247

Williamson
- Alixander 172
- Benjamin 157
- Charles 182
- Delona 167
- George 52, 151
- George Jr. 84
- Henry 250
- John 35
- John G. 103
- John P. 212, 221
- Joseph 135
- Micajah 301
- Plesant 136
- R. M. Jr. 166
- R. M. Sr. 166
- Robert 189
- Samuel 209, 234
- William 119
- William W. 247

Willick
- Earnest C. 122

Willidrus
- William 82

Williford
- Jepthe Q. 252
- John 44
- Nathan 72
- Thomas 54

Willingham
- Archibald 118
- George 127
- Hardiman 311
- Isaac 13
- Jeremiah 128, 133
- John G. 127
- Rolly 317
- Samuel 130, 175
- Thomas 309, 317
- William 141

Willis
- Ephraim .91, 138, 207
- Furnifold 267
- George 66
- Gideon 227, 259
- Hardy C. 254
- James 72, 141
- James D. 224
- John 165, 197, 208, 260, 315
- Joseph 156
- Joshua 186, 236
- Martin 265
- Paul T. 113
- Richard 148
- Richard I. 244
- Richard J. 214
- Richard T. 261
- Robert 205
- William 173
- William C. 281

Willoby
- David 215

Willson
- Benjamin H. 164
- Bennet 88
- David 243
- Hugh 185
- John 59, 187, 205, 236
- Joseph 249

Willson, cont.
  Joshua 66
  Robert 40
  Solomon 192
Willy
  James 128
Wilson
  David 216
  Elias 216, 279, 305
  Elihu 242, 267
  Fields 165
  Henry 305
  Isaiah 243
  James 160, 313
  James J. 280
  John 97, 117, 146, 265, 281
  John Jr. 112
  Joseph 174
  Josiah 105
  Lemuel 165
  Leonard 219
  Luke 67
  Robert 96
  Samuel M. 192
  Spencer 4
  William 284
  William R. 186
Wimberly
  David 233, 293
  Ezekiel .. 110, 168, 199
  Isaac 113
  James 191, 256
  Thomas 140
  Wiley 292
  William 226
Wims
  John 38
Windham
  Daniel 211
  Samuel 96

Windham, cont.
  Willis 96
Windrick
  Jones 18
Winfield
  Joel 310
Winfrey
  Reuben 111
  William 149
Wing
  George T. 303
Wingate
  Richard 77
Wingfield
  Thomas 151
Winn
  Benjamin B. 120
  George 88
  Greene 72
  John 80, 105, 110
Winston
  Thomas 150
Winter
  Jeremiah 257
  John 253
Winters
  Albert 285
  Jeremiah 279
  John 162
Wise
  Erwin 57
  John 269
  Patten 24
  Preston 121
Wiseman
  Robert 266
Wisenbaker
  Charles 259
Wisinbaker
  John 121

Wisters
  Stephen 223
Witcher
  Benjamin 134, 190, 287
Witcumbe
  Notby 12
Witeman
  Israel 291
Wofford
  Nathaniel 250
  William Jr. 159
Wolf
  Gorge 59
Womack
  John 156
  Robert 64
  William 107
Wommack
  John 214
Wood
  Aaron 33, 130
  Ashley 57, 166, 181
  Bartley 273
  Benjamin 82, 121
  Cary 178, 315
  Charles 173
  Hardy 9
  Jacob 78
  James 32
  John 137, 156, 194, 245
  Jonathan Jr. 162
  Marke K. 260
  Martin 259
  Pennell 52
  Richard 52
  Silas 204
  Solomon 48
  Thomas 143

Wood, cont.
   William 58, 85, 119, 227, 255
Woodham
   James 312
Woodley
   William 169
Woodrooff
   Richard 19
Woodruff
   Clifford 154
   Elijah 227
   James 203
   Ruben 266
   Willson 45
Woods
   Isaac 7
   Samuel 172
   William 152
Woodside
   Abraham 91
Woodson
   Simeon 243
   Simon 191
Woodward
   Francis 245
   Paschal 161
   Thomas 19, 271
Wooldridge
   Gibson 1
Woolsey
   John M. 106, 116
   Seth 78
Wooten
   Dolby 246
   Dooby 253
   Gilley 149
   Richard 218
   Thomas 186
   William 54, 183

Wooton
   John 144
   Thomas Jr. 20
Wootten
   Allen R. 277
   Thomas 122
Word
   Charles 275
Woreham
   Thomas 61
Worsham
   John 309
Wortham
   Thomas 283
   William 32
   Zachariah 229
Worthy
   William 103
Wright
   Ambrose 74, 113, 127, 205
   Asa 259
   Charles ... 96, 158, 211
   Cornelius 249
   David 189
   Gabriel 286
   George 73, 80
   James 99, 164, 219, 243, 279
   Jared 106
   John . 54, 92, 140, 254
   John C. 194
   John L. 236
   Larkin 175
   Obediah 85
   Robert 268
   Thomas 144, 231, 244, 286
   William . 73, 112, 213, 256, 291
   Wingfield 164

Wyatt
   William 308
Wyche
   George 306
   Littleton 119
   Nathan 44
   Peter 1
   Robert 49, 97
Wylee
   James 27
Wyley
   James R. 143, 163
   William 142
Wylie
   Moses 293
Wylly
   Richard 91
   William 136, 143
Wynn
   George 57
   Greene 126
   Henry 12
   John 210
   Lewis 186
   Littleton 293
   Treowetts 102
Wynne
   Henry 1
   James 267
   Peter 17, 26
   William 59

Y

Yager
   Augustine 98
Yarborough
   Ambrose 101
   Groves 143
   John 114
   Josiah 175

Yarborough, cont.
- Moses 218
- Thomas 119
- William 1, 278

Yarbrough
- Elam 26

Yates
- Burrel 75

Yeates
- Jesse 201

York
- Archibald 24
- Solomon 286
- William 146

Young
- Benjamin 129
- Enos 197
- Francis 73, 101, 210
- Harrison 117, 124, 184

Young, cont.
- Jacob 261
- James 179, 317
- James Box 8
- John 78, 183, 255
- Milas 248
- Moses 197
- Sherwood 78
- Turner 253
- Zachariah 180

Youngblood
- Charles 303
- Isaac R. 219
- Nathan 39

Yowell
- Joel 101

Z

Zachary
- Daniel 9

Zachery
- Daniel H. 81

Zachry
- Daniel H. 56
- James 81

Zant
- Joshua 33

Zelner
- Arnold 282

Zimmerman
- Philip 145

Zittrover
- Nathaniel 304

Zuber
- Jacob 116

County Index

The following counties are mentioned in commissions that pre-date the 1804 transition to a unit numbering system.

Bryan County 3, 9, 19, 31, 37, 39, 49, 50

Bulloch County 6, 11, 13, 19, 22, 37, 48, 52, 53

Burke County 1, 2, 3, 5, 6, 7, 8, 11, 12, 13, 14, 15, 16, 17, 18, 19, 21, 22, 24, 25, 26, 27, 29, 31, 33, 35, 37, 38, 39, 43, 44, 45, 46, 49, 50, 51, 53, 55, 57, 59, 61, 62, 63, 64, 65

Camden County...7, 10, 11, 13, 38, 50, 51, 63

Chatham County 5, 6, 7, 8, 12, 15, 17, 23, 24, 25, 28, 32, 34, 40, 41, 43, 47, 48, 50, 51, 52, 53, 60, 61, 62, 63, 64, 65

Clarke County 48, 52, 53, 54, 56, 60, 63, 65, 66

Columbia County.......................2, 3, 6, 9, 11, 12, 13, 15, 18, 20, 21, 22, 26, 29, 31, 35, 36, 37, 38, 39, 40, 42, 43, 45, 52, 55, 58, 62, 63, 64, 65

Effingham County 2, 4, 6, 8, 10, 11, 14, 31, 33, 35, 37, 39, 43, 44, 47, 59, 62

Elbert County 1, 6, 10, 11, 14, 19, 20, 22, 23, 24, 26, 27, 28, 29, 32, 33, 34, 35, 37, 41, 42, 43, 44, 47, 48, 49, 50, 51, 52, 53, 54, 56, 58, 61, 62, 63, 64, 65, 66, 67

Franklin County...................1, 2, 4, 5, 7, 8, 10, 11, 18, 20, 21, 24, 28, 34, 37, 38, 42, 44, 46, 47, 49, 53, 55, 58, 60, 65, 67

Glynn County 1, 12, 43, 45, 46, 51, 62

Greene County...........................3, 9, 12, 13, 14, 15, 17, 19, 21, 23, 24, 25, 26, 28, 31, 32, 33, 39, 43, 44, 45, 48, 49, 50, 55, 58, 59, 60, 61, 62, 63, 64, 65, 66

Hancock County 1, 2, 4, 5, 6, 7, 11, 12, 13, 14, 15, 16, 17, 18, 19, 20, 21, 23, 24, 25, 27, 29, 31, 32, 33, 34, 36, 37, 38, 39, 40, 41, 43, 44, 46, 47, 48, 50, 51, 52, 53, 54, 55, 56, 58, 60, 62, 63, 64, 65, 66, 286

Jackson County................................2, 4, 16, 19, 20, 28, 29, 32, 33, 34, 35, 36, 37, 38, 39, 40, 41, 42, 44, 45, 46, 48, 49, 50, 54, 55, 56, 57, 58, 59, 60, 62, 64, 67

Jefferson County 4, 5, 10, 13, 14, 16, 17, 18, 19, 20, 23, 25, 27, 28, 31, 32, 33, 34, 35, 37, 38, 39, 40, 41, 42, 44, 45, 46, 48, 49, 50, 52, 53, 54, 55, 56, 57, 58, 59, 61, 63, 64, 67

Liberty County 8, 10, 18, 24, 25, 27, 28, 31, 54, 58, 59, 65, 67

Lincoln County 1, 4, 14, 17, 18, 22, 24, 27, 31, 32, 34, 45, 46, 52, 56, 59, 65, 66, 72, 111

McIntosh County 4, 5, 10, 11, 16, 22, 27, 31, 45, 48, 52

Montgomery County...........................2, 3, 4, 5, 7, 9, 14, 15, 18, 20, 21, 26, 28, 36, 37, 41, 42, 44, 49, 50, 51, 53, 55, 56, 57, 61, 63

Oglethorpe County 1, 2, 3, 4, 5, 10, 12, 15, 16, 18, 19, 20, 21, 24, 33, 34, 40, 41, 43, 45, 46, 47, 52, 55, 58, 59, 60, 63, 64, 66

Richmond County.... ....1, 3, 4, 5, 6, 10, 16, 17, 18, 20, 21, 22, 24, 33, 34, 35, 46, 49, 50, 53, 55, 57, 58, 62, 63, 64

415

Screven County 5, 13, 14, 15, 24, 28, 29, 31, 33, 40, 50, 55, 56, 59, 60, 66, 67
Tattnall County 51, 61
Warren County 1, 2, 5, 9, 12, 13, 18, 20, 21, 23, 24, 27, 28, 29, 31, 33, 34, 38, 40, 43, 44, 45, 46, 48, 49, 50, 52, 55, 56, 57, 60, 64
Washington County 1, 2, 3, 4, 5, 6, 9, 10, 14, 16, 18, 22, 23, 24, 25, 27, 28, 29, 31, 32, 34, 35, 37, 38, 39, 40, 41, 44, 46, 48, 50, 52, 53, 54, 55, 56, 61, 62, 63, 65, 66
Wilkes County 1, 2, 4, 5, 6, 8, 9, 10, 11, 13, 14, 15, 16, 19, 20, 21, 22, 23, 24, 25, 26, 27, 28, 29, 33, 34, 35, 37, 38, 41, 43, 44, 45, 47, 51, 52, 53, 57, 58, 59, 60, 61, 62, 63, 64

Militia District Index

District 1 .... 79, 84, 91, 101, 110, 112, 136, 142, 150, 153, 177, 191, 216, 246, 249, 297
District 2 .... 84, 101, 105, 107, 124, 190, 227, 275, 300, 312
District 3 .... 101, 106, 107, 111, 116, 142, 153, 158, 160, 179, 213, 273, 283, 310, 312
District 4 .... 89, 105, 106, 112, 116, 160, 184, 194, 195, 232, 249, 293
District 5 .... 107, 116, 142, 165, 181, 187, 211, 219, 220, 231
District 6 ....74, 82, 91, 105, 109, 116, 124, 136, 156, 177, 207, 213, 224, 229, 238, 244, 251
District 7 ....142, 164, 180, 199, 205, 226, 230, 240, 242, 244, 253, 256, 261, 272, 274, 285, 305
District 8 ....84, 89, 105, 106, 107, 173, 179, 186, 189, 193, 198, 202, 221, 237, 240, 260, 282, 301
District 9 .... 73, 91, 107, 121, 149, 163, 181, 198, 217, 253, 259, 283, 301, 312
District 10 .... 107, 121, 140, 165, 178, 202, 283, 304
District 11 .... 82, 107, 121, 143, 165, 197, 219, 236, 290, 304
District 12 .... 91, 143, 149, 165, 177, 211, 237, 241, 258, 305, 310
District 13 .... 76, 82, 107, 143, 165, 201, 208, 224, 242, 257, 267, 313
District 14 .... 84, 105, 130, 144, 156, 242, 248, 261, 262
District 15 ....80, 105, 120, 158, 300
District 16 .... 101, 111, 120, 130, 150, 153, 176, 210
District 17 .... 67, 90, 110, 120, 146, 181, 197, 206, 220, 239, 243, 248, 284, 294
District 18 ....96, 170, 248
District 19 .... 71, 124, 155, 169, 188, 192, 218, 242, 254, 267, 268, 271, 280, 302
District 20 .... 80, 91, 105, 124, 141, 142, 154, 198, 213, 220, 237, 251, 260, 262, 294
District 21 .... 67, 91, 113, 152, 164, 197, 225, 260, 282, 294
District 22 ....67, 87, 107, 152, 187, 207, 245, 279
District 23 .... 72, 107, 143, 146, 201, 213, 281, 285
District 24 ....74, 143, 211, 257, 275
District 25 ....82, 84, 91, 113, 143, 307, 314
District 26 .... 84, 106, 111, 120, 133, 143, 251, 267, 276, 314
District 27 .... 78, 88, 91, 107, 120, 138, 170, 185, 238, 251, 280, 281, 305, 316
District 28 .... 67, 78, 161, 179, 192, 223, 239, 257, 304
District 29 .... 67, 68, 82, 92, 108, 142, 158, 196, 216, 218, 279
District 30 ....74, 105, 118
District 31 .... 68, 101, 118, 142, 153, 213, 227, 238, 261, 281, 312, 314
District 32 ....68, 118, 142, 175, 269, 288
District 33 .... 68, 107, 118, 171, 183, 187, 215, 233, 244, 283, 289, 302
District 34 ....96, 233
District 35 .... 75, 76, 84, 117, 159, 183, 217, 232, 242, 269, 291, 298
District 36 .... 68, 84, 117, 149, 172, 175, 231, 236, 244, 250, 279, 296, 308, 316

District 37 .... 77, 84, 148, 166, 206, 281
District 38 .... 107, 110, 137, 160, 181, 189, 237, 255, 263, 299, 313
District 39 .... 97, 148, 170, 188, 265, 302
District 40 .... 106, 119, 141, 212, 250, 252, 253, 306
District 41 .... 97, 150, 172, 216, 279, 287, 293, 310
District 42 .... 71, 84, 130, 131, 170, 187, 220, 248, 286, 299, 300
District 43 .... 84, 92, 152, 158, 169, 299
District 44 .... 71, 82, 108, 121, 138, 157, 172, 181, 214, 240, 260, 269
District 45 .... 71, 100, 101, 121, 134, 156, 231, 268, 292
District 46 .... 68, 82, 121, 148, 159, 222, 223, 248
District 47 .... 71, 104, 121, 138, 146, 153, 195
District 48 .... 71, 76, 96, 142, 152, 153, 172, 173, 207, 248, 269, 301, 314
District 49 .... 68, 82, 89, 111, 138, 214, 243, 289, 305, 309
District 50 .... 75, 134, 167
District 51 .... 73, 85, 139, 146, 205, 228, 262, 263
District 52 .... 75, 84, 90, 139, 164, 202, 225, 250, 279, 285, 291, 312
District 53 .... 73, 82, 90, 91, 138, 207, 284
District 54 .... 75, 81, 141, 186, 207, 245
District 55 .... 75, 82, 91, 141, 186, 220, 283
District 56 .... 74, 91, 141, 179, 207, 231
District 57 .... 75, 89, 90, 146, 169, 182, 189, 207, 243, 265, 279, 312
District 58 .... 73, 85, 139, 239, 268, 285, 286, 294
District 59 .... 73, 75, 148, 154, 174, 191, 215, 244, 261, 315
District 60 .... 68, 97, 102, 124, 138, 142, 167, 171, 184, 189, 218, 235, 245, 290
District 61 .... 68, 102, 105, 168, 176, 186, 192, 224, 261, 290, 294
District 62 .... 98, 109, 113, 138, 182, 213, 224, 238, 241, 251, 253, 254, 273, 288, 315
District 63 .... 74, 98, 165, 284, 293, 317
District 64 .... 98, 141, 154, 207, 227, 244, 256, 275, 299
District 65 .... 73, 138, 141, 160, 172, 173, 227, 250, 255, 261, 284
District 66 .... 74, 85, 138, 155, 267, 283, 288, 306, 317
District 67 .... 73, 92, 101, 105, 110, 169, 175, 186, 190, 226, 272, 292, 304, 313
District 68 .... 76, 138, 178, 188, 254, 298, 305
District 69 .... 77, 104, 106, 107, 140, 142, 174, 178, 202, 215, 260, 266, 282, 294
District 70 .... 68, 72, 109, 141, 160, 178, 202, 282, 287, 317
District 71 .... 84, 98, 107, 124, 159, 182, 187, 188, 206, 232
District 72 .... 68, 81, 83, 98, 113, 148, 154, 177, 198, 206, 207, 211, 224, 251, 256, 280
District 73 .... 80, 98, 110, 113, 128, 152, 161, 164, 177, 227, 246, 285
District 74 .... 68, 77, 78, 80, 81, 88, 98, 106, 109, 138, 141, 154, 155, 163, 166,
    177, 195, 203, 241, 244, 257, 263, 274, 283, 290, 297, 308
District 75 .... 68, 75, 79, 98, 106, 128, 138, 141, 145, 155, 170, 178, 251, 281, 291, 298

Militia District Index

District 76............. 77, 80, 85, 92, 106, 109, 145, 155, 189, 228, 240, 242, 245, 260, 268, 270, 287, 294, 305
District 77 ...... 76, 80, 97, 121, 136, 137, 162, 166, 178, 211, 221, 229, 232, 240, 248, 298
District 78 .... 89, 104, 129, 145, 150, 185, 222, 248, 278, 302
District 79 ....80, 89, 106, 110, 115, 134, 136, 145, 148, 150, 180, 192, 205, 221, 227, 239, 259, 267, 276, 290, 304, 309, 313
District 80 .... 82, 136, 163, 168, 172, 174, 191, 207, 248, 289
District 81 .... 73, 80, 92, 110, 155, 157, 164, 196, 228, 238, 260, 261, 271, 273, 304
District 82............. 73, 74, 85, 92, 104, 106, 110, 112, 125, 145, 177, 182, 205, 230, 232, 243, 271, 277, 279, 291, 298, 309, 315
District 83 .... 76, 80, 109, 115, 145, 167, 184, 201, 241, 251, 253, 259, 271, 287, 295, 298
District 84 .... 70, 81, 107, 114, 115, 145, 155, 166, 201, 236, 240, 245, 278, 288, 298, 315
District 85 ....71, 74, 85, 104, 114, 115, 121, 134, 145, 152, 179, 202, 231, 241, 252, 254, 265, 273, 288, 312
District 86 .... 93, 113, 148, 150, 169, 176, 196, 254, 260, 277, 303
District 87 .... 101, 110, 114, 147, 164, 180, 196, 233, 239, 275, 307
District 88 ....114, 123, 156, 214, 274, 313
District 89 .... 93, 152, 164, 171, 174, 204, 230, 288, 296, 304, 308
District 90 .... 80, 81, 113, 136, 174, 182, 240, 257, 262, 274, 287, 296, 313
District 91 .... 102, 113, 137, 150, 154, 168, 180, 196, 197, 209, 287, 289
District 92 ....80, 180, 245, 248, 262, 309, 313
District 93 .... 93, 148, 155, 178, 184, 201, 240, 248, 251, 293, 311
District 94 .... 93, 192, 209, 220, 241, 275, 309, 313
District 95 .... 93, 102, 148, 189, 218, 257, 263, 272, 281, 287, 309
District 96 .... 76, 92, 101, 114, 178, 209, 282, 299, 312
District 97 .... 81, 101, 114, 135, 153, 267, 272, 289, 313
District 98 .... 78, 113, 136, 137, 158, 168, 238, 275, 284, 292, 303, 305
District 99 .... 81, 93, 102, 122, 134, 159, 162, 175, 224, 238, 241, 283, 284, 300
District 100 .... 73, 101, 102, 113, 148, 155, 185, 205, 217, 262, 284, 316
District 101 .... 77, 80, 83, 108, 110, 159, 231, 256, 265, 285, 288, 314
District 102 .... 99, 116, 136, 148, 153, 159, 166, 173, 177, 199, 220, 224, 257, 314, 318
District 103 .... 80, 102, 117, 144, 155, 178, 197, 234, 253, 272, 295, 313
District 104 .... 76, 83, 99, 114, 126, 141, 179, 182, 204, 219, 234, 237, 240, 307, 313
District 105 .... 83, 100, 107, 138, 159, 163, 164, 168, 173, 189, 195, 218, 292, 303, 316
District 106 .... 71, 80, 91, 107, 131, 144, 175, 204, 255, 265, 280
District 107 .... 79, 99, 117, 132, 168, 175, 208, 227, 253, 259, 308, 316
District 108 ....74, 80, 84, 100, 117, 154, 175, 177, 181, 192, 202, 253, 276, 284, 295, 308, 317
District 109 ....77, 102, 108, 144, 153, 155, 160, 173, 180, 205, 232, 243, 250, 269, 270, 286, 308
District 110 .... 82, 83, 99, 152, 158, 163, 186, 204, 222, 251, 257, 281, 293

District 111............89, 92, 115, 144, 156, 177, 185, 204, 206, 214, 244, 259, 295, 302, 304
District 112........................80, 90, 111, 126, 144, 159, 178, 189, 204, 208, 234, 244, 256, 260, 298, 308
District 113................................76, 102, 108, 130, 131, 169, 189, 253, 271, 283, 301, 314
District 114..90, 108, 150, 176, 191, 225, 238, 261, 283
District 115...............85, 98, 107, 108, 141, 154, 174, 175, 176, 194, 204, 216, 225, 249, 251, 267, 270, 275, 278, 296, 308
District 116...80, 98, 123, 137, 192, 240, 257, 303
District 117..97, 98, 144, 165, 219, 240, 244, 300, 301
District 118................................79, 92, 136, 153, 158, 165, 189, 228, 239, 254, 294, 303
District 119...........................81, 91, 100, 108, 109, 147, 161, 166, 203, 214, 224, 225, 274
District 120.................75, 81, 92, 123, 132, 147, 153, 157, 176, 178, 226, 235, 238, 255, 258, 276, 286
District 121..................................89, 104, 131, 179, 186, 197, 219, 260, 265, 287
District 122......................81, 108, 126, 132, 147, 153, 157, 172, 176, 178, 194, 213, 223, 226, 227, 229, 238, 243, 270, 274, 289, 292
District 123..........................97, 132, 147, 168, 180, 246, 260, 274, 278, 298, 306
District 124.............................92, 97, 105, 112, 132, 147, 150, 159, 185, 198, 232, 238, 257, 279, 290
District 125...79, 80, 111, 116, 162, 168, 202, 209, 291, 294, 307
District 126.................................87, 92, 116, 142, 156, 169, 183, 203, 224, 255, 259, 286
District 127.................................77, 103, 111, 118, 119, 184, 203, 237, 272, 294
District 128......................................103, 104, 111, 137, 148, 176, 235, 239, 261, 282, 307
District 129................................96, 116, 135, 157, 160, 180, 207, 255, 258, 281, 294, 317
District 130.......................75, 87, 115, 124, 135, 142, 178, 179, 186, 193, 203, 227, 255, 257, 297, 305
District 131...............................127, 135, 157, 176, 201, 257, 284, 294, 309, 317
District 132...75, 119, 142, 149, 179, 212, 242
District 133..................96, 111, 115, 135, 142, 167, 177, 188, 201, 220, 230, 248, 249, 263, 274, 281, 296
District 134.................74, 86, 87, 103, 111, 116, 135, 142, 148, 162, 187, 195, 209, 216, 221, 225, 241, 273, 279, 303, 310
District 135................................74, 103, 127, 140, 142, 160, 163, 179, 203, 214, 287, 310
District 136...............102, 113, 134, 148, 161, 175, 199, 228, 237, 241, 253, 263, 268, 290
District 137....................78, 95, 100, 110, 133, 143, 159, 181, 204, 207, 227, 263, 273, 305
District 138.................96, 106, 115, 163, 173, 179, 202, 222, 225, 252, 257, 267, 290, 300
District 139..............95, 100, 122, 143, 144, 179, 207, 235, 245, 246, 254, 255, 265, 282, 284, 288, 295, 301, 317
District 140................................92, 106, 112, 150, 161, 176, 191, 239, 254, 257, 273, 316
District 141...............104, 131, 132, 150, 157, 172, 193, 220, 270, 273, 297, 305, 309, 314

Militia District Index

District 142 ....83, 89, 102, 108, 143, 155, 160, 166, 177, 197, 248, 256, 259, 261, 275, 277, 302
District 143 .... 83, 89, 100, 108, 122, 127, 151, 164, 168, 209, 254, 267, 268, 285, 296
District 144 ....95, 126, 157, 213, 260, 293, 307
District 145 .... 81, 83, 96, 99, 122, 144, 171, 203, 238, 257, 261, 275, 287, 296, 303
District 146 .... 78, 89, 107, 126, 144, 181, 203, 216, 233, 248, 255, 257, 295, 311, 314
District 147 .... 126, 215, 218, 240, 256, 258, 270, 274
District 148 .... 108, 111, 126, 144, 153, 216, 230, 243, 246, 265, 292, 298, 312, 316
District 149 ....77, 82, 126, 219, 229, 244, 246, 266
District 150 ....98, 107, 147, 220, 238, 239, 272
District 151 .... 80, 99, 127, 129, 147, 160, 194, 274, 285, 305, 310, 311
District 152 ....82, 243, 261, 271, 303, 307, 313
District 153 ....78, 89, 103, 113, 209, 256, 272, 292
District 154 .... 79, 81, 131, 147, 165, 195, 227, 232, 236, 272, 280, 297, 300
District 155 .... 81, 96, 128, 131, 136, 137, 172, 174, 239, 241, 272, 284, 303, 312
District 156 .... 78, 81, 107, 118, 134, 150, 173, 183, 192, 202, 234, 276, 292, 305
District 157 .... 81, 96, 98, 110, 179, 222, 238, 265, 304
District 158 .... 87, 110, 137, 158, 176, 186, 205, 230, 232, 277, 279, 288, 289, 296
District 159 .... 82, 97, 98, 110, 158, 187, 206, 232, 235, 237, 245, 267, 281, 293
District 160 ....83, 117, 136, 143, 162, 166, 188, 194, 196, 216, 218, 238, 246, 253, 255, 261, 274, 309, 317
District 161 .. ..96, 108, 116, 150, 155, 181, 189, 194, 213, 219, 228, 234, 236, 248, 265, 267, 275, 305, 312
District 162 .... 83, 111, 144, 153, 174, 206, 225, 255, 274, 277, 280, 284, 299, 314
District 163 .... 83, 89, 115, 133, 153, 162, 163, 173, 182, 201, 220, 229, 266, 310, 314
District 164 .... 78, 81, 99, 134, 150, 164, 202, 208, 210, 213, 256, 259, 274, 288
District 165 .... 93, 116, 150, 151, 155, 171, 176, 203, 223, 262, 268, 275, 291, 300, 311
District 166 .... 78, 86, 128, 161, 180, 197, 269, 275, 291, 318
District 167 .... 103, 104, 160, 172, 177, 212, 219, 243, 253, 262, 273, 302, 306, 313
District 168 .... 86, 134, 148, 181, 189, 206, 214, 220, 223, 224, 265, 268, 282, 305
District 169 .... 99, 105, 136, 158, 163, 188, 206, 224, 234, 257, 277, 293, 294, 314, 315
District 170 .... 86, 99, 129, 175, 188, 201, 219, 235, 266, 303
District 171 .... 85, 93, 148, 156, 162, 191, 196, 240, 260, 274, 297, 302, 307
District 172 .... 85, 103, 144, 186, 223, 252, 275, 276, 297, 316
District 173 ....78, 86, 253, 262, 309
District 174 .... 86, 93, 113, 138, 150, 162, 166, 203, 221, 234, 282, 286, 317
District 175 .... 98, 125, 148, 160, 166, 186, 194, 203, 236, 241, 282
District 176 .... 85, 112, 113, 159, 183, 197, 220, 236, 259, 276, 300, 315
District 177 .... 78, 86, 148, 150, 163, 175, 177, 217, 253, 260, 291, 302
District 178 .... 122, 173, 225, 246, 248, 249, 266, 277

District 179............86, 93, 122, 163, 181, 182, 206, 232, 240, 248, 260, 266, 270, 280, 287, 299, 303
District 180................85, 86, 99, 122, 152, 166, 192, 193, 197, 239, 260, 271, 277, 300
District 181................................93, 122, 150, 190, 196, 224, 246, 261, 289, 293, 317
District 182........................79, 89, 96, 101, 121, 157, 198, 224, 271, 298, 299
District 183................................83, 96, 157, 195, 215, 232, 236, 257, 289, 299
District 184...79, 82, 150, 178, 203, 282
District 185..77, 146, 171, 190, 253, 286, 305
District 186..103, 146, 169, 198, 203, 215, 229, 315
District 187...............83, 96, 103, 146, 153, 166, 202, 207, 220, 232, 237, 270, 275, 277, 297, 302
District 188..101, 106, 208, 219, 265, 294, 300
District 189..140, 151, 163, 188, 252, 265, 269, 270, 292, 302
District 190.............95, 124, 130, 154, 176, 196, 197, 220, 226, 243, 269, 273, 276, 294, 298, 308
District 191..95, 130, 185, 206, 288, 295
District 192..122, 140, 148, 239, 299, 302
District 193.......100, 111, 130, 180, 184, 201, 212, 242, 259, 276, 282, 292, 306, 317, 318
District 194..95, 121, 130, 179, 187
District 195..................................95, 118, 149, 152, 191, 201, 244, 245, 248, 274, 279, 313
District 196..190, 246, 267, 268, 302
District 197................................95, 100, 118, 149, 162, 241, 252, 253, 266, 303, 317
District 198................................95, 151, 170, 236, 237, 276, 286, 294, 306, 310, 312
District 199..100, 130, 143, 191, 229, 284, 286
District 200..85, 95, 121, 156, 175, 220, 276, 313, 314
District 201........................113, 121, 143, 149, 177, 228, 245, 255, 274, 283, 286, 303, 310
District 202............................100, 121, 140, 170, 184, 201, 236, 245, 271, 281, 295, 301
District 203........................113, 121, 129, 134, 166, 223, 235, 242, 245, 253, 259, 273, 304
District 204............................121, 158, 172, 202, 235, 245, 249, 252, 280, 289, 293
District 205................................128, 159, 190, 209, 235, 273, 281, 292, 301
District 206..78, 85, 167, 168, 203, 270, 276
District 207..103, 167, 177, 214, 279, 308
District 208................................95, 129, 137, 168, 187, 194, 201, 219, 223, 230, 250, 289
District 209.........85, 108, 129, 137, 149, 156, 167, 184, 185, 189, 191, 224, 236, 293, 314
District 210................................85, 93, 103, 149, 167, 175, 203, 225, 241, 244, 296
District 211................................129, 130, 143, 156, 182, 193, 238, 262, 279, 292
District 212...............120, 154, 156, 175, 189, 193, 207, 235, 242, 250, 266, 276, 283, 303
District 213..136, 170, 175, 191, 230, 244, 271, 275, 278
District 214................................85, 149, 163, 185, 206, 213, 215, 237, 258, 302
District 215..130, 143, 212, 225, 250, 298
District 216................................82, 87, 92, 135, 149, 157, 178, 215, 219, 261, 294, 308

Militia District Index

District 217 ....81, 82, 92, 134, 142, 155, 169, 190, 192, 228, 232, 236, 240, 270, 292, 302, 317
District 218 .... 87, 92, 104, 112, 141, 142, 183, 189, 194, 240, 285, 288, 294
District 219 .... 87, 137, 167, 170, 175, 199, 245, 261, 283
District 220 .... 79, 82, 104, 135, 156, 171, 184, 193, 228, 244, 248, 285, 288, 293, 306
District 221 .... 82, 87, 101, 132, 161, 178, 190, 214, 226, 232, 238, 254, 272, 310
District 222 .... 135, 158, 189, 213, 254, 256, 279, 284, 301, 302, 312, 317
District 223 .... 94, 95, 142, 207, 215, 223, 268, 284, 286, 310, 316
District 224 .... 112, 138, 158, 191, 225, 238, 278, 299
District 225 .... 82, 94, 135, 166, 185, 191, 199, 218, 244, 284, 297
District 226 .... 88, 98, 147, 150, 162, 167, 183, 188, 228, 236, 259, 303, 310
District 227 .... 88, 98, 104, 147, 185, 230, 248, 250, 253, 266, 285, 292
District 228 .... 79, 155, 195, 197, 218, 265, 282, 314
District 229 .... 88, 104, 119, 156, 162, 185, 228, 256, 259, 276, 280, 295, 299, 310, 316
District 230 .... 93, 151, 183, 190, 208, 257, 284, 295, 296, 299, 310, 314
District 231 ....93, 116, 119, 147, 157, 160, 171, 177, 188, 192, 214, 242, 248, 269, 270, 296, 310, 314
District 232 .... 104, 147, 172, 179, 201, 214, 244, 254, 256, 278, 296, 301, 302
District 233 .... 79, 93, 105, 106, 161, 176, 182, 223, 250, 252, 276, 281
District 234 .... 93, 147, 160, 189, 197, 211, 239, 240, 259, 292, 310, 314
District 235 .... 88, 100, 119, 155, 168, 226, 254, 258, 260, 273, 280, 296, 314
District 236 .... 154, 163, 187, 190, 197, 227, 256, 259, 266, 286, 289
District 237 .... 87, 88, 104, 119, 147, 150, 152, 156, 179, 190, 194, 225, 245, 303, 312
District 238 .... 79, 119, 146, 147, 154, 169, 182, 189, 214, 239, 297
District 239 .... 94, 112, 170, 225, 236, 254, 262, 281, 284
District 240 .... 87, 94, 149, 152, 158, 210, 229, 234, 238, 268
District 241 .... 94, 95, 135, 149, 159, 228, 235, 238, 251, 292, 313
District 242 .... 78, 86, 99, 130, 156, 166, 175, 186, 196, 209, 226, 258, 267, 274, 307
District 243 ....95, 96, 130, 196, 203, 224, 259, 312
District 244 ....96, 99, 130, 137, 138, 145, 154
District 245 ....78, 86, 99, 111, 144, 145, 176, 198, 227, 231, 266, 287, 289, 297, 299, 306, 310
District 246 .... 79, 86, 99, 130, 151, 235, 258, 259, 284
District 247 .... 78, 129, 145, 179, 251, 253, 273, 308, 310
District 248 .... 78, 135, 196, 223, 229, 246, 253, 284, 317
District 249 ....86, 96, 167, 179, 197, 225, 252, 287
District 250 ....145, 184, 193, 206, 228, 246, 288
District 251 .... 87, 99, 102, 109, 145, 185, 218, 229, 235, 248, 287, 295
District 252 ....96, 111, 130, 140, 159, 162, 175, 195, 214, 234, 259, 274, 298
District 253 ....87, 158, 285
District 254 .... 87, 99, 102, 130, 151, 158, 197, 203, 229, 250, 297

423

District 255.................87, 111, 162, 165, 166, 176, 181, 192, 198, 221, 253, 284, 289, 313
District 256......................................87, 99, 125, 133, 180, 249, 280, 281, 302
District 257...96, 111, 159, 164, 190, 199, 246, 301
District 258...99, 135, 158, 194, 201, 233, 244, 301, 308
District 259........................84, 117, 136, 171, 176, 186, 216, 231, 243, 272, 290, 303, 307
District 260..................................84, 86, 166, 167, 195, 228, 238, 278, 291, 300
District 261......................135, 149, 156, 173, 179, 193, 214, 224, 245, 290, 301
District 262................................130, 149, 151, 230, 241, 249, 303, 310
District 263................................172, 192, 196, 209, 231, 232, 234, 268, 311
District 264......................129, 130, 156, 172, 180, 185, 189, 251, 268, 281
District 265................................130, 137, 151, 226, 285, 309, 314, 317
District 266................................130, 208, 227, 235, 246, 271, 292, 306
District 267......................130, 143, 161, 172, 185, 214, 222, 241, 254, 273, 288
District 268......................................135, 179, 194, 250, 280, 301, 308
District 269................................146, 159, 196, 206, 226, 228, 235, 267, 280, 308
District 270...142, 154, 294
District 271................................143, 198, 205, 231, 235, 288, 293, 303, 304
District 272...179, 213
District 273..133, 138, 153, 154, 162
District 274......................129, 131, 142, 157, 164, 203, 224, 226, 266, 276, 281, 283, 294
District 275..141, 172, 188, 209, 226, 266
District 276......................149, 159, 169, 171, 184, 195, 220, 240, 260, 273, 302
District 277................................145, 161, 178, 206, 237, 267, 303, 309, 313, 315
District 278................................145, 166, 185, 187, 209, 236, 258, 261, 289, 293, 295
District 279......................135, 136, 158, 176, 195, 216, 223, 265, 266, 295, 302, 304, 308
District 280......................133, 149, 153, 174, 192, 215, 270, 295, 298
District 281......................140, 148, 166, 185, 194, 206, 241, 308
District 282......................145, 149, 185, 189, 190, 227, 267, 273, 286, 289, 304
District 283......................138, 149, 171, 198, 228, 233, 236, 237, 270, 271, 281, 288, 314
District 284......................133, 135, 146, 153, 174, 205, 261, 266, 284, 295
District 285..146, 169, 183, 205, 208, 285
District 286......................133, 161, 176, 187, 198, 204, 207, 262, 269, 271, 275, 316
District 287......................146, 161, 173, 179, 181, 185, 206, 209, 258, 271, 293, 317
District 288......................146, 153, 174, 175, 196, 224, 226, 229, 239, 243, 254, 257, 274
District 289..152, 186, 192, 251, 275, 281, 299, 303
District 290......................133, 146, 164, 206, 219, 224, 229, 237, 248, 311
District 291..156, 187, 195, 210, 277, 296, 315
District 292..156, 165, 191, 242, 245, 258, 308, 316
District 293..136, 165, 222, 232, 277
District 294......................95, 155, 156, 204, 214, 246, 255, 271, 295
District 295......................146, 190, 191, 194, 233, 234, 244, 273, 276, 302, 312

Militia District Index

District 296 .... 146, 195, 205, 240, 246, 285, 287, 302, 312
District 297 .... 148, 208, 215, 292, 304, 309
District 298 .... 136, 159, 186, 191, 215, 244, 248, 269, 277, 289, 306
District 299 .... 135, 158, 164, 191, 227, 243, 259, 261, 271, 275, 309, 316
District 300 ....140, 159, 171, 180, 217, 222, 226, 227, 248, 273, 277, 296, 297, 305, 306, 307
District 301 .... 140, 164, 174, 183, 198, 214, 228, 256, 293, 300
District 302 .... 141, 150, 204, 222, 230, 249, 261, 282, 284, 290, 293
District 303 .... 170, 176, 180, 188, 248, 259, 262, 267
District 304 .... 151, 156, 170, 171, 184, 191, 207, 230, 236, 262, 272, 273, 291
District 305 .... 148, 164, 186, 206, 221, 262, 271, 278, 301, 305
District 306 ....137, 151, 164, 175, 183, 196, 224, 230, 232, 246, 249, 265, 302, 305, 313, 316
District 307 .... 134, 139, 154, 159, 174, 183, 209, 240, 257, 278, 286, 287, 293
District 308 .... 137, 140, 146, 153, 155, 187, 198, 265, 272, 276, 293, 308, 313
District 309 .... 149, 173, 188, 204, 254, 256, 272, 285, 303, 311
District 310 .... 132, 139, 149, 157, 162, 181, 202, 273, 296, 312
District 311 ....146, 185, 250, 258
District 312 .... 149, 157, 168, 178, 198, 219, 231, 243, 262, 288, 289, 299, 314
District 313 .... 135, 156, 180, 183, 197, 241, 257, 267, 289, 296
District 314 .... 163, 190, 226, 244, 259, 278, 289, 294
District 315 .... 130, 149, 180, 205, 226, 236, 273, 280
District 316 .... 160, 161, 208, 277, 278, 285, 299, 310, 313
District 317 .... 139, 170, 195, 199, 218, 239, 266, 272, 287
District 318 .... 160, 161, 174, 175, 194, 245, 246, 255, 265, 271, 290, 312
District 319 .... 139, 156, 193, 198, 217, 231, 251, 252, 266, 270, 273, 293
District 320 ....141, 168, 171, 172, 173, 178, 195, 215, 230, 232, 239, 240, 244, 259, 285, 286
District 321 .... 142, 143, 160, 164, 172, 208, 220, 235, 277, 308
District 322 .... 183, 215, 226, 229, 239, 274, 277, 317
District 323 .... 151, 177, 197, 227, 291, 299
District 324 .... 137, 162, 204, 267, 277, 313
District 325 .... 163, 165, 214, 220, 224, 256
District 326 .... 163, 181, 205, 213, 224, 230, 258, 280, 299
District 327 ....239, 258, 269, 288
District 328 .... 161, 190, 215, 219, 244, 260, 285, 300, 310
District 329 .... 158, 166, 195, 207, 214, 225, 235, 236, 276, 298, 315
District 330 .... 165, 194, 233, 243, 251, 252, 275, 296
District 331 .... 148, 195, 209, 229, 282, 291, 292, 307
District 332 .... 169, 171, 225, 238, 271, 274, 284, 293
District 333 164

District 334...186, 234, 243, 253, 283
District 335...183, 213, 228, 249, 266, 283
District 336...231, 235
District 337...181, 218, 231, 242, 256, 274, 284, 302
District 338...228, 253, 305
District 339...193, 205, 242, 281
District 340...214, 231, 233, 242, 251, 296
District 341...179, 201, 202, 216, 223, 224, 229, 306
District 342...191, 226, 245, 262, 276, 303, 307
District 343..198, 227, 245, 285, 306
District 344...197, 220, 290, 291
District 345...204, 230, 238, 258, 277, 288, 302, 303
District 346...187, 204, 208, 221, 228, 282, 285, 292
District 347...181, 206, 210, 238, 258, 261, 283
District 348...201, 211, 244, 249, 269, 282, 301, 315
District 349...187, 245, 315
District 350...205, 219, 243, 266, 278, 285
District 351...187, 237, 289, 307
District 352...183, 209, 259, 270
District 353...182, 224, 258, 310
District 354...186, 191, 204, 229, 246, 255, 266, 276
District 355.............................192, 211, 214, 236, 245, 255, 258, 267, 290, 306, 313
District 356...188, 191, 206, 244, 253, 271, 299
District 357...202, 218, 220, 231, 253, 265, 278, 295
District 358...176, 206, 227, 235, 242, 245, 258, 280, 305
District 359...190, 191, 207, 236, 274, 312
District 360...174, 209, 222, 238, 248, 268, 283, 309
District 361...196, 231, 248, 250, 272, 298, 312, 316
District 362...175, 196, 211, 232, 270, 273, 292, 295, 302, 308
District 363...178, 219, 234, 258, 276, 286, 288
District 364...185, 192, 202, 217, 225, 241, 255, 286, 295, 298
District 365...189, 199, 201, 243, 275, 277, 302
District 366...176, 196, 213, 224, 269, 273, 299, 317
District 367...183, 188, 212, 226, 244, 261, 268, 269, 273, 299
District 368...............................175, 186, 207, 223, 237, 259, 262, 278, 287, 288, 292, 314, 317
District 369...178, 186, 197, 223, 270, 276, 278, 292, 299
District 370...196, 265, 268, 274, 278, 288, 317
District 371...175, 185, 285
District 372...176, 181, 193, 204, 219, 226, 243, 255, 274, 303
District 373...183, 188, 206, 239, 265, 267, 275, 292, 317
District 374...185, 186, 198, 208, 229, 249, 273, 280, 313

Militia District Index

District 375 .... 187, 214, 225, 232, 245, 277, 290, 296, 318
District 376 .... 197, 209, 222, 259, 275, 300, 307, 313
District 377 .... 191, 206, 225, 254, 259, 277, 281
District 378 .... 191, 192, 209, 229, 234, 255, 262, 280, 295, 305, 313
District 379 .... 193, 216, 219, 227, 241, 258, 268, 271, 288, 292, 306
District 380 .... 194, 254, 256, 279, 281, 282, 289, 293, 304
District 381 .... 194, 218, 250, 271
District 382 .... 257, 280, 308, 312
District 383 .... 268, 278, 309
District 384 .... 206, 207, 240, 241, 255, 278, 289, 309
District 385 .... 232, 296, 302
District 386 .... 208, 209, 233, 237, 268, 278, 297, 298, 307
District 387 .... 208, 219, 253, 284, 299, 316
District 388 .... 219, 296, 299
District 389 .... 219, 235, 265, 271, 308
District 390 .... 228, 246, 267, 287, 312
District 391 .... 233, 272, 282, 293, 295, 313
District 392 .... 231, 238, 257, 280, 286, 301
District 393 .... 244, 278
District 395 .... 239, 252
District 396 .... 278, 293, 312
District 397 .... 280, 290, 308
District 398 286
District 399 291
District 400 .... 291, 309, 313
District 401 306

District-to-County Cross Reference

District 1	Chatham County
District 2	Chatham County
District 3	Chatham County
District 4	Chatham County
District 5	Chatham County
District 6	Chatham County
District 7	Chatham County
District 8	Chatham County
District 9	Effingham County
District 10	Effingham County
District 11	Effingham County
District 12	Effingham County
District 13	Effingham County, then abolished
District 14	Effingham County, then abolished
District 15	Liberty County
District 16	Liberty County, then Long County
District 17	Liberty County
District 18	Liberty County, then abolished
District 19	Bryan County
District 20	Bryan County
District 21	McIntosh County, then abolished
District 22	McIntosh County
District 23	McIntosh County, then abolished
District 24	Liberty County, then Long County
District 25	Glynn County
District 26	Glynn County
District 27	Glynn County
District 28	Glynn County, then abolished
District 29	Camden County
District 30	Camden County
District 31	Camden County
District 32	Camden County
District 33	Camden County
District 34	Screven County
District 35	Screven County
District 36	Screven County
District 37	Screven County
District 38	Screven County

District 39	Montgomery County, then Tattnall County, then Toombs County
District 40	Montgomery County, then Tattnall County
District 41	Montgomery County, then Tattnall County
District 42	Montgomery County, then Tattnall County, then abolished
District 43	Montgomery County, then Tattnall County, then Toombs County
District 44	Bulloch County
District 45	Bulloch County
District 46	Bulloch County
District 47	Bulloch County
District 48	Bulloch County
District 49	Montgomery County, then Emanuel County
District 50	Montgomery County, then Emanuel County
District 51	Montgomery County, then Toombs County
District 52	Montgomery County, then Laurens County
District 53	Montgomery County, then Emanuel County
District 54	Montgomery County, then abolished
District 55	Montgomery County, then Johnson County
District 56	Montgomery County, then Johnson County
District 57	Montgomery County, then Emanuel County
District 58	Montgomery County, then Emanuel County
District 59	Montgomery County, then abolished
District 60	Burke County
District 61	Burke County
District 62	Burke County
District 63	Burke County
District 64	Burke County
District 65	Burke County
District 66	Burke County
District 67	Burke County
District 68	Burke County
District 69	Burke County
District 70	Burke County
District 71	Burke County
District 72	Burke County
District 73	Burke County
District 74	Burke County
District 75	Burke County, then Jenkins County, then abolished
District 76	Jefferson County
District 77	Jefferson County
District 78	Jefferson County
District 79	Jefferson County

District-to-County Cross Reference

District 80	Jefferson County
District 81	Jefferson County
District 82	Jefferson County
District 83	Jefferson County
District 84	Jefferson County
District 85	Jefferson County
District 86	Washington County, then Laurens County
District 87	Washington County, then Laurens County, then abolished
District 88	Washington County
District 89	Washington County
District 90	Washington County
District 91	Washington County
District 92	Washington County
District 93	Washington County
District 94	Washington County
District 95	Washington County
District 96	Washington County
District 97	Washington County
District 98	Washington County
District 99	Washington County
District 100	Washington County
District 101	Hancock County
District 102	Hancock County
District 103	Hancock County
District 104	Hancock County
District 105	Hancock County, then Baldwin County
District 106	Hancock County
District 107	Hancock County
District 108	Hancock County
District 109	Hancock County
District 110	Hancock County, then abolished
District 111	Hancock County
District 112	Hancock County
District 113	Hancock County
District 114	Hancock County
District 115	Hancock County, then Baldwin County
District 116	Hancock County
District 117	Hancock County
District 118	Hancock County
District 119	Richmond County
District 120	Richmond County

Georgia Military Commissions, 1798–1818

District 121   Richmond County
District 122   Richmond County
District 123   Richmond County
District 124   Richmond County
District 125   Columbia County
District 126   Columbia County
District 127   Columbia County, then abolished
District 128   Columbia County
District 129   Columbia County
District 130   Columbia County, then abolished
District 131   Columbia County,
District 132   Columbia County, then McDuffie County
District 133   Columbia County, then McDuffie County
District 134   Columbia County, and also McDuffie County (duplicate)
District 135   Columbia County
District 136   Washington County
District 137   Greene County
District 138   Greene County
District 139   Greene County, then abolished
District 140   Greene County
District 141   Greene County
District 142   Greene County
District 143   Greene County
District 144   Greene County
District 145   Greene County
District 146   Greene County
District 147   Greene County
District 148   Greene County
District 149   Greene County
District 150   Warren County
District 151   Warren County, then abolished
District 152   Warren County, then McDuffie County
District 153   Warren County
District 154   Warren County
District 155   Warren County
District 156   Warren County, then abolished
District 157   Warren County
District 158   Warren County
District 159   Warren County
District 160   Greene County
District 161   Greene County

District-to-County Cross Reference

District 162	Greene County
District 163	Greene County
District 164	Wilkes County
District 165	Wilkes County
District 166	Wilkes County
District 167	Wilkes County
District 168	Wilkes County
District 169	Wilkes County
District 170	Wilkes County, then abolished
District 171	Wilkes County
District 172	Wilkes County, then Taliaferro County
District 173	Wilkes County, then abolished
District 174	Wilkes County
District 175	Wilkes County
District 176	Wilkes County
District 177	Wilkes County
District 178	Wilkes County
District 179	Wilkes County
District 180	Wilkes County
District 181	Wilkes County
District 182	Lincoln County
District 183	Lincoln County
District 184	Lincoln County
District 185	Lincoln County
District 186	Lincoln County
District 187	Lincoln County
District 188	Lincoln County
District 189	Elbert County
District 190	Elbert County
District 191	Elbert County
District 192	Elbert County
District 193	Elbert County
District 194	Elbert County, then abolished
District 195	Elbert County
District 196	Elbert County
District 197	Elbert County
District 198	Elbert County, then abolished
District 199	Elbert County
District 200	Elbert County, then abolished
District 201	Elbert County
District 202	Elbert County, and also Jones County (duplicate)

District 203	Franklin County, then Madison County
District 204	Franklin County, then Madison County
District 205	Franklin County, then Madison County
District 206	Franklin County
District 207	Franklin County, then Banks County
District 208	Franklin County, then Banks County
District 209	Franklin County, then abolished
District 210	Franklin County
District 211	Franklin County
District 212	Franklin County
District 213	Franklin County
District 214	Franklin County, then abolished
District 215	Franklin County, then Stephens County
District 216	Franklin County, then Clarke County
District 217	Franklin County, then Clarke County
District 218	Franklin County, then Clarke County
District 219	Franklin County, then Clarke County
District 220	Franklin County, then Clarke County
District 221	Clarke County, then Oconee County
District 222	Clarke County, then Oconee County
District 223	Clarke County, then Oconee County
District 224	Clarke County, then Oconee County
District 225	Clarke County, then Franklin County, then Oconee County
District 226	Oglethorpe County
District 227	Oglethorpe County
District 228	Oglethorpe County
District 229	Oglethorpe County
District 230	Oglethorpe County
District 231	Oglethorpe County, then abolished
District 232	Oglethorpe County
District 233	Oglethorpe County
District 234	Oglethorpe County
District 235	Oglethorpe County
District 236	Oglethorpe County
District 237	Oglethorpe County
District 238	Oglethorpe County
District 239	Jackson County, then Oconee County
District 240	Clarke County, then Oconee County
District 241	Jackson County, then Clarke County
District 242	Jackson County
District 243	Jackson County, then Barrow County

District-to-County Cross Reference

District 244   Jackson County, then abolished
District 245   Jackson County
District 246   Jackson County, then Barrow County
District 247   Jackson County, then abolished
District 248   Jackson County
District 249   Jackson County, then Barrow County
District 250   Jackson County, then Walton County
District 251   Jackson County, then abolished
District 252   Jackson County, then abolished
District 253   Jackson County
District 254   Jackson County, then abolished
District 255   Jackson County
District 256   Jackson County, then abolished
District 257   Jackson County
District 258   Jackson County, then abolished
District 259   Screven County
District 260   Screven County
District 261   Jackson County, then Clarke County, then Oconee County
District 262   Franklin County, then Madison County, and also Jasper County (duplicate)
District 263   Franklin County
District 264   Franklin County
District 265   Franklin County, then Banks County
District 266   Franklin County, then abolished
District 267   Franklin County, then Stephens County
District 268   Franklin County, then Hall County
District 269   Lincoln County
District 270   Camden County
District 271   McIntosh County
District 272   McIntosh County, then abolished
District 273   McIntosh County, then abolished
District 274   Warren County, then McDuffie County
District 275   Montgomery County
District 276   Morgan County
District 277   Morgan County
District 278   Morgan County
District 279   Morgan County
District 280   Morgan County
District 281   Morgan County
District 282   Morgan County
District 283   Morgan County

District 284   Franklin County, then Banks County, and also Morgan County (duplicate)
District 285   Morgan County
District 286   Morgan County
District 287   Morgan County, then abolished
District 288   Jasper County
District 289   Jasper County
District 290   Jasper County
District 291   Jasper County
District 292   Jasper County
District 293   Jasper County
District 294   Jasper County
District 295   Jasper County
District 296   Jasper County
District 297   Jasper County
District 298   Jones County, then abolished
District 299   Jones County
District 300   Jones County
District 301   Jones County
District 302   Jones County, then abolished
District 303   Jones County, then abolished
District 304   Jones County
District 305   Jones County
District 306   Putnam County
District 307   Putnam County
District 308   Putnam County
District 309   Putnam County
District 310   Putnam County
District 311   Putnam County
District 312   Putnam County
District 313   Putnam County
District 314   Putnam County
District 315   Elbert County
District 316   Gwinnett County, then Barrow County
District 317   Pulaski County, then Dodge County
District 318   Baldwin County
District 319   Baldwin County
District 320   Baldwin County
District 321   Baldwin County
District 322   Baldwin County
District 323   Twiggs County

District-to-County Cross Reference

District 324	Twiggs County
District 325	Twiggs County (consolidated with District 425)
District 326	Twiggs County
District 327	Wilkinson County
District 328	Wilkinson County
District 329	Wilkinson County
District 330	Wilkinson County
District 331	Wilkinson County
District 332	Wilkinson County
District 333	Wayne County
District 334	Wayne County, then Brantley County
District 335	Wayne County, then Brantley County
District 336	Wayne County, then abolished
District 337	Telfair County, then abolished
District 338	Telfair County, then abolished
District 339	Telfair County, then abolished
District 340	Telfair County, then abolished
District 341	Laurens County
District 342	Laurens County
District 343	Laurens County
District 344	Laurens County
District 345	Laurens County
District 346	Laurens County, then abolished
District 347	Jones County
District 348	Pulaski County, then Bleckley County
District 349	Pulaski County, then Dodge County
District 350	Pulaski County, then abolished
District 351	Tattnall County
District 352	Wilkinson County
District 353	Wilkinson County
District 354	Twiggs County
District 355	Twiggs County
District 356	Twiggs County
District 357	Twiggs County, then abolished
District 358	Jones County
District 359	Jones County
District 360	Jones County
District 361	Jones County
District 362	Jasper County, then abolished
District 363	Jasper County

Georgia Military Commissions, 1798–1818

District 364 Pulaski County, then Dodge County, and also Jasper County (duplicate)
District 365 Jasper County
District 366 Jasper County, then abolished
District 367 Putnam County
District 368 Putnam County
District 369 Putnam County
District 370 Franklin County
District 371 Habersham County, then Banks County
District 372 Twiggs County
District 373 Jasper County
District 374 Putnam County
District 375 Putnam County
District 376 Twiggs County, then abolished
District 377 Jones County
District 378 Jones County
District 379 Jasper County
District 380 Jasper County
District 381 Camden County, then abolished
District 382 Madison County
District 383 Madison County
District 384 Pulaski County, also Dodge County (split)
District 385 Hall County
District 386 Pulaski County, then Bleckley County
District 387 Pulaski County, then Bleckley County
District 388 Pulaski County, then Bleckley County
District 389 Putnam County
District 390 Putnam County
District 391 Laurens County
District 392 Hall County
District 393 Montgomery County, then Wheeler County
District 395 Montgomery County, then Wheeler County
District 396 Morgan County and also Twiggs County (duplicate)
District 397 Morgan County
District 398 Richmond County, then abolished
District 399 Morgan County
District 400 Morgan County
District 401 Tattnall County, then Evans County
District 394 Montgomery County, then Wheeler County

County-to-District Cross Reference

Baldwin County	District 105	District 320
	District 115	District 321
	District 318	District 322
	District 319	
Banks County	District 207	District 284
	District 208	District 371
	District 265	
Barrow County	District 243	District 249
	District 246	District 316
Bleckley County	District 348	District 387
	District 386	District 388
Brantley County	District 334	
	District 335	
Bryan County	District 19	
	District 20	
Bulloch County	District 44	District 47
	District 45	District 48
	District 46	
Burke County	District 60	District 68
	District 61	District 69
	District 62	District 70
	District 63	District 71
	District 64	District 72
	District 65	District 73
	District 66	District 74
	District 67	District 75 (abolished)
Camden County	District 29	District 33
	District 30	District 270
	District 31	District 381 (abolished)
	District 32	

Chatham County	District 1	District 5
	District 2	District 6
	District 3	District 7
	District 4	District 8
Clarke County	District 216	District 223
	District 217	District 224
	District 218	District 225
	District 219	District 240
	District 220	District 241
	District 221	District 261
	District 222	
Columbia County	District 125	District 131
	District 126	District 132
	District 127 (abolished)	District 133
	District 128	District 134
	District 129	District 135
	District 130 (abolished)	
Dodge County	District 384 (split)	District 349
	District 317	District 364 (duplicate)
Effingham County	District 9	District 12
	District 10	District 13 (abolished)
	District 11	District 14 (abolished)
Elbert County	District 189	District 197
	District 190	District 198 (abolished)
	District 191	District 199
	District 192	District 200 (abolished)
	District 193	District 201
	District 194 (abolished)	District 202
	District 195	District 315
	District 196	
Emanuel County	District 49	District 57
	District 50	District 58
	District 53	
Evans County	District 401	

County-to-District Cross Reference

Franklin County	District 203	District 217
	District 204	District 218
	District 205	District 219
	District 206	District 220
	District 207	District 225
	District 208	District 262
	District 209 (abolished)	District 263
	District 210	District 264
	District 211	District 265
	District 212	District 266 (abolished)
	District 213	District 267
	District 214 (abolished)	District 268
	District 215	District 284
	District 216	District 370
Glynn County	District 25	District 27
	District 26	District 28 (abolished)
Greene County	District 137	District 146
	District 138	District 147
	District 139 (abolished)	District 148
	District 140	District 149
	District 141	District 160
	District 142	District 161
	District 143	District 162
	District 144	District 163
	District 145	
Gwinnett County	District 316	
Habersham County	District 371	
Hall County	District 268	
	District 385	
	District 392	

Georgia Military Commissions, 1798–1818

Hancock County	District 101	District 110 (abolished)
	District 102	District 111
	District 103	District 112
	District 104	District 113
	District 105	District 114
	District 106	District 115
	District 107	District 116
	District 108	District 117
	District 109	District 118
Jackson County	District 239	District 250
	District 241	District 251 (abolished)
	District 242	District 252 (abolished)
	District 243	District 253
	District 244 (abolished)	District 254 (abolished)
	District 245	District 255
	District 246	District 256 (abolished)
	District 247 (abolished)	District 257
	District 248	District 258 (abolished)
	District 249	District 261
Jasper County	District 262 (duplicate)	District 297
	District 288	District 362 (abolished)
	District 289	District 363
	District 290	District 364 (duplicate)
	District 291	District 365
	District 292	District 366 (abolished)
	District 293	District 373
	District 294	District 379
	District 295	District 380
	District 296	
Jefferson County	District 76	District 81
	District 77	District 82
	District 78	District 83
	District 79	District 84
	District 80	District 85
Jenkins County	District 75 (abolished)	
Johnson County	District 55	
	District 56	

County-to-District Cross Reference

Jones County	District 202 (duplicate)	District 305
	District 298 (abolished)	District 347
	District 299	District 358
	District 300	District 359
	District 301	District 360
	District 302 (abolished)	District 361
	District 303 (abolished)	District 377
	District 304	District 378
Laurens County	District 52	District 343
	District 86	District 344
	District 87 (abolished)	District 345
	District 341	District 346 (abolished)
	District 342	District 391
Liberty County	District 15	District 18 (abolished)
	District 16	District 24
	District 17	
Lincoln County	District 182	District 186
	District 183	District 187
	District 184	District 188
	District 185	District 269
Long County	District 16	
	District 24	
Madison County	District 203	District 262
	District 204	District 382
	District 205	District 383
McDuffie County	District 132	District 152
	District 133	District 274
	District 134 (duplicate)	
McIntosh County	District 21 (abolished)	District 271
	District 22	District 272 (abolished)
	District 23 (abolished)	District 273 (abolished)

Georgia Military Commissions, 1798–1818

Montgomery County	District 39	District 54 (abolished)
	District 40	District 55
	District 41	District 56
	District 42 (abolished)	District 57
	District 43	District 58
	District 49	District 59 (abolished)
	District 50	District 275
	District 51	District 393
	District 52	District 394
	District 53	District 395
Morgan County	District 276	District 284 (duplicate)
	District 277	District 285
	District 278	District 286
	District 279	District 287 (abolished)
	District 280	District 396
	District 281	District 397
	District 282	District 399
	District 283	District 400
Oconee County	District 221	District 225
	District 222	District 239
	District 223	District 240
	District 224	District 261
Oglethorpe County	District 226	District 233
	District 227	District 234
	District 228	District 235
	District 229	District 236
	District 230	District 237
	District 231 (abolished)	District 238
	District 232	
Pulaski County	District 317	District 384
	District 348	District 386
	District 349	District 387
	District 350 (abolished)	District 388
	District 364 (duplicate)	

County-to-District Cross Reference

Putnam County	District 306	District 314
	District 307	District 367
	District 308	District 368
	District 309	District 369
	District 310	District 374
	District 311	District 375
	District 312	District 389
	District 313	District 390
Richmond County	District 119	District 123
	District 120	District 124
	District 121	District 398 (abolished)
	District 122	
Screven County	District 34	District 38
	District 35	District 259
	District 36	District 260
	District 37	
Stephens County	District 215	
	District 267	
Tattnall County	District 39	District 43
	District 40	District 351
	District 41	District 401
	District 42 (abolished)	
Telfair County	District 337 (abolished)	District 339 (abolished)
	District 338 (abolished)	District 340 (abolished)
Taliaferro County	District 172	
Toombs County	District 39	District 51
	District 43	
Twiggs County	District 323	District 356
	District 324	District 357 (abolished)
	District 325 (see 425)	District 372
	District 326	District 376 (abolished)
	District 354	District 396
	District 355	

445

Georgia Military Commissions, 1798–1818

Walton County	District 250	
Warren County	District 150	District 156 (abolished)
	District 151 (abolished)	District 157
	District 152	District 158
	District 153	District 159
	District 154	District 274
	District 155	
Washington County	District 86	District 94
	District 87 (abolished)	District 95
	District 88	District 96
	District 89	District 97
	District 90	District 98
	District 91	District 99
	District 92	District 100
	District 93	District 136
Wayne County	District 333	District 335
	District 334	District 336 (abolished)
Wheeler County	District 393	District 395
	District 394	
Wilkes County	District 164	District 173 (abolished)
	District 165	District 174
	District 166	District 175
	District 167	District 176
	District 168	District 177
	District 169	District 178
	District 170 (abolished)	District 179
	District 171	District 180
	District 172	District 181
Wilkinson County	District 327	District 331
	District 328	District 332
	District 329	District 352
	District 330	District 353

446

www.ingramcontent.com/pod-product-compliance
Lightning Source LLC
Chambersburg PA
CBHW081331080526
44588CB00017B/2591